INDIAN ESOTERIC

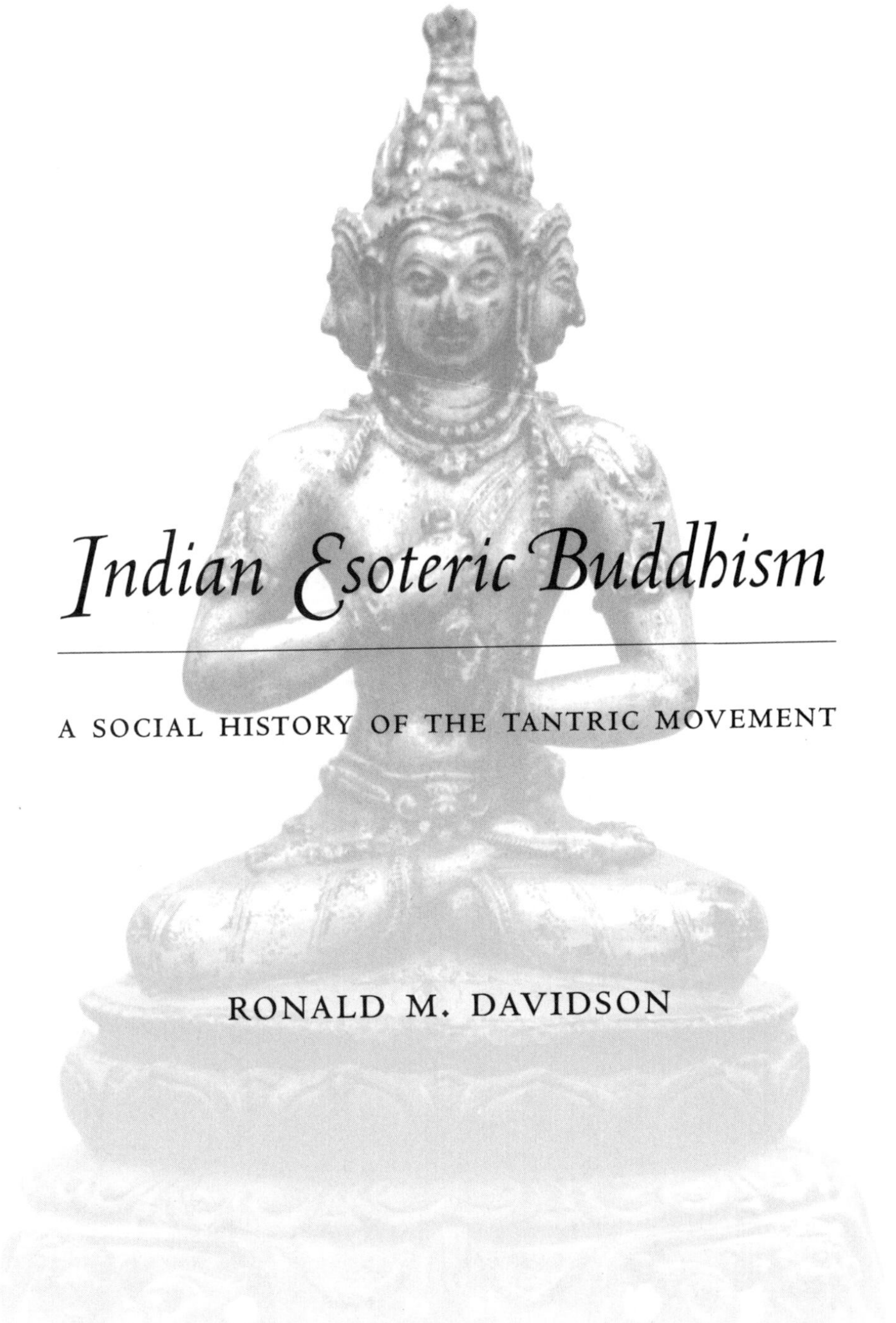

Indian Esoteric Buddhism

A SOCIAL HISTORY OF THE TANTRIC MOVEMENT

RONALD M. DAVIDSON

COLUMBIA UNIVERSITY PRESS / NEW YORK

COLUMBIA UNIVERSITY PRESS
Publishers Since 1893
New York Chichester, West Sussex

Library of Congress Cataloging-in-Publication Data

Davidson, Ronald M.
Indian esoteric Buddhism : a social history of the Tantric movement /
Ronald M. Davidson
p. cm.
Includes bibliographical references and index.
ISBN 0-231-12618-2 (cloth) — ISBN 0-231-12619-0 (paper)
1. Tantric Buddhism—India—History. I. Title.

BQ8912.9.I5 D38 2002
294.3'925'0954—dc21 2002067694

Columbia University Press books are printed
on permanent and durable acid-free paper.
Printed in the United States of America

c 10 9 8 7 6 5 4 3 2 1
p 10 9 8 7 6 5 4 3 2 1

Contents

Maps and Illustrations

MAPS

FIGURES

Preface

Similar to other works of extended scholarship, this work has taken far too long to write. Like many authors in a similar position, having completed the manuscript, I cannot understand why such a work has not yet been attempted, nor can I comprehend why it took me as long as it did. In writing the work, I sometimes feel like an apprentice illusionist seeing practiced conjurors seducing the unwary—their manipulations of reality appear so easy in the practiced hand, and I can only aspire to such apparent felicity.

I have attempted this text with a goal that appears somewhat quaint and perhaps ill conceived: I wished to honor those Indian Buddhist masters who have constructed esoteric Buddhism in their own time. The quaintness stems from my dissent from the modern proclivity of writers to find fault when our forebears do not measure up to a conceptual architecture erected after their time. My ill-conception is that I have approached those of saintly aura and sought humanity where others seek holiness, having looked for the fragile edges of their personalities while the tradition affirms the impenetrable core of their personas. My compulsion to extend praise to these gentlemen proceeds despite our differences, for much that they did I have found disturbing or even, at times, dishonorable. Yet they produced a form of Buddhist praxis and identity that sought sanctity in a world unraveling before their eyes. So, perhaps as an extension of my American heritage, I have searched for the well-tamped earth of common ground, finding a meeting place on the horizon of history, one that displaces the sublime hierarchy of their preferred environment. Those of the Buddhist tradition will fault me for my critical, historical method, while those on some form of ideological crusade will castigate me for my lack of doctrinal rigor. I am at peace with either dissatisfaction.

It is normative for authors to thank their professional colleagues first, but I wish to defer the task, for I have never been able to express sufficiently my gratitude to my family. Since she first began to work on medieval English manuscript microfilm in the kitchen, my mother, Marie Davidson, has been an important, supportive presence in my life. She labored over my English prose when I wanted to study Sanskrit grammar and has assisted in ways beyond measure. My late wife, Law Young Bao, sacrificed her own health and, ultimately, her life, through the most difficult years of my career, believing in me when few others did. Our daughter, Stephanie, has continued to grapple with the challenge of her mother's untimely death and to blossom in ways unforeseen. My second wife, Dr. Katherine Schwab, has become my confessor and confidant, revealing to me the importance of art history and material remains in a manner I could but dimly perceive, and whose patience in the face of my brash archaeological reductionism is for ever treasured.

Among my teachers, first and foremost must be Ngor Thar-rtse mkhan-po, whose death in 1987 robbed me of both friend and teacher. As all relationships do, ours ran the gamut of emotions, but I can never repay the years he spent reading with me through the treasures of his Sakya tradition. I also wish to thank my professors, Padmanabh Jaini, Lewis Lancaster, Barend A. van Nooten, Fritz Staal, Michel Strickmann, David Snellgrove, Katsura Shoryu, Steven Beyer, and others, who have provided me guidance, support, and consideration. My other Tibetan and Indian teachers—including rGya-sprul mDo-mang Rin-po-che, mDo-grub chen, Kun-dga' Thar-rtse zhabs-drung, Jagannath Upadhyay, and Padma 'Byung-gnas—cannot go unmentioned for their generosity and instruction.

This book could not have come to pass without the extraordinary support of my colleagues. David Germano provided me a forum at the University of Virginia to inflict various stages of the manuscript on his students, who suffered through its growing pains. He has consistently helped through diverse phases and made penetrating suggestions. Phyllis Granoff at McMaster has been a true friend and supporter, even while she has had so many other duties and obligations. Without her attention to detail and assistance above and beyond the call of duty, this work would have been very much poorer. I am also indebted to Matthew Kapstein, Janet Gyatso, Anne Klein, Leonard van der Kuijp, Steven Goodman, Kenneth Eastman, Paul Groner, Fred Smith, Douglas Brooks, and Gregory Schopen for their suggestions and ideas. John Thiel and Paul Lakeland and my other colleagues at Fairfield University have been invariably supportive.

I have been fortunate enough to receive support from the Council for the International Exchange of Scholars, the United States Information Service, the American Institute of Indian Studies, United States Educational Foundation in India, Fairfield University Humanities Institute, Fairfield University

Research Committee, and Dean (now Academic Vice President) Orin Grossman of Fairfield University. While in India, I have had the pleasure to be associated with Sampurnand Samskrit Vishwavidyalay, the Central Institute of Higher Tibetan Studies, and have received great kindness from the Library of Tibetan Works and Archives. My guides and colleagues in these establishments, Laksmi Narayan Tiwari, Professor Samdhong Rinpoche, the late Dr Jagannath Upadhyay, Dr. Banarsi Lal, and Losang Shastri have sped my journey. My friend Virendra Singh has made my trips to India both enjoyable and memorable; he taught me the Hindi I actually learned. I was treated well by the Indian Museum, the National Museum, the Bihar State Museum (Patna), the Archaeological Survey of India, the Anthropological Survey of India, the Asiatic Society, Sahitya Akademie, Orissa State Archaeological Department, Tibet House, and the Tribal Research Institute (Bhubaneswar). Indian anthropologists, especially Mr. S. C. Mohanty, Dr. R. K. Bhattacharya, and Dr. J. Sarkar have been exceptionally helpful in understanding India's tribal realities. I have also received exemplary assistance from Dr. Klaus-Dieter Mathes of the Nepal Research Centre and from the Nepal National Archives.

Finally, I am indebted to the many reviewers of this book in its various stages, most especially to Phyllis Granoff, David Germano, their students, two anonymous reviewers, and Cynthia Reed. Their efforts have made this an infinitely better book, although all too many errors of fact and interpretation no doubt remain, for which I alone am responsible. I am especially indebted to Wendy Lochner at Columbia University Press, who has sped this manuscript along faster than I imagined possible, all the while remaining gracious and temperate. Her staff has been invariably kind and considerate. My cartographic assistant, Rich Pinto, took my rudimentary drawings and turned them into professional illustrations, relieving me to worry about words. In retrospect, it seems to me that there were friends, colleagues, and helpers as numerous as the proverbial sands of the River Ganges; to each and all those who have assisted, I give my heartfelt thanks.

Ronald M. Davidson

FAIRFIELD, CONNECTICUT

Acknowledgments

All the maps and figure 3 are courtesy Ronald M. Davidson and Richard Pinto.

Figure 1 permission of the Archaeological Survey of India.

Figure 4 is by permission of Dr. Lokesh Chandra and the International Academy of Indian Culture.

Figures 5, 10, 13, 20, and 21 are courtesy of the American Institute of Indian Studies, Art and Architecture Library.

Figure 15 courtesy of Katherine A. Schwab.

Figures 2, 12, 14, 16, and 19, courtesy of the Cleveland Museum of Art.

Quotations from the following works are by permission of the publishers:

P. A. Brunt, trans. (1976) *Arrian: History of Alexander and Indica,* Loeb Classical Library, no. 236 (Cambridge: Harvard University Press).

Morris Bishop (1966), *Letters from Petrarch* (Bloomington & London: Indiana University Press).

Colette Caillat, ed. (1989), *Dialectes dans les Littératures Indo-Aryennes,* Publications de l'Institut de Civilisation Indienne, Fascicule 55 (Paris: Éditions e. de Boccard).

Georges B. J. Dreyfus (1997), *Recognizing Reality—Dharmakīrti's Philosophy and Its Tibetan Interpretations* (Albany: State University of New York Press).

Thomas M. Green (1982), *The Light in Troy: Imitation and Discovery in Renaissance Poetry* (New Haven and London: Yale University Press).

Philip Jacks (1993), *The Antiquarian and the Myth of Antiquity: The Origins of Rome in Renaissance Thought* (Cambridge and New York: Cambridge University Press).

Keith N. Jefferds (1981), "Vidūṣaka Versus Fool: A Functional Analysis," *Journal of South Asian Literature* 16.

John Keegan (1993), *A History of Warfare* (New York: Alfred A. Knopf).

Philip Lutgendorf (1991), *The Life of a Text: Performing the* Rāmcaritmānas *of Tulsidas* (Berkeley: University of California Press).

John Morrell (1983), *Taking Laughter Seriously* (Albany: State University of New York Press).

Harmut Scharfe (1993), *Investigations in Kauṭalya's Manual of Political Science* (Wiesbaden: Harrassowitz).

Roberto Weiss (1969), *The Renaissance Discovery of Classical Antiquity* (Oxford: Basil Blackwell).

Joanna Gottfried Williams (1982), *The Art of Gupta India: Empire and Province* (Princeton: Princeton University Press).

All of the balance of the quotations fall within the Fair Use Clause for copyrighted material.

Pronunciation and Orthographic Guide

The pronunciation of Sanskrit should provide few problems, except that even authorities on some of the Buddhist systems continue to pronounce the names incorrectly. Generally, a long mark over a vowel should be treated as equivalent to a stress mark, and inappropriate stress is surely the greatest failing in Sanskrit pronunciation in the United States today (e.g., Madhyamaka continues to be incorrectly pronounced in the United States as Madhyāmaka, although it is never spelled that way). There is also the general problem is differentiating ś from ṣ (both sounding to us like "sh") or differentiating the various retroflex (ṭ, ṭh, ḍ, ḍh, and ṇ) from their corresponding dentals (t, th, d, dh, and n). Americans tend to pronounce our sounds between these, not quite retroflex (which sends the tongue farther back) and not quite dental (requiring the tongue farther forward).

Out of consideration for general readers, I have rendered Tibetan into a semblance of English pronunciation, and the correct orthography is found in the notes or in the bibliography, except in the case of some well-known names (e.g., Trisong Detsen). However, I intended this book as a tool for access to India, and I certainly hope that Indian students will be stimulated to learn Tibetan and to seek out Tibetan references. The romanization system for Tibetan orthography is the now-standard "modified Wylie," although David Snellgrove appears to actually be the first to have proposed the system. The reader will also notice that I have used the somewhat out of date Wade-Giles romanization system as well, rather than the more modern Pinyin. I have done so for one primary reason. The standard Pinyin system runs all the words in a title together, so that the *I tsu fo ting lun wang ching* would be romanized *Yizifodinglunwangjing*, a linguistic catastrophe for the neophyte. Until an acceptable alternative occurs, I have elected to retain the more accessible form.

INDIAN ESOTERIC BUDDHISM

I

Introduction: A Plethora of Premises

But now, I will speak of those among the twice-born laymen, virtuous in the Dharma, who, through their persistent employment of mantras and tantras, will be engaged in the functions of the state.

There will be in the whole world at a calamitous time, the best of the twice-born, and his name will be pronounced with a *Va*.

Wealthy and completely familiar with the Vedas, let him wander all of this earth—girdled by three oceans—for the purpose of polemical eloquence.

He will love to fight with those non-Buddhist partisans [*tīrthika*].

Yet he always keeps the bodhisattva visualized before him, and recites the six-letter mantra, restrained in speech.

Thus, he will be a prince bearing the song of Mañjuśrī because of his motivation for the welfare of beings.

Indeed, celebrated for his accumulated performance of rituals, his intellect is superb.

There will be Jaya and the famous Sujaya, and also Śubhamata. They will be from a well-placed family, along with the righteous, ennobled, excellent Mādhava. There will be Madhu and Sumadhu as well.

There will be Siddha and thus *Madadahana (Destroyer of Pride).

There will be Rāghava the Śūdra, and those born among the Śakas.

They will all in this life recite mantras of the prince Mañjuśrī, with their speech restrained.

They will all be esoteric meditators, learned and intelligent.

They will be present among councilors of state [*mantrin*] for they will be completely based in the activities of government.

—*Mañjuśrīmūlakalpa*, LI.955a–963b.[1]

The *Mañjuśrīmūlakalpa*'s obscure Mr. *Va* and his peers are enticing examples of the intersection of the religious and the sociopolitical realms in early medieval India. Rhetorically dedicated to the welfare of all beings, Mr. *Va* evidently employed his energy, wealth, and intelligence to travel over much of India to haggle, debate, and generally harass the adversaries of the Buddhist Dharma. Espousing a doctrine leading to the end of passion, he and the others were passionately involved in the affairs of state, employing the newly evolved tools of the vehicle of secret spells (Mantrayāna or Vajrayāna) to gain a hearing in the courts of kings and at the tables of tyrants. While the authors of the *Mañjuśrīmūlakalpa* clearly believed Mr. *Va* to be an outstanding exemplar of the virtuous layman at the middle of the eighth century C.E., there can be little doubt that he was both an emblem and culmination of the profound shift of Buddhist public life from the seventh century forward.[2] Around this time, India fragmented politically and saw the rise of regional centers in a manner unprecedented and unexpected after the stable gravity of the Imperial Guptas and the Vākāṭakas (c. 320–550 C.E.). Pressed by military adventurism, populations moved across the subcontinent, while Buddhist coalitions sustained crippling setbacks in various parts of South Asia. The changes of fortune and the generation of new Buddhist institutions have remained almost as obscure as our quasi-anonymous Mr. *Va*, even if there can be little doubt that the contested domains of Indian political, military, and religious life profoundly affected Buddhist activity and self-representation.

This work discusses the factors in the formation of esoteric Buddhist traditions in the cauldron of post-Gupta India. Its thesis is that esoteric Buddhism is a direct Buddhist response to the feudalization of Indian society in the early medieval period, a response that involves the sacralization of much of that period's social world. Specifically, this book argues that the monk, or yogin, in the esoteric system configures his practice through the metaphor of becoming the overlord of a maṇḍala of vassals, and issues of scripture, language, and community reflect the political and social models employed in the surrounding feudal society. Our investigation accordingly explores selected forms of Indian Buddhism that flourished in the early medieval period, here taken as the time from c. 500 C.E. to 1200 C.E. Ultimately, medieval Buddhist systems became fatally wounded in the profoundly altered Indian culture that coalesced in the fractious aftermath of the founding of Muslim states in the late twelfth and early thirteenth centuries. Yet these same systems and institutions had demonstrated successful strategies of survival through more than five centuries in the volatile world of medieval South Asia and had served as the platform for the profound Buddhist cultural transmissions to the surrounding societies of Southeast, Central, and East Asia. Our primary concern in examining the evidence is the tension that developed between forms of esoterism that evolved within the hallowed walls of Buddhist monasteries and those forms synthesized by the peripatetic figures of the Buddhist "Perfected" *(siddha)*. These latter were reputed saints—mostly laymen like our Mr. *Va,* as opposed to monks—who conducted themselves in a wide variety of venues and who were frequently agonistic in their interactions with the non-Buddhist world.

The received hagiographies of both monks and siddhas are constructed from the interaction of romantic literature, religious inspiration, vernacular literary movements, and institutional and noninstitutional developments in Indic Buddhism and were principally brought into focus by the serendipitous arrival of Tibetans in early eleventh-century India. Most of these historical trajectories are still refractory to precise chronological placement, and we have no early archaeological or early datable non-Buddhist references to most of the protagonists found in the traditional hagiographies of its saints. Indeed, one of the problems of this era's historical presentation has been scholars' willingness to rely on certain Buddhist compendia of the saints' lives, especially the *Caturaśītisiddhapravṛtti* (Lives of the Eighty-four Siddhas), attributed to Abhayadattaśrī. This work must be handled carefully, however, and the present work emphasizes instead the far greater number of individual hagiographies that have circulated in India, China, and Tibet.

As conceived, therefore, this work is an analysis of factors and contexts in the generation of the vehicle of secret spells, a movement specifically grounded in the Buddhist experience of the sixth to twelfth centuries in India. Even though the development of this form of Buddhist spirituality was clearly influenced by the manifold and dramatic transformations in India's culture, the complexity of the context has not been fully considered to date. Certainly, several excellent studies have been written on its literature, ritual, and meditative praxis. However, Buddhological writing on India has sometimes neglected the context, a lament about the discipline rightly voiced by other Indologists. Thus a complete assessment requires that we consider the sociopolitical matrices of the Indian environment and their influences on the persons, texts, and traditions that came to constitute the new, ritually oriented Buddhist system.

To this end, chapter 2 covers the military and political background of early medieval India, with a view to Keegan's thesis that a culture of belligerence is the result of many factors and becomes itself the agent of social transformation, such that all facets of culture are subsequently influenced. We are fortunate that in the past several decades this period has received much attention, through the work of both Indian and European historians. Like esoteric Buddhism, the early medieval period has been something of an orphan of historians' sustained interest in the Gupta era, which is widely portrayed as India's golden age. In response, the chapter situates medieval India in its dynastic and military developments from the fall of the Guptas to the rise of the Delhi Sultanate, from around 500 to 1200 C.E. The chapter seeks to demonstrate that, precipitated by the idealization of the universal conqueror, medieval Indian politics and literature recast kingship into a form of divinity. One consequence of the kings' apotheosis was a concomitant feudalization of the gods in religious literature, such that the divinities become reformulated as royalty.

Chapter 3 addresses the Buddhist institutional and individual responses to the disintegration of previously supportive consortia in Indian society and its consequences for the Buddhist subculture. This chapter is concerned with the background of esoterism as a result of the convergence of both events external to Buddhist monasteries and decisions made within the Buddhist Mahayana intellectual and contemplative communities. The evidence reveals a declining capacity of Buddhists to direct political agendas or even establish parameters for much of their own discourse. The chapter identifies eight changes that mark the early medieval Buddhist cosmos, including the loss of guild-based patronage, the loss of the Kṛṣṇa River Valley and the lower Deccan plateau to Buddhist institutions and the decline of women's participation in Buddhist activities at almost all levels. They further extend to the development of philosophical skepticism, the espousal of non-Buddhist epistemological axioms, and the rise of large Buddhist monastic establishments. Finally, we find the development of an institutionally based form of Buddhist esoterism and the phenomenon of the Perfected *(siddha)*, the new variety of Buddhist saint. Chapter 3 examines the first six of these changes in the context of the medieval Indian world.

Chapter 4 continues with a consideration of the emergence of institutional esoterism. It argues that esoteric Buddhism is the most politicized form to evolve in India. This chapter proposes that the defining metaphor for esoteric Buddhism is that of the monk or practitioner becoming the Supreme Overlord *(rājādhirāja)* or the Universal Ruler *(cakravartin)*. An examination of the issue of consecration rites providing ritual access to maṇḍalas, and their origin in the realpolitik of the seventh century, forms much of the discussion in this chapter. The position of Vajrapāṇi as the mythic guardian and military agent of the new doctrine is examined through the lens of literature. The chapter proceeds with an brief discussion of the new canon accepted by Buddhist institutions, the *vidyādhara-piṭaka* (Sorcerer's Basket). A paradigmatic example of the new monk, in the eighth century person of Buddhaguhya, is viewed through a fragment of his surviving letter to a Tibetan king and his received hagiography. Finally, esoteric Buddhism is seen as an attempt to sacralize the medieval world, with the Buddhists seeking to transform the political paradigms into vehicles for sanctification.

Chapter 5 begins to investigate the world of Buddhist Perfected *(siddha)* and its ideological and cultural landscape. The chapter examines the background of sainthood in Buddhism and related systems. Previous models of this variety of Buddhist saint are considered, but alternative models are presented to explain the complex interaction between Śaivas, Śāktas, and the emerging Buddhist siddha subculture. The development of the new siddha goal—articulated in an ideological context that included outcaste, village, and tribal peoples—is examined through the surviving documents, epigraphy, and modern tribal ethnography. In the area of religion, particular attention is given to the successful Śaivite and Śākta orders: the Lakulīśa Pāśupatas, the Kāpālikas and the Kaulas, in terms of their contributions and discontinuities. The siddhas understood themselves placed within arrangements of imagined and real geography, and these schematisms are briefly discussed. The question of variety is considered as well, with the siddhas revealing a greater behavioral variation than monks, probably as a consequence of their irregular involvement with the socializing milieus of the Buddhist monasteries or princely courts.

Chapter 6 addresses the questions of language and scripture. The rise of new forms of Buddhist literature, principally that classified as *mahāyoga* and *yoginī tantra*, is examined, especially with regard to its use of sexual images and coded language. I look at the earliest siddha narratives of scriptural revelation and argue that siddha scriptural composition is best described by interactive and social, rather than individualistic, models of authorship. The earliest document on the myth of Indrabhūti is featured, demonstrating lay siddhas' scriptural transmission and their proclivity for ritual performance. A classic instance of extreme language in the *Buddhakapāla-tantra* is taken as a test case for the apologetic that all esoteric language is secret, with the commentators' lack of hermeneutic consensus as indicative of this position's difficulties. The communication through secret signs and coded language is discussed in light of the multiple sources, such as the *Sarvabuddhasamāyoga-tantra*, that discuss such materials, and a Dravidian or tribal element is posited. Moreover, because of the siddhas' employment of new languages, sociolinguistic issues of function, bilingualism, diglossia, and related questions are broached. The chapter concludes with a discussion of models of humor and play in siddha scriptures and hagiographies.

Chapter 7 examines siddhas and monks in communities, both imagined and, so far as we can understand, real. As an idealized community, the maṇḍala form is reexamined, and one variety of siddha maṇḍala appears drawn from earlier goddess temple arrangements. The idealized communities are also seen in the layout of the eight cemeteries. This latter, in turn, precipitates questions of numbering, particularly the emphasis on the number eighty-four, which is seen in some of the compendia of siddha narratives. This curious number, and most other siddha formulae, appears to have their grounding in village organizational units, which were developed for the purpose of political administration and taxation. In view of ascertaining real communities, Vitapāda's record describing the early ninth-century congregations experienced by Buddhajñānapāda is presented, as well as an early eleventh-century description of Nāropā. The chapter continues with the codes for siddha socialization and Indrabhūti's discussion of the sacramental process of the tantric feast. Internal critiques of siddha behavior are also examined. Finally, the chapter tests the model of esoteric Buddhism fielded in chapter 4 and seeks to demonstrate that a shift of signification occurred. Analogous to the metaphor of the practitioner's becoming the Supreme Overlord, Buddhist siddhas seemed to espouse a goal of kingship and dominion over the sorcerers *(vidyādhara)* and the gods themselves.

Chapter 8 offers a summation about the nature of Buddhists' contested domains. Its survey seeks to reintegrate the Buddhist developments into the period's wider culture. The book concludes with an appendix listing the important early medieval Pāśupata sites with their approximate dates.

At the outset, I have been encouraged to disclose the topics not included in this work, and this seemed good advice. Many readers might naturally expect that a book on esoteric Buddhism would include a detailed discussion of its rites and yogic practices. Other works, however, have provided excellent descriptions of specific rituals and their rationales, and we may anticipate many more studies in the near future. The available coverage is particularly good in the case of late Indian works popular with Tibetans, such as the *Hevajra Tantra*, the *Guhyasamāja*, the *Kālacakra*, and the six yogas attributed to the siddha Nāropā.[3] Increasingly, too, works dedicated to the esoteric forms found in medieval China and Japan have been written at a very sophisticated level. Likewise, individual textual studies and translations have been compiled with excellent results, and we can anticipate even better examples as more Sanskrit texts are brought to light. Discrete ritual systems, such as the fire sacrifice *(homa)*, have been given some consideration and examined in specific studies of lineages and terminology.[4] However, since the genesis for all these activities, ideas, doctrines, rituals, and behaviors arose in the context of early medieval India, it would seem important to provide a frame story for the vehicle of these interesting and influential Indian masters.

HABITS OF THE HEART, DEDUCTIVE PREMISES, AND BUDDHIST INHIBITIONS

Such an attempt at religious history is not without difficulties. The documentation available is elusive, difficult, incomplete, and highly charged in metaphysical presuppositions. Modeling the genesis, development, efflorescence, and success of the esoteric system will challenge our understanding at virtually every level. However, some of our best tools have been called into question through a variety of factors. Three categories of theoretical obstacles have impeded our understanding of esoteric Buddhist history. The first might be called a habit of scholarship, the way that Buddhist studies research has tended to avoid the historical evaluation of early medieval Buddhism, despite a plethora of sources and evidence. Second, the rhetorical statements of some modern theoreticians, especially those questioning the epistemological or ethical validity of historical inquiry, have disquieted classical Indology. Finally, the epistemological claims to exclusivity by the Buddhist tradition itself have caused some serious scholars to pause in their inquiry, often in hopes that the tradition will respond to the challenge of critical method with an indigenous alternative. These three factors appear to have cast a pall over the historiography of medieval Indian Buddhist traditions generally. As a result, I would like to employ the balance of the introduction to discuss a few observations on both theory and methodology. The purpose of this analysis is simply to suggest the strengths of the humanist historical methods generated during the Florentine Renaissance of the fourteenth to fifteenth centuries and their bearing on the contemporary study of other cultures.

Scholarly habits, once ingrained, are difficult to modify, especially when they have yielded such apparent treasures in the study of Indian and Buddhist history: edited texts, linguistic descriptions, lexicons, and the like. One of the most pervasive habits is the search for origins, however these origins are identified or articulated. Source privileging is perhaps an outgrowth of the Judaic heritage and the position of *Genesis* in religious literature. It may also be the result of a similar fascination found in Greek literature, at least since the *Theogony* of Hesiod. Beyond these, the emphasis on beginnings in Indian historiography was fueled by the curious assessment of India as essentially "unchanging" since time immemorial. This stance has been supported by both the Brahmanical doctrines of eternal religion *(sanātana-dharma)* and by the colonial recasting of the Hellenistic dictum concerning the transport of enlightenment to the benighted barbarians.

In the case of the Buddhist tradition, it was exacerbated by the European post-Enlightenment ideology of a religious decline over time and valorized by the indigenous Buddhist doctrine of the degradation of the true law *(saddharmavipralopa)*. Paradoxically, according to this reading, India was a static society, but one in which the great religious figures—Buddha, Śaṅkara, and so on—had been increasingly misunderstood by their followers, revealing a presumption that religious change can only be for the worse. Thus the purportedly unchanging nature of Indian society was being gradually eroded by the obtuse and ritual-bound excesses of those followers of the great religions who perverted the true message of the founders, misled the masses, and caused the disintegration of society. Behind this scenario is the equally sustaining perspective that civilizations either progress or decline in the face of superior cultures—all good social Darwinism. As actually applied, the model precipitated the search for the least corrupt level of culture. Consequently, British and European historiography has emphasized the *Ṛg Veda* (the oldest scripture), the life of the Buddha (the founder of Buddhism), the activities of Aśoka (the first emperor of South Asia), the composition of the Pāli canon (purportedly the oldest scripture), the advent of Islam, and so forth.

Specifically Buddhological writing has occasionally suffered from the supposition that the rise of literary and institutional systems occurs with scant concern for the social world. According to this model, developments in the doctrines or meditative traditions of Buddhism occur principally or exclusively because of internal circumstances. So, the reasons for the occurrence of the doctrine of emptiness espoused in the *Prajñāpāramitā* (Perfection of Insight) scriptures or the elaborations on meditative practice concomitant with the bodhisattva vow are simply Buddhist considerations without recourse to non-Buddhist discourse or the sociopolitical context. Such assessments are an understandable reaction to the earlier proclivity of some authors—Jean Przyluski as an example—to seek for indigenous developments primarily as the result of the influence of other religious traditions.[5] In this reductive line of thought, Maitreya, for example, must have been the recast Mitra; Amitābha (or Vairocana) was the reformulation of Ahurā Mazda, and so forth. These directions are developments of a diffusionist paradigm, in which portions of religious expressions—doctrines, ideas, or rituals—are presumed to be taken as whole pieces from other systems. Diffusionist models were the stuff of nineteenth-century anthropology, with Franz Boas and his followers the primary exponents, and they had an electric effect on religious studies since the time of Frazer's *Golden Bough*.

The understandable response to such unsophisticated diffusionist models was to accept the idea of indigenous development as the *sine qua non* of Buddhological writing, and certain undeniable realities motivated these directions. First, the Buddhist scriptural corpus is simply enormous and unwieldy. The principle of social economy suggests that internal causation be examined before external causation. Since the received canons have not been entirely explored, some feel safe in simply continuing the arduous procedure of understanding internal Buddhist systems. There is much to be said for this philologically sound and historically fundamental procedure, especially as the canons are still terra incognita in so many areas. Thus we can all profit admirably from the astute philological work of those who attempt the difficult and frustrating task of textual editions, sources, and relations.

Second, Buddhist texts were uniquely the objects of the greatest translation efforts humankind has ever witnessed. There is simply no precedent for or analogue to the translations made into Chinese and Tibetan during more than a millennium of effort. Concomitant with these translations, moreover, is an enormous quantity of historical material, chronological data (true and suspect), putative authorship, differing recensions, textual strategies, and so forth. Buddhist studies has only begun to unravel some of the thorny issues relating to the translation of the texts, canon relationships, authorship questions, to but begin a long list of desiderata. Yet it is equally clear that, out of all the vast wealth of religious composition produced in India before the solidification of Islamic power, Buddhist texts and authors enjoy a far greater sense of chronological identity than those of any other Indian tradition.

The irony of these trajectories is that the period of greatest chronological confidence, the medieval period, is paradoxically the era most neglected. Although this period has received attention from Sinologists, Tibetologists, and Singhalese specialists, little analogous exploration has been found in the history of Indian Buddhism. Indeed, the emphasis has been almost entirely on the first or the second half-millennia (500 B.C.E. – 1 – 500 C.E.) of Indian Buddhist history, rather than on the period in which the manuscripts, translations, authorities, and scriptural formulae were, in so many cases, actually produced.

This neglect appears grounded in the assessment that the forms of Buddhism made popular in medieval centers were questionable, if not degenerate, as their opponents have claimed. Here, the diffusionist model is sometimes accepted and posed as a presumptive textual question: to what extent do Buddhist esoteric scriptures *(tantra)* rely on Śaiva compositions? This question is posed in a text-critical manner, which presupposes the unilateral borrowing of Buddhist materials from Śaiva systems and has been recently reaffirmed by Alexis Sanderson.[6] However, while the study of Buddhist esoterism can sometimes localize the composition of a text to within decades, Śaiva tantras can, in most cases, be speculatively placed in the neighborhood of centuries, with Abhinavagupta's *Tantrāloka* (c. 1000 C.E.) being the major watershed in determining the evidence for a specific Śaiva work.

Little wonder that attempts at the history of esoteric Buddhism, as seen in the efforts of David Snellgrove and MATSUNAGA Yukei, de-emphasize the diffusionist ideal. In their excellent descriptive works, they endeavor to explain the received system found in the documents, yielding an analysis with a diminished Indian historical—social, economic, political—horizon.[7] The primary direction taken by these and other scholars is to discuss the connections between the various texts of the tradition, to our collective benefit in understanding these works. The traditional form of textual analysis is concerned with the relationships of Buddhas in maṇḍalas, the identity of mantras, and the stratification of texts. However, to date this direction has often yielded textual descriptions with a curiously disembodied sense of authorship, and we are left asking questions of audience, language, teaching environments, or patronage. Yet these compelling questions cannot be entirely ignored, and YORITOMI and Strickmann have shown that even their limited movement in this direction can yield extraordinary results.[8]

Moving beyond data analysis, forms of historical writing embedded in literary ideals have come to influence much of the humanities in Europe, the United States, and India. Although earlier systems were structuralist in nature, later authors espoused poststructuralist or postmodernist ideals. Extreme proponents of both have been less concerned with evidence than establishing hegemony and creating a space in which the fundamentals of historical epistemology have negotiated authority.[9] For such authors, the affirmation of objective validity is suspect and objects—such as epigraphs, texts, manuscripts, and material finds—lack foundational realities.[10] Instead, they speak of power differentials and the arrangement of the episteme. This is because postmodernists articulate a turn to the subject, some to the point that Dirlik—himself a postmodernist—has written of the "crisis of historical consciousness" in our ability to speak with validity about the past.[11]

Moreover, it has become part of one intellectual trend to assume that the eighteenth to twentieth centuries were dedicated to the purpose of providing us with a distorted perception of the world, so that Euro-American colonialism could move forward in its need for universal power. This proposal supposes that all traditional academic writing is grounded in, and tainted by, an imperialistic civilization whose discourse embodies its method of securing power over the colonial objects. Such rhetoric, particularly among intellectuals from the Middle East and India, employs the position of the Orientalist critique, a manner of dismissing Western critical evaluation of non-Western realities, particularly historical realities. Motivated by the works of Edward Said and others, critics of Orientalism have defined it as including the academic persons (Orientalists), the style of thought, and the corporate institution of the academy. Irrespective of method or direction, we are informed, those of the West cannot help but express the power differential between India and the Euro-American academy. During the empire, this was done to define the West as essentially different from and legitimately in dominion over the Orient. Since history and Indology arose at this time, neither can be extracted from a discourse of modernity that expresses power over Asia, if only because of the media and geopolitical realities of the present. Members of the Subaltern Studies collective like Chakrabarty have furthermore maintained that "'Europe' remains the sovereign, theoretical subject of all histories."[12] According to this idea, any discipline claiming all of humanity as its domain is by definition Eurocentric. Thus not only the person of the foreign historian but the very discipline of history itself colonizes India.

Characteristically, the disciplines of religious studies and Buddhist studies have lagged behind other disciplines in their engagement of these issues.[13] So, while Brennan can confidently mark the passing of Orientalist critiques in other areas, such is not the case for the study of Indian religion, in part because religion remains at the heart of the modern nationalist agenda.[14] The immediate consequence of many of these challenges is a turn toward the subject, in which the character or intentions of the historian become the topic of discussion. At its best, this procedure can result in a productive reflexiveness on the process of historical composition. Too often, however, the redirection has meant that European or American scholars working in the field of Indology or religious studies have been called on to justify virtually every aspect of their discipline.

Indeed, some historians of Indian thought and culture, excited by new ideas and interested in the application of usable theoretical systems to the data at hand, find the politicizing rhetoric of the current field unhelpful. The problem is not that new theories of historical writing, however challenging, are not welcome. Theoretical systems—structuralist, postmodernist, critical, or some other flavor—often provide the opportunity to reassess our sources, our methods, our areas of investigation, to mention but a few of the many fields made richer by the discussion.[15] Some of these are used in this study to examine the intertextuality of several of our documents and the larger literary field.[16] Interesting new directions—including Subaltern Studies—have made our discussion more nuanced in its revisiting of the issues of agency and authority. The dismantling of essentialist formulations of group structure and identity is most welcome, although some authors seem to erect other monoliths in their place. Moreover, issues of iconicity and symbolic representations have fundamentally profited by the observations forwarded in poststructuralist works.

However, we must also admit that theoreticians' sweeping claims to authority have inhibited aspects of the historical investigation of medieval India. Sheldon Pollock, for example, has written on the malaise of purpose afflicting Indologists as a result of Orientalist critiques.[17] Those of us wishing to employ whatever ideas and methods that we may, have found ourselves rebuffed for not committing ourselves to a position. Patterson, for instance, has maintained that historiography without theoretical commitment is equivalent to criminal assault and armed robbery.[18] Yet we can also see problems with such claims to authority, for even Abou-El-Haj has called attention to the fact that some theory-based scholars lack the linguistic ability to evaluate their texts in the primary languages.[19] Seemingly, then, one consequence of the new authority of theory is found in a concomitant erosion in practice, so that we find in some theory-based scholars a weakened comprehension of the original documents in the languages of their composition.

In the cases of both structuralist and postmodernist systems, Richard Evans and others have provided a balanced response. He has affirmed that historians should remain open to the discussion while seeing that sometimes certain authors demonstrate a confusion between their theories, on the one hand, and method and evidence, on the other.[20] In postmodern diction, we frequently hear of an author's methodology, when in fact a theoretical agenda is being specified. As Richard Etlin observes in the realm of artistic value, poststructuralist authors sometimes project their claims into a frame of their own creation.[21] Conversely, Murray Murphey has taken a different approach, by providing a systematic review and defense of historical epistemology, based on the findings of cognitive science.[22] Here, we see that some categories appear natural to us as a species and are cross-culturally part of our perceptual process. Thus relativist agendas seem weakened in their criticism about the foundations of knowledge, for humans appear to have some common categories of perception.

Similarly, analyses of Said and his followers have showed that many Orientalist critics are engaging in an action that precludes the possibility of knowledge or the representation of cultural entities, particularly by foreigners.[23] In the hands of nationalists, the agenda has been extended to guard the history or topics of non-Western cultures from critical assessment.[24] Orientalist critiques sometimes have as their covert agenda the preservation of traditional hierarchies, with the sense of history as cultural property. Whereas some British colonial authors, to use an example drawn from the literature on Orientalism, certainly treated India as the colonial Other, that capacity assisted the maintenance of the critical distance required to engage in crucial historical research. This has given us the disciplines of historical linguistics and sociolinguistics, developed the first Indic library catalogues, inaugurated excavations, begun a rigorous examination of Indic epigraphy and a systematic numismatics, and developed both a typology of the history of architecture and the stylistic classification of sculpture, to name but a few areas enriched by their efforts.[25] The individual personas of these pioneers were not universally laudable—they were sometimes fraudulent and occasionally criminal—but their results constituted the basis for much of later Indology.[26] Moreover, with the commodification of the postcolonial critique by Indians and others in academic positions in the West, we might wonder whether ethical questions are those of foreigners alone.[27] At some point, it would seem advantageous to dissociate the personality issues of British, French, and German Orientalists from the discipline of Indology, but that remains anathema to some critics, who propose an essentialism in the discipline while denying it in their own culture.[28] Even those promoting a renovation in the study of Indian religion, such as Richard King, have found themselves struggling against the categories of postcolonialist discourse.[29]

Analogous in scope is the opinion—sometimes voiced by Buddhists—that we are not in the position to really understand the ideas and propositions of Buddhist scripture or representative Buddhist authors unless and until we experience complete awakening. The argument is predicated on the ideology that the experience indicated by the texts in question is so profound that only a meditator passing through the "lightening-like concentration" *(vajropama-samādhi)* could possibly comprehend the true import of the material. This idea holds that the Buddhist scriptures are a natural expression of the enlightened condition, so only those partaking of that condition can understand their meaning. We are instructed that great scholarship is but a step leading to higher knowledge, and the best model of scholarship is to learn the texts accurately, but not to question such historical incidentals as authorship, composition, contradiction, discontinuity, and so forth. Especially, we are encouraged to consider all scripture as true scripture, so that scriptural works remain as canonical in Los Angeles as they were in Lhasa or Beijing.

Apologetic statements to the contrary, Buddhist exegetic systems themselves provide us with the rationale for understanding scriptural materials before our own awakening, if we are ever so blessed. We may recall that virtually all schools of Buddhism uphold the trifurcation of insight: insight is constructed of learning, reflection on the learned material, and finally its cultivation until the terrace of omniscience is attained *(śruta-cintā-bhāvanā-mayī prajñā)*. This trifurcation indicates that both a thorough grounding in the textual tradition and a critical reflection on its propositions are held to be of exceptional value. Indeed, Mātṛceta lauds the Buddha for his ability to withstand the scriptural imperative to test all doctrines, and *Dṛḍhramati reinforces Āryadeva's observation that doubt is the vehicle for entering the Mahayana.[30] Most Tibetophiles, for example, are unaware that there is an entire genre of Tibetan literature from the eleventh century forward that attempts to discuss and adjudicate what is legitimate Dharma and what is not *(chos dang chos min rab 'byed)*. Much discursive consideration and actual debate went into the articulation of canonical criteria and resulted in the exclusion of selected works from the canon. These discussions simply relied on the consensus and understanding of scholarly opinion, with minority voices being represented—in some ways similar to academic discourse today.

With or without orthodox approval, however, we should engage this material with the critical faculties at our disposal. We might separate this mode of address from that required by traditional Buddhism by understanding that reflexive historical awareness is different from direct spiritual experience. Historical understanding has the capacity to evaluate according to specific logical and linguistic structures, structures that are not transhistorical but are durable. These procedures are neither Buddhist nor specifically religious, but humanistic in origin and are elicited to some degree by the textual and artistic materials at our disposal in Tibet, India, Central Asia, and China. In its monastic or Asian context, Buddhist indigenous history and hagiography provide exemplars of behavior and sanctity for the individual communities, which could not survive without its legacy. For our purposes, though, both Buddhist literature and its related iconology demonstrate a concerted movement away from the personal to the prototypical, so that personalities are primarily considered valuable to the extent that they embody the characteristics defined by the tradition.[31] We can detect a movement toward synthetic forms approved by tradition and away from the personality of the individual.

Thus, in a sense, these three inhibitory positions are similarly essentialist: the method of addressing the early medieval material is predetermined, with little regard to the nature of the period. For those undaunted by these positions—not secured by habits of scholarship, unmoved by theoretical rhetoric, or not intimidated by traditional Buddhist disapproval—still, there is the problem of ethical viability. Philologists may wonder why historians cannot simply be content with the positivism that some presume in their manuscripts. Humanist historians are looked at askance by their more fashionable colleagues, who are only satisfied when a commitment to theory has been voiced. Finally, they are considered outside the pale by Buddhist apologists, for whom any questioning of the received tradition is an attack on the foundations of the sacred Dharma. All too often, this has left some historians apologizing for not being current, committed, or narrowly philological. Yet the curiosity of the above positions is that they are articulated without an understanding of the matrix from which the historians' craft was generated.

PETRARCH'S METHOD: *ARTES HISTORICAE* IN THE RENAISSANCE

For those of us interested in modern Indian intellectual developments, the confrontational gestures of some modernist historians is perplexing. These challenges to traditional historical representations may indeed be desirable on issues of colonial or postcolonial Indian history, but many of the most basic questions for the ancient and medieval eras have yet to be addressed. Orientalist critiques, in particular, tend to posit India as a constructed artifice, with little objective content, but such a strategy is unhelpful if the fundamentals have been systematically occluded. Authors espousing this critique identify even the fundamental epistemology necessary for a constructive contribution as irredeemably Eurocentric and colonial, for it was generated during the Enlightenment, at the moment of European expansion on the cusp of modernity. According to this assessment, the study of religion was an extension of a secular, scientific rationality that was presumed to be universalistic and value free. Yet, we are assured, the Enlightenment's discourse was really an attempt to enshrine Eurocentrism in its position of cardinal authority. Thus we are to accept that the very foundations of Indology are inspired by the colonial movement, and other civilizations need not submit to its hegemonic presumptions.[32]

However, another perspective exists that is both fruitful and constructive. One direction is to recover the intellectual ground before the eighteenth century, to see whether the Enlightenment was in fact the generative matrix of the Indology's grammar.[33] While it is true that the study of India really began during the late eighteenth century, the bases for the critical study of religion started with the foundations of historical writing and are intimately linked to it. The development of modern critical history is the direct result of the humanists of the Italian Renaissance, beginning with Francesco Petrarcha (1304–1374). Their task was to look at their own religious legacy in their own country, with a focus on the city of Rome.[34] These gentlemen did not employ the generalized sense of humanist used in the modern period, a person exercising empathy and reason in acting for the common welfare and dignity of humanity. Rather, they were scholars of *studia humanitatis:* the collective disciplines of grammar (we would say classical philology), rhetoric, history, poetry, and moral philosophy. These fields were first generated in the salons and college of Florence during the latter half of the fourteenth century and spread throughout Northern Europe. *Studia humanitatis* is most explicitly distinguished from *studia divinitatis*, a differentiation excluding theology from the humanities. The first creation of critical history (and its related methods) was begun by Petrarch and reached its conclusion in the late Renaissance with the 1566 publication of Jean Bodin's *Methodus ad facilem historiarum cognitionen.* Collectively, the authors of this period laid the foundations and surveyed the fundamentals.

Petrarch's development of humanistic historical ideals, which eventually were to be called collectively *artes historicæ,* was fostered by a romantic fascination with Roman antiquity and antiquities. He was not the first to be so enthralled. Guidebooks to the city had flourished in the twelfth century. An otherwise unknown English traveler, the "magister Gregorius," was sufficiently taken in to compile a "guidebook" to the city as it was understood through the received wisdom and legends maintained by the cardinals of the church.[35] Preeminent within this genre, however, was the composition of the canon Benedict of St. Peters, the *Mirabilia Urbis Romæ* (The Marvels of the Roman City). Benedict's task was to present Rome as the "crown of the world" *(caput mundi)*, with the remaining edifices and myths of the monuments mixed together in a blend of the legends of Rome, the works of Ovid, speculative identification, passions of the martyrs, personal observation, and hagiographies of the saints. Benedict was, by all accounts, learned after his period, but his portrayal was clearly a panegyric to the city of Romulus. Beyond the guidebooks, Petrarch's enthusiasm for antiquity was also foreshadowed by two jurists in Padua, Lovato Lovati (1241–1309) and his nephew Rolando da Piazozola.[36]

Petrarch, however, was categorically different from these precursors by his vision of a Rome in which the pagan fall was not the inauguration of the Church Triumphant. In 1337, he and his friend Giovanni Colonna di San Vito strolled through the ruins, only to begin the long process of discovery precipitated by the realization that behind both texts and visible remains lay the traces of prior, unknown remnants of civilization. Thomas Greene has articulated the process:

> To say that Petrarch "discovered" history means, in effect, that he was the first to notice that classical antiquity was very different from his own medieval world, and the first to consider antiquity more admirable. . . . Thus Petrarch took more or less alone the step an archaic society must take to reach maturity: he recognized *the possibility of a cultural alternative.* With that step he established the basis of a radical critique of his culture: not the critique that points to a subversion of declared ideals, but rather the kind that calls ideals themselves into question.[37]

Petrarch was aided in this process by the cultivation of a mental habit to look to other times for personal resolution. We can certainly be sympathetic to his proclivity, given the extravagance of Pope John XXII and the corruption of the Papal court at Avignon, to which Petrarch was attached early in his life. Indeed, his repugnance with his own period is framed by both his intermittent involvement with Papal politics and the Great Plague of 1348. In his autobiographical *Posteritati* (Letter to Posterity), he demonstrates that seldom was there a person less directly a product of the zeitgeist:

> I devoted myself, though not exclusively, to the study of ancient times, since I always disliked our own period; so that, if it hadn't been for the love of those dear to me, I should have preferred being born in any other age, forgetting this one; and I always tried to transport myself mentally to other times.[38]

Although it is not clear that anyone can be entirely extracted from his time, Petrarch's originality was not simply a negative response to his period, for this would have turned him into another crusader like Savonarola. Instead, he extended his habit of mental transportation into his literary endeavors. Not only did he write a letter to posterity introducing himself, but also he indulged his affection for the classical authors—most particularly Cicero and

Augustine—with regularly imagined dialogues between himself and them in a transport of romanticism. Yet he was equally capable of clear-sighted philology, correctly ascertaining that an ostensible donation by Caesar to the Hapsburgs was a medieval Austrian forgery.[39] And even beyond his quotations and considerations of Latin inscriptions, Petrarch established the standard for Renaissance numismatists.

The heirs of Petrarch cultivated and extended his methods in their fascination with Roman antiquities.[40] Influenced by Petrarch, Giovanni Boccaccio sought Greek and Latin manuscripts, epigraphic rubbings, and Greek instruction, high and low. A Paduan physician, Giovanni Dondi dell' Orologio, visited Rome in 1375 and was so excited by the remains that he began to make physical measurements of the ancient buildings, along with copious notes. Coluccio Salutati (1331–1406), the great humanist bibliophile, not only collected more than eight hundred manuscripts for his personal library but brought the study of inscriptions and the analysis of Latin orthography up to the numismatic standard already established by Petrarch. Salutati also convinced the Byzantine scholar Manuel Chrysoloras (c. 1350–1414) to teach Greek in Florence during 1396–1400, so that the humanists might have recourse to accomplished Greek scholarship and a direct reading of ancient Greek philosophers for the first time.[41] "Anonimo," the anonymous author of the *Tractatus de Rebus Antiquis et Situ Urbis Romæ* of c. 1411, began to employ the Constantinian regionary catalogues to understand Roman topography; these catalogues were to become more fully exploited by Signorili around 1425 in his *Descriptio urbis Romæ*.[42] In the analysis of various levels of construction, through the differentiation of materials and procedures evident in the ancient gates of Rome, Poggio Bracciolini (1380–1459) virtually invented the concept of stratigraphy and made public his results in *De varietate fortunæ* in 1448.[43]

Because of the humanist emphasis on the employment of the Latin of the classics, a foreshadowing of historical sociolinguistics—articulating levels of glossia—was considered in a controversy between positions represented by Leonardo Bruni (1370–1444) and Flavio Biondo. In 1435 these two gentlemen debated the nature of colloquial Latin of the classical period. Phillip Jacks contextualizes the circumstances of the argument:

> Biondo posited the theory that the ancient Romans had spoken a single language, of which modern Latin was an approximation. Through regional dialects it was possible to detect how classical Latin had been pronounced before the barbarian incursions. Bruni . . . reasoned that there must have been both a colloquial form of Latin *(sermo)* spoken among the plebeians, and a

> more literary form *(latine litterateque loqui)* understood only among the educated patriciate.[44]

But, if Biondo was interested in language, he was absorbed in archaeology. Through Biondo, the archaeology of the Renaissance achieved its greatest progress with his *Roma instaurata,* completed 1444–1446. Biondo's achievement is summarized by Roberto Weiss:

> Altogether, with the *Roma instaurata* it was now possible to have a reasonable idea of ancient Rome, not only from a topographical standpoint, but also as far as its growth and the functions of its buildings were concerned. Here, in this work, the historian reveals himself side by side with the archaeologist, the student of ancient institutions with the humanist who has the classics at his fingertips.[45]

Biondo's investigations were to last through the 1460s and were particularly concerned with the relationship of topography to demography and ancient institutions.

All these accomplishments of the humanists had yet to be formalized in a treatise on historiography. Cicero's definition of history was simple and expressed as the validation of a lesser discipline: for Cicero, history was "the witness of time, the life of memory, the mistress of life and the messenger of antiquity."[46] George of Trebizond, the Greek scholar who brought the study of Greek rhetorical treatises to the Renaissance, understood history as the accurate description of past events, rather than either the events themselves or their recollection. Certainly, the position of historical writing in classical antiquity, whether in the Greek of Thucydides or the Latin of Tacitus, had much to do with the emerging Renaissance awareness of models of good history, even if this understanding was not well articulated in historical criticism. The historical description, distinguished from other arts by its verisimilitude to the past, was to be chronological and to focus on causes and motivations, as well as on the consequences of acts.[47] Trebizond's sketch of history's goals—separate from rhetoric or poetry—was to be reproduced through the humanist movement of the fifteenth century.

Jean Bodin, however, provided the first systematic methodological treatise, his *Methodus ad facilem historiarum cognitionen* of 1566. A jurist by avocation, Bodin had already produced a short treatise on jurisprudence with his *Juris universi distributo* (1559), but elected to compose a better analysis of the insufficiencies of medieval law, complete with a synthesis of juridical experience, the *Methodus*.[48] In it, Bodin sought to reform juristic science into universal law, since "The best part of universal law resides in history" *(in historia juris universi pars optima est)*.[49] The procedure outlined by Bodin included reflections on the writing of history, the analysis of sources (both primary and secondary—an innovative distinction), questions of bias and partiality, as well as issues of reliability and conflicting testimony.[50]

This seemingly lengthy digression, for which I thank the reader's patience, is actually a rudimentary sketch of the development of historical and archaeological methods. The goal was not the affirmation of colonial authority, let alone Orientalism, for it began a century and a half before the Treaty of Tordesillas (June 7, 1494) enshrined the Portuguese and Spanish claims to colonial authority. The subject of *Artes Historicæ* was not Europe, but the city of Rome and, by extension, the ancient Greek and Roman world. Thus the ethical basis of historical understanding is grounded in the experience of Florentine humanists who were attempting to comprehend their own religious and cultural past. Similarly, it marked not the inauguration of modernity but the advent of the Renaissance.

It is instructive to realize that most of the above gentlemen were trained in law—either civil or Canon—or were themselves noted jurists. Their fascination with Rome was in some sense a subset of this legal and ethical involvement: Roman law provided a universalistic approach to the problems of the idiosyncratic regulations of small communities and the difficulties that travelers, businessmen, scholars, and others encountered in the morass of conflicting rules. Yet the replacement of the many standards of jurisprudence and the multiple bodies of statutory decisions by a universal Roman law would destroy confidence in local precedent and the force of individual legal decisions. Law, like good history, must be concerned with evidence, testimony, doubt, probability, uncertainty, conflicting positions, and a reflexiveness on past patterns of behavior. Like history, law also proposes an ideal of impartiality, even if realized only in its absence, as a goal never absolutely attained yet never entirely relinquished. Both history and law may be twisted to evil ends as well, and both have been turned to the purpose of oppression and enslavement. Finally, like law, history must be content with a continuing degree of uncertainty, never to claim that it has rendered the perfect decision, for new evidence may—even when all the principals are deceased—render the verdict incorrect, although it appeared an ironclad decision at the time.

Since the study of medieval Indian Buddhism has lagged so perilously behind other disciplines, it might be appropriate to reassert the bases of historical epistemology, a proposal with which postmodernist authors like Dirlik can agree.[51] Our Florentine predecessors had the good sense to identify four primary sources of evidence: first, we must consider documents, primary and secondary, and assess as required the nature of their manuscript and printing histories. Engaged as we are in the study of a religious tradition, it is insufficient to limit ourselves to the documents internal to the Indian, Chinese, or Tibetan Buddhist traditions, for these are internal documents. We must also consider the evidence that might accrue from external sources not recognized as legitimate within the religion, but authentic nonetheless. With the unbelievable wealth of documents at our disposal, of course, a degree of circumspect limitation is necessary, and herein lies the value of our accepting the counsel of both traditional and modern scholarship on essential or important texts.[52]

Second, we must consider the epigraphic remains of the period, again acknowledging the plethora of epigraphs and the reality that many are unobtainable, either because they remain unpublished or because the sources in which they were originally published have been irretrievably lost, and the original stones broken or the plates sold. Third, the archaeology of important finds should be considered, even though many of the most important sites have had the misfortune of their excavators' indolence, so excavation reports have frequently never been filed. Indeed, many is the time that Indian historians have lectured members of the Archaeological Survey of India on the necessity for excavation reports, with less than complete success. Fourth, the coins from the period may be of assistance, although, as we shall see, there is a paucity of coinage in Indian Buddhist areas during the early medieval period.

To these four sources already identified during the Renaissance, we might add a source specific to India—the sealings from the monasteries, imperial personages, and important merchants that provide so much excellent data. Finally, Petrarch and his followers did not have to investigate the modern culture of Italy to understand Rome, for they were Italians. Since the time of Herodotus' description of the Skythians in his *Histories,* however, participant-observer data have proved of extraordinary value in assessing foreign cultures, whether accrued by the historian, by anthropologists, or both, as in the case of this book. We cannot underestimate the value to the historian of learning the colloquial languages of these cultures, living in villages, or (in our case) in Buddhist monasteries. Indeed, many Indologists would affirm that they did not truly understand much of this complex society until they had lived and worked there among the descendants of those very people under investigation.

TROPES, HEURISTICS, AND OTHER DANGEROUS THINGS

If I may claim a method in my attempt to delineate the formative social factors of esoteric Buddhism in India, it is to use occasionally the model of the Renaissance recovery of the classical world as a trope for what must be done. In a real sense Petrarch, the Italian humanists, and their modern historians were wrestling with many of the same issues. They inherited a grand load of literature, much of which was indifferently understood or never examined, having lain dormant in monasteries and personal libraries for centuries. Many of the materials only survived in Latin translation; some had never been translated into any language. Their world system was inhabited by fabulous creatures and miraculous saints, witches and sacred sites, Emperors and gods, rituals and demons. The Church had skewed understanding of many translated texts—like the works of Aristotle—by appropriating them for unforeseen purposes, frequently in service of aristocratic values or noble families. The texts were written with a technical vocabulary, some of which had yet to be lexigraphically identified, while the sociolinguistics of the materials had still to be addressed. When the humanists began to examine the sources, like the *Miribilia,* for accuracy and conformity to the existing material remains, they discovered much inaccuracy and discontinuity in the process.

Mutatis mutandis, many of these parameters are encountered by one investigating medieval Indian Buddhism. The surviving texts—in Sanskrit, Tibetan, Old Bengali, Apabhraṃśa, and Chinese—have long rested in monasteries and personal libraries, seldom printed, infrequently catalogued, and read predicated on the accidents of history. Engagement of the literature has been based primarily on commitment to a lineage, and specific works are selected to the detriment of others. The printing of much of this material is adventitious: with the exception of the Chinese, no systematic printing was done before the eighteenth century, and much of it is still not effected. Little effort has been made to accurately associate the surviving archaeological sites with the literature of esoterism, and the development of historical consciousness in the tradition has been rather narrowly circumscribed. Tibetans, Newars, and Chinese have been occasionally critical in their evaluation of events within their own borders but infrequently toward India. The sociolinguistics of the materials have seldom been considered, as has the circumstance of modern ethnographic descriptions. Political and social realities, then, have been rarely applied to the formative process of much of this material, even though it has been examined in questions of its cross-cultural transmission to other countries. Systematic epigraphy of medieval Buddhist venues is virtually unknown and questions of critical assessment are held hostage to systems privileging hagiography over intelligent history.[53] Authors inquiring after Buddhist topics have sometimes examined Hindu materials only enough to refute them, as Hindu nationalists have themselves done with Buddhist texts.

In sum, I must confess that I find myself, like Petrarch, unable to take the literature at face value. Like adherents to all known religious systems, Buddhists have had a multidimensional relationship to their surrounding societies. External influences and sociopolitical realities are sometimes treated cavalierly in rhetoric, even while being incorporated through a systematic apologia of unfortunate necessity (skill in means: *upāyakauśalya*). Thus the sources for much of the doctrinal, ritual, and literary developments are hidden or ignored. Yet spirituality and its institutionalization seemingly cannot be reduced to naked politics, economics, or power. Even theory-based scholars like Dorothy Figueria and Richard King have begun to question whether prior theoretical models have not been overly reductionistic in their assumptions about some aspects of human behavior.[54] For its part, esoteric Buddhism and its hagiographical representations were not hatched on the back stairs of a Buddhist monastery a little after midnight, with the purpose of political dominion, economic gain, or the subordination of subalterns at all costs.[55]

Conversely, we should not err in the opposite direction, for esoteric Buddhism has a very strong political dimension that is occluded in the modern Buddhist apologia. We are often privy to the conversations between religious and political authorities, conversations determining the outcome of specific traditions or the exchange of ideas and power. Even a casual examination of the documents reveals that the economic and political context was influential, sometimes overwhelming so. Indeed, the records of these conversations are not the humble textual artifacts from the personal expressions of enlightened saints. When the eighth-century esoteric author Buddhaguhya, for example, replies to an invitation by the Tibetan emperor Trisong Detsen, he is not simply writing his reflections of the moment based on deep personal values.[56] Rather, he is rearticulating themes from the previous literature in Indian Buddhism on the epistles written to kings—whether by Mātṛceṭa to Kaniṣka or Nāgārjuna to the unidentified Sātavāhana monarch. These letters, in turn, are moments reflective of other discussions stretching back through the dialogues between kings and their counselors, the Buddha and Bimbisāra, the monk Nāgasena and the Indo-Greek ruler Menander. Moreover, they are indicative of the many anonymous conversations between Buddhist authorities and local tyrants or individual monks and imperial envoys since Buddhist institutions began to cast such great physical and intellectual shadows on the Indic landscape.

Similarly, kings appropriated Buddhist authority for reasons of both public authenticity and personal commitment, crowning themselves in the name of Dharma and vowing to uphold the teachings of the teacher. Such acts were performed even while the monarchs exercised a realpolitik that subverted the ethical and intellectual foundations of the tradition they evidently believed in and publicly claimed to embrace. Much of the history of Buddhism in the various civilizations of Asia revolved around monks' development of strategies to effectively counter, manage, and conform to political and economic realities that continually influenced the decision-making systems of Buddhist institutions. Even then, we should not be enticed into believing that Buddhist representatives were willing to sacrifice all ideals for the moment, or even that they were moderately successful in their endeavors. While reconfiguring their ideals and discourse in light of the models of the day, they had other competition and so frequently found themselves unwilling or incapable of soliciting the patronage that they may have desired or even desperately needed.

Indian Buddhists had, early on, developed a rhetoric of being outside the authority of the bureaucrats, rendering to Caesar that which was Caesar's only when absolutely necessary, so that canon law was supposed to supersede civil and criminal statutes in the cases of monks and nuns guilty of transgressions. Perhaps almost fatally, the Buddhist representatives believed their own doctrines of the separation of church and state, even while occasionally making exaggerated claims for royal patronage and, sometimes, catering to the whims of murderous despots. This doctrinal stance of Buddhist political and legal independence is seductively familiar to modern readers of Buddhist texts, well-schooled in Lockean ideology, even if its fundamental fallaciousness is readily apparent to those spending any length of time in Asian monasteries. Politics, economics, and Buddhism are not simply strange bedfellows but are symbolically and symbiotically related in so many aspects of intellectual and spiritual life. However, because there are no continuously surviving Indian Buddhist institutions, we all too often have believed uncritically that the Indic *Vinaya* texts have provided for us the whole picture of the religious system, even though, upon reflection, we can easily see that this is not and cannot have been true. Buddhist monasteries were not hermetically sealed and isolated from the outside world—indeed, if anything they frequently appear intensified microcosms of that very world in which they dwelt.

2

Prayers in the Palace, Swords in the Temple: Early Medieval India

[The earth itself] is being tortured by "Lords of Men"—they are specific to this era with their intrusive arrogance, crude cunning, insatiable appetites, and systematic insults to propriety in their base stupidity.[1]

—Yaśodharman's Mandasor Edict, c. 530 C.E.

And the maṇḍala of states is strewn only with allies and enemies. Yes, the world is supremely selfish—how could neutrality be found anywhere?[2]

—Kāmandaka's *Nītisāra* of the seventh to eighth century C.E.

If we are to understand the rise and victory of esoteric Buddhism, the early medieval period must be our initial focus, for this is the time—between the sixth and twelfth centuries—that mature Buddhist esoterism first appears in the available historical materials. The extent to which we can know its chronology is discussed below, but all our best indicators are in accord with the statement of the Chinese monk Wu-hsing, writing about 680 C.E., that the popularity of esoterism was a new event in India.[3] As seen in chapter 4, the Indian political systems defined models that were accepted and extended within the scriptures and rituals of the new Buddhist praxis. Accordingly, this chapter examines the political and military events of these several centuries and stresses the genesis of a climate of military and political opportunism. The importance of this new dimension is based on the observation of the military historian John Keegan that cultures of warfare fundamentally alter the nature and relationship of their component parts. Thus the activities of Indian princes were to have extraordinary consequences for all the aspects of early medieval Indian culture, from literature and ritual to government and the economy.

During the early medieval period, northern India, heretofore dominant or at least equal to the south in the military and political dynamics of the subcontinent, became for the first time subordinate in the energy and exuberance of the new period. Instead, South India and its Śaiva kings assumed center place and took the initiative in so many ways. First and foremost, this meant that northern polities were increasingly forced to submit to invidious raids on their territories, their wealth, and the safety of their cities. As a consequence, the great northern cities suffered a population decline, whereas emerging regional centers in Central and East India became increasingly important, with new families of modest roots taking control of previously tribal domains. Seeking legitimacy and identity, Indian kings from all areas began to increase their patronage of literature and to strategize their support for religion, searching for religious counselors that could bolster their political and military agendas. They also developed patronage relations with those who could validate their local aesthetics and valorize their locales. In the process, the uniformity of court culture that marked the Gupta and Vākāṭakas was seriously compromised. Finally, the early medieval period is marked by the apotheosis of kings, who assumed the positions of divinities or their incarnations and manifestations. The corollary to this was the feudalization of divinity, wherein the gods became perceived as warlords and the rulers of the earth.

THE OCCLUSION OF THE MEDIEVAL

"Early medieval" here identifies the period after the final demise of the Imperial Guptas around 550, and especially following the death of Harṣa in 647, with the subsequent collapse of the Puṣyabhūti dynasty. This time is now gaining attention after its previous neglect, and our understanding of its dynamics has accelerated in the past several decades. Principally, the evidence is based on the data available in land grant proclamations *(śāsana)*—usually in copper or stone—and augmented by information from literature, coins, and the archaeological record. As a consequence, there is a growing awareness of the fundamental contours of these centuries' events. The sudden appearance and disappearance of aristocratic families, visions of armies in conflict, the vicissitudes of cities, the transformation of economies, the religious background of the period, the position of belles lettres and art—all of these are now understood with much greater clarity than before.

Part of the problem in understanding the medieval has been an undue emphasis on selective great empires in Indian history. This emphasis has inhibited our comprehension of the sometimes more ephemeral but no less important cultures that survived in duration from several decades to more than two centuries. Accordingly, the third-century B.C.E. Mauryan domain of Aśoka has been the focus of much research, and the continued search for India's identity tacitly begins with understanding India as the area encompassed by Aśoka's edicts.[4] After Aśoka, historians have been fascinated with the Gandhāran epoch, particularly from the time of the Indo-Greeks until the conquest of Gandhāra by the Sasanians, inclusively c. 160 B.C.E. to 225 C.E. Indic history after the Gandhāran Kuṣānas and before the complete Turkic control of the north around 1200 C.E. has emphasized the Gupta and Vākāṭaka period and dominions (c. 320–550 C.E.). We need only observe that four of the first five tomes of the massive *Corpus Inscriptionum Indicarum* were dedicated to the Aśokan, Kuṣāna, Gupta, and Vākāṭaka inscriptions. Yet we certainly have an abundance of epigraphs from the Gurjara-Pratīhāras, the Pālas, the Coḷas, and many other polities. Therefore, the attractiveness of the Mauryan, Gandhāran, and Gupta dynasties to European aesthetics seemingly had much to do with their selection and presentation to date.

By contrast, the early medieval period, approximately from c. 500 C.E. to 1200 C.E., is messy and confusing and has been perceived as uninteresting and chaotic. It is the period of the rise of cultural forms that British and continental authors loved to hate and that some Indians acknowledge with chagrin: tantrism, *bhakti,* excessively sophisticated poetry, *satī,* the solidification of the caste system, and the rapacious appropriation of tribal lands, to mention a few. The historiography of these centuries is enveloped in the language of decline and fall, of degeneration and decay. This language persists despite the fact that some of the dynasties—for example, that of the Gurjara-Pratīhāras (c. 725–1018 C.E.) or the Pālas (c. 750–1170 C.E.)—lasted as long as or longer than the Guptas. A language of chaos does not acknowledge the reality that the Rāṣṭrakūṭas dominated India in a manner that the Guptas never achieved.

A contributing element has been the social or political agendas of those writing Indian history. British authors of the nineteenth century posited a moral basis in Alexandrine historiography for their appropriation of power on the subcontinent.[5] Indian authors, having limited critical models for indigenous history, have both followed and reacted to the British lead.[6] Moreover, some have employed their own history to search for a period of (Hindu) unification that could serve as a counterpoint to the colonial enterprise of the Ghaznivids, the Maliks, the Mughals, and the British.[7] In both the Indian and the British camp, there has been a tendency to search for a "golden age" of India, in which the aesthetic, literary, or political values have defined the best in the civilization. Influenced by British historiography, the fundamental paradigm was either Periclean Athens or Augustan Rome—although the imperial image of Macedonian Hellenism was also influential—and the temporal locus frequently selected to be the golden age was the period of the Imperial Guptas. Alternatively, the Guptas have occasionally become the basis for tendentious quests: postindependence north Indian nationalism and linguistic hegemony, claims for the superiority of Indian civilization, modern nationalistic definitions of "Hinduness" *(hindutva)*, and a multitude of other purposes.

The reliance on British historiography has influenced some historians to invoke the periodization strategies of Europe in the assignment of categories to Indian history. Analogous to the decline and fall of Rome, effected by the Hunic invasions, the decline and fall of the Guptas was seen as precipitated by the Ephthalite Huns between 460 and 530 C.E. According to this model, the ancient world is followed by the medieval, which occupies the period until the rise of the modern, and the medieval is dominated by the political institution of feudalism, variously interpreted. The similarities between the two appeared to some to provide India with a status equal to that of Europe, and a teleological vector toward the modern as well.

Despite some interesting similarities between European and Indian developments, we must be wary of carrying the analogy too far. India did not experience a series of events similar to the Renaissance, for example, nor did it have a highly structured Church that a reformation could contest. Nor did claims to universality under any analogue to the Holy Roman Empire appear with confidence. The model is further problematized by the extraordinary changes in the subcontinent induced by the gradual colonization of India from the first Islamic raid on Thāna in 644 C.E. to the solidification of Muslim power with Mu'izzu'd Din's victory at the Second Battle of Tarain in 1192 C.E. Nonetheless, the relative acceptance of the medieval designation for this period of Indian history shows that many in the scholarly community find it a useful, if troubling, term.

There may be nothing inherently wrong with applying European periodization to Indian history, although such application comes with much baggage and can become a tool for dubious strategies: disinformation, cultural imperialism, or the search for nationalistic legitimacy. Such a state of affairs is especially true when presumptions concerning the nature of the medieval period or of feudalism have inhibited our understanding of changes over time in Europe, within India, and concerning the fundamental differences between the two. To the degree that we employ the nomenclature of periodization as a convenient rubric—and nothing more—we may facilitate an understanding of these matters.[8] Most particularly, a judiciously employed periodization demonstrates a commitment to envisioning India as a society in which change was the rule.

In counterpoint to the apparent unification of India under the great empires, in the medieval we encounter the value placed on region and locality. During these centuries, there was no one center for anything: politics, religion, economics, or culture. Instead, we see new core areas of authority asserting their independence, their own aesthetics, their religious authenticity, their ways of doing business, and their languages and individual stories, embedded in literary systems and political models. The period witnessed the generation of regional styles of sculpture and monumental architecture, the profusion of literary languages in the four corners of the land, the struggle of royal houses for imperial hegemony, the efflorescence of literary forms, and the proliferation of castes and classes. All these developments were made possible by the crystallization of a sense of spatial identity and local valorization never before seen. Each place becomes valuable, consecrated by gods and heroes, visited by saints, enraptured by famous lovers, immortalized by poets, and contested by warlords.

Yet this same movement toward regionalization contributed to much of the literary culture, and the medieval is the source of so many Indian literary genres, an observation particularly true of religious texts. In terms of Buddhist works, the majority of the final edited versions of scriptures in the Pali Canon stem from the work of Buddhaghosa and his contemporaries, coming at the cusp of medieval Buddhism. Mahayanist texts gained ground, especially philosophical works but also scripture and literature. Such learned medieval dynamism was to influence much of Buddhist activity. Almost all of the translations into Tibetan and most of those into Chinese, a high proportion of surviving manuscripts, many of the important commentaries, independent treatises, canonical formulations, lists of scriptures, and historical discussions are from the early medieval period as well. In terms of personalities, so many essential authors, the preponderance of Chinese Buddhist pilgrims (with their records), and many of the Buddhist saints derive from the medieval era, not from the earliest centuries of the Indian Buddhist order.

In the wider Indian culture, this process was even more obvious. Monarchs sponsored or supported many of the great plays, romances, and epics of Sanskrit and Prakrit literature, as well as the development of massive Śaiva and Vaiṣṇava temple complexes. Their activity was so compelling that Southeast Asia saw the creation of Indianized states, where Sanskrit was an official language. All these factors and more speak of a richness that is poorly served by a language emphasizing decline and ignoring creativity and opportunity. Indeed, the problem with the medieval centuries is not an absence of activity but a surfeit. There are too many lineages, building programs, claims to authority, and challenges to the previous paradigms; there is too much military adventurism, literary activity, and inscriptional and documentary evidence. The excessive richness of our material—increased almost daily by excavations and epigraphic finds—makes this perhaps the most intellectually challenging epoch of Indian history. The wealth of disparate political strategies, literary cycles, military events, religious formations, and the ever-shifting dynamics of allegiance and behavior, all these present us with a bewildering montage of rapidly developing relationships between geographic locales and social formulae.

And yet, there is an undeniable malaise to parts of this period, something of a continuing struggle for power and position that speaks, not of a collapse of culture, but of a paucity of public discourse on the responsibilities of power. There is a sense of license and adolescent willfulness to many of these dynasties, a willfulness that is both pervasive and corrosive. We have only a modest sense of alternative voices or agendas in our records. Anticipating the issueless politics of some leaders in postindependence India, the early medieval period leaves us with a disquieting sense of intellectual and religious personages in the process of abandoning cultural criticism. Sycophancy and patron-client relations appear to seize the field, and the entire society suffers as a result. Thus the locales not only became sites of provincial valorization and divinity but fortresses against the onslaughts of armed men and often were rendered perilously parochial in their horizons.

EARLY MEDIEVAL POLITICAL AND MILITARY EVENTS

500–650 C.E.

Our primary concern—the area of greatest esoteric Buddhist activity—is North India and the Deccan, from the Kṛṣṇa River valley to the Himalayas and from Bengal to Gujarat. Consequently, this discussion initially concentrates on the events that brought down the two great empires governing this area toward the beginning of the sixth century C.E. The first was the Imperial Guptas in the modern Indian states of Rajasthan, northern Madhya Pradesh, Kashmir, the Punjab, Uttar Pradesh, Bihar, and Bengal. The Guptas were on a cultural continuum with the Vākāṭakas in southern Madhya Pradesh (south of the Nārmadā and Son Rivers), Maharashtra, Orissa, Chhattisgarh, Jharkhand, Andhra Pradesh, and parts of Karnataka. Loosely, these areas respectively define northern India and the Deccan plateau.

It is appropriate to begin the discussion with the fierce assault on the north waged by the Ephthalite Hūṇa peoples. The Ephthalites (or Hephthalites), who probably came from the Wakhan area of the Amu Darya River in the eastern region of what is now Afghanistan, had been enormously successful, seizing Gandhāra from the Kidāra Kuṣānas sometime in the mid-fifth century.[9] They destabilized Buddhist institutions during that century and defeated the Sasanian emperors Yazdigird in 454 and Firoz in 480. Skandagupta apparently engaged the king of the Ephthalites, possibly Toramāṇa, in battle between these dates. Skandagupta's Junagaṛh rock inscription in Gujarat—on the same boulder inscribed by Aśoka and Rudradāman before him—identifies that he had conquered otherwise unidentified foreigners *(mleccha)* by 455–458. This announcement is normatively interpreted to indicate his defeat of the Hūṇa army.[10] The Ephthalites, however, continued to be active. A little-known chieftain of Mālava named Prakāśadharman of the Aulikara lineage claims to have once again turned back Toramāṇa in an engagement sometime before posting his stone inscription of 515–516.[11] This may have temporarily stopped the southern advance of the Ephthalites, but they pressed east and around 520 conquered Kashmir. They were finally prevented from overrunning all of North India by another Aulikara, Yaśodharman, apparently the successor to Prakāśadharman, around 530.[12]

Yaśodharman's Mandasor inscription, written in 533–534, states that this Aulikara monarch held sway throughout North India, from the Brahmaputra River valley, in modern Assam, to the far west. His claim was probably an exaggeration, but one with a simple significance: the Imperial Guptas were no longer important in the military affairs of their ancestral lands. Indeed, there is only one further Gupta inscription available, a land grant in the Koṭīvarṣa area made in 542–543, by the last of the imperial line, Viṣṇugupta.[13] This chronology for the demise of the Guptas is supported by the Jaina version of the *Harivaṃśa* epic of Jinasena, which maintains that the Guptas were recognized as surviving for 231 years, from c. 320 to 551.[14] Thus the end of the great imperial line occurred, as so often seen in India, through a simple absence in the inscriptional record.

Yośodharman himself, and his Aulikara clan with him, seem not have to survived much beyond his epigraphic self-promotion. Yet in the wake of the Gupta's loss of position, a horror vacui in North Indian polity facilitated the precipitous rise and sudden decline of noble lineages and bloodthirsty princes for the next fifty years. What is remarkable is that much the same process occurred in the Deccan, where the main Vākāṭaka house in Vidarbha (around modern Nagpur) and their subsidiary branch in Vatsagulma (Washim, Maharashtra) had held power at least since the beginning of the fourth century C.E. Their contributions to religious life were particularly noteworthy—the main house special-

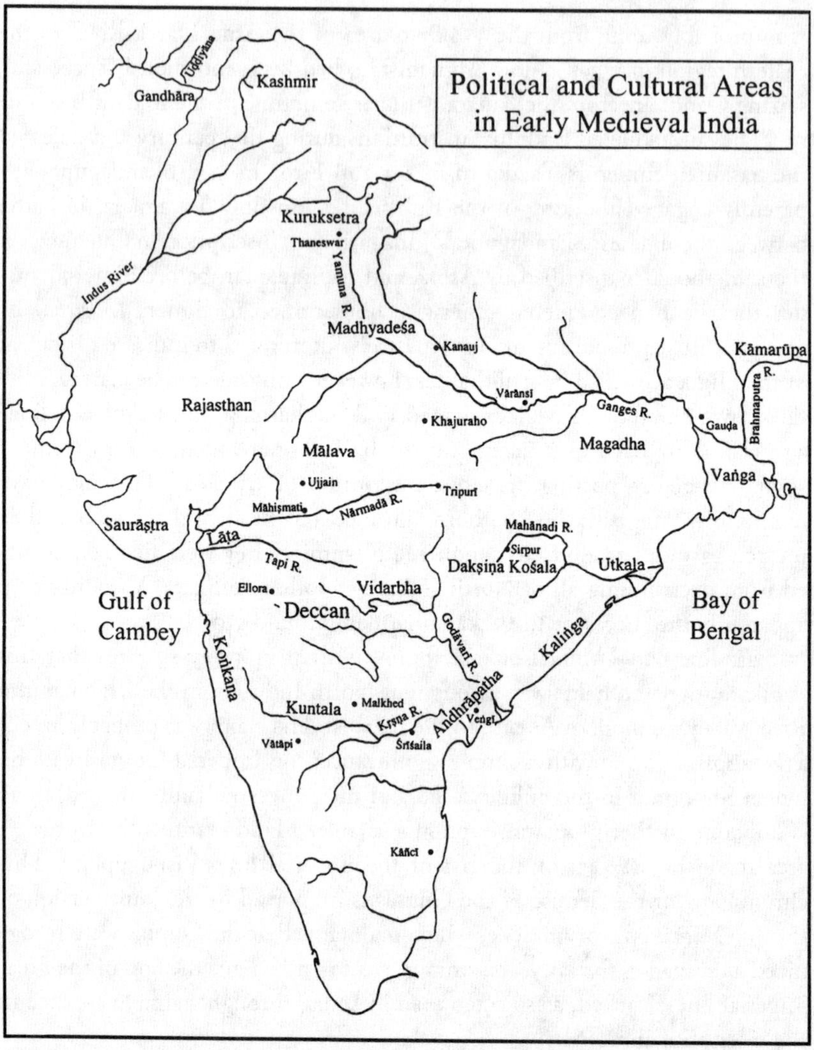

MAP 1 Political and Cultural Areas in Early Medieval India.
Ronald M. Davidson and Richard Pinto

ized in erecting Hindu temples while the Vatsagulma branch was responsible for much of Buddhist Ajantā construction.[15] For reasons that are still not clear, however, the Vākāṭaka dynasty did not survive much into the sixth century.

Thus, by the middle of the sixth century, the Guptas, Vākāṭakas, and Aulikaras had surrendered the field, while the Hūṇas had been successfully stymied in the Indus basin, leaving much of the subcontinent—from the Kṛṣṇa River to Kaśmīra and from Bengal to Gujarat—accessible to opportunistic appropriation. In a pattern that would recur after the fall of great states, two kinds of groups came to power: clans that already had gained authority as feudatories of the previous great dynasties, and those houses that seemingly came from nowhere, gaining control through speed, ingenuity, ruthlessness, and luck. Available positions were finite in number and to some degree dictated by geographical parameters. For our purposes, seventeen regions exhibited sustained importance during the era (Map 1). Along the Gangetic valley, active areas include the delta of Bengal (historically known as Vaṅga/Samatāṭa), the Brahmaputra River valley (historically Kāmarūpa), the Ganges up to the doab (Magadha), the area around the Ganges-Yamuna doab (Madhyadeśa), and the fertile plain of the modern Punjab and Haryana states (Kurukṣetra). Elsewhere in the north, vital zones include the valley of Kashmir, the western border of the desert in modern Rajasthan, the plain between the Nārmadā and the Chambal rivers (Mālava), and the Kathiawar Peninsula (Saurāṣṭra). In central India, the strategic regions are the plain around the upper Godāvarī extending to the Nārmadā (Vidarbha), the upper Mahānadi valley (Dakṣiṇa Kośala), the combined Tapti and Nārmadā deltas (Lāṭa), the Koṅkan coast on the west, Utkala/Tosalī in northern Orissa and Kaliṅga on the south Orissan coast in the east. Finally, toward the south, we will be concerned with the combined deltas of the Godāvarī and the Kṛṣṇa (Andhrāpatha/Veṅgī), and the upper Kṛṣṇa valley (Kuntala).[16]

The historical designations I have given for these places are simply the best known during the period, but alternate names are encountered with alarming suddenness in epigraphs and literature. Just as disconcerting, geographical terms are used in a hazy and imprecise manner, such that Uttarāpatha (the north) means one thing to a soldier from Kanauj, while it means something entirely different to a poet from Kuntala. The problem of the relationship between designation and locale can be acute, especially in medieval Buddhist literature.

However indicated, these areas became the sites for much of the action in medieval India and, *mutatis mutandis*, have continued to dominate much of Indian cultural geography down to the present. The struggle for these areas began almost as soon as the Guptas and Vākāṭakas ceased to be important, and military adventurism was dominated initially by the Later Guptas of Magadha, the Maukharis of Madhyadeśa, the Gauḍas of Vaṅga, the Varmans of Kāmarūpa, the Maitrikas of Saurāṣṭra, Kāḷachuris of Mālava, and the Chāḷukyas of the city of Vātāpi in Kuntala. Because Indian historical writing has traditionally presented a confusing series of partial pictures with little effort at depicting a coherent continuum of events, the present discussion attempts to present the military-political interaction between the major players as a whole.[17]

TABLE 2.1 Chāḷukyas of Vātāpi

Pulakeśin I (c. 543–566)
Kīrtivarman (c. 567–597)
Maṅgleśa (c. 597–609)
Pulakeśin II (c. 609–654/5)
Vikramāditya I (654/5–681)
Vinayāditya (c. 696–733/4)
Vijayāditya (c. 696–733/4)
Vikramāditya II (c. 733/4–744/5)
Kīrtivarman II (c. 744/5–753)

Almost simultaneously, around 550 C.E., Maukhari Īśānavarman (reigned c. 550–565) and the founder of the Chāḷukyas, Pulakeśin I (c. 543–566) began to move against their neighbors.[18] Pulakeśin sought to extend the boundaries of his rule east against the Kadambas, a group farther up the Kṛṣṇa, and against the Nalas, a group living along the Tuṅgabhadrā, which is a Kṛṣṇa River tributary. While he was accomplishing these ends, Īśānavarman was also involved in a series of raids to the east, against the Gauḍas, and south, where he encountered the Chāḷukyas.

Whereas the Chāḷukya king made efforts to solidify his domain, the Maukhari lord was apparently in search of temporary bragging rights, with little concern for permanence. This difference of agenda—between kings in search of domain versus those more dedicated to personal promotion—is seen time and again in the early medieval period.

TABLE 2.2 Maukharis of Madhyadeśa

Harivarman
Ādityavarman

Īśvaravarman
Īśānavarman (c. 550–565)
Śarvavarman (c. 560–575)
Antivarman (c. 575–600)
Grahavarman (c. 600–605)

Part of Īśānavarman's problem was close to home, where the Later Guptas were beginning to exercise their own search for dominance. The Maukharis, who comprised an old aristocratic house, had been important vassals of the Imperial Guptas, and Īśānavarman was probably the nephew of Viṣṇugupta, the last of the Imperial Gupta line. Clearly, the Maukharis moved to claim the crown, but Kumāragupta (c. 550–560) stood in their way. His house had perhaps been vassals of the imperial line, and although they employed the designation "Gupta," they were apparently unrelated to the Imperial Guptas. All we know for certain is that they enjoyed status as aristocracy (*sadvaṃśa*) in the early sixth century and that they used titles similar to those employed for Gupta vassals.[19] Kumāragupta encountered Īśānavarman sometime around 560 C.E. and stopped the Maukhari leader in the field of battle. So great were the stakes, and so incomplete the outcome, however, that on the Aphsaḍ stone it is inscribed that Kumāragupta committed suicide at Prayāga, perhaps because his vow of conquest remained unfulfilled.[20]

TABLE 2.3 Later Guptas of Magadha

Kṛṣṇagupta
Harṣagupta
Jīvitagupta
Kumāragupta (c. 550–560)
Dāmodaragupta (c. 560–562)
Mahāsenagupta (c. 562–601)
Mādhavagupta (c. 601–655)
Ādityasena (c. 655–680)
Devagupta (c. 680–700)

In a manner well known in Indian history, the Maukharis found themselves fighting on two fronts, since the Hūṇas had used this opportunity to come into conflict with them, as they had done to so many other rulers before. After stopping the Ephthalite army, either Īśānavarman or his son, Śarvavarman (c. 560–575), engaged the next Later Gupta ruler, Dāmodaragupta, around 562 C.E. Although the Later Guptas claimed victory for their forces, their king, Dāmodaragupta, was evidently killed in the fight. The Aphsaḍ inscription indicates that he had temporarily passed out on the field of battle, only to be awakened by the touch of the lotus hands of heavenly damsels in his new heavenly abode.[21] The real outcome, though, was the Maukharis' realization that their belligerence had not succeeded; for the moment, Magadha was safely in the hands of Mahāsenagupta (c. 562–601), the young son of Dāmodaragupta.

TABLE 2.4 Maitrikas of Saurāṣṭra

Bhaṭāraka
Dharasena I
Droṇasiṃha
Dhruvasena I
Dharapaṭṭa
Guhasena
Dharasena II
Śīlāditya I (c. 590–615)
Kharagraha I
Dharasena III
Dhruvasena II
Dharasena IV
Dhruvasena III
Kharagraha II
Śīlāditya II (c. 648–662)
Śīlāditya III
Śīlāditya IV
Śīlāditya V
Śīlāditya VI

We have little information on the next two decades, and the sense is that the rulers of most areas were solidifying control—this is clearly indicated in inscriptions from such disparate areas as Vaṅga, Utkala, Dakṣiṇa Kośala, and Saurāṣṭra.[22] The former three represented newly coalesced rulerships of a Gauḍa kingdom, the house of Māna (Utkala), and the aristocratic Pāṇḍuvaṁśīs, while Saurāṣṭra was governed by an established aristocratic house that had served as feudatories of the Imperial Guptas, the Maitrikas. Sometime in the beginning of the last quarter of the sixth century, however, individual princes began to test the waters to see whether conquest could be achieved. The Kāḷachuris, who had already controlled much of Maharashtra, under Kṛṣṇarāja (c. 550–575) extended their domain to the Koṅkan coast, subjugating the Mauryas of the area and continuing on into Vidarbha.[23]

TABLE 2.5 Kāḷachuris of Mālava

Kṛṣṇarāja (c. 550–575)
Śaṅkaragaṇa (c. 575–600)
Buddharāja (c. 600–620)

Chāḷukya Pulakeśin's successor, Kīrtivarman (c. 567–597) began a raid or series of raids up the coast of the Bay of Bengal, from the mouth of the Kṛṣṇa River to the Gauḍa kingdom.[24] About the same time, the Magadhan monarch Mahāsenagupta mounted a more sustained campaign against Kāmarūpa, defeating its king, Suṣṭhitavarman (c. 570–590), along the shores of the Brahmaputra River. It is likely that part of Bengal also became temporarily included in Mahāsenagupta's domain at this time. The Gauḍas, though, had come into their own, uniting under Jayanāga (c. 570–600). Eventually, the Later Guptas found themselves surrounded on three sides by very strong and belligerent adversaries: the Maukharis in the north, the Varmans of Kāmarūpa and the Gauḍas in the east, the Pāṇḍuvaṁśīs and the Mānas in the south, with the Chāḷukya raids adding to the problem. Around 585, then, the Later Guptas left Magadha and took up residence in Mālava, probably settling in its most important city, Ujjain. Why Mahāsenagupta elected to move there is an open question, but Devahuti has suggested that he may have had relations in Mālava.[25] Gauḍa Jayanāga apparently used this opportunity to extend the Gauḍa influence. He followed up on the Later Guptas by invading Kāmarūpa around 595, capturing Suṣṭhitavarman's sons soon after his death, but releasing them to govern as Gauḍa vassals.[26] However, if Mahāsenagupta thought his problems were over by moving to Ujjain, he was dreadfully wrong. The Kāḷachuris evidently resented the presence of the Later Guptas so close to their capital, Māhiṣmati, on the Nārmadā River. Kāḷachuri Śaṅkaragaṇa (c. 575–600) marched north to take Ujjain in 595–596.[27] As a consequence, the Later Guptas apparently became "guests" of a Kāḷachuri vassal, even if the accommodations were not to their liking.

TABLE 2.6 Varmans of Kāmarūpa

Puṣyavarman
Samudravarman
Balavarman
Kalyāṇavarman
Gaṇapativarman
Mahendravarman
Nārāyaṇvarman
Mahābhūtivarman
Candramukhavarman
Sthitavarman
Suṣṭhitavarman (c. 570–590)
Supratiṣṭhitavarman
Bhāskaravarman

At this low ebb to Later Gupta fortunes, the Vardhanas of Thaneswar came to the rescue. They were initially established in Thaneswar by the semi-mythical ancestor, Puṣyabhūti (var. Puṣpabhūti), and their house has frequently been identified with the designation Puṣyabhūti/Puṣpabhūti as well as Vardhana. Thaneswar (Sthāṇvīśvara) itself is now the relatively insignificant town of Kurukshetra in Haryana, about 100 miles north of Delhi. The curious part, however, is that it was apparently no more politically significant then than it is now, and the Vardhanas, who were members of the merchant caste *(vaiśya),* had gained political and military power. Somehow, Mahāsenagupta's sister, Mahāsenaguptā, had been married to the Thaneswar monarch, Ādityasena (c. 555–580), some years before, establishing an alliance between mutual foes of the Maukharis in an exercise of classical Indian political strategy.[28] Their son, Prabhākaravardhana (c. 580–605), became the first of the Vardhanas to establish complete independence and was noted for his belligerence and adventurism, so Bāṇa (Harṣavardhana's court poet) describes this ruler's militarism with unmistakable language.[29]

TABLE 2.7 Vardhanas or Puṣyabhūtis of Thaneswar

Puṣyabhūti
Ādityasena (c. 555–580)
Prabhākaravardhana (c. 580–605)

Rājyavardhana (c. 605–606)
Harṣavardhana (c. 606–647)

Thus engaging so many of the local lords of North and West India, Prabhākaravardhana made a name for himself and his court and became capable of encountering the Kāḷachuri's vassal, Devagupta. The moment they chose probably coincided with Devagupta's sudden loss of reinforcement, since the Chāḷukya monarch Maṅgleśa (c. 597–609) invaded the Kāḷachuri domain in 601, seizing the Kāḷachuri's treasury.[30] Around the same date, Mahāsenagupta appears to have passed away and his sons Mādhavagupta and Kumāragupta become wards of the Thaneswar court and friends to the heir apparent, Rājyavardhana, and the younger Harṣa, who became particularly attached to Mādhavagupta.[31] The elevated fortunes of the Vardhanas did not escape the notice of the Maukharis, who offered (or were coerced into) diplomacy in the form of a marriage alliance between the new ruler, Grahavarman (c. 600–605) and Harṣa's younger sister, Rājyaśrī. This was quite a distinction for Prabhākaravardhana's provincial merchant clan, to be aligned with the ancient aristocratic lords of Kanauj, a far older and more prestigious family than the Later Guptas. The grand wedding occurred around 603–604, and Prabhākaravardhana sent his sons hunting Hūṇas in the Himalayas as a reward, no doubt cognizant that the prestige of his family rested securely on the force of arms.

Unfortunately, the good times were soon to be over, and events in the next few years would entirely change the political landscape of North India. In 605, Prabhākaravardhana fell ill and quickly passed away. At the moment of the announcement of his death, Devagupta—seeking revenge for the humiliation at Prabhākaravardhana's hands—moved on the Vardhana/Maukhari alliance and killed the young king, Grahavarman, sending his young widow, Rājyaśrī, to flee into the woods to seek refuge with a Buddhist hermit. Harṣa had come back to Thaneswar in time to hear his father's last testament, and his brother Rājyavardhana—learning of Devagupta's opportunism—sought out the Mālava king and killed him in battle. Devagupta, though, apparently had entered into an alliance with a new figure on the military landscape, the Gauḍa lord, Śaśāṅka (c. 605–625). Śaśāṅka had taken over Bengal following the death of Jayanāga and was perhaps a vassal to Grahavarman's father, Antivarman (c. 575–600), using that position to solidify control over Bengal and throwing off the yoke of vassalage with the death of Grahavarman.[32] Whatever the precise nature of his relationship with the central Indian states, certainly Śaśāṅka used the opportunity to put forth his own agenda and saw the Thaneswar brothers as his primary opponents. We can understand the opportunity, with the Maukharis heirless, Mālava leaderless, the Kāḷachuris recovering from the onslaught of the Chāḷukyas (who were themselves entering into a war of succession), and the peripheral states of Kāmarūpa, Utkala, Dakṣiṇa Kośala, and Saurāṣṭra in the hands of weak or disinterested rulers.

Clearly, the Vardhanas were susceptible to marital alliances, so Śaśāṅka offered his daughter in marriage as a ploy. The offer was duplicitous, however, and while Rājyavardhana was in the Gauḍa king's camp discussing arrangements, Śaśāṅka murdered him, apparently by his own hand.[33] Śaśāṅka fled back to Gauḍa, and Harṣa made arrangements to follow him, first proceeding to Kāmarūpa to form an alliance with Bhāskaravarman, who agreed to be Harṣa's vassal. Together they assaulted Bengal in 606–607, going as far as the great city of Puṇḍravardhana to encounter Śaśāṅka, but the engagement was inconclusive.[34] Harṣa's punitive expedition certainly did not stop Śaśāṅka from entering North Orissa in 608 or taking all of Utkala and parts of Kaliṅga by 611, even if Harṣa did manage to thwart Śaśāṅka's designs on Magadha and Madhyadeśa.[35]

While these events were unfolding in the east, Kāḷachuri Buddharāja had recouped his strength from the Chāḷukya incursions—mostly because of the Chāḷukya war of succession that resulted in Pulakeśin II's ascension around 609. Buddharāja used this opportunity to move against Vidiśa in 608–609. Unfortunately, the reemergence of Kāḷachuri expansionist designs, and the preoccupation of Harṣa with the east and the Chāḷukya's involvement in the south, no doubt assisted the Maitrikas in entertaining their own plans. Around 610, the Maitrika king Śīlāditya I (c. 590–615) invaded the Mālava country, appropriating it from the Kāḷachuri's vassals and eliminating Kāḷachuri influence north of the Nārmadā River.[36] The Maitrikas were to occupy Mālava and its principle city, Ujjain, for the balance of the next decade.

Detecting an opportunity to complete the beginning made by Maṅgleśa before he was deposed, Chāḷukya Pulakeśin II invaded the Kāḷachuri land from the south in c. 620, and eliminated the influence of this family in West India for more than two hundred years; they would reemerge as the rulers of Tripurī in the mid-eighth century. Pulakeśin II subjugated Lāṭa, Mālava, and part of the Gurjara kingdom, which had extended its domain into southern Rajasthan. He drove the Maitrikas back into Saurāṣṭra and coerced them into an alliance. Much of this area was to remain in Chāḷukya possession until the death of Pulakeśin II in 642.

In the east, though, in about 625 Śaśāṅka's dreams of conquest were ended by his death. Harṣa, who could not defeat the murderer of his brother in life, invaded Gauḍa after his death, issuing grants there in 628 as his royal prerogative.[37] Harṣa controlled much of North India by this time, but decided to extend westward, where he had not previously gone. With Śaśāṅka safely dead, Harṣa tried to expand the empire to the extent enjoyed by the Imperial Guptas, and Saurāṣṭra was in the Chāḷukya political maṇḍala. Thus, around 630, Harṣa pressed westward and encountered the young Maitrika Druvasena II with such ferocity that the Maitrika monarch took refuge with the Lāṭa ruler and founder of the Gurjara house there, Dada II, who was himself directly supervised by the Chāḷukyas. Pulakeśin II could not stand by and see his territory so dramatically diminished, so the great Chāḷukya army—already in possession of most of the Deccan plateau—met the Thaneswar monarch on the field of battle. Unfortunately for the Vardhanas, Harṣa had overestimated his ability to wage war in the Deccan, and his elephants were overthrown by the southerners.

Flushed with victory and with the issue of the west decided, Pulakeśin II extended his family's domain eastward as well and shortly thereafter established the "Eastern Chāḷukyas" in Andhrāpatha (Kṛṣṇa and Godāvarī River valleys), where they were to remain a force for several centuries. Not satisfied with his accomplishment, the Chāḷukya monarch also began a series of campaigns up the Bay of Bengal, bringing Kaliṅga under Chāḷukya rule. To celebrate his victories, Pulakeśin II commissioned the poet Ravikīrti to compose the exuberant Aihole inscription of 634–635, which is explored in more detail below.[38] Not to be outdone, Harṣa began a series of campaigns against Orissa between 637 and 642, campaigns that once more brought him up against the area claimed by the Chāḷukyas. Harṣa interrupted his southern policy only with a brief threat to Kashmir.

Pulakeśin II had not just focused on the north, but had conducted campaigns in the south as well, particularly against Kāñcīpuram, the capital of the dynamic and powerful Pallava kingdom. This latter aggression brought the Chāḷukyas to grief, however, for what Harṣa could not do, the Pallavas accomplished. In 642, the Pallava prince Narasimhavarman marched north with his military might and laid waste to the Chāḷukya capital of Vātāpi, killing Pulakeśin II.[39] Even then, the Chāḷukyas remained a force in Vātāpi for the next century. Indeed, despite their eventual loss of power in their traditional homeland, in a manner similar to that of the Kāḷachuris of Madhya Pradesh, branches of the house of Chāḷukya continued to operate in various milieus throughout the early medieval period.

Harṣa by this point had moved his capital to the metropolis of Kanauj, claiming the Maukharis' city by virtue of authority, a claim he enforced as his sister was the widow of the last Maukhari lord. Yet the rapacious Harṣa never was able to defeat either of his two nemeses: Śaśāṅka died of a debilitating illness and Pulakeśin II was to be conquered by another southern ruler. Still, when Pulakeśin II's Aihole edict records his enemies, Harṣa stands out as a significant figure in the Chāḷukya desire for universal conquest. The Vardhana prince was only able to outlive his nemesis by five years. By 647, Harṣa was dead, and his empire was unraveling before the eyes of his courtiers. Thus, in all, the 150 years between 500 and 650 were enshrined in elaborate verses by poets north and south: Ravikīrti among the Chāḷukyas and Bāṇa in the Kanauj court. Beyond their capacity in composition, both lesser poets and the Chinese Buddhist pilgrim Hsüan-tsang have praised the rulers of the regions of India, even while articulating their patrons' rapacious conduct. Others, however, were not so laudatory of this endless warfare, and the T'ang dynasty's imperial annals, *Chiu T'ang shu*, noted that the period 617–627 was one of profound disturbances in India, with ceaseless bloodshed.[40]

650–750 C.E.

A similar statement was appended in the T'ang annals after the death of Harṣa, but the other years visible to us through the faulty lens of epigraphs and literature appear no less troubled or difficult. Moreover, we have a less complete record of the military and political machinations of Indian dynasts in the century following the deaths of Harṣa and Pulakeśin II. We should not, however, infer that there was a reduction of adventurism—much of the behavior exhibited by the major actors during the periods of the Chāḷukya and Puṣyabhūti dominion also was manifest on a smaller scale after their collective demise.

This period started off badly, with the Pallavas occupying Vātāpi and with Kanauj embroiled in a battle for succession. The Chāḷukyas, though, were able to regain the throne of Vātāpi, and Vikramāditya I (654–681) assumed control in 654–655 with the assistance of his relatives and vassals, the Gaṅgas of Mānyapura (Mysore district).[41] The course of events in the Deccan and the south during the next few years appears confused, with breakaway attempts by the vassals of the Chāḷukyas and corresponding efforts at domination by Vikramāditya I. Clearly, by c. 670, Vikramāditya I had reestablished Chāḷukya dominion over much of the western Deccan, up to Koṅkan and Lāṭa. These gains were solidified with a branch of the Chāḷukyas becoming one of the great forces in the Gurjara-Mālava area for the next few centuries. One of their traditional foes, the previously Puṣyabhūti feudatory Maitrikas, was overcome during this operation, and Śīlāditya II (c. 648–662) seems to have been the lord defeated by the new Chāḷukya house, headed by Dharāśraya Jayasiṁha.

The great bane of the Chāḷukyas of Vātāpi, however, remained the Pallavas, centered in Kāñcī. Pulakeśin II's two efforts at humbling Kāñcī were again tried by Vikramāditya I, with little better results, and the balance of the latter's reign is taken up with struggles in the south; both Vātāpi and Kāñcī suffered sacking by opposing forces during the last decades of the seventh century. Indeed, the Chāḷukya-Pallava conflict continued to consume the south of India for the first half of the eighth century, and Vikramāditya II was noted as having humiliated the Pallavas by taking Kāñcī thrice during his life, once as the agent of his father Vijayāditya (c. 696–733/4), and twice during his own reign (c. 733/4–744/5).[42] The only entertainment available to the Vātāpi Chāḷukya rulers was to maintain their hold on the Deccan. Chāḷukya edicts toward the end of their dynasty depict the princes of the realm holding court in military encampments over a vast area, from Ellora in Maharashtra to the far south.

We know little of the events in Kanauj, although it is evident that Harṣa made insufficient allowance for his succession. In all likelihood, the various areas of India once administered by the aristocratic Puṣyabhūti vassals were now claimed as their own by those same houses. The Maukharis appear to have gained control over Madhyadeśa, with its capital Kanauj. Magadha had been put into the hands of Mādhavagupta, the Later Gupta scion who had come to the Thaneswar court in 601 as a boy. He evidently did not, however, command the area north of the Ganges, for a strange episode unfolded there between the T'ang envoy, Wang Hsüan-tse, and the prince of Tīrabhukti, *Arjuna.[43] The event—in which *Arjuna took Wang Hsüan-tse into custody—resulted in the intercession of Tibet and Nepal into Indian life and the presence of foreign troops on Indian soil, some measure of the unsettled conditions of the period. This nominal subaltern status of northern Magadha to Tibet lasted until perhaps 703.

Harṣa's previous vassal, Bhāskaravarman of Kāmarūpa, used Harṣa's death as a pretext to invade Gauḍa, which had no effective leadership at that time.[44] Also adopting this strategy, Mādhavagupta's successor, Ādityasena (c. 655–680), extended the Later Gupta control into parts of Uttar Pradesh, the Chota Nagpur Plateau, southern Bihar, and parts of Bengal.[45] He was able to make a marital alliance with the Maukhari Bhogavarman—whose exact position is unknown, but probably was a ruler of some variety—in recognition of the importance his dynasty had assumed. Power attracts power, of course, and the Chāḷukya king Vinayāditya (c. 680–696) began a series of raids on the north at this time, coming into conflict with Ādityasena's son, Devagupta (c. 680–700), to the defeat of the latter around 695.[46]

The seventh century marks the initial intrusion of Islam into South Asia, beginning with the unauthorized raid on Thāna (close to Mumbai) in 644 and followed by the attack of the Arab general Ismā'īl on the port of Ghoghā in 677.[47] From then on, regular attacks on the trading cities of western India occurred, leading up to the wholesale invasion of the Sindh section of the lower Indus valley (current Pakistan). The offensive was launched by Al-Hajjāj, the governor of both Iraq and much of the old Sasanian domains, as part of the great expansionist movement that took them into Kabul and Transoxiana as well.[48] In 711, six thousand Syrian cavalry and soldiers with six thousand more camel-riders, support troops, and catapults, attacked the city of Debal, where the inhabitants were slaughtered over three days as a lesson. In succeeding months, principally combatants were killed, while the much of the population of defeated cities were sent back to Al-Hajjāj as slaves, a common Muslim practice. The Arab conquest continued to send out raiding parties, but their forward movement appears initially to have been checked in Gujarat by the allied forces of the Lāṭa Gurjara ruler, Jayabhaṭa IV, and the Maitrika king Śīlāditya V (c. 710–735) around 725, and in Mālava by the Gurjara-Pratīhāra founder, Nāgabhaṭa.[49] The Arabs, however, tried to avenge their loss, and attacked Lāṭa, overrunning it and went as far down the coast as Navsari, between modern Surat and Mumbai. There—as the Navsari Plates proclaim with gory graphic details—Avajinajāśraya-Pulakeśirāja defeated the "Tājika army."[50] From this point on, the Gujarat branch of the Chāḷukyas became the great power from Lāṭa to Saurāṣṭra, and into Mālava.

Dramatic changes in power were taking place elsewhere in the north, however. In Kashmir, the Kārkoṭa dynasty had established itself as supreme in the valley but were feeling themselves extraordinarily pinched by the Arab aggression in the Indus valley. Moreover, Central Asia had become the battleground between the Tibetan imperium, the T'ang Chinese, the Arabs, and the Turks.[51] Evidently invoking the Indian theory of the politicomilitary maṇḍala, in 713 the Kārkoṭa king Candrāpīḍa (c. 711–720), had asked the new T'ang ruler, the Hsüan-tsung emperor, for assistance in defense against the Arabs. The Chinese were the geographically remotest enemies of the two powers—Tibetans and Arabs—immediately threatening him. Candrāpīḍa received something of a respite while waiting for his reply, since in 715 there was a change of Umayyad caliph in Damascus.

TABLE 2.8 Kārkoṭas of Kashmir

Durlabhavardhana
Pratāpāditya
Candrāpīḍa (c. 711–720)
Tārāpīḍa (c. 720–725)
Lalitāditya Muktāpīḍa (c. 725–756)
Kuvalayāpīḍa
Vajrāditya
Pṛthivyāpīḍa
Saṃgrāmāpīḍa
Jayāpīḍā Vinayāditya (c. 779–810)
Lalitāpīḍa
Saṃgrāmāpīḍa II
Cippaṭajayāpīḍa
Ajitāpīḍa
Anaṅgāpīḍa
Utpalāpīḍa

The immediate consequence of this change was that the great conqueror of the Amu Darya basin, Qutayba bin Muslim, rebelled against his new lord and was killed by his own troops.[52] The new caliph also began a diplomatic initiative in 717 to solidify gains in Transoxiana in the name of Islam. In response to both these realities, the Hsüan-tsung emperor did not send aid to Candrāpīḍa, but in 720 did offer him the status of vassal state, which was part of a larger Chinese effort at containment of Tibetan and Arab imperial forces. Kashmir's recognition had been preceded since 717 by China's own diplomatic initiatives to many of the countries in the western Himalayas, Pamirs, and the Hindu Kush.[53] This Chinese policy primarily meant that Kashmir's back was covered from Tibetan imperial aggression, a fact made clear with the destruction of a Tibetan garrison on the Wakhjir pass in 722 and the capture of a sizable Tibetan force.

If the new Kārkoṭa king, Lalitāditya Muktāpīḍa (c. 725–756), felt himself secure, he had little time to enjoy his status. Once again a young belligerent with designs of conquest arose, by the name of Yaśovarman, who initially seemed as if he would follow in the footsteps of Yaśodharman and Harṣa before him. Yaśovarman apparently came from a branch of the Maurya aristocratic family, and he usurped the throne of Kanauj about 720.[54] Thereafter, he cut a swath through North India, defeating and killing the last of the Later Guptas around 725–730. His "world conquest" *(digvijaya)* is celebrated in the Prakrit poem, *Gaüḍavaho* (Slaughter of the Gauḍa King), by one of his illustrious littérateurs, Vākpatirāja. In a fictionalized account, Yaśovarman is represented as defeating the kings of Magadha, Gauḍa (whence the epic's name), South India, and, after crossing the Malaya Hills at the southern tip of India, the king of Persia (poet's geography).[55] His victories over the Magadha king, probably Jīvitagupta II of the Later Guptas, and the Gauḍa rulers were almost assuredly authentic, but Yaśovarman certainly did not progress to the lower Deccan, where Chāḷukya Vikramāditya II was at the height of his power.

In the wake of Yaśovarman's conquest of the Gangetic valley—coupled with the reality that the Gurjaras, Maitrikas, and Chāḷukyas were all tied up with the Arab threat to the western Deccan until 737—Lalitāditya decided to pursue and defeat Yaśovarman. Using his status as a Chinese vassal and enemy of the Arabs, Lalitāditya recruited from border areas and obtained his magician/general Caṅkuṇa from Tokharisthan.[56] Lalitāditya then launched an attack on Yaśovarman's forces, taking Kanauj in 733 and proceeding through much of the Madhyadeśa/Magadha area, before finally returning to Shrinagar in 747. Between these dates, Lalitāditya is credited with conquering most of the areas of the Deccan, the Koṅkan coast, Broach, and Rajasthan. As in the case of other poets, we have to temper the enthusiasm of Kalhaṇa's Kashmiri boosterism, although, given the uncertainty of the military situation between 733 and 747, it might be closer to the truth than the depiction rendered for Yaśovarman by Vākpatirāja.[57] Whatever his actual sweep of the Deccan and West India, Lalitāditya eventually began a campaign against northern areas—Baltisthan, western Tibet, and the Tarim Basin. This was to be his final march, for it was his fate to die in the deserts of the Tarim Basin around 756, a victim of his own aggressive aspirations and the swiftly changing geopolitical circumstances of eighth-century Inner Asia.[58]

750–900 C.E.

One of the more remarkable facts of the early medieval period was the rather dramatic simultaneity of dynastic instability. The Gupta and Vākāṭaka houses fell within a relatively short period in the mid-sixth century. Likewise, in the eighth century the Vātāpi Chāḷukyas rapidly disintegrated in the south and the

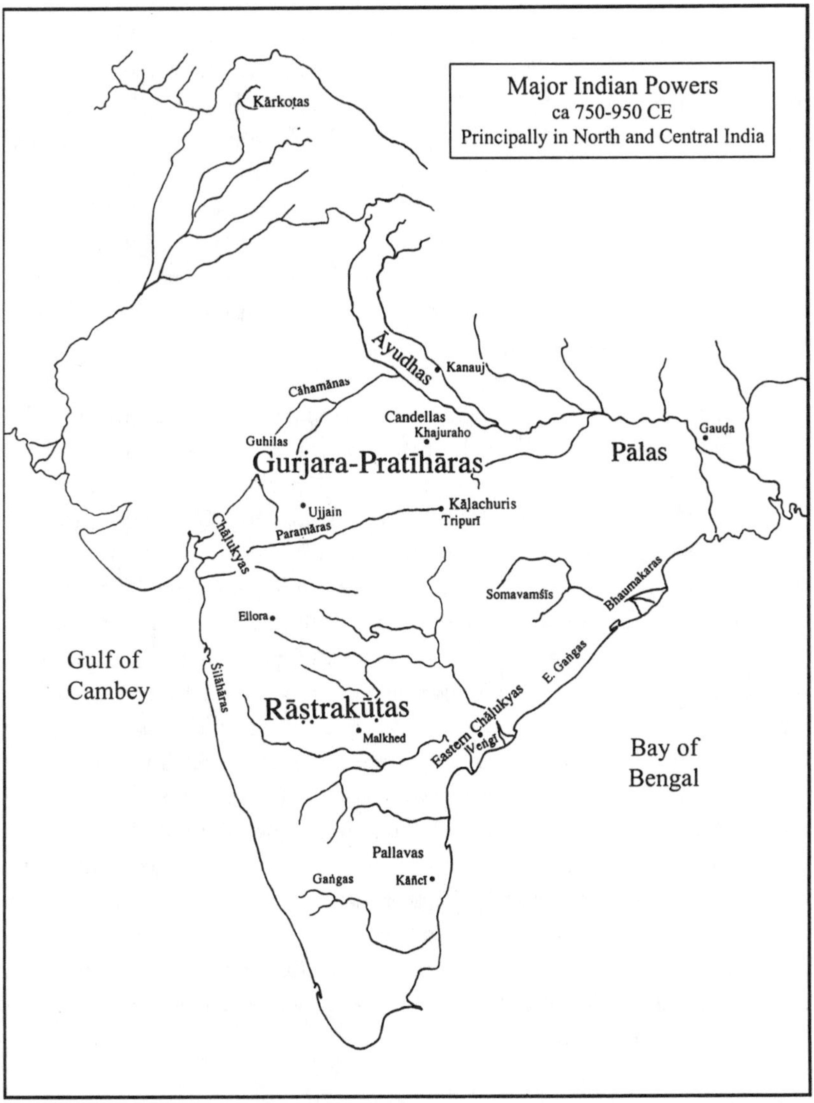

MAP 2 Major Indian Powers, c.750–950 C.E.
Ronald M. Davidson and Richard Pinto

new powers of the north—Yaśovarman and his Kārkoṭa nemesis—swiftly declined. These aristocratic clans seldom entirely disappear, however—the Maurya and Maukhari, the Chāḷukya and Kāḷachuri, as well as a host of lesser lineages, continued to submerge from historical perception and resurface later throughout these centuries. Sometimes they acted as vassals to a temporarily ascendant clan; sometimes they were lost to any records for a century or more; sometimes they fragmented into multiple lineages and operated as subalterns in multiple locales in diverse capacities. Many lines were analogous to these, and one of the most confusing aspects is trying to control the nomenclature of clan designations and their hydralike immortality.

About the middle of the eighth century, though, another great change in Indian history occurred. Simultaneously, three major dynasties emerged, dynasties that were to control much of the political and military history of the subcontinent for the next two centuries: the Rāṣṭrakūṭas of the Deccan, the Gurjara-Pratīhāras of Mālava-Rajasthan, and the Pālas of Bengal (Map 2). The geographical designations should be familiar, since the areas involved were quite similar to those governed by Pulakeśin II, Harṣa, and Śaśāṅka over a century before. The durability of the Kṛṣṇa-Bhīma-Godāvarī River valleys of the Deccan, the area between the Nārmadā and the Ganges-Yamuna doab, and Gauḍa in the east at sustaining major military/imperial forces is intriguing. These eighth-century dynasties and their ever-shifting kaleidoscope of vassals continued to function from the time of the major Arab incursions until just after the middle of the tenth century. Only the Pālas retained a continued, but limited, venue until the arrival of Muhammed ibn Bakhtyār Khaljī at the beginning of the thirteenth century. One of the ironies of the political history of this period is that each of these dynasties' capacity to wage war made the unity of the subcontinent practically impossible for any one of the imperial houses. Their collective collapse provided the occasion for the adventurism of Muhammed of Ghazni in the eleventh century and ushered in the Turkic-Muslim conquest of North India.

In the power vacuum of the Deccan after the defeat of the Arabs in 737, two leaders managed to put together sufficient military organizations to make use of the opportunity: Nāgabhaṭa I (c. 725–760) of Ujjain and Dantidurga of the western Deccan.[59] We may recall that Nāgabhaṭa had participated in one of the decisive battles against the Arabs, probably around 725. He was witness to the manner in which weak aristocratic houses were destroyed when his own relations, the Gurjaras of Lāṭa, were routed by both the Arabs and the Chāḷukyas in 737, never to gain authority again.[60] With the Chāḷukyas keeping a close watch on the west, however, Nāgabhaṭa chose first to pursue the path of least resistance. He began to strike eastward, particularly as there was no imperial authority after the withdrawal of the Kārkoṭas from the Ganges/Yamuna valley in 747. His eastward movement, though, was brought up short by Karkarāja, the ruler of the area around Bhopal, so neither he nor his nephews, who ruled after him, were very successful in the east.[61] They retained their seats of government in Ujjain, where it remained at least until 800.

TABLE 2.9 Gurjara-Pratīhāras

Nāgabhaṭa I (c. 725–760)
Devarāja (c. 750–)
Vatsarāja (c. –790)
Nāgabhaṭa II (c. 790–833)
Rāmabhadra (c. 833–836)
Mihira Bhoja (c. 836–885)
Mahendrapāla (c. 890–910)
Mahīpāla (c. 910–?)
Bhoja II (c. ?–914)
Vināyakapāla (c. 930–945)
Mahendrapāla II (c. 945–950)
Vināyakapāla II (c. 950–959)
Vijayapāla (c. 960–1018)
Rājyapāla (c. 1018–1019)
Trilocanapāla (c. 1020–1027)
Mahendrapāla II

By contrast, Dantidurga (c. 735–755), the founder of the Rāṣṭrakūṭa line, immediately embarked on a widely successful strategy of conquest even while still a vassal of the Chāḷukyas.[62] Within a few years, he had gained the submission of the rulers of Kośala, Kaliṅga, and Śrīśaila, probably representing his victories in the name of his suzerain. Following this, he continued southward, attacking Kāñcī around 743 and asserting a victory over the Pallavas. Then turning northward, he established his authority over parts of Gujarat, the Gulf of Cambay, and the lands along the rich Nārmadā River valley, seizing Ujjain itself for a short time.[63] This action was probably contemporary with Nāgabhaṭa's action in the east. When Nāgabhaṭa returned, however, the Pratīhāra king clearly could control both his capital and the Nārmadā, since the Hansot plates indicate that by 756 he was able to promote the Cāhamāna house as his vassal in Lāṭa.[64]

TABLE 2.10 Rāṣṭrakūṭas

Dantivarman I
Indra I
Govinda I
Karka I
Indra II
Dantidurga (c. 735–755)
Kṛṣṇa I (c. 755–772)
Dhruva Dhārāvarṣa (c. 780–793)
Govinda III (c. 793–814)
Amoghavarṣa (c. 814–880)
Kṛṣṇa II (c. 878–914)
Indra III (c. 914–928)
Amoghavarṣa II (c. 928–929)
Govinda IV (c. 930–935)
Amoghavarṣa III (c. 936–939)
Kṛṣṇa III (c. 939–967)
Khoṭṭiga (c. 967–972)
Karkka II (c. 972–973)

The period 745–760 is certainly unclear, with claims and counterclaims made by poets in boastful epigraphic panegyrics for their royal patrons. In any event, the Rāṣṭrakūṭas seemed destined to clash with their Chāḷukya lords. This conflict finally materialized around 750, when Dantidurga overthrew the last overlord of the Vātāpi Chāḷukyas, Kīrtivarman II, ending the two centuries of domination this house had enjoyed in the Kṛṣṇa River valley. Subsequent charters indicated that Kīrtivarman II continued to exercise power in a limited venue for sometime thereafter, and Dantidurga's uncle and successor, Kṛṣṇa I (c. 755–772), also claimed victories over this last of the Chāḷukya monarchs.[65] Kṛṣṇa I continued Dantidurga's vision of an imperium, asserting control of the Koṅkan coast, perhaps in at attempt to shore up the Rāṣṭrakūṭa fortunes after the loss of Lāṭa and Mālava to the Gurjara-Pratīhāras. Around 765–770, Kṛṣṇa I took his conflict to the south, where he engaged and defeated the Gaṅgas close to Bangalore, and then to the east, where the Eastern Chāḷukya branch ruled the Kṛṣṇa and Godāvarī delta area of Andhrāpatha. Both these aristocratic houses submitted to the Rāṣṭrakūṭa lord, turning Kṛṣṇa I into the supreme ruler of a third of India.[66]

TABLE 2.11 Bhaumakaras of Orissa

Śivakaradeva I (c. 736–780)
Śubhakaradeva I (c. 780–800)
Śivakaradeva II (c. 800–820)
Śāntikaradeva I (c. 820–835)
Śubhakaradeva II (c. 835–838)
Śubhakaradeva III (c. 838–845)
Tribhuvanamahādevī (c. 845–850)
Śāntikaradeva II (c. 850–865)
Śubhakaradeva IV (c. 865–882)
Śivakaradeva III (c. 882–890)
Tribhuvanamahādevī II (c. 890–896)
Tribhuvanamahādevī III (c. 896–905)
Śāntikaradeva III
Śubhakaradeva V
Gaurīmahādevī
Dandimahādevī
Vakulamahādevī
Dharmamahādevī

Source: Adapted from YORITOMI *1990, pp. 142–143.*

The reason eastern India was not affected in this process was that it had only just achieved a degree of political unity and affluence. In Orissa, the Bhaumakaras solidified control of Utkala around 736 and were to maintain this position for approximately the next two centuries. Yet they were scarcely involved with the wider political matrix, except in their interactions with Dakṣiṇa Kośala and Bengal. Bengal, conversely, began to emerge from a lawless period described in the literature as "the manner of fishes" *(mātsyanyāya)*, which is a metaphor analogous to the English "law of the jungle," indicating the rule of the mercilessly powerful.[67] The chaotic period—which had begun about a hundred years earlier with the deaths of Śaśāṅka (c. 628) and Harṣa (647)—was brought to a close by one individual gaining control, Gopāla (c. 750–775), the founder of the

Pāla dynasty.[68] He is said to have been elected by a community of his peers, an appropriation of the old myth of Manu, the lawgiver. However he came to power, it is clear that he achieved control in Gauḍa and extended it into other areas of Bengal, which had not seen order since the time of Śaśāṅka. Gopāla's effectiveness is all the more curious, since he came from a family described as scribes *(kāyastha)* by the later Arab author Abul-i-Fazl or as belonging to a menial caste *(dāsajīvinaḥ)* by the authors of the *Mañjuśrīmūlakalpa*.[69] We know little of Gopāla's reign, except that one of the authors of the *Mañjuśrīmūlakalpa* had a rather dim view of his ability to sustain even a rudimentary government.[70] In about 775 he was succeeded by Dharmapāla, who, perhaps more than anyone else, is responsible for the fame of the dynasty. Since we know little of the actual extent of Gopāla's domain, we have little knowledge of how Dharmapāla increased its extent or solidified Gopāla's prior gains.

TABLE 2.12 Pālas

Gopāla (c. 750–775)
Dharmapāla (c. 775–812)
Ḍevapāla (c. 812–850)
Mahendrapāla (c. 850–865)
Śūrapāla (c. 865–873)
Vigrahapāla (c. 873–875)
Nārāyaṇapāla (c. 875–932)
Rājyapāla (c. 932–967)
Gopāla II (c. 967–987)
Vigrahapāla II (c. 987–992)
Mahīpāla (c. 992–1042)
Nayapāla (c. 1042–1058)
Vigrahapāla III (c.1058–1085)
Mahīpāla II (c.1085–1086)
Śūrapāla II (c. 1086–1087)
Rāmapāla (c. 1087–1141)
Kumārapāla (c. 1141–1143)
Gopāla III (c. 1043–1058)
Madanapāla (c. 1158–1176)
Govindapāla (c. 1176–1180)
Palapāla (c. 1180–1214)

Source: Adapted from Huntington and Huntington 1990, p. 542, chart 1.

By the 780s, though, it had become clear that the great powers of India were headed toward a military engagement. The precipitating event was trouble in Madhyadeśa, and Kanauj remained everyone's first prize. Then ruling in Kanauj was a relatively weak dynasty known as the Āyudhas, obscure in origin. Vajrāyudha, the first known king, became the target of an attempt by the Kashmiris to recapture lost glory. In about 780, Lalitāditya's grandson, Jayāpīḍā Vinayāditya (c. 779–810), made a raid from the north, conquered Vajrāyudha, and captured his throne.[71] With this dramatic demonstration of weakness in the center, the Pratīhāra monarch Vatsarāja elected to try for the entire state, ill content with capturing a glorified chair. After Vajrāyudha's death—perhaps as a result of the Kashmiri war—a succession dispute had broken out in Kanauj, and in about 784 Vatsarāja marched in and defeated the sitting king, Indrāyudha, allowing him to remain on the throne as a vassal. The Pālas must have considered Madhyadeśa part of their propreitary domain, and Dharmapāla took on the cause of the other disputant to the throne, Cakrāyudha.[72] Following the standard medieval mode of settling disputes, the Pratīhāra and Pāla leaders brought their armies to battle close by Prayāga, the confluence of the Ganges and Yamuna Rivers. Unfortunately for the Bengali contingent, Dharmapāla's army was defeated, and the two white umbrellas that he used as his imperial standards were seized by Vatsarāja on the field.

The Rāṣṭrakūṭa king, now Dhruva Dhārāvarṣa (c. 780–793), had been following the troop movements of his two greatest competitors with personal interest and used the opportunity to invade Mālava in Vatsarāja's absence.[73] In about 786 Dhruva moved his army along the same path as Vatsarāja's army had followed, from Ujjain to Kanauj, for much the same reason. There, he encountered the Pratīhāra monarch and took from him the two umbrellas he had earlier taken from Dharmapāla, sending Vatsarāja to seek shelter in the desert. By then, Dharmapāla had moved up his re-equipped and reinforced army to encounter the Rāṣṭrakūṭas on the field, only to have his newly acquired white umbrellas taken away by Dhruva as well. Dhruva now had four of the Pāla umbrellas and was in possession of virtually all of India, but elected to abandon the north, which remained hostile to the southern invader.

Despite the distressing loss of four of his best umbrellas, Dharmapāla actually became the beneficiary of these engagements, all of which he had lost. Dhruva contracted his forces to the south and, after his death in 793, his four sons became involved in a decade-long succession battle.[74] The Pratīhāras were trying to put their shattered country back together during the continued occupation of its southern sector by the Rāṣṭrakūṭas. Vatsarāja died disgraced around 790 and was succeeded by Nāgabhaṭa II (c. 790–833). Dharmapāla used this opportunity to advance to Kanauj for the third time, depose Indrāyudha, and place Cakrāyudha on the throne as the Pāla vassal. Thus, for a brief period of almost a decade at the end of the eighth century, the Pālas were the undisputed lords of the north. Their satisfaction was, however, short-lived. Nāgabhaṭa II was interested in retrieving his family's fortune and reputation. He organized another army in the interim and had established several of the Deccani kings—now no longer involved with the Rāṣṭrakūṭas—as his vassals. In about 795 he moved on Kanauj and conquered Cakrāyudha, the Pāla puppet. Dharmapāla responded, as he had to, and engaged Nāgabhaṭa II on a broad front on his home ground, apparently culminating in a battle at Monghyr, now in modern Bihar. Alas, the noble Bengali king was again defeated by a Pratīhāra army, doubtless losing more umbrellas in the process.

Govinda III (c. 793–814) had emerged from the Rāṣṭrakūṭa succession battles around 796 completely confident and in charge of much of the south, having conquered twelve great southern kings, who had sided with one of his brothers.[75] Not content to rest on these laurels, he elected to march northward as his father had done and once again seize the fruits of the Gangetic valley, since the warring north again provided the same fertile field for southern aggression. Govinda's loyal younger brother, Indra, now governor of Mālava, paved the way for his brother to come up through the Nārmadā valley, much as his father had done. The Deccani army encountered Nāgabhaṭa II, probably south of Kanauj, and utterly routed the Pratīhāra army, as his father had done to Nāgabhaṭa's parent. Then Govinda proceeded to Kanauj, where he received the submission of Cakrāyudha, who had already been almost everyone else's vassal and demonstrated remarkable survival skills. Accurately assessing the course of events, Dharmapāla evidently joined Cakrāyudha in this process of submission, and, now shockingly short of umbrellas, he offered an image of Tārā to Govinda III as a token of his subordinate status. Govinda III, having claimed the authority to attack anyone on the subcontinent, retreated to his source of power in Ellora.

The ninth century thus began with the complete dominion of the Rāṣṭrakūṭas over everyone; they were enjoying the height of their power, an illusory position, as Govinda III was to find to his chagrin. In his approximately two-year absence from the south, his client states formed alliances and rebelled against their suzerain, a pattern that was to occupy the Rāṣṭrakūṭas for most of the ninth century.[76] In 802 the Eastern Chāḷukyas had rebelled and were suppressed by Govinda. Immediately thereafter, a confederation of the Gaṅgas, Pallavas, Karṇātas, and others challenged Rāṣṭrakūṭa supremacy, an uprising that took the better part of two years to quell.

However, whereas the last ten years of Govinda's reign were relatively peaceful, the north was beginning to heat up again. Nāgabhaṭa II had used the opportunity of Dharmapāla's death around 812 to occupy Kanauj again, solidifying his position by 815.[77] The Pratīhāras would occupy Madhyadeśa for most of the ensuing 150 years. Dharmapāla's successor, Devapāla (c. 812–850), wisely did not challenge the Pratīhāras for Kanauj, avoiding his father's error. Instead, he used his time in strategies of encroachment against Nāgabhaṭa's regime, gaining ground slowly and establishing vassal states in Assam and Orissa as well. Nāgabhaṭa II died in 833, and his son Rāmabhadra (c. 833–836) was poorly suited for the medieval military life. Devapāla, realizing his chance, struck out against the Pratīhāra occupation of Madhyadeśa, obviously pursuing a successful military strategy.[78] Devapāla's adventurism, coupled with Rāmabhadra's ineffectual leadership, caused a crisis among the Pratīhāras, and in 836, Rāmabhadra was murdered by his own son, Mihira Bhoja (c. 836–885), who was to become the Pratīhāras' most dynamic and ruthless tyrant.

The Rāṣṭrakūṭas also had a new ruler, Amoghavarṣa (c. 814–880), who ascended the throne as an adolescent, after the death of Govinda III. Again the Eastern Chāḷukyas rebelled, and Amoghavarṣa fled the throne from 818 to 821, when he was restored by the combined military sagacity of his uncle and a succession dispute among the Eastern Chāḷukyas. For approximately a decade, Amoghavarṣa had the opportunity to grow up, and this may have been the time during which the capital was moved from Ellora to Malkhed, in the modern state of Karnataka. His respite was not to last. His greatest challenge emerged from his own Rāṣṭrakūṭa relatives in Gujarat, who had been placed there initially by his father after the successful northern campaign. This internecine conflict was to last from around 835 to 860 and created considerable internal problems for the Rāṣṭrakūṭas.[79]

Back in the north, the new Pratīhāra leader, Mihira Bhoja, and others used the situation to their advantage. The Arabs had embarked on a new series of raids and were repelled by Bhoja's vassals, the Cāhamānas, in 842.[80] With this behind him, Bhoja engaged Devapāla shortly thereafter, defeating the Bengali king with the assistance of Pratīhāra vassal states, particularly the Kāḷachuris, who had resurfaced in Tripurī, close to modern Jabalpur.[81] Disposing of these threats to his security, Bhoja elected to use the Rāṣṭrakūṭas' problems to his advantage. In about 860, Bhoja moved his army down along the Nārmadā valley toward Lāṭa and engaged those vassals loyal to Amoghavarṣa even while they were fighting the Gujarati Rāṣṭrakūṭas.[82] Unexpectedly, the appearance of the Pratīhāras as a common foe caused the various Rāṣṭrakūṭa factions to quickly settle their differences and unite. With their collective strength, they repelled Bhoja's army back north and brought to an end the lengthy Rāṣṭrakūṭa civil war.

Amoghavarṣa used the settlement to turn again to the rebellious Eastern Chāḷukyas, who continued to have the temerity to desire independence. In about 860, Amoghavarṣa again took Veṅgī, to the discomfiture of Vijayāditya III (c. 849–892), the Eastern Chāḷukya king. The Chāḷukyas, though, did not take their defeat lying down. During the end of Amoghavarṣa's life, the contentious Gujarati Rāṣṭrakūṭas in the west were replaced by the hostile Eastern Chāḷukyas as the main source of trouble for the Malkhed imperium. From 870 off and on until around 899, past the death of Amoghavarṣa in 880, the war between Malkhed and Veṅgī continued, having been taken up by their heirs, Kṛṣṇa II (c. 878–914) and Bhīma.[83] With the death of Amoghavarṣa, Vijayāditya III took the conflict to the Eastern Gaṅga and Kāḷachuri vassals and allies of the Rāṣṭrakūṭas, establishing his military capacity through the agency of his redoubtable general, Paṇḍaraṅga. Although the Chāḷukyas did achieve independence, it was not to last. Kṛṣṇa II refitted his forces after the death of Vijayāditya III and even briefly captured the Eastern Chāḷukya successor, Bhīma (c. 892–921). Bhīma, however, continued his uncle's struggle and around 899 finally claimed victory and independence from the Rāṣṭrakūṭas after thirty years of conflict.

One of the reasons for the Rāṣṭrakūṭa's protracted problems was that Kṛṣṇa II in reality had to fight on two fronts, since Pratīhāra Mihira Bhoja's age had not brought him indolence. From around 870 to 880, Bhoja had been involved in a series of conflicts with the Pālas, who had to suffer through succession disputes that brought two brothers and a cousin to the throne within approximately twenty-five years: Mahendrapāla (c. 850–865), Śūrapāla (c. 865–873), and Vigrahapāla (c. 873–875).[84] Bhoja evidently tried to use the Pāla's own strategy of encroachment to obtain some ground, although its success is not entirely clear. After Vigrahapāla's abdication in favor of his son, Nārāyaṇapāla (c. 875–932), however, the circumstances stabilized, and Nārāyaṇapāla's reign was long enough to re-establish confidence in the court. Then, Amoghavarṣa's death around 880 provided Bhoja with the opportunity to attempt again the domination of Lāṭa that he had not achieved in 860.[85] Assisted by his Cāhamāna vassals, he once more moved his troops down the Nārmadā valley, this time successful in his bid to dominate the eastern shore of the Gulf of Cambay. Kṛṣṇa II, having lost the battle, elected instead to win the war. With fresh reinforcements, he drew his troops back, moved to the east, crossed the Nārmadā, and took Ujjain from the Pratīhāras, dealing Bhoja a political and psychological setback deep in the Pratīhāra homeland and causing his retreat from Lāṭa. Bhoja's failure in the west was exacerbated by problems later, at the end of his life, and the Kashmiri king Śaṅkaravarman used Bhoja's failing years to annex part of the northern areas around 886.[86]

Bhoja's death in 888 did not end the Pratīhāra desire for a resort on the Gulf of Cambay. His son Mahendrapāla (c. 890–910) once again invaded around 900, but this time the campaign was successful, ending the Rāṣṭrakūṭa dominance there.[87] The consequences for the Rāṣṭrakūṭas were several: Gujarat—with which they now had no overland communication—was taken from the subsidiary branch of the Rāṣṭrakūṭas and administered directly from Malkhed, perhaps because of its perilous position. The loss in the west of the Lāṭa vassals, and especially the Lāṭa vassal forces, contributed to the Rāṣṭrakūṭa's loss of the Eastern Chāḷukya lands.[88] Unfortunately, the next century would see the eclipse of two of the three dominant states, and the rise of new forces from all sides.

900–1000 C.E.

Undaunted by the erosion of Rāṣṭrakūṭa territory, Kṛṣṇa II bided his time, and around 910, when Pratīhāra Mahendrapāla died, he used the ensuing struggle between the three heirs as an opportunity to invade the north. Mahendrapāla's three sons—Bhoja II, Mahīpāla, and Vināyakapāla—all competed for the throne, in a conflict similar to the one among the Pāla rulers half a century before. The exact course of events is not clear, but it is likely that for a very short time Mahīpāla achieved dominance.[89] This may have been the point that the Rāṣṭrakūṭas intruded on the north, as part of a confederation with the Tripurī Kāḷachuris to back the placement of Bhoja II on the throne.[90] Kṛṣṇa's campaign was little more than a humiliating raid, though, and Bhoja II did not last past 914. By then, however, Kṛṣṇa II had died, and his grandson Indra III (c. 914–928) assumed the Rāṣṭrakūṭa mantle. With Bhoja II gone, Indra III realized that the Rāṣṭrakūṭas had lost their authority in the north, and, in 916–917, Indra III mounted an extensive campaign of invasion, which resulted in the temporary occupation of Kanauj and left behind a trail of corpses.[91] Mahīpāla survived, thanks to the assistance of the increasingly powerful Candella clan of Khajuraho; these Gond tribal rulers assisted reinstating their increasingly nominal overlord on his tarnished throne.

Having tested the waters, Indra III decided to attempt the retaking of Eastern Chāḷukya domains, lost by his grandfather after so much strife. The opportunity came in 921, when Kṛṣṇa II's nemesis, Chāḷukya Bhīma, died.[92]

Bhīma's eldest son held firm, even if it cost him his short life, for he died on the field. The Eastern Chāḷukya victory was Pyrrhic in more ways than one. Like the destabilizing succession battles that afflicted the Pālas and the Pratīhāras before them, the Eastern Chāḷukyas were to go through six rulers in the next few decades, severely limiting their capacity to maintain their position. This eventually resulted in their being taken over for twenty-seven years by the Telugu, Jaṭā Choḍa Bhīma (c. 973–1000).[93]

For the Pratīhāras, the succession dispute was temporarily resolved with the ascension of Vināyakapāla around 930, whose reign of approximately fifteen years was undistinguished. Their problems re-emerge around 945, with multiple claimants to the throne, and the Pratīhāra empire suffered through divided rule and succession battles for some years. During the reigns of Mahendrapāla II (c. 945–950), Vināyakapāla II (c. 950–959), Vijayapāla (c. 960–1018), Rājyapāla (d. 1019), and Trilocanapāla (c. 1020–1027), the Pratīhāras declined precipitously.[94] Trilocanapāla was to be the last of the Pratīhāra emperors, a line of potentates whose domain was eroding by the year. These final Pratīhāra rulers faced not only internal dissention but the aggressive rise of their previously subordinate vassal states: the Candellas of Khajuraho, the Paramāras of Mālava, the Guhilas of Rājaputāna, the Cāhamānas of Sakambhari, and others. Indeed, Rājyapāla was to lose his life at the hands of Candella Vidyādhara, who came to despise the Pratīhāra's cowardice in the face of the new threats from Mahmud of Ghazni, the feral Turkic prince. So, too, the Pratīhāras not only were diminished by the loss of previously loyal client states, but were caught between the Ghaznavid onslaught (c. 1000–1027) and the opportunism of long-term hostile forces in the Deccan.

Among them were the Pratīhāra's old nemesis, the Rāṣṭrakūṭas of Malkhed, who had experienced their own succession battles after the death of Indra III in 928. The first in line, Amoghavarṣa II (c. 928–929), possibly was murdered by his brother Govinda IV (c. 930–935). Govinda IV, considered too dedicated to the women of his seraglio, was deposed by a confederation of Rāṣṭrakūṭa and his uncle, Amoghavarṣa III (c. 936–939), who assumed the throne under duress.[95] It was Amoghavarṣa's son, Kṛṣṇa III (c. 939–967), who seemed to revive the martial spirit of the Rāṣṭrakūṭas.[96] He subdued the Tripurī Kāḷachuris in 938, even before he assumed the throne. Once in power, he led blitzkrieg raids on the Coḷa kingdom in the south in 943, eventually conquering the Coḷa army in 949. Clearly now emulating the great Rāṣṭrakūṭa warlords of the past, such as Indra III, Kṛṣṇa III captured Veṅgī, subdued the Eastern Chāḷukyas, and placed his puppet on the throne. The newly powerful Candellas had evicted some of his northern garrisons, and Kṛṣṇa III responded with a northern expedition in 963–964. There, he defeated the Candellas and moved on the diminished Pratīhāra army, probably under Vijayapāla. They were routed, and Kṛṣṇa III continued on to gain victories in Mālava against the Paramāras, as well as in Gujarat.

These final raids ended up costing the Rāṣṭrakūṭas dearly. Sīyaka, the Paramāra monarch, was not one to accept the inevitable fact of Rāṣṭrakūṭa domination, as had so many of the northern lords in the past. Instead, Sīyaka put together another army, in confederation with princes who had also suffered from Kṛṣṇa III's conquest. In 972, after a series of engagements, Sīyaka gained Malkhed and sacked the Rāṣṭrakūṭa capital.[97] Kṛṣṇa III had already passed away, leaving his son Khoṭṭiga (c. 967–972) to hold the throne. Khoṭṭiga died as a result of the war, however, and his successor, Karkka II, lasted little more than a year as the Rāṣṭrakūṭa monarch. In the end, the Rāṣṭrakūṭas were brought down by their continual oppression of their predecessors: the Chāḷukyas. Seeking to end his subordinate status, Taila II, a local chieftain tracing his lineage back to the royal Vātāpi Chāḷukyas, put together a confederation of states—the Kāḷachuris, the Yādavas, and other Chāḷukya houses—to bring the Rāṣṭrakūṭa empire to utter ruin by December 973.

The last of the three great empires was the only one capable of maintaining itself, the Pālas of Magadha and Bengal. They had managed to stay out of much of the conflict after the time of Devapāla, and the last half of the ninth century saw them consumed with their contentious succession problems. Nārāyaṇapāla's lengthy reign, c. 875–932, contributed to stability there even as others were rent by internal dissension. In the interests of stability, the Pālas had attempted to make multiple diplomatic alliances by marriage to the Kāḷachuris and the Rāṣṭrakūṭas, although these never came with guarantees of peace. Indeed, both the Kāḷachuris and the Candellas began a series of raids on Pāla territories, from the middle of the ninth century on, contributing to the climate of instability.[98] Moreover, the problem of ambitious vassals plagued the Pālas, as it had everyone else. We often see the capacity for a new leader to come in, act as a dutiful subject during a period of power consolidation, and then set up an independent principality at his lord's expense.

In this manner, Nārāyaṇapāla's son Rājyapāla (c. 932–967) had to contend with the fragmentation of Bengal, through the agency of the Candras, who took over the eastern and southeastern sections of Pāla territory and ruled there until the middle of the eleventh century.[99] Whereas the Candras appear indigenous to Bengal, that was not the case for the Kāmbojas, who were evidently a tribal group from the Bengal-Burma border.[100] The ability of tribal leadership to coalesce and take control during the early medieval period was astonishing, a fact that had great consequences for the period. Previously, the Candellas had been a tribal band, evidently members of the larger Gond ethnicity, who had been supremely successful in establishing their credentials. The Kāmbojas appropriated both the Gauḍa principality of western Bengal around 975, during the reign of Gopāla II (c. 967–987), and even filched the names of the Pālas themselves. Thus not only do we find that the Pratīhāras had adopted Pāla names for themselves (Mahendrapāla, etc.), but the Kāmbojas mimicked the cognomen "Pāla" as well. As a result, they are frequently identified as the "Kāmboja Pālas" of Gauḍa.[101]

By the end of the tenth century, the old Pāla domain had been eroded on all sides and was mostly confined to the modern state of Bihar below the Ganges. Not until the time of Mahīpāla (c. 992–1042) did the Pālas begin to regain sections of Bengal that had been lost. His most serious problems were to occur from the south, with the Coḷa invasion of 1021–1023 and the Kāḷachuri occupation of Banaras in 1034.[102] Unfortunately for the dynasty, Mahīpāla was to prove the last great Pāla emperor, and his death marked the beginning of the end for this royal house, which was to sputter on until its subordination at the hands of the Senas in the mid-twelfth century.

1000–1200 C.E.

For our purposes, a concise summary of the succeeding two centuries will suffice to configure the course of events. In the Deccan, the takeover of the Rāṣṭrakūṭas and the occupation of Malkhed by Taila II with his Chāḷukya confederation in 973 marked the beginning of a new dynasty. This was the Chāḷukyas of Kalyāṇī, named for the capital that they constructed upriver from Malkhed in the middle of the eleventh century.[103] Their major conflicts over the next two centuries were with the Coḷas and other peoples of the Deccan and south of the Kṛṣṇa River. The Chāḷukyas of Kalyāṇī were finally brought down by much the same institutional problem that had destroyed the Gurjara-Pratīhāras before them: the rebellion of previous vassal states. In the last quarter of the twelfth century, a group of former feudatories—led by the Kāḷachuris, Yādavas, and Hoysalas—repeatedly engaged the remnant of the Chāḷukya house and removed it from power around 1190.

In the north, the previous domain of the Pratīhāras was divided into multiple smaller states: the Cāhamānas, Guhilas, Paramāras, Tomaras, and so forth. Most of these are classified by historians as Rajput houses, a loose category that includes various military clans from Gujarat to Bihar. Many of them claimed descent from Agni *(agnikula)*, tracing their lineages to a myth of the creation of a race of warriors in a fire altar by the sage Vasiṣṭha at Mount Abu (Arbuda). This was in distinction to houses descended from the Sun *(sūryavaṃśa)* or the Moon *(somavaṃśa)*, in the manner of previous Kṣatriya families.[104] Much of Gujarat was still under the control of the remnants of the Chāḷukyas who had been instrumental in turning back Arab aggression in 737. Similarly, they bore the brunt of the initial assaults of Muhammed of Ghazni from 1000 to 1027. His destructive raids marked the dramatic renewal of the thrusts of Islamic armies into India, which culminated with the loss of the north to the Ghurids of Afghanistan and the founding of the Delhi Sultanate with the ascension of Shams al-Dīn Iltutmish in 1210.[105] Analogously, a greater part of the western Deccan plateau was under the Yādavas while the Paramāras remained in power in Mālava until their subjugation to the Kāḷachuris in the mid-eleventh century. Indeed, two dynasties of very different circumstances were to emerge as major forces in the north: the Kāḷachuris of Tripurī and the Gāhaḍvālas. Under the adventurism of kings like Gāṅgeya (c. 1015–1041) and Karṇa (c. 1041–1073), the Kāḷachuris became the dominant power of central and northern India during the eleventh century.[106] In Kanauj, the Gāhaḍvālas had taken power in the absence of authority with the fall of the remnants of the Pratīhāras. They solidified control of Madhyadeśa while the Kāḷachuris were involved with the Candellas and the Paramāras, eventually extending their hold into areas of northern Bihar.

Thus the Pālas were increasingly surrounded by forces of agonistic rulers—east, west, and south. From the east, the Kaivartas challenged the Pāla hold on north Bengal, while the Candras (and later the Varmans) controlled the eastern sections of Bengal.[107] The biggest threat, though, came from the Senas, who dominated southern Bengal.[108] Following the lead of an adventurous warrior from Karṇāṭaka, the Senas were to expand their control of areas of Bengal until virtually the entire area was theirs. The Pālas were confronted on the west by the Gāhaḍvālas, who had begun encroaching on Pāla territory and eventually took all of northern Uttar Pradesh and Bihar.[109] From the south, the Kāḷachuris invaded multiple times, but their interest was in the spoils of war, rather than in long-term dominion. The end of the Pālas finally came in the second half of the twelfth century, around 1170, when Madanapāla could no longer hold off the combined forces of the Gāhaḍvālas in the west and the Senas in the East. Thus one of the longest-lived dynasties in Indian history came to an end, with the Pālas continuing as only a minor house subservient to the Senas until the Muslim conquest of Magadha by Muhammed ibn Bakhtyār Khaljī around 1204/5.

This review of the political and military history of India is highly defective in at least one respect: scale. We have concentrated on the large battles, the major changes, the subcontinent-wide movements of men and forces. Yet for each of the large changes, there were many more conflicts between the vassals of a major power. Since these were not perceived as determining the direction of important events, the major powers of India elected to allow their feudatories almost unlimited scope for low-level conflict in the early medieval period. Such localized conflicts in fact had an overwhelming impact. The feudatories attained positions of importance by appropriating lesser princes and rose to challenge their overlords at an opportune moment. The battles extracted their tolls, not simply on the warrior class, but on the entire population, as shown in more detail below. Beyond that, the license to engage in conflict that does not encroach on the major powers meant that, at the level of local chieftains, skirmishes over villages, borders, and resources happened with predictable regularity. Consequently, small princelings could work their way up the ladder of political-military hierarchy by sanguinary callousness. Thus our review of the conflicts must be understood to have been mirrored at lower levels with much greater frequency.

THE CULTURE OF MILITARY OPPORTUNISM

Both inscriptions and documents preceding the opening of the early medieval era suggest that the rulers were broadly divided between two kinds of persons. The first kind were those who followed the older chivalry *(rājadharma)* espoused in the *Mānava Dharma Śāstra,* the *Śāntiparvan* of the *Mahābhārata,* and related texts. The author of the *Mānava Dharma Śāstra* identified the king as an entity whose primary function was protector of the populace (I.89) and dispenser of justice (VII.10). Because of the compilatory nature of the text, there is no uniform message about military aggression from this author. In one place (VII.198) he advocates that the king should exercise three of his four means *(upāya)* for overcoming an adversary: offering the adversary conciliation, offering him gifts to solicit his favor, and sowing rebellion within his camp. Never, the verse tells the reader, should a king overcome his enemies by resorting to the fourth means, that of war *(na yuddhena kadācana).* Yet elsewhere the text offers triumphal homage to a king's military virtue:

> Engaged on the fields of battle, the Lords of the Earth seek each others' death. Never diverting their faces from being fought with supreme strength, they ascend to heaven (upon their mutual destruction). (VII.89)[110]

This form of chivalry is analogous to that found in the *Rāmāyana*, where Rāma is depicted as the ultimate self-effacing prince—he is willing to do anything, including relinquishing power, to protect his father's word and therefore his sense of justice.

In distinction to this chivalry was the attitude exhibited by the Pāṇḍavas in the *Mahābhārata*, where they precipitated the destruction of their kinsmen for personal vindication. Their complicity in so much devastation for its own sake is recognized as an ethical dilemma both before the battle—for example, in the opening chapters of the *Bhagavadgītā*—and after the actual conflict itself. It has been long understood that the *Śāntiparvan* is a lengthy treatise motivated by Yudhiṣṭhira's profound unhappiness at his and his brothers' behavior during the conflict, in which many of their relatives had died. The *Śāntiparvan* begins with the simple statement to the ṛṣi Nārada about the evils the five brothers have brought on their world (12.1.13–44). It is ultimately up to Bhīṣma—the paradigmatic warrior who is ridiculously depicted as skewered by Arjuna's arrows so completely that he rests not on the ground but on the protruding tips of the arrows—to teach Yudhiṣṭhira the reasons for such carnage. The balance of the *Śāntiparvan* is Bhīṣma's extended treatise on both Kṣatriya behavior *(rājadharma)* and liberation *(mokṣadharma)*. Along with the *Arthaśāstra* and the *Mānava Dharma Śāstra*, the *Śāntiparvan* represents a base line that we may use to assess the development of the early medieval culture of military adventurism, since the bulk and direction of these three works were produced during or before the time of the Imperial Guptas.[111]

If Yudhiṣṭhira's literary persona is concerned about the behavior of the Indian military in battle, some modern authors have been less apologetic. For a variety of reasons, it has been common to depict ancient and medieval Indian warfare as a benign event in which only the chivalrous combatants lost their lives.[112] Those adopting this position most frequently appeal to the single testimony of Megasthenes, as recorded in Arrian's *Indica* and Strabo's *Geography*. In his discussion of the castes, Megasthenes maintains that "if there is an internal war among the Indians, it is not lawful for them to touch these land workers, nor even to devastate the land itself; but while some are making war and killing each other as opportunity may serve, others close by are peacefully ploughing or picking fruits or pruning or harvesting."[113] Megasthenes' information, however, suggests the proclivity of some Indians to misrepresent themselves to foreigners.[114] Megasthenes' report also shows that those traveling to India frequently have their own agenda, and he employed India as a stage for the fabulous. Megasthenes, for example, presents the genealogy of Candragupta Maurya, the founder of the first pan-Indian state, as the 153d generation descending from Dionysus and denies that Indians have slaves—clearly an inaccurate reporting of both Indian ideas and Indian behaviors. While his testimony is valuable in some areas, our Greek ambassador was also the victim of his own credulity by reporting that he had seen mouthless humans living on vapors (? Gandhārvas), unicorns, gold mining ants, and a host of fabulous beasts. His testimony was questioned by his peers and was dismissed by Strabo and other Greek historians.[115]

Our evidence suggests that war in ancient and medieval India was not a benign affair. We can surmise this from the requirements of similar warfare elsewhere and from the epigraphs, procedural manuals, and explicit concerns of those who had to clean up in the aftermath. Curiously, most of the damage to the society was *not* the direct result of the narrow conflict of armies on an assigned battlefield. Ancient pitched battles were seldom more than a few hours long, were relatively ritualized in nature, and entailed a loss of life that was minimal compared to the wider pattern of destruction.[116] Predominantly, the devastation of the environment and citizenry was the result of military foraging, the violence inflicted on crops and citizens outside the battlefield, and such practices as burning of cities, poisoning wells, and enslavement of populations. Moreover, the pollution of water supplies by battlefield runoff, the spread of disease and famine, and the violence of renegade soldiers all contributed to the long-term population declines in cities targeted in such conflicts.[117]

Foraging was and is required for armies in the field. The difficulty was that, for most of the history of warfare, soldiers have been capable of carrying only about seventy pounds per man, including weapons, armor, clothing, and food.[118] The balance of provisions, medicine, weapons, tools, and so forth must be either transported or secured in the target area. The enormous distances covered by these armies involved in pitched battles meant that the primitive transportation systems of India must have concentrated on irreplaceable items, and certainly de-emphasized food for the soldiers and fodder for the cavalry, chariot, and elephant corps. These developments are evident from the archaeological record, epigraphs, and the major contemporary sources for political systems and military expediency—the *Arthaśāstra* (first to second century C.E.) and the *Nītisāra* of Kāmandaka (seventh to eighth century C.E.).[119] Such sieges meant that armies initially relied on local produce, later to be replaced by goods from a larger area of supply. These supplies required well-organized units, and we can infer that they eventually evolved into supply specialty groups, such as the Bañjaras of the Mughal period.[120] To offset the effects of the siege, a ruler might poison the wells or burn the standing crops, practices validated in the *Nītisāra* under the recognized doctrines of deceitful strategies *(kūṭayuddha)*.[121] Even in the *Arthaśāstra*, recommended methods included the employment of tribal peoples to act on behalf of the invading force: they might poison the cultivators, burn their crops, or set fire to the fortifications.[122] We can also surmise that they would be motivated to take revenge for intrusion into traditional tribal lands or for the suppression of tribal peoples, as in the case of the Guhilas over the Bhillas.[123]

The results of these and other practices were manifold, but principally entailed the erosion of the difference between private and public violence, so that conscripts both learned the skills of organized butchery and became desensitized to its consequences.[124] Whether in the heat of battle or in the lives of surviving participants, war is a paradoxically private affair, but with grave public consequences on noncombatants in its immediate proximity and on the citizenry when the soldiers return home.[125] The effects of such practices on the unarmed populace was articulated in Aśoka's Shabazgarhi inscription, where he writes that the battle of Kaliṅga resulted in 150,000 enslaved, 100,000 combatants killed in the battle itself, and many times that number losing their lives in the aftermath as a direct result of the conflict.[126] Although the absolute figures might be inflated, as has been frequently suggested, the ratio of combatants, slaves, and slaughtered innocents appears appropriate. Many among the populace lost their lives because of militarily engineered famine or through poisonings, hatreds by third parties, and reprisals by military commanders.

The conflagration of medieval cities was common enough for Hira Lal to remark, "The burning of capital towns seems to have been a favorite form of annoyance to unfriendly rulers and was perhaps regarded as a great achievement."[127] Religious tracts acknowledge the burning of cities as a subset of belligerence, and works like the Buddhist *Siddhaikavīramahātantra* specify rituals for the pacification of agonism and conflagrations.

> This king of mantras is recited to pacify all strife, antagonism, argumentation, misfortune and destitution, and they all become pacified with the *homa* sacrifice using rice chaff. Whatever flowers may be obtained, say the mantra over them, and release them into water. Then all peace and victory will be obtained, have no doubt. When a city is burning, stand facing the fire and address praise to seven handfuls of water, then throw them on the fire. One desiring to protect his home from incineration will thus preserve it.[128]

Many of our sources warn commanders against such activities for Machiavellian reasons—they would turn the populace against them. However, such arguments are appropriate only when territorial gain is the primary goal, which was only one of many reasons for battle.[129] For the conquerors, though, who did not seek further domains, few of these inhibitions are evident. So, when Karkarāja defeated Nāgabhaṭa, the Bhopal Rāṣṭrakūṭa prince is depicted by the court poet as laughing in the devastated city of his enemy.[130]

Thus the great cities of Kanauj, Vārāṇasī, Gauḍa, and so forth had difficulty retaining primacy as centers of culture, for their preeminence had revealed their attractiveness to opportunistic invasion. Kanauj frequently became the goal of armies, and this reality forced such rulers as the Pratīhāras to found a series of subsidiary palaces and regional centers in the periphery, well outside the actual path of potential invasion.[131] Armies tended to approach cities along established trade routes, so the greenbelts of those cities could be sources of supply. Conversely, overland routes, which may have been shorter, were not preferred.[132] An aggressive force approaching the regional capital might not only seize the offices of government and, if possible, members of the royal house. They might also avail themselves of the copperplate records (from which they can get information on vassals), the treasury, the wealth of the large banking houses, and other potential sources of revenue. Following this, the burning of cities in the aftermath of the invasion was a means of dispersing the populace and dissuading counterattacks, particularly if the invading force did not wish to establish a new confederate on the throne or to acquire the territory for itself. Thakur and Jha have reviewed the list of twenty-one mercantile cities found in the eighth century Prakrit story, the *Samarāiccakahā*, and have found that, for those having had some level of archaeological examination, virtually every one experienced rather dramatic decline during this period.[133]

Moreover, as has been discovered by China in the aftermath of the Cultural Revolution, the United States in the wake of the Vietnam war, and the Soviet Union after its conflict in Afghanistan, not all returning soldiers become law-abiding citizens. Having learned the business of slaughter and intimidation, the demobilized conscripts sometimes form criminal gangs, where they apply their training in the use of armament and military tactics. The aftermath of conflicts provides them a perfect series of abandoned buildings to employ as hideouts. Requiring revenues to make up for the losses during the campaign, the central government will just as frequently turn a blind eye to the intrusion on civil authority and accept from the pirates whatever payments of tribute that might serve its purposes.

This process assisted the transformation of the feudal practice of gift giving and rewards into corruption and rapacity. Indeed, much of the discussion of the reigns of previous dynasties in Kalhaṇa's *Rājataraṅgiṇī* (1148–1149) is taken up with the corruption of kings and officials (to which even Manu agrees). Kalhaṇa demonstrates the cruelty of such behavior when he shows rulers like Jayāpīḍa (c. 779–810) seizing the entire harvest of Kashmir for three years running.[134] This conduct was also in evidence on the coasts, where piracy was endemic—sometimes conducted directly by a local warlord, sometimes by privateers surrendering part of their booty to the prince.[135]

As a consequence of the emergence of this culture of military adventurism, decentralization and the coalescence of fiefdoms became primary characteristics of the period.[136] These in turn yielded the castelization of parts of India with the development of fortresses and armed encampments in various locales. By the early medieval period, Indians had developed all three normative forms of fortifications: refuges, strongholds, and large strategic defenses. Keegan notes that the castelization of a country is the sign of its lack of centralized authority. As he observes, "Strongholds are a product of small or divided sovereignties; they proliferate when central authority has not been established or is struggling to secure itself or has broken down."[137]

The sage Kāśyapa in the *Śāntiparvan* graphically articulates the experience of a kingdom falling into lawlessness by the metaphor of the emergence of Rudra, the personification of evil and destruction:

> Where the treacherous obtain confirmation in the assembly, even when they have killed women or Brahmans, and appear without fear in the presence of the king—the Ksatriya lives in terror of that estate.
>
> For there the god Rudra emerges at the moment when treachery is outrageously crafted by rogues. Through these evil deeds, those rogues produce Rudra, indiscriminately harming both the virtuous and venomous alike.
>
> Rudra is the soul lurking in the hearts of vicious men, killing each of their own bodies as well as the bodies of others. They say Rudra is like cruel catastrophes by the winds of the world. His form looks like clouds and conflagrations.[138]

We will catch up with Rudra—recast as Maheśvara—again in later chapters, but I emphasize Keegan's fundamental argument that war is not, as Clausewitz has classically claimed, an extension of political intercourse by other means.[139] Clausewitz's proposition was based on the reductionism of Aristotle and his followers, who maintain that man is a political animal, indicating that all behavior is essentially political, despite the clear evidence that political goals and institutions are frequently subverted and destroyed by war, as they are by other cultural systems. Rather, Keegan argues that war is an extension of cultural forms, an activity in which all the elements of the culture come into play and by which all these elements are themselves are affected and transformed. The lengthy list of the recognized causes of war given by Kāmandaka around the seventh to eighth centuries—including everything from the abduction of women and the arrogance of leaders to divine guidance—seems to support Keegan's model.[140]

AESTHETICS AND THE APOTHEOSIS OF KINGSHIP

Perhaps the most telling aspect of warfare, and the strongest verification of Keegan's thesis in this culture, is the early medieval period's substantial change in the representation of rulers and their military belligerence.[141] War became depicted as a facet of the erotic play of the king, who was understood as the manifestation of a divinity. Such representations were embodied in verse panegyrics *(praśasti)* that had become part of mainstream epigraphic statements, at least by the time of Hariṣeṇa's verses in honor of Samudragupta, written around 350 C.E.[142] Poets certainly had been part of the Gupta courts, and we find Hariṣeṇa emphasizing the importance of poetry in Samudragupta's court, especially by claiming that the king himself was a "poet king" *(kavirāja)* with his own command of poetic literature.[143] Yet the simple presence of poets did not immediately invoke the erotic sentiment on behalf of kingship, a process that required time to mature. Skandagupta receives a rather prosaic epigraph in his Bhitari Stone Pillar Inscription, despite the mention of the songs and adulation *(gīta, stuti)* generated by *vandanajana* (panegyrists) on his behalf.[144] In fact, though, the Guptas' epigraphic panegyrics were, for the most part, indicative of value systems familiar to the great epics, and we find the frequent invocation that a concern for the country's citizens was the model of kingly behavior.

The first indication of a new direction is seen in Vatsabhaṭṭi's 473–474 C.E. verses in praise of Bandhuvarman, who was governing the city of Daśapura on behalf of Kumāragupta.[145] There Vatsabhaṭṭi demonstrates a trend that will become obligatory during the early medieval period: the divine erotization of kingship and, ultimately, of warfare. This trajectory took some time to develop, however, and Vasula's praise to Yaśodharman is relatively toned down in the c. 530 C.E. Mandasor inscription, again demonstrating concern for the welfare of the world.[146] Yet the 533–534 epigraph of his subordinate Viṣṇuvardhana emphasizes the eros of kingship and belligerence, and mentions the role of poets singing in Sanskrit and Prakrit in praise of one of the king's ancestors.[147]

From this time forward, we find an idealization of warfare and the apotheosis of kingship in Indian inscriptions and literature. Living monarchs would be accorded the same level of panegyric previously reserved for incarnations of divinity, with whom they would be incessantly compared. Bringing with them their training in poetic sentiment, the court poets increasingly constructed verses of praise to the monarch and his ancestors *(praśasti),* inspired by the canons of poetry as these latter developed. In their verses, belligerence is recast in the language of eroticism *(śṛṅgāra-rasa)* and heroism *(vīrarasa)*—exactly the sentiments afforded divinity. War is no longer the assembly and slaughter of frightened men for dubious purposes, but the seizure and seduction of the goddess Fortune (Śrī: wealth) from the cities of the enemies into the harem of the conqueror. In Ravikīrti's 634–635 C.E. Aihole lineal panegyric *(praśasti)* to the Chāḷukyas, for example, Jayasiṃha-vallabha, the first Chāḷukya monarch identified there, won through battles and "by his bravery made Fortune his own, even though she is suspected of fickleness."[148] The conquering king carries out his agenda, not by force—although the battlefields drip with gore ("thousands of headless bodies" in the epigraph)—but by dint of his divine virility, so that the wealth of the target kingdom helplessly throws herself at his feet. Even more, Pulakeśin II in a later verse in the paean simply has Fortune obsessed with him at birth. His conquering of Vanavāsī is rendered in language that portrays the city as a coy woman and the warlord as her ardent lover; their embrace depicted as the dalliance of idle courtiers, not the bloody pillaging of a terrified populace.[149] Examples could be multiplied from the inscriptions and literature of the Kāḷachuris, Puṣyabhūtis, and others in the north as well, although Śaiva kings and poets over all seem to be particularly susceptible to this variety of diction.[150]

In the hands of such noted authors as Ravikīrti, Rājaśekhara, Bāṇa, and Vākpatirāja—to name only the most famous of medieval poets—the cultured folks at home were treated to the elaborate descriptions of the seductiveness of their lords in the field of battle. These court poets invoked the diction of the heroic and erotic sentiments—sometimes allied with the ferocious *(raudra)*—in Sanskrit and Prakrit poetry, so warfare become draped with language of play *(vilāsa)* and games *(krīḍā)*, as if between lovers. Our warlords, seen as extensions of the divinities they accrued during their coronations, demonstrate their lack of seriousness of purpose, as did Rāma or Kṛṣṇa in their destruction of demons for the welfare of mankind. Kielhorn has shown, for example, that the Aihole panegyric is closely modeled after Kālidāsa's epic poem dedicated to the life of Rāma, the *Raghuvaṃśa.*[151] Likewise, the Bilhari Stone Inscription of Kāḷachuri Yuvarājadeva II makes pointed comparison between its composition and the work of the famous poet Rājaśekhara.[152] It is just this intersection of the belligerent, the erotic, and the sacred that motivated Johan Huizinga—first trained as an Indologist—to articulate his model of humanity as *homo ludens* (the playful man).[153]

We will return to the element of play later, but here it is sufficient to note that the erotization of warfare served the purpose of sanctioning belligerence: it was now the divine play of gods. The depiction of war as play allowed the rulers of early medieval India to establish a sense of their own action as both divinely inspired and without the serious consequences that would mitigate its being just good fun. This is exactly the attitude warned against in works on law and polity, for their Brahman authors were all too often required to flee from burning cities and the devastations of cruelly armed men.

The impact on Brahmans, in fact, was unprecedented. As a result of the ensuing medieval warfare on a large scale, the period became a time of great Brahmanical migration, in which the highest caste not only sought patronage and protection but also spread the values of caste and ritual into the new regional centers. When these priests and their families would arrive in a new area, they would be given (if they were lucky) land that was considered "waste" *(bhūmicchidranyāya)*; they were granted areas that were wild and in need of clearance for farming purposes. Our records indicate that Brahmans crisscrossed northern India during most of the period in question, emigrating from Madhyadeśa, Bengal, Magadha, Gujarat, Rajasthan, Kashmir, and other locales at various times to seek employment in regions such as Madhya Pradesh, the Deccan, and, preeminently, Orissa. Their individual reasons for relocating, though, are not inscribed in the land grants they received. Swati Datta, who has studied the phenomenon, became convinced that Brahmans emigrated to escape the military adventurism of the period and the lawlessness that followed in its wake.[154] Singh has studied the Oriya circumstances in some detail, however, and has pointed out that the possibility of free land was doubtless a contributing factor, so the émigrés were part refugees, part opportunistic homesteaders.[155] Whichever may be the case, there can be no question that Brahmans served the interests of monarchs by spreading normative, caste Hindu values, acting as de facto propagandists for the new order, Hinduizing the immediate area contiguous to their farmland by their influence on tribal religious systems, and so forth.

Our sources suggest that the primary beneficiaries of royal largess were those Brahmans whose specialties included the rituals associated with their lineages *(gotra)* or those with an expertise in the legal literature *(dharmaśāstra, smṛti)*. The former specialty was clearly part of the symbiotic relationship between those who represent the sacred power *(brahma)* and those who invest that power in the social order *(kṣatra)*. Monarchs during the early medieval period unquestionably required the presence of Brahmans to assist in coronation and related rituals, which assured the divine authority of the ruling house. Indian polity required that the law be administered—in the idiom of the day, the staff of coercion *(daṇḍa)* be held—by a king representing the sacred order and embodying its capacity for protection and dominion. Brahmans conferred this sacrality by their presence in the kingdom, and it served the interests of both parties for them to locate in the royal proximity.

Legitimacy was a central concern for these new regional rulers, since many of the ruling houses did not derive from traditional Kṣatriya lineages. Some were tribal in origin, some were from other castes, and some were simply indeterminate, since the caste system was besieged by new clan designations and ethnonyms that had no direct correspondence to traditionally affirmed categories. The result of these phenomena was technically known as the doctrine of the "mixture of the castes" *(vārṇasaṃkara)*, in which new groups were identified as having been brewed from inappropriate unions between members of existing lineages. This designation represented a convenient prevarication but one that brought a significant indeterminacy about correct relations—food, marriage, or employment, to name the most important. But even beyond ritual, the knowledge of polity *(nīti)*, legal literature, and administrative systems *(arthaśāstra)* was a boon to any new ruling house, and the new rulers needed both the talent and learning of Brahmans who found themselves looking for such opportunities. The freshly empowered rulers of the newly developed order—installed in the position of divinities on earth at their coronation—required all the assistance they could obtain. The rulers' survival required that any informed bearers of the emerging social order be turned to the valorization of the warlords' clans, their domains, and their political aspirations.

FEUDALIZATION OF DIVINITY

In the medieval militarized culture, the apotheosis of the king served his strategy of divine right to the assumption of power, irrespective of his actual lineage. However, the process of divine royalty conversely implied the royalty of divinity, so the apotheosis of rulers entailed the feudalization of the gods. Kulke and Rothermund have pointed out that the gods began to have hierarchies, and the imperial divinity *(rāṣṭradevatā)* favored by an overlord became the divine overlord for the family and village divinities worshiped by the monarch's vassals. They called this process the "royalization of divinity"—the gods became part of the political process and advanced in their public aura as their royal patrons succeeded in their strategies to obtain vassals and dominion. For our purposes, though, it might be understood as the "sāmantization" of the gods, a term they applied to the development of Indian feudalism in the political sphere.[156] By sāmantization of the gods, I mean that the great and local deities of the period became feudalized as lords and ladies, with their personalities assuming the position of the paradigmatic feudal lord *(sāmanta)*. They occupied positions in metaphysical space analogous to the positions controlled by their devotees in terrestrial space, with all the attendant rights and responsibilities. At the same time, lesser divinities became understood as representatives of the imperial divinity, who protected and them in a complex exchange of divine services, just as the vassals owed allegiance and loyal to the monarch through the exchanges of goods, services, land, and booty.

Eventually, this phenomenon became thoroughly worked out in the early medieval literature. Its emerging synthesis was based on the erosion of categorical differences at the apex of human and celestial societies. If kings could become divine in their playful belligerence, the mythology and ritual respect eventually accorded divinities in the new grand temple complexes would reinforce the conception of a deity's imperial status. Thus Rāma, portrayed as a supremely heroic king in the Vālmīki *Rāmāyana*, became an incarnation of Viṣṇu in the Purāṇas, and even members of his retinue, like Hanuman, eventually attained godlike status. Likewise, Śiva, heretofore an ascetic, became married to Pārvatī, so the new Ruler of the World (Lokeśvara) was revealed as a domesticated emperor with children. With his minions *(gaṇa)*, Śiva engaged in battle with demons and accordingly was recognized as the Destroyer of Three Cities. His activity became the model for medieval terrestrial monarchs, because of both his violent manifestations and the erotic nature of his aesthetics and iconology.

The emergence of the new Purāṇic literature at this time embodied the understanding that gods were in competition for hegemony over the cosmological and ritual landscape, so that the previous battle between gods and demigods now included divine competition. Whether Śiva or Viṣṇu, Durgā or Kālī, the theological protagonists of Purāṇic narratives became involved in their own divine military culture, in which they would make alliances, fight the challenges to their authority, and subvert the domains of their neighbors. Domestically, they were royalty as well, with palaces and gardens, children and attendants. Thus Purāṇic divinities lived in fortresses, married, received guests, held court, supported poets, and feasted their favorites.

As a consequence of this confluence of imperial and sacred spheres, coupled with the rise of the emerging regional centers, a new dynamic in religious art and architecture developed as well. The period saw a very rapid buildup of temple construction, most frequently for reasons of political expediency and cultural authority. Without an urban cultural center of gravity, the early medieval period saw an efflorescence in regional styles. With the fall of the Guptas, as Williams has noticed:

> Finally, in both architecture and sculpture, a new pluralism of regional styles appears, which means that some of the above generalizations are not fully borne out in certain areas. We no longer see the old *koine* of style [under the Guptas], including both motifs and their treatment, that had stretched from Gujarat to Bengal and from the Salt Range to the Vindhya Mountains. The development of regional styles, familiar in later medieval architecture, is also apparent in the less plentiful and less well-preserved structures of the late sixth and seventh centuries.[157]

Williams's observation on pluralism can be integrated into our models only by acknowledging that the previous metropolitan centers of culture—Vārāṇasī, Kanauj, and Avanti (Ujjain)—had, by the sixth- and seventh-century perceptions, become dramatically eroded in their authority.[158] Regionalism is an exuberant expression of locality for artists and is the means for integrating styles normatively outside the canon—preeminently tribal and folk representations—into media of permanency (stone especially). These durable media are not standard for local artists until patrons from that area wish to represent themselves as being on a par with remote authorities. This entails a loss of aura for those in Pāṭaliputra, Vārāṇasī, Kauśāmbī, or Mathurā, so that they can no longer command taste and establish standards of connoisseurship in areas far distant.

In erecting the new temple complexes, kings became patrons to the new divinities that commanded the areas under the rulers' political control. Thus the new temples satisfied many different functions. They became testaments to royal legitimacy, with the rulers using the temple walls as a *tabula rasa* for the epigraphs that communicated royal piety, regal decisions on legal matters, imperial conquests, formal alliances with other houses, and a host of matters rendering them archives for a ruling house. For example, the temple of Bhīmeśvara at Drākṣārāma, close to the mouth of the Godāvarī River, was used as an Eastern Chāḷukya place of public pronouncement, after its tenth-century construction.[159] As soon as it was seized by the Coḷas in 1076 C.E., they also inscribed their statements of piety on its hallowed walls. Similarly, the Mukhaliṅgam complex (Kaliṅga) between c. 600 and 1100 C.E. and the Varāha Narasiṃha temple at Siṃhācalam (N. Andhra) between 1000 and 1600 C.E. both served as the centers of religious culture and as the sites of regal pronouncements.[160] The net result was that the sacred zones became the palaces of the gods and the temples of the kings, with both enjoying feudal privileges over the domain under temple control.

CONCLUSION: EARLY MEDIEVAL VITALITY

The turn of events after the fall of the Gupta and Vākāṭaka dynasties supported the emergence of a new culture of military adventurism, which became increasingly the reference point for the other facets of Indian society. Contrary to the received language of chaos, the period is rich in specific kinds of institutions and structurally embedded systems that emphasize decentralization and regionality. Many of these institutions and systems arose as a response to the uncertainty of safety in the large metropolitan centers, which lost population to an increasing number of regional locales that achieved importance through the influx of new talent and the clearing of tribal lands for agriculture. The new political and military ideology of the universal conqueror is evident in the use, appropriation, and dissemination of culture through the agency of the royal courts and by the eclipse of alternative systems of cultural maintenance. During this period, there was a weakening of support for some previously strong systems (Vedic ritualism, Buddhism), but there was also the rise of elaborate temple building and the development of regional schools of art. We see the coalescence of schools of poetry and the emergence of Sanskrit and Prakrit connoisseurship, with its articulation of ideas of appropriate literature and standards of criticism. Poets not only became the mechanism for royal propaganda but served to bring local aesthetics into conformity with the Sanskrit high culture.

With the valorization of regional identity came the apotheosis of kings and their new lineages, contributing to the discourse of divine power. Ultimately, this would lead to the feudalization of divinity as well, so that the gods became kings even as the kings became gods. Religious edifices not only supported the kingship claims by clans of indistinct or even disreputable lineage but resulted in the rise and development of regional styles of art and architecture and the recognition of local gods as important. These new temples became the showpieces of royal self-representation and the tableaus for epigraphs indicating statements of royal piety and naked power. It is in this new world of rapidly changing feudal alliances and evolving religious orders that the great Buddhist monasteries and lay associations would find themselves challenged on all sides.

3

The Medieval Buddhist Experience

> Then there will be renunciates—firmly committed to the dispensation of Śākyamuni and always attached to the pronouncement of mantras—who will work for the benefit of the teaching.
>
> I will speak of them, O Prince, those who will live when the best of sages, the Excellent Unique Eye of the World, has passed away—so listen attentively!
>
> Yes, have no doubt that, with the eon's denouement, in the devastation of the Teacher's message, there will be monks influential within political domains.
>
> —*Mañjuśrīmūlakalpa*, XXXVII:933–935[1]

The weight of early medieval India fell on all its institutions, but in an uneven manner, affecting some much more than others. Certain facets of society, such as the Jaina traditions and the secular military systems, responded with resilience, having developed coping strategies. Some forms of culture entered a period of efflorescence, especially institutions surrounding the courts of local lords. These groups participated in the development of an international ideology of refined culture and its political reflex.[2] Buddhist congregations, however, found themselves under attack from without and challenged from within. The vitality that the monastic and lay institutions had demonstrated before and during the Gupta period appeared to falter in the face of successive challenges at both the institutional and ideological level. Our sources indicate an attrition in external support and an erosion of confidence inside the Buddhist communities, so that Buddhists no longer could point to the obvious benefits of participation in their activities. Little wonder, then, that medieval orthodox representatives, like Śaṅkara, could successfully depict the dispensation of the Buddha as an intentional deceit, misleading the masses and ushering them down the path of delusion.[3]

This chapter aims to articulate the Buddhist experience in the midst of the early medieval ebb and flow of political, economic, and religious cultures. The frame of reference is reduced from that of chapter 2, so that we can examine how the larger sociopolitical realities affected the minority Buddhist culture. Subsequent chapters will cover the development of esoteric Buddhism within this reduced frame of reference. As shown below, this new form of Buddhist praxis evolved both as a response to the eroding sociopolitical environment and as a strategy for religious reaffirmation in the face of unparalleled challenges to Buddhist institutions. The evidence suggests that the rise and development of the Buddhist esoteric forms were the result of a complex nexus of external social forces and internal Samgha dynamics. Consequently, it appears that the Mantrayāna was at once the most socially and politically involved of Buddhist systems and the variety of Buddhism most acculturated to the medieval Indian landscape.

In the course of our investigation, we might keep in mind questions of agency and authority, for the esoteric turn was accompanied by changes in decision systems at the social level. In this respect, three groups appear at the center of medieval Buddhist decision-making—the monks of the orthodox Samgha, the informed Buddhist laity, and the new form of Buddhist personality represented by the Perfected *(siddha)*. However, the narrowly Mahayanist-type informed laity became less influential as the medieval period progressed, for they were the first to experience the radical alteration of Indian life in the economic and political arenas, and consequently they became the first casualties of the era. Thus authority shifted to an uneasy alliance between the monastic community, on the one hand, and the increasingly radical siddhas at the margins of Buddhist society, on the other. Accordingly, the following chapters consider this distinction between institutional and noninstitutional esoterism, the former based on decisions predominantly made within the monastic community, and the latter the product of the Buddhist siddha culture. This chapter explores the circumstances that define and circumscribe the medieval Buddhist experience and, by extension, that of the Mantrayāna.

The present chapter concerns six specific realities of the post-Gupta Buddhist world. Several were consequences of the transformation in cloister/lay involvement, while others were primarily monastic in nature. First, the older Buddhist patronage system lost its bearings and required the search for new directions of support. Second, because these new directions were of limited success, Buddhist institutions experienced a contraction in both the number and the geographical distribution of sites. Monasteries fundamentally ceased operation in the Kṛṣṇa and Godāvarī River valleys and became concentrated in the northern and southern corners of India. Third, the nature of women's participation in Buddhist activity changed, seen both in the lack of resources available to fully ordained nuns (assisting the demise of nuns' orders during this period) and in a net contraction of the number of women involved in Buddhist lay practice of any variety. Fourth, some Buddhist intellectuals developed a radical form of skepticism, the Prāsaṅgika Madhyamaka, which claimed the intellectual high ground and was successful, in part, by virtue of its extremism. Fifth, other Buddhist intellectuals became engrossed in the development of a Buddhist version of Brahmanical epistemology, with a concomitant degradation of traditional Abhidharma-based Buddhist scholasticism. Sixth, with the simultaneous change of patronage and rules of survival, many Buddhist monasteries began to assume the position of landed fiefdoms, with a growth in the net size of some of the great monasteries and the new development of the "supermonastery" *(mahāvihāra)*. These great institutions, in turn, generated a curriculum that supported the new intellectual turn of the tradition.

GUILDS, COMMERCE, AND POLITICAL LEGITIMACY

Central to the altered dynamic of medieval Indian Buddhism was the destabilization of guilds and their roles in national and international commerce. Buddhist institutions may have received their great impetus from Aśoka, but their capacity to spread through multiple language and ethnic groups and their ability to elicit patronage generation after generation depended as much on their symbiotic relationship with the guilds of Indian tradesmen and merchants as on their attractiveness to princes needing access to the advances of Indic culture. Ever since the myth of the first Buddhist laymen—Trapuṣa and Bhallika—and the first grand monastic patron, Anāthapiṇḍada, Buddhist institutions have relied on the largess and prestige of commercial patrons. In return, monks taught merchants' sons, ministered to their medical needs, lent them capital, provided them with temporary residences at specific points in their journeys, made them amulets, provided them with linguistic feats of translation, and introduced them to local personages.[4]

Guilds were either concerned with manufacturing or involved with distribution, although there was invariably some overlap between the two, and both were held in high esteem during the Gupta hegemony.[5] Both types had intermittently supported the Buddhist cause, although the involvement of national and international trading cooperatives and service guilds with the Teaching of the Teacher was far more dramatic than those whose purpose was light manufacturing. The company of monks is evident in the petroglyphs along the Indus trade routes, where stūpas and icons of the Buddha are engraved along with the names of merchants, princes, and local personages of means.[6] We even find evidence of monastic financial instruments, like a promissory note written in Kuchean, evidently written from one Śīlarakṣita to his associate Āryavarman—one Buddhist monk to another—to buy various types of copper straps.[7]

As Buddhists altered the perceptions of the importance of trade, they were themselves affected in the process; monks embedded the images of merchants and guildsmen in their own diction. We find, for example, a trade-influenced ordination lineage inscribed along a Gilgit caravan path, with the monks Satyaśreṣṭhī and Dharmaśreṣṭhī—Guildmaster of Truth and Guildmaster of the Dharma—engraving their names in rock.[8] In the scriptures, as well, the leader of the caravan *(sārthavāha)* and analogous figures become powerful metaphors for awakened activity. In the *Gaṇḍavyūha*, for example, Vasantī, the goddess of the night, explains that, as a bodhisattva, she may appear in the guise of a caravan master or other personage, to lead to safety those lost and in danger, whether in forests, on mountains, on the oceans, and so forth.[9] There is a commercial expansion of earlier mythic and ritual directions, and Ray has shown that myths of bodhisattvas (ultimately Avalokiteśvara) as protectors of mariners represent strong trajectories in earlier Buddhist scriptures; conversely, the contemporary Hindu Dharmaśāstras discourage or forbid maritime travel.[10] Caravan leaders eventually become the model for bodhisattvas in the *Daśabhūmika-sūtra*—a bodhisattva is to be as dedicated toward the goal as the caravan master—and the caravan master becomes an apt metaphor for the Buddha himself in panegyrics over time from Mātṛceṭa to Śāntideva.[11]

In the political arena, Buddhist monks gave legitimacy to royal patrons, especially those outside the Gangetic valley. Whether in Gandhāra or Kaśmīra (Indo-Greeks, Śakas, Kuṣānas, Ephthalites, Shahis), in the Sindh, in quasi-tribal areas like Orissa (Bhaumakaras, etc.), and analogous polities in Central and Southeast Asia. For these royal patrons, Buddhist monks first inscribed foreign languages (Kuchean, Khotanese, Gāndhārī, etc.), acted as scribes for court proceedings, and encouraged both capital expenditures by courts and the value of artistic enterprise. These services allowed the mercantile community to prosper in a way unforeseen without Buddhist monastic assistance and entitled royal patrons to reap the benefits of the first Asian foray into a globalized culture. As a result, Buddhist monks spread their Dharma by extending the domains of such services to the fertile Indus valley, the oases of Central Asia, the ports of Southeast Asia, and eventually to China.[12]

Even before the early medieval period, patronage patterns had been changing, as demonstrated in the transformation of language from the Middle Indic Prakrits to Sanskrit. For example, the brothers Mahāpanthaka and Cūḷapanthaka—well-known arhats and standard personalities in the *Avadāna* literature—are considered illegitimate sons of a wayward daughter of a banking guildmaster *(seṭṭhi)* in the versions found in the Pali canon.[13] Yet when their stories are rendered into Sanskrit or languages appropriate for the movement into Central Asia, they become the sons of Brahmans.[14] Such surprising alterations of narrative contents are comprehensible only in the face of equally dramatic transformations of sociolinguistic expectations and audience appeal. The narrative changes, in this case, are reflective of the ability of Sanskrit to transmit sociopolitical values and indicative of the social composition of those versed in this language.[15] In North India and Central Asia, the merchants apparently supported these changes, for Buddhist monks were actively involved in the commercial transactions, as is evident from the records in the Sanskrit or Hybrid Sanskrit *Vinayas* of the Sarvāstivāda, the Mahāsāṅghika, and the Mūlasarvāstivāda, their Chinese analogues, and within materials in regional languages like Gāndhārī.[16]

The geopolitical realities of the early medieval period, however, had extraordinary consequences for guilds at both the national and the international level. Nationally, Indian merchant guilds began to emulate the political structure by turning into landed feuda, resolving their prior national trade network into a system of personal allegiances to local lords. In this, they had little choice. The guilds represented a reservoir of available assets for those intent on military adventurism, and the paucity of minted monies during the era only served to increase the attractiveness of these guilds as temporary resources. The medieval decline of both trade and artisan guilds in North India is to some degree tied to their perception as a consistent source of income for sovereigns, beyond the royal booty secured from war. Military campaigns are both extraordinarily expensive and an unreliable source of funds, so guild and temple treasuries represented a manipulable base of revenue and subject to "special" taxes. The *Rājataraṅgiṇī*, in particular, provides many episodes of official rapacity in the history of the period, and the tendency for kings to take what is not theirs is frequently noted in the seventh–eighth-century *Nītisāra* and elsewhere.[17] Even then, such special taxes were not always successful, and the financial burden of military adventurism is suggested by the consistent pattern of coin debasement for many of these dynasties.[18]

Guilds and temples both represent potential challenges to Kṣatriya power, since dynasties may be founded by either militarized merchants (e.g., Puṣyabhūtis) or armed Brahmans (as the Parivrājikas possibly were) or influential Śūdras (Pālas). Guilds even would go to the extent of arming the ascetic orders, and the eighth-century *Bṛhatkathāślokasaṃgraha* mentions the Śaiva order of the Pāśupatas acting in exactly that capacity.[19] One means of controlling guilds, then, was to provide them with a land grant, requiring continual involvement with the structure of government and investing them in a specific place at the rulers' discretion. Long-distance trading guilds in particular experienced erosion of their position. Their eventual displacement by Arabs in much of the south under the Rāṣṭrakūṭas simply made good sense by the standards of the day. Arabs could be easily isolated, heavily taxed, and removed at any time, for the south was at that time under no direct threat by Islamic armies.

As a result, much of the wealth that had previously been in the hands of long-distance merchants and caravan directors became accrued by those in positions of political power. This is probably the greatest single economic difference between the Gupta and the medieval and was one of the causes for the paucity of coinage and its replacement by trading in kind for small purchases or by bullion and gold dust for larger ones. Only a few of the long-distance mercantile guilds *(śreṇi, goṣṭhika)* managed to sustain a pattern of success. South India was home to the infamous Vīra-Baṇañjas of the Ayyāvoḷe guild—who brag in their epigraphs about being heavily armed and beholden to no one—and in Rajasthan were the horse-dealing Heḍāvikas, who make an analogous claim.[20] Other areas of the north show a noticeable decline in inscriptions and a quick disappearance of sealings, indicating that northern trading activity became deinstitutionalized, with some kinds of trade being handled through government agencies acting in the administrative capacity of guilds.[21]

In the long run, few of the great North Indian trading guilds seemed to have survived. For their part, the manufacturing cooperatives frequently had to relocate with the shift in population from the previously large metropolitan areas to smaller cities in the hinterlands, with much more problematic roads and systems for the transportation of goods.[22] Nationally, after the seventh century we find the greatest evidence for South Indian trading guilds—the various groups claiming the name Ayyāvoḷe—which became armed, landed, and not supportive of Buddhist causes, at least until the eleventh century.[23] Already, the *Siṃhavyūha-rāja-bodhisattva-paripṛcchā*, translated into Chinese in 663 C.E., demonstrates the change of religious affiliation. The text—probably from South India or Śrī Lāṇka—depicts the bodhisattva Vijayasambhava trying to convert a guildmaster or merchant named Uttaradāna, who neither believed in the Dharma nor had respect for the Buddha.[24]

Internationally, the mid-seventh to mid-eighth centuries brought on the greatest alteration in the manner of the disposition of commercial enterprise since the opening of the silk trade in the second century B.C.E. The role of Islam in the destruction of Buddhist sites from the eleventh century on has been well documented and, some would say, excessively emphasized. However, the extraordinary changes in international patterns of trade brought about by the simultaneous rise of Islam and the coalescence of the T'ang dynasty in China has not been well examined by those concerned with Indian Buddhism. Perhaps this is because the relatively benign influence of the Sasanians in the area from Gandhāra to Transoxiana has seldom been acknowledged, but it definitively provided the background for the change under Islam. Sasanian governorship of the area provided some of the greatest support for Buddhist mercantile practices and the spread of the religion, which was only interrupted with the Ephthalite incursions in the fifth to sixth centuries. After the death of Yazdgird III in 651 C.E. at Merv in eastern Khorasan, the Sasanids came to an end and the Umayyads spent the next century trying to suppress the fractious Iranian peoples and their continued uprisings.

In Bactria and Afghanistan, Buddhist sites like Tepe Sardār in Ghazni, Bāmiyān, Haḍḍa, Balkh, and Kāpiśa experienced a measured resurgence of vitality.[25] Transoxiana, as well, shows signs of new Buddhist activity in Adjina Tepe by Kurgan-Tyube (Tajikistan), at Kuva in Farghāna (Uzbekistan), and at Ak-Beshim near Bishkek (Kyrgyzstan), which demonstrated Buddhist building programs after the sixth century. Yet all this activity, with the exception of that at Bāmiyān and Haḍḍa, was relatively insignificant in both scale and duration. In reality, we find no Buddhist site activity after the ninth century and most is eclipsed by the arrival of Islam in the mid-eighth century.[26] As Frye has noted, "The medieval world was a brutal world, but the [Islamic] conquests in central Asia seem to have been exceptionally rough. One finds many notices in the sources about the harsh treatment of the local people."[27] The slave markets of Kufā, Basra, Balkh, and Merv were filled with the human chattel that resulted from the Arab presence in Afghanistan and Transoxiana, where both non-Arab converts to Islam *(mawālī)* and nonbelievers *(kafir)* would languish until sold to a buyer. Indeed, the consequence of the 'Abbassid rapacity was the ninth-century rise of their nominal subjects, the Tahirids in Iran and the Samanids in Turkharistan and other areas of Central Asia, under whom these oases experienced an Islamic resurgence in the ninth and tenth centuries.[28]

Until then, Sogdian merchants, already powerful in the Tarim long-distance trade, would temporarily become supreme. With them, their forms of religion, especially the Dēnāvarīya sect of Manichaeism, would prevail in the hunt for patronage, at least through the eighth century. Manichaeans fled from the Amu Darya basin in advance of the Arab armies, and in eastern Turkestan Manichaean Sogdians came to provide many of the same benefits to new Tarim groups that the Buddhists had offered half a millennium before.[29] They acted as scribes, provided technological advice based on agrarian experience in Transoxiana, and served as architects, military advisers, and diplomatic consultants. Their financial ability, international connections, and technical expertise were not lost on the Uyghurs, among others. The Chinese first saw Manichaeans in Ch'ang-an in 694, but the court was eventually to proclaim in 732 that Manichaeism was "a basically evil doctrine which deceives the people by falsely calling itself Buddhism," an allusion to its notoriously syncretic character.[30] The Uyghurs, however, understood the value of Sogdian knowledge and Mou-yü Qaghan made Manichaeism a state religion in 762 for perhaps the only time in its history.[31]

Moreover, if the overland trade routes became increasingly problematic for Buddhist-affiliated merchants, the sea lanes proved no better. During the Umayyads, Arab merchants maneuvered themselves through the sea trade to Indonesia and China. This was even more true after 749, with the transfer of the caliphate to Baghdad under the 'Abbassids, whose interest in stimulating maritime traffic was directly proportional to their reliance on international trade for the maintenance of their hegemonic position in the Arab world. Both Arab and Persian seafarers found numerous ports favorable to them, from India to China. The anonymous *Akhbār al-Ṣīn w-al-Hind,* circulated in 851, indicates that the Rāṣṭrakūṭa monarch—probably Amoghavarṣa (c. 814–880)—was the friendliest of kings to the Arabs, while the Gurjara-Pratīhāra king was irredeemably hostile.[32] If barter in kind or in bullion was most common, at least one economic historian maintains that Arab dominance was such that, when coinage was used, Arab dinars were the preferred currency.[33] The Rāṣṭrakūṭas apparently did not even bother to mint their own coins, for no examples of their imprints survive. Arab and Persian ubiquity extended into China; when the foreign community in Canton was attacked in 878 during Huang Ch'ao's rebellion, abu-Zayd of Sīrāf claimed that 120,000 Muslims, Christians, Jews, and Magians were killed.[34] The net result of these exchanges was that much of the wealth of South, East, and Southeast Asia was manipulated by Arab and Sogdian merchants, with the surplus flowing back to the Middle Eastern Islamic caliphate.

Merchants allied with Buddhist institutions would no longer be central to the trade between Bengal and Indonesia, but became relegated to second-rate small businessmen, if they got any business at all in the face of the larger volume of Arab and Persian traffic. The communities of Śrīvijaya, Burma, Nepal, and Tibet were still partly or wholly Buddhist, however, with the result that the relations between some areas of India and foreign rulers remained viable. We note the donative inscriptions concerning of Balaputradeva of Suvarṇadvīpa to Nālandā in the ninth century, of the King Kyanzittha of Pagan in 1084, 1112, and the repairs of Letyāmengnan of Arakan between 1112 and 1167, all these latter concerning the Mahābodhi temple in Bodhgaya.[35] Yet the foreign interest is notable for two factors—their involvement is for the purpose of revitalization or repair, and it is not done by merchants or those with guild affiliation. Indeed, the principal sense we get of international merchant involvement with Buddhism from the eighth to the tenth centuries is that found in Nepal and Tibet. This is especially visible during the period of the Tibetan Royal Dynasty's interest in Buddhism and their extensive ties to sites in Central Asia, which they secured through military prowess.[36] By the tenth to eleventh centuries, the improved economic climate evidently stimulated mercantile construction of Buddhist institutions once again, as is evident in inscriptions in Bihar and around Vātāpi.[37]

POLITICS, PATRONAGE, AND ETHICS—THE LOSS OF KUNTALA AND ANDHRĀPATHA

The result of these developments were threefold: funding, the ethics of patronage, and the contraction of Buddhist institutional range. With regard to the first, it became clear over time that Buddhists could no longer rely on a symbiotic relationship with merchant guilds to fund their large and costly institutions, and that their positions in state ceremonies associated with kingship also became threatened. The late seventh-century economic climate—formerly conducive to the relatively quick accrual of capital and concomitant social position—now became difficult for those seeking the financial avenue to legitimacy. With Arabs in the sea lanes and Sogdians in Central Asia, economic pathways no longer seemed to privilege Indians. Only the possibility of military adventurism remained open for newly developed groups, an approach that some elected to employ. Consequently, economic opportunity fell increasingly into the political sector, which meant that Buddhist monasteries were secure primarily in those areas where the Buddhist tradition was not seen as the adversary of the state or state-sponsored social systems. Yet this was a difficult proposition for Buddhists, as Hindu divinities and

Purāṇic ritual systems appeared to offer a closer fit in needs and values espoused by medieval states.

There can be little doubt that, traditionally, the alliance with commercial representatives had allowed both merchants and monks the opportunity to challenge received systems of power in a critical and effective manner. Scriptures like the *Mātaṅgī-sūtra*—more recently relegated to the position of an introductory story in the *Śārdūlakarṇāvadāna*—articulated the authenticity of the disempowered, in this case an outcaste woman who becomes an arhat.[38] These narratives indicated the Buddhist commitment to a theoretically egalitarian soteriological structure and quasi-egalitarian social system. Backed by such affirmations of legitimacy, the Brahmanical schematism was forced to adopt a series of ad hoc strategies, like paradigms of the "confusion of castes" *(vārṇasaṃkara)*, which declared all new castes result from cross-caste marriage. This allowed them to cope with such peculiar circumstances as the sudden rise of the number of people (formerly tribal or otherwise outside the system) now claiming or being required to claim caste affiliation. Conversely, Buddhist institutions affirmed that these peoples did not inherently require Brahmanical legitimacy for their authenticity, but the Buddhist position relied on tangible methods—especially financial—for their demonstration of the putative noninherence of social valorization.

Alternatively, Buddhist monks had been very successful in legitimizing new groups that had established themselves in positions of political or military authority, and which sought affirmation of their position by some religious or ritual means. One of the rituals that Buddhists had employed with overwhelming success throughout India was the cult of the stūpa, which was one of the royally sponsored rites whereby kings—of whatever persuasion—would establish themselves in positions of imperial authority. Stūpa sanctification, elaborate donations to monastic centers, and the performance of one or more of the great Vedic śrauta ceremonies were used in complementary but nonintegrated roles for the affirmation of regal potency. As Inden indicates:

> Before the eighth century, the Buddha was accorded the position of universal deity and the ceremonies by which a king attained to imperial status were elaborate donative ceremonies entailing gifts to Buddhist monks and the installation of a symbolic Buddha in a stupa. . . . This pattern changed in the eighth century. The Buddha was replaced as the supreme, imperial deity by one of the Hindu gods (except under the Palas of eastern India, the Buddha's homeland) and the performance of śrauta rituals as separate ceremonies was largely abandoned.[39]

While we may not know the extent to which such rituals were actually employed, Buddhist political rites were, with few exceptions, eventually eclipsed by the development of Purāṇic coronation *(rājyābhiṣeka)* ceremonies. This ritual transformation in the public sphere was to have a profound influence on esoteric ritualism, as seen below.

Even in the case of marginal peoples, Buddhists began losing their privileged position of patronage. The previous Buddhist monopoly on dealing with barbarians, outcastes, foreigners, and other ne'er-do-wells was effectively countered in the early medieval period, first by Pāśupata missionaries and then by Brahmans who appeared willing to travel and populate the countryside in return for land. The Pāśupatas, in particular, were the first semiorthodox group of renunciates *(saṃnyāsin)* capable of emulating the zealous Buddhist proselytization among both marginalized Indians and non-Indians. Even Buddhist monarchs supported this variety of Śaiva ascetic, as shown in the Bhagalpur plate of Nārāyaṇapāla of about 900 C.E.[40] These ascetics seemed to work in conjunction with Brahmans in a manner as yet poorly studied. If Pāśupatas appear to have been the focus of royal temple building and institutional patronage, Brahmans were given uncleared land in proximity to the temples. We can surmise that, in these instances, the Brahmans actually assisted as the priests and kept the temple the focus of the lay population by instituting and performing Brahmanical rites of passage, although sometimes Pāśupatas are also specified as the ritual officiants. While this interaction is broadly demonstrated through India from the sixth century on, it is in Cambodia that Brahmanical religious culture most evidently usurped the position Buddhism enjoyed in other societies.[41] The early religious inscriptions (604 and 624 C.E.) are by a Brahman, Vidyābindu, but succeeding inscriptions of 627 by Vidyāviśeṣa and 639 by Vidyāpuṣpa indicate the dedication of liṅgams and footprints of Śiva and declare that Pāśupatas were to maintain ritual prerogatives at the sites.[42]

We can only imagine how alarming this series of events was to Buddhist institutional managers. In the course of a few decades in the mid-seventh century, the most effective strategies for Buddhist support had come unraveled and were being appropriated by others who successfully represented themselves as the successors to the original Buddhist initiatives. Both the Sogdian Manichaeans and the Indian Śaiva system of the Pāśupatas appropriated aspects of Buddhist nomenclature and iconography for their own use. We have seen how in China the Hsüan-tsung emperor's government felt it necessary to limit Manichaeism in 732 C.E., with the observation that they presented themselves as Buddhists. Pāśupata iconography, similarly, presented its mythic founder Lakulīśa in exactly the representation of "turning the wheel of the Dharma" *(dharmacakrapravartanamudrā)*, sometimes completely equipped with the close curls and coronal dome *(uṣṇīṣa)* of the Buddha, clearly a usurpation of Buddhist iconography.[43] With their previously secure social and economic niches rapidly eroding in a culture increasingly dedicated to *sāmanta* feudal forms and military adventurism, Indian Buddhists attempted to beg, borrow, or steal new foundations for institutional survival.

Unfortunately for the monks, feudal cultures engaging in opportunistic belligerence presumed that religious groups receiving patronage would valorize their behavior and vindicate their authority. This brings us to the second point, the problems Buddhists had with the evolving ethics of patronage. While it is true that certain warlords who succeeded in putting together a confederation of belligerents ultimately found their way into the Buddhist fold, this was relatively rare. Some of the chief names stabilized their regnal positions via the Buddhadharma, but it is by no means clear that they began as Buddhist supporters. Perhaps most definitively, this path was taken by the members of the Pāla dynasty, around 750 C.E. Certainly, they had no claim to Kṣatriya status when they first appeared, and contemporary evidence indicates that they may have been Śūdras or even outcastes. The *Mañjuśrīmūlakalpa*, for example, contains two descriptions of Gopāla; the first, from the viewpoint of a Madhyadeśa monk, is quite favorable, while the verses presenting the opinion of monks from Gauḍa is very pejorative.[44] Evidently the diversity of Buddhist opinion reflected the degree to which the Pāla monarch was conducting himself along approved Buddhist lines in specific locales. The Madhyadeśa monks liked his building of monasteries and bringing justice, while the Gauḍa monks simply declared that the time was unrighteous and the Buddha's dispensation in trouble.

Overall, Buddhist institutions could not effectively compete for patronage from militaristic princes, who increasingly found that they were best represented by Śaiva values and rhetoric. Śaiva systems made allowance for forms of behavior that Buddhist syntheses could not support, since even the most syncretic Buddhist systems were not as open to negotiation about issues of violence, power, and self-aggrandizement as were the medieval Śaiva representatives. A comparison of inscriptions written at the dedications of religious buildings by, respectively, Buddhist and Śaiva potentates shows how the ethical positions of each religious tradition configured the rhetorical gestures of their respective supporters. Although many examples could be found, I have selected two for comparative purposes. The first comprises excerpts from an inscription by Devapāla (r. c. 812–850 C.E.) affirming the construction of reliquaries and monasteries by his friend Satyabodhi, the contemporary abbot of Nālandā. The second is part of a proclamation by the Kāḷachuri prince Yuvarājadeva II (r. c. 980–990 C.E.), who is dedicating part of the tax of a market town to the support of his friend Aghoraśiva and the monastery of Hauhaleśvara. The royal and religious figures in both dedications are highly distinguished and of profound importance for their respective lineages—whether sacred or secular. The representation of the activities and qualities of the kings is our primary concern here in either instance.

Gohsrāwāñ Inscription of Devapāla

Then staying here for a long time, he, the quintessence of intelligence, being treated with reverence by the lord of the earth, the illustrious Devapāla shone like the sun, endowed with splendor, filling the quarters with his daily rising, and dispelling the spread of darkness. He who, a friend like the monks' own self, as if the very arm of the holy monk Satyabodhi, by the decree of the assembly of the monks was permanently steadfast in the protection of Nālandā and firm in the stability of the Saṃgha. Practicing the generosity of those who are friends of beings, by offering up his all as well as manliness, eagerly directed toward the attainment of perfect wisdom and vying with his other excellencies, residing here while his high holy office was continuing, he hoisted the banner of his fame on the two poles of his family in the northern region. Whatever merit has been acquired by the erection of this edifice which is, as it were, the staircase to the city of salvation, may through that the whole assemblage of men, headed by the circle of his elders and including his parents, attain to perfect wisdom![45]

Bilhari Inscription of Yuvarājadeva II

(Describing an ancestor, Keyuravarśa) Even when his forces marched for vanquishing the guardians of the quarters, sporting as at the time of world-destruction, so as to rouse the apprehension of the three worlds, no mass of dust could rise from the ground, inundated as it was with the streams of tears flowing from the eyes of the wives of his enemies who were again and again taken captive. . . . He strew the battle fields all over with the heads of his proud enemies who, exasperated with rage attacked him—their heads, with skull bones falling off, being pressed by the machine-like hands of the exulting female ghouls (vetālīs), eager for the blood dripping from the parts struck by his vibrating swift arrows, and which were honored with the side-glances of heavenly damsels moving in the sky. "Our king is Rudra incarnate . . . our king is an iron fetter for curbing the wayward princes!" When the multitudes of excellent poets continuously uttered such brilliant words of flattery, the minds of his enemies present in his hall of audience were incomparably afflicted.[46]

We should avoid the conclusion that these kinds of inscriptions represent actual reality, especially since prudence is even indicated at the end of Yuvarājadeva II's panegyric with the ascription of these public verses to poets writing for flattery's sake. Thus it is by no means clear that Buddhist kings were necessarily less bloodthirsty than non-Buddhist kings. These inscriptions were rhetorical in principle for the purpose of public presentation and collectively have a tenuous relation to reality. Although Buddhist kings might hold up certain ideals associated with the Buddhadharma, that does not mean that they were capable of adhering to the precepts of nonviolence in an increasingly militaristic culture. Indeed, in the Nālandā copperplate charter Devapāla is described as "acting as the guru for the initiation of all his enemies' wives into the state of widowhood."[47] Similarly, Nārāyaṇapāla's Bhagalpur plate describes his "sword, which was actually blue like a lotus, appeared yellow and red to his enemies out of fear (as it had drunk their blood), while it was flickering in the forefront of battle."[48]

Nor was the earlier Buddhist message on nonviolence unequivocal. Demiéville long ago called attention to the section in Asaṅga's *Bodhisattvabhūmi* that allows a bodhisattva to engage in the slaughter of thieves or brigands who are about to commit one of the five sins of immediate retribution, so that the bodhisattva could go to hell rather than the criminals.[49] The same section also allows a bodhisattva to overthrow or otherwise remove a king, warlord, or evil minister who oppresses his people.[50] Such actions are justified under the rubric of the bodhisattva's "skill in means" *(upāyakauśalya)* and are to be undertaken solely for the service of beings, so that the bodhisattva replaces himself for the other and suffers in his stead. This same rubric allows for a wide latitude in questionable behavior, with the single mandate that all actions must by no means be undertaken on the bodhisattva's own behalf *(svahitāya)* but only for the benefit of others (*parahitā*ya). Evidently this doctrinal basis was used by Buddhist representatives to justify belligerence on the part of their favorite monarchs. The Chinese monk Hsüan-tsang, in particular, repeats a lengthy mythological justification for Harṣa's extensive and debilitating campaign against Śaśāṅka in the early seventh century.[51]

Yet there must have been some relationship between the nature of these pronouncements and the actual proclivity of royalty to military aggrandizement at the expense of both opponents and their subjects. The configuration of identity, in particular, appears to have been central to this process. Vaiṣṇava kings had panegyrics to themselves written, which articulate their emulation of the righteous violence of Viṣṇu's incarnations, taking their cues from the expanding corpus of Purāṇic literature. For example, the Bhitari Pillar inscription depicts Skandagupta running to his mother to happily report on the death of enemies, just like Kṛṣṇa did, although other Vaiṣṇava inscriptions appear to emphasize the violence of the Man-Lion (Nṛsiṃha) incarnation.[52] And, as can be seen from the Kāḷachuri inscription of Yuvarājya II, above, the Śaivas are often the ones who indulge in the expostulation of their attempts at turning the world into the charnel ground of Maheśvara. In reality, the Śaiva regal inscriptions are collectively the most extraordinary documents for the combination of religious fervor, erotic sentiment, and graphically violent images.

Perhaps the best index of the differences, though, is the alteration of epigraphic diction when a noble house exhibits a change of religious allegiance. This happened at times to both the Pālas and the Bhaumakaras; the former is the well-known Magadha-Gauḍa house while the latter clan ruled the area around much of Orissa from c. 736 to 930 C.E., before being displaced by the Somavaṃśis' extension of their domain from Dakṣiṇa Kośala. In the Pālas' instance, it is instructive to reflect that the Śaiva devotee Vigrahapāla (r. c. 1058–1085) is described as acting as the "Lord of Death for the clan of his enemies," in a manner beyond the pale of his predecessors.[53] In the Bhaumakara's case, we might compare the Neulpur Grant of Śubhakaradeva (r. c. 790–810)—very indicative of traditional Buddhist values—with the much more aggressive Talcher plate of his descendent, Śivakara (reigned c. 885–894).[54] Whereas the former king has "the protection of his subjects as his highest aim" and "has pacified the affliction of the world caused by the doings of his kinsmen," the latter bragged that his older brother "was beyond delicacy in the matter of crushing the lotus-like heads of irresistible foes."

Buddhist identity, then, reinforced—minimally—the posturing of the compassionate activity accorded bodhisattvas. When Devapāla, for example, gains the throne, he repeatedly states that he does it as a bodhisattva obtains the position of a Buddha, following the parinirvana of the previous teacher of the world.[55] This ideology was, moreover, shared by Buddhists and non-Buddhists alike, and throughout the literature of the early medieval period Buddhists are depicted as notably compassionate toward other beings. In Bāṇa's *Harṣacarita* (c. 630 C.E.), the Buddhist monk Divākaramitra becomes the vehicle for the denouement of the saga. Harṣa is in search of his sister, Rājyaśrī, whose husband, Grahavarman, and brother Rājyavardhana were slaughtered by Śaśāṅka in the belligerent politics of the period. He learns that she has taken refuge with his old Brahman friend-turned-Buddhist monk, Divākaramitra (Indian literature can be *so* Victorian), because Buddhists are noted for their compassion toward beings in distress.[56] Similarly, the good eldress Kāmandakī is the primary agent for the welfare of the hero and heroine in Bhavabhūti's classic, *Mālatīmādhava* (c. 730 C.E.), the play named after these two. She organizes the nuns and her friends to keep Mālatī from marrying the wrong man, persuades soldiers to find her when she has been captured by a murderous Kāpālika ascetic, and acts as a point of humane moral reference throughout the plot. The Buddhist reputation for kindness was sufficiently well known that Malladeva-Nandivarman—a Śaiva king of the Āndhra-maṇḍala (Central Andhra-Karnataka)—maintained in 339–340 C.E. that "in reputation for the highest compassion toward all beings in the triple world, he was like a bodhisattva."[57]

Buddhist virtues like these did not present compelling reasons for patronage, when a king could just as easily reformulate his image in favor of the model of Śiva, who was, after all, represented as a killer divinity with a permanent erection. It appears, however, that wherever they received patronage, Buddhists injected (or attempted to inject) the rhetoric of ethical responsibility into their political dialogues. Perhaps the best example is the scathing indictment of the behavior of kings found in the "Prophecy of Kings" section of the *Mañjuśrīmūlakalpa*. The authors of the chapter, written around 750 C.E., are obviously eager for royal attention to Buddhist institutional needs. At the same time, they are utterly scandalized at the real behavior of many of the monarchs they describe. Yet all they can offer is a mythology of long life and time in heaven for the righteous kings and significant time in the lowest of hells for those whose behavior harms the Buddhist religion.[58] What is missing from Buddhist discourse, however, is any intelligible, nonsectarian rationale for the formal renouncement of military adventurism. Buddhist monks appear never to have been successful in articulating a broad-based ethical system with a compelling narrative that would motivate Indians to bring into civil society the consideration and decorum delineated within the monastic sphere.

Indeed, from the seventh century on, wherever there is Śaiva patronage, Buddhist institutions withered, especially in the Deccan and in the Kṛṣṇa and Godāvarī River valleys. Between the Chāḷukyas, the Pallavas, the Gaṅgas, and the Rāṣṭrakūṭas, the entire range of area between Mukhaliṅgam, Kāñcī, and Vātāpi were largely dominated by aggressively Śaiva monarchs. The Kṛṣṇa River valley, in particular, had been the site of so many Buddhist institutions over the previous thousand years: Nāgārjunikoṇḍa, Guntupalli, Amarāvatī, Gurubhaktakoṇḍa, and Jaggayyapeta, to name but a few.[59] There, new schools had flourished, famous saints lived, and whole new directions were taken in sculpture and architecture. By the sixth century, though, the region's Buddhist population was in serious decline. Vātāpi and Aihoḷe both have single Buddhist sites, developed toward the end of the sixth or beginning of the seventh century and apparently abandoned shortly thereafter. The sites occupied later appear to be solely those of Jaggayyapeta (until the seventh century), Guntupalli (until the beginning of the eighth century), Gummadidurru (eighth century), and perhaps Amarāvatī.[60] It was not until the religious activity of the late tenth to early eleventh century—for example, the queen Akkādevī's Buddhist praxis in 1021 C.E. and the rebuilding of monasteries by Vīra-Baḷañja guildsmen in 1095–1096 C.E.—that Buddhists appear to make a modest return to the Kṛṣṇa River valley.[61]

Buddhist monastic activity appears to survive primarily in the east (Magadha, Utkala, Baṅgala, Kāmarūpa, and Samatāṭa), in the west (Lāṭa, Saurāṣṭra, Sindh, and Koṅkana), in the north (Kaśmīra, Oḍiyāna, Jālandara, and parts of Madhyadeśa), and at the southern end of the subcontinent (Nāgapattinam). Although Buddhist activity continued elsewhere, that does not mean it was unaffected by the southern developments. Since the Deccan continued to produce the wealthiest and most powerful of the dynasties during the early medieval period, the influence of their religious selections had a pervasive potency born of prestige. Throughout much of India, Buddhism no longer held the pride of place previously accorded, and the monks felt themselves under pressure to conform to the dominant paradigm—the Varṇāśrama Dharma, the affirmation of caste and the stages of life.

MEDIEVAL WOMEN'S BUDDHISM— HIDDEN FROM VIEW OR MISSING IN ACTION?

Conformity and reconfiguration are something religious traditions are continually required to negotiate. Buddhist institutions could not capitulate to certain aspects of the Varṇāśrama model, but other facets were seen as definitively negotiable, particularly if it brought them closer to sources of support and social legitimacy. The decline of women's participation was part of this process, and from the seventh century forward we see an erosion of women's involvement, most particularly in the virtually total eclipse of the office of the nun *(bhikṣuṇī)* in North India. More broadly, though, the early medieval period saw the dramatic deterioration of support for and involvement of women in Buddhist activities at any and every level, whether in the monastery, in the lay community, or in the newly evolving siddha systems.

While many feminist historians have proposed nuanced models of Indian religion, a few have challenged this perception of women's declining participation and have proposed a theory of "androcentric record keeping."[62] I understand this terminology to invoke the principle that women were half the population and therefore must have been half of those involved in all forms of religious practice. According to this model, we do not see women's participation because—as was certainly evident in nineteenth-century anthropological explorations of tribal religion—men were keeping the records and ignored the activities of female participants. Thus the argument is that women were victims after the fact of their participation and not during their actual lifetimes. Individual authors point to the disparity between archival records available in Europe and their representation within standard histories of European periods, noting that women's participation has been excluded from those later histories. They have argued by analogy that this must have been the case in early medieval India as well.

Yet such models are, when viable at all, based on selected archives where the records of women's activities have still been kept. Although it is true that men kept the records, the model of androcentric record-keeping cannot account for several realities. We find discrepant accounts of women's involvement over time, specific archaeological data about women, the actual preservation of women's documents either alongside men's or even in preference to them (e.g., *Therīgāthā*, the hybrid Sanskrit text of the *Mahāsāṃghika Bhikṣuṇī Vinaya)*, and other phenomena. The record-keeping model as proposed actually relies on the astonishing logical fallacy that the absence of evidence is itself evidence for presence. This is a modification of Fischer's "furtive fallacy," which "begins with the premise that reality is a sordid, secret thing; and that history happens on the back stairs a little after midnight."[63] It is not clear, moreover, how women would have been active in everything except the archives of a tradition, especially since—according to the model—they should have been half the active population, present in all areas of human endeavor. It does not follow that women in the early medieval period had no religion—that would be unintelligible and contraindicated by the evidence.[64] The evidence merely suggests that women, like all humans, were excluded from some varieties of religious activity, were persuaded with respect to other forms of behavior and actively selected certain methods of religious expression, based in part on their sense of support and fulfillment. In this instance the evidence is relatively uniform—increasingly, medieval Indian women did not participate in Buddhism and most particularly in esoteric Buddhism.

Our sources suggest that, even while individual women exercised power and authority in political and economic affairs in specific regions during the medieval period, they did not extend that involvement into Buddhist institutions. We have many ways of determining the approximate percentages of women participating in Buddhist activities; particularly important are epigraphic, ethnographic, and textual sources. These sources show a remarkable convergence: women probably constituted between approximately 1 percent and 20 percent of individuals acting in most religious capacities from the medieval period to the present. The data are sketchy, but they indicate that women's numbers precipitously declined during the period of esoteric Buddhism, particularly in high status and authoritative religious positions. Far from being supportive of women's participation, the Mantrayāna was decidedly deleterious to the religious aspirations of those women desiring participation as independent and equal persons. Just as evident is the clear message that, although occasionally presented with higher-status options, Indian women from the medieval period on have predominantly participated at lower levels of religious status. This is true even while those women from selected families enjoyed high-status participation in political and economic venues outside Buddhist communities.

Archaeological materials can be particularly useful in the exploration of marginal or marginalized figures. The depersonalization essential to the hagiographical process is part of a larger ritual and literary field, for Indian hagiography appears to require that the process of legitimacy extend from either an ancestral lineage or its immediate analogy, the religious lineage. Our epigraphic sources, which are not as subject to these factors—particularly the retrospective, explicit, or implied forms of signification endemic to hagiography—show the greatest variation in women's position in Buddhism over its duration. Clearly, the early traditions evident in Sāñchī, Amarāvatī, Barhut, Taxila, Gandhāra, Sarnāth, Vajrāsana, and the other great sites demonstrate flourishing nuns' communities.[65] These are sites where bhikṣuṇīs commanded sufficient resources—or sufficient prestige to act as a cipher for others' resources—to have erected railings and have their names inscribed in dedication statues.[66] In Mathurā, for example:

> In the year 39 of mahārāja devaputra Huviṣka, in the 3rd (month) of the rainy season, on the 5th day, on this date, the bodhisattva was set up by the nun Budhadevā, the female pupil of the nun Puśahathinī, together with her parents for the welfare and happiness of all sentient beings.[67]

If we consult Bühler's list of epigraphs at Sāñchī, conveniently tabulated in his discussion, we can see just how significant these inscriptions really were. Bühler lists names for 141 monks, 104 nuns, 250 men who are not designated as ordained, and 150 women not designated as ordained.[68] This tabulation has some degree of uncertainty. Some of the names are repeated, up to three times, while others contain some question as to the actual name. For our purposes, however, it is significant that the ratio of nuns to monks exceeds the ratio of undesignated women to men. The former is 104 : 141, or about 3 : 4, while the latter is 150 : 250, or 3 : 5. Thus, in Madhya Pradesh, early Buddhist institutions apparently enjoyed a great vitality of women's participation—they respectively represented 43 percent of the total clerics in inscriptions and 38 percent of the laity. Even though Indian nuns and laywomen at this time (as at other times) were relegated to a secondary status, they actively involved themselves at both householder and monastic levels to an extraordinary degree.[69]

A review of the epigraphic materials for the medieval period, however, does not indicate the enthusiastic participation of women at this level, and it has already been observed by Falk that nuns were increasingly in short supply.[70] Her observations are affirmed by surviving inscriptions. For example, Huntington's review of seventy-seven inscribed and dated sculptures from the "Pāla-Sena" schools—both Buddhist and Hindu—lists no nuns at all. The only inscription by a woman claiming even religious affiliation as a committed laywoman *(upāsikā)* comes from a pre-Pāla fourth-century image.[71] Of the other Buddhist images, inscriptions record donations by two queens, a princess, the wife of a chieftain, a vintner's daughter, the wife of a wealthy donor, a monk's mother, and four otherwise undistinguished wives of gentlemen of means.[72] All the women listed in these inscriptions identified themselves through their relations to men. This information is reinforced by the data from the Kurkihar bronze hoard, a group of specifically Buddhist statuary. Of the ninety-three inscriptions listed, forty-two provide names of donors: nine are clearly donated by women (no nuns), while thirty-three are by men (ten clearly by monks), yielding 22 percent women, the highest archaeological percentage I have seen in the early medieval period.[73]

These findings reinforce the suggestions available from the numerous personal sealings found in Nālandā. As many as 173 personal sealings were listed by Hirananda Sastri as the complete excavated inscriptions up to 1942 for the flagship monastery of the medieval Buddhist educational system. Of these, only three identify women—Śrīmat-Sīyādevī, Śrī-Ijjādevī, and Śrīdevī—and all of them well-respected ladies, as is indicated by their names.[74] Among the largest class of other personal material from Nālandā, the 109 "unhistorical votive inscriptions," only one name could possibly be construed as feminine, Kṛṣṇātukā, and is otherwise unspecified religiously.[75] We need not be suspicious that Sastri was overlooking females; in fact he was assiduously seeking them and misrepresented one name as feminine, which had to be corrected by the editor, Chakravarti.[76] This hunt for nuns and Buddhist laywomen in modern archaeology has been expressed to me many times by Archaeological Survey of India or other excavators, who have almost uniformly indicated their disappointment at not finding bhikṣuṇī epigraphs at their digs. The Nālandā data appear to confirm the statements of the Chinese monk I-ching that nuns were allowed no specific provision in monasteries of his acquaintance. His rather cavalier attitude that women should just do as they were told appears a reinforcement of the late seventh-century unwillingness to engage women's participation.[77]

As the esoteric system appropriated and negotiated the values and behavioral systems of some of the non-Buddhist Śaiva and other clerical traditions—as examined in the ensuing chapters—it is germane to propose analysis by analogy: what do we see in the respective level of Indian women's involvement in the ethnography of contemporary systems of renunciation *(samnyāsa / bramacharyā / tantra)*? Again, we most frequently come up with the 1–20 percent figure. For example, Sinha and Saraswati noted in 1978 that two of the 239 Daṇḍisaṃnyāsīs in Vārāṇasī were women.[78] Miller and Wertz's study of Bhubaneswar identified two women among the forty-one that they found in the twenty-two monasteries of the city in 1963–1964.[79] Parry could not locate any women among the estimated fifteen Aghori (extreme tantric) ascetics he knew from 1976 to 1978, although he heard of one woman who had died a few years before.[80] In the most complete study to date, though, Denton recorded 134 women among the estimated thirteen hundred ascetics in Vārāṇasī in 1981.[81] The great majority of these had not entered into the formal level of renunciate *(saṃnyāsinī),* which pertained to only about a quarter of the 134 ascetics. The preference was clearly for the office of celibate ascetic studentship *(brahmacāryā).* Only about a dozen of the 134 were pursuing an active life of tantric ritual.

Even the above figures might prove misleading or somewhat generous in their assessment, since in most cases we do not know their relative status within the larger community. For example, in 1988, while reviewing Sinha and Saraswati's figures in light of his own fieldwork, Sawyer found that the two reported women among the Daṇḍiswāmis were not formal members of the community. They neither carried a staff *(daṇḍa)* nor sat on the throne *(gaḍḍi)* but acted as devoted disciples of the community, not their peers.[82] The two women in the Miller and Wertz sample as well were widows who took care of the monastic leader Jagadānanda as if they were his mothers *(gurumā),* not his peers. This is particularly an issue in Barrow's nineteenth-century census figures, for "in the official *Census Returns* for 1881, which enumerate 93 (51 male and 42 female) Aghori followers in the Central Provinces and 2,121 males and 1,046 females in the N.W. P. (Azimgarh District). In the Ballia District there were 68, of whom fully half were women."[83] Yet he later reports that the 1881 *Punjab Census Report* shows 316 Aghori individuals, all apparently male.[84]

Our textual sources of the period are solely those of esoteric hagiography, a topic pursued in detail in the next several chapters. Yet the percentages for most, but not all, of these sources mirror our findings in both epigraphy and ethnography. Esoteric hagiography is the most problematic of our materials, as might be expected, and reflects the greatest degree of variation. The difficulty is exacerbated by the suspect nature of so many of the hagiographical sources—they are universally represented as Indic, but many clearly speak of Tibetan issues and some certainly appear to be Tibetan compositions. Even then, the hagiographical reporting of feminine presence is relatively modest, yielding ratios of women to men of 0 : 85 (0 percent), 3 : 81 (4 percent), 1 : 50 (2 percent), 4 : 38 (10 percent), 4 : 80 (5 percent), and 3 : 81 (4 percent).[85] The exceptions to these ratios are from a group of three texts to come out of Ding-ri and are ascribed either to the mythic siddha Phadampa Sangyé or to the translation of his revelation by the Tibetan translator, Shama Lotsāwa. These texts show an emphasis on women's involvement with esoteric Buddhism and express a discordant note (compared to the rest of the literature) because of it. For example, one of these texts is entirely on stories *(avadāna)* about thirty-five Ḍākinīs, representing them in standard mythic Buddhist form.[86] The other two represent hagiographical ratios of 19 : 60 (24 percent) and 136 : 245 (36 percent).[87] We may conclude, however, from a variety of factors that these texts are Tibetan reformulations and represent the accelerated involvement of women in esoteric Buddhism in eleventh- to twelfth-century Tibet. This increased involvement may be seen in Tibetan lineage lists and was invoked in an observation made bitterly by Shama Lotsāwa's sister, Shama Machig, to Indian Buddhist men she refused to teach because she was "from a border country and, even worse (by Indian standards), a woman!"[88]

Indeed, the surviving literature shows the fallacy of assuming equal participation of women in the Indian esoteric system. Clearly, the literature configures the ritual system as directed toward males and privileging male responses. Out of the hundreds of ritual manuals from the esoteric period surviving in Sanskrit, translated into Tibetan, Chinese, Newar, Uyghur, and other languages, out of the hundreds of exegetical works describing the ritual systems in those several languages, out of the lineages—living and dead—in Tibet, Nepal, Burma, Nan-chao, China, Japan, Mongolia, Śrī Lāṅka, and many other places, esoteric specialists have yet to uncover a single text or lineage that preserves instructions about yogic or sexual practices that relate to women's position. Those texts treating specifically sexual rituals describe them in a manner anatomically impossible for women to perform, if they were to be the primary agents.[89] Beyond that, the several texts surviving that are reputedly authored by women (and we have little cause to doubt such authorial ascriptions) all discuss the ritual and meditative system from the viewpoint of the male. Perhaps the best example of this is the *Vyaktabhāvānugata-tattva-siddhi*, a text that has been lauded by one feminist as "a gemlike treatise" because it ostensibly articulates an affirmation of the female body.[90] Yet the first chapter of the work actually affirms not the female body but how that body might be manipulated and employed by a yogin in search of his own goal.[91]

Moreover, the inapplicability of modern sisterhood models for this period of Indian history is evident in light of the donative inscriptions of Indian queens.[92] Many individuals occupied that exalted position in various locales, and some of them founded or donated to Buddhist monasteries. There is the example of the well-known Duḍḍā-vihāra, founded by the Maitrika monarch Dhruvasena I in the mid-sixth century C.E. on behalf of the princess Duḍḍā, or again the Gāhaḍvāla monastery of Kumāradevī at Sārnāth in the mid-twelfth century.[93] I have not located a single inscription, however, demonstrating early medieval benefaction by a Buddhist queen or a Buddhist laywoman to a Buddhist nunnery, despite their sometimes extensive, even excessive, donations to monks. The very few nunneries recorded during the period seem to have been constructed by kings, rather than queens, such as the institution established by the Bhaumakara king, Śivakaradeva, in 888 C.E. at the request of the local chieftain, Rāṇaka Śrī Vinītatuṅga.[94] This was chronologically the final inscription that has yet surfaced mentioning Buddhist nuns in India.

How can we make sense of the evidence at our command? Theory has tended to depict women's religion either as the result of their unequivocal oppression or as a vehicle for their assertive self-empowerment.[95] I propose that, in the case of early medieval India, it was neither of these two extremes, for they imply an essentialization of and binary structure between agency and accommodation.[96] In the *Harṣacarita*, Harṣa's sister, Rājyaśrī, has found assistance and refuge in the peacefulness of the forest with the Saṃgha under the aegis of the compassionate monk Divākaramitra. After she is persuaded not to burn herself on a pyre in grief over the loss of her father, husband, and older brother, she begs Divākaramitra to allow her (and, we expect, all her ladies in waiting) to take the red robe of a nun. The good monk launches into a moving soliloquy about the virtues of the monastic estate. Still, Divākaramitra ends his paean to renunciation by observing that her brother seems to have reservations on this matter and that she should now follow his lead. Were it not for Harṣa's reticence, who would deny her the robe?[97] If we contrast this story with the aggressive defense of the outcaste woman's renunciation in the *Śārdūlakarṇāvadāna*, or similar episodes in early Buddhist literature, we obtain a clearer view of the delicate web of medieval Indian social relations.[98] Neither is Divākaramitra shown insisting on Rājyaśrī's vocation, nor does she herself try to resist her brother. While this is admittedly an epic poem, Bāṇa's vignette may provide a degree of insight, especially when observed in light of the other records.

Divākaramitra's hesitation shows that Buddhist monks—whether Mahayanist or of the esoteric persuasion—were not enthusiastic about receiving women into the order or even making room for their participation in the tradition. As indicated by the warning issued by the *Subāhuparipṛcchā-tantra* (translated into Chinese in 726 C.E.), the presence of a female body continued to be a trial for some monks:[99]

> Smiling, they walk along in conversation, glancing aside with their eyes.
> Every limb of their forms steals one's mind.
> The body of a woman is just like a beautiful sword—
> It attacks a man's mind.

We must conclude that, overall (and with notable exceptions), medieval Indian women were persuaded to leave Buddhist religious life behind and retreat to the home, as their society (and, increasingly, their religion) exhorted them, and frequently forced them, to do. In this they were neither passive pawns nor independent agents, but, when they could, they made decisions for themselves based on the influences of their time and society. Buddhist authors and institutions—male and female—internalized, articulated, and espoused these Varṇāśrama Dharma paradigms, since there appeared to be neither another option nor an alternative sense of direction. The ritual focus of surviving literature attributed to women of the period simply reinforces the virtual unanimity of this decision and provides us with little recourse but to assume that they accepted this position as they saw the doors of the Buddhist religion grow narrower before their eyes.

A LOSS OF FOOTING: THE AGENDA OF SKEPTICISM

In view of the decimation of the patronage base and the internalization of fundamentally non-Buddhist social models, the concomitant erosion of an independent Buddhist intellectual agenda should come as no surprise. Before this, the wealth of specifically Buddhist philosophical positions, supported by a technical Buddhist language, was one of the highlights of the word of the Buddha. Neither the Ābhidharmikas, nor the Yogācāras, nor the Vijñānavādins, nor the Sautrāntikas, nor many other Buddhist doctrinal schools seriously called this philosophical and doctrinal process into question. They presumed the right and responsibility of the monastic intellectuals to define a technical vocabulary and to support that vocabulary through an analytical apparatus that posited a Buddhist address of reality. Typically, that apparatus included the composition of new scriptures, which cast this technical vocabulary as the word of the Buddha *(buddhavacana)* or the teaching of the Teacher *(śāstuḥ śāsanam)*. Yet, by the end of the seventh century C.E., certain influential Buddhist teachers and thinkers had adopted positions whereby no new technical vocabulary was at all acceptable *(prāsaṅgika-madhyamaka)* or could be derived only from the pan-Indic discourse *(pramāṇavāda)*.

How could this extraordinary paradigm shift in intellectual values have taken place? As with the other changes in the early medieval era, the disestablishment of Buddhist technical terms had its roots in an earlier period, but came to define the discourse only during the seventh century. It really began with the crystallization of Buddhist skepticism at the hands of Nāgārjuna, with his affirmation in the *Vigrahavyāvatanī* XXVIII–XXIX that no proposition may be adopted in the middle way.[100] Only the level of truth available in the world *(samvyavahāra)* is the proper basis for speaking and communication. Clearly directed toward those proponents of early Indian epistemology, the text attempts to establish the priority of conventional usage, which Nāgārjuna makes the basis for both the teaching of absolute truth and the realization of nirvana in *Mūlamadhyamakakārikā* XXIV.10.[101]

Similar to the Greek philosophical movement of Skepticism, the Madhyamaka position appears really an affirmation of the most basic fundamental structures of the Buddhist path: karma, rebirth, and so forth. Clearly, it implied that the defining characteristics of these structures should not be subject to metaphysical discourse or contentious debate. They refused to expose the ethical parameters of the doctrine to the kind of minute examination that had already been turned toward philosophical positions and accordingly tried to communicate a return to prethematic ethical purity. Both the Indian and Greek traditions, however, had problems with the public perception that they represented extreme forms of nihilism, even though their religious agendas were actually central in their presentations. Although there is some uncertainty about whether the authors of the *Mūlamadhyamakakārikā* and such works as the *Ratnāvalī* were the same person, it is clear from the testimony of later authorities that the Madhyamaka system supported a strong affirmation of the monastic regimen.

However, the eventual consequences of Nāgārjuna's epistemological skepticism became worked out in the Prāsaṅgika school. In this form, Buddhapālita and, especially, Candrakīrti (c. 600–650 C.E.), dismissed any effort among Buddhists to justify any independent philosophical voice or technical nomenclature. In this regard, the Prāsaṅgika Madhyamaka may be most clearly compared to the method emphasized by Parmenides, the ostensible founder of Skepticism. Similar to Parmenides' denigration of the "backward-turning path of ordinary reasoning" *(palintropos keleuthos)*, Candrakīrti presumed that every statement implicated the contrapositive, so that nothing could be said without implicating *(prasaṅga)* its simultaneous antithesis.[102]

At its advent, the strong affirmation of worldly conventions, and especially the Prāsaṅgika criticism of Buddhist-constructed ideologies beyond such conventions, may have been a neotraditionalist response to internal and external pressure on Buddhist intellectual systems during the early medieval period. Yet the unintended result was a validation of an ethical standard established by the lowest common denominator in Indian society and the restriction of vocabulary to a common-language assessment of reality. Both in *Madhyamakāvatāra* VI.166–178, with its autocommentary, and in the lengthy *Prasannapadā* commentary on the *Mūlamadhyamakakārikās*, Candrakīrti consistently assails the capacity of anyone to articulate an independent analysis outside of that accepted in the ordinary perception of the world at large.[103] By the eighth century, the definition of relative truth—the only kind capable of being enacted in the world and the basis for the realization of the absolute—consisted of three elements. As has been shown by Eckel, relative truth is satisfactory when *not* analyzed, it consists of dependent origination, and it demonstrates efficiency in cause and effect.[104] It would be difficult to construct intentionally a doctrine more inhibitory to intellectual enquiry and ethical values, yet this was not the purpose but the unintended result of the Prāsaṅgika negation of all prior Buddhist agendas.

Such a doctrine clearly had consequences for the religious institutions, a difficulty already foreseen by Nāgārjuna in *Mūlamadhyamakakārikā* XXIV.11.

Here he proposes the metaphor that when emptiness is poorly comprehended it annihilates the individual, like a snake incorrectly handled or a spell improperly cast. Yet exactly this corrosive force came to bear against two of the primary facets of Buddhism: its ethical regimen and its doctrinal structure. Although Nāgārjuna may have castigated literally minded individuals as dimwitted *(mandamedhas)*, it is clear that he constructed the ideal justification for the morally indolent to buttress their unwillingness to adhere to the precepts. Such indolence was ever lurking in the background, and the early convocations of Indian monks in the centuries preceding Nāgārjuna had been seen as a response to a laxity of the rules. Buddhist monasteries relied on clerical virtue to assure the laity that their donations would reap extraordinary rewards, yet the history of Buddhist monasticism is a narrative about the extended testing of preceptorial boundaries by the morally challenged.

By the medieval period, this tendency fed on the erotized compositions of the Sanskrit and Prakrit poets, and medieval literature contains several acknowledgments that Buddhists were being led astray. Kalhaṇa mentions in his chronicle a purportedly sixth-century monastery in Kashmir, founded by a subsidiary Kashmiri queen, Yūkadevī. The monastery had to be divided into two sections: one for monks adhering to the rules of discipline, the other dedicated to monks with the accoutrements of householders—wives, children, cattle, and property.[105] I-ching further remarked in 692 C.E. on his trip to India, "Some observing one single precept on adultery say that they are free from sin, and do not at all care for the study of the *Vinaya* rules. They do not mind how they swallow, eat, dress, and undress. Simply directing their attention to the Doctrine of Nothingness is regarded by them as the will of the Buddha."[106]

In undermining the idea that ethical statements were to be taken as veridical *as stated,* Nāgārjuna and Candrakīrti clearly provided an avenue for those seeking a ready-made authoritative voice for the neglect of the Buddhist precepts. The most famous literary example of this direction is found in the seventh-century farce the *Mattavilāsa,* by the Pallava monarch, Mahendravikramavarman (c. 650). Here Śākya Bhikṣu Nāgasena—the Buddhist monk—is shown actively searching for the "true scriptures," which allow to the clergy the pursuit of women and the drinking of alcohol.[107] He bitterly complains that the elders in the community are hiding them from him to keep him ignorant about these sacred texts. Yet it was not only Hindu dramatists that noted that medieval Buddhist ideology problematized the ethical system. Śaṅkara openly declared that there could be no possibility of an intelligible path that was socially approved, since the disparate elements in the Buddhadharma, and especially that of the Madhyamaka, rendered all such attempts puerile nonsense.[108]

Apparently many both within and outside the Buddhist tradition understood that walking the line of nonfoundational praxis was hazardous to the vows.

LOOKING ELSEWHERE FOR DIRECTION: THE TURN TO EPISTEMOLOGY

Doctrinally as well, statements by Mādhyamikas contributed to the disempowerment of normative Buddhist intellectual standards and assisted the headlong rush into the Buddhist appropriation of epistemology.[109] Earlier Buddhists had relied on the statements in the scriptures and had followed a well-worn process of consensual affirmation of Buddhist doctrine. In the medieval period, however, these same fundamentals apparently lacked the resonance and strength previously accorded them. Contributing to this perception of weakness were the concerted physical and intellectual assaults on the Buddhist order from their Brahmanical antagonists, as seen above. As a medium for intellectual challenges, orthodox antagonists employed the epistemological vocabulary that had become the language of the wider Indian world. For whatever reason, Buddhist intellectuals were grappling with the need to articulate their own reliable sources of understanding. Eventually, they turned to the larger Indian intellectual community to affirm their own standards by means of pan-Indic values. Among other consequences of this change of direction, many intellectual monks took a turn toward epistemology in an unprecedented manner, seeking philosophical assurance in the standards developed in the non-Buddhist epistemological circles.

Although the initial forays into the discussion of epistemological standards are as old as Buddhism, with the work of Dharmakīrti (c. 650 C.E.) this form of discourse moved from interesting marginalia to center stage. Asaṅga (c. 350–400 C.E.) had already included some epistemological material in the *Śrutamayī* and *Cintāmayī Bhūmis*. There, he discussed the issues of *hetu-vidyā*, which was primarily concerned with syllogistic reasoning, valid and invalid proofs, and many of the questions later to be classified under reasoned discourse *(parārthānumāṇa)*.[110] Yet the inclusion of this material into the larger corpus of the *Yogācārabhūmi*, and abbreviated in the *Abhidharmasamuccaya*, was not indicative of epistemology's centrality to Asaṅga's exegetical direction.[111] Rather, like the lengthy section on the sixteen varieties of opponents' claims in the *Savitarkādibhūmi*, the purpose of the *hetu-vidyā* presentation was ancillary to the domain of meditative praxis and supplementary to the intellectual facets of the system. We may presume that it was included primarily for the purposes of completeness in education.[112] Indeed, the *Abhidharmasamuccaya* finishes its discussion of epistemology by warning that one desiring his own benefit (i.e., liberation) will simply recognize the different varieties of verbal expression but will not waste his time disputing with others.[113] This dictum resonates with the fundamental Buddhist value that monks should follow gnosis but not those forms of perceptual consciousness required in the pursuit of epistemology.[114] Clearly this warning by the doyen of Buddhist meditative systems was not heeded in later centuries.

The results of the epistemological turn are immediately seen in the work of Dignāga, which finds its fulfillment in Dharmakīrti. Dignāga apparently could not verify the significance of the word of the Buddha simply by the standards of authenticity that had motivated Buddhists in the past.[115] Because he was focused on the criteria that had been introduced by non-Buddhists, Dignāga came to vindicate the scriptures—and their forms of praxis—in light of commonly held Indian values, rather than verifying them through ideals such as dispassion, nirvana, and so forth. He was therefore called on to reverse a long-standing Buddhist tradition concerning the value of the teaching of the teacher, which was admirably summed up in the categories of the *Adhyāśayasañcodana-sūtra.* This scripture claims that anything well-said—so long as it is endowed with significance, is in accordance with the teaching, eliminates defilements, leads to nirvana, and not the opposites of these—could be understood as the word of the Buddha.[116] All of these values were subservient to the ancient Buddhist ideal that the Dharma was not dependent on the Buddha or any other individual. Monks, therefore, should rely on the Dharma and not on individual personalities.

Because Dignāga could not enter into pan-Indic discourse based on this model, he appropriated another instead. For Dignāga, the Buddha became the embodiment of valid reasoning *(pramāṇabhūta)*, an indication that the individual as the source of the message was rapidly becoming more important than the message itself. This personalization of philosophy became valid even within intellectual communities, which had been resistant to the pressures of popular Buddhism until then. Dignāga's position had short-term gains and long-term consequences. In the near term, the Buddha became important for Buddhist epistemologists because he was the source of valid cognition. Dharmakīrti refined this and dedicated an entire chapter to the definition of the Buddha as the source of uncontradicted truth, thus placing him as a personality on a par with the personalities of the Vedic seers and the lawgiver Manu. Thus, according to this new expression, the Buddha's understanding and speech remained uncontroverted by any element of observable or inferable reality *(pramāṇasiddhi).*

In the long term, however, the assumption of these positions was arguably detrimental to Buddhist institutions. Dreyfus has both summed up the challenge represented to Buddhists by epistemology and glossed over the consequences it had for them:[117]

> Starting from the discussions of the *Nyāya-sūtra* and Vātsyāyana's commentary, great attention was paid to argumentation and the theory of inference. This resulted in the establishment of a logic that gained wide acceptance, so much so that it provided intertraditional standards of validation. These developments created the relatively neutral framework within which competing claims of Indian philosophical schools, such as Nyāya, Mīmāṃsā, Jain and Buddhism, could be assessed.

But, even as Dreyfus is forced to admit later, these standards were neither neutral nor supportive of the traditional Buddhist path, although they provided the criteria whereby that path came to be assessed in the public forum. Perhaps more indicative of the crisis, however, within the Buddhist intellectual community was the fact that, after Dharmakīrti, virtually all scholastic forms of intellectual discourse seemed propelled toward the use of his nomenclature.

From this point on, the questions asked in India would not be, for example: is this text the word of the Buddha. Instead they are: do you mean that the Buddha is in error or that the ideals of the Buddhist tradition do not live up to the standards established for normative discourse in pan-Indian intellectual circles? All these changes resulted in Buddhists' adopting reference points that were not initially developed within the tradition but emerged instead from systems antagonistic to Buddhist ideals. To their credit, the Buddhist epistemologists fused the doctrines of Vijñānavāda idealism to the systemic requirements that discussions of perception and syllogistic argumentation invoke. However, the result was that the vocabulary and diction of Dharmakīrti and his successors are more familiar to those trained in the treatises of the Naiyāyikas than to one versed in the Abhidharma or earlier Mahayanist works.

In engaging non-Buddhist systems, monks evidently overlooked the principle that negotiations are successful from positions of strength. To be influential, to capture the direction of the discourse, to configure the categories of reality in one's favor—all of these depend on the ideal that the message projected is taken by its believers as confidently true. The public presentation of the Buddhadharma from the seventh century on became resolutely epistemological and given to quibbling about shades of gray. This was a form of presentation that those in positions of political and military authority would not hear and could not comprehend. What they did understand was that Buddhist scholars had adopted as their primary standards of validation the systems generated in and matured by the Varṇāśrama Dharma.

It must again be emphasized that the potential for each of these two directions (skepticism and epistemology) existed in Indian Mahayana for some centuries before they overwhelmed the centers of monastic instruction. Neither of their progenitors—Nāgārjuna and Dignāga—lived in the early medieval milieu. However, both of the primary institutionalizers—Candrakīrti and Dharmakīrti—were most influential from the mid-seventh century C.E. forward, precisely when economic destabilization and political uncertainty became the prevailing nature of Indian social life. Thus we may rely equally on evidence and inference to affirm that the sociopolitical events of the time propelled the voices of Buddhist self-skepticism and non-Buddhist intellectual self-promotion to emerge into the normative discourse of Buddhist institutions. The two voices worked well in concert, skepticism eroding confidence in a specifically Buddhist intellectual language, and epistemology developing a language acceptable to the mundane world. These voices took control of the normative discourse and erected widely approved standards of viability whereby Buddhist doctrines either were clothed in epistemological language or were simply unacceptable.

BIG IMPORTANT MONASTERIES—ADMINISTRATORS IN MAROON ROBES

By the seventh century, the grand vessels of the Buddhist monasteries found themselves in narrow straits and shallow waters. Their most reliable traditional sources of support—the merchant guilds and minority kings—were experiencing extraordinary distress. While the North Indian guilds were being depleted, tribal and other minorities were being vigorously proselytized. Buddhist strongholds, the great urban centers of North India, were simultaneously experiencing population loss as they increasingly became the targets for Deccan based raids and internecine strife. These large urban environments were being replaced with a relocation of population into rapidly appearing smaller centers that were not located on the traditional trade routes, and operated as market centers rather than the sources for goods traded by guilds with national and international connections. Śaiva kings were displacing Buddhists in the Deccan, and the greater Buddhist dynasties of the Pālas, Bhaumakaras, or Khadgas had yet to coalesce or to declare their Buddhist affinities in the east. In the west, the forays of Islamic armies were the harbingers of future unhappiness, and Buddhist promoters like the Maitrikas were in dire straits.

As they experienced the retrenchment of their populations into the narrower ranges of Northeast, West, and South India, Buddhist monasteries began to emulate the very political forms that caused them their distressing decline in the subcontinent—the sāmanta feudal system. From the seventh century until the complete collapse of Buddhist monasteries in the fourteenth century, Buddhist institutions became feuda for the abbots and the monks. They administered their estates and established loyalties in a manner closely analogous to members of the circle of vassals *(sāmantamaṇḍala)* of an overlord *(rājādhirāja)*. Monasteries relied on these great kings for their land grants and the maintenance of law beyond the borders of their grants. Nationally, the new "Great Monasteries" *(mahāvihāra)* managed to establish branch institutions, which appeared to act as their extensions in other areas, much as sāmantas acted as their lord's representatives. The primary difference was easy to understand and represented the central service of the new monasteries: their retainers were monks and laymen being educated by these feudal cloisters, rather than military retainers in service of the state. The simultaneous process of the growth of institutions, the decline of their absolute numbers, and the close relationships established between them all had consequences for the *Vinaya* and for the architecture of the monastic buildings.

In *Vinaya* terms, I-ching's testimony seems clear: he interpreted the four more popular *Vinayas*—Mahāsāṃghika, Sthaviravāda, Mūlasarvāstivāda, and Sammitīya—as having been original and the others as having evolved as their branches.[118] With the increased connections between parts of the country, selected *Vinaya* schools thus successfully established hegemony in areas of greatest patronage. The net result was that these traditions, with their increased authority and prestige, displaced less popular schools through the hermeneutic that smaller groups were but subsets of the "older" systems and therefore less authentic. This displacement process is well attested to in the more complete historical record of the Mahāvihāra Sthaviravāda of Śrī Lañka, and our incomplete Indian data support that model as well. In particular, I-ching saw the increasingly popular *Mūlasarvāstivāda Vinaya* as the source of the Dharmaguptaka, the Mahīśāsaka, and the Kāśyapīya, despite the probability that these latter were actually earlier in development and codification than the Mūlasarvāstivāda.[119] The result of this evolution was the slow eclipse of the other *Vinayas*, so that none but the Mūlasarvāstivāda was introduced into Tibet from the eighth to the thirteenth centuries, probably because of its successful adaptation to the life of large institutions.[120]

In architectural terms, Buddhist monasteries in North India during the early medieval period began to resemble one another much more closely than before. The differences of layout seen between Nāgārjunakoṇḍa, Sāñcī, Taxila, and Ellora (representing multiple *Vinaya* schools) are seldom encountered. From the vantage of the later megamonasteries, the variety observable in these earlier communities seems to be struggling toward the grand synthesis of the monumental edifices of Somapura or Nālandā. However, the earlier buildings demonstrate a wider spectrum of local forms, a creative investiture in the organic process of development rather than the uniformity of large institutions. In one sense, the mahāvihāras of the medieval world appear curiously like Buddhist versions of neoclassical office buildings or an Indian version of university gothic architecture in its repetitive systematization. Such systematization also shows up in the formalization of monastic sealings; during this period virtually all monastic sealings represent their monasteries as "Dharmacakras" and have a glorified wheel of the Dharma—frequently set between two deer—immediately above the institution's name.[121]

We are still in the dark on almost all facets of these large monasteries, which are sometimes misleadingly referred to as universities, as if the circumstances of their establishment and curriculum were analogous to the universities of Italy and France begun some centuries later. Their daily operations, the composition of the monks and laity engaged in study and practice, the manner of teaching and instruction, and, especially, the changes of curricula or texts used for the various examinations—almost all internal practices are obscure to us. The number of monastic sites known to us are slowly increasing as the Archaeological Survey of India and other archaeological bodies in state and university departments are forced to contend with site destruction due to severe population pressures. To date, however, we have no thorough survey of the extant sites and their locations. My discussions with Indian archaeologists lead me to believe that many, perhaps a majority, of medium-size medieval monasteries remain unexcavated and unstudied, and—even if excavated—the results remain unpublished. Thus we have no good estimation of the total monastic population of India at any point in the early medieval period, since we do not know the absolute number of monasteries.

Concerning the size of the great monasteries, our best evidence is from the written legacies of Hsüan-tsang and I-ching, both of whom have been accused of inflating their estimates. Hsüan-tsang's statement is simple: Nālandā has "several thousand" monks, hundreds of whom are known in other countries.[122] I-ching is more specific, evaluating the number of monks in Nālandā as "more than three thousand" in his *Nan hai chi kuei nei fa chuan,* and "three thousand

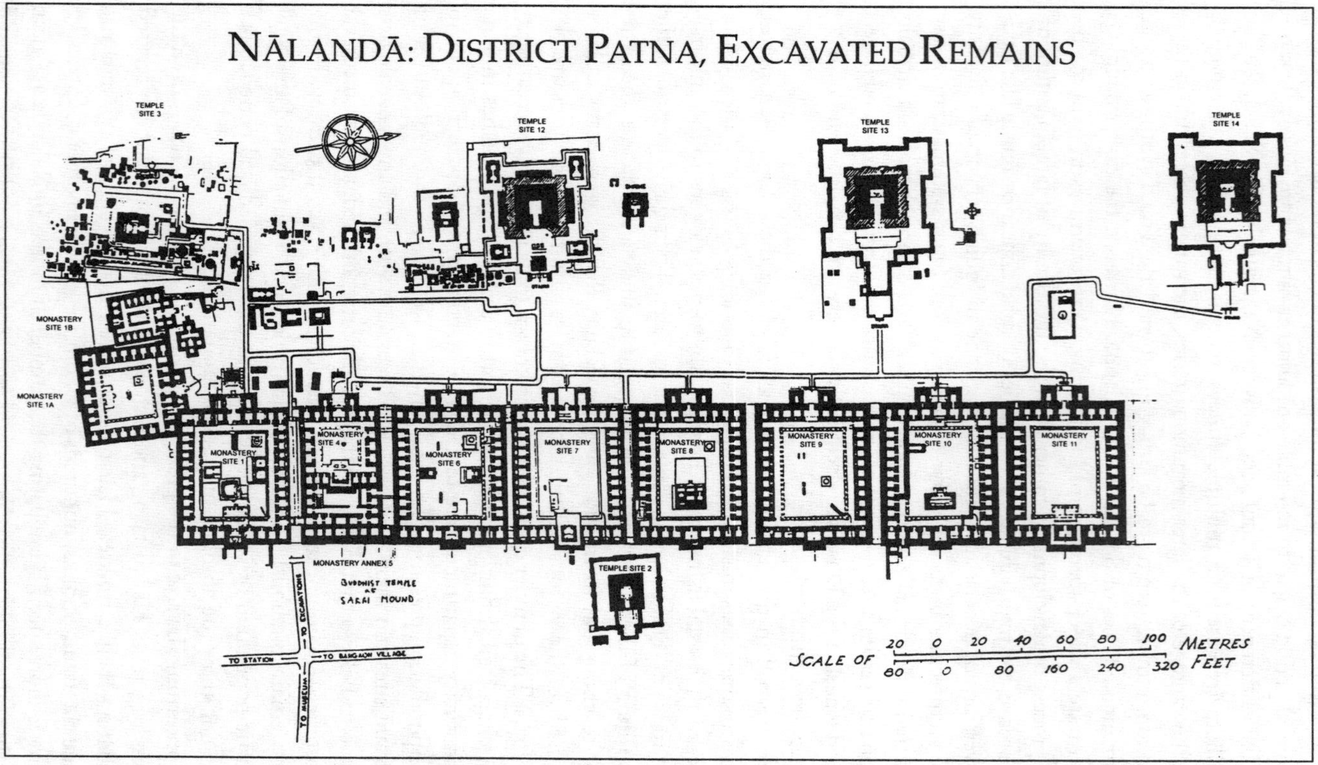

FIGURE 1 Nalanda: District Patna, excavated remains. *Site plan courtesy of the Archaelogical Survey of India*

five hundred" in his *Ta t'ang hsi yü ch'iu fa kao seng chuan.*[123] How realistic are these estimates? The surviving site (Figure 1) has eight large monasteries (monasteries 1–11, in the eccentric numbering of the site) and two smaller ones (monasteries 1A and 1B); these latter are most probably the oldest monasteries built in association with the old "Original Perfumed Chamber" *(mūlagandhakuṭī*: Stupa 3).[124] I-ching twice indicates that the principal buildings numbered eight, but it is not clear whether the other two, earlier monasteries were functioning as well.[125] The published plans indicate that each of the eight large monasteries has between thirty-two and thirty-seven potential "cells," although it is not clear that all of them were used as such. I-ching speaks of nine cells to each of the four walls, leading to thirty-six for the four sides of each floor in each building.[126] It would be safe to say that, at its maximum, approximately thirty-five of the cells on each of the lower floors were occupied at any one time. Monasteries 1B and 1A, by contrast, have thirteen and twenty-six cells, respectively.

The *Mūlasarvāstivāda Vinaya*—probably the dominant *Vinaya* during the ninth-century Devapāla period that the current site represents—allows for either a three-story or a five-story construction.[127] I-ching seems to describe construction of three stories "or more," which is not as clear as we might like.[128] Because the walls of Monastery 1B were excessively narrow, it is unlikely that it could have been five stories, but that does not apply to the other nine monasteries. Given the inscriptional panegyrics to the "lofty spires" of Nālandā's famous cloisters, so that they resemble the snowy peaks of Mount Sumeru, it would be difficult to argue that they were short in height.[129] If each cell was occupied by two monks (I have witnessed three modern monks living in rooms this size, but not happily), then we would end up with approximately seventy monks on each floor of the eight large monasteries. Thus the height becomes the crucial variable; there would be about 210 monks per monastery if the monasteries had three stories, 280 monks if four stories, and 350 if they had five stories. The individual administrators—abbots, etc.—traditionally have occupied the penthouses of these centers, so we might consider that the top floor was not fully used in this manner. If we take the approximate total of the eight large monasteries with three floors (210 times 8 = 1,680) and add the two smaller centers (Monastery 1B, perhaps 70 monks; Monastery 1A perhaps 150 monks), we arrive at a figure of 1,900 monks, give or take an abbot or a famous guest. However, if we use the five-story model (350 times 8 = 2,800 + Monastery 1B + Monastery 1A), we still end up with a figure of about three thousand, and it is difficult to see in either case how the total of 3,500 monks could be ascertained. We must consider, for example, that any model would have to allow for surges during pilgrimage or great lecture/ritual times, when monks might have to triple-up, and specific areas of monasteries could be closed when not needed. In a pinch, monks could also occupy the large temples outside the walls, clearly placed for lay use. There was likely a class of monks specializing in devotional activity who lived in these sites as well, but it is not clear that they would be counted among the Nālandā monks.

We are better informed of the relations between these domains of Buddhist praxis and the immediate environment, primarily because of the combination of the written legacy and the excavated clay sealings. Among the several hundred sealings, and beyond those of undistinguished individuals, the clay impressions left in the rubble of this edifice indicate an elaborate series of relations with attached villages, officers of the courts in the area, and other monasteries.[130] Monasteries of this variety would frequently be given jurisdiction over the proximate area as an extension of their endowments and part of the feuda assigned to them. The consequence was that monasteries had the responsibility for the maintenance of law and the settling of litigation, not simply over their own clergy, but over the villagers under their aegis as well. Thus the extraordinary number of sealings from village offices *(grāmikajanapada)*, royal agents *(adhikaraṇa)* attached to this or that village, and the occasional police station *(sthāna)* must be connected with more than economic functions. Collectively they represent the detritus of documents, bundles, various warrants and writs of the courts all under the authority of the monasteries.

Similarly, the remarkable number of sealings from other monasteries indicates close relations and occasional formal ties. For example, we find construction in honor of the martyrdom of the eminent monk Karuṇāśrīmitra, who went to the Buddha's heaven after having been burned to death by a Baṅgāla army while he was trying to save his monastery of Somapura. A disciple in his line constructed statues and monasteries in several locales around North India, including a monastery specifically dedicated to his *Vinaya* lineage, the Mitras.[131] The interesting part, though, is the inscription celebrating this in the proximity of the Nālandā grounds, where it was set up so that its message might gain greater response and achieve the public appreciation that was its due. These records indicate that monks of specific monasteries became associated with other specific monasteries, either because they established them as extensions of the *Vinaya* and curricular systems of the home cloisters or because the areas were naturally affiliated.

The personal relations, dedication, and loyalty that represent the glue of medieval social and political systems clearly played as important a part in the great Buddhist monasteries as it did elsewhere. Sharma recognized this in his classic work on Indian feudalism, and any discussion of the early medieval period certainly should take into account that political and land-tenure relations sometimes worked on a continuum—particularly in the cases of religious emoluments—rather than being utterly disparate.[132] Certainly, Buddhist monasteries were not required to provide troops to the granting dynasty, but they provided other labor services—ritual, educative, cultural, and so on. These were considered of such value that the securing of scholars, religious statuary, or learned priests was recognized as a valid cause for military belligerence.[133]

Likewise, the consequences of being involved with the wrong faction meant that monasteries were set aflame with some frequency. This became an issue in discussions of retrieving and preserving Indian literature during the construction of libraries for Royal Dynastic Tibetan monasteries, and the record indicates that Nālandā library had been burned down at least once in the mid-eighth century.[134] Allegiance was maintained by the services monks performed for the lord of the area. One received text of the *sBa-bzhed* (Testament of the Ba Clan) indicates that the Buddhist clergy of Magadha set up a special reliquary *(caitya)* named "Dharatu-caṃda" (apparently Prakrit for "moon of support") in front of the Pāla king's palace. Inside it contained "bones and relics of the Tathāgata," as well as "the fortune of enemies of the king who had yet to be born."[135] If true, the strategy must have been simple and convincing—if the enemies of the king were kept pacified with the relics of the Tathāgata, then they would harm neither the kingdom nor the clergy. At a time when clerics took seriously their duty to curse offenders of the Dharma, the agonistic ritual response by virtuous monks was held as the potential threat to those seeking to overthrow the monarch or harm the order. Thus the relationship between monastery and state was based both on a system of mutual identity and on an ideology of magical performance. As we examine the development of esoteric Buddhism, we see that this metaphor is carried to the extreme.

CONCLUSION: A TRADITION UNDER DURESS

The medieval experience for Buddhists in India represented a dramatic change from their position of centrality in Indian life during the Gupta. Previous sources of support and prior areas of strength became eroded and, occasionally, eclipsed. As the great trading guilds became crippled in the internal military situation and hobbled in the external geopolitical events, donations to the monasteries began to evaporate. The search for new kinds of patronage placed monasteries in the position of assuming many of the characteristics of the society around them. They gained stature as landed feudal lords, collecting rents and taxes and exercising judicial powers in their domains. As a result, the monasteries began to internalize many of the same value systems that the external society reflected. They affirmed a greater esteem for political power and began to see power as an avenue for the advancement of their agenda. They furthered the weakening of support for women's religious expression, withdrawing resources from nuns and dissuading women from donning the red robe. They became enamored of the new authority of non-Buddhist epistemological discourse and placed it in a position of prominence in the curriculum of the large teaching monasteries.

In sum, early medieval Buddhist institutions assumed the dynamics of the Indian life around them. While monks and monasteries had always claimed a separate judicial and religious space from the Indian town and village, in reality no monastery had ever been hermetically sealed from the events around it. At times, the interval between the world at the monastic gate and the temple inside appeared distant indeed, but this was continually (re)negotiated in the strategies of monastic decorum and religious requirements. As the world changed, the relationships between monks and their families, between the preceptors and the novices, between the bursars and the suppliers, and between the abbot and the feudal lord all changed as well. The esoteric system became an internalization of many of these factors and clearly evolves out of the medieval experience.

4

The Victory of Esoterism and the Imperial Metaphor

The Buddha, together with Vajradhara,
Indeed, all the Buddhas have consecrated you.
So you will be, from this day forward,
Great Kings of the triple world,
Lords among the Victors *[jinādhipati]*.
From this day on, you are victorious over Māra;
You have entered the most excellent city;
And you will, from this day on,
Obtain Buddhahood, of that there is no doubt.

—Mañjuśrīmitra's *Nāmasaṃgītimaṇḍalavidhyākāśavimala*[1]

Our survey of the background vicissitudes of India and the somewhat reduced frame of reference for aspects of medieval Buddhism have so far set aside a specific discussion of esoterism and its development, but we now turn fully to this issue. As the most ritually evolved form of Buddhism, esoteric Buddhism had its genesis in the Buddhist experience of the medieval Indian horizon. The emergence of the esoteric dispensation is both a response and a strategy on the part of facets within Buddhist communities: it was a response to the difficult medieval environment and a strategy for religious reaffirmation in the face of unprecedented challenges to the Buddhist social horizon. Central to my investigation is the proposal that esoteric Buddhism was not generated exclusively from the many sources traditionally depicted. In deference to humanistic criteria, I cannot presume that the esoteric system is the direct message of a/the cosmic Buddha—whether Vairocana, Vajradhara, Samantabhadra, Nairātmyā, or some other figure—which is the orthodox Vajrayāna position. Nor does the evidence support the model that Buddhist esoterism is the pale imitation of Śaivism, as it has sometimes been described. Finally, it is clearly not the result of narrowly internal forces in Indian Buddhism.[2] All three positions have been embedded in the various models proposed to date.[3]

Rather, the evidence suggests that the rise and development of the esoteric form of Buddhism is the result of a complex matrix of medieval forces, both those dynamics generated within the Samgha communities and other factors over which the communities had no control. The evidence supports a position that is curiously both astonishing and reassuring: the Mantrayāna is simultaneously the most politically involved of Buddhist forms and the variety of Buddhism most acculturated to the medieval Indian landscape. Briefly, the mature synthesis of esoteric Buddhism—the form defined as a separate method or vehicle employing mantras—is that which embodies the metaphor of the practitioner becoming the overlord *(rājādhirāja)*. In this endeavor, the candidate is coronated and provided with ritual and metaphorical access to all the various systems that an overlord controls: surrounded by professors of mantras, he performs activities to ensure the success of his spiritual "state." The process represents the sacralization of the sociopolitical environment, as it was seen on the ground in seventh- to eighth-century India.

The analysis presented here distinguishes between two different Buddhist sociologies of knowledge. On one hand are monks practicing these forms in the great Buddhist monastic institutions; their parameters and horizons of expectations are assessed in this chapter. This variety of Mantrayāna arose in support of, and provided maintenance to, the monastic estate, allowing it to interact with the warlords and princes, the military generals and the emerging tribal leaders. In view of its primary focus and generative nexus, this can be called "institutional esoterism." Institutional esoterism was the form that succeeded wherever esoteric Buddhism prospered. This form was principally the domain of monks, who wrote and preached in a hermeneutical method that emphasized the development and integration of esoteric ideas and models into institutional requirements. In this guise, esoterism became part of the socialization system that turned laymen from disparate backgrounds into members of a culture unified by monastic rule, ritual, cosmology, and doctrine.

On the other hand was the somewhat anarchical domain of the Perfected *(siddha)*, those sometimes scruffy, long-haired denizens of the margins of the Indian social institutions. Siddhas are examined in the succeeding chapters, but it suffices to note here that they and the monks represent symbiotic estates in the politicization of Buddhism. Although the siddha tradition seemed in some ways a logical conclusion to the Vajrayāna, neither did it exist in a vacuum (religious, intellectual, ritual, or social), nor did it arise without a necessary tension between it and other facets of the Buddhist path embodied in disparate Buddhist institutions. While the siddhas are portrayed as noninstitutional or even anti-institutional, they actually played an important position in the lives of

Buddhist and non-Buddhist social forms. Yet the conundrum was that siddhas, in all likelihood, were far fewer in number than monks, even if the Perfected had a higher visibility. Both monks and siddhas cultivated political patronage and authored apologia, so they are equally essential to a discussion of the maturation of the Mantrayāna.

Esoteric Buddhism may thus seem astonishing, in that it directly reflects the internalization of the medieval conceptual and social environment, rather than being the revealed system that orthodoxy portrays. By the same token, the sociopolitical nature of esoteric Buddhism appears reassuring, thanks to evidence from the introduction of this form of Buddhism into other cultures, such as China from the time of Śubhakarasiṃha, Vajrabodhi, and Amoghavajra. In this context, Mantrayāna is both highly political and culturally sensitive, having become a favorite of the court during the T'ang dynasty and especially during the reign of the Tai-tsung emperor (762–779) in the aftermath of the An Lu-shan rebellion.[4] Likewise in Japan, with the rapid acceptance of the esoteric tradition during the Heian under the advocacy of Kukai (774–835) and Saicho (767–822), the position of the Shingon and Tendai sects at court became proverbial. It has been said that the former was the special provenance of the imperial family and the latter the particular interest of the aristocratic clans, both patronage sources demonstrating the strength of their political associations. Closer to India, similar circumstances are encountered during the Royal Dynastic period in Tibet, particularly during and after the reign of Trisong Detsen (755–797).[5] Likewise, the rulers of the Ta-li kingdom in the aftermath of Nan-chao were noted patrons of the Mantrayāna.[6] The finds of bronzes of esoteric divinities in Thailand, the importance of similar representations in the kingdom of Pagan in Burma and in Cambodian Angkor all reinforce this conclusion.[7] There appears no exception to the rule that, when the Mantrayāna becomes culturally important outside India, it is principally through the agency of official patronage, either aristocratic or imperial.[8] Given these circumstances, it would be extraordinary if the military and political culture of early medieval India had not shaped esoteric institutions, doctrines, literature, rituals, and iconography, at least to some degree.

In fact, the degree is compelling, and central aspects of esoteric Buddhism came to embody directly and unequivocally the structure, aesthetics, and ideology of medieval Indian feudalism. In short, esoteric Buddhism is the form of medieval Buddhism that internalized, appropriated, reaffirmed, and rearranged the structures most closely associated with the systems of power relations, ritual authentication, aesthetics, gift-giving, clan associations, and sense of dominion that defined post-Gupta Indian polities. However, by no means should we be seduced into believing that these changes came directly from a single caste or strata of society, either high caste or low, as has been sometimes affirmed.[9] Rather, esoteric Buddhism was generated by groups that were constituted in a variety of discrete social levels and tended to define the esoteric system based on the relationship between the needs of the institution or small group and the models of authority developed in the society at large. In this regard, Buddhist monasteries evolved regional institutional cultures, analogous to the specific cultures seen in large corporations or educational institutions in the modern period. Individuals became socialized into these cultures and began to reflect the values developed by the consensus and history of the institution.

While Indian Buddhism had a change of direction that appears radical in many respects, it also exhibits aspects of a synthetic and, even at times, syncretic approach. However, opportunistic syncretism is seldom as unprincipled, destabilizing, or symptomatic of incompetence as it sometimes has been depicted. Frequently, the opportunistic appropriation of a behavioral facet, ideology, or aesthetics of a proximate culture becomes the key for renewal and dynamic revitalization. Certainly, one could not accuse neo-Confucians, like Su Shih (1037–1101), of either a lack of principle or debilitating lassitude in their articulation of Confucian syntheses of Buddhist and Taoist doctrinal or meditative paradigms. Indeed, the neo-Confucian model became the vehicle for the complete victory of a renewed Confucianism in East Asia, even if it surreptitiously emulated very un-Confucian ideas, whose central procedures were nevertheless interpreted in a compelling Confucian manner. Accordingly, syncretic systems are often indicative of an ideological mesne—a stratum of potential occupation that is not exclusively the purview of any one religious tradition. Yet the dynamic properties of opportunistic syncretism appear to require a perceived duress within the parent tradition, in this case, Mahayana Buddhism. Thus the Mahayana moved toward multifaceted development after the fall of the Guptas, being pressed on by a sense of urgency and of crises within and without. Many of the directions taken were consistent with fundamental Buddhist principles, but in the rapidly changing environment of the new political and military realities, they took on forms of signification unforeseen by their progenitors.

CHRONOLOGY: THE SEVENTH-CENTURY BEGINNING

In our examination of its birth, we should differentiate between the employment of mantras, maṇḍalas, fire sacrifice, and other specific ritual items, on one hand, and the mature esoteric system, on the other. Such a rationale is useful, for the expression of powerful phrases in Indian culture, the arrangement of altars, the references to scepters *(vajra)* are older than Buddhism itself. Even within the Buddhist sphere, as has already been pointed out, most Buddhist traditions employ sacred phrases for various purposes, especially in protection and healing rituals.[10] For their part, many Mahayanists defined other kinds of phrases as expressive of "supports" *(dhāraṇī)* in the contemplation or propagation of the Dharma and even defended their use.[11] Yet the employment of these specific rituals within monastic environments was not set apart from other avenues, if the available literature is any indication. Until it matured, such esoteric materials were individual aids, not a unified system. They were not considered constituents of a self-contained path and did not contribute a sense of identity within the community, either to set the individual apart or to bring others into the fold. The ritual secrecy, the transmission of separate precepts, the intimate connection between master and disciple—these had not come together in a self-aware manner.

The mature esoteric synthesis that arose then was emblematic of the new formulation: it insisted on an immutable master-disciple bond, employed royal acts of consecration, and used elaborate maṇḍalas in which the meditator was to envision himself as the Buddha in a field of subordinate Buddhas. Proponents of the system composed a new class of scriptures that taught the transmission and recitation of secret mantras. Calling themselves "possessors of mantras or scepters" *(mantrin / vajrin)*, they developed rituals (particularly fire sacrifice) for the purpose of a codified series of soteriological and nonsoteriological acts and ultimately institutionalized this material in Buddhist monasteries where texts were copied, art produced, and rituals performed. In this regard, the self-description of mature esoteric Buddhism as the way of secret mantras *(guhyamantrayāna)* is analogous to the Mahayana's self-description as the way of the bodhisattva *(bodhisattvayāna)*. The nomenclature and ideology of bodhisattvas (Siddhārtha, Maitreya) had been around long before it became embedded in a different ritualized "way," with new vows and a new path topography. In a similar manner, the identification and use of mantras (or *dhāraṇī* or *vidyā)* had existed for centuries before there arose a new ritualized synthesis of different factors.

It is only in the second half of the seventh century that the definitive esoteric system emerges, and we have several verifications of this dating. Literature designated "proto-tantric" (a term I believe to be somewhat misleading) was still the exclusive form of Buddhist esoterism through the middle of the seventh century.[12] Examples of this are the Gilgit manuscript of the *Kāraṇḍavyūha-sūtra*, which was written sometime around or before 630 C.E. and the 653/54 composition and translation of the *Dhāraṇīsaṃgraha* of Atikūṭa.[13] In addition, the Ch'an monk Wu-hsing remarked around 680 C.E. that the popularity of the esoteric path was a new and exceptional event in India, observable even while he was in residence.[14] He reputedly brought back with him the earliest version of the *Mahāvairocanābhisambodhi-tantra*, although he did not translate it.[15] Then there is the difference in attitude evident between Hsüan-tsang's dismissal of ignorant users of spells in 646 C.E. and I-ching's personal involvement with esoterism during his Indian sojourn between 671–692 C.E.[16] Finally, we note Bodhiruci's career, perhaps the most neglected of the early esoteric translators. His early translations into Chinese from 693 to around 700 were almost exclusively normative Mahayana materials (*Mahāratnakuṭa*, etc.), but the period from around 700 to 710 was taken up with the emerging esoteric corpus of texts.[17]

The new system came into being quite swiftly, a demonstration that incrementalist presumptions on the emergence of new Indian systems are problematic. It is evident that the synthesis was effected in decades, not centuries, although it eventually took centuries to work through all the consequential developments. Even then, it appears that the overwhelming majority of esoteric Buddhist literature was written in the space of about four hundred years, from the mid-seventh to the mid-eleventh centuries. This is true of the siddha documents as well, for they appear on the scene only a few decades after the mature synthesis is clearly evident. As shown below, Buddhist siddha presence was already attested in both Buddhist and non-Buddhist literature by 720–730 C.E., and in the third quarter of the eighth century extraordinary evidence emerges for authority being granted to the most radical of the new forms of literature—the *yoginī tantras*.[18] To understand these developments, it is helpful to set aside the traditional explanations for eventual reconsideration and instead ponder whether the esoteric development is not better represented as an extension of the medieval milieu.

BECOMING THE RĀJĀDHIRĀJA— THE CENTRAL MANTRAYĀNA METAPHOR

One of the long-lived points of controversy on the nature of the Mantrayāna is its definition. Modern efforts have been sometimes either sectarian or nationalistic, such as the attempts of occasional East Asian scholars to discredit later Vajrayāna as corrupt and to portray their own tradition as pure.[19] Ideological definitions have lasted for some centuries. Some definitions of esoterism—or, more broadly, tantra—include the presence or absence of mantras, of the yogins' self-visualization as a divinity, of the presence or absence of maṇḍalas, and so forth. The problem with these traditional efforts is that they tend to rely on monothetic appraisals, such as Tsongkhapa's very popular definition that everything identified as "tantra" must involve the visualization of oneself as the Buddha.[20] This particular formula was questioned almost as soon as it was voiced. Already in 1420 C.E., Ngorchen Kunga Sangpo (1389–1456) challenged this model in two works dedicated to the examination of texts classified as *kriyā-* or *caryā-tantra.*[21] Ngorchen was able to show that a great many works, both simple and complex, do not mention such a visualization yet still must be included in the esoteric canon. Also somewhat misleading are etymologies of *tantra* as derived from the root √*tan* (to stretch or weave). Although the word certainly can mean this, other semantic values are more applicable to the period and matrix of activity.

It should be clear from developments in cognitive science that polythetic category constructions (or analogous models) are the primary vehicle for human decision systems. Thus we should find a *set* of variables that both meets tests of the evidence and fits the historical context for the rise and development of tantric Buddhism.[22] Polythetic categories may be used to describe a single genus, but they are constructed to identify prototypical examples that operate as cognitive reference points. They provide an interrelated web of parameters that serve in aggregate to define specific kinds of category. So, the category "bird" is defined by prototypical birds—perhaps jays, robins, or cardinals—and observes the variables of feathers, beaks, flight, warm-blooded, clawed feet, laying eggs, and so on. The important contribution of polythetic category construction is that the presence or absence of a single variable does not defeat the inclusion of an item into the category. Thus we have flightless birds (penguins), nonprototypical birds (emu), and so forth. In addition, other animals lay eggs (snakes, platypus) or have beaks (octopi), but their dissatisfactory relationship to the prototype or their possession of insufficient variables precludes their inclusion in the category.

Sometimes such categories are constructed around a specific metaphor, such as the articulation of airplanes imitating the function of the bird. Thus there are prototypical airplanes (perhaps, *Spirit of St. Louis,* Douglas DC-3, Spitfire), but the category is elastic enough to include early types (biplanes/triplanes) or atypical examples (B-2). Interestingly, these patterns demonstrate that the early instances of the category (archaeopteryx, *Wright Flyer*) are overtaken by later examples that come to constitute the prototypical forms in cognitive category formation and linguistic expression. Moreover, in this analysis we must be careful not to confuse the metaphor with the entity emulated, as the unsophisticated have sometimes, upon seeing an airplane at a distance, referred to it as a funny bird. Nor should we extrapolate on the social base that generated and developed such a metaphor, for ornithologists do not build airplanes nor do aeronautical engineers discuss the mating behavior of birds. Within the metaphor, other models or functions may also be implied or included in a shifting series of negotiations, as in the case of passenger jets or reconnaissance aircraft. An airline passenger may never reflect on the aviary inspiration of aircraft and see herself simply as a tourist on a bus or a ship that flies. These do not negate the metaphor, but they do compromise its purity and obscure its basic themes, even when there is no question of its inspiration. Finally, metaphor development can occur incrementally or quickly, depending on the social circumstances. The technological and ideological distances between Leonardo da Vinci's flying machine (1498) and the *Wright Flyer* (1903) were slight, despite the lengthy chronological span of over four hundred years. The reverse is the case for the distances between the *Flyer* and the Me 262 (1942), the first production jet aircraft; ideologically they are quite distant but chronologically they are less than forty years apart. Yet the subsequent development of airplanes following the Me 262 resumed its incremental pace.

Prototype theories have been challenged by alternative models of category formation.[23] Wittgenstein, for example, in discussing the formulation of universals, fielded the analogy of "family resemblances," in which the members of a family collectively share characteristics that are identifiable despite the individuals involved.[24] In a different direction, cognitive psychologists have articulated the manner in which features might be bundled together into categories. Developmental psychologists, for their part, have indicated that the causal relationships between the features of a category play an overwhelming role in child development. In an interesting series of experiments, Keil was able to show that children tend to build categories by examining causal relationships that are domain specific and understand that the difference between a category and its metaphorical representation is a difference of causal domains.[25] Just as important, as a child matures, the features associated with a concept increase as well, so that a rich relational association develops. The net result of these theoretical and experimental positions is that esoteric Buddhism could be examined for a conceptual framework that invokes a rich web of causal and relational associations, one that grows and becomes increasingly refined and complex as time passes.[26]

Fortunately we only need read the texts and examine the rituals to determine that Mantrayāna has built into it a sustaining metaphor, one that has been somewhat neglected by both traditional and modern scholars outside India. Yet it appears that the central and defining metaphor for mature esoteric Buddhism is that of an individual assuming kingship and exercising dominion. Thus the understanding of such terms as tantra in Buddhist India would invoke, first and foremost, the idea of hierarchical power acquired and exercised through a combination of ritual and metaphysical means. Based on this power, the varieties of understanding and of personal relationships become subsumed to the purposes of the person metaphorically becoming the overlord *(rājādhirāja)* or the universal ruler *(cakravartin).* It is the Buddhist version of the early medieval feudalization of divinity seen in the Purāṇas and elsewhere, applied to the Buddhist path by its ritual enactment in which either monks or laity may participate.

As the central forms are explored in some depth—consecration, self-visualization, maṇḍalas, the esoteric acts—we will see that many had their origins elsewhere. In its coalescence around the metaphor, though, esoteric authors drew from and redefined many ritual and meditative structures. The consequence is that the different practices were synthesized into a nexus whose overarching narrative was that of divine kingship in the early medieval feudal world of India. This nexus and narrative as a defining metaphor satisfies polythetic (or feature bundle) category construction, since the elements of assuming kingship work in coordination, while no one of them is essential to the definition. Thus neither self-visualization nor the use of mantras nor the coronation ritual nor the actions of the initiate nor any of the other attributes of the esoteric path have in and of themselves the capacity to sustain or defeat the category. Such a definition is necessary, for many texts or rituals lack one or another of these attributes, but are decidedly esoteric in tone and performance. Conversely, almost every attribute occurs in some way in texts and rituals that are not esoteric, but that in retrospect may be understood to have contributed to its formulation.

It is astonishing to realize that so many significant terms found in the standard esoteric ritual manuals and the Buddhist tantras have political and military significance as well as religious, and the bivalence or paronomasia of these terms in aggregate is extraordinary. Indians of the era certainly must have understood this fact. We should recall that this is the period in which poets like Daṇḍin would demonstrate their skill by composing such double-entendre works as the *Dvisandhāna.* This work was so paronomasic that it supposedly embodied the storyline of the *Rāmāyana* and the *Mahābhārata* simultaneously.[27] Likewise,

Rājaśekhara and his early tenth-century contemporaries valued paronomasic words *(dvyarthapada)* to the point that they were exempt from faults of poetic use applying to other kinds of words.[28] Thus the metaphor of the esoteric meditator becoming the Rājādhirāja is sustained through the multiple forms of ritualization that are equally applicable to kings and tantrikas. Let us for a moment juxtapose the operative terminology in both the act of securing kingship and the esoteric metaphor:[29]

The monk obtains consecration *[abhiṣeka]* from his preceptor *[vajrācārya]* so that he takes pride in himself as a divinity *[devatābhimāna]* and will be given dominion over a circle of divinities *[maṇḍala]*, of different families *[kula]*. He comes into the company of yogins with spells *[mantrin]* so that he can employ their secret spells *[guhyamantra]*. He is protected by Vajrapāṇi, the general of secrets *[guhyakādhipati]*. He becomes authorized to engage in ritual behavior *[karma]* that varies from pacific *[śāntika]* to destructive *[abhicāraka]*.	The prince obtains coronation *[abhiṣeka]* from his priest *[purohita]* so that he is recognized as composed of fragments of divinity *[devāṃśa]* and will be given dominion over a circle of vassals *[maṇḍala]* of different lineages *[kula]*. He comes into the company of his counselors *[mantrin]* so that he can make use of their confidential counsel *[guhyamantra]*. He is protected by the head of the army *[tantrādhipati]*. He becomes authorized to engage in royal behavior *[rājakarma]* that varies from pacific *[śāntika]* to ritually destructive *[abhicāraka]*.

Before we continue to explore this metaphor, a word of caution may be expressed. It appears to me that, especially in the case of the siddhas, other metaphors come into play as well. Even in the monks' cases, though, the imperial model is associated with other metaphors: cleansing the body, the inspiration of celestial goddesses, the Buddhist soteriological path, life in the monastery, the creation of art, and so forth. After all, the monks retained their status as monks, with the requirement that they adhere to the vows of the *Vinaya*, the recitation of rules every fortnight, ordination, and so on. As Mahayanists, they also took the vows of the bodhisattva, received bodhisattva ordination, and envisioned themselves as saving all beings through their practices. The esoteric system acts as a third level to the monastic life, in which the others are not discarded, but all are somehow integrated into the regimen.

In my reading of the material, however, I have been consistently impressed by how these other issues are subordinated to the paradigm of dominance, hierarchy, and regal power. They are placed in a relationship to a paradigm of power, most fundamentally expressed in medieval feudal form. It is not so much that other models are not brought into play from time to time but, rather, that the point of reference for the different themes continues to be the feudal monarch. In some ways, this is similar to the manner in which other events and groups within medieval society were required incessantly to negotiate with the king in his domain and become subsumed under his aegis. As a Buddhist form of the sāmantization (or feudalization) of divinities exhibited in Purāṇic literature, so we may recall that the divinities remained gods even while they became represented as kings, just as kings remained rulers even while they were declared divine.

CORONATION (*ABHIṢEKA*)

The relationship between the initiatory ritual of the *abhiṣeka* and the coronation ritual of kingship is explicit and, in many ways, determinative of the implicit political model of the Mantrayāna, although neither ritual system has received the attention it merits. In the Buddhist case, part of the problem has been the nature of the sources, which survive principally in manuscript form or in published Tibetan and Chinese texts.[30] In the case of secular coronations, the few documents from the early medieval period have been generally neglected in favor of Vedic materials, with notable exceptions.[31] Law's survey, for example, indicates that the *Agni-purāṇa* breaks coronation into rituals performed the day before the actual coronation *(aindrī-śānti)* and the coronation day itself. The latter rituals include (a) *homa*; (b) bathing of the prince with earth from places in the kingdom *(mṛttikā-snāna)*; (c) sprinkling by ministers; (d) sprinkling liquids by *Ṛg-veda* and *Sāma-veda* Brahmans and the *rājapurohita*; (e) sprinkling of water from a pitcher by the *rājapurohita*; (f) rites by *Yajur-veda* and *Atharva-Veda* Brahmans; (g) being shown auspicious items; (h) crowning; (i) presentation of officials to the prince; (j) payment of fees to the Brahmans and a coronation feast; (k) the royal procession through the capital; and (l) the return to the palace and distribution of gifts to the people.[32]

Substantially the same ritual is presented by Bhaṭṭa Lakṣmīdhara, the chief minister of the Gāhaḍvāla monarch Govindacandra, in the *Rājadharmakāṇḍa* volume of his *Kṛtyakalpataru*, a legal digest composed in the second quarter of the twelfth century. There, the old Kashmiri **Ādipurāṇa* is taken as the primary source, with an alternative version using Rāma's coronation in the *Rāmāyana* as the model.[33] A similar structure is also exhibited in the *Viṣṇudharmottara-purāṇa*, studied by Inden, as this text provides the most lengthy treatment of *abhiṣeka* in Purāṇic literature.[34] Inden's analysis is especially clear in showing the appropriation of sections of the old Vedic Rājyasūya rite, their transformation and integration into the larger Purāṇic cosmos, so that the king is the centerpiece of the ceremony. He is not the passive patron of a Brahmanocentric performance of a lengthy Soma fire ceremony, as the Vedic system had emphasized.[35]

Not all Buddhist *abhiṣeka* rituals, however, are indicative of the coronation paradigm. It appears that the earliest use of *abhiṣeka* as a meditative ritual is in the visualized form of a purificatory baptism. The fifth–sixth century "Yoga Treatise from Qïzïl," as it has been called for lack of a surviving title, indicates in many places that a meditator *(yogācārabhikṣu)* visualizes or receives visions of various seated and standing Buddhas sending out light rays. These are often mediated through a woman formed of the various elements, such as space *(ākāśadhātumayā strī)*. The light rays return to strike the fontanel of the yogin's head, pass through his body, and reemerge to encounter the world.[36] This brings pleasure and purification to the meditator and cleanses the world. Likewise, a text reputedly translated by the famous Kuchean translator Kumārajīva between 402 and 412 C.E., but probably composed in China, the *Ch'an mi yao fa ching* (Scripture Teaching the Secret Essence of Meditation), discusses an analogous visualization. Here the meditator sees the Buddha's mysterious "true body" of the thirty-two marks and eighty characteristics, holding a vase filled with water that looks like nectar in five colors. The water is poured on the head of the meditator, filling his body, purifying it of afflictions, and leading his mind to liberation.[37] Similarly, the apocryphal *Kuan fo san mei hai ching* (Scripture on Contemplating the Ocean of Buddhas) has meditators visualize the entry of medicine into their bodies, so that they are purified of afflictions and physical difficulties.[38] None of these fourth–sixth century texts so much as mentions the analogy of the prince's receiving his coronation from a king. Rather, like the bathing (also termed *abhiṣeka*) of the Buddha's statue during the celebration of the Buddha's birthday in the month of Vaiśāka, the bathing of the disciple during *abhiṣeka* demonstrates the cleansing of adventitious impurities from a form inherently pure. Even in the context of proto-tantric texts like Atikūṭa's 653/54 *Dhāraṇīsaṃgraha*, the model employed for consecration is either purificatory or mythic, rather than secular.[39]

About the same time as these cleansing rituals, if not before, the coronation ritual became part of Buddhist discourse but in the mythic context of a bodhisattva's becoming the successor to a Buddha. The Lokottaravādins in the *Mahāvastu* understood Maitreya to be the crown prince *(yuvarāja)*, following in the footsteps of Śākyamuni, who is the Dharmarāja. With the early Mahayana scriptures—particularly the *Laṅkāvatāra* and *Daśabhūmika-sūtra*—the mythic coronation ritual became firmly embedded in the narrative of a bodhisattva's assuming the tenth stage. There, he becomes "one who has obtained his coronation" after a truly cosmic event, in which all the Buddhas of the ten directions shower him with light.[40] The myth builds on the idea that a crown prince exercises power even while waiting to become the ruler of the kingdom, but the myth is also completely embedded in the cosmological time periods that the Mahayana saw as the era of maturation for such a bodhisattva. The metaphor, however, remains incomplete in Buddhist praxis, since it was entirely relegated to the bodhisattvas at the tenth level. There was no actual ritual that recreated the narrative relation of the Buddhas to the bodhisattvas. Curiously, it was the late fifth-century *Consecration Scripture,* as Strickmann called the *Kuan ting ching*, that is our earliest source for the Buddhist employment of this myth in the lives of real masters and disciples, even though this text is clearly a Chinese apocryphon.[41] We can surmise, based on the mythic precedents and the form of the coronation ritual, that Indians had employed a similar form at some point, but the finding of a Chinese first instance is intriguing. Here there can be no doubt about the metaphor involved, for the text is explicit that the ritual is performed for the disciple in exactly a manner analogous to the investiture of a prince into the affairs of state.

Within the esoteric texts of the late seventh and early eighth centuries, the coronation ritual is articulated in short chapters that frequently appear as supplementary to the larger ritual agenda. The texts tend to emphasize the use of mantras and the elaboration of fire ceremonies *(homa)* for the purposes of the four esoteric activities. For example, one of the earliest—if not the earliest—description of the consecration ritual in a maṇḍala is found in the *I tsu fo ting lun wang ching (? *Ekākṣarabuddhoṣṇīṣacakravarti-sūtra),* reputedly translated by Bodhiruci in 709 C.E.[42] The consecration contains elements normative to the later ritual systems—throwing the flower in the maṇḍala, obtaining the mantra and image of a divinity, and so on—but much of the ritual paraphernalia and explicit metaphorical identity is missing. Indeed, the consecration is but a member of the list of essential rituals for the transfer of spirituality between master and disciple.[43] Closely analogous is the entry for the *abhiṣeka* in the *Susiddhikara*, said to be translated by Śubhakarasiṃha in 726 C.E.[44] The primary purpose is association with the *homa,* so that the rituals that will overcome the various obstacles to ritual action can be performed, especially the ferocious ritual of the magical murder of enemies *(abhicāraka)*. Again, the explicit metaphors associated with kingship are missing, as well as the items that this metaphor requires.

By the early eighth century, however, we gain a sense of the increasing importance of the consecration and a relatively systematic development of the metaphor it holds. Perhaps most indicative is the naming of an entire scripture in honor of the relatively brief mythic and ritual associations of a consecration episode related below. The *Vajrapāṇy-abhiṣeka-mahātantra* is a text mentioned by Haribhadra (who lived during the reign of Dharmapāla, c. 775–812), by Buddhaguhya, and entered into the surviving Tibetan imperial register of the library at the Denkar palace.[45] The work is far more developed in its articulation of the importance of the consecration ritual and explicit in the metaphor involved and why:

> Now, O possessor of the vajra, this Dharma of vajra has been explained [for] you, and the vajra arisen from meditation has been actually placed in your hand by all the Buddhas. So, from today, all the magical ability of Vajrapāṇi in the world is just yours. It is yours to tame those insufferable beings harming the Dharma and to kill those afflicted with anger—that is why the guides of the world have given you the vajra. In the way a Universal Conqueror *[cakravartin]* is coronated that he might achieve dominion, in this same sense it is said that you have been consecrated Adamantine Intellect so as to be King of the Dharma.[46]

Other early esoteric works, such as *Mahāvairocanābhisambodhitantra*, also supported the explicitly imperial significance of the *abhiṣeka*, and mid-eighth-century commentators like Buddhaguhya interpreted the text accordingly.[47] The panoply of imperial coronation was eventually to find its way into the ritual process as its metaphorical matrix became increasingly emphasized. Buddhaguhya's approximate contemporary, Mañjuśrīmitra, articulated a number of consecratory moments in the larger coronation ritual: consecration with water *(jala)*, with a crown *(mukuṭa)*, with a vajra, with a bell *(ghaṇṭa)*, with the adamantine discipline of Mañjuśrī *(mañjuśrīvajravrata)*, with the mantra, to become a teacher *(ācārya)*, through the elimination of defilement, with gnosis *(jñāna)*, in body/speech/mind, and through the conferral of a new adamantine name *(vajranāma)*. Thus the successful candidate emerged as the Buddha himself and became the King of the World, as seen in the statement at the beginning of this chapter.[48] Even the standard admonition that those having secured *abhiṣeka* should continue to receive this ritual often—either physically or in meditation—also has its roots in normative Purāṇic strategies. The *Viṣṇudharmottara* indicates that the king is to receive a shortened version of the coronation ritual daily before holding court and seasonally before battle.[49]

The initiate's *(mantrin)* accouterments were fundamentally royal as well, and it will come as something of a surprise to those familiar with the modern Shingon and Tibetan ritual equipment that at least some medieval Indian esoteric masters employed medieval-sized implements in the performance of these ceremonies. In the most lengthy discussion I have seen, the early eighth-century *Subāhuparipṛcchā* indicated that vajras were to be between ten and twenty inches in length (about 25–50 cm.), and made of heavy metals (gold, silver, copper, iron), stone, human bone, and so on.[50] These "thunderbolt scepters" were therefore formidable weapons *(kuliśa)*, as vajras were consistently termed in esoteric literature, and they closely resembled the size of vajras depicted both in the Gandhāran sculptures of Vajrapāṇi and in an eighth-century Vajrapāṇi statue from Kashmir (Figure 2).[51] In these venues, weapons the length of the forearm are frequently depicted, and the musculature of the Herakles/Vajrapāṇi iconography leaves little question but that he was to represent the foremost of heroes in Gandhāran Hellenistic representations. One statue, the Haḍḍa Herakles/Vajrapāṇi, has even been shown to reflect Alexander's imperially sponsored school of Lysippos.[52] The subsequent episode of Vajrapāṇi's *abhiṣeka* in later esoteric literature is one of the most widely recognized mythic events in the esoteric corpus, and the *Vajrapāṇyabhiṣeka-tantra* builds on this recognition. All these isolated instances suggest a wider ritual understanding of vajras as representing the staff of martial office *(daṇḍa)* for Vajrapāṇi and for those who follow in his footsteps in their own coronations. While we must defer examination of the subsequent development of *abhiṣeka* in the noninstitutional texts, it is clear that in the consecration ritual of institutional esoterism, the imperial paradigm was supreme.

With the *abhiṣeka,* many of the esoteric scriptures—particularly those designated as *yogatantra*—maintain that the disciple is to envision himself as the Buddha. Again, we see a practice whose early form was protective rather than royal, and again the search leads to Chinese apocryphal literature. The seventh chapter of the fifth-century *Consecration Scripture* is apparently the earliest text that explicitly asks a meditator to envision himself as the Buddha, with all the thirty-two marks and eighty characteristics; this teaching is there called the "Mahārṣidharma," the teaching of the Great Sages.[53] The

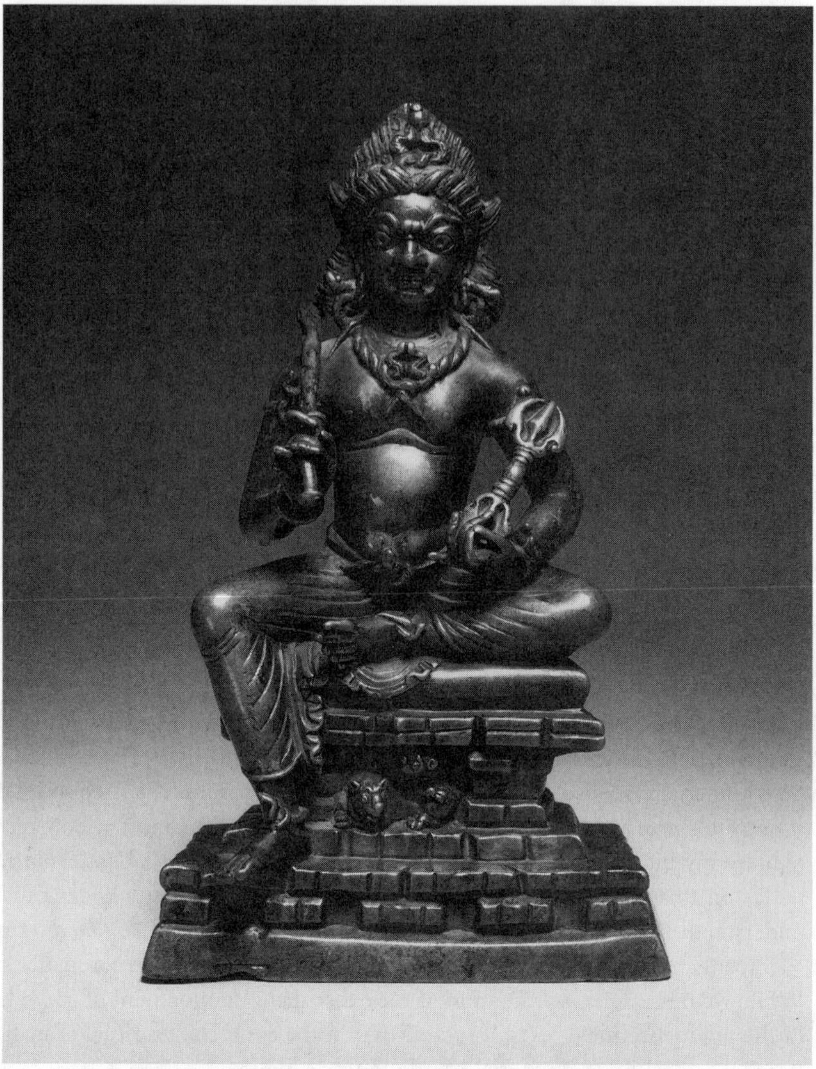

FIGURE 2 Vajrapāṇi with the Ritual Vajra of Royal Office.
Kashmir, c. eighth century. Brass with silver inlay, 8 3/4 × 5 in.
© The Cleveland Museum of Art, 2001, Gift of George Bickford, 1971.
Reproduced by permission.

practice, however, was a subterfuge to get the five great spirit kings of the different directions to protect the monk, rather than constituting an emphasis on the spiritual identity of monk and Buddha. Unfortunately, there seems to be some discontinuity between the system articulated in the *Consecration Scripture* and that found later, in terms of both content and time, as Indic materials on self-visualization do not reemerge for another two hundred years. With respect to content, the balance of our normative descriptions of self-visualization indicate that the individual conceives of himself as the sacramental person *(samayasattva)* while the gnostic person *(jñānasattva)* is drawn from the realm of space; the two persons generally have the same form, particularly in the later materials.[54]

Where did this system of self-visualization come from and why is it not present in all forms of esoteric ritual? I initially had considered that self-visualization might be a particularly civilized form of spirit possession, especially since siddhas had close connections with both tribal and lower caste peoples where possessive behaviors are frequently encountered. However, none of the practices associated with spirit possession—ecstatic behavior, shaking of limbs, loss of consciousness, self-mutilation—are encountered in descriptions of self-visualization within the tantras or other esoteric texts. Despite the records of spirit possession *(āveśa)* by young children employed in Buddhist rituals, there can be no doubt that these practices were strongly distinguished from the formal meditation of the Mantrayāna *(utpattikrama)*.[55] Moreover, the descriptions of self-visualization as the Buddha or other tantric divinity are encountered in esoteric texts before the rise of siddha literature, by two or so decades (c. 700 C.E.). We conclude here that a connection with marginalized populations or tribal peoples cannot be affirmed on the evidence.

Instead, the introduction and employment of self-visualization in the tantras appear to stem from the consequences of the imperial model: a king becomes divine when he is coronated and given dominion over a circle of vassals *(sāmantamaṇḍala)*. According to Manu, for example, a king is made of "parts" *(aṃśa)* of the various divinities: "Since a king is magically emanated from the various bits of the lords of the gods, he thus has dominion over all beings, through his brilliance."[56] During the early medieval period, India and Southeast Asia saw the rise of the "devarāja" cult, in which the king claimed to be a form of Śiva whose "subtle inner self" *(sūkṣmāntarātman)* was found in a divinity housed in the royal temple, established in the center of the capital. Kulke, who has done the most extensive work on this royal cult, maintained that kings ruled in the name of Śiva as the Lord of the World *(lokeśvara)* to establish legitimacy, particularly necessary in the case of kings who had usurped the throne and could rely only on the "charisma of office," in Max Weber's terminology. Once the relation of being a part of the deity through coronation had been accepted, the mythos of divinity extended to the king, so that an "attack on the king would be tantamount to an attack on the rule of Śiva."[57] In his critique of Kulke's theoretical structure, however, Pollock pointed out that multiple levels of culture are implicated. The spread and development of divine identity rituals might be understood as a central moment in the larger process of investment in the aesthetics, literature, art, and other aspects of a cultural model of embodied divinity in the form of a king.[58]

Although Kulke's data are primarily drawn from the eleventh century, evidence for this extension is at least as old as the *Mānava Dharma Śāstra* and is visible in inscriptions from the seventh century, such as in Ravikīrtti's 634–635 C.E. panegyric to Pulikeśin II's Chāḷukya lineage. There, divine attributes are accorded the Chāḷukyas: they are beyond human *(amānuṣatva)* and equal to Indra *(Śakrakalpa)*, and they do not die but, instead, desire the riches and power of the lord of the gods *(sureśvara-vibhūti-gatābhilāṣa)*.[59] Likewise, seventh–eighth-century Kāmandaka describes the king as "divinity on this good earth."[60] Twelfth-century Lakṣmīkara justifies all this to his lord Govindacandra with a quotation from the *Nāradapurāṇa*, "How could he not be divine—for with his speech a king turns an impure man pure, and each day he is with both the pure and impure?"[61]

If divinity of the king was placed and verified through his coronation ritual at the hands of his priest, so too the apotheosis of the monk came about through his consecration at the discretion of the esoteric master. Some of the esoteric scriptures neglected to affirm this apotheosis—as diligently noted by Ngorchen Kunga Sangbo—but not for ideological reasons in the construction of esoteric categories about the tantras and their meditative manuals. Rather, the neglect was a simple consequence of the rapid development of the literature (and their attendant practices), as well as the high degree of regional and personal variation in their evolution. Not all of the consequences of the appropriation of the coronation ritual were understood with the first performance of the ritual, and we still observe ambivalence in some literary materials, which vacillate between a system of regal empowerment and a hermeneutic of cleansing the candidate's defilements.

> Whoever should but see this maṇḍala, the nature of Dharma, he is released from all fault, even if he has committed the five heinous crimes of immediate retribution, even if he is of bad character or weak-minded.
>
> *Mañjuśrīmūlakalpa*[62]

Purification of these faults neither required nor suggested the divinity within coronation, and Buddhist monks' skepticism about the ostensibly "divine" behavior of real monarchs may have been a factor in these texts as well. However, even in Purāṇic coronation manuals the themes of the king's liberation from fetters and his purification from defilements are expressed.[63]

MAṆḌALAS AND FIELDS OF PLENTY

If the critical investigation of esoteric Buddhism has been hampered by an excessive emphasis placed on the postenlightenment doctrine of spiritual/temporal duality, perhaps this is most evident in the study of maṇḍalas. The idealization of the maṇḍala has become part of popular cultural parlance in Europe since the time of Carl Gustav Jung's absorption of early medieval Indian and related Tibetan or Japanese forms of religious iconography. Yet Jung, even though so affirmative on these visual representations, warned of the actual study of Asia. Since Jung, many scholars have been seduced by his explicit gnosticism, which maintained that the spiritual plane influences mundane reality, and not the reverse. While we may be sympathetic with one raised in the atmosphere of religious strife in and around nineteenth-century Switzerland, we cannot afford to emulate Jung's disinterest in the historical development, form, and employment of maṇḍalas since the second half of the seventh century.

Institutional Buddhist esoterism, in particular, can both accept the credit and bear the responsibility for the development of the meditative maṇḍala form. Maṇḍalas are implicitly and explicitly articulations of a political horizon in which the central Buddha acts as the Rājādhirāja in relationship to the other figures of the maṇḍala.[64] In their origin and evolution, religious maṇḍalas represent a Buddhist attempt to sanctify existing public life and recreate the meditator as the controlling personage in the disturbing world of Indic feudal practice. The other Buddhas and bodhisattvas live within or in proximity to his palace *(kūṭāgāra)*. They assume their positions based on his will and through the agency of his bestowing coronation on them. They reflect his entourage in their own segmentary entourages, and they are ultimately dissolved into him, demonstrating their subordination to the veracity of his existence. At the borders of some maṇḍalas live the demons, snakes, and other beings of marginal existence in the great charnel grounds. When a monk receives his coronation into the maṇḍala, therefore, he receives explicit authority to engage and manipulate phenomenal existence. His action represents the Buddhist institution placing an agent into the idiom and metaphor of public life, embodying the monastic institution's reaction to a predatory feudal system by emulating its form while subverting its goals. Thus the maṇḍala represents a spiritual "state," a word that exhibits the paronomasia of both a mystical condition and a political reality in English as maṇḍala does in Sanskrit.

Previous scholars have observed that the idea of the maṇḍala was in some sense already implied in the mythology of the pure land in which Buddhas and bodhisattvas reside. The *Susiddhikara* maṇḍala, for example, depicts the relationship between three Buddha families *(kula)* (Tathāgata, Vajra, and Padma) in a manner that mirrors the Mahayana scriptures' assignment of direction to the Buddhas and their fields—Śākyamuni in the center, Akṣobhya in the east, and Amitābha in the west.[65] The earliest maṇḍalas provide a schematic synthesis and formalization of their respective Buddha fields. Moreover, YAMADA has demonstrated that the language in the Mahayana scriptures discussing the pure lands of the Buddhas has been developed based on prior statements of heavenly paradises *(svarga)* found in some of the older *Upaniṣads*, like the *Śvetāśvatara*, *Kaṭha*, and *Muṇḍaka Upaniṣads*.[66] Schopen has also determined that the pure Buddha fields—especially Sukhāvatī of Amitābha in the west—may function as a generalized religious goal (or result), somewhat independent of a cult of devotion normally associated with these Buddha fields in East Asia.[67]

However excellent their Buddhological discussions may be, most scholars have avoided the meaning of *kṣetra*, the "field" in Buddha field. Contrary to the neutral and sanctified sense offered to date by the designation field or land, the term *kṣetra* clearly indicates a domain in which political power and influence are wielded. Perhaps the most widely distributed discussion of a field *(kṣetra)* in Buddhist works is found in a passage, incorporated into different scriptures in both Sanskrit and Pali, that discusses the origin of kingship in the formation of the world. The myth depicts beings from the Ābhāsvara heavens gradually becoming dissatisfied with their ethereal existence, becoming attracted to food and clothing, and ultimately ending up born on earth. However, they lack order. They then elect a king, Mahāsammata, so as to avoid chaos, and devote a portion of their produce for his maintenance. At this point. the etymology of "noble" *(kṣatriya)* and "king" *(rājā)* are offered, since Mahāsammata was the first of each; it was said that a *kṣatriya* is one who is the lord of the fields, since he protects them from harm.[68]

The etymology is a play on the words "noble" *(kṣatriya)*, "field" *(kṣetra)*, and "protect from harm" *(kṣatāc trāyate)*, and at first seems specious, as do so many of the Indian hermeneutical etymologies. Yet this is different, for the terms *kṣatriya* and *kṣetra* are linked to another term, *kṣatra*. *Kṣatra* is the universal potential for political or military power invested in *kṣatriyas*, much as the cosmic power behind mantras *(brahman)* is invested in Brahmans. *Kṣatra* is that which authorizes the warrior class to rule and legitimizes their exercise of power. It is the reason that the nobles may accept a portion of the goods and services of other castes; *kṣatra* also bears with it the responsibility for the maintenance of law and order in a specific domain. Edgerton has already noted, in fact, that the association of *kṣatra* and *kṣetra* is so close that one is frequently interchanged with the other in Buddhist texts.[69] So *kṣetra* should be understood in the sense of the "domain" (rather than field) over which the Buddha—as the preeminent *kṣatriya* and lord of that domain—presides with the dominion *(kṣatra)* of his Dharma. The utopian world of the "pure Buddha domain" is accordingly articulated, not through the values of liberal modernity but, rather, through a model already invested in feudal systems and in which all domains require dominance. The Buddhist pure domain is actually much more similar to the autocracy of Plato's *Republic* than to the blithe anarchy of Marx's utopia.

The relationship of pure lands to the esoteric maṇḍala, therefore, supports the identity of maṇḍalas as articulations of the Buddhist response to the early medieval military and political situation. Even in its external form, a maṇḍala expresses a much modified form of the ancient Indian theory of polity: the proper relationship between a would-be conqueror *(vijigīṣu)* and his proximate states. Our earliest surviving document on state maṇḍalas is the *Arthaśāstra*, ascribed to the Mauryan theoretician Kautiliya, but most probably composed in the first or second centuries of the common era (Figure 3).[70] In that work, the prospective conqueror is admonished to consider the states in immediate relationship to him: those in front alternate between those that are his enemies or their allies *(ari, arimitra, arimitramitra)* and those that are the conqueror's allies *(mitra, mitramitra)*.[71] Behind is a similar situation with enemies *(pārṣṇigrāha, pārṣṇigrāhāsāva)* and allies *(ākranda, ākrandāsāva)* alternating. To one side (which is not specified in the text) is the middle *(madhyama)* state, which can be influenced in one or another direction, and the neutral state *(udāsīna)*, which can also either stand aside at times of belligerence or be brought into the equation by procedures extending from diplomacy to sedition. Beyond the rather transparent affirmation that the *Arthaśāstra* depicts somewhat paranoid kings ruling states continually struggling with one another, it is excessively theoretical in that it fundamentally conceives of state relations among bordering states as solely antagonistic.

In distinction to this early model, actual medieval Indian political practice rewarded states that erected relations with vassals *(sāmanta, rājā, maṇḍaleśa)* who governed client buffer states between the powerful patron state and its

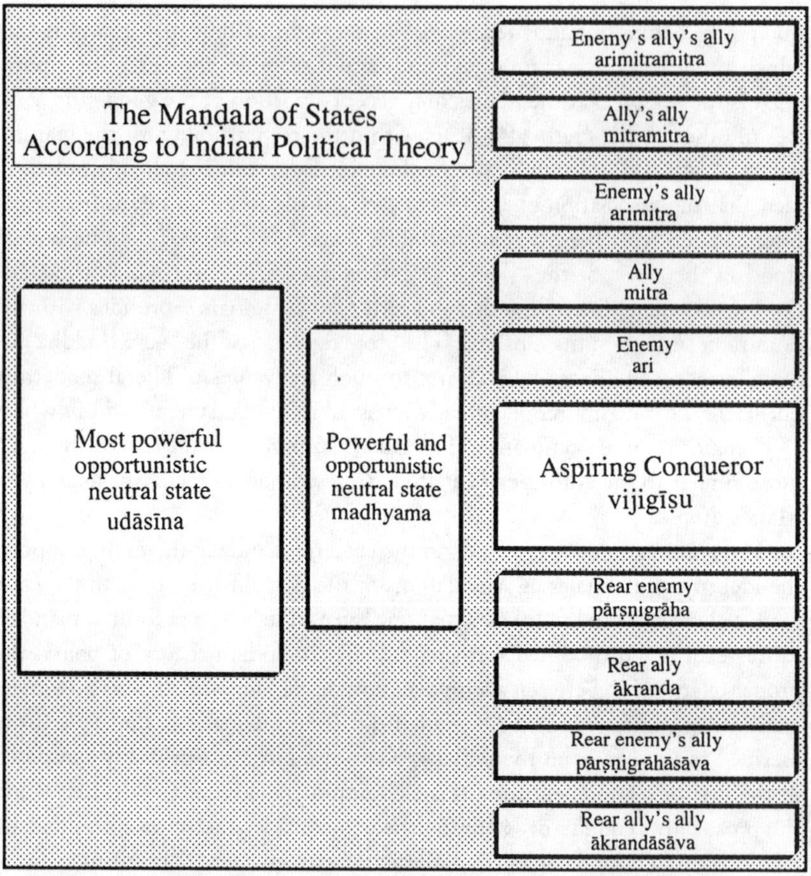

FIGURE 3 The Maṇḍala of States According to Indian Political Theory.
Courtesy Ronald M. Davidson and Richard Pinto

real antagonists. As a standard of comparison, the Imperial Guptas had a more centralized bureaucracy, where governors of the various provinces *(kumārāmātya)* were appointed, served for a term, and were reappointed from the capital, although this system was not always applied through the entire domain. They were attempting to move in the direction of the modern nation-state, with its civil apparatus, chain of command, and loyalty to the centralized national purpose, as had the Mauryas before them.

However, in contrast to conditions under the Gupta, regionalization and decentralization were hallmarks of early medieval polity, wherein a powerful nation was equipped with a surrounding maṇḍala of vassal states.[72] For example, the Bhaumakaras in Orissa surrounded themselves in the eighth century with the vassal states of the Śulkis, Tuṅgas, Nandobhavas, Bhañjas, and perhaps the Nalas (Map 3). This group of vassals was both subordinate to the Bhaumakaras and dependent on them for support and protection. Similarly, the defeat of Harṣa by Pulakeśin II in about 632 C.E. was proclaimed a great Chāḷukya victory. Harṣa's "lotuslike feet were touched by the light emitting from the jewels in the crowns of his armies of vassals, rich in unlimited power," and when Harṣa was defeated, so was his maṇḍala of vassals.[73] Thus the supreme ruler or overlord was bounded not by enemies, as depicted in the Indian theoretical system, but by a supporting network of polities that fan out and are tied to the principal state and one another through systems of loyalty, exchange, services, and so forth. Not all vassals were the recipients of territory—except perhaps in a ritual sense—and some seem to have allied themselves with superior powers as a means of self-preservation.[74] In this way, the most powerful states are buffered from direct contact with one another; it is the subordinate princes that must suffer the continual low-level conflicts at their borders.

The problem of the early theoretical description of state relations has become mirrored in modern ideas contested in the past few decades. Sharma articulated a model in which the early medieval period is described as feudal, a description that has been disputed ever since.[75] Because of the difficulties with the terminology of feudalism, Fox proposed the application of Southall's model of a "segmentary state" to cover state organization and relations during the medieval era. A segmentary state is a political system with numerous centers, each of which has separate administrative systems, frequently clan-based; power is wielded by a single overlord whose subordinates in the lesser centers recognize his authority through ritual means.[76] Perhaps the principal contribution of the segmentary model is the demonstration that subsidiary centers of political authority each have their own executive apparatus, so that the governmental functions are individually administered by these centers, with no direct control by the overlord's own administration. Because of their relative autonomy, these subsidiary centers may segment off and form new alliances with related states or may even reverse the relationship, becoming the overlord to its former ruler. The recognition of this reality has motivated political historians like Stein to discuss the difference between "core" or "nuclear" areas and "periphery" vassals. Thus, the sāmantas' allegiance to a specific overlord in any direction is purely opportunistic and subject to subversion by another power. Indeed, the *Arthaśāstra* describes as desirable the separation of a maṇḍala of vassals and allies from a king, to be seized by the conqueror.[77] The paradigm

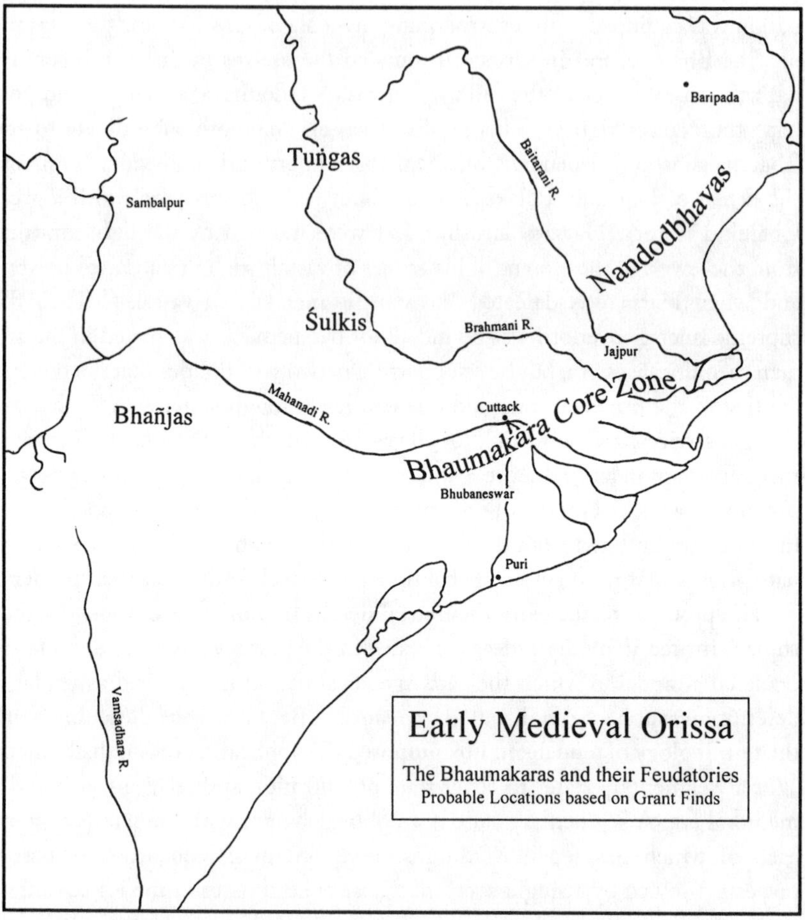

MAP 3 Early Medieval Orissa.
Ronald M. Davidson and Richard Pinto

occasionally functioned in real life, with various twists. For example, the Candellas had been vassals *(sāmantas)* of the Pratīhāras, yet turned their lords into their own vassals when the opportune moment arose.

The segmentary representation has certain advantages and disadvantages. In some respects the segmentary state appears to be internally analogous to the model of the administrative circle *(prakṛtimaṇḍala)*, as found in the *Arthaśāstra*, the *Mānava Dharma Śāstra*, the *Nītisāra*, and elsewhere. Authors like

Kāmandaka maintained that every country possessed seven essential elements: the king, ministers, kingdom, forts, treasury, military forces, and allies.[78] Theoreticians declared that each country had all seven of these, and the relationships between superordinate and subordinate states were based as much on their similarity as on anything else. However, like the segmentary model, the administrative circle is an essentialist paradigm, which does not recognize differentiation, modification, development, decline, or division. The historical insularity of both representations should not be surprising. The segmentary explanation derives from anthropological literature, where historical awareness is secondary, while the administrative circle is a product of Indian traditional culture, which understands itself as embodying eternal legal structures. Beyond that, the segmentary model has the theoretical difficulty, already recognized by Chattopadhyaya, that it is a better tool to explain the fragmentation of relations between states than their enduring associations throughout difficult periods.[79]

One of the distinct advantages of the term feudal, as it turns out, is that it is a legal term and identifies not simply political arrangements but land tenure and authority as well, something the segmentary model was not designed to do. Yet the term feudalism carries such historiographical baggage that it seems to require some qualification, and Chattopadhyaya has brilliantly suggested the term "sāmanta-feudalism" to indicate the political structure of early medieval society. The term sāmanta is standard nomenclature within the epigraphs and literature of this period, and Chattopadhyaya's suggestion certainly has the merit of integrating indigenous terminology into our historiographical lexicon. In reality, the designation sāmanta is only one of many employed—also including hierarchical levels—such as *mahāsāmanta*, *mahāmaṇḍaleśvara*, *maṇḍaleśvara*, *mahārāja*, and *rāja*.[80] These were all used to indicate various levels of subordination to a lord, who was often given the title Great King of Kings *(mahārājādhirāja)* or Overlord *(paramabhaṭṭāraka)*, and who maintained a circle of subordinate quasi-states *(sāmantacakra, sāmantamaṇḍala)*. As a hybrid term, moreover, sāmanta-feudalism has the further merit of extending beyond simple polity and of embracing the larger cultural horizon, where guilds and priests were invested with both land and legal authority on their territory, further indicating the process of regionalization or localization of power.

When we turn from these developments to Buddhist maṇḍalas, the similarity is obvious (Figure 4). Buddhist maṇḍalas involve a central or nuclear system, yet the subsidiary sets in the various directions (four, eight, or more) each contains its own internal order and each is capable of becoming the center item if

FIGURE 4 Trailokyavijaya Maṇḍala, showing the arrangement of Buddha families. *Courtesy of Loskesh Chandra and the International Academy of Indian Culture.*

the need should arise, sending the previous center to the periphery.[81] Thus if the candidate during the coronation ceremony throws his flower onto Akṣobhya, then he would become a member of the adamantine family *(vajrakula)* and Akṣobhya would assume the central place in the maṇḍala for the practice of that individual. The *Sarvatathāga-tatattvasaṃgraha*, as well, describes the production of the first maṇḍala shortly after Vairocana had become Buddha, that is, almost immediately after he himself had been consecrated. Vairocana then attracts a number of personages, beginning with Samantabhadra, who is coronated with a crown whose jewels are the bodies of all the Buddhas and is subsequently consecrated with the name "Vajrapāṇi" (scepter-holder). After this, all the other thirty-six figures of the maṇḍala are consecrated with names conferred on them by Vairocana, before they are placed in their position in the maṇḍala.[82] A closely similar process is related in the *Sarvadurgatipariśodhana-tantra.*[83]

This is precisely the method observed by an overlord towards his well-respected vassal: the coronation ceremony for the sāmanta is performed with the Rājādhirāja in the position of patron *(yajamāna)* while the vassal is the one being coronated. By this means, the vassal is ritually installed and secured in a locale under the authority of the Rājādhirāja. Such a pattern is quite different from that observed when a prince assumes the position of Rājādhirāja, for then the overlord is both patron and central performer of the coronation rite. Examples of exactly this ritual relationship are found widely in the early medieval period. The sixth-century Maitrika king Droṇasiṃha, for example, was consecrated as the vassal of his overlord, who was probably one of the latest of the Imperial Guptas.[84] Likewise, Cakrāyudha was installed as the king of Kānyakubja by Dharmapāla in the late eighth century, as a symbol of the Pāla's supremacy over North India. In both instances, the Rājādhirāja acted as the patron while the sāmanta was coronated at his pleasure and under his authority. The subordinate vassal sometimes operated under the direction of the crown prince *(yūvarāja)*, who was also coronated with his father as patron—this is analogous to the position played by various figures in Buddhist maṇḍalas, such as Vajrapāṇi or Mañjuśrī with respect to the Buddhas Akṣobhya or Vairocana.

Accordingly, Buddhists derived their maṇḍala forms and functions, not so much from the theoretical treatises of Indian polity as from their immediate observation at the disposition and execution of realpolitik in their environment. They did not take direct recourse to the ideology of the *Arthaśāstra* and analogous literature. Instead they obtained this vision of reality by observing the actual relationship of the overlords and their peripheral states, which incited this vision of reality. Indeed, the Buddhist maṇḍala is a classic analysis of the system of sāmanta feudalism in early medieval India, all sufficiently sanctified for the monastic community. The application of this model at the intersection between the political and religious domains is well illustrated in the 629 C.E. Boṭād copperplate grant of Dhruvasena of the Valabhī Maitrikas.[85] There, Queen Duḍḍā's penchant for the construction of monasteries is described in terms of her having constructed a "maṇḍala of monasteries." The application of this term indicates that the political diction of a circle of vassals in the seventh century was coming to be applied to a circle of religious structures. Queen Duḍḍā occupied the center of the circle, while the monasteries protected her periphery and were sustained by her authority.

Construction details and vocabulary for the maṇḍala are directly connected to the architectural heritage of palace construction as well. Indeed, the term for the residence of the divinities of the maṇḍala is exactly that employed for palaces and pavilions in medieval architectural manuals, with the architectural terminology for them almost identical. The central Buddha resides in a pavilion *(kūṭāgāra)*, which has entrances in the four directions and ornamented corners in the intermediate directions. The entrances are dominated by arched gateways *(toraṇa)*, in the shape of scepters *(vajra)*, and guarded by an adamantine wall—a fortress of religiosity. Internally, there is an adamantine redoubt *(vajrapañjara)* protecting the lord and his families. Although the term *vajrapañjara* came to be interpreted by Tibetans as an impenetrable canopy *(rdo rje gur)*, the term initially indicated a cage or citadel that could not be penetrated, and the *Harṣacarita* uses the term as a metaphor in its identification of Harṣa's body with specific parts of the citadel.[86] The clear association of Buddhist maṇḍala terminology with palace architecture is equally evident when we compare maṇḍala ground plans with those depicted in such medieval treatises as the *Mayamata*. Here, the arrangement of the palaces, pavilions, and halls closely resembles the Buddhist maṇḍala idealization. Their similarity is obvious when set against the structure and terminology of temples *(mandira)* dedicated to Brahmanical divinities or monasteries *(vihāra)* for Buddhist monks.[87] Not only are these latter designs dissimilar to maṇḍalas, but the terminology could not be more distinct. Meister's review of medieval North Indian temple architecture establishes a lexical base for dissociating these temple plans from the Buddhist maṇḍala architecture.[88] Nowhere in maṇḍala discussions are found descriptions of a sanctum sanctorum *(garbhagṛha)*, a single entrance through an assembly hall *(jaṅghā)*, or other specifics evident both in the literature for the period or in surviving temples from the seventh to eleventh centuries.

We might wonder whether sufficient attention has been given to the value of some of the terms associated with a maṇḍala as well. For example, the designation "family"—observed in the Buddha families in the center and cardinal directions of the maṇḍala—is not a precise rendering of the Sanskrit word *kula*. Although there is some variation according to locale, in the Gangetic valley a *kula* indicates not just a clan *(gotra)* or a specific lineage *(vaṃśa)* but a clan or lineage situated in a specific residence. In the medieval period, the term *kula* specifically had the value of direction and locality attached to it, to the point that the term was extended even earlier in the *Mānava Dharma Śāstra* to identify the plot of land a *kula* could cultivate.[89] Similarly, Brahmanas of the same *gotra* belong to different *kula*, depending on where they have their residence—indicating a determinative sense of place-specificity.[90] Seventh-century Buddhist usage may even have applied this designation to small funerary stūpas where lay supporters located the ashes of their deceased, which would indicate their postmortem residence according to familial association.[91]

In the Buddhist maṇḍala, a *kula* is not just a family with specific characteristics but one located in a certain area and in a specific direction. That area occupies a section of the great "palace" *(kūṭāgāra)* of the king of the domain, and the king provides consecration to others so that they might be placed in a specific area of the domain, with their own entourages, identities, and so forth. One statement on the relationship of family to place is found in a chapter expressing a ritual of time and domain of activity *(kṣetrakālavidhi)* in the *Mañjuśrīmūlakalpa*:

> Thus, the mantras appropriate to the eight families are situated in the eight directions. Indeed, mantras from the Buddha family are accomplished in the north.
>
> Mantras from the Lotus family find their accomplishment in the east. Based on the southern direction, mantras from the Vajra family succeed.
>
> There is a treasury in the west, so that the Jewel family is in the intermediate direction. Success is considered among the places in the northwest.
>
> Moreover, there is the yakṣa family in the southwest. In the southeast is seen the family of the heroic Śrāvakas, for accomplishment (of their mantras) is achieved in those places there.
>
> In the northeast direction, the highly esteemed family of the Pratyekabuddhas is located, for accomplishment is achieved for them in the places there.
>
> In the lower direction, all the worldly mantras achieve success. And these mantras enter the earth's plane among the eight families (bringing success to them).
>
> Above are broadcast the supermundane mantras of Uṣṇīṣa. Those mantras there come to accomplishment spoken by the Cakravartin Buddha.[92]

This array contains many curiosities, such as the nonstandard assignment of families and directions, when compared with materials achieving popularity in lineages of greater currency in Tibet and Japan. However, the importance of these kinds of statements is clear: specific mantras bestow success on definite populations principally in special locales. Thus, *kula* are families indelibly associated with spatial arrangements and their placement in certain areas.

The localization of qualities and behavior is an important way to view the world, and in India it is aligned with ritualized conduct. This relationship between direction and conduct is frequently voiced in the tantras and schematized in terms of both positive and negative qualities. Thus persons falling into the Vajra family tend to have an especially violent nature, as opposed to the greater benevolence in the Padma family, and so forth. Even the directional associations are open to a shift in perspective, and the discussion changes from scripture to scripture. The Vajra family is normally placed in the east, for example, but in this quotation the *Mañjuśrīmūlakalpa* specifically locates it in the south. The author of this section did not care for those southerners, evidently, and elsewhere in the chapter the author specifically locates the sinful brethren *(pāpakarmin)* in the southern direction.[93] All the qualities associated with the directions may be altered and transmuted as well, but the method of change is entirely determined by the assignment of family and direction.

Going beyond the normative family designations, at the periphery of the maṇḍala we find those on the margins of society, often depicted in the polluted zones of the cremation grounds that are considered in detail below. Here, though, the worldly beings and the cemeteries represent those in early medieval India on the periphery of caste life—those without a noble family.[94] They were condemned to live beyond the borders of the encampment or of the city, near the cremation ground or even beyond it.[95] Accordingly, these polluted zones of potential chaos defined the borders of the spiritual state of the maṇḍala, even as they defined the boundaries of regional cities or polities. And just beyond the polluted borders, the entire maṇḍala is surrounded by a wall of flaming vajra. This protective and impenetrable wall of vajra is the extension of the scepter wielded by the king to demonstrate dominion against those demonic beings who would disrupt the law *(Dharma)* of the lord. The vajra wall is the limit of order, which extends outward from the lord in the center and ensures the correct conduct of those in family congregations, and the worldly beings included in the circle of protection.

In service of this kingdom, the lord has recourse to the various activities of a king: the four tantric karmas or ritual events—the pacification of problems *(śāntika)*, the augmentation of supporters' wealth *(pauṣṭika)*, the subjugation and control of enemies *(vaśīkaraṇa)*, and the execution of criminals by magic *(abhicāraka)*.[96] Normally, these are effected by the fire sacrifice *(homa)* ritual, and in the esoteric canon the *homa* rite establishes a ritual bond between the officient, the divinities propitiated, and the beings affected by the ceremony.[97]

Some authors consider these four tantric karmas the lesser of mystical accomplishments, strongly differentiated from the great accomplishments examined below.[98] As time progressed, certainly, virtually all the esoteric ceremonies became described as really soteriological in essential nature, and the *homa* was no exception. Like the transformation of wood into ash, this interpretation emphasized the simultaneous transmutation of the personality afflictions into forms of awakened being, by means of their purification in the fire of gnosis.[99] Another direction, however, was to internalize the fire sacrifice, so that it became an inner visualization in which the yogic practices associated with psychic heat or sexual yoga were described in a manner invoking the terminology and associations of the *homa*.[100] This latter direction was seen very early, but apparently became especially valued by siddha exegetes in their discussions of yogic meditation and breathing.

Ferocious activity, such as that implicated in the rituals of magical execution, are in particular delegated to Vajrapāṇi. In his description, the use of military metaphors is explicit and sustained: he had always been called the "general of yakṣas" *(yakṣasenādhipati)*, those ambivalent tree spirits that continually vacillate between specter and aide.[101] He also assumed the title Lord of the Mysterious *(guhyakādhipati)*. This title initially indicated that Vajrapāṇi was the leader of a class of yakṣas that were mysterious *(guhyaka)*, although later it came to denote that he was the lord of the secret mysteries.[102] In some works, the title is taken to indicate his activity in collection, recitation and protection of the *Sorcerers' Basket* of esoteric scriptures *(tantra, vidyādharapiṭaka)*. He guards against those inimical to the Buddhadharma, and his designations clearly resonate with the medieval inscriptional Sanskrit use of the term "lord of the tantra" (= master of deployment, *tantrādhipati)* for a general officer of the military.[103]

Vajrapāṇi is also the guardian of the vehicle of secret spells, so he protects those possessing secret spells *(mantrin)*. In this role, the yakṣa general uses his secret spells as a king employs secret counsel *(mantra)*, and it is noteworthy that the king's counselors are identified as mantrins in Indian political nomenclature. Thus the secretaries associated with peace and war, the counselors of state, and many of the royal inner circle were designated mantrins. The topic was important enough for Lakṣmīdhara to devote a chapter to secret counsel in his compendium of Kingly Duty *(Rājadharma)*, where he assembled quotations from the legal and epic literature on the importance of the security of state secrets, including Yājñavalkya's affirmation that the kingdom has its basis in secret state policy *(mantramūlaṃ rājyaṃ)*.[104] Indeed, most medieval treatises on statecraft, for example, the policy section from Bhūlokamalla's 1131 C.E.

Mānasollāsa, include discussions of the qualities required of the king's mantrins.[105] This pun on the paronomasia of the term "mantra"—indicating both the spells of the priest and internal decisions of a court—was sufficiently significant to be repeated by the early medieval *Nītisāra* at least twice for its (possibly humorous) simultaneous applicability to both the religious and political domains.[106]

BECOMING THE INSTITUTION

This analysis of ritual remains incomplete without a consideration of the issues of scriptural composition and institutionalization. The question of composition is discussed elsewhere, but it is fair to say that the nature of Buddhist institutional life inhibited composition in some individualistic form. Some of the models proposed for Mahayana to date, such as that by Ray, have emphasized visionary individuals in forests propounding new scriptures.[107] In the case of esoteric literature, it is unlikely that isolated scriptures were developed outside a social world, with monks—and eventually siddhas—composing works autonomously. Virtually all our materials on esoteric composition emphasize the social environment, even in the cases of visionary revelation and inspiration. Unfortunately, the majority of these references come in the form of siddha hagiographies, so we must put off for now consideration of the manner of composition of the new scriptures. Instead, we turn to the quintessential monkish endeavor: canonical compilation and exegesis.

The monks who were creating institutional esoterism evidently considered their scriptures central to the longevity of their institutions and needed to articulate the values of authority and duty that could ensure scriptural transmission. This latter implies the issue of a canon of sacred authenticity, a body of the holy law that guards against the negation of propriety and defends the palace of the Dharmarāja against the attacks of those dedicated to its defeat. The Mantrayāna was the last version of Indian Buddhism to develop and sustain a canon of scripture, long after the canons of the early schools or of the Mahayana were verified as received authority by a larger or smaller segment of the Indian community. Consequently, esoteric monks were required to build on the previous models to the extent that they could, but the foundations of their new categories of scripture required them and others representing the institution to formulate a new mythology of revelation.

The first esoteric canons were apparently little more than collections of spells *(mantra-* or *dhāraṇī-piṭaka)*, and both the Mahāsāṃghikas and the

Dharmaguptakas among the early schools have had such collections attributed to them.[108] It is further clear that the early canon of spells was strongly associated with the areas between Kashmir and Swat—the latter being the land of Uḍḍiyāna or Oḍiyāna. Even the language of the surviving early literature affirms its association with places employing birchbark for manuscripts, notably employed in these areas.[109] The *Abhidharmakośabhāṣya* contributes to this sense of locality, mentioning two kinds of spells, one from the area of Gandhāra *(gāndhārī vidyā)* and one bringing visions of the future *(īkṣaṇikā vidyā)*.[110] We have no indication that any other area of the subcontinent managed to represent its ritual phrases so effectively at such an early period.

These mantra or ritual collections were doubtlessly put together somewhere between the fifth and seventh centuries, although collections of spells continue to be gathered down until the present.[111] This is the material that will come to be designated as "proto-tantric" in critical literature, although it provides us with a misleading sense that somehow these collections understood that they were anticipating the later, mature system, which was certainly not the case. Be that as it may, the nature of the early collections may be inferred from surviving works entitled the *Dhāraṇīsamgraha* (Collection of Spells), and the introduction to *Atikūṭa's **Dhāraṇīsamgraha* indicates that is was considered a fraction of a much larger *Dhāraṇī-piṭaka*.[112] *Atikūṭa's work is an interesting accumulation of rituals of protection, rituals relating to Amitābha's pure land, the consecration of disciples, and so forth. One or another of these compendia may have been alternatively titled the *Vidyādhara-piṭaka* (Sorcerers' Basket), for a spell from this latter work is quoted in Śāntideva's *Śikṣāsamuccaya*.[113] A *Sorcerers' Basket* seems to have been the source or inspiration for other surviving collections, like the *Vidyottama*, although several of these texts, again like the *Vidyottama*, show affinities with siddha literature.[114]

By the mid-eighth century, some conception of an esoteric canon with eighteen titles had evolved, although the precise nature of the earliest version of this ostensible collection remains obscure.[115] Contained in the Chinese Tripiṭaka is a work attributed to Amoghavajra, a work that purports to identify eighteen works of an esoteric compendium (*Chin kang ting ching yü ch'ieh shih pa hui chih kue,* T. 869). The list declares that they are from the *Vajraśekhara* (or *Vajroṣṇīṣa,* Tip of the Vajra Scripture), indicating that the complete text had eighteen subsidiary texts or sections within it. Apparently, the collection was conceived along the lines of the great Mahayanist collections, like the *Prajñāpāramitā* (Perfection of Insight), which also contains multiple works. Many of the items from the earliest list of eighteen remain obscure, but it is evident that the list was supposed to include a few works that are relatively well known. Among these are the *Sarvatathāgata-tattvasaṃgraha*, the *Sarvabuddhasamāyoga*, some form of the *Vajraśekhara* itself, the *Ardhaśatikāprajñāpāramitāsūtra*, some form of the *Guhyasamāja*, and the *Śrīparamādya*.

Many questions arise as to the relationship of these works to the ones currently represented by the canonical translations or in surviving Sanskrit manuscripts. The descriptions given by Amoghavajra between 746 and 774 C.E. leave much uncertainty about their correspondence to texts of the same or similar titles. Most of the existing translations of these titles are from the eleventh century or later, and few examples have survived from Amoghavajra's list that are actually rendered into Chinese during the T'ang dynasty. Amoghavajra's descriptions, for example, often indicate the number of maṇḍalas in each text, but the uncomfortable reality of many esoteric scriptures is that the maṇḍalas are described only partly or merely suggested in the received works. We are often left relying on the ritual manuals of later authors to assist us in understanding the maṇḍalas, but most of these works were written long after Amoghavajra's life. Thus many of the entries by Amoghavajra simply do not provide sufficient information to ascertain the extent of the scriptures they purport to describe or the texts closest to the sources he was representing.

Beyond the nature of the available scripture lists, we can see the Indian construction of scriptural categories, for our lists do not completely agree, except on the magical number eighteen. The esoteric ideology of a version of a canon in eighteen scriptures was an interesting and an instructive development of the Indian fascination with organizing numerology, for the number eighteen is seen in epic and Purāṇic literature as well.[116] However, we should not be seduced into believing that the various lists of the eighteen actually represented any universal esoteric canon that may have been collected, recited, ritualized, and transmitted as a whole. Rather, each of the lists identifies an esoteric canon according to representative proponents of the system in specific locales or at selected times and operates as an ideology of canon, working off the earlier Buddhist ideal.

Embedded in the idea of a canon in Buddhism is the mythology of the Buddha's realization, scriptural preaching, its collection after his death, and continued recitation by succeeding generations. Earlier Buddhist movements had conceived of a scripture on the model of the Buddha realizing the truth at the moment of awakening, following his defeat of Māra, the tempter. He then took this awakening and preached a scripture to an audience at a specific time in a specific place; the story of each preaching was attentively attached to the preface of each scripture. Immediately after the demise of the Buddha, we are assured, the community recited the scriptures at Rājagṛha, with Ānanda responsible for the Sūtras, Upāli reciting the *Vinaya*, and (in some versions) Mahākāśyapa relating the *Abhidharma*.[117] Mahayanists build on this model, so that the Buddha realized the truth of the Mahayana in a different world system and generally in a different lifetime far earlier than the historical Śākyamuni's time. New circumstances for the preaching of the scriptures were articulated as well, so that the word of the Buddha was received by an appropriate audience composed of the great bodhisattvas, like Mañjuśrī or Avalokiteśvara. Mahayanists also fashioned various alternatives to the standard scriptural recitation. One popular version depicts the convocation of a million bodhisattvas at the cave Vimalasvabhāva, where Mañjuśrī recited the Mahayanist *Abhidharma,* Maitreya recited the Mahayana *Vinaya,* and our old friend Vajrapāṇi recited the Mahayana *Sūtra.*

Perhaps the greatest problem with these competing mythologies was that they were, at their roots, fictive. While most scholars agree that there was a rough body of sacred literature (disputed) that a relatively early community (disputed) maintained and transmitted, we have little confidence that much, if any, of surviving Buddhist scripture is actually the word of the historical Buddha. More persuasively, the Buddhist order in India might be considered the greatest scriptural composition community in human history. Given the extraordinary extent of the material passing at any one time under rubric of the "word of the Buddha," we might simply pause and acknowledge that Indian Buddhists were extraordinarily facile litterateurs. Indeed, perhaps the interesting characteristic of Indian Buddhism is its ability to develop and sustain a culture of scriptural composition. This is no easy task, for it requires that the standards of authentic scripture be flexible enough to be met throughout the changing history of the subcontinent. Yet these same standards must be sufficiently conservative as to provide a sense of institutional continuity. We should acknowledge the ability of Indian Buddhists to provide a balance between these incommensurate requirements over the course of two millennia, producing in the process what is arguably the world's most extensive scriptural corpus. Institutional creativity of this order, at this level, over this length of time, is sheer inspired genius.

In the case of esoteric Buddhism, however, the institution ran into some difficulties. For reasons that are now obscure, masters of the new revelation did not elect to delineate a single myth for the authentication of the esoteric scriptures. Instead, competing myths, often tied to individual scriptures, were put forward. In fact, this may have been the strategy of the earlier Mahayanist and Abhidharmika communities. If true, though, the process has become clouded by the filtering device of a coalescence of the stories into a greater narrative, perhaps representing the manner in which consensus is eventually developed between monastic communities in India. In any event, two esoteric mythologies were eventually to succeed beyond most others, although we still have many individual scriptures claiming an independent origin. One of the myths of preaching involved King Indrabhūti of Oḍiyāna (an early version of this story is examined in chapter 6, as it is also an early siddha hagiography). The story of the tantras' preaching that was to have greatest resonance in institutional literature, however, was the myth of Maheśvara's subjugation by the most important esoteric bodhisattva, Vajrapāṇi.

Because it is an esoteric myth, it was appropriate for it to begin with a rite of authentication, in this case the consecration of Vajrapāṇi into his position as protector of the Dharma and the forceful converter of recalcitrant foes. As a mark of the esoteric method, the consecration of Vajrapāṇi as protector and collector became a literary event, closely tied to the preaching of the esoteric scriptures. It occurred in an episode celebrated in several scriptures, most notably the *Sarvatathāgatatattvasaṃgraha* and the *Vajrapāṇy-abhiṣeka-mahātantra.* Moreover, while Vajrapāṇi had a lengthy literary history in Indian Buddhism since the time of his conversion by the Buddha in the area of Gandhāra, for the esoteric system, an entirely new story is revealed.[118] In the changed narrative, Vajrapāṇi is in fact the transformation of the bodhisattva Samantabhadra, so well known in Mahayanist literature for his vows and aspirations on behalf of all beings. Soon after the cosmic Buddha Vairocana (Figure 5) achieved his awakening, he issued from his heart the "heart mantra" of all the Buddhas: *vajrasattva.* Then, impelled by the benediction and miracles of all the Buddhas, there formed a new bodhisattva in the form of Samantabhadra:

> Out of the *vajrasattva* concentration, because it is exceedingly firm and entirely good, formed a uniquely hard body in the form of Samantabhadra. Then, having assumed its place in the heart of Lord Vairocana, it disclosed this pithy verse,
>
> Aho! I am Samantabhadra, the hard being of those self-originated.
> For, even though bodiless from my hard nature,
> I have attained the body of a being.
>
> So now the body of Samantabhadra, the great bodhisattva, descends from the heart of Vairocana and appears seated on a lunar disk in front of all the Tathāgatas, requesting their command.
>
> Then, the lord Vairocana entered into the concentration called "the pledge scepter of all the Tathāgatas." He acted so that every experience of

FIGURE 5 Sarvavid Mahāvairocana from Nālandā.
Eighth to ninth centuries. Guilded bronze. National Museum, no. 47.48.
Photo courtesy of the American Institute of Indian Studies.

happiness and ease and all sovereignty would occur to protect those in the realm of beings without exception or exclusion. He even acted so that they would gain the fruit of attainment of the highest accomplishment in the unsurpassed Mahayanist comprehension, which leads to the supernormal cognition of the gnosis of equanimity of all Tathāgatas. He did this with a vajra leading to the accomplishment of all those Tathāgatas, a vajra that was the pledge of all Tathāgatas' great means, power, heroism, and great gnosis so that, for the welfare of beings, there would be the turning the Dharma wheel of virtue, concentration, insight, liberation, and the vision of liberation's gnosis. Having consecrated that Samantabhadra with the coronation of the turban and the jeweled crown composed of the bodies of all the Tathāgatas, Vairocana coronated him into the state of being the Cakravartin of all Tathāgatas and placed that vajra in his two hands.

Thus, all the Tathāgatas consecrated him with the name consecration, by exclaiming, "Vajrapāṇi, Vajrapāṇi!"

Then, the bodhisattva, the great bodhisattva Vajrapāṇi, proudly brandishing the vajra in his left hand, carried the vajra at his heart with the yoga of elevation, and disclosed this pithy verse:

> This is the unexcelled vajra of accomplishment of all those Buddhas.
> It is I. It is the vajra consecrated into this vajra in my hand.[119]

Vajrapāṇi's consecration was most particularly a prelude to his subjugation of the preeminent of evil beings, Maheśvara (Śiva), whom he kills in combat any number of times in any number of scriptures.[120] The most important source of the myth, the section in the *Sarvatathāgatatattvasaṃgraha*, has been translated several times, so a simple summary here may suffice. The story opens with the cosmic Buddha, Vairocana, requesting that Vajrapāṇi generate or emit his adamantine family *(vajrakula)*. Normally, this would be the beginning of the establishment of a maṇḍala, wherein the perfection of the Buddha's law can be understood. This time, however, Vajrapāṇi refuses the request. Different versions of the story provide variations on the rationale, but the basic line is that Maheśvara (= Śiva) is deluding beings with his deceitful religious doctrines and engaging in all kinds of violent criminal conduct. So, Vairocana asks Vajrapāṇi to bring this evil character and his entourage into compliance. He utters a mantra that drags them to his palace at the summit of Mount Sumeru. Vajrapāṇi orders them to comply with the Buddha's doctrine, and all but Maheśvara submit. Maheśvara replies that he is the lord of the universe and Vajrapāṇi is but a pathetic tree spirit. The two challenge each other to acquiesce, and they engage in magical combat. After successive battles, eventually Vajrapāṇi is successful by means of his superior mantras and righteousness. Maheśvara and his wife, Umā, are tread on by Vajrapāṇi's feet, which is the greatest insult in India as the feet are the most polluted limb. As a result of his victory, all of Maheśvara's retinue, including his wife, agree to become part of Vairocana's maṇḍala, and they are given back their names but with the word "vajra" placed before each to denote their new Buddhist status. They are bound by new vows and accept the pledge to quit their evil ways and become good Buddhists. Maheśvara is the sole exception, for he will not relent. Accordingly he is killed, and his life transferred to another realm, where he becomes a Buddha named Bhasmeśvara-nirghoṣa, the Soundless Lord of Ashes. In honor of the great victory over the demonic Maheśvara, a new maṇḍala is created of the gods and goddesses formerly in Śiva's service. The new maṇḍala is entitled Trailokyavijaya, the Victory over the Triple World, with Vajrapāṇi appearing in the center as the divinity Trailokyavijaya.

The popularity and longevity of this myth of Śiva's humiliation and assassination is extraordinary and must be related to its context. An Indian Buddhist of the eighth century would certainly have recognized this kind of episode, in which the defeat of a demonic figure by a divinity occurs, for it is the stuff of epic and Purāṇic literature. Whether the defeat of the buffalo demon Mahīśa by the goddess Durgā or the destruction of the ten-headed ogre Rāvanā by Rāma, the active defeat of a violent opponent is normative in Indian narratives. This is, in fact, quite different from the passive defeat of Māra by the Buddha, for Śākyamuni is depicted in Buddhist hagiography as overcoming his nemesis by equanimity, not through force. The snappiness of the dialogue employed in the scriptures suggests that the Maheśvara subjugation myth has been much influenced by Indian storytellers who continue to travel around, alone or in small troupes, and describe mythic combat using painted pictures on cloth hung behind them.[121] The fact that the story is sometimes explicitly associated with the painting of its maṇḍala reinforces this possibility.[122]

Indians, then, would read or hear the narrative with similar narratives in mind. They would also have received the story with many of the terms suggesting the structure of the ritualized combat in their world, with its challenges, self-aggrandizement, and disparagement of the opponent's virtue. After the conclusion of the combat, the maṇḍala of one lord is captured and subsumed into the maṇḍala of the victorious lord by the activity of his general. Then, the new prince of the expanded maṇḍala establishes the law (Dharma) within the new territory, much as Vairocana teaches the tantras at the end of the *Sarvatathāgatatattvasaṃgraha*, once the territory is safe for Buddhists.

After hearing the story, disciples would be consecrated into this new spiritual state, in which they could meditate on themselves as identical to Trailokyavijaya, with their feet treading on Śiva's deceased head and Umā's breasts.[123] This meditation recreates the total victory of the prince on the field of battle, dishonoring his slain enemy and taking the queen for his own.

For our purposes, the most important factor in the consideration of these myths is the recognition that they articulate a form of belligerence that is quintessentially early medieval Indian. The narrative use of violence in the context of Buddhist institutions allowed institutional esoterism to compete with Śaivism, to appeal to the worst instincts of the warlords of the medieval period and yet to delimit the nature of approved violence, in some ways approaching the description of a "just war" found within Aquinas. Buddhaguhya is adamantly positive about the nature of violence perpetrated on the difficult to tame by the members of the scepter family *(vajrakula)*, but the good *vajrācārya* took myth as veridical and ritual as its reenactment.[124] The result of the narrative is the reemergence of Dharma, after all—the release of obstructions to the pronouncement of the scriptures and the reaffirmation of universal salvation.

If the myth of the preaching of the esoteric canon was relatively well established, its actual canonical parameters were not. The different lists of eighteen (sometimes thirty-six) tantras remain artifacts of numerology and provide only a moderate sense of the esoteric scriptural horizon. Perhaps another avenue to understanding, though, would be through a simple examination of texts as they were invoked in literary or ritual appeals to authority. In fact, whatever the ideology of canon articulated in the various lists, the canon as it was actually employed in eighth-century institutions might best be termed the *canon in use*. That is, there was a body of texts that were identified by acknowledged bearers of the culture at discrete points in the hermeneutic process—based on reference, commentary, and translation. Although each of these works eventually found its way into some canon, they do not appear as a group in any specific list. However, they certainly are individually identified as important in reference by some of the more influential monks of the eighth or early ninth centuries. Such an esoteric *canon in use* in the eighth century doubtless included the *Sarvatathāgatatattvasaṃgraha*, the *Mahāvairocanābhisambodhi*, the *Vajrapāṇyabhiṣeka*, the *Subāhuparipṛcchā*, the *Amoghapāśa*, the *Vajravidāraṇa*, the *Susiddhikara*, the **Ekākṣarabuddhoṣṇīśacakravarti-sūtra*, the *Sarvadurgatipariśodhana*, the *Vajraśekhara*, the *Ardhaśatikāprajñāpāramitāsūtra*, the *Prajñāpāramitānaya-śatapañcaśatikā*, the *Śrīparamādya*, and others.[125] Most of these were to be classed as *kriyā*, *caryā*, or *yoga* tantras by the tenth century, but such classifications are part of the selection process and remain *ex post facto*, seldom demonstrated in the texts and rarely apparent in the composition of any one of them. Each, in its own terms, proclaims its own importance and unequivocal status as supreme within the esoteric dispensation.

MONKS AND THEIR RITUALS

It should be emphasized that the scriptures and rituals of institutional esoterism were supported, performed, interpreted, and transmitted by Buddhist monks. Although the obvious success of these scriptures (and their proponents) must be acknowledged, the scriptural classifications often applied to the canon in use can inhibit our understanding of the process of composition and are valuable primarily to determine later reception and employment. Thus the problematic issue of how these texts came to be propounded remains obscure, especially as it is apparent that the fountainhead for many of the practices and doctrines of institutional esoteric Buddhism was outside the purview of the institutions themselves. Indeed, the affirmation of purity sometimes taken by East Asian esoteric representatives is belied by some of the content of their own canonical scriptures, which reflect the siddha proclivity to cemetery rituals, seduction rites, virginal spirit possession, and other varieties of antinomian behavior. Rather, institutional esoterism both acted as a part of the composition process and defined the hermeneutic of selection while the other sources (siddha, tribal, lay, political) often lacked the sacred authority to pronounce on behalf of a potential scripture.

If the sources for many ritual systems were external to the monastic institutions, it is also obvious that monastic techniques were employed to make the aggregate of the statements palatable. The above scriptures are frequently framed or introduced with specifically elite monastic philosophical materials, and the doctrinal or ethical statements certainly must have been composed inside the hallowed walls of Buddhist monasteries.[126] Indeed, esoteric scriptures and related treatises became some of the few places where specifically Buddhist terminology and the development of new doctrines can be seen in the eighth and ninth centuries. Yet, despite their continued proclamation of ethical purity and condemnation of lapses of morality within the community, monks also became increasingly attracted by the structures of Indian medieval life. The texts themselves introduce to monks the themes of power, personality, eroticism, violence in defense of the Dharma, spells, and the mythology of absolute supremacy.

Perhaps the greatest curiosity in all of institutional esoterism is the monks' utter disinterest in themselves as literary personas. Almost all of our hagiographical literature is about and by siddhas (some of this literature is explored in detail below). But this literary direction did not extend to the Buddhist monks. By and large, we know their names, and, in a few instances, we know where they lived. Almost none of our resources, though, indicate the employment of an esoteric ritual program at a specific monastery. We do not know, for example, whether the great monasteries of Nālandā or Vikramaśīla employed esoteric literature and rituals in community-wide celebrations or in the postmortem ceremonies of their abbots or munificent patrons. It is clear that some reliquaries of selected individuals at Ratnagiri, for example, display images of Heruka, Mārīcī, or some other esoteric figure.[127] Some temples were dedicated to esoteric divinities, such as the Saṃvara temple in Nālandā.[128] But we know neither how early such rituals were exercised nor the aggregate involvement of the samgha. At most, we can determine that certain monks, wherever they were, favored specific scriptures and inscribed these tantras into commentaries.

Probably the best exemplar of the new, emergent institutional esoterism is Buddhaguhya. He not only became the preeminent exegete during the second half of the eighth century but also, more than any other single individual, represented the confluence of spirituality, esoterism, political insight, and promotional skill. His ability both to attract and to decline an invitation from the most powerful Buddhist ruler of the eighth century, Trisong Detsen of Tibet, is a testament to his institutional aura.[129] We do have some hagiographical accounts of Buddhaguhya retained by Tibetans, the earliest probably being the mention in versions of the *sBa-bzhed* (Testament of the Ba Clan).[130] In fact, the text opens with the very brief mention that there was a failed mission to get two scholars, Buddhaguhya and Buddhaśānti, but that they were meditating on Kailāsa and could not be brought. Certainly, we know that the attempt to lure the good monks was sincere. A letter, purportedly the reply of Buddhaguhya to Trisong Detsen, has been preserved in the Tibetan canon. At the beginning, the famous scholar relates his apologies for being unable to accept the august invitation:

> You have sent [the religious envoys] Era Aro, Mañjuśrī, and retinue, with the best of wealth—silver and gold—to seek the Holy Dharma of India, so that they might open a window to illuminate the deep darkness of Tibet.
>
> As the veritable Buddhaguhya (one whose secret is the Buddha), it gladdens my heart that the Meridian of Royal Authority in the world, the one

who has straightened the crooked ways of power within his administration, the Supreme Lord in an unbroken stream of divine manifestations, the Lord Trisong Detsen should order thus:

"Ride the high plain of Dharma, human and divine!" So he informed Mañjuśrī and Murita not to regard the great diseases forming through the concentration of wind, bile, and phlegm in this heap of the blazing bejeweled body, or through the obstructions of 80,000 demons.

They have persevered, coming from such a high place to invite me there, but I am powerless to go. The Bodhisattva, Ārya Mañjuśrī himself admonished me, "If you go to Tibet, you will lose your life!" Even though I cannot make the journey, I am sending the meditative instruction, my *Yogāvātara*, in response to the King's presents.

Bhoṭasvāmidāsalekha, 1.6–9[131]

Both this letter and the content of Buddhaguhya's works in the catalogue of the Denkar Palace Library indicate that the scriptures he preferred were exactly those supporting Buddhist institutional life.[132] Moreover, the received hagiography of Buddhaguhya is maintained in the annals literature of the Nyingma sect, this group having the strongest claim to the esoteric systems translated into Tibetan in the eighth to ninth centuries. Buddhaguhya's hagiography is employed to secure the legitimacy of one of their eight esoteric lineages, designated the eight streams of early translations. The story works around the importance attached to the eighth-century Tibetan king's petition and his attempt to lure the great scholar to the halls of his palace. As it is encountered in a mid-fourteenth-century history, the hagiography promotes this Nyingma version of the Royal Dynastic agenda:

The Third Stream of Nyingma Translations

The Dharma taught when Ācārya Buddhaguhya went to Kailāsa. As to the chronicle of this great person:

There was an important kingly *[kṣatriya]* lineage in West India. At one time there was born to the king of this lineage a son. But the king thought, "This son of mine is not a person worthy of acting in the world as the teacher [Ācārya] of men. Therefore, he should be put to the propitiation of Ārya Mañjuśrī, who is the Lord of Knowledge. He must beseech Mañjuśrī to make him an Ācārya."

The prince was accordingly given a physical support in the form of a cast statue about a cubit in height. He was given a vocal support of a lotus flower, and a mental support of a container filled with milk. The king then imparted to him the text of Mañjuśrī's meditation and sent him on to practice. Because the king had accumulated great merit, and because the boy was of the kṣatriya lineage, the prince accomplished his goal in only six days. The cast image of Mañjuśrī smiled and laughed, and so forth. The lotus flower kept fresh as if newly sprouted, and the milk seeped as if it were boiling.

The prince thought, "I've been here propitiating Mañjuśrī, but is it better if I take this as some sort of accomplishment [siddhi]?" So he had his doubts. Finally he said, "This god is nothing more than the Māra named Kālodāyin!" Just then, a large black bird emanated from the statue. It dipped one wind in water, mixed it with earth and threw the mud next to where the teacher [prince] was sitting. The boy then lost consciousness for a while. When he regained his awareness, and took a look, the statue had faded to black, the lotus had become old, and the container of milk seemed all dried out.

[The prince thought,] "Now, this is the result of not accepting siddhi at the appropriate time for it to be accepted. So, what was the fault? It was the experience of doubt. From what was this the result? It was the result of having learned too little. If there is too little learning, then it should be understood as the action of Māra!" Aloud he said to himself, "This is I or someone like me." So he asked permission of his father, and went to East India, where he studied with five hundred scholars. Because his family was good (being *kṣatriya)* and as he had already propitiated Mañjuśrī, he absorbed without impediment all the learning of these five hundred Paṇḍitas.

Now, because his family was good and by virtue of his learning, he collected many goods and a great entourage, so that the distractions became overwhelming.

In response, he felt a feeling of renunciation. "If there is too much learning (so that all manner of people are attracted), then that should also be known as the work of Māra. And that is I or someone like me." In Kailāsa, there is the rookery in the golden cliff of the Raven Headed [God]. He went there to practice meditation.

At this same time, in Tibet there resided the Dharma protector, the Lord Trisong Detsen. He heard that there was a learned Paṇḍita from India in residence at Kailāsa. So he sent about three liters of gold dust with four messengers with an invitation: Lotsāba Wa Mañjuśrīvarman, Chim Shākya Prabha, Drenkara Mukhendra, and Tsangte Lektra.

Buddhaguhya, however, replied, "I've made a vow to practice, and so will not go to Tibet with you." Still, they asked if they could receive the Dharma, as he would not go back. "I'll have to ask my chosen divinity if the time has come for me to teach or not," Buddhaguhya replied. So he prayed to his chosen divinity for three days and asked his question. The divinity prophesied that the time had come and he may preach the Dharma.

Buddhaguhya told his four Tibetan disciples, "Before the explanation of the Dharma of the secret mantras, one requires the consecration." So the Ācārya, by simply striking a few lines on the surface of Lake Manasarovar that was laid out like a turquoise maṇḍala, all of a sudden there was the peaceful Vajradhātu maṇḍala of the forty-two divinities clearly radiant, appearing in the sky before them. All the great disciples personally saw it. Then the Ācārya asked, "Do you want to ask the divinity for the consecration or me?" In their minds, they thought, "Since the god can disappear, perhaps we should ask the god first?" But then the Ācārya snapped his fingers, and the entire group of divinities merged into his heart.

"You red-faced demons from Tibet! You have such little interest in the pledge between master and disciple! Only because there is something of a connection leading to the teaching of Dharma that I will explain it to you."

Having said this, he taught the *Vairocanābhisambodhi-tantra*, the *Sarvadurgatipariśodhana* together with its practical manuals, his own *Yogāvatara,* along with the teachings of yoga. Furthermore, he transmitted the internal esoteric works of the *Net of Illusion*, especially the *Guhyagarbha* with its commentary. He also bestowed the *Stages of the Path with their Instructions*, and his own *Stages of the Vajra Path with Instructions*. He also conferred on many specific lesser instructions, such as the *Great and Smaller Nets of Peace*, *The Medium*, etc. He also gave them the *Dhyānottara* along with his commentary. In short, many of the teachings of the inner and outer secret mantras were translated.

All the great disciples taught these to the king Trisong Detsen, and he in turn taught them to Ma [Rinchenchok] and Nyak Jñāanakumāra. After this, the lineage is said to be basically the same as the Düpado.[133]

This very interesting hagiography is reflective of both Indian and Tibetan themes, and it is difficult to separate them from time to time. Some differentiation between the two can be seen in the contrast between this fourteenth-century version and the 1608 version of Tāranātha, which is less historically reliable and more emphatic on the miraculous.[134] There can be no question, though, that the description of his early life is a later addition, whether written in India or Tibet. Moreover, some of the titles mentioned at the conclusion of the story play no part in the normative materials by and about Buddhaguhya. The names of the Tibetans sent to obtain his services are somewhat different from those mentioned in the letter, but the letter itself has some difficulties. Even the identity of Kailāsa as his residence cannot be verified. One colophon mentions that he stayed in the Himālayas, but we do not know when Indian Buddhists began making pilgrimage to that specific sacred mountain.[135] We know that seventh-century sites, such as Jagreśwar, outside Almora, were erected before Buddhaguhya, and one of these may have been his goal.[136]

The special accord given to Buddhaguhya's family status in the work is more difficult, because we do not know the level to which caste played a part in Indian monasteries. I know of no work or inscription that supports the idea that caste invaded monasteries sufficiently to segregate monastic orders, as it has done in Southeast Asia. We also do not know whether a proprietary custody of esoteric rituals was secured by caste, as has occurred in Nepal. However, the presence of Tibetans, Chinese, Nepalese, Burmese, and Indonesians at the flagship monasteries of later Indian Buddhism suggests that the importance attached to caste, whatever it may have been, was not yet overwhelming. In all likelihood, Indians offered those of high caste greater access to education, rituals, and authority, as much because they came to the monasteries with a better background in all these skills and connections through their caste affiliation as for any other reason.

Most important for our purposes, though, is the recognition that Buddhaguhya's syllabus was (even in the voice of later Nyingma apologists) associated primarily with the texts that are represented in his surviving corpus. Although the *Yogāvatāra* does not appear to be extant, the other materials by and large survive. It is unlikely, though, that he had much to do with the works of the *Māyājāla*, including the *Guhyagarbha*. These works were around—as were other, more radical scriptures—but the selectivity of authoritative works endorsed by Buddhaguhya is part of the dynamic that made monastic institutions so strong, for his writing by and large affirms monastic identity. Buddhaguhya is attributed authorship of works on the *Sarvadurgatipariśodhana*, on the *Vairocanābhisambodhi*, on the *Subāhuparipṛcchā*, on the *Dhyānottara*, on the *Sarvatathāgatatattvasaṃgraha*, as well as others of the same focus. Beyond the works he had commented upon, the texts he cites are as central to this facet of the esoteric movement as those receiving the benefit of his exegesis.[137]

In fact, Buddhaguhya's pattern of commentarial elaboration and textual citation appears to define in some very basic way the category of institutional esoterism. It was the process of scriptural appropriation, affirmation, and commentary that made the works acceptable to the larger monastic community. He assiduously ties ritual elements to the standard nomenclature of the Buddhist path, elaborating performative patterns in light of Buddhist philosophical systems.[138] Furthermore, his ritual texts, based on these same scriptures, ensured them a place in the menu of rites that stabilized the social relations in the grand edifices of later Buddhism. These ritual systems established performative tracks that the monks could follow and, if the testimony of eleventh- to twelfth-century Tibetan translators is reliable, increasingly occupied an important position in the monastic life.[139] By that time, monasteries were to admit of smaller units—temples, really—in which the performance of specific ritual systems were maintained: Saṃvara at Nālandā, Heruka at Ratnagiri, and so forth. The beginning of this movement can be seen in the rites to Mahākāla as the kitchen protector, as reported by I-ching in the late seventh century.[140]

Another major figure for whom some sense of identity is available was certainly Śākyamitra. Assuming that it is the same author, the end of the commentary to the classic Mahayana expression of aspiration, the *Bhadracaripraṇidhānarāja*, provides a hint as to his identity. The verse of benediction indicates that the commentary was written by the intelligent Śākyamitra for the purpose of augmenting the Śākya lineage.[141] It is not clear from this reference whether he is simply doing this transfer of merit as an act of piety to the lineage of the historical Buddha or he himself was actually born into that family. I am inclined to the latter interpretation, for the Śākyas were given a privileged position through much of Indian Buddhist history and medieval monks certainly had no compunction about identifying themselves as from that clan (Śākyabhikṣu) from time to time.[142]

The other data available on Śākyamitra are from the beginning of his enormous commentary on the *Sarvatathāgatatattvasaṃgraha*. It is entitled the *Kosalālaṃkāra* (Ornament of Kosala), perhaps indicating the country of his origin. Assuming that he and the *Bhadracaryā-praṇidhānarāja-ṭīkā* author were the same, then he must have been from the late eighth or early ninth century. He was definitely one of the more important figures of that period who connect several different personalities and their lineages. At the beginning of the *Kosalālaṃkāra* is a most unusual autobiographical statement.

> At the good city [? Bhadranagara], with great faith I first pleased the highest guru, Buddhasena, who has obtained great fame. I received his permission [to practice] and obtained the rituals and vows. From him, I learned much and reflected on many teachings.
>
> At Koṅkana, Dramiḍa, Īśvaraśrīsamāja *[dbang phyug dpal 'dus]* I happily served Dharmasena, and Dharmākara.
>
> At Sahya [Western Ghats], I prayed to Dharmavajra, of most excellent name, and gave much service to Uṣṇīṣavajra.

> I then went to the source of qualities, Oḍiyāna in the north. There I served King Indrabhūti, holder of the reality of the tantras' meaning.
>
> At Tagkye City [?] I happily relied on the Kośalācāra *Sthiramatibuddhyākara-śīlajña. But a fraction of method of the scripture that I realized directly from the teacher's own mouth, I have contemplated so that the gradual worldly ritual of yoga, in accordance with the teacher's [instructions] will remain for a long time.[143]

In this instance, our confidence about its authenticity is greater, simply because it is from the scholar's personal statement. Not only is his general exegetical method quite conservative, but the above record accords well with what is known from the few other surviving personal accounts. The activity in Koṅkana, the importance of Oḍiyāna and the Western Ghats, and the foray into the south all resonate with other late eighth- and early ninth-century sources.

The net result of these and the other few indications of monks investigating the esoteric tradition are simple. First, the few exegetical personalities are important exemplars of a much larger population of seminal figures from the seventh to tenth centuries, all too few of whose names survive. We will continue to encounter important monks and siddhas about whom we know nothing other than that their disciples were extraordinarily influential in the spread of the new esoteric doctrine. Second, it is highly likely that some of these names represent the actual identities of the authors of the Buddhist tantras, for they were clearly central personalities in exactly the right places at the right times. If we are seeking prototypes for those composing the new esoteric scriptures as the Word of the Buddha, we need to begin with the teachers of the first commentators. Finally, the aggregate information on all of these individuals is so meager as to be pathetic. In contrast to the more extensive hagiographical works on the siddhas, our esoteric monks were disinterested in self-promotion and certainly never captured the imagination of either monastic or lay storytellers. This latter point is important, for if there were many more esoterically inclined monks than siddhas, then the public personas of the relatively few radical siddha figures became overwhelmingly important in the popular presentation and proclamation of the esoteric dispensation.

SACRALIZATION OF THE DOMAIN

In our assessment of esoteric Buddhism as internalizing the political models of medieval India, we should be wary of being seduced into a comfortable reductionism, concluding that the esoteric movement diminished the Buddhist leaders into sycophantic actors imitating the domain of mere politics. Instead, we might observe the great litterateurs and teachers of North Indian monasteries trying to sanctify the world as they received and accepted it. This is not to diminish the importance of patronage issues or the influence of the sāmanta culture, but simply to affirm that the mission of Buddhist cloisters was a consensual effort at sanctifying society, much as the esoteric ritual system sacralized the political metaphor. These monks tried to take, in another trope of esoterism, the poison of belligerence and transmute it into the nectar of welfare. They attempted to transform power and hierarchy into community and congregation. Swimming in the sea of sāmanta feudalism, they tried to see it as an ocean of gnosis and to engage it in the creation of merit for all beings. At least three factors were important in the sacralized esoteric formulation—the Buddhist ideology of skillful means, the Indian understanding of metaphor, and the Mahayanist conception of radical transformation. Esoteric Buddhists extended these items far past the previous Mahayanist parameters, and this extension marks some of the difference between the exoteric and esoteric directions. At the same time, esoteric monks brought the feudal rituals into a world already governed by monastic rules and bodhisattva vows, so that the initial development of esoteric precepts was not dramatic or crucial, but instead a modest supplement to the existing pledges.

When we look at Buddhist notices of skillful means, two things are striking. First, the appropriation of popular forms was driven by sociological realities. So, as informed Indian laymen become important in the religious life of Buddhist India, contravening the earlier exclusive reliance on monks, Buddhist scriptures are being written to reflect these realities. Thus, at about the same time as Fa-hsien observed the authority and learning of the lay teachers Rādhāsvāmin and Mañjuśrī in fourth-century Pāṭaliputra, personalities like them became embodied in the literary personas of Vimalakīrti and Śrīmālā.[144] These figures could become learned, and ultimately accepted as Buddhist teachers, for they were the end-product of the many changes in Indian economic and political life over the preceding centuries. In this end, they stand in contrast to previous virtuous laymen, from whom monks would never have studied the Buddhadharma. However, the process of the Buddhist appropriation and reformulation of phenomena emerging in the Indian sociopolitical world appears to take at least some decades, even a century or more.

Second, the doctrines of skillful means are posed as the recovery of what had always been or the rectification of a straying from the authentic reality.[145] Frequently, this is done with the idea that the authentic reality is eternal, as in the modern definition of Hinduism as the "eternal Dharma." Moreover, we also find the idea that the straying from the norm has been accomplished by the sequestering of the clergy from the larger movement; such is the supposition behind the "unique vehicle" of the *Lotus Sūtra*. There the Śrāvakas are depicted as separating themselves from the great congregation, as they cannot stand to hear the doctrine of this great Buddha Vehicle. Informing many of these concepts is the fact that India did not really develop a model of the disaffected intellectual as the cultural critic, as happened in Europe since the time of the Renaissance. What we know of Indian Buddhist monks is that they tended to affirm aspects of popular culture, whether in the early Buddhist acceptance of the doctrine of karma or the appropriation of *homa* as a viable avenue of religion. Monks not valorizing popular culture and secluding themselves from the Indian cultural horizon were understood as unskillful in technique and inattentive to their missionary duty. Buddhaguhya himself spent some of his exegetical capital demonstrating that the preaching of the tantras had everything to do with attracting people of different temperament:

> "Most excellent work for the benefit of others" means that the Buddhas taught the various means by the entryways of the hand gestures, the mantras, and the maṇḍalas, all of which had been blessed by their inexhaustible emanations.[146]

Nor was there a concomitant rejection of intellectuals by the Indian popular culture, as has occurred in Europe and the United States since the Enlightenment. Rather, our evidence suggests that there was a closer connection between Indian popular and elite culture, and this extended to the acceptance of cultural cues from the political as well as the religious domains. We see this even in the formation of the early Samgha, and it is well established that the organization of the community was based in some part on the rules of order already employed by the smaller republics, like the Licchavis and the Śākyas.

And many of these same ideas were also institutionalized as ritual metaphors. Certainly, in the above instance, emulating the constitution of a small republic did not give the Buddhists political authority. Yet the special relationship of the Buddha to his Śākya clan spilled over into the organization of the order and privileged the position of that clan in the ensuing history of Indian Buddhism. Just as true, the visualizations and meditations of esoteric Buddhism did not make a monk the overlord, but the developing relationship between the great monasteries where feudal law was exercised and the lords of the land made the metaphor all the more resonant. Monks found this image or ritual trope of power, authority, and freedom irresistible. They took it, though, and filled it with the content of the Buddhist path. Thus the monk still progressed on the path, but he did so as a hero, he did it like a king, he did it like an elephant in procession, for the road to awakening was like an inexhaustible treasury, and the path lead to the impenetrable citadel of Vairocana. All these metaphors were specifically employed by Buddhaguhya to explain the esoteric turn.[147]

Indeed, throughout Indian Buddhist life, figures of speech, similes and metaphors, metonymy and synecdoche, and all the other aspects of the sophisticated Indian literary world have played a part.[148] Especially in the Mahayanist literature, where such figures or examples are rife, Buddhists were attentive to their use. Whether with respect to the nine metaphors for the embryo of the Tathāgata embedded in the mundane or the dozens of images on the empty nature of phenomenal reality, Mahayanists have employed metaphors or similes frequently to illustrate their messages.[149] Often they used poetic principles to explain questions of doctrine or its understanding, and just as often these figures of speech were subject to rather subtle analysis. Sthiramati, for example, engages in a rather abstruse discussion on the exact applicability of a poetic fancy in identifying two dissimilar items (a boy and fire) into a single image (an irascible [fiery] boy). The purpose is not to discuss or demonstrate poetic sensibility but, instead, to vindicate the relationship between the underlying consciousness *(ālayavijñāna)* and the misconception of self in either the individual person or the elements of reality, for the imperceptible continuum must somehow resemble the falsely imagined soul.[150]

For esoteric Buddhists, though, the difference is the ritualization of their metaphors. They have viewed the external obsession with military prowess and the manipulation of vassals whose loyalty might be justifiably questioned in the shifting sands of medieval alliances. They have seen how princes decimated the guilds, moved much of the population to the countryside, erected castles and fortifications, and brought in Śaiva ascetic orders to legitimize their self-obsessed actions. Monks understood that others in the religious landscape supported in ritual and literature the apotheosis of the king and the sāmantization of the gods. For them, the Buddhist path was still the content—and most of the institutional tantras are explicit in this—but its ritualization put that content in a new vessel, with the accoutrements of power and a new, self-confident authority. And because it was much the same content, and since it was constructed using building blocks largely present in advance (mantras, maṇḍalas, *homa*s, etc.), the transition was relatively smooth, with a remarkable lack of protest from others in the Buddhist community about the new turn to ritual.[151]

A cynic might point to the appropriation of these models by monks as a validation of his worst opinions about religious degradation over time. However, it appears that the actual lesson is different. If one is to bring a conscience to the system, then an engagement with the lethal forces of self-aggrandizement is the only possible avenue. In his commentary to the *Vairocanābhisambodhitantra*, for example, Buddhaguhya expounds on the virtue of the practice:

> The fruit for some, in their virtuous action in propitiating the mantras, is that they perfect the world into something other than it was. For others, by the power of their reflection and application, they are ripened [to Buddhahood] in this very life.[152]

Therefore the ritualization of the public persona of the overlord is, among other things, an attempt to impress it with a consensual sense of responsibility, replacing the license previously accorded. So Buddhaguhya could discuss the blessing of the Buddhas in the same breath as validating the hierarchy of the medieval world.

Thus, for the monks—and, I would argue, for all Buddhists—the fundamental reason they could engage the world in this way is that they believed in the transformation of personality. This ideal, called "fundamental transformation" *(āśrayaparivṛtti)* in Yogācāra nomenclature, was expressed philosophically and doctrinally long before the advent of the esoteric system. However, with the accelerated engagement of monks in the ideology of the feudal universe came an equivalent acceleration of the employment of this or similar terminology in meditative ritual.[153] Whereas a total of perhaps two dozen important statements on the idea exist in Yogācāra and related literature, I have not been able to count the number of esoteric scriptures and commentaries that employ the notion—certainly many times the Yogācāra total.[154] We must keep in mind that the reason for such a distribution is that the idea is displayed widely through the manuals of practice. Each time, for example, a meditator is asked to visualize himself as a Buddhist divinity, the stages of generation include a movement from a seed-syllable *(bījamajtra)* to a divine symbol to the fully formed deity. At each moment of transformation, the idea is that this represents a fundamental transformation, so reality—even at the most exalted level—is subject to manipulation by the mind of the meditator. For example, Śākyarakṣita, in his *Pīṭhādinirṇaya*, describes the phenomenon in the transmutation of internal veins into internalized forms of the external pilgrimage zones:

> From the transformation of the letters like PUṂ, etc., we are to envision the places—the pilgrimage seats *[pīṭha]*, etc.—inside the empty spokes of the cakras located in the head, etc. We should furthermore meditate that both the pilgrimage seats and the veins inside them are fundamentally transformed by the form of the divinity. This is similar to the way that pilgrimage seats in the external world are revived (and therefore transformed) by the waters of rivers in their proximity. And in the same way the veins revive the fingernails, and so forth.[155]

Here we find a convenient association of many of the elements needed in the emergence of esoteric Buddhism: the ritualization of external circumstances, the identity of internal and external, the employment of metaphors in the process, and transformation as the procedure for sanctification.

The last method for the sacralization of the feudal world was the simple act of bringing its rituals into the monastic compound, where the rules of the *Vinaya* and the vows of the Bodhisattva provided a sense of formal authority, to which the new rite must be accommodated. Because monastic esoterism was already based in an institution, dramatic new rules and legal procedures were not required for the culmination of the new rites. For example, the *Mañjuśrīmūlakalpa* provides a rather lackluster statement of guidance to candidates after their consecration:

> So! The secrecy of the pledge of the Great Bodhisattva, the True Prince Mañjuśrī, is never to be transgressed. You are never to produce great demerit. Nor are any of his mantras to be repudiated. No Buddha or Bodhisattva is to be contradicted and your master is to be propitiated. Otherwise, there will be a transgression against the pledge, and the mantras will not lead to accomplishment, where there may be found great merit.[156]

This kind of modest list of commitments is found reinforced elsewhere, as in the esoteric instruction on the bodhisattva's virtue by Śubhakarasiṃha, and they share a broad range of values that support and promote the monastic path.[157]

When such modest lists of requirements are contrasted with the highly formalized and well-defined series of vows articulated in siddha communities—examined in chapter 7—some of the differences in their organizations are evident. Because the siddhas had no overarching institutional culture in which to become socialized, they appeared to need a much more structured agenda of vows and restrictions. Not so the monks. The very act of moving the consecration and related rituals from the regal court to the monastic courtyard did not absolve the monks of their monastic vows, even if they may sometimes have been little more than a public posture. Nonetheless, Buddhist monastic culture had erected an institutional dynamic that spoke of the need for restraint from erotic behavior and aggression, and all the monks would have received instruction to that effect.

Yet there is no denying that modeling the new meditative practices after systems of political power was a perilous enterprise. Both the monastic engagement of the feudal world and the meditative engagement of its ideal were invitations to corruption by complicity. Most especially, the problem was that of capture. How often can a monk visualize himself as King of the World, erotic and powerful, without being captured by the fantasy of his own vision? When the new scriptures explicitly proclaim that the individual can become all-powerful in this one life, what perspective can be expected of a semiliterate monk from a small village that has just been burned and had its wells poisoned by the local warlord in a dispute over tribute? Faced with the burning of the library at Nālandā, would not the monks have wished for dominion and authority in their world?[158] What would the newer disciples of Karuṇāśrīmitra, the martyr of Somapura, have said after their master was burned to death and the monastery destroyed by the invading Baṅgāla army?[159] They would surely ask whether there were not some way to harness the power of Vajrapāṇi, the General of Secrets, to overcome these armies and to rectify the barbaric displays of inhumanity. In the process they would, as the *Mahākālatantra* teaches, try to use magic and visualization to engage in battle with the forces of evil and obtain success to rule the state.[160] Perhaps some Buddhists engaged the practice of maṇḍala and deity visualization in order to tame the fires burning in the time of the Kaliyuga, and some of them just as evidently became scorched in the heat of their own imagined realm.

CONCLUSION: ESOTERIC BUDDHISM AS SACRALIZED SĀMANTA FEUDALISM

Esoteric Buddhism coalesced in the special circumstances of the rise of sāmanta feudalism in the seventh century C.E., a rise that was eventually reflected in the new Buddhist terminology and ritual systems. The fact that the political environment providing the basic model for esoterism did not itself emerge until the late sixth to early seventh centuries assists the chronology of the mature esoteric movement. Reinforcing our temporal parameters are the appearances of Buddhists in non-Buddhist literature, the translation of esoteric works into Chinese, the testimony of Chinese monks, and the lack of any prior notice of the mature esoteric system before the seventh century. Thus the Buddhist tantric movement is a consequence of the new culture of military adventurism, which brought the apotheosis of kings and their maṇḍalas of vassals, with the concomitant feudalization of all forms of Hindu divinities.

Esoteric Buddhism, though, was not simply a reaction to the new environment, but stemmed from the palpable sense of institutional duress. The decline of guilds and international trade relations, the rise of militant Śaivism and its capacity to appropriate patronage, the decline of women's involvement in Buddhist praxis, and the loss of a specifically Buddhist intellectual center all set the institutions adrift. Institutional Buddhism responded by contracting into regions of strength and into edifices mimicking feudally grounded fortresses, which mirrored in legal behavior the activities of the kings they cultivated. Little wonder that the esoteric tradition should emulate in ritual form and ideological substance the most potent narrative of the period—becoming the Supreme Ruler of a circumscribed spiritual state. They imitated the structures and rites of those who were the first Lords of the Maṇḍalas, the petty lords and regional rulers of the newly empowered fiefdoms that gained power and authority as the old order eroded in the former centers of culture.

In this process, the decision systems had shifted along with the cultural landscape. Unlike the durable message evident in the introduction of Buddhism into such places as Gandhāra, early medieval Buddhists elected to substantially modify their message.[161] Among their reasons was a search for patronage by new class of rulers, a shift in perspective that paradoxically had more benefits in proselytization outside the borders of India than within it. Employing the hermeneutics of skillful means, to survive they must adapt, but in adapting they flirted with the forces that rendered them subordinate in the first place. Yet, as institutions with specific socialization goals and a highly structured corporate existence, these new grand monasteries had few alternatives. Once fully institutionalized, Indian esoteric Buddhist traditions appropriated the socialization process that brought a specific Buddhist valence and uniformity to the monastic personas. Their training conveyed a commonality to their experiences so that, irrespective of their backgrounds, the monks comfortably assumed the demeanor of the monastic regimen. From this point forward, North Indian monks envisioned themselves as rulers in the grand domains of their metaphorical spiritual states, embedded in a community with ritual systems that ensured their integration into their own society.

Thus institutional esoterism sought to sacralize observable reality, employing the techniques that had always been successful. Here, the Buddha was depicted as a king with a crown, clothed in all the ornaments of royalty. Here, the monks received the ritual of coronation and became divine in the process. Here, they envisioned the spiritual state filled with Buddhas and bodhisattvas, with worldly beings and families of divinities. Here, they acted as agents for the Dharma, for the law. They performed the ceremonies that—in their minds—would bring peace where there was war, wealth where there was poverty, control where there was chaos, and destruction to the enemies of religion. Yet, ironically, because Buddhist monks became enmeshed in the same web of relationships that defined the world of sāmanta feudalism, they came to be perceived as a weak imitation of the authentic imperial tradition, a system that had successfully subverted most forms of religion to its own naked purposes. In all these dynamics of medieval Indian culture, institutional esoterism played a part, even when marginalized by the structure of its own ethical ideals. Throughout the era, esoteric institutions continued to develop, stimulated by both a need for survival and a sustaining belief in their new self-representations.

We know little of the reception these texts found outside the monasteries in India. It is evident, however, that the maṇḍalas found in the institutional works were accepted and supported by the monarchs on the Indian borderlands, for they understood that Buddhist institutions had provided them with exactly the right combination of political and religious authority.[162] Coming from outside India, they and their representatives received from institutional esoterism some of its many virtues: access to the great intellectuals of the tradition, elaborate ritual systems, training in Indian monasteries, spells of undoubted power and potency, astrology, and medicine. All these topics found in the scriptures might be used in service to the authenticity of the monarch and his state. Buddhist monks were only too glad to initiate these non-Indian lords into the maṇḍalas of their scriptures, and the magic of Buddhist social symbiosis once again guaranteed monks a place at the table, even if so many of the tables were foreign.

5

Siddhas and the Religious Landscape

Riding on the best of buffaloes within the domains of the great forest tribes, he is ornamented with snakes and carries an iron vajra.

His hair colored ocher with bezoar and tied upwards in just the right way, with skulls around his head, let him apply ocher to his beard.

He exclaims the mantras HRĪḤ ṢṬRĪ, etc., brandishing his iron vajra.

This lion's roar should be done that way because it is the vajra practice of Yamāri.

And if he has developed the ability, let him enter a city playfully. In an auspicious dance, he sings "sweet confection" and other kinds of songs.

—*Kṛṣṇayamāri-tantra,* XI.9–12[1]

It might seem that the "Great Perfected" *(mahāsiddha)* of esoteric Buddhism collectively defeat the proposal that the Vajrayāna is the most feudalized form of Buddhism. Based on siddha images, it is questionable whether the Mantrayāna is actually constituted by those responding to the increasing importance of political systems and authority in the period around the death of Harṣa in 647 C.E. The siddhas, one may suppose, were unconcerned with allegiance of any variety, preferring the untrammeled existence of a psychic world in which ritual systems, social rules, lineage concerns, scriptural continuity, and the other paraphernalia of institutional Buddhism were simply jettisoned for personal liberation. Going naked along their own paths, devoted solely to their own subjective experiences, the siddhas—in this argument—represented a purity of religious expression devoid of scholastic hairsplitting or legalistic wrangling, which was so much the obsession of the great monasteries of the medieval period. The new variety of saint cannot have been on a continuum of sacrality with the rigidly observant arhat, the self-sacrificial bodhisattva, or even the monk employed in the mythology of institutional esoterism: he must have been above them. With their ornaments of human bone, carrying skullcaps and tridents, conquering demons, flying to the land of the ḍākinīs, copulating in graveyards, these personalities could only be associated with the heterodox Śaiva figures, like the Kāpālikas, the Pāśupatas, or analogous antinomian personalities.

Although the romanticism of these images—to some degree generated by and sustained within siddha hagiographical literature—might be briefly enjoyable, there can be no question that siddhas were not exclusively or even principally the self-absorbed saints represented in some materials. The engagement of these sources to date has been somewhat limited, with a tendency toward excessive reliance on the text of the *Caturaśītisiddhapravṛtti* (Lives of the Eighty-four Siddhas) ascribed to Abhayadattaśrī. Curiously, this emphasis has sometimes been accompanied by a concomitant denial that the behaviors described in that text or in the tantras closely associated with the siddhas could be taken literally. Such narratives must be symbolic and interpreted through the use of coded or "twilight" language *(sandhyābhāṣā)*. The overwhelming conclusion of these contradictory and confusing assessments is that the Buddhist siddhas were indeterminate saints occupying some indefinite space at some vague time.

Such depictions are most often the result of inattention to the available historical and archaeological records. Our sources indicate that, among other aspects, the siddhas were the form of Buddhist saint demonstrating the greatest diversity, occupying an extraordinary spectrum of activities and attitudes, even if their absolute numbers were probably rather modest at any one time. Though relatively few in number, they captured the imagination of Buddhist India and managed to generate a vast and sustaining literature.

This chapter examines the rise of noninstitutional Buddhist esoterism, which emerged by the early eighth century C.E. The focus here is the landscape of siddhas, by which is meant the ideological topography that these personalities inhabited in the fractious world of medieval India. They derived from the older model of siddhas found in political and romantic literature, at least beginning in the first few centuries of the common era. In their public personas, siddhas occupied a space between institutional esoterism and the larger world of Śaiva and Śākta personalities, especially the Śaiva movements of the Kāpālikas and the Pāśupatas. However, the first evidence for Buddhist siddhas occurs in the first decades of the eighth century, and it has strong continuities with the archetype of a sorcerer *(vidyādhara)*. For siddhas, the fundamental issue was the manner in which they may succeed to the powers accorded the sorcerers and, in the process, overcome the gods themselves. Because they drew from a very broad background, and as they did not rely on a specific educational and socializing institution, siddhas exhibited far greater variations in behavior than did either esoteric monks or Buddhist laymen adhering to the older bodhisattva model. Yet they had clear involvement with kings and courts, both personally (some were aristocrats) and mythically (as rulers of the sorcerers). This investigation includes an examination of the geography of the movement—both the imaginary geography of the "seats of power" and the real landscape of actual pilgrimage sites. Moreover, because they are so frequently referenced in siddha literature, siddha relationships with tribal and outcaste peoples are also considered.

SOME SIDDHA SOCIAL MODELS

The question of the origins and relations of both siddhas in general and Buddhist siddhas in particular has been taken up by many authors, but with less than satisfactory models proposed, primarily because their sociocultural matrices have not been sufficiently taken into account. Because siddhas exhibit a distinct continuity with non-Buddhist behaviors, they might be viewed as part of a larger field of Buddhist/non-Buddhist reciprocity, yet this has been a contested topic. In his general discussion of the appearance of non-Buddhist divinities in Buddhist maṇḍalas, for example, Ruegg has suggested that Buddhist esoterism generally employed certain elements of Indian religion. According to Ruegg, these are not taken from specific systems, but from the "pan-Indian religious substrate" of lore, from which all Indic religions draw their images.[2] This pan-Indic substrate is represented as a common store of identical formal structures that were employed for different functions in the various traditions, and Buddhists tended to include divine personalities from this religious substrate into their narratives or maṇḍalas as "worldly deities." So, although Śiva has a specific iconography, which may be employed in several different traditions, his function profoundly changes from one tradition to another. According to this model, the deities are not identified as specifically Śaiva or Vaiṣṇava but were taken without reference to their affiliation, and Ruegg is particularly doubtful about articulating a system of borrowing from one religion to another.

However, Sanderson, reviewing the origin of the Vajrayāna, was not entirely convinced by Ruegg's argument.[3] He takes some pains to point out that evidence is absent for a nonaffiliated religious system—all the personalities, both human and divine, are associated with specific institutionalized lineages and not simply free-floating forms. Whether the topic is the gods or the saints of the systems, they are represented within specific lineages and traditions. When Buddhist texts are concerned with theological objects, these come into view at specific locales and under sometimes peculiar circumstances, as shown below in the case of Heruka. Thus Sanderson properly moves the discussion from a proposition about religious icons to the analysis of specific religious agents.

Unhappily, Ruegg's model cannot entirely account for the spectrum of specifics, based on caste, gender, locale, affiliation, and other variables. It appears not entirely applicable, especially because of its postulation of a Platonic plane wherein resides the forms iterated in specific religious systems. His position seems analogous to Saussure's *langue/parole* model, wherein the entire potential of a language *(langue)* is never expressed in the particular speech of a person *(parole)*.[4] Because of their structuralist formulations, neither Saussure's nor Ruegg's models—and this is part of Sanderson's criticism—can easily take into account regional variation, incomprehensible idioms, place-specific identity, and the sudden emergence of a new prototype that overwhelms some parts of a religious system but not others.[5] Yet Sanderson's observation of the specificity of lineages seems also excessively reified, for it would be difficult from his model to determine whether there were unique local personalities or specific movements even within these broad heterodox groups.

In an entirely different direction, White postulated that human siddhas appropriated the designation "siddha" in order to emulate the behavior and to obtain the powers of their celestial heroes.[6] According to this line of reasoning, the celestial band lived on mountain peaks, and the earthly siddhas attempted to secure their services, their females, and—ultimately—their powers. Again we might wonder if this is not excessively reified. Whatever its applicability to other traditions, White's position does not accord well with the primary data on the Buddhist goal, which seem to speak of supremacy over the Vidyādharas (sorcerers, human or divine) rather than celestial siddhas. Certainly for Buddhists, human siddha behavior was not in imitation of the celestial Perfected, but sought to gain power through decidedly different means.

Since the term does not apply to Buddhist saints until the medieval period, we might look to non-Buddhist sources for some degree of inspiration, especially in view of the astonishing variation and vitality of Indian religion during the ancient and medieval eras.[7] For the present purposes, though, this discussion is limited to those non-Buddhist systems with an observable clergy or group identity, rather than unfocused popular movements. Buddhist documents consistently specify the interaction between Buddhists and others at this level—especially their involvement with Brahmans or Śaiva/Śākta ascetics. It has frequently been an object of scholarly consternation, for example, that Hsüan-tsang did not utter a word about the rise of the devotional *(bhakti)* movements, despite his travel around 642 C.E. through South India, where they clearly were the most vital force.[8] The probable answer to this anomaly is that Buddhist monks have seldom considered non-Buddhist popular religion a matter of concern: its doctrinal content is limited; it is noncontemplative; and it has no specific behavioral agenda, but predominantly relies on affective states, generally combined with song and dance. Devotees *(bhakta)* who fit into established patterns, viz. Śaiva *bhaktas*, the Buddhists tended simply to see as representing an older tradition. Hsüan-tsang and others were probably unaware that they were dealing with a new phenomenon developing in South India.

In distinction to popular devotional movements, the available evidence suggests that a contribution to siddha ideology derived from local, tribal, and outcaste groups existing in a fluid state outside the formal institutions of religious authority. At the beginning of the medieval period, India was only starting to encounter the full range of tribal cultures, local groups, autochthonous cults, site-specific divinities, and other phenomena. Indeed, the data available suggest that much of the prehistory of noninstitutional yogins dedicated to full-time praxis is messy, is not easily classified, and probably includes a plethora of lost systems, either group-based or totally personal *(svatantra)*. In the case of the designation "siddha," the title seems to progress through India by two primary means. First, the designation is appropriated by one group from another unrelated group, although their discontinuity is by no means certain. Second, related behaviors and identities develop between two or more closely patterned groups.

FIRST MOMENTS IN SIDDHA IDENTITY

Apparently the earliest Indian use of the term "siddha" to specify a successful group of saints is found in Jaina quarters and evinces only partial continuity with the Buddhist or Śaiva application. In terms of firm chronology, this is perhaps the easiest to specify, for the term is used in the homage at the beginning of the Hāthigumphā cave inscription of Khāravela, who is post-Mauryan and generally assigned to the second or first century B.C.E.[9] Inscribed in a cave on the Udayagiri hill north of Bhubaneswar in Orissa, the inscription simply begins with the homage to the arahants and the siddhas *(namo arahantānaṃ namo savasidhānaṃ)*. The nature of these siddhas is not specified, yet we have little reason to doubt that it indicates Jaina saints who became successful in their practices, but who were not identified with the other Jaina designations: arahant and Tīrthaṅkara.[10] The inscription does not appear to reference a classification of saints concerned with the accomplishments of magical powers *(siddhi)*, and we might recall that names from the early period included marks of success (such as Siddhārtha) without the supernatural connotation implied in the powers claimed by the medieval siddhas.

A different direction is found in the Mandasor stone inscription of Bandhuvarman, composed by the local poet Vatsabhaṭṭi and dated February–March of 474 C.E.[11] There, siddhas are described as among those who worship the sun and, specifically, those who propose to obtain magical powers *(siddhyarthin)*. The old solar cult was at one point quite widespread, and its association with power is noticeable even in the southern recension of the *Rāmāyana*, where Rāma is instructed by the Ṛṣi Agastya in a hymn to the sun, so as to gain its assistance in his contest with his archnemesis, the ten-headed demon king Rāvaṇa.[12] Various similar references to siddhas have caused Fleet and others—both ancient and modern—to identify a class of demigods or quasi-divine beings designated as "siddhas," and these were understood to be different from humans carrying the same name. Celestial siddhas became the stock in trade for many episodes in poetry, and such figures have become notorious for the amorous behavior exhibited between siddhas and their female companions.[13]

However, we need to acknowledge that the application of "siddha" to humans is well developed in early Indic political literature, an employment that suggests both the environment in which siddhas received patronage and the group to which the name may be legitimately applied. These many references call into question White's proposal that human siddhas modeled themselves after the celestial archetype. In particular, the first- to second-century *Arthaśāstra* specifies almost a dozen situations in which an individual might masquerade as a siddha using their specific practices to accomplish the ends of realpolitik. Some of the figures are called *siddhatāpasa*, the accomplished ascetic, and many of the citations depict them as skilled in magic *(māyāyogavid)*.[14] Agents of the state might be employed to impersonate such siddhas, using various devices to entrap criminals through the criminals' own spells, or to entice tribals to rebel against an adjacent state.[15] These agents could formulate real or bogus rituals—especially rites concerned with love, power, or money—and assassinate the king's enemies by infusing their magical concoctions with poison.[16] The *Arthaśāstra* proposes many deceptive activities to be employed exclusively in the destabilization of neighboring states, and these actions frequently involve agents posing as siddhas or other religious characters to lure monarchs to secluded spots while promising them wealth, horses, or sex, not necessarily in that order.[17] Those suspected of treason could be enticed into criminal complicity in the death of an adult or infant by a "siddha" (agent), who would lead that person to a burial site where money is found on a corpse. This money (placed beforehand on the corpse) would then be entrusted to the suspect, only to have him apprehended by the king's police officers later.[18] The king's revenue agents might also make use of the "siddha" subterfuge, by faking miraculous appearances of divinities and asking for donations to increase the king's revenues and, we suspect, to line their own pockets.[19]

Such activities are on a continuum with the behavior of other personalities claiming to obtain siddha status in Indian literature, most notably Viśvāmitra in the Vālmīki *Rāmāyana*. We may recall that Viśvāmitra becomes a siddha by performing sacrifice *(yajña)* at Siddhāśrama on the banks of the Kauśikī River, close to the Himālayas.[20] The *Rāmāyana* is explicit that the name of Viśvāmitra's residence comes from the identity of siddhas as "those who perform great ascetic practice."[21] Unfortunately, Viśvāmitra cannot complete the sacrifice because, each time he tries, demons of every description and of extraordinary strength displace the sages who assist him in the rite. Accordingly, he requests that the brothers Rāma and Lakṣmaṇa assist him in their protection of the ritual environment. Ultimately, Viśvāmitra accomplishes his goal—invincibility—and, having made the retreat title "residence of siddhas" *(siddhāśrama)* true in fact rather than in name only, he can go forth a siddha *(Rāmāyana,* I.30.14: *gamiṣyāmi siddhaḥ siddhāśramād aham).* This successful career is in accordance with images of siddhas in the approximately contemporary *Milindapañha* (Questions of the Indo-Greek King Menander). In this work, siddhas are noted for their capacity to "sing truth" *(siddhā saccam anugāyanti)*—that is, perform acts of truth *(saccakiriya).* By the power of their truth statements, siddhas make the rain fall, cause fire (the god Agni) to be turned back in its course, and even transform the dreadful Halāhala poison—which stained blue the throat of Śiva himself—into a medicinal antidote.[22]

Later literature expresses a continuity with the *Rāmāyana's* symbiosis between king and ascetic. Its most famous literary expressions are revealed in episodes about the ferocious ghoul *(vetāla)* rites conducted by evidently Śaiva figures, like those seen in such masterpieces as the *Harṣacarita* and the *Kathāsaritsāgara*. In the earliest of these, the mid-seventh-century *Harṣacarita*, the pattern is already well established.[23] The terrifying Bhairavācārya, with the assistance of Harṣa's legendary ancestor Puṣpabhūti, seeks to obtain success in the magical powers of the sorcerers/vidyādharas. He needs the king's strength and, to seduce him into assistance, equips the monarch with a charismatic sword named Aṭṭahāsa (Śiva's laugh) to overcome the demonic personality who will ultimately appear—the Nāga Śrīkaṇṭha. The ascetic, dressed in black, builds a fire in the mouth of a corpse on the cremation ground and summons the undead. After an epic struggle, the king defeats the demon with his bare hands, only to have the fiend disappear and the goddess Fortune (Śrī) appear on the blade of his sword. She bestows on Bhairavācārya the ornaments of the sorcerer/vidyādhara—special hair lock, diadem, pearl necklace, armlet, belt, hammer, and sword.[24] She also confers on Puṣpabhūti the magical property of a strong line of royal descendants, which eventually leads to the poet's own patron, the Emperor Harṣavardhana.

Literature from the eighth to the eleventh century, for example, the *Bṛhatkathāślokasaṃgraha*, the *Mālatīmādhava*, and the *Kathāsaritsāgara*, also mention cemetery rites to gain control over a ghoul or *vetāla*, who is the peculiar source for access to the divine realm of the Vidyādharas. All these works describe situations in which rituals are performed by ascetics of various stripes to gain power. Each ascetic apparently requires the extraordinary protection extended by a king or great warrior. In most of the stories the warriors guard the various directions, while in some of them the heroes are both the guardians and the intended victims. The kings protecting specifically evil siddhas are to be ultimately offered to the demon or divinity that will come out of the sacred circle. This latter plot twist was to become so popular that the story literature of the "twenty-five *vetāla* legends" *(vetālapañcaviṃśati)* was eventually to separate, so that the stories could be further elaborated using the king/siddha/vetāla interaction as a frame for the narratives.

In other literature, the evil siddha's cemetery rites are interrupted in their course. The earliest version of which I am aware is in the seventh-century *Avantisundarīkathā*, wherein the young prince Mantragupta intervenes on behalf of a damsel in distress, about to be sacrificed by a corrupt ascetic *(dagdhasiddha)*.[25] The clear expression of many of these romance novels is that the realm of the divine sorcerers *(vidyādhara)*, whose spells empower their thaumaturgical ability, is directly approached through the cremation and charnel grounds at the margins of civilization, wherein are found outcastes *(mātaṅga)* and tribal peoples.[26] The ethical nature of the siddhas attempting to secure these supernormal abilities is at best dubious, however, and at worst constitutes the most excessive form of criminal. Thus it takes a king or great warrior to ensure the stability of the law *(dharma)* in the face of such powerful and self-absorbed individuals.

ŚAIVA AND ŚĀKTA ASCETIC ORDERS

For Buddhists, the single most influential clerical development during the early medieval period was the rise of Śaiva/Śākta ascetic orders, an extension of the influence of South Indian patronage of Śaiva traditions and South India's intrusion into the north from the sixth century forward. This is not to say that all the Śaiva/Śākta orders were southern in origin or even that they experienced their greatest influence in the south. It is important to note, though, that even the northern denominations enjoyed heightened power and prestige because of the systematic preference for Śaivas in the courts of the Chāḷukyas, the Pallavas, and the Coḷas, among others. In part, their popularity stems from the capacity of Śaiva teachers to sacralize the behavior of the most bloodthirsty warlord—he was acting in the manner of Mahākāla (Great Death), a form of Śiva. Thus the vindication of military adventurism worked best with the Śaiva orders that came with a discourse of the legitimization of otherwise illegitimate conduct. Brahmanical authors of most of the *Dharmaśāstras* were not themselves enthusiastic about belligerence, and adventuristic monarchs frequently employed Brahmans for the development and authentication of orthodox activities while their self-indulgent behavior was left to the approval of Śaiva/Śākta ascetics.[27]

As compensation, these kings would build temples and monasteries *(maṭha)* for their ascetics and promote Śaiva/Śākta interests in the kingdom. Consequently, the early medieval period became the great era of Hindu temple building, and the majority of the temple complexes still standing—Bhubaneswar, Khajuraho, Jagreśwar, Aihole, Brahmaur, Baṭesarā, Alampur, to mention a few—had their foundations between the sixth and the ninth century. Many verifiable Śaiva/Śākta denominations became heavily patronized during this time, and we might wonder whether there was some coming and going of allegiance. It is probable that, while an ascetic might be concerned with Śākta cults at some times, he would be absorbed in specifically Śaiva rituals at others, for these two were not seen so entirely separate at the ascetic level as they appear in stable temple ritual venues. The discussion below concerns the Kāpālika, Kaula, and Lakulīśa Pāśupata denominations, for these are the three most observable in medieval literature, epigraphy, and archaeology, with the correspondingly greatest influence on Buddhist siddha practice.

The Kāpālikas were clearly the most notorious of the ascetic systems, having been roundly rebuked in much of dramatic literature and poetry for excesses of conduct, which included ritual intercourse and the sacramental ingestion of substances running the gamut from intoxicating to lethal.[28] They were continually accused—probably with intermittent correctness—of the ritualized slaughter of victims offered to goddesses such as Caṇḍikā, the deity Bhairava, or even local demons like the Vetālas. It is their sanguinary behavior that has reaped the greatest of opprobrium for the Kāpālikas, and their early mythology celebrates the mythic killing of the god Brahmā by Śiva in a fit of pique. Because Brahmā's skull attached itself to Śiva, the lord of the cemetery was required to engage in extensive penance to be freed of the adhesive cranium. Kāpālikas celebrated the penance of their deity by displaying several (Rāmānuja lists six) primary signs and two secondary indicators. Rāmānuja's six consist of a necklace *(kaṇṭhikā),* a neck ornament *(rucaka)*, a large earring *(kuṇḍala)*, a jewel in their hair *(śikhāmaṇi)*, ashes, and a sacred thread.[29] The two "secondary" indicators actually came to represent their defining characteristics: the possession of a skull (ostensibly a cranial cap for eating) and a type of slender staff called a *khaṭvāṅga.* This latter might be topped with a skull and hung with their small, double-headed drum *(ḍamaruka).* Kāpālikas were also known to carry a trident *(triśula)* in place of a *khaṭvāṅga.*

Part of the problem in identifying a Kāpālika is that none of these items by themselves authenticated an individual as a Kāpālika. Jewelry of various varieties, especially large, round earrings pierced through the cartilage of the ear, are noted for many of the ascetic traditions and were associated in literature with sorcerers *(vidyādhara).* Smearing oneself with ashes is ubiquitous among Śaivas and is certainly not even an exclusively ascetic practice. The use of staffs of various kinds—in association with types of begging bowls—is noted with most ascetic traditions. Sanderson has indicated that various varieties of Śaiva traditions also carried staffs with skulls on them.[30] Indeed, the carrying of staffs was not particularly Śaiva, since it is enjoined in the *Samnyāsa Upaniṣads* and found among other groups as well. Even the Buddhist clergy have used their own version of mendicants' staffs *(khakharaka).*[31] Although carrying a skull bowl might seem to be the defining characteristic of a Kāpālika, its entire mythology comes from the literature of penance in the Dharmaśāstras. Manu, for example, indicates that the use of a skull bowl or a corpse's head as a flag is not simply enjoined for killers of Brahmans, but might be given as a twelve-year penance *(prāyaścita)* for those who had killed a fetus, a sacrificer, or a woman who is newly purified after cessation of her menstrual period. It might even be given as a penance for one who has perjured himself in court or opposed his teacher, or who has killed a woman or a friend.[32] The legal tradition speaks of the practice's *temporary* nature—that is, it was done for a specified length of time in response to a specific act. Indeed, the difficulty of tracing Kāpālika traditions outside of a few texts could be inherent in the ephemeral nature of their behavior.

Given these concerns, it is unsurprising that medieval Indians expressed bafflement in separating Kāpālika from Kaula systems, as seen in a commentary to Kṛṣṇamiśra's farce/allegory, the *Prabodhacandrodaya*.[33] Both traditions have a heavy Śākta component, and both have proved difficult to differentiate in their practices, being primarily distinguished by internal self-definition rather than any categorical distinction of behavior. Sanderson has identified, for example, the *Jayadrathayāmala* as a lengthy Kāpālika scripture, but it is clear that the greatest of the Kaulas, Abhinavagupta (c. 975–1050 C.E.), accepts the authority of this work as well.[34] Perhaps the best indication of the public parameters of the Kaula ideal is summed up by a well-known, scurrilous piece of Prakrit poetry from Rājaśekhara's *Karpūra Mañjarī*. There, the Kaula antihero of the play, Bhairavānanda, delivers a half-parody of his own practice:

> I don't know mantra from tantra,
> Nor meditation or anything about a teacher's grace.
> Instead, I drink cheap booze and enjoy some woman.
> But I sure am going on to liberation, since I got the Kula path.
> *What's more,*
> I took some horny slut and consecrated her my "holy wife."
> Sucking up booze and wolfing down red meat,
> My "holy alms" are whatever I like to eat,
> My bed is but a piece of human skin.
> Say, who wouldn't declare this Kaula Religion
> Just about the most fun you can have?[35]

If the Kaula system has given trouble to those wishing to differentiate it from the Kāpālikas, the entire edifice of "tantrism" has been difficult to separate from tribal religions, for several reasons. First, tribal systems represented the historical "Other" for much of Indian religion, orthodox and heterodox alike. Second, tribal systems engaged in blood sacrifices, including human sacrifice, so those denominations relieving ennui with the beheading of their fellow man (Kāpālikas) were poorly distinguished from the tribal systems. For example, Vākpatirāja's *Gaüḍavaho,* written 730–750 C.E., describes as a Kaula the tribal woman engaged in human sacrifice to the goddess.[36] Although this may have indicated a local usage or may have meant that they belong to the family of that place, most likely these were identified in the poet's (and public's) mind with all other sanguinary Śākta practitioners, irrespective of ethnicity or religious affiliation.

Archaeological findings may assist here, and Dehejia has studied temples to the cult of the yoginīs, groups of feminine goddesses—traditionally sixty-four in number—to which unique circular and rectangular temples have been erected.[37] Dehejia has located the remains of fourteen of these intriguing sites (see Table 5.1) and has proposed that several more are capable of being adduced from the literature and probable finds, but in the face of a paucity of evidence they must remain conjectural.[38] All of these are medieval (ninth- to fourteenth-century) sites. Dehejia contends that all these temples were governed under the Kaula system. Thus she maintains that they represented the systematic practice of sexual congress at the sites as offerings to the yoginīs and that such practices did not implicate human sacrifice.

TABLE 5.1 Yoginī Temples

Kañcīpuram
Khajuraho
Dudahi (by Lalitpur, Madhya Pradesh)
Naresar (by Gwalior)
Badoh (by Lalitpur, Madhya Pradesh)
Bheraghat (by Japalpur)
Mitauli (by Gwalior)
Ranipur-Jharial (Orissa)
Rikhiyan (Banda District, Uttar Pradesh)
Lokhari (Banda District, Uttar Pradesh)
Shahdol #1 (Shahdol District, Madhya Pradesh)
Shahdol #2
Hinglajgadh (Gandhi Sagar)
Hirapur (by Bhubaneswar)

It is difficult to follow Dehejia on her Kaula connections, even if she has done great service in identifying and illustrating these sites. Kaula manuscripts certainly discuss the cultus of the sixty-four (or eighty-one) yoginīs, but we have not found any Kaula text that mentions these kinds of sites in their pilgrimage guides (*pīṭhanirṇaya*) or that discusses their use. Beyond the fact that most Kaula works appear composed after the sites were constructed, there are problems in assuming that the smallest of these, Hirapur, could physically accommodate the Kaula cultic activity. There is certainly little enough room in this tiny hypaethral temple (Figure 6), which measures only about twenty-five feet in inside diameter, and group sexual congress in the manner described would appear difficult because of its physical limitations.[39] Furthermore, there

FIGURE 6 Interior of Hirapur Yoginī Pīṭha in Orissa.
Ronald M. Davidson

is no sexual representation at all in any of the sculptural programs associated with the sites, although erotic motifs have been seen on contemporary temples from the same geographical area.[40] In reality, the primary activity depicted at these sites—beyond the figures of the yoginīs—is the display of severed heads (Figure 7), indicating that the sanguinary rites were probably the principal activity practiced. The location of these temples in areas dominated by tribal peoples that were involved in sanguinary rituals suggests that they were constructed with a similar ritual in mind. The major problem is a lack of evidence for undomesticated tribal peoples building in stone, even if the yoginī temple at Khajuraho was identifiably the product of a branch of the Gond tribe.

We also have evidence of other temples in which the representation of yoginīs has continued: the Causathyayoginī mandirs in Banaras and Ujjain, the Siddhbhadra mandir in Maṇḍi (Himachal Pradesh), the Bābā koṭ Mandir in the Damdama Palace in Maṇḍi. In addition, yoginīs are interpreted as part of the sculptural program in the Śaktidevī Mandir at Chattrarhi (Himachal Pradesh) by those in the village. With the exception of the Śaktidevī Mandir, which is not clearly yoginī in execution, the others are from the seventeenth century or later. In the two Mandi temples, the yoginīs are represented by sim-

FIGURE 7 Yoginī from Hirapur displaying human sacrifice.
Ronald M. Davidson

ple slabs of stone with sixty-four pairs of footprints. Because of their simplicity, there are doubtless many others in North India and the Deccan that I have not noted. These sites are not evidently Kaula, and Dehejia maintains that the yoginī cult became separated from the Kaula practice because of Muslim influence, a curiously modern hermeneutic of foreign pollution. Early medieval inscriptions about the construction of temples associated with yoginīs, such as the Siyān inscription of Nayapāla or Udayāditya's Mominābād inscription, seem to have escaped Dehejia's notice.[41] In tone and content they are similar to the much earlier (424–425 C.E.) Gaṅgdhār Stone Inscription of Viśvavarman, which declared the construction of a "ferocious dwelling, filled with ḍākinīs" *(ḍākinīsamprakīrṇam | veśmātyugram)*.[42]

Perhaps the most widespread and important development in early medieval ascetic orders, however, has been understudied and underemphasized.[43] The rise and spread of the Lakulīśa Pāśupata system of Śaivism appears to be the earliest organized Hindu ascetic response to the śramaṇa systems of Buddhism, Jainism, and cognate traditions. While modern historians have focused on the Daśanāmi organization of Śaṅkarācārya and his followers—with its four leaders in the four directions of India—there can be little doubt that the Pāśupatas were far more successful and widely distributed during the sixth to the tenth centuries. Regardless of whether they were founded by an individual of disputed dates (perhaps second to fifth centuries C.E.) named Lakulīśa, the Pāśupatas followed a form of religious behavior attributed to him as the purported author of the *Pāśupata-sūtra.*

There, the Pāśupata is enjoined to follow five levels of practice *(sādhana):* In the first, he emulates the distinguished state (with normative Śaiva appearance, *vyaktāvasthā),* wherein the normative ascetic practice of a Śaiva in a monastery is expected; thus they were to inhabit temples and conform to rules. In the second, the yogin conforms to the undistinguished state (without a Śaiva appearance, *avyaktāvasthā),* in which the follower acts in a manner calculated to reap ridicule; here they were to act insane in public and court dishonor. In the third, the Pāśupata cultivates the stage of victory *(jayāvasthā),* during which he achieves victory over the senses; here they were to dwell in empty caves and contemplate Paśupati through muttering mantras. In the fourth, the yogin achieves the stage of severing *(chedāvasthā),* in which he severs the root of defilement in the world; here they were to dwell in cemeteries while recollecting Rudra. In the fifth and final stage *(niṣṭhāvasthā),* Pāśupatas were to dwell in Rudra while enjoying his grace, concluding the process of ending suffering.[44] Of these, the second is exceptional and distinctly Pāśupata, since it involves seeking unmerited social disapproval, so that those in the immediate environment are tricked into their vocalization of their moral outrage by the Pāśupata yogin. Since the Pāśupata is only imitating disreputable behavior—for example, behaving like a dog—the castigation is unmerited and the yogin accordingly is relieved of previous negative karma, which now passes onto the unwary critic. The entire system is a response to the marked proclivity of high-caste India to favor public confrontation and censorious remarks.

In fact, possibly the earliest Śaiva mention of the stage of "siddha" as a goal is found in the *Pāśupatasūtra*—perhaps a second- to third-century text—ascribed to Lakulīśa. There a *siddhayogin* is described as one who is not touched (literally smeared) by either ethical action or guilt.[45] This refers to the result of the practice of temporarily courting disfavor, for which the siddha was not considered at fault in passing his negative karma to his critics. Like so many other similar adjectives in Sanskrit (e.g., Buddha), siddha here is used as an adjective (accomplished) but moving toward becoming a title (Perfected), similar to the early employment of *siddhatāpasa* in the *Arthaśāstra*, and these texts apparently were composed within a few centuries of each other. Just as evidently, the *Pāśupatasūtra* simply justifies the behavior of siddhas with a hermeneutic of "higher purpose," which is very familiar to esoteric exegesis, whether Śaiva or Buddhist.

There can be little doubt that the Pāśupatas were extraordinarily successful in associating themselves with powerful patrons. The appendix contains a list of the probable sites I have been able to identify from published materials by archaeologists, architectural and art historians, based on the presence of Lakulīśa images (Figure 8) or of inscriptions. Certainly there are more sites that have not been so identified, and the list is more representative than exhaustive, but as yet there is no systemic survey of Pāśupata sites in India. Earlier sites have been claimed, especially the third-century Caturmukha-liṅga at Nand and the Mathura pillar of Candragupta II. Both of these, like all the other earlier images and possible sites, are problematic and dubious. In the latter case, the 380 C.E. Mathura pillar is the record of a dedication to a teacher of Māheśvaras, a certain Uditācārya who is descended from a Kuśika, and depicts a figure holding a club. Some historians have jumped to the conclusion that this depicts Lakulīśa and that Kuśika is the famous disciple of his mentioned in later inscriptions. Unfortunately, the pillar mentions neither Lakulīśa nor Pāśupatas, and the iconography of the club-wielding figure is fairly different from known Lakulīśa representations.

However, I cannot confidently declare that every site in the appendix actually represents an edifice of Pāśupata affiliation. It is clear, for example, that temples from Bhubaneswar to Narayanapura, including Mukhalingam and

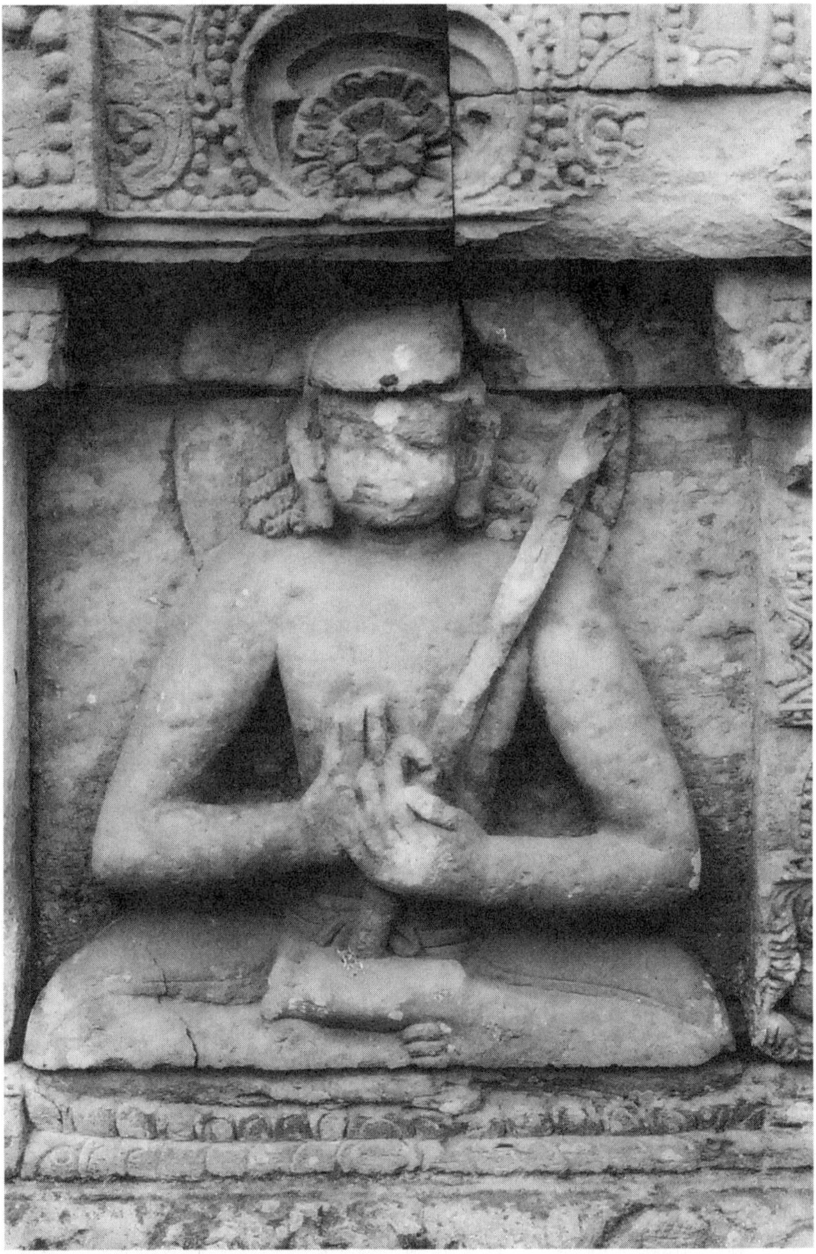

FIGURE 8 Lakulīśa from Paraśurāmeśvara Temple. Bhubaneshwar, Orissa, seventh century. *Ronald M. Davidson*

Jayati, have been subject to broadly similar canons of iconography in the selection of Lakulīśa for one of the standard figures placed in niches. This activity carries over into decidedly non-Pāśupata temples in some areas, and it might be noted that the Mālādevī temple in Gyaraspur (Vidisha District, Madhya Pradesh) is a Jaina institution sporting a Lakulīśa sculpture. For our purposes, though, it is sufficient to see that such representations are unlikely in the absence of Pāśupata activity in the immediate neighborhood, and—short of an epigraph—there is as yet no way to determine the relationship between the presence of Lakulīśa on a temple and Pāśupatas in the courtyard. Yet some measure of their zealous missionary activity does exist since, even beyond India, the Pāśupatas were the first non-śramaṇa ascetic system to challenge Buddhist proselytism of non-Indian peoples. By the seventh century, Pāśupata teachers had been able to secure a place for themselves in the court of Bhavavarma II, and Sanskrit epigraphs for the next two centuries note the importance of this form of Śaivism in Cambodia.[46]

We might reflect on the contrast between sites associated with Lakulīśa and, presumably, the Pāśupatas, on one hand, and those associated with Kāpālikas or Kaulas, on the other. Whereas we have *many* representations of Lakulīśa—often associated with his disciples—we have very few of Kāpālika teachers, and these are found mostly in Bhubaneswar or Khajuraho. Even then, as in the case of the Kāpālika depicted on the Tāleśvara mandir in Bhubaneswar, they might be represented as in attendance to the Lakulīśa image. It is possible that the image of Śiva as the prototypical penitent begging with a skull bowl *(bhikṣāṭanamūrti)* represents the presence of Kāpālikas, but it is difficult to say, since this legend is so strongly associated with Purāṇic literature that has no direct relationship to the most extreme sect of Śaivism. If anything, the Purāṇas have come to represent much of Pāśupata teaching, and it is clear that many of the great Purāṇas associated with Śiva have espoused the Pāśupata dualistic perspective on the nature of the god of yogins. Thus, while the Kāpālikas became well distributed in dramatic literature as the villain of choice, the Pāśupatas certainly became the most widely spread Hindu ascetic tradition. They offered a celibate challenge to the missionary Buddhists and supported Brahmanical traditions of caste and the subordination of women. Pāśupatas, moreover, appeared to have introduced dramatic conventions into temple cultus, and Pāśupata teachers were noted for their virtuosity in both vocal music and dance. The espousal of their perspective in the great literary productions of early medieval Hinduism, the Purāṇas, served to solidify their popular position as the most important and best organized of the Śaiva ascetic lineages.

MARGINAL SIDDHA TOPOGRAPHY

Thus the literary and epigraphic evidence suggest that the term "siddha" indicated a spectrum of religious practices and related behaviors in premedieval and medieval India. Much of the conduct may be ascetic *(tapas)* in pursuit of personal dominion, either over karmic impediments (as the Jaina) or over other groups (as in most traditions). None of these narratives necessarily involve cults to quasi-divine siddha figures who enjoy residence in a realm beyond the senses and above the clouds, although divine goals appear from time to time primarily under the rubric of Vidyādhara, rather than siddha. Instead the sources reveal a subculture of individuals whose apparent purpose is to gain power or authority and to provide services of a dubious ethical nature to kings, generals, and councilors in search of dominion, gifts, lucre, or women of easy virtue. The services include prophecy, spirit possession, demonic control, love potions, wealth generation, magical killing or actual murder, and a host of other practices that do not entail the supermundane culture of liberation. We get no sense that they are necessarily involved in any specific cultus to Śiva, Buddha, Viṣṇu, Devī, Sūrya, or any other single transcendent or pan-Indic divinity, although any of these may appear associated with them. Rather, their chosen objects of ritual propitiation are the demons *(rākṣasa)*, ghosts *(piśāca)*, [un]dead *(preta)*, tree spirits *(yakṣa/yakṣī)*, and ghouls *(vetāla)* of the charnel grounds, the forest, and the periphery of the kingdom. Beyond their exotic appearances before their patrons in the court, the siddhas are commonly associated with criminals *(māṇava)*, tribal peoples *(āṭavī)*, alchemists *(dhātuvādin)*, dramatic troupes *(nārtikas)*, and spies. In this sense, the category of "siddha" is the logical consequence of a civilization whose medieval expression is a concern for (and sometimes obsession with) status, hierarchy, political power, religious authority, and personal indulgence. Accordingly, the goal of turning into a siddha frequently becomes the aspiration of those excluded from status and hierarchy, either by birth or by accident.

This is not to say that these siddhas did not have an idea about their own religious affiliations, and no data support the model that siddhas represented a modern, nonsectarian, quasi-Unitarian idea of religion as extrapersonal and transcultural. Such figures, even if they occasionally change their religious identities, often support a vociferous allegiance while they are members of one group or another. If we were to draw similarities (which I believe we might), siddhas were often contentiously in support of their respective factions of the moment—Śaiva, Bauddha, Vaiṣṇava, Kaula, Jaina, Saura, tribal, or caste-based. Their individual allegiances should not be underestimated, and the tantras contain much strong and potentially lethal polemics. Even when tolerance of other traditions is espoused, the evidence suggests that personal validation comes through fidelity to the religious lineage, and the (most often male) yogin attains his accomplishment by virtue of his dedication to the opportunistic use of others for his own benefit.

That opportunism also makes the siddha in turn the object of devotion and the source of protection, since the power of the siddha (unencumbered by impersonal ethical standards) might be turned to the benefit and protection of others, particularly those sharing a local or ethnic affiliation. Because of their special capacity over ghosts and other spirits, siddhas have become the protectors of choice against the diseases inflicted by all the ghoulish phenomena of Indian folklore. Both current and historical practice have emphasized the relationship of saints, amulets, and the protection from disease, as well as bringing general auspiciousness to locales. In many places in North India, the association of several diseases—particularly malaria, understood as a disease of "fever"—with ghostly phenomena makes the protection of siddhas especially compelling.[47] Historically, siddhas have assisted the diagnosis of diseases and provided solutions to local difficulties by means of using young children (especially virgin girls: *kumārī)* as subjects in spirit possession *(āveśa),* practices already described in texts attributed to Amoghavajra in the eighth century.[48] Siddhas thus used children as mediums for the control, direction, and subjugation of disease-bearing ghosts.

Especially during the early medieval era, "siddha" became an element in personal names. Such a use reflects the proclivity of Indians to appropriate powerful and sacred designations for personal protection, benefit, or emulation. These names are particularly evident for patrons, workmen, or scribes featured in epigraphs. Moreover, they reverse the earlier use of "siddha" as an adjective (e.g., Siddhārtha) to a noun in names like Sanasiddha—perhaps meaning Primal Siddha—the husband of the Buddhist laywoman who endowed a series of offerings in 450–451 C.E. in a Sāñchī stone inscription.[49] Similarly, a 1204 C.E. inscription from the Kangra Valley temple of Baijnath indicates that one of the members of the family was a certain merchant Manyuka, the son of Siddha *(siddhaputra).*[50] Other names reflect the disposition of medieval Prakrit to contract an honorific suffix, -pāda to -pa/pā, a usage seen in Buddhist rendering as well. Thus the 946 C.E. Partabgarh Inscription, which records the gifts of various fields and endowments to the use of one or more temples, is inscribed by Siddhapa, the son of Satya.[51] Likewise, the Śujunīdevī Bust *(mohrā)* of the Nirmand temple of Paraśurāma in Himachal Pradesh records its manufacture in 1026 C.E. by Siddhapa, evidently a skilled brass- and bronzesmith.[52] It is interesting to note the social reality of these individuals

FIGURE 9 Siddh Śrī Bābā Bālak Nāth of Himachal Pradesh. New Delhi street shrine, c. 1985. *Ronald M. Davidson*

bearing the designation siddha; apparently, they were not driven by the normative Brahmanical aesthetic, which abhors physical labor. Their name designations evidently seek to attribute to the bearer an authenticity derivative from the saints, before whose power and sanctity they stand in awe.

The eventual disposition of the siddha paradigm is found in various areas of modern India, and I am particularly familiar with the cultus of the "sidhs" of Himachal Pradesh. Sidhs—the modern, North Indian vernacular rendering of siddhas—are unexceptionally understood to be saints who have mastered the great powers, although a great many of these "saints" are entirely mythic.[53] More to the point, however, is the use to which Sidhs are put in Himachal Pradesh, such as the important figures of Bābā Bālak Nāth or Bābā Deot Sidh. While the former is illustrated figuratively in Figure 9, the latter primarily "is represented throughout Kangra by a square stone upon which the image of two feet has been carved," according to Campbell, although I have seen such footprints elsewhere in North India. Campbell indicates that "his domain is particularly human fertility, cow's milk, and general health, i.e., protection from attacks by ghosts and evil spirits. For this last purpose there are special amulets (called *asinghi)* which are worn by devotees and put on children, often containing an appropriately blessed and dedicated written mantra."[54] Other sidhs' footprints are ubiquitously observable in Himachal Pradesh, the Punjab, Rajasthan, Gujarat, and Uttar Pradesh. Sidhs may also be called Birs (hero: Sanskrit, *vīra)* as well and alternatively celebrated with conical vermilion mounds that were one to two meters high; sometimes a mask or bust *(mohrā)* representing the sidh is placed on the mound during festivals.[55] Both the footprints and masks have become the reference markers for the intersection of folk art, sedentary tribal communities, saint's cults, amulet forms, and oral literature.

Some sidhs, however, are represented with a well-developed iconography, and elaborate hagiographical or mythic cycles of literature coalesce around their frequently humorous activity.[56] One of my favorite is Bābā Koṭ, the sidh of the Damdama palace in the old kingdom of Maṇḍi in Himachal Pradesh and the protector of the quasi-nomadic Gaddi tribal peoples who form much of the demographic base of the area.[57] Bābā Koṭ, whose name means "Father Fort," appears to be an entirely mythic synthesis of real siddhas and has become the god/saint mediating between the people of the region and their future fortune or luck. His oral literature represents him as habitually traveling with his comic sidekick Narsingh, and their statues currently reside in the temple on the upper story of the Damdama palace, which was built in the seventeenth century by Suraj Sen, king of Maṇḍi. The two have become the protagonists for an entire series of Gaddi tribal legends and ballads, in which the valor and bravery of Bābā Koṭ is set against the comic antics of his friend. Bābā Koṭ is depicted as a divine Gaddi Śaiva saint *(bīrbābā)*, with a crown on his head, a trident on one arm, and a skull in his hand; a snake hangs around his neck, along with a garland of skulls. In immediate proximity is a circular stone with sixty-four tiny pairs of footprints representing the yoginīs. He smokes a hookah while not on errantry, can be placated by offerings of marijuana or liquor, and may be visited on selected days of the week. In return, Bābā Koṭ guides people who have lost their path (literally and figuratively) and keeps ghosts at bay, ensuring the health of the retinue of the palace.

RELIGIOUS RELATIONS: THE AGONISTIC LANDSCAPE

The clear Buddhist appropriation of non-Buddhist designations and practices appears to reflect the adventurism of the medieval Indian world, rather than the ecumenical atmosphere of recent Euro-American discourse. Our evidence suggests that all the religious traditions—Buddhist siddhas not the least—arrogated others' religious activities when they appeared popular in court or on the street. This sometimes surreptitious appropriation was born not from respect for the religious competitors but, rather, from a sense of urgency in the face of potential extinction in the fluid medieval environment. Yet our investigation of such practices is somewhat hampered by the conflicting claims of modern authors writing about the medieval dynamic. Some historians have proposed that India was always a land of religious toleration, as seen in the proclivity of kings and counselors to patronize multiple religious traditions.[58] As evidence of this, we are informed that this broad liberal toleration is to be found in *Bhagavadgītā*, IX.23, which proclaims:

> Even all those devoted to other divinities, making their offerings, filled with faith—
> They are all worshiping only me, Kaunteya, but just not in exactly the right way.[59]

Perhaps somewhat occluded in the discussion is an alternate reading. This verse is actually a recipe for ignoring the content of other religious traditions (since the correct way of worship is Vaiṣṇava) and seizing their sites of worship (since the real god is Kṛṣṇa). Instead of being an affirmation of liberal values, statements like this raise a question as to whether models proposing a benign syncretism in fact account for the opportunistic and agonistic appropriation of rituals, organization, sites, and doctrines from other religious systems. Such acts would be done for the purpose of success in the face of religious competition for status, patronage, and resources. Fortunately, developments in historical writing in the past few decades have made the unsupportable ecumenical position much rarer, with a gratifying increase in the understanding of actual religious relations.[60]

In fact, our documents about the religious traditions from this period, like many of our epigraphs, reflect a range of attitudes toward other religious systems, with mutual antagonism the most frequent posture. Relations in South India, with its affluence and position as the source of many religious movements, appear to have set the stage. As Stein observes:

> During the seventh and eighth centuries, the tolerant relations among religious sects in South India had clearly come to an end. Mahendravarman I persecuted Saivites until his conversion; then he turned on Jainas. Later, the Saivite saint Sambandar who converted the Pandyan ruler, is celebrated in an annual festival at Minaksi temple of Madurai which commemorates the impalement of 8,000 Jaina heads at the young saint's urging. Still later, in the eighth century, Nandivarman II Pallavamalla, an ardent Vaisnavite, carried out persecution of Jains and Buddhists, and his contemporary, the Vaisnavite hymnist Tirumangai is said to have plundered the Buddhist vihara at the town of Nagapattinam using the golden image to finance the construction of walls around the principal shrine in Srirangam and other benefices.[61]

Instances of mutual suspicion and hostility could be multiplied ad infinitum, although most did not appear to result in such lethal outcomes. Yet Buddhists were sometimes themselves the recipients of homicidal action. Oriya literature reports one instance of the slaughter of more than six hundred Buddhists during the time of the Somavaṃsīs and the murder of others under the reign of Choḍagaṅgadeva.[62] Just as clearly, not all felt such great antipathy toward other systems of devotion, and we do find glimmerings of a consideration of others' traditions from time to time, although they are decidedly a minority voice in the period.[63] Political involvement may have been a factor as well, for the patronage of many kings toward multiple religious traditions could be viewed in part as an attempt to keep them all beholden to the ruler—and divided from one another—rather than a dedicated catholicity among Indian monarchs.

Buddhists generally were not much better at ecumenical graciousness than others. Granoff has pointed to references that appear generous to others' rituals, but in the same manner as in the *Bhagavadgītā:* others' rituals are true because they were really pronounced by the/a Buddha or bodhisattvas.[64] There are several instances of lesser acceptance, usually along the lines that even a Tīrthika's mantras can be acceptable, so long as they are done in a Buddhist manner or before Mañjuśrī or some other Buddha/bodhisattva. Allowance is made for the otherwise morally challenged, as well. Some siddha materials state that success will come even to those without consecration or to murderers, to those committing the five sins without expiation, to eaters of meat and fish, to those attached to liquor and sex, to those with "vows of denial" *(nāstikavratin),* and so on, if only they will follow some specific path.[65] We also find various admonitions not to disparage either one's own or another's tradition, expressed as the standard esoteric vow to avoid such behavior.[66] However, the tone of such expressions is frequently guarded and indicative that relations with other traditions were often difficult.

Conversely, Buddhist siddha literature is replete with castigations of those outside the Buddhist fold *(tīrthika).* For example, the *Vajrapañjara* includes the following statement.

> The Lord replied, "We cultivate in the mind the indivisibility of emptiness and compassion. This is called the doctrine of the Buddha, the Dharma and the Saṃgha. Concentration is known as disputing with Tīrthikas, rooting out those who dispute with you, and firmly announcing the texts of one's own school.[67]

We also find the denial that the gods are correct objects of worship. As Tilopa sings in his *dohā.*

> Brahma, Viṣṇu, Maheśvara. Hey, bodhisattva! bodhisattva! Do not
> worship these gods!
> Don't make offerings to the gods, or go to the external places of
> pilgrimage!
> There's no liberation in offertories to these deities.[68]

Even more aggressive are statements about the use of magic to restrain or destroy those of other paths. For example, the *Guhyasamāja tantra* states,

> Now, as to the concentration named the "vajra that paralyzes all the non-Buddhist teachers":

> One meditates on [Vajradhara] with the visage of the Wrathful, and all [his retinue] at the point of a three pronged vajra, like the King of Mountains, on the head of the enemy.
>
> Even if this enemy could paralyze the Army of the Buddha, he will die, have no doubt.[69]

These kinds of statements are found in several places in the literature, including in the *Vajramahābhairava-tantra*.[70] Consistently, we see a perceived need to formulate a defense of the Dharma that takes into account the aggressive action of the opponents, whoever they might be. One of the more interesting—not to say disturbing—aspects of this defense is the aggressive affirmation of the Buddha's Army *(buddhasainya)* as a rather consistent theme. Whatever this means, and the commentators are not very forthcoming, the Buddhist siddha literature begins to include the conception of an organized militant response on behalf of the Buddhadharma.[71] Visible in the hagiographic literature are several stories, such as those about the siddhas Virūpa or Kāṇha, relating accounts of the destruction of non-Buddhist religious sites, ostensibly in response to the well-authenticated attacks on Buddhist institutions.[72] Archaeology occasionally verifies such records with discoveries of the Buddhist appropriation of others' sacred edifices—such as the Soro liṅgam inscribed with the classic Buddhist statement of "those elements . . . " *(ye dharmāḥ. . .*).[73] Such examples are far less obvious than the reverse, however, and the destruction or appropriation of Buddhist statuary and sites are encountered more frequently.

BUDDHIST SIDDHAS AND THE VIDYĀDHARAS

As discussed above, medieval literature, such as the *Harṣacarita*, declares the goal of many non-Buddhist siddhas to be ascension to the realm of the Vidyādharas (Sorcerers). This is done through cemetery rituals said to confer the powers and signs of this class of beings—the special hair lock, diadem, pearl necklace, armlet, belt, hammer, and sword (Figure 10). Curiously, though, Buddhist literature is arguably the earliest to discuss the Vidyādharas at all, and this designation is applied to those who manipulate incantations *(vidyā)* for the purposes of personal power and gratification.[74] For example, in the *Śārdūlakarṇāvadāna*, a text composed in the early centuries of the common era, an outcaste or tribal woman *(mātaṅgī)* is described as a great sorceress *(mahāvidyādharī)* when she casts a love spell to cause the Buddha's cousin, Ānanda, to fall hopelessly in love with her

FIGURE 10 Vidyadhara from Nalanda, flying with emblematic sword in hand. Vedibandha of north face of temple site 2, seventh century. Granite.
Photo courtesy of the American Institute of Indian Studies

daughter.[75] The *Ratnaguṇasañcaya-gāthā,* the early, versified form of the *Prajñāpāramitā* (Perfection of Insight) literature, relates that a bodhisattva is like a sorcerer *(vidyādhara),* for both of them can do what others cannot. Whereas the bodhisattva situates himself in the realm of emptiness beyond existence and nonexistence, the sorcerer may fly up into the empty sky like a bird or cause blossoms to appear out of season.[76] Elsewhere, Mahayanist literature describes yogins or bodhisattvas who may be Vidyādharas and places them in the company of siddhas and physicians.[77] Thus siddhas—like sages (ṛṣi), Vidyādharas and other saintly individuals—became located in both mythic celestial and mundane human realms: in the sky, on mountains, in caves and forests, in cemeteries, and at the margins of civilization.[78]

Traces of these issues appear in the earliest Buddhist use I have encountered that identifies the Buddha himself as one who is perfected and a sorcerer, as well as a physician. In the *Varṇārhavarṇastotra* of the early second-century poet Mātṛceta, who employed a wide field of metaphors for his paeans to the Buddha, the poet appropriates these terms:

Homage to you,
Who have eliminated the disease of every defilement,
Who have removed every arrow [of ignorance],
Who is a perfected sorcerer *[siddhavidyādhara]*,
Who is the greatest of physicians.

Varṇārhavarṇastotra, II.33[79]

Here, I have translated *siddha-vidyādhara* as an adjective and a noun, as I believe was the usage of Mātṛceta's period. However, the late tenth–early eleventh-century Tibetan translator Rinchen Sangbo and his Indian Paṇḍita Padmākara understood the compound as two nouns, indicating that the Buddha was both siddha and sorcerer *(rigs sngags 'chang ba grub pa po)*. Their interpretation reveals the evolution of the category siddha from adjective to noun. Perhaps most interesting, however, is that this early invocation demonstrates the durable association of terms for siddhas, sorcerers, magicians, and physicians throughout Buddhist literature. This association is evident from the hagiography of the Kuchean Fo T'u-teng (active 310–349 C.E.), through the late fourth-century *Bodhisattvabhūmi*, and into the rise of esoteric Buddhism.[80] Yet we should by no means be lured into believing that this constitutes a textual verification of early noninstitutional Buddhist esoterism. Indeed, we would be hard-pressed to find a monk more supportive of normative early Buddhist institutions than Mātṛceta, whose poetry became standard liturgy in the great Buddhist monasteries of the early medieval period.

If institutional Buddhist esoterism was sociologically and historically defined by the person of the scepter-carrying monk, though, the siddha represents a new form in Indian Buddhism, one that ultimately came to mark a movement that began on the periphery and eventually worked its way into the heart of Buddhist institutions. I have chosen to designate it as noninstitutional only with respect to its sources and period of formation, although it continually represented a hazard for the structures of the monasteries and their surrounding communities.[81] Buddhist siddhas' language and literature were inherently destabilizing, for they challenged the ideological bond of Buddhist institutions—lay merit-making by donating to celibate monks who were fields of merit by virtue of their adherence to the elaborate codes of the *Vinaya*. Although institutional esoterism had already formulated a hermeneutic of violence and defense, of political order and hierarchical status, siddhas brought to the table images of sexuality and eroticism, of charnel grounds and ghost rituals. These were the erotic means whereby siddhas achieved the status of the Vidyādhara monarch, for the erotic sentiment was for them the vehicle to the highest realization.

Esoteric monks, for example, tended to represent the vajra in the Vajrayāna as a thunderbolt-scepter: this was the adamantine vehicle, which could penetrate anywhere and destroy all its enemies. The eighth-century *Vajraśekhara-tantra* is the *locus classicus* for the standard definition: a vajra is "that which is firm, hard, and non-empty, its character is impenetrable and unsplittable; since it is thus unburnable, indestructible and emptiness, it is called vajra."[82] In this avenue, the vajra represented the king's right to force—the metaphorical legal "staff" *(daṇḍa)*, which legal literature claimed as the essence of kingship—and therefore the symbol of the Buddha's Law (Dharma). The enforcement of the law was left to Vajrapāṇi (Vajra in Hand), who ensured that criminal elements (mythically represented by either Māra or [Śiva] Maheśvara in the esoteric system) would not overwhelm the monasteries. The Maheśvaras of the world were stubborn, and Vajrapāṇi was represented as the "best of those subduing the difficult to tame" *(durdāntadamakaḥ paraḥ)*.[83] This definition may be compared to the erotized one found within some siddha literature: the vajra is now frequently described as the male member, and Vajrasattva (recast Vajrapāṇi) is eros embodied. Accordingly, the Vajrayāna becomes the vehicle for ritualization of the erotic sentiment.[84] As the *Guhyasamāja* proclaims, "[We speak of] ignorance, anger and desire; but desire always is found in the Vajra [penis]. Thus the skillful means of the Buddhas is understood as Vajrayāna."[85] This erotic aspect of the siddha culture reframed so much of the esoteric movement and extended the erotic sentiment *(śṛṅgārarasa)* of medieval poetry into the domain of Buddhist ritual. The aestheticization of the esoteric scriptures—their description in terms of poetic sentiments—was marked by Amoghavajra with his early notice of the first *yoginī-tantra*. There, the *Sarvabuddhasamāyoga* is described as employing the nine aesthetic sentiments *(rasa)* of Sanskrit literature as part of its message. [86]

In this light, the distinction between the consecration *(abhiṣeka)* rituals (examined in chapter 4) and those of the new system become all the more important. Two erotized and one interpretive consecration rituals were added to the others in an unwieldy fusion of fissiparous rites. While the entire wealth of institutional rituals were collectively categorized under the rubric of the pot consecration *(kalaśābhiṣeka)*, the other three consisted of the secret consecration *(guhyābhiṣeka)*, the gnosis relying on "insight" consecration *(prajñājñānābhiṣeka)*, and the fourth consecration *(caturthābhiṣeka)*. The secret consecration involved the disciple bringing a female sexual partner *(prajñā/mudrā/vidyā)* to the master, who copulated with her; the combination of ejaculated fluids, termed the "thought of awakening" *(bodhicitta)*, was then ingested by the disciple as nectar. This qualified the disciple to practice the internal yogic system of "self-consecration" *(svādhiṣṭhānakrama)*. This latter denotes a complex series of physical and mental exercises in which the body is visualized as having a series of internal maṇḍalas, which are consumed in a psychic fire. With the insight/gnosis consecration, the disciple copulated with the female partner under the master's tutelage. This sexual act is for the purpose of obtaining the proper method of the "centers of the internal maṇḍala" *(maṇḍalacakra)* to realize the four joys *(ānanda)* during the four moments of the ritual orgasm.[87] Finally, the fourth consecration varied considerably, involving either a symbolic revelation in a highly charged charismatic environment or, more frequently, lengthy instruction about the nature of reality in which the experiences of the previous twosexual consecrations were to be integrated into a larger Buddhist philosophical context.

However, the new consecrations embody an association of ritual behavior and yogic meditation that is a later fusion. The earliest siddha literature simply speaks of a sexual ritual that is sacramental rather than yogic. It is found in such scriptures as the *Guhyasamāja*, the *Sarvabuddhasamāyoga*, the *Laghusaṃvara*, and others that became understood as proposing the path of "highest yoga" *(anuttarayoga)*. These materials are unassailably from the eighth century, with references to them by well-known eighth- and early ninth-century figures like Amoghavajra, Vilāsavajra, Jñānamitra, and Śākyamitra.[88] Although not always separately titled, the name of this rite, when identified, is variously given—sometimes "seal rite" *(mudrāvidhi)*, sometimes *maṇḍalacakra*-rite. However, the descriptions are sacramental, without the yogic associations of later *maṇḍalacakra* instructions that specify internal psychophysical centers, letters, and the manipulation of winds.[89] The earliest notice appears in the *Subāhuparipṛcchā Tantra*, which specifies that the monk or yogin will attract a "nonhuman" (generally a *yakṣī*) in the forest or other secluded spot, and their copulation yields worldly benefits, especially magical flight.[90] Buddhaguhya, in his earliest of the surviving commentaries on this work, is straightforward that this rite is done by one (such as a monk) who might desire a non-Buddhist woman for sexual pleasure but cannot be self-indulgent toward humans.[91] However, any female attracted by mantras to a secluded place, we are assured, can only be a nonhuman like a *yakṣī*.

The net result meant that, in association with other sacraments *(samaya)* and in a secluded site, the purpose of the ritual was for the adept to experience sexuality while in relationship to a divinity, often visualizing himself and his partner as the divinity and its consort. The consequent ejaculate was taken, then, to have the mystical properties of the divinity, so that it was, quite literally, the seed of divinity. Since the divinities most frequently represented, such as Heruka, had their iconology taken from rural, tribal, or Śaiva contexts, the point was the recreation of divine attributes (*siddhi, jñāna, mokṣa,* etc.) in the ritualist by reenactment of the divine behavior. Thus the goal was the ritual experience of sanctified copulation, with partners either human or nonhuman almost equally acceptable, so long as the sacramental structure of the event was maintained. Some early esoteric literature, such as the *Dhyānottarapaṭalakrama,* certainly taught yogic breathing and other practices, but there was nary a hint of sexual rituals associated with its psychophysical yoga, and the two do not come together until the late eighth or early ninth century.[92] Even then, the sexual sacrament, by that time called the "consort vow" (*vidyāvrata*), continued to be practiced separately. The ninth-century author Padmavajra dedicates two chapters of his classic, the *Guhyasiddhi* (Secret Accomplishment), to the description of this activity.[93] Certainly, solid monastic figures like Mañjuśrīkīrti supported the consort vow as an important phase in the mantrin's spiritual development, to be undertaken for six months or so.[94]

These new consecratory systems were sufficiently alarming that attempts were made by Buddhist monks—abbots and exegetes—to frame their ritual narrative, deny their necessity, or extract their physicality. The first was accomplished by the requirement that they be understood as extensions of the imperial metaphor of the institutional consecration rites. Although the imperial metaphor is not as applicable—and not frequently applied—to the three later consecrations, some authors at least continue this line of thought.[95] Implied in this application (although I have not seen it explicitly worked out), the disciple becomes the master because he inherits (ingests, uses) the genetic potency of the thought of awakening (semen) from his parents (his own master and partner). They share the same partner and therefore interact with the seal (*mudrā*) of office or the insight (*prajñā*) of kingship or its potent knowledge (*vidyā*). It is obvious, though, that the new rites represent a difficult synthesis of disparate models. As a consequence, our several theoretical consecration texts generally emphasize the first and fourth consecrations, being the most Buddhist, while the second and third are given very short shrift.[96]

Thus the domestication of erotic rituals required that they be framed with the imperial rituals at the beginning and Buddhist philosophical thought at the end. One major exception to an abbreviated treatment of the second and third consecrations is found in Ratnākaraśānti's *Abhiṣekanirukti.* However, the esteemed commentator applies his hermeneutics to a fourth consecration-style (Buddhist) discourse on the logical and epistemological implications of these two, rather than on their specific ritual praxis. Beyond this, he teaches that the goal is the attainment of the citadel of Vajradhara, using an older Mahayanist image to extend the imperial metaphor into the goal of the new path.[97] This renewed emphasis on the imperial metaphor as the ritual framework allowed Atiśa simply to deny that the three subsequent initiations were appropriate for Buddhist monasteries—they were to be performed by the laity and no one else.[98] Alternatively, the entire process could be internally visualized, rather than physically enacted, and this was the path eventually chosen by most Tibetan traditions.

The immediate goal of the erotic and other rites was the obtainment of psychic powers (*siddhi*), often understood as the mark of success as a sorcerer. Again, the 726 C.E. translation of the *Subāhuparipṛcchā Tantra* provides the earliest notice of these powers. The siddha was to obtain eight forms of power divided into three levels.[99]

Superior Siddhis	**Mantra** Mantra siddhi means delighting both the super mundane and mundane divinities through one's practice of mantras.
	***Asuraguhā** Demigod's Cave siddhi is of two kinds: one is able to achieve the treasures of the gods or one meets a daughter of the demigods, and goes to their palace to live for an aeon.
	Rasāyana Elixir siddhi means ingesting medicines that arise from the elements, from the veins, from beings' bodies, or from viscous liquids. One lives a long time without disease, remains young and with sharp faculties.
Middling Siddhis	**Anardhyaratna** Priceless gem siddhi means that there will be a bestowing of gems continuously.
	Nidhi Treasure siddhi is the ability to find treasures in the earth. The two kinds of treasure are human and divine. Human treasure is simply caches of gold, silver or gems. Divine treasure includes pills, malachite, magic boots, and books; these will allow one to fly into the sky, become invisible, run swiftly, and immediately penetrate the content of any text.
	Ākara Cornucopia siddhi means that one arrives at wells of gold and silver.
Mediocre Siddhis	**Rasa** Alchemical siddhi means that there is a kind of mercury that looks like gold. One measure [*phala*] of it will transmute a thousand measures of iron into gold. Others say not iron, but a drop of rasa that looks like

ordinary mercury can transmute a thousand measures of copper into gold.

Dhātuvāda Lesser alchemy is the collection of drugs and using them to transform lead, etc., into gold.

The list is initially presented in a somewhat different order in the scripture but is explained in both the scripture and its commentary in the above manner. Although these siddhis represent the earliest list I have found, it was not the enduring one. Perhaps by the mid- or late eighth century, another list of the "great perfections" *(mahāsiddhi)* was to become the standard. These are the sword siddhi, ocular medicine (giving supernatural vision), ointment of fast walking, invisibility, elixir, flight, the ability to pass through earth and to have dominion over the underworld.[100] This latter list is still malleable, though, and Abhayākaragupta (c. 1100 C.E.) provides an "et cetera" after the last item.[101] We get a sense that the self-imposed structure of eight "great perfections" is an artificial limitation, for new accomplishments continue to be proposed as new rituals are created to secure the desired powers.[102]

This list, as elsewhere, shows an obsession with materia medica, with elixirs and finding items lost or buried. This latter circumstance, certainly, may simply extend from the fact that in the sociopolitical dislocation of medieval India, those fleeing a site will frequently bury their goods and fail to find them when (or if) they return. Coin and silver hoards from periods of unrest are one of the most important archaeological and numismatic sources, and they provide the primary origin of "treasure" described in the scripture. Moreover, many of the siddha scriptures discuss ointments and drugs, especially those applied to the eyes or feet. The use of the various species of datura (especially *datura fastuosa)* is particularly evident. Sometimes termed the "crazy datura" *(unmattadhattura)* or "Śiva's datura," it was generally employed as a narcotic paste or as wood in a fire ceremony and could be easily absorbed through the skin or the lungs.[103] The seeds of this powerful narcotic, termed "passion seeds" *(caṇḍabīja)*, are the strongest elements and contain the alkaloids hyoscine, hyoscyamine, and atropine in forms that survive burning or boiling. In even moderate doses, datura can render a person virtually immobile with severe belladonna-like hallucinations. The drug has been used by Indian criminal gangs like the Thugīs to incapacitate unsuspecting travelers. This may have something to do with the siddha fascination with flying or perhaps inform their iconography, for a common report from the use of datura is the sensation of aerial transport or the feeling of being half-man and half-animal.[104]

CHRONOLOGICAL CONCERNS AND ŚAIVA EXCHANGES

Because of its thematic and textual continuity with some Śaiva scriptures, Sanderson has proposed that the more extreme branch of the new siddha literature, the *yoginī tantras*, represented an appropriation of Kāpālika tantric literature by Buddhists. Based on his examination of mostly unpublished Sanskrit manuscripts, he has concluded that this level of Buddhist scriptures was entirely dependent on prior Śaiva tantras:

> The Yoginī tantras have indeed drawn on the Śaiva Tantras. Specifically, there are extensive parallels between these texts and the group of Tantras classified as the Vidyāpīṭha of the Bhairava section of the Śaiva canon. . . . A comparison of the two groups of texts shows a general similarity in ritual procedures, style of observance, deities, mantras, maṇḍalas, ritual dress, Kāpālika accoutrements, specialized terminology, secret gestures and secret jargons. . . . Dependence on the Śaiva literature is also apparent in passages in the Tantras of Saṃvara . . . that teach the sequences of the pīṭhas or holy places that figure prominently in the ritual and yoga of this system. . . . Examination of the texts reveals these similarities to be detailed and pervasive. It also enables us to explain them as direct borrowings by redactors producing what was obviously intended to be a Buddhist system parallel to the Śaiva Kāpālika cults but, of course, superior to them.[105]

Certainly Sanderson is correct about many parts of the picture: the quick and dramatic formation of the extreme practices of the Vajrayāna is inexplicable without taking into account the influence of the Kāpālikas. There can be little doubt that items essential to the literature of the *yoginī tantras*—such as the use of skulls, the employment of the specialized club *(khaṭvaṅga)*, and the later *Cakrasaṃvara*-based rhetoric of Heruka's subjugation of Maheśvara—cannot have arisen without sustained Kāpālika influence. In the myth, Heruka becomes the emanation of Vajrapāṇi, and Bhairava is the form Maheśvara takes. The twenty-four locales are sites where Bhairava and his consort, Bhairavī, are situated causing trouble for everyone. Heruka destroys Maheśvara, redefines the Bhairava/Bhairavī couples as Buddhists, and establishes his maṇḍala by taking his place at the summit of Mount Meru. In some versions of the myth, Heruka is said to take on the image of Maheśvara—the wearing of skulls, ashes, and other adornments—so as to attract to the noble Buddhadharma those of the lowest moral level.[106]

It is not surprising, therefore, that selected tantras of esoteric Buddhism present an aspect of intertextuality with received Kāpālika scriptures. Yet it is open to question whether the *received* Kāpālika texts are actually the sole or primary sources for the *yoginī tantras*. Although we must await the publication and detailed consideration of the Śaiva and Buddhist Sanskrit texts to which Sanderson alludes, there are certain problems with his formulation that might mitigate his rather extreme version of a unilateral appropriation, without alternative sources or mutual influence. These problems may be summarized as chronological difficulties, a lack of examination of the sources of Śaiva formulations, and an excessively narrow definition of materials available to Buddhists.

The earliest Buddhist siddha material comes into evidence around the 720s–730s C.E., give or take a decade. The *Mālatīmādhava* of Bhavabhūti presents us with the earliest Buddhist siddha personality—uncharacteristically a woman, Saudāminī—who is noticed in non-Buddhist literature. Saudāminī represents a Buddhist nun who had trained with one of the female protagonists of this unusual literary work, the nun Kāmandakī. However, Saudāminī is portrayed as one who had given up her robes to pursue the study of the Kāpālika path in the esoteric center of Śrīparvata; this may be the same locale referred to in Śaiva literature as Śrīśaila or Kaumāraparvata.[107] She has gained the siddhis, most particularly that of flight *(khecari)*, and has come to assist the Buddhists in their struggle with the evil Kāpālika siddha, Aghoraghaṇṭa, and his female companion, Kapālakuṇḍalā.[108] As it turns out, the hero of the play (Mādhava) quickly dispatches Aghoraghaṇṭa, and the play turns into a contest of wills between the nun Kāmandakī and her archenemy, Kapālakuṇḍalā. If Kāmandakī represents the Buddhist antithesis of Kapālakuṇḍalā's Kāpālika propensity for violence, Saudāminī indicates the redemption of its potential. She moves its brute force away from an obsession on personal gratification at any price to an impulse for compassion toward all beings. Bhavabhūti is the first to chronicle one direction taken by Buddhists in the early medieval period and to acknowledge that one specifically Buddhist contribution to extreme ascetic practice was restraint in service of a moral direction.

Extraordinary siddha behavior is apparent in early eighth-century Buddhist scriptures as well, even if its presence has been sometimes glossed over by apologists. The *Subāhuparipṛcchā*, whose first translation is attributed to Śubhakarasiṃha in 726 C.E., is the earliest example of this known to me; several siddha or Kāpālika rituals are found in this text.[109] Sections of the scripture—especially chapter 7—invoke the cemetery-based ghoul *(vetāla)* practices, the employment of corpses in the center of the maṇḍala, the selling of human flesh, and its use in ferocious homa rituals. As seen above, it also specifies the attraction of female tree-spirits (*yakṣī*) as sexual partners to confer siddhi and specifies which clothing is appropriate for the rite.[110] Since the well-dressed mantrin wears blue to the ritual, we may suppose that this is the earliest datable attestation of the notorious "blue-clad" (*nīlāmbara*) mob, whose sartorial preferences became the insignia of their infamous behavior.[111] They are possibly connected to the extremely popular cult of Nīlāmbara-Vajrapāṇi (blue-robed Vajrapāṇi), a system enjoying a plethora of Buddhist texts and ritual manuals. As we have seen above, the *Subāhuparipṛcchā* develops the first lengthy discussion of the source, nature, and number of siddhis.[112] The use of bones is also enjoined, specifically the use of a bone vajra when the mantrin engages in rituals of magical murder.[113]

The evidence of the *Subāhuparipṛcchā* is chronologically reinforced by the presence in the eighth century of two texts that eventually came to be classified as *yoginī tantras:* the *Sarvabuddhasamāyoga-ḍākinījāla-saṃvara-tantra* and the *Laghusaṃvara*. A form of the name for the first of these appears in the list of eighteen *Vajraśekhara tantras* that are said to constitute the earliest esoteric canon.[114] Although it is uncertain that the reference there is to the same scripture currently found in the Tibetan canon, the slightly later mention of this title by Jñānamitra (c. 800) as a member of "the canon of eighteen" gives a measure of credence to a continuity with the text known to Amoghavajra (active 746–774).[115] The sense of authenticity is reinforced by the presence of two recensions of the *Sarvabuddhasamāyoga*, a longer one included in the normative Tibetan canon and a shorter version found only in the *rNying-ma rgyud 'bum* (Old Tantric Canon) of the Nyingma tradition.[116] These two are related, and their organization speaks of the possibility of a still earlier version, perhaps the one known to Amoghavajra, although the two surviving commentaries address the longer recension and neither of them know of the received shorter *Sarvabuddhasamāyoga* in eleven chapters.[117] The Tsamdrak (mTshams-brag) and Tingkyé (gTing-skyes) manuscripts of the *Old Tantric Canon* contain both recensions and classify them as *mahāyoga-tantra*—indicating its earlier placement—while the editors of the standard canon included only the longer version and identified it as a *yoginī-tantra*.[118] Probably, then, some Indic text used as the basis for the Tibetan translation(s) was formalized during the eighth to ninth centuries.[119]

Unfortunately for the proposal that Kāpālika scriptures are the exclusive source of Buddhist works, the chronology of the Vidyāpīṭha tantras is by no means so well established. We may legitimately question the somewhat speculative chronology that has been proposed.[120] Most affirmations of the earliness of Śaiva materials, for example, rely on the Sdok Kak Thoṃ inscription, an important Cambodian bilingual inscription in both Khmèr and Sanskrit.[121] The inscription, broken at the end, records various dates, the last being 1052 C.E., probably close to the actual date of composition. Most important, for the history of Śaiva tantras, it maintains that, at the moment of independence of Kambujadeśa from Java, King Jayavarman II (now proclaimed an independent *cakravartin*) had rituals performed by one Hiraṇyadāma based on the text of the *Vināśikha*. He then had his favorite priest, Śivakaivalya, learn three texts—the *Vināśikha*, the *Nayottara Saṃmoha*, and the *Siraścheda*—from the oral recitation of Hiraṇyadāma, that they would be passed down in that family. Śivakaivalya and his family would be the only ones allowed to perform the ritual according to the *Vināśikha*. Śivakaivalya initiated all his relations into the form of worship and died during the reign of Jayavarman II. The date given for Śivakaivalya is in the early ninth century, and scholars of Śaiva tantra have taken this date as veridical, indicating that the texts included therein (at least one of which has been maintained as also within the Vidyāpīṭha) must have been composed well before that time.[122]

Yet what the Sdok Kak Thoṃ inscription really says is that three texts, of sufficient importance in the middle of the eleventh century to be included in a Cambodian inscription, were part of a family's representation about their position in the foundation of a state and proof of their religiopolitical stature. We might have more confidence in the inscription's content if the texts were not described as entirely oral, if the occasion were not concerned with the origin myth of Khmèr independence or if these texts had shown up in any other inscriptions. This latter might be considered when we see that a certain Śivasoma appears in the Sdok Kak Thoṃ inscription as an inheritor of Śivakaivalya's position as the royal preceptor and the guru of Śivakaivalya's grandnephew, Vāmaśiva. Śivasoma is featured in at least one inscription earlier than 1052, the Pràsàt Kantāl Dom north inscription of Indravarman. We might expect that his proximity to the throne (he was reputedly the grandson of Jayavarman II) and position in Śivakaivalya's family would afford him access to the same texts, even if he did not have the prerogative in their ritual.[123] However, not only are all of the many Cambodian inscriptions before 1052 mute about these Śaiva tantras, but there is also no indication that Kāpālika behavior had ever been employed by the principals, which would be expected if the works were as central as the eleventh-century inscription claims. Śivasoma himself is described as eternally of the "right" behavior *(sadā dakṣinācāra)*, expected in a Pāśupata disciple but utterly foreign to Kāpālika decorum.[124] Beyond this, the eleventh-century Sdok Kak Thoṃ inscription itself has problems in projecting later events to the earliest period. As Chakravarti noted in his study,

> In the Sdok Kak Thoṃ inscription the people of Anreṃ Loṅ are said to have belonged to the Karmāntara caste even in 894 Śaka (=A.D. 972) i.e. two years before the alleged date of the creation of the caste by order of Jayavarman V as narrated in the Koṃpoṅ Thoṃ inscription.[125]

In reality, the available evidence suggests that received Śaiva tantras come into evidence sometime in the ninth to tenth centuries with their affirmation by scholars like Abhinavagupta (c. 1000 C.E.); all chronologies affirming their extreme antiquity remain problematic.[126] Other models of their historical formation require sustained special pleading about single reference citations, a questionable method of arguing history. Were there other, earlier tantras? We certainly have indications that such was the case, and there were assuredly earlier examples of Śaiva heterodox practice. In his autocommentary to the *Pramāṇavārttika*, Dharmakīrti in the mid-seventh century specifies that he was familiar with the *Ḍākinībhaginītantras* and others.[127] No titles or specific contents are given, beyond his mentioning them in a discussion of the deconstruction of the exact relationship between ethical action and its result, depending on the state of the mind of the individual. This is, of course, the central argument of the esoteric method: a person with superior capabilities can employ dangerous methods for transcendental ends. It is possible that the term "tantra" there simply means ritual rather than text, for that is how the *Kālikāpurāṇa* is seen using the term.[128] However, this remains to be demonstrated, and the context appears to point to received texts, rather than simply to known rituals.

INDIAN SACRED GEOGRAPHY

In all probability, the postulation of two and only two possible categories of sources for the Buddhist *yoginī tantras*—Buddhist and Śaiva—will prove unsustainable and appears to suppose that all cemetery or antinomian rituals must, by definition, be Śaiva. Perhaps the greatest problem with the model is that it closes discussion about other potential sources of esoteric Buddhism. One need not postulate a pan-Indic religious substrate (as did Ruegg) in order to acknowledge that Buddhist authors might have drawn on other sources. The two instances cited by Sanderson, that of the secret signs *(chomā)* for the recognition of intimates in the esoteric gathering and the twenty-four sites of praxis *(pīṭha, upapīṭha,* etc.) are, in reality, excellent examples of why the Śaiva scriptures are improbable as unique sources, although they were clearly contributory. The issue of secret signs, understood as an alternative form of communication, is explored in chapter 6. The present discussion concentrates on the list of pilgrimage sites.

The question about the filiation of such sacred sites (as opposed to lists of them) is their professional clientele. Based on his fieldwork, Gross has shown that modern Indian sādhus congregate and encounter one another at sites of mythic importance, and it might be expected that such was formerly the case as well.[129] The twenty-four sites represented in the *Cakrasaṃvara* recasting of the eighth-century legend of Vajrapāṇi's conquest of Maheśvara are certainly not particularly Buddhist, nor are they uniquely Kāpālika venues, despite their presence in lists employed by both traditions. Briefly, one list of the twenty-four sites is arranged in the following manner:[130]

> Four pīṭhas: uḍḍiyāna, jālandhara, pullīyamalaya, and arbuda.
> Four upapīṭhas: godāvarī, rāmeśvara, devīkoṭa, and mālava.
> Two kṣetras: kāmarūpa and oḍra; and two upakṣetras: triśākuni and kośala.
> Two chandohas: kaliṅga and lampāka; and the two upacchandohas: kāñci and himālaya.
> Two melāpakas: pretapuri and gṛhadevatā; and two upamelāpaka: saurāṣṭra and suvarṇadvīpa.
> Two śmaśānas: nagara and sindhu; and the two upaśmaśānas: maru and kulatā.

Although there are many variations in the items, in the received form and by any standards, this list is quite peculiar. For example, none of the major Buddhist pilgrimage areas are mentioned (Mahābodhi, Rājagṛha, Kapilavastu, etc.) even though these were of clear concern to esoteric Buddhists. Because the Buddhists pretended that they were claiming the locales from Śaivas, we might expect that they would be Śaiva, and specifically Kāpālika, pilgrimage venues. A well-attested practice of the Kāpālikas, however, is the *Mahākālahṛdaya*, which evidently focused on the Mahākālapīṭha in Avanti (Ujjain), a known Kāpālika stronghold.[131] Yet neither Mahākāla nor Avanti are listed among the twenty-four sites, but only the broader area of Mālava, and even then it is not given a position of importance. Similarly, Vārāṇasī, Tripurā, Khajuraho, Bhuvaneśvara (Figure 11), and Śrīparvata are all well attested as strong Kāpālika sites, but are not identified in the list.[132] This contrasts with other Śaiva tantras, which are much more pointed in listing specifically Śaiva sites as their sacred locales.[133]

FIGURE 11 Vaitāldeul temple: probable Kāpālika site. Bhubaneshwar, Orissa, mid-eighth century. *Ronald M. Davidson*

Among the four great *pīṭhas* often found in this list, Oḍiyāna is now verified as the Swat valley by the inscriptions published by Kuwayama, and it was clearly a Buddhist site, with little in the way of Śaiva representation and none whatsoever of Kāpālika that we can determine.[134] Certainly, it was Buddhist earlier than any other formalized Indian tradition, and similar problems arise with many of the other sites in the list of twenty-four. Kāmarūpa, for example, indicates the Kāmākhyā-pīṭha and its environs and is listed as a pīṭha in the alternate *Hevajra* list.[135] Yet its prior history as a tribal site of the Kirātas is fully acknowledged by the *Kālikā-purāṇa*, which indicates that caste Hindus simply took the expedient of driving out the tribal occupants and pursued the worship of the goddess along the lines established before the Hindus arrived.[136]

Likewise, Jālandara-pīṭha, where the goddess Mahāmāyā (Vajreśvarī) is worshiped in the modern town of Kangra; it was probably a Gaddi tribal site before Brahmans and Śaiva sādhus took possession. We have yet to locate the exact position of another of the pīṭhas, Pulliya-malaya (sometimes identified with Paurṇagiri). However, its name *(malaya)* seems to indicate that it was located in South India and was probably a Buddhist name for all or part of the Agastya Malai, the southernmost mountain range of India and very close to the fabled Buddhist pilgrimage site of Potalaka.[137] This is in line with Rājaśekhara's list of four "malaya" mountainous areas in South India/Śrī Lāṅka, with the sacred one among them being made pure by Agastya's proximate abode.[138]

Arbuda is also included in the *Cakrasaṃvara* lists and is the well-known Mount Abu, approximately 100 kilometers west of Udaipur. While Eklinjī, to the north of Udaipur, was a Pāśupata locale, the area around Mount Abu was originally associated with the Bhilla and Ābhīra tribal peoples.[139] The language spoken there was peculiar enough to warrant a mention of its imitation by actors in Bharata's *Nāṭyaśāstra*.[140] The Gurgi Stone Inscription of Kokalladeva II (end of the tenth century C.E.) identifies Arbuda as a place name, and no precise religious associations for the site are specified.[141] Even when it became more closely associated with Sanskrit culture, it was apparently first Vaiṣṇava and Jaina, rather than Śaiva, and it remains today a predominantly Jaina center. Its only mention in the twelfth-century *Kṛtyakalpa-taru*, for example, was in a quotation from the *Nṛsiṃha-purāṇa*—where the site was recommended for all Vaiṣṇavas—and Lakṣmīdhara was seemingly unable to place it in a Śaiva context, despite his obvious interest in doing so.[142] Since Lakṣmīdhara was familiar with the *Skandapurāṇa* of his time, the eventual inclusion of a pilgrimage guide to Arbuda-tīrtha as the next to the last section of the final book *(khaṇḍa)* in some redactions of the *Skandapurāṇa* is verified as being exactly what it appears, a rather late medieval addition.[143]

As will be seen in chapter 6, the centerpiece of the *Cakrasaṃvara* recasting of the eighth-century myth is the placement of Saṃvara on the pinnacle of Mount Meru. With this in mind, it might be thought that this is actually the replacement of Śiva by Saṃvara on Mount Kailāsa, the well-known Śaiva pilgrimage site just inside the Tibetan border. All the other pīṭhas, upapīṭhas, and so forth were to be governed by the divinity from the Mount Meru vantage point, and we might be tempted to see the Buddhist appropriation of the Śaiva site as indicated by the myth, especially since current Tibetan understanding is that Kailāsa is the home of Saṃvara. However, McKay has shown that the literary sources are not so neat as this; Kubera—not Śiva—was the original inhabitant of Kailāsa, and Kubera was "originally associated with outcasts and criminals."[144]

How should we assess this record? Long ago, Sircar had already noted the tribal affiliation of many of the sites, while for others, "Names of the tirtha, Devi and Bhairava were often fabricated by the writers . . . [who] had only vague ideas about some of the tirthas and often took resort to imagination."[145] This is particularly the case for Uḍḍiyāna/Oḍiyāna, which was lost to Islam precisely in the tenth to eleventh centuries, when it became a popular item in *pīṭha* lists, a most curious phenomenon. Moreover, many different lists of sacred sites were distributed throughout the *yoginī-tantras*, and the good scholarly monk Śākyarakṣita is forced to go through elaborate hermeneutical gymnastics to try somehow to correlate them all with Buddhist doctrinal and meditative categories in his *Pīṭhādinirṇaya.* [146] After trying to explain away the profound inconsistencies in the various lists of *pīṭhas* found in the *yoginī tantras*, he addresses the obvious question.

> So, are not these various lists mutually contradictory? In the establishment of these places as a *pīṭha* or *upakṣetra*, do we not have mutually incommensurate temperatures, properties or absences thereof? In answer—no, the lists are not in contradiction. This is because for one place there may be many identities. So we say here that this place may be called Nagara, or Pāṭaliputa or Mālawa, yet they are the same place and it is an *upakṣetra*.[147]

Śākyarakṣita is being both a good exegete and utterly disingenuous, for there can be no question that there are far more places than twenty-four specified even in the lists he employs, with very few points of commonality among them. The major similarity is that they are unified by the number twenty-four, another demonstration of the general Indian emphasis on numerical form over actual content, as seen in the case of the "eighteen" tantras of the early esoteric Buddhist canon.

The Śaiva *Jayadrathayāmala* list generated to define one version of these sites is as yet indeterminate in origin, even though it may prove to be a Śaiva appropriation of an earlier Kaula or other Brahmanical list, or generated by either Kāpālikas or Buddhists. Certainly Buddhists had long since shown their willingness to pursue rigorous demonology by their elaborate schematism of various and sundry nonhumans in the *Mahāmāyūrīvidyārājñī-sūtra*, but by this time they were not the only ones doing so.[148] Buddhists, however, were among the major proponents of specifying a site wherein was located a divinity with specific properties (such as his family) and specific mantras. The *Mañjuśrīmūlakalpa*, for example, also has a long list of places, beginning with Cīna and Mahācīna.[149] In these two locales, the bodhisattva Mañjuśrī's mantras may be recited for success (siddhi) to occur and the eighth-century text continues on through other geographical areas, many of which appear on the *Cakrasaṃvara* roster.

SIDDHA DIVINITIES—BHAIRAVA AND HERUKA

The site question is closely related to the issue of the deity Bhairava and his Buddhist counterpart, Heruka. Bhairava is unattested in the early Śaiva literature, such as the *Pāśupatasūtras*, which mentions many other names for Śiva.[150] Even in the seventh-century drama the *Mattavilāsa,* which is supposed to identify Kāpālikas, Bhairava is not mentioned. At the same time, in the *Harṣacarita,* the Śaiva character of Bhairavācārya clearly has a relationship to the divinity, even if he is not explicitly identified as a Kāpālika. The myth of the twenty-four Bhairavas occupying sites attacked by Vajrapāṇi (or Heruka) and his retinue appears simply to be an articulation that these *pīṭhas*, and so on, started as place-specific sacred areas, and Bhairava seems to have been little more than a local ferocious divinity at one time. He was eventually appropriated by Śaivas, much as they aggressively appropriated so much other tribal and outcaste lore for their own ends (Figure 12). By the time of the *Kālikā-purāṇa,* a *liṅgam* called Bhairava was identified on the side of Durjaya hill, in Kāmarūpa (here = the area around Guwahati), and the text provides two birth stories for this figure. The first is that Bhairavas (plural) are manifestations of the middle part of the Śarabha body of Śiva, the Śarabha being a mythic eight-legged beast.[151] The other birth story provides a discussion of the origin of the two brothers Bhairava and Vetāla, who are both monkey-faced sons of Śiva and are possessed of ghostly essence *(vetālatva)*.[152] Animal-headed divinities are frequently indicative of tribal origins, perhaps again from the Kirātas, who were among the original inhabitants of Assam and are identified

FIGURE 12 Bhairava holding *khaṭvāṅga* club in his left hand and a *ḍamaruka* drum in his right. South India, thirteenth century. Stone, 113.36 × 49.23 cm. *© The Cleveland Museum of Art, 2001, John L. Severance Fund, 1964.369. Reprinted with permission.*

by Shafer as having been speakers of a Tibeto-Burman language.[153] They are possibly ancestors of the Bodo-Kachāris of modern Assam.[154]

The use of Heruka to destroy Maheśvara and Bhairava is similarly comprehensible. While Heruka is formed in imitation of Maheśvara in the myth contained in the *Sarvatathāgata-tattvasaṃgraha*, the 726 C.E. translation of the *Subāhuparipṛcchā* contains an apparently earlier reference to Heruka, there depicted as a local demon like a ghost *(piśāca)*.[155] This is in close consonance with the *Kālikā-purāṇa*, which identifies Heruka as the divinity of a cremation ground *(śmaśāna)*.

> And there is a cemetery called Heruka, ferocious and red in color. He carries a sword and human skin, angry, devouring human flesh. Festooned with three garlands of heads, all oozing blood from their severed necks, he stands on a ghostlike corpse, its teeth falling out from the cremation fire. Ornamented with weapons and his vehicle, let him be worshiped only with your mind.[156]

The description of Heruka as a cemetery is also consistent with the curious translation of his name into both Tibetan and Chinese: blood drinker *(khrag thung)*. This is probably not derived from his iconography or from some hermeneutical reading of his name; instead, it is an extension of the fact that cemeteries absorb the blood of the deceased. In December 2001, I visited Kāmākhyā-pīṭha, to see if I could locate the Heruka cremation ground. It appears that the *Kālikā-purāṇa* refers to the cremation area found approximately two hundred meters east of the current location of the main temple and around three hundred meters from the oldest site on the Nīlagiri hill, where Kāmākhyā was located before the most recent temple was built. None of the priests at the site knew of the name Heruka, but the cremation ground is now called Masān-Bhairo (Śmaśāna-Bhairava), and a small temple there is dedicated to the ferocious divinity of the site. The name change should not surprise us, and by the time of the composition of the *Yoginī-tantra* or the *Kāmākhyā-tantra*—the other two Sanskrit texts closely associated with Guwahati—the Heruka designation appears to have become occluded. Although this cemetery may have migrated some, as did the parent Kāmākhyā site itself, I feel confident that it is the lineal descendent of the śmaśāna that the *Kālikā Purāṇa* describes as serving those who came with their deceased to the sacred area of the goddess.

In the *Kālikā-purāṇa* description, Heruka is clearly divine, yet is to be worshiped only mentally, rather than with great physical offerings. Moreover, the

Heruka origin myth, as recounted in the longer *Sarvabuddhasamāyoga*, describes Heruka in the manner of a cemetery divinity, rather than specifically either as the tamer of Maheśvara or as his imitation. In this mythic beginning, Māra and other criminal elements are more clearly specified as his opponents.[157] Thus the Buddhists apparently appropriated a local term for a specific Assamese ghost or cemetery divinity and reconfigured it into the mythic enemy of evil beings in general. Because Śiva and Māra were at the head of the very long list of criminal gods, they were included and subordinated to Heruka's establishment of his maṇḍala. His local and possibly tribal background suggests that there may have been a tribal affiliation as well.

The analogous entity of Śaṃvara—or Saṃvara/Sambara, often called Heruka—further illustrates the complexity of the situation. Śaṃbara, as the name of a quasi-divinity, is well known in the *Ṛgveda* as the fundamental enemy of Indra and Agni; he was also a leader of the Dasyus and a demander of ransom.[158] In particular, he has many fortresses or castles—either ninety-nine or a hundred—which are conquered by Indra in one of those mythic struggles that make Vedic literature so interesting.[159] In the course of the struggle, Indra assaults Śaṃbara from a high mountain.[160] Evidently, Śaṃbara was still alive enough by the first to second century for him to be noticed in the *Arthaśāstra*, where he is described as a divinity who possesses a hundred illusions *(śatamāyam śaṃvaram)*.[161] I have no intention of arguing that the Dasyu leader in the *Vedas*, the divinity in the *Arthaśāstra*, the Śaiva employment of the designation as a name for Śiva, and the Buddhist Vajrayāna divinity are somehow "the same." It is remotely possible that a cult to a local god of this identity survived for two millennia; I know of no evidence for this, however. It is probable, though, that the resonance of opposition to the Hindu Varṇāśramadharma was sustained in this name, which was still available to the literate, and that the designation was eventually used by Buddhists in the eighth century, when the figure of Śaṃvara was described. The earliest employment appears to be in the *Sarvabuddhasamāyoga*, where the author discusses the term as Śaṃvara, the highest bliss.[162] At the same time, the author introduces the name as the application or involvement of all illusion *(māyā)*, which works well in the context, yet also resonates with the *Arthaśāstra's* employment of the name. So, although Buddhists clearly abstracted from Śaiva sources certain iconographic features for the composite Śaṃvara, it is likely that other sources were also tapped (Figure 13).

Finally, Śaiva literature was heavily influenced by other forms of Hindu and non-Hindu myth and ritual and was as involved in opportunistic appropriation as the Buddhists. Indeed, the Buddhist emulation of Śaiva principled oppor-

FIGURE 13 Saṃvara from Ratnagiri, Orissa. Eleventh century. Bihar State Museum. Arch no. 6505. *Photo courtesy of the American Institute of Indian Studies*

tunism may prove to have been the most sustained contribution of the Śaivas to Buddhist ritual. Evidently village or tribal divinities like Tumburu have been appropriated by both the Śaiva tantras and esoteric Buddhist works.[163] Buddhist practices are paralleled in such places as the end of the *Vīṇāśikhatantra*, where we encounter the doctrine of a unique syllable *(ekākṣara)* other than OM; in esoteric Buddhism the ideology and attendant practices of *ekākṣara* developed around the figure of Mañjuśrī at least since the 702–705 translations of several *dhāraṇī* scriptures.[164] In the middle of the Śaiva tantra the *Rudrayāmala*, moreover, are four chapters on Vaiṣṇava worship—not the hallmark of a self-contained Śaiva corpus.[165] In addition, the *Kālikā-purāṇa* relies heavily on Vaiṣṇava forms and frequently references a *Vaiṣṇavītantra*.[166]

In the area of myth as well, Bhattacharya long ago pointed out that the *Tārātantra*, the *Brahmayāmala*, and the *Rudrayāmala* all depict discussions about how Vaśiṣṭha received instruction from the Buddha on esoteric ritual, and the received texts of these demonstrate a concerted awareness of the Buddhist contribution to Śaiva practices.[167] It would be remarkable, indeed, if some Vidyāpīṭha literature were to prove the sole exception to this Śaiva syncretism, particularly since the practice of penance by carrying a skull precedes the formation of the Kāpālika lineage, which must therefore be minimally based on *Dharmaśāstra* decision systems. In reality, one of the *Kālikā-purāṇa* myths of the origin of Bhairava—the result of Śiva's having split his Śarabha body—is shown as following a lengthy struggle with Viṣṇu. The Vaiṣṇava connection is further emphasized in a later version of the twenty-four pilgrimage sites' origin as found in the *Gorakṣasiddhāntasaṅgraha:*

> Why was the Kāpālika path proclaimed? To answer this question, it has been said that the twenty-four enumerated incarnations of Viṣṇu were born and, at the completion of their tasks, they each went crazy. How is that? Creatures born into the womb of animals end up playing around without purpose, and the same happened to the incarnations—the boar incarnation, the man-lion incarnation—who ended up creating fear of their habitats, the earth, jungle, and forest. Some attacked cities and villages, while others fell on the ocean. Kṛṣṇa, especially, went around indulging in seduction. Paraśurāma destroyed many Kṣatriyas because of the fault of a single Kṣatriya. So, the Lord [Śiva] became angered by all this degenerate activity, and the twenty-four Kāpālika forms were sent onto the twenty-four incarnations of Viṣṇu. They struggled together, and the Kāpālikas cut off the heads of all the incarnations and carried them around in their hands. Thus the Kāpālikas were born.[168]

Like the other forms of the origin myths, this late one has no great claim to an accurate record of *the* source of the Kāpālika tradition, even though Vaiṣṇava influence is occasionally quite visible. It simply demonstrates that Śaiva traditions—after all, this is a Nāthpanthi explanation of the Kāpālika origins—engaged in the hermeneutics of superiority with the adversary of the moment, not because it is an articulation of the actual foundations of the system. We might expect that the Buddhists acted similarly in their description of iconographic and ritual sources, which communicate a plethora of involvements and interactions. Thus it is premature to jump to the conclusion that the received Śaiva tantras were formulated without appropriating any material from the Buddhist tantras (or tantric oral traditions). A more fruitful model would appear to be that both heavily influenced the final formulation of the agonistic other and that each had alternative sources as well.

KĀPĀLIKA-BUDDHIST CONVERSIONS

What evidence is there that Buddhists and Śaivas exchanged materials? As indicated above, Gross' fieldwork shows that ascetics meet (and discuss the relative merits of their paths) at specific pilgrimage sites. Some of the well-known sites were locales where Buddhists and Śaivas certainly met: Devīkoṭa, Kāmākhyā, Bhubaneśvar, Vārāṇasī, Jālandhara-pīṭha, and others, even though many of these were places where Buddhists would also have met a wider variety of ascetic. More explicitly, there are occasional records of Buddhists becoming Śaivas, for example, the nine Nāthas mentioned in the *Kubjikāmata* system, as noted by Schoterman.[169] This would probably be the reason that the *Jayadrathayāmala*—one of the works claimed as the origin of Buddhist *yoginī-tantras*—possibly cites the Buddhist *Guhyasamāja*, suggesting both its dependence on Buddhist tantras and its probable final editing well after the middle of the eighth century, when the *Guhyasamāja* was composed.[170] We also have records of Śaivas becoming Buddhists, reflecting the fact that the Buddhist proselytization of ascetic traditions had been going on at least since the mythic conversion of Urubilvā Kāśyapa and his five hundred dreadlocked followers by the Buddha.[171] What is different with the Buddhist siddha system of the early medieval period is that these converts no longer necessarily gave up their previous modes of behavior. Whereas Urubilvā Kāśyapa and his companions abandoned their defeated magical snake, shaved their heads, and donned the yellow robe, the new method of conversion did not require this extreme change of conduct or appearance.

In honor of the deconstruction of a specifically Buddhist relative truth by the Mādhyamikas, the siddhas could represent themselves as good Buddhists who just happen to like skulls, tridents, and cremation ground ashes as a fashion statement. They might even describe themselves as Kāpālikas of the Buddhist flavor, as has been frequently noted in the case of Kāṇhapa and in the case of Saudāminī in the *Mālatī-mādhava* of Bhavabhūti. Another example of this conduct is the self-description of the siddha Acinta in his **Tīrthikacāṇḍālika.*

> The woman's pīṭha is the Crest-Jeweled Mother; my family becomes the Caṇḍālī-kula. And the triple world is scorched—the tongue of flame pervades the sky. Acintaśrī will dance; he will beat the ḍamaru in the sky and on the ground. (1)
>
> Let the vajra fire desiccate the ocean, yet preserve both the sun and moon. Acinta the Kāpālika is a glorious dancer; he will beat the ḍamaru in the sky and on the ground. (2)
>
> Gods, demigods, and men, Īśvara, Umā, and so forth; they are all scorched by the fire of gnosis. Acinta the Kāpālika is a glorious dancer; he will beat the ḍamaru in the sky and on the ground. (3)
>
> I lead a yoginī and I put her in the Lord's pīṭha; I have sung this sort of maṇḍala in song. Acinta the Kāpālika is a glorious dancer; he will beat the ḍamaru in the sky and on the ground. (4)[172]

This and other evidence suggests that the Buddhist-Kāpālika connection is more complex than a simple process of religious imitation and textual appropriation. There can be no question that the Buddhist tantras were heavily influenced by Kāpālika and other Śaiva movements, but the influence was apparently mutual. Perhaps a more nuanced model would be that the various lines of transmission were locally flourishing and that in some areas they interacted, while in others they maintained concerted hostility. Thus the influence was both sustained and reciprocal, even in those places where Buddhist and Kāpālika siddhas were in extreme antagonism.

THE OTHER ŚAIVAS: THE PĀŚUPATAS

Yet there were other Śaiva influences beyond the Kāpālika system, a fact that might be expected given that neither the political nor the economic patronage of Kāpālikas is well attested, and the archaeological record suggests that Kāpālika sites were actually somewhat rare. Evidence for other influence is found in the temporary practice of feigning madness—that is, possession by spirits or ghosts—as espoused by the Pāśupatas, whose social horizon was far better known and whose attested sites are spread throughout Buddhist areas (see the appendix). As noted above, the Pāśupatas were to practice five stages in their ascetic endeavors. In the first, the distinguished state (*vyaktāvasthā*), they were to inhabit temples and conform to rules. In the second, the undistinguished state (*avyaktāvasthā*), they were to act insane in public and court dishonor. In the third, they were to dwell in an empty cave; in the fourth, they were to dwell in a cemetery; and in the fifth, they were to dwell in Rudra.[173] The second stage is of particular interest here. Ingalls has studied this material in some detail and has already noted that *Pāśupatasūtra* III.11 requires that, for the purpose of cultivating dishonor, the undistinguished yogin is to "act like a ghost" (*pretavac caret*).[174] Kauṇḍinya's commentary elaborates:

> Here, the verse indicates an expression about a person, not about someone deceased. Why? Because it concerns instruction about correct conduct (to which real ghosts do not adhere). The term "like" [*vat*] indicates that it is a variety of metaphor, and it is to be understood that this conduct is to be cultivated by a yogin acting like a homeless man, as if completely insane. His body is smeared with filth and his beard, nails, and hair are completely grown out, as if he had abandoned all the ritual impressions of life. Cut off from all the castes and stages of life, he becomes powerful in renunciation and perfects his purpose: reveling in the disgust exhibited toward him.[175]

Pāśupatas considered that the founder of the most noted version of the system, Lakulīśa, was in reality an incarnation of Śiva, who came to the rescue of Brahmans by entering into a corpse abandoned in the charnel ground, a story repeated in both the *Vāyu-* and *Liṅgapurāṇa* and in the 971 C.E. Ekliṅgjī inscription.[176] So, Lakulīśa was the form of Śiva as a reanimated body. It is noteworthy that corpse revival was the provenance of another form of demon: the *vetāla* (ghoul). As already seen above, Bhairava had the essence of a ghost (*vetālatva*), and apparently the Kāpālika espousal of Bhairava's ghostliness can be traced to the influence of prior systems of religious madness. Accordingly, the literature supports Pāśupata Śaiva models of saints acting like ghosts and ghouls, specifically in imitation of an incarnation of the great god. Again, this ascetic (*śramaṇa*) practice probably preceded the Pāśupatas. In this vein, the fifth-century Harwan tiles from a Buddhist monastery in Kashmir (Figure 14) show an individual usually interpreted as a non-Buddhist śramaṇa, but could just as easily be a ghost—its potential for ambivalence is indicative of ascetics' ghostly masquerade.

FIGURE 14 Seated Ascetics. Kashmir, fourth century. Terracotta, 50.80 x 30.60 × 5.20 cm. *© The Cleveland Museum of Art, 2001, Edward L. Whittmore Fund, 1959.131. Reprinted with permission*

Yet, even if the ascetic practice anticipates the Pāśupatas, these Śaivas were the first to institutionalize it in a codified strategy that established a rapprochement with normative Brahmanical values. Following them, this form of behavior was appropriated by both radical and mainstream ascetic *(saṃnyāsin)* traditions. Crazy behavior is approved in the *Svacchandatantra* and also becomes recommended in the late *Nāradaparivrājakopaniṣad*, which describes this life as "his behavior without evidence of caste, he goes as a demon, as a madman, as a child."[177] While Olivelle, who has studied and translated this material, believes that it indicates a general approval of such states, it is clear from the context that various opinions have arisen on how to integrate the Pāśupata's form of conduct into the system of renunciation.[178] The *Āśramopaniṣad*, for example, also allows this form of conduct, but restricts it to one form of Forest Retiree *(vānaprastha)*, the "Foam-drinkers" *(phenapa)*, and to the highest variety of Samnyāsin, the "Great Geese" *(paramahaṃsa)*.[179]

Thus, for Śaiva yogins, this conduct is "like a ghost" *(pretavat)*, "like a demon" *(piśācavat)*, or "like a ghoul" *(vetāla)* because the yogin has left behind the ritual impressions that form a human being. This is done explicitly during the ceremony of renunciation, called by Bharati the "sacrifice of dispassion" *(virajāhoma)*, in which the renunciate celebrates his own death.[180] The force of the metaphor, "like a ghost/demon," then, is that the yogin is fundamentally a ghost—a ghost without ritual impressions—that just refuses to go away. He cannot be dead, since he still needs food and acts in the world; he cannot be living, since he is utterly outside the structure of ritual obligations and gift giving, which define one's existence in Indian caste society. By his nonobservation of food prohibitions, he is irretrievably polluted, all the more so because ascetics court the very things people strive to avoid—proximity to corpses, pain, and sexual continence. And in the Pāśupata's case, the yogin also courts social disapproval. He is thus a contradiction in terms, a living paradox. In this context, there is no great semantic difference between acting like a ghost and acting like a demon. Frequently the terms have overlapping significance in ritual conduct, especially in places like Banaras, where the tank of Piśācamochan is a place to go to liberate the spirits of the dead.

Buddhists were as obsessed as other Indians with ghost lore, even if most of the available studies on Buddhist ghost rituals focus on East Asia. For Indian monks, ghosts represented both problems and opportunities. They were problems because, before the nineteenth-century influx of modern medicine, ghostly influence was identified as the cause of many illnesses, especially malaria and other causes of fever. Freed and Freed, who have provided us with a fascinating study of ghosts and medical lore in modern India, indicate that the realm of the undead continues to play an extremely important place in the ideology of illness and health throughout the subcontinent.[181] For their part, Buddhist monks were concerned with the possibility that individual monks would become ghosts after their cremation, and the *Mūlasarvāstivāda Vinaya* considers steps to be taken on their behalf.[182] Ghosts were, however, also ritual opportunities, for Buddhist meditators developed (and continue to develop) rituals for the liberation of the newly departed *(preta)*, who may be wandering the earth confused and in need of compassionate assistance. Thus a ghost may represent the chance to accumulate merit, and it is likely that the early Buddhist practice of the transfer of merit to specific departed—a monk's parents—became the source for the Mahayanist practice of the transfer of merit to all sentient beings. The widespread East Asian lore of Mahāmaudgalyāyana liberating his mother from hell must be seen as an extension of Indic obsession with ghostly possibilities, not solely or even principally as a Chinese indigenous development.[183] Mahāmaudgalyāyana's task in the story became a Buddhist specialty throughout Asia, with ghost rituals in efflorescence everywhere Buddhist monks took on the responsibility of beings' liberation.

After the development of the esoteric Buddhist siddha paradigm, the older practices associated with ascetic *(śramaṇa)* traditions began to be included in the spectrum of approved behavior. For example, the conduct of subduing females for sexual favors, controlling demons and ghosts, and the performance of cemetery rituals are noted from the mid-eighth century on, and allusions to these behaviors appear in such diverse texts as the *Vajrapāṇyabhiṣeka-tantra* and the *Subāhuparipṛcchā*.[184] More developed practices arise as well, and much of the ninth-century *Guhyasiddhi*, particularly chapter 6, is dedicated to the explanation of how a successful Buddhist is to undertake the Insane Vow *(unmattavrata)*. As summarized in the *Subhāṣitasamgraha*,

> Assuming the image of insanity, he remains silent, in deep contemplation. Thus he wanders around *like a demon*, through contemplation on his personal divinity.
>
> The vowtaker doesn't carry a bowl when wandering in search of alms but takes instead the remains of food already eaten in a plate or broken bowl on the street.
>
> Wandering around, he strives for food, and consumes it. Having eaten, he might be content—but this is also to be rejected.
>
> The loincloth might be worn, whether split or decayed. Or he may be naked and wander as he likes.[185]

The language of this extract is almost exactly that of the Pāśupata and related materials given above, including the vowtaker's behavior being modeled after that of a ghost/demon. The Pāśupatas were so influential on esoteric Buddhists, in fact, that Avalokiteśvara is depicted wearing the dress and attributes of Paśupati (Śiva).[186] By the late twelfth century in Tibet, Drakpa Gyeltsen specifically cites the "insane practice" under the rubric "avadhūtacaryā" *(kun 'dar spyod pa)*, recommending it in his *Great Jeweled Tree of Tantric Practice.* [187] This latter text remains the classic arrangement of topics for the Sakya tradition and the most complete indigenous Tibetan compendium of esoteric practice to that time. Thus the practice was not simply peripheral to the system, but a form of yogic behavior recommended to those well advanced along the path and considered integral to success in the esoteric method.

Finally, the Pāśupatas are the probable source for the employment of song and dance in the Buddhist forms of worship, which is ubiquitous in *yoginī-tantra* literature. Although others, particularly devotional movements *(bhakti)*, used singing and dancing in their ritual systems, theirs were primarily folk forms with a minimum of structure to interfere with the experience of ecstasy. The Pāśupatas, by contrast, particularly enjoined the use of song and dramatic forms in the worship of Śiva, and this emphasis occurs from the earliest documents right through the life of the order.[188] These were not folk forms, for Kauṇḍinya's commentary to *Pāśupatasūtra* I.8 indicates that when worship is performed using song, it should be done according to the *Gandharvaśāstra*; and when veneration is by dance/drama, it should be accomplished in consonance with the *Nāṭyaśāstra*, the latter presumably Bharata's classic text.[189] Their virtuosity in vocal song and structured forms of dance were perhaps an extension of their involvement with court life and missionary activity. Indeed, inscriptions about one of the Pāśupata successor movements, the Kālāmukhas, are replete with references to the musical and dramatic accomplishments of its representatives, including the employment of temple girls *(devadāsī)* for their performances.[190]

Likewise, Vajrayāna siddhas were, for all appearances, the first of Buddhists to employ singing (not chanting) and dancing (not simple hand gestures) in the acts of offering before images. Such acts were frequently enjoined in the *yoginī-tantras*, right from its earliest expression, and sometimes brought with them the values espoused in Śaiva/royal court affiliation, as seen in the longer *Sarvabuddhasamāyoga.*

> Having subdued the great kingdom of the triple world by one's own courage, in order to conquer all the beings [in that triple world] one teaches with the horse dance.[191]

Similarly, specific forms of singing are enjoined in the same text.

> The excellent song of the manifestations of the Buddha, for those knowing these mudrās, is the excellent cause of perfection, accomplishes all the esoteric acts, continually brings all the physical necessities, and thus all the forms of increase of goods. So, having sung the songs with six varieties of tunes, sing the divinity's song.[192]

A dedicatory inscription from Gayā (not Bodhgayā) indicates that sophisticated song and dance forms were eventually used in Buddhist temples as well, albeit at a later date and in somewhat different circumstances. Around the twelfth century, a local prince, Puruṣottamasiṃha, erected a "perfumed chamber" *(gandhakuṭī)* to the Buddha, on behalf of his grandson, Māṇikyasiṃha. Three times a day, formal offering was made "by means of instrumental music in the highest key *(pañcamagata)* together with Rambhā-like Bhāvinīs and Cheṭīs dancing round wonderfully with mirth and singing and so on, in a way appertaining to the unions of Anaṅga (Kāma)—(worship) increased by hospitable entertainments."[193] Although the exact nature of their participation in other activities of the temple is unclear, the specification of two types of women—primarily *bhāvinī* (noble women) and secondarily *ceṭī* (attendants)—making offerings through sophisticated forms of song and dance is suggestive. Their activity seems to be a development from the earlier introduction of these forms by siddhas and used in the singing of Apabhraṃśa songs in both earlier and contemporary *yoginī-tantras*. What was different about the early Buddhist use, compared to the Pāśupata and Kālāmukha employment of these forms, is exactly this use of non-Sanskritic language systems in various circumstances. However, our inscription, written in relatively good Sanskrit, does not specify the language of offerings. Instead, its court relationship (it is, after all, a court-sponsored temple in Gayā) appears to preclude the use of Apabhraṃśa in this instance, and the temple supervisor specified in the inscription was a monk, Dharmarakṣita. Accordingly, the institutionalization of initially siddha-related practices, at least in this case, apparently involved the shift to Brahmanically approved language and (no doubt) vocal and dance systems.

SIDDHAS IN THE TRIBAL LANDSCAPE

Understanding the relationship between heterodox systems—like the Kaulas and Kāpālikas—and the tribal rituals systems has been made even more problematic by the promiscuous use of the term "tantric" when some historians of India discuss either these indigenous peoples or their practices.[194] The political events and military adventurism of the post-Harṣa period not only destabilized the guilds and caused urban areas to experience a dramatic population loss. These events also precipitated the intensive interaction of tribal groups with those representing normative Indic civilization, as families became refugees and would-be conquerors crossed tribal lands. However, the term "tribal" has been applied to widely disparate ethnicities, including pastoralist nomad groups, semiagrarian confederacies, and the indigenous (Adivasi) people of Orissa, Assam, Madhya Pradesh and Maharastra, who have retained hunter-gatherer practices down to the present. In the latter case, it is not easy to see how an orally based, hunter-gatherer culture is directly related to religious scriptures (tantras) that are generated in an agrarian society. What is clear from the ethnographic and historical record is that Hindus of every stripe—Śaiva, Śākta, Vaiṣṇava, and Smarta—have engaged in aggressive Hinduization of tribal peoples, beginning in the early medieval period. Hinduization has normatively taken the form of the seizure of sacred sites by Brahmans, the appropriation of tribal deities by Śaivas, Śāktas, and Vaiṣṇavas, and the investiture of specific peoples with a caste identity, the supposedly "mixed" birth groups *(samkarajāti)*.[195] Sometimes, tribal rituals are also captured for continuation at the site, with a degree of modification, but with Brahmans or Śaiva/Śākta ascetics now in charge.[196]

The goals of these and other practices included the "pacification" of threatening groups, control of their produce, identification of their ignoble *(anārya)* divinities with the great Hindu gods, and the subordination of their lifeways to that of normative Hinduism. Rituals based on tribal usages were not the same as the tribal rituals themselves but, instead, were imitative and exploitative in nature. Indeed, Hinduization has most concretely resulted in the alienation of tribal lands from these peoples, and the contest between tribal peoples and caste Hindus over religion, land, and usage rights continues to this day. The blanket representation of tribal peoples as "tantric" by certain modern Indian authors merely extends the process of appropriation into the early twenty-first century, much as the exploitation and subjugation of tribal peoples in the United States has been capped by the imitative exploitation of their religious systems in New Age religion.[197]

As Indians became increasingly scattered to forest tracts during the medieval period, their representations of the indigenous inhabitants appeared to change in some areas of literature. Earlier literature, such as the *Mahābhārata*, had not described the autochthonous foreigners *(mleccha)* in favorable terms, providing origin myths that showed them descended from such unsavory characters as the wicked Vena.[198] The *Arthaśāstra* considers tribal peoples worse than thieves, for they set themselves up as kings against correctly (Brahmanically) coronated kings.[199] Likewise, earlier Buddhist literature had not looked favorably on Indian indigenous peoples, for they were notorious robbers of caravans, and Buddhist sympathies (and patronage) were with the trading guilds. Thus the *Daśabhūmika-sūtra* twice uses these people as a metaphor for problems on the spiritual path: in same the way that either tribal depredations or armed fortresses might impede the caravan leader from reaching the trading city, the bodhisattva's progress is arrested by spiritual impediments.[200] The medieval change is striking, beginning with the favorable assessment of indigenous peoples in Bhāravi's sixth-century romance, the *Kirātārjunīye,* which depicts help provided to the Pāṇḍava brothers by Kirātas and Yakṣas.[201] Likewise, around 730 C.E. Yaśovarman wandered through a tribal sacrificial site in the military romance *Gaüḍavaho*, and the poet depicts him commenting on the beauty of the tribal couples.[202] Such a change is in keeping with the rise of tribal power and the feudalization of indigenous clans.[203] Not only did the Candellas of Khajuraho come from Gond tribal stock, but the grandfather of great Pāṇḍuvaṃśi king Tīvradeva (c. 800 C.E.)—ruler of Dakṣiṇa Kośala kingdom centered in Sirpur (Raipur District, Chhattisgarh State)—had been a Śabara tribal chieftain.[204]

In the case of esoterism there emerge several shifts of representation. This might be expected, for in reality the geographical convergence of tribal peoples and esoteric Buddhism—measured through the historical record and archaeological sites—is more pronounced than the convergence of the Vajrayāna and Kāpālika Śaivism. We find not only esoteric sites like Malhar, Sirpur, and Ratnagiri in areas that are thoroughly tribal during this period but canonical and exegetical references to tribal and their closely associated outcaste peoples almost at every turn.[205] For example, the obscure words of coded language found in the *Hevajra-tantra* and elsewhere are often designated "foreign speech" *(mleccha-bhāṣā)* or "the language of Oḍiyāna."[206] The affiliation of these words and coded language is examined more closely in chapter 6, but it is important to remember that "foreign" in early medieval India did not simply designate "extraterritorial." As a term, it also applied to the plethora of tribal peoples found throughout the areas now known as Madhya Pradesh, Chhattisgarh, Jharkhand, Orissa, Gujarat, Koṅkana, Bengal, Assam, Kashmir, and Swat—precisely in all the strongholds of esoteric Buddhism.[207]

Beyond the geographical convergence and the possibility of indigenous loan words, the esoteric tradition supported several formulae that valorized indigenous peoples as icons. For instance, there emerged a hermeneutic of primitiveness, naturalness *(sahaja, nija)*, or nonartificiality *(akṛtrima)*.[208] Since ritually affirmed virtue was no longer the sine qua non of the path—irrespective of whether it was from a Buddhist ceremony or impressed by Brahmanical rites of passage—the natural human condition was regarded as a symbol for innate awakening. Moreover, individuals began appropriating the designation "Śabarapāda/Śabareśvara/Śabaripa," which may indicate their status as actual, tribally born siddhas or (more likely) their assuming this designation by having lived in tribal areas for a period. The ethnonym Śabara designates a historically important tribe, most frequently identified with the modern Saora (Śabara > Savara > Saora) in Orissa, Chhattisgarh, and Madhya Pradesh.[209] Together, these trajectories brought a strong sense of affiliation between esoteric Buddhist siddhas and the peoples of the forest, secured in part by the Buddhist appropriation of divinities of supposed Śabara origin.

Evidence for the identification with tribal peoples comes especially through the Prakrit poetry generated by selective siddhas. Serendipitously, some of these are preserved in the original language—or something very close to it—and they are especially dramatic in the *Caryāgīti* collection.

> Higher and higher, in the mountain the Śabara girl lives. This Śabara nymph flaunts a peacock's feather; around her neck a garland of guñja berries. [1]
>
> [She scolds her husband,] "You crazy Śabara! You drunken Śabara! Don't raise a ruckus or cause such a commotion! I am your own wife—Ms. Naturally Beautiful!" [2]
>
> Branches from the canopy of the diverse excellent trees stroke the sky. Bearing earrings and a vajra, the Śabara girl rambles around this forest. [3]
>
> The Śabara lays down his triplex bower—a bed thatched through with great ecstasy. For this Śabara is a real Casanova; with Lady Nonself as his whore, love illuminates the night. [4]
>
> [Afterward] he chews his essential betel and camphor with great ecstasy. Thus receiving empty Nonself in his throat, great ecstasy illuminates the night. [5]
>
> Hey, Śabara! With the conclusion of the teacher's direction, pierce your mind with your arrow! Nocking one arrow, pierce, pierce highest nirvana! [6]
>
> That crazy Śabara! Because of anger he's wandered into the ravine between high mountain peaks. How's this Śabara ever going to get out? [7][210]

The significance of the verse is clear enough, indicating a familiarity with the degree of sexual freedom and the use of intoxicants continually reported of tribals in India. Moreover, the verse is a relatively transparent allegory, in which the Śabara stands for the esoteric yogin, engaging in promiscuous intimacy with emptiness. Yet the commentator Munidatta cannot leave it there, for his tortuous explanation runs the spectrum from excessive to obsessive, interpreting each item as if it must denote some aspect of the yogic process. The point remains, however, that the Śabara became a cipher of both tribal peoples and the attainment of ultimate reality. Similar values are evident in one of Kāṇhapa's Apabhraṃśa dohās.

> A sage at the summit of the best of mountains, the Śabara makes his home.
> As his position is inviolable by even the "five-faced" [lion], the aspiration (to obtain the summit) of the best of elephants is very distant.[211]

The surviving anonymous Sanskrit commentary is exceedingly blunt: the Śabara is Vajradhara himself on the top of Mount Meru, and the five-faced (which can be either a lion or Śiva) cannot begin to approach him.[212] Thus the Śabara becomes an icon for the Buddhist esoteric divinity Saṃvara and assumes the position of a metaphor for the myth of Maheśvara's humiliation and death.

Although Munidatta's commentary views two *Caryāgīti* verses (nos. 28 and 50) as the composition of one of the Śabarapādas, there is little evidence for the ascription beyond the content. However, at least three and perhaps more of the Buddhist siddhas are said to have appropriated this name (or similar designations) for themselves; their hagiographies are found in disparate sources. Perhaps the earliest use of this appellation is for the late tenth-/early eleventh-century teacher of the siddha Maitrīpāda, and the Sanskrit Sham Sher manuscript published by both Lévi and Tucci indicates that, after Maitrīpāda's change of identity into Advayavajra, he studied with a Śabareśvara in the south.[213] It is open to question whether this is the personality introduced in Abhayadattaśrī's *Lives of the Eighty-four Siddhas*, who is referred to as Śabaripa and for whom no connection to Maitrīpāda is imputed, since neither the latter scholar's name nor his nom de plume Advayavajra occurs in Abhayadattaśrī's work. The literature also includes mention of a Śawari who was of the Brahman caste and who taught the early eleventh-century Shangpa Kagyüpa founder, Khyungpo Neljor.[214] There is furthermore a late eleventh-century Śabareśvara identified as both the teacher of Phadampa Sangyé Kamalaśīla and the author of an intriguing and difficult poem on the secret nature of the mind.[215] In addition to these individuals is a much later Śavaripa acting as the esoteric preceptor for Vibhūticandra, the late twelfth-/mid-thirteenth-century Indian scholar of the *Kāla-*

cakra.[216] The accepted explanation seems to be that Śavaripa is immortal and still wandering the world, a revival of the old "eternal sage" myth found applied in Buddhism to saints as diverse as Mahākāśyapa and Vimalamitra. For our purposes, however, it is instructive to consider that the tantric directives for siddhas to practice in tribal areas no doubt fueled both a fascination with and the appropriation of their identity, all with more than a dash of Rousseauean romanticism of the noble savage thrown in.

The poetry most closely associated with the Śabareśvara/Śavaripa persona tends to play off the behaviors attributed to indigenous groups in the medieval world. As seen above, medieval tribal peoples were depicted drinking, making love, and sleeping frequently. One of the Śavaripas employed these activities as ambivalent tropes for the realization of emptiness.

The Vision of Emptiness

The reality of mind's highest realization is declared as a seed in the realm
of space.
I embrace the nubile nonself by the throat and remain in the state of
awakening.
"Reject!" "Take!" — these delude the self.
Hey! Śavari plays with all the fetters within great bliss. I embrace the
Empty Lady.
Hey! Body, speech and mind are matured.
By inspection throughout all times, Śavari will become drunk.
In every form of joy, Śavari falls asleep,
Passes out in the realm of space.
Hey! My reality is declared a seed in the realm of space.
The fruit shines like the Morning Star.
"Reject!" "Take!"—these delude the self.
I kill the elephant of mundane fetters and make an offering cake of the
five senses.
I reject all of my suffering.
"Reject!" "Take!"—these delude the self.
Not sleeping day or night, I act as the watchman of my own mind.
The woman born from it, stays alone, having gone to a secluded spot.
The chieftain is said to be Lokanātha.
"Reject!" "Take!"—these delude the self.
So I embrace the Empty Lady—Śavari plays in great bliss.[217]

FIGURE 15 Śabara woman. Hoysala, Mysore, twelfth century. National Museum no. 2/5/1249. *Photo courtesy of Katherine A. Schwab*

Beyond their occasional mythic affirmation of indigenous peoples, the Buddhist record on ritual appropriation is also mixed. Associated with the tantras are several rituals, with attendant iconography, that focus on two feminine divinities: Parṇaśabarī and Jāṅgulī. The former clearly derives her name from one standard reference to the Śabaras—the "leaf clad" *(parṇa)* Śabaras—which was explained by an origin legend that lasted, according to Russell, well into the nineteenth century for the Bundelkund Saora (Figure 15).[218] Similarly, the Jāṅguli goddess is indicative of her origin in the jungle *(jaṅgala)*, a designation for "forest" that is in fact a loanword in English through Hindi. Both of these goddesses enjoy well-distributed literature and are sometimes, as in chapter 15 of the *Kṛṣṇayamāri-tantra*, invoked in the same ritual.[219]

> So now, I will pronounce the ritual meditation on the Noble Jāṅguli. By merely visualizing her, one could cross over water. (1)
>
> Visualize her with three faces, and six arms. She is yellow, and forms from the seed mantra Phūḥ. She holds a snake in her hands and is of enormous form.[220] She loves to ride on her peacock vehicle. (2)
>
> To the east, paint Mayūrī, with Bhṛkuṭī to the south. To her west is Parṇaśabarī, and Vajraśṛṅkhalā to the north. (3)
>
> Peacock feathers, a gourd, a branch and a chain[221]—visualize these (for the other goddesses) and their colors: yellow, red, dark, and blue. (4)
>
> The intelligent one will visualize them thus, and recite the mantra: OṂ PHŪḤ JAḤ (5)
>
> Place (visualize) Mudgara, etc., at the doors (in the cardinal directions) and Puṣpa, etc., in the intermediate directions. Then, by the Noble Jāṅguli yoga, you can always cross over water. (6)[222]

These rituals obviously invoke peacocks or peacock feathers, sometimes flowers, and other "jungle-like" ritual paraphernalia. The siddhis they convey are principally overcoming poison, either from snakes or flowers, and able magically to cross over water. Jāṅguli's capacity to cure poison was sufficiently important for the Tibetan translators simply to render her name as Dug-sel (ma) (the clarifier of poison). These jungle goddesses are described as two-, four-, or six-armed, with one to three heads, and in different colors. Parṇaśabarī's mantra describes her as a *piśāci*, in this case not necessarily a ghost, since the name was from an early period applied to tribal peoples as well.[223]

Although the extent of the Buddhist interest in seemingly tribal—especially Śabara—goddesses is impressive, the process of appropriation and incorporation of these figures was by no means straightforward. Actually, the distance between these divinities and their putative origins needs to be assessed as well, and one way to do that is to observe the difference between tribal and Buddhist iconography. All the tribal gods/goddesses for which there is much evidence indicate that they are depicted as wide-eyed figures of a decidedly rudimentary character, either as barely recognizable anthropomorphic figurines or as simple pieces of rock or wood. None of the tribal goddesses appear to employ the elaborate iconography described by our Buddhist rituals, and real tribal divinities are much more closely mirrored by such statues as the wooden Jagannātha group, which is thought to be an actual Śabara effigy that has been somewhat Hinduized in the process.[224]

Even more important in the current instance is the question of gender, since the contemporary Saora are one of the few tribal groups that have no central goddess figures, calling into question either the accuracy of Śabara = Saora or the Buddhist capacity to understand the tribal source of its representations. This latter is the more likely conclusion, since other tribes in Madhya Pradesh, Chhattisgarh, Jharkhand, Orissa, and Bengal have a fundamental mother goddess (e.g., the Kond earth goddess Tari). As Verrier Elwin observed in his fieldwork, "There is no Earth Mother in the Saora pantheon. How extraordinary this is can only be appreciated when we reflect on the enormous influence of this conception over the whole of eastern India, and particularly among the Saoras' nearest neighbors, the Konds."[225] Tari (and the Gond equivalent) has been represented by a post or stump and serves as the probable ritual source for the Śākta cults of Khambeśvarī, Subhadrā, Danteśvarī, and a host of other figures in the Orissa/Madhya Pradesh area.[226] Moreover, if the esoteric Buddhist masters did not succeed in correctly identifying the tribe, they were not alone in the early medieval period. Vākpatirāja's eighth-century *Gaüdavaho* specifies that a Caṇḍikā figure—probably identifying the site of the current Vindhyāvāsinī in Mirzapur—was worshiped by "Śabara kaula" women, but the statue was doubtless built on a Śākta appropriation of a Gond site.[227] Even though apparently in error, the ascription of sanguinary goddesses to Śabaras is well attested in early medieval literature in both Sanskrit and Prakrit, and the literary convention is almost certainly behind the Buddhist articulation of the same phenomenon.

Even beyond tribal peoples, many Buddhist siddhas affirmed a strong continuity with outcaste or lower-caste groups. As already seen, the earliest surviving text assigning the use of mantras to the historical Buddha, the *Mātaṅgī-sūtra* section of the *Śārdūlakarṇāvadāna*, depicts the Buddha's ritual combat with a woman who is of the Mātaṅga group. Similar to the phenomenon of Śabareśvara/Śavaripa, several individuals employed outcaste ethnonyms for their personal names: Caṇḍālaja, Ḍombīheruka, Ḍombi, and so on. The presence of animals expressing outcaste aesthetics, especially dogs, is found in the hagiographies of the various yogins appropriating the designation Kukuripa/Kukurāja. Likewise, many of the goddesses of siddha maṇḍalas, as seen in chapter 7, indicate outcaste affiliation: Ḍombinī, Caṇḍālī, and so forth. Finally, even the proper name for the flame of psychic heat in esoteric Buddhist yoga is given an outcaste identity. Perhaps the most frequently quoted verse from the *Hevajra Tantra* describes the visualization.

> Caṇḍālī ignites in the navel. She burns the five Tathāgatas.
> She scorches Locanā and the other goddesses.
> When *haṃ* is burned, the moon melts.[228]

All told, the Buddhist valorization of indigenous peoples and outcaste groups is a theme well articulated in esoteric Buddhist works. Yet it should be viewed as a piece of a larger picture, in which the rhetorical or actual presence of these peoples is but one of the many social levels included in select communities. They may include siddhas from princely houses, like Indrabhūti, with merchants and Brahmans also represented. Although their hagiographical presence may sometimes be suspected as more ideological rather than real—it is doubtful that many of the Śabareśvara/Śavaripa figures were born tribal—the overall effect is that of a much broader affirmation of ethnic identity than at any other time in Buddhist history. Some of our many questions on the actual linguistic and community contributions of autochthonous peoples are examined in the subsequent chapters.

CONCLUSION: A COMPLEX TERRAIN

In the period between their appearance in the early eighth century and their demise some six to seven centuries later, Buddhist siddhas captured the imagination of Buddhist communities in North India, Nepal, and elsewhere, even while they were probably few in absolute numbers at any one time. The new ideal arose both from the Buddhist appropriation of elements of the much older siddha tradition and from the aggressive intrusion of non-Buddhist elements into the Buddhist milieu. Here, siddhas took as their primary goal the acquisition of supernormal powers (*siddhi*) and, ultimately, dominion over both gods and sorcerers (*vidyādhara*). The means to do so involved magical rites in cemeteries or forests in conjunction with persons of authority, especially kings, using their aid to subjugate various kinds of nonhuman beings. Frequenting both cemeteries and the palaces of the new lords of the land, they practiced every form of magic, from love potions to ritual slaughter. With a political awareness as to the perquisites of royal patronage, siddhas acted as the kings' agents, engaged in secret signs and elaborate disguises, and provided their royal patrons with sacred entertainment through sophisticated temple song and dance. However, for siddhas the earthly political sphere was but a pale imitation of the ultimate celestial political environment, even though they made provisions for their appropriation of mundane political authority. In fact, siddhas desired nothing less than power over the divinities themselves and the underlying forces of reality. They represented the limitations of worldly ethics and morality as applicable only to incompetents, for siddhas must be above such concerns.

Accordingly, Buddhist siddhas have both continuities and discontinuities with siddhas in other, especially Śaiva, lineages. In some ways, Buddhist siddhas demonstrated the appropriation of an older sociological form—the independent sage/magician, who lived in a liminal zone on the borders between fields and forests. Their rites involved the conjunction of sexual practices and Buddhist maṇḍala visualization with ritual accouterments made from parts of the human body, so that control may be exercised over the forces hindering the natural abilities of the siddha to manipulate the cosmos at will. At their most extreme, siddhas also represented a defensive position within the Buddhist tradition, adopted and sustained for the purpose of aggressive engagement with the medieval culture of public violence. They reinforced their reputations for personal sanctity with rumors of the magical manipulation of various flavors of demonic females *(ḍākinī, yakṣī, yoginī)*, cemetery ghouls *(vetāla)*, and other things that go bump in the night. Operating on the margins of both monasteries and polite society, some adopted the behaviors associated with ghosts *(preta, piśāca)*, not only as a religious praxis but also as an extension of their implied threats.

Thus Buddhist siddhas represented a new social prototype that provided regional centers and disenfranchised groups with a model of autonomous power outside the artifice of caste Hinduism. They also offered sophisticated religious approval that did not require the abandonment of regional identity, in this way different from the depersonalization that Buddhist monks experienced. Siddhas became the first line of temporal involvement with tribal and outcaste peoples, appropriated and imitated cult practices, objects, and sites, and set up preferred siddha religious activities in distant provinces and foreign lands. This is not to say that they were all of a piece, for many Buddhist siddhas were at the very least notoriously contentious, castigating other traditions with ridicule and intimidation. Siddhas also argued and fought with one another and with the powers that be, proving the most fractious group of Buddhist ascetics to inhabit the subcontinent during the medieval period. In their behavior, they consistently represented themselves as outside the normal ethical strictures, for they were becoming kings of the Vidyādharas. The voluminous literature they generated has only begun to be examined critically, and many surprises about this new form of saint await us. It is to the issue of literature and language that we now turn.

6

Siddhas, Literature, and Language

Thus have I heard. At one time, the Lord was residing in the vaginas of the women who are the adamantine body, speech, mind, and heart of all the Tathagatas.	*Evaṃ mayā śrutam | ekasmin samaye bhagavān sarvatathāgata-kāyavākcitta-hṛdayavajrayoṣid-bhageṣu vijahāra ||*

Now, having clearly explained the succinct meaning of this introductory statement of the *Guhyasamāja-tantra*, I will hereafter interpret it according to the oral instruction of the Ācāryas. So, the letter *E* means the sacramental seal *[samayamudra]*. The letter *vaṃ* indicates the great seal *[mahāmudrā]*. As for *ma*, it is the Dharma seal, and *yā* is the action seal *[karmamudrā]*. *Śrutaṃ* provides the sense of commitment. Or again, the letter *E* means . . .

—Vilāsavajra, *Śrī Guhyasamājatantra-nidāna-gurūpadeśana-vyākhyāna*.[1]

Creating their ideological ground between the grand, feudalized institutions of orthodox esoterism and the emerging and sometimes agonistic religious and political landscape of the early medieval period, Buddhist siddhas formulated literature that reflected their own concerns. These issues, however, were as diverse as the siddhas themselves. While some siddhas were absorbed in scriptural composition, others were obsessed with its domestication and inclusion into the monastic syllabi, with selected individuals pursuing both tasks. Yet the obstacles to curriculum inclusion were among the most formidable any emerging Buddhist system had ever faced. As the opening of the *Guhyasamāja* above indicates, siddhas developed new forms of scripture that depicted an erotized Buddha at the center of a retinue of beguiling damsels. Siddhas also included in their pantheon tribal and local goddesses, murderous blood-drinking gods, and a host of illicit characters, from ghosts to snakes.

They used erotic descriptions that framed in explicit language a series of rituals extolling everything from group sex to ritual homicide to cannibalism. Buddhist siddhas employed varieties of language that were inauthentic by any aesthetic standards of the day: regional (some say barbaric) Sanskrit, Apabhraṃśa, and Old Bengali. In their nonscriptural works, siddhas spoke in the first person and employed forms of versification most closely allied with folk theater, wandering poets, and images of the countryside. However, the sheer outrageousness of their texts emphasized the humorous discontinuities of Buddhist existence, providing an extreme version of literary play. It is no exaggeration to state that the reader never really knows where the lines are drawn in siddha literature.

This chapter examines the development of the new siddha scriptures and as much as possible of the sociology of their articulation, including the office of the wandering siddha storyteller. It looks at the two principal and some subsidiary myths for the preaching of the *mahāyoga* and *yoginī tantras*, especially the important Indrabhūti myth as related in the earliest surviving document on the propagation of the new scriptures. The chapter discusses the hermeneutics of scriptural authentication and briefly examines the questions of coded language, finding the probability of a tribal or Dravidian component. Based on coded language, it explores the overarching question of secret signs, which included coded language under its aegis at one time. As an extension of both coded language and secret signs, the rhetoric of naturalness is again broached, and the sociolinguistics of the language forms that appear in the new scriptures, especially the issues of regional Sanskrit and vernacular literature, is analyzed. In addition, the siddha sense of humor and play is discussed. The chapter concludes with the idea of autobiographical voice in the *dohā* form of poetry.

REGIONAL TOWNS AND THE LAY SIDDHA

The historiography of Indian Buddhist scriptural production has tended to suggest, as in the case of Ray, that Mahayanist scriptures were composed in the confines of forest monasteries by an elite class of visionaries.[2] Their understanding of the scriptures, according to this model, was refined after decades of individual meditation and personal reflection. Inspired by the visions of various Buddhas and bodhisattvas, the revelation of a new doctrine or idea extended from the collapse of cognitive categories and was precipitated by a vision of truth. This experience resulted in a new synthetic, creative vision of reality, one that the forest meditators put into the voice of the Buddha as an acknowledgment of its visionary source. Each individual rendered into an appropriate language the content of his vision. These visions were collected and compared, finally producing a canon.

The applicability of this model to Mahayanist scriptures has yet to be determined, but I believe that this could not be the case for Indian esoteric Buddhism. Indeed, our evidence, both social and scriptural, supports the idea that the esoteric (especially siddha) scriptures arose as preeminently social events. Despite the evidence for a rhetoric of inspiration and isolation, as seen in the instance of tribal deities in the forests, the context for the development of scriptures appears to be the regional centers of social and political authority. This is where analogues to the kind of Sanskrit employed in the siddha scriptures are found; this is where vernacular languages are applied to literary styles; this is where the kings in their regional courts talk to wandering siddhas or take tribal and outcaste peoples into their discussions. Most of the place names represented in siddha literature—with the exception of holy cities like Vārāṇasī—are well-known locales outside the large metropolitan zones, yet not in the deep forest.

If this social model is true, then it would explain the extraordinarily *performative* nature of the new holy texts. The new scriptures of the siddhas, the *mahāyoga-* and the *yoginī-tantras*, are overwhelmingly dominated by ritual, song, dance, and storytelling—all blended together. Even when the forms of yoga are observed, the emphasis is on the fluidity of language and on the performative functions of letters and groups of sounds. Thus one source of the new scriptural authors might be sought from a social strata composed of, or at least exposed to, singers, performers, players, street preachers, and touring theater troupes. Although their narratives may invoke images of birds and snakes in the deep forest, none of these groups dwell there or develop their performances in solitude. This proposal is supported by the observation that groups still employing siddha vocabulary, such as the Bauls, tend to live and wander on the margins of the cities. In his study, Dimock traced the two older centers of Vaiṣṇava-sahajiyā activity to the relatively small towns of Śrīkhaṇḍa and Kuliyā, both in West Bengal.[3] Barrows's observation on the Aghoris in the nineteenth century is similar: their centers at that time were at Mount Abu and Girnar.[4] Gross's fieldwork among the wider population of sādhus indicated a pilgrimage path that went from regional center to regional center—Rishikesh, Pashpati, Kullu, Chitrakut, and so forth—although he observed that many sādhus preferred the major holy cities of North India, such as Āyodhyā and Ujjain.[5]

Chapter 7 pursues more extensively the questions of Buddhist siddha communities. If our model is true, however, then their sociology suggests that medieval siddha methods of composition would probably have been similar to those forms employed by preachers of the Purāṇas and the Epics, even if their religious identities were different. As such, siddhas specializing in scriptural composition would have been like the *sūtas* or the *vyāsas* associated with the Purāṇic and the Epic genres, and all of them would have engaged in composition as a social event, rather than an individually inspired system.[6] Thus in the course of explaining a point or teaching a ritual, a new variation on the form would occur in the instructional process. Collections of such instructional variations attributed to India siddhas have been found preserved in Tibet.[7] These variations would be then collected into small scriptures, and the latter would be further grouped into the larger tantras, which in turn might be summarized or completed with a "conclusive tantra" *(uttaratantra)*. We certainly see collections of smaller scriptures, such as the very short tantras that Gayādhara and Candramāla brought to Tibet in the mid-eleventh century.[8] Moreover, the majority of chapters found in the extreme *yoginī* scriptures—like the *Hevajra*, the *Ḍākārṇava*, or the *Vajraḍāka*—are actually quite short and seldom more than a few folia, even when fifty or more chapters are aggregated into a single work.[9] Analogous observations could be made on the *mahāyoga-tantras*, such as the *Guhyasamāja* or the *Kṛṣṇayamāri*, each of which is a mixture of verse and prose and constituted by abbreviated rituals in rather short sections. This is unlike works with a much greater sense of overarching composition, and the *Kālacakra* is one work that stands aside from others in this regard.[10]

THE HIDDEN SCRIPTURES

The dangerous nature of the various practices performed by the Buddhist siddhas—and their strong non-Buddhist ritual associations—meant that their codification into acceptable scriptural systems required extraordinary interpretive devices. Even then, these strategies were not entirely successful in accomplishing either the smooth development of new varieties of esoteric literature or their easy integration into institutional curricula. Their limited successes should not be surprising, given the nature of the requirements. Buddhist hermeneutics in service of the siddha-related literature had to accomplish several arduous goals. First, under the rubric of secrecy, it had to explain why the new literature diametrically contradicted the fundamental Buddhist values of virtuous restraint, since restraint and discipline *(vinaya, śīla)* were the starting points to Buddhist institutional life. Second, siddha hermeneutics needed to generate a systematic interpretation of difficult passages, especially those tying erotic behavior to the Buddha himself. Finally, the exegesis needed to be sufficiently flexible both to reassure the conservative monastic community, while continuing to incorporate new developments in Indian religious life. These are very demanding parameters, for they require an incredibly wide narrative and doctrinal spectrum, all the while making it believable to at least some of the greater Buddhist community. As a result of these and other obstacles, interpretive strategies ultimately took some extraordinary twists and turns.

Because the siddha material was alternatively either toxic or erotic (or both), the most persuasive hermeneutic developed was that the time had sufficiently degenerated to the point that people needed these methods to attract them to the path of awakening. An alternate explanation, however, was that previous assemblies were simply not worthy of receiving the new formulae.[11] Whatever the justification, no longer could the Buddha's message be that pristine virtue was rewarded with undeniable benefit. Instead, disciplined eroticism was now the means to liberation. At the same time, the siddhas successfully argued for the superiority of their teachings. They taught the "highest yoga," leading to awakening in a single lifetime; no other path could possibly lead to this stage.[12] And, as the *Hevajra Tantra* points out, those who do not believe it could be considered the real heretics among the Buddhists.[13]

As seen above, institutional esoterism relied primarily on the narrative of the subjugation and displacement of Śiva as Maheśvara to provide the precipitant moment for the preaching of its esoteric literature. The integration of Maheśvara's retinue into a cosmic vision of reality provided a sense of the sacralization of sāmanta feudalism, valorizing the very monasteries themselves as powerful sacred zones. Although the earliest institutional works did not explicitly recognize the need to embody a new preaching occasion, later literature took up the story with a vengeance. In so many later scriptures, in so many commentaries, Maheśvara is always battling Vajrapāṇi, and the Lord of Secrets is always winning the day. It was to become one of the most important and popular literary events in the developing system of the secret mantras.

For the siddhas, though, the story was to some degree a conflicted or ambiguous statement. Certainly, the *Cakrasaṃvara* system was eventually to appropriate the narrative as a conversion scenario, turning the imaginary geography of the twenty-four Bhairavas into Buddhist seats of power. Although they may have approved of the suppression of the Destroyer of Three Cities, as Śiva was known, their own scriptures had evolved in ways that did not admit of the grand synthetic visions of reality that the institutional systems erected. The multiplicity of esoteric Buddhas/divinities, each with his/her own retinue, sacred zone, occasion of preaching, and ritual statement mitigated against the single preaching model acceptable to institutions. In that sense, the siddha tantras reflected their heterogeneity of source locales and lack of a unifying institutional culture. Instead, we find a preference for the individual expressions about the teaching of each tantra and a privileging of the local account of the transmission of its consecrations and other rites.

The problem with these individual narratives, however, is that they pushed the boundaries of religious imagination. Most Indian Buddhist communities were aware of the written record, even if many individuals could not actually read it themselves. But others could read, and the stories of preaching, collection, and recitation of the Buddhist canon, as well as the standards invoked to affirm authentic scriptures, were relatively well known. There seemed little room in that record to place the more flagrant compositions. By the prior standards of scripture acceptable throughout Buddhist communities, new scriptures were expected to "conform to the sutras, be reflected in the vinaya, and not contradict reality."[14] It is hard, for example, to reconcile the affirmative eroticism of the *Sarvabuddhasamāyoga*'s opening statement—"The illusory seal of all women is the highest non-dual vehicle for awakening"—with the rigorous morality incumbent on ordained monks.[15] Thus another strategy for the integration of this new material needed to be developed. The new avenue was suggested by much earlier Indian Buddhist precedents.

A legend of filial piety reproduced in several sources, such as the *Divyāvadāna*, shows the Buddha preaching to his mother, Mahāmāyā, in the Heaven of the Thirty-three. *Abhidharma* scholars employed this mythology for their own purposes by imbuing it with some content. For them, the scholastic works that constituted the new *Abhidharma* basket of their canon were proposed as the message that the Buddha taught his mother in heaven.[16] Similar narrative systems also became important for Mahayana monks, as they were seeking to establish a broader understanding of the Buddhadharma than the conservative elders of the various orders could admit. Among their other devices, a myth of the preaching of the *Prajñāpāramitā* (Perfection of Insight) scriptures had evolved, in which the Buddha had entrusted them to the subterranean snake spirits, only to be retrieved by Nāgārjuna at a later date.[17] Other scriptures also articulated a mythology of hidden caskets or the Buddha's discourses buried in the element of space itself.[18]

These scenarios were informed by and supported an Indian indigenous theme of suspicion that the truth or the real story is purposely being hidden by those in positions of power. The best early medieval representation of this consistent mistrust of the received archive was found in the *Mattavilāsaprahasana* (Farce of the Fool's Play), by the mid-seventh-century Pallava king, Mahendravikramavarman. There a Buddhist monk, identified simply as Śākyabhikṣu Nāgasena, begins his Prakrit monologue by expostulating on how terrible it was that the elders where hiding the real scriptures wherein the Buddha extolled the benefits of drinking wine and making love to nubile women.[19] Certainly, the play expresses one perception of the clergy as discontent with the received canon. However, if the seventh-century monk could not find the scriptures that he suspected his superiors had kept from him, by the eighth century siddhas had successfully located the holy texts through the act of composition.

The narrative of Indrabhūti's receiving the hidden scriptures became arguably the most widely accepted of the siddha transmission stories. As shown in its earliest surviving version, it is incorporated into an important commentary on the *Prajñāpāramitā-Nayaśatapañcāśatikā* (150 Line Perfection of Insight Sutra) that was included into the institutional esoteric canon. Jñānamitra, the author of the commentary, provides an interesting mythology of the preaching of the esoteric scriptures and their recovery and transmission in a complex social and geographical world.

The Explanation of the Scriptural Annals

> Previously, the Buddha lived eighty years in the human realm. However, at that time there was in this Jambudvīpa no fit human vessel worthy of conversion to the path of the esoteric scriptures like the *Sarvabuddhasamāyoga* or the *Guhyasamāja,* etc. Therefore, the four Great Kings caused the scriptures to reside in the realm of the Thirty-three, Tuṣita, etc., or wherever there were gods and bodhisattvas of the good aeon who were fit vessels for the teaching.
>
> Much later, after the Buddha passed into nirvana, the King of Zahor and his entire retinue miraculously conceived of a pure faith in the Dharma. Thus they became vessels fit for conversion to that esoteric vehicle. By the grace of Vajrapāṇi, the eighteen classes of esoteric scripture, the *Sarvabuddhasamāyoga*, etc., came to that country of Zahor. Then the king of Zahor, Indrabhūti, saw those scriptures and could not explain their sense. However, by the power of previous virtuous action he had obtained supernormal cognition, thinking, "In Madhyadeśa, in the country of Mālava, there is the Ācārya Kukura. During the day he teaches the Dharma to approximately a thousand dogs. During the night, he enjoys the sacraments

> with those dogs. Thus, he is the dog guru *[kukkurācārya]*. I wonder if I have become fit to be converted as a worthy vessel for that path?" So he sent an official messenger to request the Ācārya to come to Zahor.
>
> Now the Ācārya, by the power of previous virtuous action had obtained all five forms of supernormal cognition. So [after receiving the messenger] he thought, "Well, has that king become fit for conversion or not? Moreover, have I become a vessel for those scriptures or not?" And [by virtue of his supernormal cognition] Kukura concluded, "He has become fit for conversion and I am a worthy vessel for the scriptures. Now I will be able to clarify the king's doubts. However, if I am not able to see those scriptures in advance, then in a hundred ways I will not be able to clarify the king's doubts and that will be very unfortunate."
>
> So he sent a reply back with the official messenger, "I request that the king allow me to see these scriptures in advance, so please send them here." When the scriptures arrived, Kukura took one look at them and he became turned upside down, uncertain on where to look. Throwing himself down in front of the books, he cried out, "I have no Lord! I have no Refuge!"
>
> Vajrasattva then physically appeared before him asked, "Just what do you want?"
>
> Kukura replied, "I want to be able to understand these deep scriptures merely by looking at them."
>
> Then Vajrasattva pronounced his blessing, "So I give it to you!"
>
> Then, without even opening the texts, all the meaning of the *Sarvabuddhasamāyoga* and so forth directly became clear in his mind. So then, the Ācārya went to Zahor and preached the Dharma to the king and his retinue. As Vajrasattva had prophesied, he set the king and his retinue to meditating in manner of the Vajradhātu maṇḍala.[20]

The chronicle continues to discuss how Kukura divided up the queens and the court, each placed at a physical direction in the maṇḍala. They and the princes and princesses all took their place on an enormous maṇḍala board, in a physical enactment of the Vajradhātu maṇḍala by the members of the court. Jñānamitra assures us that, at the end, not only did Indrabhūti become a Vidyādhara but so did all the thousand members of the court. Even the heir apparent, Śakraputi, and his seven hundred courtiers, as well as his sister, with her hundred ladies-in-waiting, all became Vidyādharas.

Almost every aspect of this story is interesting and instructive. It is extremely early, for one thing, with Jñānamitra's commentary finding a place in the imperial catalogue of the Denkar Library of c. 810 C.E.[21] The language of the commentary verifies its early date, for it uses syntax and expressions that were not common translation Tibetan during the later period of translation from the tenth to the thirteenth centuries. Moreover, it clearly represents an orthodox attempt to integrate the newly evolving scriptures into the canon and has a hermeneutical agenda. The conclusion of the story describes the physical arrangement of the court as members of the Vajradhātu maṇḍala, which is the maṇḍala from the *Sarvatathāgatatattvasaṃgraha,* rather than from the *Sarvabuddhasamāyoga.* The sense of orthodoxy is further affirmed by Jñānamitra observing that if the *Perfection of Insight* is the mother of all the Buddhas, then the *Sarvatathāgatatattvasaṃgraha* is the father.[22] This gender-laden line of textual categories eventually matures into the classification of *mahāyoga-tantras* as Father Tantras and the *yoginī-tantras* as Mother Tantras. I know of no other source so early, though, that applies gendered categories to esoteric scriptures.

The perennial importance of the Northwest, where Zahor has been sometimes located, is also evident. Other versions of the Indrabhūti mythology almost invariably attach him to Oḍiyāna, and it appears that the two were at one time considered either in proximity or actually identical.[23] In an example of the siddha reiteration of a single name, Indrabhūti became a designation attached to several figures, some of them prolific authors. The Sakya order of Tibetan Buddhism, for instance, retains a memory of three Indrabhūtis—a greater, middle, and lesser—all kings of Oḍiyāna.[24] The other tension is between Mālava and Zahor, between the Buddhist stronghold in the Northwest and the new northern power of the Gurjara-Pratīhāras, where the Kāpālikas had their most important pīṭha of Mahākāla in the city of Ujjain.

More to the point, the story is entirely about laymen, a king on one side and an outcaste preacher on the other. Kukura's living habits—and the bestiality subtlely implied in his night time sacramental involvement with the thousand dogs—make him as extreme in one social direction as the king is in the other.[25] In a sense, they are images of each other; Kukura has his dogs as his retinue and Indrabhūti conducts himself with his queens, courtiers, prince, and princess. Yet they meet in their mutual lack of comprehension on the meaning of the new scriptures. It is only through the intervention of Vajrasattva (our eros embodied and an extension of Vajrapāṇi) that Kukura is capable of understanding the significance of the scriptures and able to teach them to Indrabhūti and his court. Furthermore, the story also depicts laymen teaching one another in the medieval Buddhist ritual system. This they do without any basis other than divine inspiration, for neither is represented as having other teachers. Yet the inspiration and understanding extends from their mutual contact. Indeed, themes of social context at the moment of inspiration continue to inform so many of the siddha narratives, as seen in the cases of Virūpa's inspiration by Nairātmyā and other examples.[26] Social context is also central in the *sahaja-siddhi* lineage story related by another Indrabhūti, who was the receptor of a teaching on *sahaja* that began in Oḍiyāna. There, a princess *Śrī-Mahā-Līlādevī received the teaching on the perfection of natural reality *(sahaja-siddhi)* through her encounter with an unnamed black-haired Ṛṣi in the forest monastery of *Ratnālaṃkāra.[27] In Jñānamitra's narrative, transmission of the siddha lineage is handed from Kukura to Indrabhūti based on their mutual quandary over a poorly understood text, and both protagonists become siddhas in the process.

FROM TRANSMISSION TO RECEPTION

Our investigation of the initial transmission has actually led toward the category of reception: the manner in which claims proposed or literature developed by one group were received by the wider community. In such an investigation, I do not specifically intend the question of literary aesthetics—as discussed by Jauss, Iser, and the Universität Konstanz school of reception theorists—but, rather, its application to the intellectual and social history of Buddhist India.[28] All our evidence indicates that Buddhists were very aware that they lived in highly fluid historical circumstances. In these, they saw and anticipated the continual emergence of claims to authority and power, especially spiritual authority modeled in ways that challenged institutional fundamentals.

Most Buddhist Mahayanist and esoteric scriptures explicitly acknowledge the question of reception with the introductory chapters *(nidāna)* affording scenarios in which different communities are assembled, followed by their haggling over the meaning of the Buddha's message. The hermeneutics of reception, in fact, contributed to one of the great paradoxes of Indian esoteric Buddhism: the employment of secrecy for the purpose of propagating extensively the esoteric practices within multiple communities and subcultures. The esoteric method is arguably the most successful Indian Buddhist ritual system to market itself throughout both the traditional and modern worlds. Given the extraordinary spread and viability of the esoteric persuasion, it appears that one aspect of its popularity is exactly its claims to superiority by virtue of selectivity. Few themes fan the flames of desire like restricted access and an aura of incomparability. In their emphasis on secrecy, esoteric Buddhists shared systems of transmission with other institutions that required secrecy in the pursuit of hegemonic status: governments, trade societies, criminal conspiracies, and ritual specialists.

In recognition of these requirements, the rhetoric of esoterism directed that new material typically be introduced through the agency of a scriptural pronouncement that is presented as a challenge to the status quo. The language of the introductory chapters *(nidāna)*, introductory sections of threatening chapters, and sections on coded language *(sandhyābhāṣā)* often represent their content as causing grave doubts, sometimes about their referents, sometimes about the nature of the Buddha's message itself. Many of the literary techniques had already been introduced in Mahayana sutras, especially the *Saddharmapuṇḍarīka,* but were used now to justify decidedly different content.[29] For example, in chapter 2 of the *Saddharmapuṇḍarīka*, the chapter on Skillful Means, a new pronouncement of the single vehicle is proposed for all those grasping after separate vehicles. The monks, nuns, laymen, and laywomen who cannot withstand the new message are allowed to leave, for the new system would sow doubt and confusion in their hearts, causing them to lose their confidence in the Buddha's dispensation. The teacher's real message is difficult to understand *(durbodhyaṃ tathāgatasya saṁdhābhāṣyam)*, but consists of the articulation of a single vehicle. Because of the limitations of the various assemblies, though, he had to couch his message in a skillfully coded series of graded ideas. Yet behind these statements lurks a doctrine often alluded to in Buddhism: the intention of the teacher has not been exhausted by the current understanding of the existing community. As new events and conditions in the world unfold, the teacher's intention becomes clearer in some measure as well. New material, then, represents the liberation of the teacher's intention from literalness *(saṃdhinirmocana)*.

The rhetoric of degeneration in the early medieval period meant that the new practices could be envisioned as both a sign of the times and an opportunity to harness formerly inaccessible energies. For example, in an alternative Indrabhūti narrative, the Oḍiyāna monarch begs the Buddha for a set of scriptures that embody the means to liberation for those who could not withstand the requirements of monastic renunciation, but who wanted to use the senses for the purpose of awakening.[30] This story had the advantage of employing the Mahayanist idea that liberation (or the embryo of the Tathāgata) existed as a specific element in the six senses of beings or that the fundamental purity of consciousness was concomitant with gnosis. Using beings' proclivities (even sex and death), then, was another example of the Buddha's skillful means of leading them to awakening. Yet neither the Maheśvara subjugation myths nor the Indrabhūti preaching stories exhausted the inspired speech of Buddhist preachers, who continued to develop new and exciting descriptions about the preaching of this or that tantra. Sometimes these were related in the introductory chapter of a tantra, as shown in the *Buddhakapāla-yoginī-tantra-rāja*, or in the commentarial materials dedicated to the interpretation and propagation of that work, as in the *Kālacakra-tantra*.

The other great strength of skillful means' rhetoric lay in the Buddhist experience of teaching—monasteries understood the principle of graded instruction, so that novices would be led to knowledge by degrees. Indeed, the "graded ideas/audience quality" issue plays an important position in the tantras, where the introduction of new material had to work that much harder because of the quantum leap in erotic language. Recent apologists for the Buddhist tantras have concentrated on linguistic deconstruction through the artifice of "coded language" *(saṃdhā/saṃdhyā/saṃdhāya-bhāṣā)*, which had been used by selected commentators to take some of the spice from the brew. According to this idea, all the language of the tantras is figurative, not literal. Thus the eros and thanatos of the esoteric scriptures are to be understood as indicative of a secret coded form of language, referring to internal experiences. The key to such language was revealed in the esoteric transmission from master to disciple, and only uninformed outsiders considered that the statements might be simple declarative pronouncements.

Unfortunately, as shown below, the invocation of the various strategies of textual hermeneutics—of which "coded language" is only one—is highly idiosyncratic and lacks any uniform method of application.[31] Only in the modern public presentation has there developed the myth of uniform tantric hermeneutics, a single key or approved method of interpretation for passages involving erotics or violence. Yet actual practice is dramatically different from this modern rhetorical position. A single section of a tantra may be taken as literal or variously figurative by different commentators in India (or China, Tibet, or Japan), even with the same commentator sometimes adopting different explanations mid-stride. This disparity was acknowledged in traditional discourse. Thus the argument against literalness appears to lose a degree of force in the absence of hermeneutic unanimity. Moreover, there is even doubt that "coded language" had a well-defined semantic value, let alone a systematic application.

THE BUDDHA'S TALKING SKULL EXCITES WOMEN, KILLS SNAKES, AND BELCHES A BOOK

The single most outrageous opening scenario of any Buddhist text with which I am familiar is found in the *Buddhakapāla-yoginī-tantra-rāja*, a ninth-century or later work that self-consciously has included material in imitation of Kāpālika Śaivism. It is classified as a *yoginī-tantra* and in many ways represents an excellent corrective to the rather limited consideration of *yoginī-tantra* material to date. In view of the available archive, there has been an excessive emphasis on the *Hevajra Tantra* or the *Cakrasaṃvara* corpus, based in part on the Tibetan esteem for these lineages. The *Buddhadkapāla*, though, continues to enjoy a strong traditional reputation and popularity. Its exegetical and ritual visibility signifies that its status as an esoteric text was taken seriously by its Indian authors and commentators as well as by the Tibetans who have preserved its translation. The *Buddhadkapāla*'s introductory scenario relates the narrative of its own preaching and the spiritual source of its text. That inaugural direction is not exceptional in itself, but the *Buddhadkapāla* unfolds its story in a manner virtually guaranteed to shock its listeners or readers. After the short, initial description of the Buddhas, their consorts, and their retinues in language familiar to readers of the *yoginī-tantra* literature, the text moves to the precipitating dramatic moment.

> Then the Bhagavān—having correctly explained the mantras and all the tantras by means of adamantine words in the great adamantine site—this lord of all the Tathāgatas placed his vajra in his consort's lotus, and promptly entered final nirvana [dying] in the lady's vagina. Having seen the Lord pass away in that manner, all the bodhisattvas and all the yoginīs were astonished. Looking to one another, they all exclaimed, "Oh, my! How is it that the Bhagavān, the Lord of all the Tathāgatas, should pass away in this Great Jeweled Maṇḍala?"
>
> So the bodhisattva mahasattva Vajrapāṇi turned to the yoginī Citrasenā and asked her the following question: "Devī, is there some slight method whereby those beings of lesser merit may ascend to power *[*śaktyārohaṇopāya]*?"[32]
>
> "For it is said that there are sixty million [methods] in the *yogatantra*. There are 160 million in the *yoginī-tantra*. There are 800 million in the various *sūtrāntas*. In the same way, there are 500,000 krores [$(5 \times 10^5) \times 10^7$] within the perfection vehicle *[pāramitāyāna]*. All of these methods have been expounded by the Munīndra [Śākyamuni]. If any are separated from mantras, then the power of tantra *[tantraśakti]* will not appear."
>
> "Now within some of the tantras, according to the mantra, recitation up to ten million times is proposed. Those of medium merit, however, are said to achieve siddhi quickly by reciting the mantra one hundred thousand times. Likewise, those of great merit will become accomplished very quick-

ly in ten thousand recitations. In that way, the Great Vajrin, the Chief of the Tantric Lords has spoken. Those of little merit, though, must recite ten million times. Yet it is said that those of little application may recite the mantra a hundred thousand times. Actually, ones attached to meditation might recite only ten thousand mantras."

"So the question remains: How is the recitation of those beings mired in desire? How many recitations for those who belong to families of morons and idiots? How does one who has lost his goal recite the mantras? For it would seem that mantras recited by those engaged in idle gossip will have their accomplishment occur elsewhere. And if the recitation is done in accordance with the emotions of retarded troglodytes—well, they can recite for as many tens of millions of aeons as there are stars in the sky and get no powers at all."

Now the yoginī Citrasenā, having heard this, looked at the face of the [deceased] Lord, ogling him with desire and languorous sidelong glances [*sakaṭākṣa*]. Then enraged and ferocious, with a mind full of compassion, she destroyed Māra's army. Consequently, ogled in that way by this Mahādevī—the Lady and mistress of all the tantras[33]— the head [of Śākyamuni] opens up and out pops a mantra: OM BUDDHE SIDDHE SUSIDDHE AMṚITA ARJE BUDDHA KAPĀLA SPHOṬANIPĀTAYA TRĀSAYA HŪṂ HO PHAT |[34] Resounding in this way, the supreme mantra goes forth and conquers the nāgas below the seventh level, reducing them to dust. The mantra then comes back and enters the mouth of Citrasenā, only to emerge from her vagina and returns to the Buddha's skull.

As all the nāgas were being destroyed by the power of this mantra, they became afraid and began to sweat heavily. So the great magical snakes, like Vāsuki, assembled, as did all the rest of the poisonous tribe: Karkoṭaka, Śaṅkhapāla, Takṣaka, Ananta, Padma, Mahāpadma, and so forth. Turning toward the yoginī Citrasenā, they implored her, "Devī, say what you want and we will do it!" She replied, "Do whatever is in accordance with the Buddha's experience!"

As soon as this was heard, in the middle of the Great Jeweled Maṇḍala, the Buddha's skull opened its mouth wide and out of it emerged a text. The skies resounded with the verse,

"O Goddess Citrasenā—take the book! It will benefit all beings.
This tantra is a great king of tantras, for there is no yoginī [tantra] superior to it.
It is called *Buddhakāpāla*. It will benefit all beings."

Having heard this, Citrasenā took up the text and entrusted it to Vajrapāṇi.[35]

This peculiar opening is an excellent vehicle to test to position that the tantras embed within the secret scriptures a coded language accessible only to the masters. If so, the surviving commentaries would be expected to provide some degree of continuity between their positions and their language, for all three Indian commentators are acknowledged masters. Conversely, if the commentaries are actually independent moments in the domestication of the tantra, then they will instead each display their author's proclivities. According to this latter model, the primary purposes of the commentaries will be to lessen the force of the scripture's extreme content and to move the text into a symbolic realm approachable by normative Buddhist praxis.

Three commentaries are available for the opening chapter of the *Buddhakapāla:* the *Śrī-Buddhakapālatantrapañjikā Jñānavatī* ascribed to Saraha,[36] the *Buddhakapālatantrapañjikā Tattvacandrikā* ascribed to Padmavajra,[37] and the *Śrī-Buddhakapālamahātantrarājaṭīkā Abhayapaddhatiḥ* of Abhayākaragupta.[38] In reality, the commentaries are so different one from the other that it is sometimes hard to believe that they comment on the same text or belong to the same tradition. Collectively, they might act as a paradigm for the difficulties in the homogenization of Buddhist hermeneutical strategies, since they all address this singular episode in quite different ways.

The Saraha commentary is either the most creative or the least linear, depending on whether any degree of consistency is desired. Having described the teacher and retinue in a relatively standard fashion, Saraha declares the yoginī Citrasenā as an emanation of the Buddha, not too different from the kind of grand solipsistic hermeneutics found in the *Hevajra Tantra,* wherein all the elite members of his retinue are the Tathāgata's manifestations.[39] However, the balance of the retinue is described in standard terms, identifying Ānanda and Avalokiteśvara as members of the Arhatsaṅgha and Bodhisattvasaṅgha, respectively, all residing together in the maṇḍala. When the Buddha suddenly enters nirvana, though, the Bodhisattvas all become the faculties of vision, hearing, and so on.[40] From this point on, most of the characters are simultaneously explained as internal components—especially the various yogic channels (*nāḍī*), forms of gnosis, or the Buddhas of the yogic "perfecting process" (*sampannakrama*)—as well as being the external agents. The description leaves the student with the queasy feeling that not only is the Buddha's physical body inhabited by the various "perfecting process" internal maṇḍala figures, unexceptional in itself, but that they are individually and collectively active characters in the drama of the tantra. Consequently, the reader courts the uncomfortable suspicion that the Buddha's internal soteriological diagram will break into song and dance at a moment's notice, as scriptural personalities sometimes do in the yoginī literature.

Although the other two commentators are much more prosaic, all three represent the instance of the Buddha's passing (entrance into nirvana) in different ways. Saraha maintains that, since nirvana is utterly dissociated from thought, and since this is the characteristic of the Buddha's absolute body *(dharmakāya)*, all we have to do is understand that the Buddha is demonstrating the *dharmakāya*.[41] This *dharmakāya* is somehow seen by the assembled retinue, a possibility in the case of the *dharmakāya* defined as the "corpus of instruction," which clearly identifies the issue of leading up to preaching (emitting) the tantra about to be presented. However, the definition of *dharmakāya* given by Saraha is that it is cognitively nonconceptual, so his comment appears a very curious explanation of a physical event. Padmavajra, conversely, defines the process as the pattern of sexual yoga according to the practice of *sampannakrama*. Thus the Buddha is merely demonstrating to the bodhisattvas of pure birth the way to reside in the essence of great bliss. Here, Padmavajra glosses nirvana as the highest reality *(tattva)*.[42] His definition is dependent on the specifically Vajrayāna employment of the designation "tattva" for the various elements of esoteric practice. Finally, Abhayākaragupta's text indicates that the form of nirvana is nonlocalized, a common definition of nirvana within the Mahayana. The Buddha is nonlocalized in phenomenal existence through the presence of insight derived from the adamantine seat of the Great Seal; he is nonlocalized in quiescent peace, as his great compassion motivates him for the welfare of all beings. Empowered by prior accomplishment and impelled by his nonadhesion to the extreme perspectives, the Buddha is capable of assuming whatever form may be required by beings as long as existence lasts, through his nonconceptual identity with the unlimited Tathāgatas, bodhisattvas, yoginīs, and so on.[43]

Perhaps the most interesting fact of these hermeneutic gymnastics is that all of them accomplish several things. First, the humorous non sequitur of the episode is explained away or ignored altogether. The *Buddhadkapāla* presents the disquieting image of the Buddha dying *in flagrante delicto*, surrounded by the vast retinue of spiritual beings. In the midst of this cosmic catastrophe and while the great concourse are afflicted with doubt and insecurity, Vajrapāṇi turns to some available but otherwise obscure yoginī and asks how the terminally incompetent might aspire to the awakened state? The commentators systematically dismantle the death of the Tathāgata, so that the force of his act is lost in a blizzard of philosophical terminology. Yet there can be no other explanation, for the skull of the Buddha is that which is required to release the mantra and the text of the tantra. Moreover, the commentators explain away the intriguing necrophilia of Citrasenā by the same token—if the Buddha does not really die, then the desire exhibited for the corpse of the Buddha by Citrasenā is really desire for the phenomenal body of the Buddha *(nirmāṇakāya)*. Finally, the immediately succeeding events—the survey of esoteric literature, the ecstasy of Citrasenā that results in overcoming Māra and the release of the mantra, the attack on snakes, and the exposure of the text all lose their literary force in the interpretive process. In fact Abhayākaragupta successfully turns the whole episode around and argues for the unlimited action of the Buddha in the world as a result of this episode; he does not reveal how *this* action would cause consternation in the assembly.

EVERYTHING YOU KNOW IS WRONG

The fact that there are few threads of common content should come as no surprise. Instead, the commentators demonstrate a compulsion to escort the radical scriptures into a garden of safety and innocuousness. In reality, one of the primary motivations for the above commentarial hermeneutic was as a subtle form of criticism, taking the scriptural authors to task for real or imagined transgressions of behavioral norms. The subculture of tantric composition (especially the *yoginī tantras)* exhibited clearly different values from those of the commentarial subculture: one is creative and outrageous while the other represents rapprochement with institutional norms. However, it is equally intriguing to consider that all three commentators were considered siddhas, and two of them (Saraha and Padmavajra) had their names entered into standard lists of mahāsiddhas.[44] Accordingly, we must be wary of attempts—traditional or modern—to homogenize siddhas into a single Buddhist subculture and should understand that they exhibited a wide variation of background, learning, orientation, and so forth. In the cases of Virūpa, Nāropā, and Maitrīpa, it is clear that some siddhas had passed through or were at least partially socialized in the monastic regime.[45] Conversely, others were reputed to have followed the siddha path without exposure to institutional expectations, as in the case of Ḍombīheruka (a boatman) or Lūhipa (a scribe).[46] Thus, if even the institutionally oriented siddhas are discomfited at the content exhibited here, we might wonder about its reception by others in the community, especially the more conservative monks, who might be concerned about monastic stability.

Actually, the introductory materials are often the greatest challenge for the exegetes, especially as the scriptural authors often preempt their discussion by acknowledging the reception of these scenarios as disquieting, new, and perhaps completely different from anything yet seen in the breadth of Buddhist literature. The goal of the commentators in this process is to redefine the statements, so that they will lose their unprecedented status and have their venom extracted. Consider, for example, the bald-faced declaration about the nature of the Congress *(samāja)* gathered by the Ādibuddha Bodhicittavajra in chapter 1 of the *Guhyasamājatantra.*

> Now all the Tathāgatas, having come again to the Congress, made offerings to the Lord Bodhicittavajra with clouds of jewels and elements of reality associated with the vows, so as to send forth the offerings to all the Tathāgatas. Having bowed down [to Bodhicittavajra], they declared,
>
> > "Lord, pronounce the element of reality that is the aggregate of adamantine essence, that esoteric Congress of all Tathāgatas, developed in secrecy!"
>
> Then the Lord Bodhicittavajra, the Tathāgata, said to all of those Tathāgatas, "Excellent, excellent, Lord Tathāgatas! *But [articulating that Congress] is a cause for doubt even for all the Tathāgatas, let alone for the other bodhisattvas!*"
>
> But then all the Lord Tathāgatas were amazed and astonished. So they requested of the Lord, the Master of all the Tathāgatas, the scalpel of doubts for all the Tathāgatas, "Lord, do not be indolent in teaching the secret of all the Tathāgatas' physical, vocal, and mental continua in the assembly of all the Tathāgatas, an assembly so distinguished with excellence!"[47]

This strategy for introducing new practices by maintaining that they were unknown even to the Buddhas is often seen in esoteric literature. Perhaps its earliest expression is found in the early seventh-century Gilgit manuscript of the *Kāraṇḍavyūha*, where remarkably similar language is employed to introduce the hitherto-unknown, secret, six-syllable mantra of Avalokiteśvara: OṂ MAṆI PADME HŪṂ![48]

But the commentators' purpose is hermeneutic refinement, and Candrakīrti, the author of the celebrated *Pradīpodyotana* commentary on the *Guhyasamājatantra,* clearly has a lot of explaining to do.[49] Having already appropriated the name of one of the most famous curmudgeons of Buddhist philosophical thought, the tantric Candrakīrti certainly was not one to refuse a challenge. So, instead of blithely passing over the passage as some lesser commentator might, he gamely encounters the section head on in the best apologetic style.

> So Bodhicittavajra addresses all the Tathāgatas, "Excellent, excellent" in the sense of acceptance of the task, since the question served to illuminate the idea he had in mind. But in the analysis of the literal text, "a cause for uncertainty even for all the Tathāgatas," we must see that, here, the terms "Tathāgatas" and "bodhisattvas" have to indicate yogins who are still exerting themselves [on the path]. *There can be no question of "doubt" existing for Buddhas and bodhisattvas who have eliminated the traces of defilement.* So "Tathāgatas" here really means those precious persons who have matured their good roots, have completed their hearing of the doctrines, and have well defined pedigrees *[niyatagotra]* while they are in pursuit of Buddhahood. But even for them the significance of "Congress" *[samāja]* will remain obscure without the commencement [of discussion] by the Teacher, since they will lack comprehension. How much more so for other bodhisattvas? For even when persons of the Sandalwood strata, etc.—who have matured their good roots but with little motivation—are taught this Congress, they will respond with listlessness, since it is hard to grasp.[50]

Thus, Candrakīrti redefines Tathāgatas and bodhisattvas in the text so that these esteemed categories of saintly beings could never become subject to uncertainty. Yet there can be no doubt that this is *precisely* the meaning the authors of the scriptures intended; the point is emphasized again later in the *Guhyasamāja*.[51] The original Buddha *(ādibuddha)*, Bodhicittavajra, is about to discuss the organization of reality, and the other Buddhas are as lost as freshmen in the University Registrar's office. They are afflicted with precisely the emotion least appreciated by self-righteous Indian know-it-all monks: doubt. The creation of a maṇḍala in chapter 1 of the *Guhyasamājatantra* is meaningless unless the personality of Bodhicittavajra is surrounded by the other Buddhas and bodhisattvas of the system, who are eventually to take their several places in this maṇḍala. In their brazen challenge to the received wisdom of Indian Buddhist communities, the tantra authors have issued a full warning, much as the authors of the *Lotus Sutra* had done so many centuries before: this material will offend their sense of the authority of the Buddha and might divide the community. These offenses clearly disturbed the deepest value systems of Indian Buddhists, for whom division of the community was one of the most heinous crimes possible.

Coming to our exegetical aid at this point is material drawn from sources that are seldom considered in the discussion of esoteric value systems, but that have played a central role in organizing that material for medieval Indians and Tibetans: namely, the theoretical treatises of the Vajrayāna, those many monuments to exegetical engineering that have configured, schematized, adjudicated, packaged, and promoted the otherwise bewildering mass of the esoteric scriptures. They are not exactly commentaries, although most comment on selected quotations to the various tantras. Unfortunately, the original Indic treatises have been largely ignored, and it is the fifteenth-century work of the Tibetan author Kendrup Gelek Pelsangbo that has curiously garnered the most attention, despite the publication of two of these Sanskrit works by Benoytosh Bhattacharya in 1929.[52]

Attributed to Padmavajra—perhaps the same person as the commentator on the *Buddhakapāla-tantra* whose interest in the "perfecting process" of sexual yoga was noted above—is the *Guhyasiddhi* (Secret Accomplishment). As a ninth-century understanding of the *Guhyasamājatantra*, this was to prove one of the most influential and widely quoted of the Vajrayāna technical works. Unlike Candrakīrti, Padmavajra is unrepentant in his direct address of the unprecedented statements in the *Guhyasamājatantra.* Indeed, the text begins by taking the bull by the horns.

> That condition of highest ease, released from the world's ways, pervasive yet essenceless, continually generated by the Lords of monks, it is praised by the best bulls of sages as beyond contemplation. *Unrealized even by the Buddhas,* utterly plundered of defilements by its very reality—I revere that glorious body of the Victors, so much more the excellent state, so pure by its own agency.[53]

Thus the opening contains the most Buddhist of literary conventions—a paradox. The highest state is the body of the Victors, but it is unrealized even by the Buddhas. Its transcendence of contemplation is a reasonably standard characteristic of esoteric literature and is normatively explained by recourse to definitions of nonconceptualization: where there is no idea of contemplative activity, then a self-conscious category of meditation is out of the question. The putative affirmation of the body of the Buddhas without their own realization, though, is another matter and is related to the esteem that the *Guhyasamājatantra* enjoys in the *Guhyasiddhi.* Indeed, in chapter 2 of the *Guhyasiddhi,* Padmavajra moves to explain the difficult *Guhyasamājatantra* passage on how Bodhicittavajra might understand the esoteric Congress *(guhyasamāja)* that is causing the other Buddhas in the maṇḍala such grave doubts.

Therefore, I will now elucidate something of the ritual of accomplishment—the secret occasion—by means of the path identified in the *Samāja* but not by the stages of meditation found in other tantras. (1)

Having rejected in extreme all the paths found in tantras instructing in external rituals, [the ritual of accomplishment] is announced [in the *Samāja*] exactly as it is, through the disciplined contemplation of those stages of meditation following this tradition. (2)

Now many teachers claim that the collector and cantor of the *Samāja* is the heroic leader Lokeśa, of great splendor. (3)

But, based on devotion at the feet of the teacher, only *we* maintain that in the *Śrīsamāja* there is no other collector and canter (4)

Than the author of the tantra, Hṛdvajra [= Bodhicittavajra]. He alone is the speaker and the teacher. Thus there is none other if we were to eliminate this [person of] Great Bliss. (5)

Accordingly, the statement beginning "Thus have I heard" up to the word "resided," has been pronounced by Cittavajrin himself among all the Buddhas.[54] (6)

Since this condition of residence has been declared pure and divine exactly as it is by the glorious Lord of Great Bliss, I will speak a bit about its nature. (7)

As the Master has revealed in that one highest place the true nature of the Buddhas' tantra to be simply his own great bliss, (8)

Having heard that true nature of the tantra, all the Victors' sons were shaken and, filled with anxiety, addressed the Great Lord: (9)

"What is this teaching, O Hero, which is the expression of that difficult to express, O Master, which endlessly causes terror in every way, *even within the Buddhas?* (10)

O Master, having unveiled the highest Vajrayāna, boundlessly obscure, you have expressed the essential unity of all phenomena!" (11)

Thus, the Champions of all Buddhas—frivolously chattering—trembled, arrived at stupefaction, and placed their minds in the attitude of awakening. (12)

So! This is the teaching of the surpassingly secret Vajrayāna, which has no comparison in its pure and essenceless nature. (13)

But Vajrasattva, seeing *all the Buddhas stupefied in this way*, entered the divine concentration, consisting of the pleasure of great bliss. (14)

As a consequence, he compelled all the Buddhas to employ the union of the vajra and the lotus, and in the form of the highest bliss spoke to them with the following sweet speech: (15)[55]

Unlike Candrakīrti, Padmavajra has little problem expressing the idea that the nature of the meditative system expounded in the *Guhyasamājatantra* consists of qualities that are unprecedented. For Padmavajra, not only is the message beyond the comprehension of all the Buddhas, but it is exceedingly disturbing to them, and their disturbance is rectified only if they enter into sexual congress with the female of the species. Indeed, Padmavajra ends up here with a de facto definition of tantric scripture: the expression of Bodhicittavajra's personal great bliss, which is the essence of all the Buddhas' tantras. Moreover, his great bliss is clearly a result of the unity of complements, which has as its physical expression and central technique the union of the sexual organs by masters of the Vajrayāna.

THE MAGIC DECODER: THE CONSTRUCT OF CODED LANGUAGE

These hermeneutical themes circulate around the esoteric Buddhist documents in a variety of patterns, which collectively suggest that their representatives were competing in the marketplace of Buddhist marginal institutions. Many themes articulate the ideology that, compared to other scriptures, their tantra of choice is without precedent. Occasionally, as seen above, this message was combined with the doctrine that the new dispensation was outside the prior comprehension of the Buddhas themselves, to be received from sources hitherto untapped. Most often, the specified scriptural sources are deeper levels of reality or more perfectly awakened Buddhas. In any event, we should resist the conclusion that the ideology presented is one of doctrinal progress in any modern sense.

In certain environments, all or part of these messages are allied with the formulae of coded language, alluded to above, but with a decided shift in valence. Broido has already shown that coded language in esoteric exegesis became, in a sense, bifurcated.[56] On the one hand, it was employed as a hermeneutical strategy to offer explanations to parts of texts that were socially or textually difficult. Here, coded language was a powerful interpretive tool, one that was often both used and abused. On the other hand, coded language was taken to describe a series of language acts whose exact meaning was either unknown or problematic. The words and statements were required nonetheless for reasons of ritual applications; this second form of coded language is examined below.

In its hermeneutic application, the declaration by a commentator that "this is coded" was an interpretive device sharing a commonality with the older Mahayanist usage. Its purpose, to unpack an intentional layer of significance below the surface of the language structures, was very commonly used. In such documents as the *Pradīpodyotana*, and in Munidatta's commentary to the *Caryāgītikośa*, the terms *sandhyā-bhāṣā/sandhyā-bhāṣita* have stood as categories of exegesis, along with many others.[57] The purpose of this process is to take specific words and provide them with an alternative meaning, sometimes well founded and sometimes an exercise in interpretive ballet. One example is what Munidatta does with Virūpa's drinking song, a humorous acknowledgment that the famous saint preferred to spend time in a bar rather than in religious environments.

Virūpa's Drinking Song

All alone this barmaid serves two at her home, preparing the rot-gut with neither yeast nor shredded bark.
The booze is brewed naturally strong, making my body tough—no old age or death for me!
I saw the sign at the tenth door, so I came as a customer, to get myself some.
There're sixty-four jugs set out up on the shelf. Once I make it in as a consumer, I may not leave!
Hey! There's one bottle with a real thin neck—
Virūpa says: pour me a strong one![58]

Munidatta's Interpretation

The unique Central Channel brings together the two subsidiary channels of the right and left above at the nose, to produce firmness of self-consecration. Below they are also fused at the genital organ to bind the relative thought of awakening and to produce the highest bliss.
The absolute thought of awakening is made firm through binding the relative thought of awakening with the noose of the coemergent bliss.
The yogi, like a heavenly being, enters the door of Vairocana at the tenth level, having seen its sign. He is satisfied with the drink from the lotus of great bliss.
The Central Channel unites the relative and absolute truths and is subtle in form, having destroyed duality's appearance.
Virūpa calls on the Central Channel to remain motionless.[59]

In his extraordinary reading of Virūpa's drinking song, Munidatta accomplishes several hermeneutical goals. First, he uncouples Virūpa from the kind of activity that would render him a siddha unpalatable to entire groups of prospective followers. Within India in particular, drinking is a low-status form of recreation, so Virūpa can be elevated on the social horizon by the exegetical process. Second, the poem can tie Virūpa's hagiography to the practice of various yogic meditations in the way that a simple reading of the poetry cannot. This means that the individual ritual or poetic texts attributed to Virūpa may be placed within the hagiographical continuum, so that the compositions may be understood as an extension of his awakened condition, rather than the ramblings of an alcoholic yogin.

This last point is important, for Munidatta would have us believe that the Virūpa of the drinking song in fact does not drink. Yet Virūpa's legendary alcoholic proclivities are so important to the normative hagiography that his iconography relies on a drinking episode.[60] In it, Virūpa and Kāṇha arrive at a bar with no money. Quite understandably, the barmaid refuses to serve two disreputable sādhus without some demonstration of an ability to pay. Virūpa declares that when the line between the sunlight and the shadow cast by the doorframe reaches a certain point, he will pay her. Satisfied, she serves them (pours him a strong one, in the drinking song). However, Virūpa takes a knife and nails the sunbeam on the surface of the table, causing the sun to become arrested in its path. As the sunbeam never reaches the point where they have to pay, Virūpa and Kāṇha drink up all the booze in the bar and all the liquor in the eighteen regions of that area. All the waterclocks and sundials seem broken, and everyone seems themselves as if drunk from a lack of sleep. The king eventually comes to the rescue by paying the bar tab, at which point Virūpa releases the sun and continues on his way.

This scenario was so important that it was taken as the basis for the normative iconography. In his representations, Virūpa is depicted holding onto the sun by a ray of light that comes down to his hand. The episode, like others in his hagiography, establishes that Virūpa is a mahāsiddha, one with great perfection of power. He drinks without getting drunk, all the while controlling the sun and, later, the Ganges River. In both instances, he is able to do so because he has received inspiration from Nairātmyā, the divine consort of the Original Buddha Vajradhara, in a series of revelations that brought Virūpa to the sixth level of the bodhisattva (Figure 16). Thus, consecrated by ultimate reality herself, Virūpa can overcome the gods of the natural world, which is exactly what he does. He orders the Goddess Ganges back up her course, so the river dries

FIGURE 16 *Mārga-phala lineage painting. Clockwise from upper left: Vajradhara, Nairātmyā, Kāṇha, Virūpa. Tibet, second half of the fifteenth century. Color and gold paint on cloth, 57.5 × 50.2 cm.
© The Cleveland Museum of Art, 2001, Purchase from the J. H. Wade Fund, 1960.206. Reprinted with permission.

up for a time and he can cross. In the drinking episode, he holds the god Sūrya (Sun) from continuing on his path. These are the proofs of his mastery of psychic power *(siddhi)*, and without the narrative episodes he has no siddha status.

Elsewhere we see that the interpretation of uncomfortable social realities, particularly drinking, was done through religious metaphors to such an extent that it became the source of farce. In the *Mattavilāsa-prahasana* (Farce of the Fool's Play), a disreputable Kāpālika named Satyasoma is shown rationalizing a taste for powerful drink. He shares his vision of the toddy house as a religious sacrifice with his Kāpālika consort, Devasomā.

> Satyasoma to Devasomā: Hey, Baby—check it out! This saloon imitates the riches of the sacrificial site. It's all here: the sign pole is the post of sacrifice; the booze is the Soma; the barflies are the chief priests; the glasses are the ritual vessels; the snacks, roast meat and the rest, are the special oblations; the slurred speech of the crowd is the liturgy; their drunken songs are the chants; the pitchers of white lightening are the offering ladles; the patrons' thirsty need is the mouth of fire; and the tavern-keep himself is the master of ceremonies.[61]

The differences between this and Virūpa's song are many, of course. Virūpa seems to make no apology for his recreational preference, and his hagiographers positively revel in his ability to surpass all others in quantity. It is Munidatta who feels moved to explain away the great saint's unfortunate preference in dining establishments. Satyasoma, though, has no Munidatta to do this for him and, instead, shows an alcoholic's willingness to make any excuse for his lapses. For the royal playwright, Mahendravikramavarman, the opportunity to use the widely condemned and surreptitiously practiced habit of imbibing is just too attractive to resist. The rationalization of excessive imbibing by disreputable yogins was well known enough to become a comedic moment, for the farce would have little resonance without a measure of conformity to the observable world.

In a sense, it is somewhat unfortunate that Munidatta has, in the modern period, become the exegete of choice to demonstrate the hermeneutical technique of coded language. Although many of Munidatta's readings of the *Caryāgītikośa* poems appear forced and implausible, as seen above, more commonly the process is relatively clear. For example, Anaṅga Yogin, at the beginning of his *Ḍākinījālasaṃvararahasya*, quotes two verses describing the consecration. At one point, the verses mention three "mundane" forms of bliss, contrasted with one imperishable accomplishment *(akṣarā siddhiḥ)*.

Anaṅga Yogin comments on this by saying, "The Lord spoke in code when he declared that the fourth imperishable bliss, which occurs by following the desire of the Great Seal, is thus the consecration for the perfection of the discipline [i.e., the fourth consecration]."[62] There is actually nothing particularly esoteric about Anaṅga Yogin's application of a perfectly standard exegetical device. Those familiar with the terminology of the system would arrive at exactly the same conclusion, and Anaṅga Yogin is providing here a welcome clarification of ritual language that has become a little too embedded in jargon and technical nomenclature.

Thus, at its most workmanlike level, coded language operates simply as a basic tool of interpretation for commentators attempting to unpack the practices or implications of various scriptural statements. It is well to keep in mind, however, that the *many* other categories of exegetical criticism—"direct meaning" *(nītārtha)*, "indirect meaning" *(ñeyārtha)*, and so on—afforded the opportunity for institutional siddhas to construct a series of layered significations. In this manner, each statement implicated a spectrum of other meanings, so all tantric words were polysemic by definition. Every term, however seemingly insignificant, thereby became implicated in a hierarchical web of symbol systems. The ensuing complexity turned many of the rather pedestrian ritual exercises found in the new scriptures into highly challenging intellectual enterprises. Thus tantric hermeneutics heaped thick description on thick description (to invoke Geertz's language), each embedded in the other. As a tool in the process of domestication, coded language and its analogues became invaluable assets in the architecture of criteria of meaning. It allowed siddhas to turn some of the more difficult language events into soteriological descriptions. If the forced interpretations of Munidatta are somewhat transparent, the entire spectrum of hermeneutics should be kept in mind as a corrective to the idiom of a single author.

CODED LANGUAGE AS SECRET RITUAL WORDS

In distinction to the hermeneutical usage, the other employment of "coded language" *(sandhyā-bhāṣā)* in the tantras became separated from apologetics or exegesis *per se*. It was divorced from previous attempts to explain the new doctrine as an elaboration of the prior message. Instead of justifying the new message as the unfolding of the intentional abstruse nature of Buddhist scriptures, both scriptural and exegetical authors deployed an entirely new kind of communication, consisting of both words and gestures. It was not to be justified by any of the previous literature, but stands apart from it by indicating that there were lists of terms and gestures that required specific meanings to be recognized in them.

Previous attempts to explain this kind of coded language in the esoteric Buddhist scriptures have emphasized two sources: the twenty-two terms in the *sandhyā-bhāṣā* chapter of the *Hevajra Tantra (HT,* II.iii.56–61) and the commentary to that list of coded words ascribed to Nāgārjunapāda *(Saṃdhibhāṣā-ṭīkā)*. Certainly, these are essential sources for understanding the development and application of coded language in esoteric Buddhism, yet it is not clear that all the evidence has been taken into account. For example, the introductory verses to the coded language section in the *Hevajra Tantra* emphasize that the employment of coded communication in ritualized behavior—smiling, gazing, embracing, and sexual union—is not found in the other four kinds of tantras (II.iii.54). The *Hevajra Tantra* provides glosses to its list of twenty-two terms so that their meanings may be understood by initiates who intend to engage in the practices associated with the tantric feast.

madhya = *madana*
(wine = intoxication)[63]

māṃsa = *bala*
(flesh = strength)

malayaja = *milana*
(sandlewood = meeting)

kheṭa = *gati*
(phlegm = going)

śava = *śrāya*
(corpse = resort)

asthyābharaṇa = *niraṃśuka*
(bone ornament = naked)

preṅkhana = *āgati*
(wandering = coming)

kṛpīṭa = *ḍamaruka*
(wood = drum)

dundura = *abhavya*
(emission = nonpotential)

padmabhājana = *kapāla*
(lotus vessel = skull)

tṛptikara = *bhakṣya*
(satisfying = food)

mālatīndhana = *vyañjana*
(jasmine wood = herbs)

catuḥsama = *gūtha*
(a potion of four ingredients = dung)

kasturikā = *mūtra*
(musk = urine)

sihlaka = *svayaṃbhu*
(frankincense = blood)

karpūraka = *śukra*
(camphor = semen)

sālija = *mahāmāṃsa*
(rice product = human flesh)

kunduru = *dvīndriyayoga*
(resin = union of organs)

Kāliñjara = *bhavya* (name of a mountain = potential)	*vola* = *vajra* (gum myrrh = thunderbolt)
diṇḍima = *asparśa* (small drum = untouchable)	*kakkolaka* = *padma* (perfume = lotus)

Beyond this list, the tantra indicates that yogins could make allusive references to the five Buddha families by speaking the proper names of feminine figures that could be taken as their families' defining representatives. Such an indirect reference is possible, we are assured, because the yoginīs are icons for the rites employed by Hevajra yogins. The ritual contextualization is a further affirmation of the performative aspects of *sandhyā-bhāṣā,* in that coded language was considered a vocal extension of the much larger group of secret signs articulated in the *Hevajra Tantra* and elsewhere.

These secret signs are called *chomā* in the text and are glossed as "foreign" *(milicchā)* in the *Yogaratnamālā* commentary; *milicchā* was translated into Tibetan as "a foreign language," even though it clearly means "foreign (signs)."[64] The *Hevajra Tantra* employs both the secret signs and coded language as a means for the initiates of the tantric gathering *(gaṇacakra)* to identify one another, so the signs operate as gateways for entrance into and participation within the gathering. The *Hevajra Tantra* also indicates that an individual not employing these secret signs and coded language will be subject to the wrath of the protecting *yoginīs* of the four sacred sites *(pīṭha)*, even if he is a Buddha *(HT,* II.iii.66–67). Like others, Wayman has emphasized the material found in the *Hevajra Tantra* and noted that the list of terms appearing there is identical to the list of words glossed in Nāgārjunapāda's *Saṃdhi-bhāṣā-ṭīkā.*[65] He concludes: "Nāgārjuna's commentary suggests that the *Hevajra Tantra* has given the basic list of 'twilight language.'"[66]

Unfortunately, the situation is somewhat more complex, and modern scholarship appears to have understated the broader issue of secret signs, of which coded language plays an essential part. Coded language materials are seen especially in several of the *yoginī tantra* scriptures, and lists of the fundamental texts are sometimes conveniently provided in commentarial materials. In dedicated sections of those *yoginī tantras*, the signs are divided into physical signs—including hand and facial gestures—and vocal signs, employing secret meanings apart from natural language expressions, and are not limited to the items listed above from the *Hevajra Tantra*. The scriptures convey the semiotics of the "vocal seal" *(vāgmudrā)* or the vocal part of the "seal of secret signs" *(chomāmudrā).*

This term for secret sign, *chomā* is a late Middle Indic word, the Prakrit equivalent of the Sanskrit *chadman* and other late Middle Indic words, such as *chaumā*, *chaṃḍia*, and so forth.[67] Like its other cognates, *chadman* is an interesting term: it indicates disguise, deceit, counterfeit, and deception, and certainly signifies that the appearance of an item or individual is intended to mislead and mask a real purpose. Thus *chomā* indicates not just secret codes or signs, but also the subterfuges and disguises available to spies, gang members, and adherents of secret societies. As early as the *Arthaśāstra*, secret agents were encouraged to use disguises of heterodox monks as the means to escape from difficult situations.[68] Moreover, a delightful verse from the eighth-century *Bṛhatkathāślokasaṃgraha* provides the excellent advice offered to the hero Naravāhanadatta by his friend Gomukha,

> Vārāṇasī is entirely supported by superlative thieves—really, jackdaws on holy ground—whose aegis is the secret signs *[chadman]* and who masquerade as sages with triple staff and limbs daubed in tawny paste, just to mention a few of their costumes.[69]

As the verse suggests, secret signs in India are closely related to places of pilgrimage, since the highly fluid nature of sacred locales provides the best opportunity for thieves, secret agents, criminal conspiracies, and secret societies using obscure signs to congregate and support themselves. For Buddhist siddhas, the purpose of these is most often discussed as the recognition of participants in the *gaṇacakra*, the weekly tantric feast explored below in the consideration of siddha communities.

Perhaps the earliest *yoginī tantra* movement in this direction may be found in the longest section of all concerning the esoteric meaning of specific words in the longer *Sarvabuddhasamāyoga*. There, the extensive list of words is not introduced with or identified by the term "coded language" but is simply included in a larger list of the "secret communications" *(*chomāmudrā : brda yi phya rgya)*, which begins with physical signals yet also articulates dozens of word associations.[70] Analogously, the *Samputa* devotes a section to coded language at the beginning of a long chapter on lengthening life and generating omniscience.[71] It starts with the twenty-two pairs of the *Hevajra Tantra* and segues into another series of twenty-eight terms with specific gestures or forms of ritual communication associated with them. The *Samputa* then returns to yet another series, this time of sixty-seven other terms and their ritual equivalents, before going on to discuss other esoteric rites. Many of the middle twenty-eight are shared with an analogous section of the *Catuḥpīṭha-mahāyoginī-tantrarāja*, where twenty-three terms are identified with specific gestures or other forms of communication to indicate an entire ritual system of signs.[72]

In the same vein as these other *yoginī tantras,* chapter 5 of the *Buddhakapāla* is not devoted exclusively to coded language, even though its chapter title declares this topic to be its purpose. This section begins with an announcement that it will be the alchemy *(rasāyana)* chapter and articulates an otherwise unexceptional series of practices requiring the ingestion of a lengthy set of substances running the gamut from repellent to lethal, all for the purpose of purifying the body. Then the text engages the idea of *sandhyā-bhāṣā* with the proclamation that it is difficult to find and is hidden from the other tantras. In one sense, of course, the *Buddhakapāla* does take a page from the *Hevajra Tantra* (or perhaps vice versa) since the section primarily lists terms that are glossed by other signifiers. Its list of thirty-two or thirty-three (a few are unclear) is quite different from the one in the *Hevajra Tantra.* The *Buddhakapāla's* is developed as if it were a combination of the two movements in the *Hevajra Tantra* chapter: lexical items in the world indicate personalities (divinities, yogins, yoginīs) or other proper references (sacred locales). The list completed, the *Buddhakapāla* then launches into a short exhortation on the use of coded language:

> *Buddhakapāla*-yogins should not agree that there is no coded language [even if it is difficult to locate], but should speak to each other in this great language. It is hidden within all the tantras, but in this tantra it is clearly expressed [a section identifying sites with plant parts follows]. . . . In that way the coded language *is actually unknown by the Sugatas,* is not internalized by the yoginīs, Locanā and the rest, but [is realized] by the yogin who has faith in the teacher.[73]

After this, the chapter concludes with a presentation of various relatively well known principles, such as foregoing attachment to objects in the world and specific views with reference to the absolute, all with the promise that if the yogin practices for just a half month, accomplishment will surely come.

The *Jñānatilaka's* coded-language section is different from the others in content, even though it also specifies linguistic equivalents for terms to be employed in the tantric feast.[74] The chapter appears to contain forty-six pairs of equivalents, although the Tibetan translation makes the first two difficult to interpret. The pairs begin with gender-selected items and is curious in that the male and female seminal fluids are given twice as the equivalents for other nouns. Beyond that, many of the terms are said to be codes for Buddhist technical terminology: meat is anger, cooked vegetables are ignorance, and so on.

A somewhat different direction is adopted by the *Mahāmudrā-tilaka.* Chapter 13, devoted to coded language, is introduced with the comment: "This is the secret speech in the language spoken by yoginīs when they congregate together in the Oḍiyāna and the other pīṭhas."[75] The chapter self-consciously begins with a list of sixteen of the twenty-two pairs taken from the *Hevajra Tantra,* perhaps not surprising for a commentarial scripture, even though it was not the direction taken by the *Jñānatilaka,* as seen above. This list of sixteen is taken as merely a starting point, for it is expanded to a total of ninety-seven pairs using a procedure similar to that found in the *Hevajra Tantra* and the other *yoginī tantras.*

Normally, these cursory explanations—here given a cursory treatment—would find a greater expression in the commentarial literature, but the exegetical works are not as illuminating as we might wish. For example, the *sandhyā-bhāṣā* chapter of the *Buddhakapāla* is not significantly commented on by any of the three commentators whose exegesis survives. Indeed, the only critic to note anything about the chapter, Saraha, simply glosses this section with the quip: "Of course, the section that articulates the idea of coded language is easy to understand!" He says this despite the assurance in the scripture that the Buddhas themselves have reputedly failed to achieve this comprehension![76] Instead, Saraha invests his exegetical capital in explaining the identity of the obvious lexical items. Conversely, Padmavajra's commentary is incomplete; only the first two chapters of the tantra are covered, even with protestations by the translators of its being complete. Finally, Abhayākaragupta does not comment on the coded expressions at all but, instead, concentrates on the alchemical section in the first part of that chapter.

While the *Sampuṭa* commentaries of Vīravajra and Abhayākaragupta are more direct, they are not necessarily more enlightening. Abhayākaragupta threatens that, if those who know the secret language were to employ this communication in front of those not initiated into its use, then the transgressors would be afflicted by contagion or misfortune for their revelation of secrets.[77] Beyond this, Abhayākaragupta seems again primarily concerned with issues of alchemy and the relationship of coded language to twenty-five rites concerning longevity and the use of drugs.[78] Vīravajra's *Sampuṭa* commentary provides a useful catalogue of texts in which the issue of coded language is discussed, but is also more concerned with alchemy and other ritual use of materials than with linguistics.[79] Likewise, the surviving commentary on the *Jñānatilaka* by Jñānaparama—said to be based on instructions from one of the Indrabhūtis—provides little useful direction. Jñānaparama simply affirms that this coded expression is to be used in various ritual environments, whether making offerings of food *(bali)* or other sensory objects.[80] Perhaps most interesting is Gambhīravajra's scholarly commentary on the *Mahāmudrā-tilaka*. Although he does not even explain the lexical equivalents—as the *Sampuṭa* commentaries at least do—he does provide a sense of a wider field of discussion. He indicates, for example, that Vilāsavajra thought coded language arose from the taste of bliss, perhaps a Buddhist form of glossolalia or other spontaneous language. Other teachers, however, largely considered the language a manner for determining who was qualified to come to the tantric feast and who was not.[81]

Perhaps another approach to the coded language problem may be suggested. One observation about coded language expressions in the literature is that both the gestures and the vocal secret signs were "foreign" *(milicchā)* in origin and occasionally attributed to the secret congregation of yoginīs in the mysterious land of Oḍiyāna.[82] So, when the *yoginī tantras* or their commentaries claim that the secret signs and coded language are declared by the Buddha to be foreign speech employed for the purpose of recognition in the *gaṇacakra* of yoginīs, it may relate to nonstandard language structures, whether tribal or otherwise. Even then, as seen above, the tenuous nature of coded language caused the author of the *Buddhakapāla-tantra* to castigate those who doubted its existence as a real language.

However, certain of the code words appear to be ultimately derived from Kui/Kawi/Gond or another of the Dravidian languages. Dravidian forms have a phonology much closer to the words represented than do the Munda languages. Many of the coded words are implausibly based on Sanskrit. As shown above, for example, *vola* is supposed to stand for the *vajra* (penis), and *kakkola* is to represent the lotus (vagina) *(HT,* II.iii.60). The modern interpretation is that *vola* is the word in Sanskrit that denotes the myrrh resin of the commiphora tree, and *kakkola* is a word for perfume.[83] However, the derivation of *vola* from a Dravidian root for feathers, employed as a metaphor for pubic hair *(bula/bulus/bura)*, is much more straightforward; alternatively, it may be derived from a common word for copulation *(poru/pora/pori)*.[84] *Kakkola* is likewise possibly a reflection of *kakkulāte*, a Dravidian word for love or to make love.[85] Similarly, *kunduru* indicates the coded word for sexual union and is a variety of resin in the modern interpretation. Yet it is probably derived from the Dravidian root √*kund* (to pierce, to prick, to prod).[86] While there is no question that some of the words in their current spelling are rendered into Sanskrit, it is just as likely that the vocalizations heard by siddhas were changed into Sanskrit when they were unsure of its meaning. There is even a factual testimonial of Dravidian influence in the *Vidyottama-tantra*, where Vajrapāṇi is depicted as acknowledging that some syllables of an important mantra are taken from Dravidian words.[87]

This does not mean that esoteric Buddhism is necessarily from South India; if it were, there would be little point in calling attention to the Dravidian component. Instead, the most plausible explanation is that these words and the associated gestures were formulated based both on prior experience with secret signs in pilgrimage sites as well as on the half-understood phrases of indigenous peoples or other obscure language speakers. The affirmation of its "foreign" nature would probably not have been encountered in normative Dravidian locales anyway, for southerners were not understood as foreign. Texts like the *Mañjuśrīmūlakalpa* simply describes southerners as sinful, not incomprehensible.[88] Instead, the Dravidian languages close to the north were those spoken in Orissa, Chhattisgarh, Madhya Pradesh, Bihar, and in many other areas where tribal and village Dravidian speakers were found.

SECRET SACRED SOCIOLINGUISTICS

Whether or not we accept that one contribution to coded language came from aboriginal people's native speech, the issue is associated with the clear employment of vernacular-based literary languages, such as Apabhraṃśa, Old Bengali, and Prakrit. In addition, the question of the use of nonstandard Sanskrit in the composition of many of the tantras themselves should be considered. Actually, some of these forms of linguistic use came to define the scriptural communities of the Buddhist siddha culture and in some sense differentiated it from Śaiva systems, which exhibited a weaker affirmation of vernacular-based verses. Texts edited to date show that those given the designation *yoginī-tantra* at one time or another include Apabhraṃśa verses, framed in a ritual narrative of nonstandard Sanskrit (frequently called barbaric or bad Sanskrit), and sometimes include coded language. Indeed, it has been observed that the coded language chapter of the *Hevajra Tantra* is immediately followed by the most important section in Apabhraṃśa in that tantra.[89] The only surviving Sanskrit *sādhana* in the *Buddhakapāla* system is also the locus of an important "adamantine song" *(vajragīti)* in Apabhraṃśa, to be sung by the assembled yoginīs.[90] Likewise, the *Khasama-tantra*, the *Ḍākārṇava-tantra*, the *Caṇḍamahāroṣana*, and the *Samvarodaya-tantra* all include Apabhraṃśa verses, and all of them represent *yoginī-tantra* material.[91] Although some Apabhraṃśa verses are preserved in *(Mahā-) yoga-tantras* such as the *Kṛṣṇayamāri,* they appear less frequently, and their position in the ritual life is not combined with an attempt at the systematic articulation of a coded language, either as specific terms or as an hermeneutic principle.[92] Likewise, even though the exegetical works to the *Guhyasamāja* system developed procedures for the articulation of coded hermeneutics—mostly in the environment of the "six points" *(ṣaṭkoṭika)* of the commentarial tantra, the *Sandhivyākaraṇa*—this has not been done in the context of chapters on coded language or employing Apabhraṃśa verses. Instead, it represents the hermeneutical technique already considered above.

The clearest message is that some *mahāyoga*- and many *yoginī-tantras* were concerned with alternative language systems. As a corollary, we might recognize that we are dealing primarily with forms of language, recognized as such by the principals, and not simply hermeneutical events employed by commentators. While this proposition might seem unexceptional, it has been treated differently by two authors. Ruegg has proposed that both the Buddhist and non-Buddhist usage of Prakrit and Apabhraṃśa result in some measure from the design of those authors who sought the semantic indeterminacy of this form of language: "Nevertheless, it does seem quite likely that the Siddhas employed Apabhraṃśa at least partly with a view to achieving certain aesthetic and semiotic qualities associated with Apabhraṃśa, including polyvalence and allusiveness."[93] Elsewhere, he specifically refutes Upadhye's opinion—frequently expressed by Indian specialists in Prakrit literature—that this language was used for the purposes of popularity.[94] If I understand Ruegg correctly, the difficulty of differentiating between the precise referents of phonetically similar words is the/a key to comprehending its attraction to these poets. Yet it is not clear that the difficulties we admittedly experience in reading these verses is the consequence of their intention, as opposed to modern lexical limitations in the face of the uncertain transmission of the documents.

Similarly, Newman has quoted Puṇḍarīka, the author of the grand commentary to the *Kālacakra-tantra*, to the effect that the forms of nonstandard Sanskrit encountered there have been placed intentionally for the purpose of relieving beings of their attachments to correct grammar. Thus, Puṇḍarīka indicates, the irregular forms encountered are simply for educational purposes, not because Buddhists did not know how to write correct Sanskrit.[95] Newman, pointing out that at least some Buddhists could write perfectly correct Sanskrit, has suggested taking this apologia seriously as stated, curious as it seems.

> The language of the early Kālackara literature . . . is Sanskrit into which various types of nonstandard forms have been intentionally introduced. . . .

> While some of these solecisms have pedagogic purpose, for the most part they are designed to counteract pedantic arrogance.[96]

Although this may have been the case, I find it an uncompelling proposition. Nonstandard Sanskrit is a problem more complex than either semiliterates trying to pass off their work as classical Sanskrit or a highly cultivated class intentionally writing below their audience level. As Newman has pointed out, we must refrain from associating all esoteric Buddhist authorities with nonstandard Sanskrit, and, as Ruegg has allusively suggested, the Apabhraṃśa employed by the siddhas is not a true vernacular. Yet both scholars appear reticent to acknowledge that language seems to require a linguistic community expecting this register, and sometimes several communities may be involved. These scholars' models of language use are analogous to the models of scriptural inspiration in a way: both describe compositions informed by individual decisions directed at the world. In distinction, the evidence of the texts suggests that social context—the intimate and sustained conversation between siddhas, their peers and their communities—became the overwhelmingly important principle.

In the tantric Buddhist case, at least four levels of language are employed or implied throughout siddha-related literature, in descending order of social status: good standard Sanskrit, nonstandard Sanskrit, Apabhraṃśa, and the unrecorded low-status vernacular languages of the Buddhist locales. Thus siddhas were minimally bilingual, with diglossia evident in each language, so that there is a language level associated with differing levels of status, much as modern Bengali, Hindi, and Kannada are stratified according to the degree of the background and education of the speaker. Even in the rough outline presented by our sources, sociolinguistically two languages exhibiting four major levels of glossia are unexceptional for India, and siddha religion might more profitably be described as demonstrating diglossia within Sanskrit and within the Apabhraṃśa-vernacular continuum. Thus D'souza's statements concerning the use of different glossia in modern India have resonance within our early medieval period.

> In a multilingual community the individual speaker's several languages function within a fairly well-defined system just as the styles and varieties of a single language serve the needs of the monolingual. Certain cultural contexts demand the use of a certain language while other contexts call for a different language or for silence. . . . It is clear, therefore, that in a multilingual context one finds an interplay of languages which is governed by sociocultural rules.[97]

Moreover, our evidence from modern sociolinguistics is reinforced by authors esteemed in the medieval period. In particular chapter XVII.1–63 of Bharata's *Nāṭyaśāstra* articulates the expectation that different languages are presumed from disparate linguistic communities, representing (in sociolinguistic terms) disparate glossia.[98] Not only has there developed a horizon of expectation that Mleccha languages (= tribal or foreign languages) might be represented, but Bharata also articulates the circumstances for the employment of different languages or glossia—Sanskrit, Prakrit, Mleccha-śabda, Śaurasenī, Māgadhī, and so forth.[99]

Therefore the siddha(s) contribution(s) should be examined in light of what we know about India at large; indeed, such entities as nonstandard Sanskrit and Apabhraṃśa are known elsewhere. In the latter instance, Schomer has demonstrated that Apabhraṃśa, related languages, and their use of the *dohā* verse form served a variety of community requirements during the medieval period.[100] The Buddhists were but the earliest of the various groups to demonstrate the range of applications in literary vernacular compositions. Included as well were Sants of North India, Bauls, Sikhs, Nathpanthi yogins, and a variety of other figures throughout medieval India. They used *dohās* to communicate many of the same ideas as those seen among the Buddhist siddhas: devotion to the guru, criticism of society, poetic expression of a religious path, an expression of underclass sentiments, and so forth. Schomer also shows that, while not exactly colloquial in language, their verses became part of colloquial expression, so *dohā* verses continue to be recited today by villagers and rag-pickers. They evidently were easily understood, readily remembered, sung frequently with instrumental accompaniment, and satisfied the aesthetics of the broad population. It would be, in fact, difficult to find a similar, Buddhist-inspired language and verse form that has become so very popular and so widely imitated. Under these circumstances, siddhas employed these languages, perhaps not for the expressed purpose of proselyzation, but because they represented a first moment in the Indian flowering of vernacular language use still extant today.

In the case of esoteric Buddhist Sanskrit, it is also on a continuum with other community usages, especially those found in areas where the new early medieval regional centers have obtained power. Although Śaiva tantric Sanskrit is a well-known example, it is not the only other instance of such nonstandard usages, for inscriptions contain analogous examples. Kielhorn, in his explanation of the Sanskrit in the Siyodoni Stone Inscription, could have been speaking about the language of the Buddhist tantras.

> The author or authors, though intending to write Sanskrit, had a very meagre knowledge of the grammar of that language; they were evidently influenced by, and have freely employed works, phrases, and constructions of, their vernacular. . . . The rules of *saṁdhi* have been persistently neglected. . . . As regards the treatment of nouns in general, case-terminations have often been altogether omitted; sometimes wrong cases have been employed, masculine words treated as if they were neuter, and masculine or neuter forms of adjectives and pronouns used with reference to feminine nouns, etc. . . . Moreover, the first part of the inscription contains a considerable number of words which either do not occur in Sanskrit literature at all, or for which the dictionary furnishes no appropriate meaning; and some of which undoubtedly were taken from the vernacular.[101]

Similar statements have been made by philologists examining both Buddhist and Hindu tantras, and it is not surprising to find a dramatic change in scriptural and exegetical language with a change in the sociopolitical system.[102] Thus, instead of "barbaric Sanskrit," we are dealing with a glossia that extends to political decrees and sectarian compositions and represents a clear statement of linguistic distance from the prior centers of power and socialization.

The linguistic situation is analogous to that represented by speakers of Asian languages, especially immigrants, encountering the new transcultural language of English. They must use English, for no other language will assist them in the accomplishment of their goals. But they come from a wide variety of backgrounds and cannot be homogenized. Those who have passed through the great language-refining institutions of the colleges or universities will speak standard English rather well and may have exceeded their primary-language ability in the expression of sophisticated ideas. Others will not have had the opportunity to become so well normalized in their language application, so that the syntax, grammar, and use of such items as articles and subject/verb agreement in number will be evident. Although individual idiosyncrasies are legion, generally speakers with a similar background will render English with similar forms of expressions: native Chinese speakers might find that their English is derided by elites as "Chinglish." At the same time, English is developing indigenous forms in India and elsewhere, with an emerging standard grammar and vocabulary in those locales, resulting in the development of regional Englishes. If speakers have learned some form of English as an adult, then their grasp of the primary language, even at sophisticated levels, will probably remain superior to that of English, although they will frequently employ English loanwords in their speech and writing. But many of these speakers will still look at their primary language with nostalgia and be required to employ it in certain ritual environments—weddings, funerals, holiday greetings, and other occasions.

Likewise, siddha Sanskrit exhibits diglossia because those expressing themselves in Sanskrit may or may not have had the opportunity to pass through the great language-refining institutions of Buddhist monasteries, Śaiva centers, or Brahmanical schools. Those without the training bring with them the grammar, syntax, and other peculiarities of their vernaculars, and their Sanskrit will reflect it. Nevertheless, there will be times when they must use Sanskrit, for no other language will carry the status, vocabulary, and expressive power that they need. Broadly speaking, their Sanskrit will represent loose usages of great similarity, and some will represent an emerging standard local form. Although it may not be formalized on a par with Buddhist Hybrid Sanskrit, regional Sanskrit appeared a distinct glossia in the sense that it is a comprehensible medium of communication carrying important social information.[103] In a different way, both those coming to the siddha career via the monastery and those coming straight from the village will employ the mixed Apabhraṃśa form seen in Buddhist writing: it is appropriate to specific ritualized contexts (e.g., offerings by yoginīs) and might in turn integrate Sanskrit words in the form of single lexical items.[104] Other expressions, as seen below, may also be included, so that both the Apabhraṃśa and regional Sanskrit used in siddha writings will be much more fluid than the transculturally refined Sanskrit employed by institutionally trained siddha personalities in nonritualized commentarial or technical applications. It is not necessary to agree with Pūṇḍarīka—that this regional Sanskrit was composed exclusively to teach the audience a lesson in detachment—to conclude that it was used intentionally as a language of composition. Moreover, it was employed by at least some authors who could write the classical form (as seen in their exegetical works), but who felt liberated in the loose construction and primitiveness of the new variety.

Some traditional statements in Buddhist exegetical literature emphasize the multiplicity of linguistic domains, although these have not been well explored to date. The most comprehensive statement of which I am aware is by the Kashmiri scholar *Yaśaskīrtibhadra, in his relatively extensive commentary on the *Hevajra Tantra*, the *Vajrapādasārasaṃgrahapañjikā*.[105] Although the work once briefly mentions the issue of eliminating clinging to good grammatical forms, *Yaśaskīrtibhadra's primary hermeneutics are directed to explain why so many diverse place-related glossia have been included into the esoteric canon. He explains that it has to do with the accumulated propensities of beings and that the Buddha was required to teach in multiple languages simultaneously, or the entire corpus of the law in 84,000 sections never could have been completed. *Yaśaskīrtibhadra emphasizes that this is in accordance with the old "fourfold refuges" in canonical criticism: one follows the meaning, not the letter; one follows gnosis, not consciousness; one follows the definitive meaning, not the provisional meaning; and one follows Dharma, not personalities.[106] *Yaśaskīrtibhadra's fundamental point—one that he reiterates several times—is that the employment of diverse glossia according to the places and vernaculars of India is simply good, skillful means, a position that reception theorists and educators both might commend. For our purposes, however, it is the straightforward acknowledgment that Buddhists composed their scriptures in complex and multifaceted linguistic milieus. There, the affirmation of regional identity and local empowerment played as much a role as the need to speak to high-status expectations.[107]

Finally, Apabhraṃśa Buddhist literature represents the reemergence of an autobiographical voice—the first-person singular literary cry for liberation not seen since the early canonical verse compendia of the Arhats and the Thera/Therī poetic systems. The signature line *(baṇita)* "Saraha says . . . , Kāṇha observes . . . , Tillopa declares . . ." is frequently encountered. It is curious that the development of a vernacular-based literary glossia should free authors to articulate feelings and attitudes in the literary first person (here actually the third person acting in a first-person capacity), but the otherwise disconnected languages of Pali and Apabhraṃśa share this quality. Perhaps the formalization of the bodhisattva path in the Mahayana eliminated an Indian articulation of personal viewpoint or emotional frailty; perhaps it was simply that bodhisattvas could neither do wrong nor have second thoughts. In any event, the human sentiments of aspiration and longing, of success and failure, that had been so long suppressed in Mahayanist literature had the opportunity to come to the fore once again. So, while the content of Saraha's *dohās* and the *gāthās* ascribed to Upāli render them connected only by distance, their positions as autobiographical voices in the Buddhist context bridge this seemingly irreconcilable space.

All things considered, we might understand this: the early medieval period gave rise to new forms of religious language, which included regional varieties of Sanskrit, even though the grammarians' variety of this latter continued to operate as the language of highest status. The subordinate status of regional Sanskrit is recognized in the colophons to occasional Tibetan translations, which acknowledge the inferior position of their language.[108] The regional usage, however, became an emblem of authenticity for those areas newly emerging from tribal or rudimentary agrarian peripheral polities, and the new sense of authority of regional centers relied heavily on their capacity to produce literature that spoke to their concerns. After all, they were the areas gaining control of the polity and economy of the post-Puṣyabhūti world, and upon their stability rested North India's viability. While such literatures—whether in regional Sanskrit or Apabhraṃśa—required high Sanskrit interpretive measures to be accepted in a pan-Indian religious milieu, that was of little concern to the authors or their immediate patrons, who instead reveled in the accelerating power of peripheral India's emergence from its prior netherworld. If the previous centers of influence were declining in power and prestige, Tripura, Bhubaneśwar, and Sirpur, to mention a few, were becoming the new centers of authority. Our understanding of the reasons for this shift in language, therefore, must proceed into questions of the change of group association and affiliation in parts of the Buddhist siddha subculture. Accordingly, the affirmations that coded language represent some modification of natural speech, the implications of the use of Apabhraṃśa, and the employment of nonstandard Sanskrit all indicate not only that the new system appealed to levels of society largely excluded from standard Sanskrit but that specific siddhas came from or were somehow associated with such low-caste, outcaste, and tribal groups.

Examples of Buddhist sites within early medieval kingdoms include the sites of Sirpur and Malhar, both of which represented centers in the newly emergent kingdom of Dakṣiṇa Kośala. The monastic presence at Sirpur—in the Chhattisgarh state—is affirmed by two monasteries (Figure 17), both of which were excavated in the 1950s, but no complete excavation report was filed, and now the excavator is deceased.[109] Likewise the 1976–77 excavations at Malhar, in Bastar, are also incompletely reported, with a single short monograph.[110] However, an examination of the meager reports in conjunction with the inscriptions and modern demographics indicates that these centers were swimming in a tribal sea. Both Chhattisgarh and Bastar still have a high concentration of tribal populations—Gond, Kond, Saora, Muria, and others—yet also have artistic representations in the Buddhist sites closely reminiscent of tribal art, including a Vajrasattva of a most peculiar variety.[111] Beyond that, the Sirpur inscription of Buddhaghoṣa, paleographically from the seventh to the eighth centuries, is the only Buddhist inscription I have found to mention the actual employment of mantras *(mantratattva)*.[112] Space prohibits an extensive treatment of these two locales—which deserve to be considered in relation to the more important monasteries of Ratnagiri, Udayagiri, and Lalitagiri in Orissa—but the involvement of these areas with siddha traditions is

FIGURE 17 Ānandaprabhu Vihāra, Sirpur. Chhattisgarh, early eighth century. *Ronald M. Davidson.*

reinforced by the occasional Indian claiming to have come from Dakṣiṇa Kośala, such as Vairocanavajra.[113]

EXTREME LANGUAGE AND COMEDY IN THE TANTRAS

Not only do such regional communities bring their languages to the assembly, they also inform the way in which each language is employed. If we set aside a puritanical reading of the most outrageous scriptures for a moment, we might see in them something of a playfulness and comedic expression based in the Indian aesthetics found within village or regional audiences. While reading through the extreme statements of the siddha literature, I have consistently been impressed by their level of grotesque humor. Sometimes this is quite crude, as in scatological humor, but other times it appears embedded in the simple outrageousness of the language. It has occurred to me, for example, that there could be no possible parody of siddha literature. Parody requires that the sociocultural register be reified and extended beyond the boundaries of the consistent message of the genre, whether in the case of sacred literature or poor fiction. However, there are simply no boundaries beyond which siddha literature does not go. Indeed, I have often heard a Tibetan teacher of esoteric literature—layman or monk—read some extreme statement from a scripture, burst into laughter, and exclaim that this obviously needs interpretation, for no reasonable person could possibly take such items at face value. Yet it is equally clear that many of the extreme statements were taken at face value, as the hagiographies of early Tibetan translators affirm. Rwalo Dorjé Drak (b. 1016 C.E.), for example, is represented in his hagiography as having bragged that he killed thirteen tantric scholars by black magic and had five tantric consorts, the youngest of which was the eleven-year-old daughter of a local chieftain.[114] With such mixed messages by representatives of the system, we might be forgiven for wondering how seriously this literature was intended to be taken.

Excessive language is displayed in a variety of ways. For example, the frame story for the pronouncement of the *Mahāmāyūrī-vidyārājñī-dhāraṇī*, an early esoteric text, concerns an issue of protection, but is humorous in its timing.[115]

While the Lord was staying at Śrāvastī, one of his monks, Svāti, resided with him. Now Svāti was a new monk, and he went out to collect firewood in order to heat some bath water for the Saṃgha. Just as he was wrestling with one piece, an enormous black snake slithered from out of a hole in another branch and struck him on the big toe of his right foot. Svāti crashed to the ground, foaming at the gums and rolling his eyes up into his head, out cold. Ānanda, always a good man in a pinch, immediately ran to the Buddha, paid his respects, stood to one side, and related to the Buddha that Svāti was just about dead. Never one to miss an opportunity to relate a story, the Lord told Ānanda that he should use the Kingly Spell of the Great Peacock. Who was the Great Peacock? Well, it so happens a long time ago . . . and he, the Buddha was that Great Peacock King named Suvarṇābhāsa . . . (Svāti's still down) . . . and there are these kinds of tree spirits *[yakṣa]* the spell overcomes . . . (Svāti's still out) . . . and there are these kinds of ghosts *[preta]* the spell overcomes . . . (Svāti's still dying) . . . and there are these kinds of demons *[rākṣasa]* the spell overcomes . . . (Svāti's still frothing at the mouth) . . . and, if you really want to do it right you set up a Buddha image facing east in the middle of. . . . And, by heaven, sixty pages of demon names, mantras, and instructions later, Ānanda finally got around to dealing with the very well prepared and almost entirely deceased Svāti.

In his study of the varieties of humor, Morrell has already noted that inappropriate long-windedness and a sudden excess of information may seem humorous.[116] Both circumstances apply in the interminable pronouncement of the Peacock King spell. The humorous situation, though, could be taken as unintentional. We can almost hear the thoroughly pedantic esoteric lecturer wanting to exhaust all the lists of all the demons in all the areas of the continent of Jambudvīpa, before he is willing to lead the story back to the young monk's revival from his near-death experience. Yet I would argue that the story must have struck his audience as hilarious both for the excessive verbosity and cues in the language. For example, the term "foaming/frothing" *(phena)*, used to describe Svāti's psychophysical state, is a perennially humorous word in Sanskrit. Its application to Svāti indicates both his reduced condition and his comedic representation, not to mention the great power of the Buddha's spells.

Similarly, many of the siddha hagiographical episodes are intentionally humorous, and much of that sense of humor extends to the scriptures themselves. However, it is humor with an edge, a bite of reality, and the tooth of a toxic antidote, as much good comedy in fact displays. Without the sense of appropriate boundaries, it appears that tantric humor moves back and forth between agonism and hilarity, often bringing both together at once. Humor, like hagiography, is invariably tied to social models of propriety and consistency; it frequently illuminates those models by its simultaneous acquiescence to their tyranny and subversion of their solemnity. In the esoteric frame of reference, the secret is often that the approved system of Indian Buddhist religiosity is a masquerade, a well-dressed imitation of spirituality, and the tantras easily question whether the costume is supported by anything other than air.

All this would have been communicated in the regional modalities of oral narratives, and this fact tends to become obscured in received texts. The oral proclivity of India directs our attention toward performative parameters and requires our acknowledgment that oral performances seldom can be reproduced effectively in print. Lutgendorf, who has studied the performative aspect of the *Rāmcaritmānas*, lamented the transition from spoken nuance to lifeless written materials.

> The transcription of *kathā* performances produces, to my mind, disappointing results. Performances that I experienced and described immediately afterward in my notes as brilliant and exciting appeared flat and dull when "reduced to writing." Talks that seemed highly cohesive, in which ingenious interpretations emerged one after another in sparkling strand, seemed rambling and untidy in written form, lacking any principle of organization and filled with incomplete sentences and gratuitous digressions. All oral art, of course, has an inherently "emergent" quality, which results from its being the product of a unique context.[117]

Our consideration of the humor in the Indian Buddhist context must likewise rely on its "reduced" circumstances and on the historical reality of its oral transmission to a variety of audiences. It is relevant, in this regard, that one of the great lapses in the discipline of Buddhist studies is its relative neglect of the dependence of Indian Buddhism on the communication of the preachers (Dharmabhāṇakas) to both lay and monastic assemblies. Attention to the oral form compels us to understand that the Indian expressions of all the various emotions have been developed and sustained in the telling of the tales.

The Dharmabhāṇakas, for their part, employed both formal and intuitive (creative) sources for humor and comic representation. Although the capacity for intuitive humor appears in every society, the formal sources for themes and models of funny characters often derive from the dramatic tradition. Dramatic comedy was invested in both its traveling troupes of players, which continue to proceed from village to village in modern India, as well as in formal comedies, such as would have been played at royal command or in the private halls of the wealthy. Unfortunately, folk comedies—such as the modern Tamasha of Maharastra, the Bhavai of Gujarat, or the Jatra of Bengal—by their very nature are subject to quick transformation, undercutting our ability to rely on their modern expressions and composition in the assessment of medieval materials.[118] Thus it is in the theory and practice of classical theater that an articulation of the medieval humorous environment may be somewhat understood, even while acknowledging the limitations of the written records. In the examination of hagiography, in particular, we must concur with Gitomer's plea that students of religion should consider belletristic texts, so that they may return to their own materials "with attention to literary or aesthetic values."[119]

It is well known that the earliest representation of dramatic theory is in Bharata's *Nāṭyaśāstra*, the lengthy pronouncement that is normatively ascribed to the first few centuries of the common era.[120] Likewise, the commentary on the text by the Trika rhetorician Abhinavagupta (c. 1000 C.E.) is considered definitive, though the editor has quipped that the received manuscripts of the *Abhivavabharatī* are so corrupt that even if the author himself came down from heaven, he could not easily restore the original reading.[121] It is less frequently understood that Bharata and Abhinavagupta disagreed on the theory of the comic sentiment *(hāsya-rasa)*.[122] Bharata believed that comedy depended on ridiculous fashions, features, persons, and situations. His analysis, in other words, was based on laughing *at* individuals who represent the objects and behaviors we consider inferior: buffoonery, crippled limbs, outrageous clothing, and so on—the stuff of farce. Accordingly, comedy was assigned a social position among the lower castes and women. In this regard, Bharata was quite close to Aristotle in the *Rhetoric* and *Poetics*, where both the basis of comedy (innate laughter—*hāsasthāyibhāva*) and its circumstances received similar treatment.[123] Comedy simply boiled down to getting others to laugh at the comedian *(svastha)* or at some third party *(parastha)*.

If Hephaistos, the crippled Olympian divinity of the smith's fires, served as the Greek occasion for ridicule and buffoonery, the classic expression of Bharata's theory was the person of the Vidūṣaka in Sanskrit drama.[124] Here are found all the various attributes of the subhuman—buck-toothed and ignorant—laughingly referred to as the "great Brahman" *(mahābrahmaṇa)*, a term that has an undertaker's overtones. Vidūṣakas are ugly and deformed *(virūpa)*, hunchbacks who consistently fail to do much more than feed their bellies in the never-ending quest for vittles. They also act as buffoons in their ludicrous attempts at Brahmanical virtues, such as Santuṣṭa in Bhāsa's *Avimaraka*, who protests, "Unlearned? How could I be unlearned? O.K., O.K., just listen up—there's this work on acting called the *Rāmāyana*, and just last year I learned five whole verses of it!"[125] Failing to identify even one of the two great epics of India, Vidūṣakas are the great comic sidekicks of Sanskrit dramatic literature, who befriend the hero *(nāyaka)* for incidental plot purposes, but have extraordinary effect in character construction and development. As Jefferds has noted:

> He is, in his burlesque embodiment of appetite, an antic distortion of life, a fun-house mirror that mocks but does not actually modify the original. And unlike so many of the "boon companions" of world literature—Sancho Panza and the rest—the Vidūṣaka is almost purely a figure of "fun," important not in that he qualifies the "meaning" of the main action, but for his modal impact on the whole.[126]

Several siddhas exhibit literary personas formally similar to the Vidūṣaka or other farcical characters in Indian literature. Perhaps preeminent among them is the character of Virūpa. The Virūpa hagiographies transmitted primarily by the Sakya and related systems in Tibet emphasize his comical nature. At one point in the story, for example, Virūpa and his two disciples—Kāṇha and Ḍombīheruka—encounter Śākta yogins who would like to offer our siddhas' flesh to the goddess Caṇḍikā (Figure 18):

> In the East they found a self-originated trident, called Sahajadevī, and a self-originated stone statue, called Devī Caṇḍikā. Non-Buddhist yogins would lead men there and impale them through the throat with the trident, killing them.[127] Then they would gather into a ritual circle *[gaṇacakra]*,

FIGURE 18 Caṇḍikā from Hirapur Yoginī Pīṭha. Orissa, ninth century.
Ronald M. Davidson.

> with the man's flesh as the sacrament. Virūpa proceeded there with his two disciples. The yogins wanted to eat them, so they called them into their assembly hall. The Ācārya [Virūpa] said to his two disciples, "Don't continue to release your breath—but stay here holding it inside!" The Ācārya himself entered the hall, and the yogins asked, "Where did your two friends go?" He replied, "They're outside." "Well, bring them in!" they exclaimed. "Bring them in yourself," the Ācārya replied. One yogin called them but the two did not answer. He poked them with his finger, but from the impression made by his poking, out came some foul breath—hiiissss. Then some feces began to bubble out—bloop, bloop. "This comes from rotten flesh!" he said and returned inside. The trident began to quiver and shake and, with a single clap of the Ācārya's palms, the trident was reduced to fragments and dust. Then the statue of Devī Caṇḍikā began bouncing up and down. Virūpa placed the palm of one hand on top of the image and bound up the statue between the head and the heart.[128] At that point he grabbed it by one ear and affixed a stūpa *[caitya]* to its crown. With that, all the yogins fainted. When they revived, they all asked, "If you Buddhists are greatest in compassion, why have you done this to us?" Virūpa replied, "You must cease making your offerings with warm flesh and blood from murdered beings!" They all paid homage to the feet of the Ācārya and, having taken refuge, became Buddhist yogins.[129]

It would be hard to argue that this episode and the many others like it were not understood as humorous. In the story we are presented with three Buddhist yogins, their leader Virūpa having received direct transmission and authentication from the embodiment of feminine wisdom, Nairātmyā.[130] Virūpa has performed miracles—turning the Ganges back in its path, holding the sun at knifepoint—that demonstrate his superiority to the gods themselves, for both the river and the sun are gods. And yet, when his two disciples are prodded by the flesh-hungry Śākta yogins, out bubbles fecal matter and rotten flesh. Contrary to the doctrines of the Adamantine Body *(vajrakāya)* or analogous doctrines of yogic purity, in place of the divine inner form that is supposed to be the property of the awakened siddha, here we find bodies that are walking bags of stinking filth.[131] At the heart of this episode is the inversion of expectations, the discontinuity between juxtaposed images. Whereas the non-Buddhists may be polluted from eating human flesh, the Buddhist yogins ooze and bubble.

Buddhist esoteric humor thus finds additional expression in discontinuity and incongruity, over and above its Indian emphasis on the humor of physical malformation and debased personality. This is validated in the theoretical domain as well, even though Bharata's emphasis is on ridicule as a dysfunctional imitation of the erotic sentiment. Indeed, one primary theoretical difference between Bharata and Aristotle is Bharata's subordination of comedy to the erotic sentiment,

> Among these eight sentiments, four are the cause of the arising of the other four—the erotic, the ferocious, the heroic, and the disgusting. Thus: VI.43
>
> > Comic sentiment arises from the erotic, the pathetic from the ferocious, the marvelous from the heroic and the terrifying from the disgusting. VI.44
> >
> > The imitation of the erotic is the comic. VI.45ab[132]

By contrast, in his commentary on Bharata's *Nāṭyaśāstra*, Abhinavagupta, through all the tricks of the Sanskrit commentator, effectively manages to redefine comedy. For Abhinavagupta, the comic sentiment is not strictly related to an imitative version—and therefore dysfunctional form—of the erotic sentiment. On the contrary, it may either include or be generated from any of the eight sentiments.[133] This is the case because the nature of comedy is not, as Bharata claims, the appearance of "defective" *(vikṛta)* items, such as dress, ornaments, expressions, or limbs—defects embodied in the Vidūṣaka. Rather, Abhinavagupta declares, the nature of the comic sentiment is found in the inappropriateness of dress or facial expressions or inconsistent psychological states. Since inappropriate elements may occur in conjunction with any of the dramatic sentiments, the result may be laughter.[134]

Abhinavagupta has admittedly articulated an incongruity theory of comedy. Morell has summed it up well.

> The basic idea behind the incongruity theory is very general and quite simple. We live in an orderly world, where we have come to expect certain patterns among things, their properties, events, etc. We laugh when we experience something that doesn't fit into these patterns. As Pascal put it, "Nothing produces laughter more than a surprising disproportion between that which one expects and that which one sees."[135]

Abhinavagupta's genius was in seeing that any of the various dramatic experiences can provoke laughter unless handled exactly, or, as Schopenhauer would have it, without indicating a paradoxical relationship between the idea and the actuality.[136] Bharata may have hinted at incongruity in his description of the "imitation of the erotic," and the Vidūṣaka clearly represents an imitation of a Brahman—being a Brahman by birth but not by language or deportment. Yet Abhinavagupta was explicitly identifying comedy as the distance between metanarrative representation and the actuality encountered on the ground. The ultimate incongruity, however, is that between the living and the dead, between the beneficial saint and the disaster-bearing ghost. Since siddhas include both functions in their public personas, this is exactly the paronomasic position of these saints.

In Virūpa's case, his similarity to the Vidūṣaka is primarily formal, rather than functional, and moves toward the inversion of categories that expresses the incongruity of expectations. Like Vidūṣakas, Virūpa speaks in the ostensible vernacular (Apabhraṃśa and Old Bengali), not in the Sanskrit of elevated discourse. His name (Virūpa = deformed or ugly) is an apt descriptive applied to the Vidūṣaka, as is his marginal status in society. Virūpa's deformity, however, is ecclesiastical—he has abandoned his position as the abbot, has returned the robes that were symbols of his status, and wanders forth naked. Both his Prātimokṣa and his Vajrayāna vows are depicted as shattered, for he has abandoned both the monastic estate and the recitation of mantras. Actually, though, we know that they have been rendered useless, because his depth of realization supersedes any need for such vows. Like the Vidūṣaka's imitation of Brahmans, Virūpa imitates Śaiva practitioners, but the comedy that results comes directly from Virūpa's position as the protagonist of the story, not a position that the Vidūṣaka has traditionally held, since every Vidūṣaka is continually assigned a part in the supporting cast.

Yet the mundane reality of Virūpa's iconography is that he is rendered in the image of a fat *sādhu*, holding the sun in place (Figure 19) and being served wine by the barmaid, whom he just might take home after the king pays his bill. Grossly obese, he follows the much more ancient iconography of the humorous figure in India, such as the Vidūṣaka jester, and the typology of Virūpa in statues is similar to that of those prior funny followers of Śiva—the gaṇas who scramble for sweets offered the great god and generally resemble buffoons in their antics. Even more directly, Virūpa is foreshadowed in the image of the tree spirit *(yakṣa)*, such as the magnificent early Kubera from Mathura in the National Museum (Figure 20).[137] In the exaggerated anatomy of Kubera's belly, his excessively large head on his shoulders with virtually no neck intervening, his left leg under him and his right half-raised, he is almost identical to our standard images of Virūpa.[138]

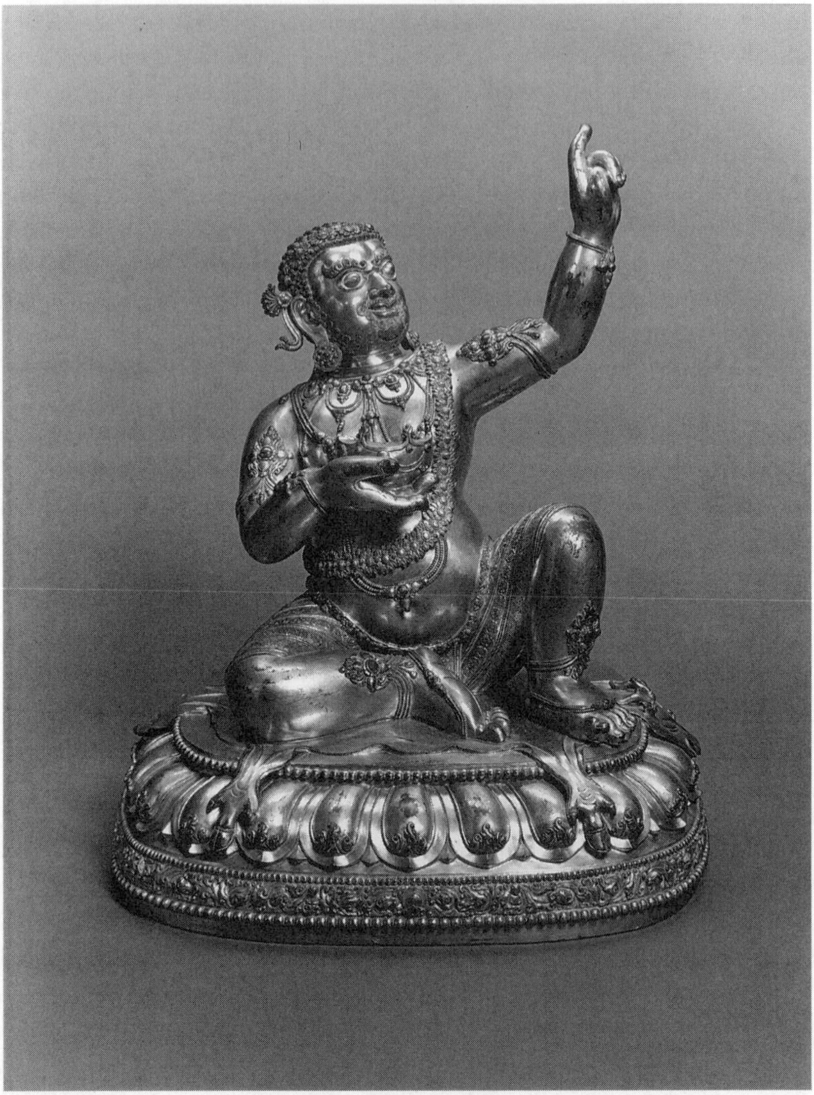

FIGURE 19 Mahāsiddha Virūpa. Chinese, Ming dynasty, Yung-lo mark and period, 1403–1424. Guilt bronze, 43.6 cm. high. *© The Cleveland Museum of Art, 2001, Gift of Mary B. Lee, C. Bingham Blossom, Dudley S. Blossom III, Laurel B. Kovacik, and Elizabeth B. Blossom in memory of Elizabeth B. Blossom, 1972.96. Reprinted with permission.*

FIGURE 20 Kubera. Ahichchhatra, second century. National Museum Acc. no. 59.530/2. *Photo courtesy of the American Institute of Indian Studies.*

Actually, placing figures like Virūpa in the larger field of siddha representations leads us to a festival of the grotesque. Both Indians and Tibetans have taken great glee in depicting Buddhist siddhas as deformed or irretrievably eccentric, so that they are given exaggerated hair, beards, eyebrows, noses, ears, and other peculiarities as attributes of their spirituality. In their artistic representations, they are on an esthetic continuum with the Chinese flair for the misproportioned iconology of the arhat, so that the halls of the five hundred arhats in Chinese monasteries resemble nothing so much as medical museums of physical deformities. A similar sentiment in modern Thailand allows the insistence of Upagupta's ugliness to be an attribute of the enlightened arhat's popularity and serves as a vehicle to critique the putative equation of physical attractiveness and spiritual capacity.[139] The humor behind these images is explicit and contagious, implicating extraordinary spirituality in the absence of either normative esthetics or approved canons of beauty. Accordingly, both Kagyüpa and Ch'an/Zen painting were eventually to excel in articulating new contortions or bizarre excesses of the human frame in the saints' portraits.

They were not alone in such associations, and Bakhtin has shown that Rabelais' love of the grotesque was grounded in part in the legends and stories of "Indian wonders" that had been the stock in trade of descriptions of the East since the time of Ctesias in the fifth century B.C.E.[140] Thus the affirmation of extreme forms of conduct and physicality—so much a part of the Indian sense of spirituality—fueled the religious imagination of the Orient as well as the Occident. For Bakhtin, Rabelais was giving a voice to the folk culture of carnival, which he strongly distinguished from the official culture and its approved festivals. In Virūpa and his like, Bakhtin would see the clowns and fools who "celebrated temporary liberation from the prevailing truth and from the established order."[141] Thus Bakhtin believed that all folk celebrations indulged in overthrowing the official ideology of the hierarchical system by means of defilement and the celebration of the grotesque body.[142]

This social body of the grotesque was celebrated, according to Bakhtin, in the medieval and renaissance carnivals, such as the "Dance of the Noses" or the "Feast of Fools." The overriding movement is the leveling of the social system, invoked by the celebration of such acts as defecation, urination, abusive language, comic dialogues, parodies of important figures, and mocking songs. Carnival, for Bakhtin, represents the isolated victory of the oppressed classes over the hegemonic dynamic of the dominant political culture. It invokes the temporary suspension of hierarchy in an all-consuming egalitarian expression of gross physical functions and the coarsest of humor.

Many of Bakhtin's observations ring true in the confines of siddha literature in general, although it is clear that he seems not to recognize that social inversion replaces the rules of one social strata with those of another. So, both carnival and the siddha tradition employ established hierarchies, rather than invoking Bakhtin's ideology of egalitarian physicality. Yet it is also true that, in siddha literature, the emphasis on exaggerated physical functions finds its way into many aspects of its narratives, whether in the indulgence in liquor or in the siddhas' stated preference for brothels and bars. Siddhas' employment of the low-status glossia of Apabhraṃśa resonates with their challenges to Brahmanical religion, court-sponsored Śaivism, and Buddhist monastic decorum. Their actions almost invariably exceed the bounds of karma and good taste, not to mention their hagiographical destruction of Śaiva religious sites and the violation of monastic rules with impunity. All these place them beyond the pale, acting as heroes *(vīra)* in the farce of reality.

From another vantage point, van Buitenen has maintained that the standard pattern for the Indian hero is the Vidyādhara, the sorcerer or celestial traveler, closely resonant with the siddha model of becoming the Vidyādhara emperor.[143] Certainly, heroic images abound in Vajrayāna literature—invoking the typology of "heroes and heroines" *(vīrāvīra)* as the paradigmatic Buddhist esoteric adepts—but just as clearly these characters are not merely heroic, but also comic and even ludic. Their activity is part-heroic, part-agonistic, and part-playful, as is much of the behavior of the divinities in Purāṇic literature or the other narratives of medieval India. Thus siddhas are often comic heroes, whose activity is rhetorically for the welfare of beings, although there are times when their behavior incongruously appears merely powerful self-indulgence. In this way, siddhas as comic heroes seem to personify the ambivalence felt by both Indian society and the Buddhist hierarchy toward powerful personalities with a dubious ethical foundation.

Incongruity might even be precisely the point of some esoteric Buddhist literature. The clear and insistent discontinuity between the forms of virtue espoused by early Buddhist traditions and the antinomian behavior affirmed in the Vajrayāna has caused some early British and European readers of this literature to take it as an imitative and exploitative form. The imitative theme could have been humorous to these readers but for their Victorian aesthetics. In his edition of the *Subhāṣita-saṃgraha*, Bendall expressed the sentiment well.

> I have printed text, and even, where extant, also commentary on this extraordinary phase of soi-disant Buddhism, thinking it well that scholars at

> least should know the worst. To me it all reads like an obscene caricature of the teachings both of earlier Buddhism and of legitimate Yoga.[144]

Yet caricature is also a form of comedy, even if Christian Europe of the day (or any day) had difficulty accommodating the idea that the sacred could be hilarious. These scholars did not learn the Indian message that, as in the figure of Hanuman, laughter is not necessarily ridicule but the honest correction of a distorted perception, a rectification that can be afforded only by an acknowledgement of truth. This seems to be part of the intimation about siddhas in their early reference in the *Milindapañha*, that siddhas sing truth.[145]

Thus esoteric scripture might convey the perception that, in all probability, Buddhist monks and reverend laity were unlikely ever to have been as sanctified as their Mahayanist hagiographical representations depict them. Esoteric literature is likely in some measure to be both shocking and compensatory: it tells a story as extreme in the direction of unmeritorious conduct as the earlier Buddhist ideal depicted on the positive side of the ledger. Certainly, neither representation could have been entirely accurate. It is unlikely that siddhas could have survived in India for half a dozen centuries acting in a wholly barbaric manner, and it is equally unlikely that Buddhist monks were, as a group, as saintly as their literature represents them. The symbiotic relationship between esoteric advocates of both institutions appears to reinforce their actual commonality, as shown in chapter 7, on community.

CONCLUSION: THE LITERATURE OF PERFECTION

The development and elaboration of Buddhist scripture employed a new application of language that had both continuities and discontinuities with earlier Buddhist usage. These scriptures were revealed, as in earlier Buddhist times, but the manner of their revelation was decidedly different, privileging laity rather than monks or the celestial bodhisattvas of the Mahayana. The tantras were probably composed in the social horizon of ritual instruction, moving smoothly from supplemental instruction to the articulation of new meditations, to full blown scriptural texts. Their language was challenging, even hostile at times, and the tantras' consistent representation of the Buddha in erotic environments cannot have provided Buddhist Indian communities with much confidence in the new scriptures' authenticity.

Perhaps the answer to the issue of the new scriptures is that they represented new linguistic and aesthetic communities, ones that arose as a result of the sociopolitical events from the seventh century forward. Because of a consistent pattern of population dislocation and the influx of newly proselytized tribal and village peoples, Buddhists developed new constituencies. In the process they drew from a much broader spectrum of social backgrounds, linguistic bases, and performative sensibilities. They sang in songs composed in different languages or in idioms representative of the aesthetics and images employed and expected by these new groups. Siddhas affirmed the importance of local culture with tribal-related rituals, the naturalness of the jungle, the perimeter, the mountain, and the edge of the field. They used images and told stories that violated Brahmanical ideals and must have both shocked and delighted their audiences. Their concern for storytelling became canonical in the *yoginī-tantras*, and they freely played with language as children play with toys, sometimes irresponsibly, with potentially disastrous results. Many of their patrons came to the Buddhist fold because it offered them the status and access to intellectual services that Brahmanical allegiance could not. Yet, at the same time, their commitment to the Buddhist community was but a way-station on the path to legitimacy. In the process, however, the Buddhist scriptural syntheses were changed because of the influx of new forms of Sanskrit, Apabhraṃśa, Prakrit, and coded languages.

The institutionalization of some siddha literature by the more conservative siddha and the monastic community relied heavily on the most developed hermeneutical strategies that Buddhism has ever seen, with limited success. At the same time, both the wide variation in interpretation and the broad application of the principle of coded language resonated with the ideology that makes esoteric Buddhism esoteric. Everything is obscure, hidden, and secret—a mask or deception behind which the real meaning may be dimly perceived. Initiates converse in the language of signs and use speech that is filled with double entendres. Words are never what they seem and may even be beyond the understanding of the Buddhas themselves. Under this strategy of exegesis, virtually no text ever says what it means. And this attitude is extended to the self-consciously outrageous language invoked by the tantra authors, through a system of commentarial apologetics that seeks out the authentic meaning of the scriptures "that seek out the real meaning," a most tortuous search. Thus the tantras self-consciously laugh at the prior experience of their audience—showing the Buddha sowing doubt in the mind of his listeners and letting them know that everything they know is wrong, since even the Buddhas themselves do not know this material. Conversely, the goal of many commentators is to assure the institutional communities that everything they know is *not* wrong. They are there to bring the extreme scriptures back into the fold, to revisit the standards of scriptural authenticity that had heretofore served the Buddhist community so well.

Even then, these two trajectories, in reality, represent symbiotic subcultures in esoteric Buddhist India. Without the scriptures, the commentators have no grist, while the grain served up by the scriptural authors remained unpalatable until prepared by the exegetes. Between these two, the theoreticians of some esoteric works, as seen in Padmavajra's *Guhyasiddhi,* continually offer voices that side with one, then with another, and occasionally propose multiple alternatives just to keep life interesting. Thus the final message of language is that the culture of Buddhist scriptural composition was alive and well, even if freshly sprouted in the new soil of regional centers and marginal peoples.

7

Siddhas, Monks, and Communities

> There was one Caṇḍālaja ["born an outcaste"], who was a disciple of Mahācārya Kukuripa and who meditated on the absolute mind. Because he exclusively cultivated the perfecting process yoga, he developed an obsession for the nonfoundational nature of all elements of reality. Then he went to Jālandhara, and a plague erupted so that many people died. The harvest was destroyed by hail. For five years, no rain fell. A Brahman who knew secrets *[mantrin]* was asked about the disturbance. He replied, "In this place there is a Buddhist residing who has turned surreptitiously to expounding a non-Buddhist doctrine. Since he resides here, all of these misfortunes have arisen. In this world, he will ruin others, but in the future, he himself will be ruined." Śrī Kukuripa heard this and went to Caṇḍālaja to teach him all over again.
>
> —Nāgabuddhi, **Ardhapañcamagāthā*[1]

Nāgabuddhi's **Ardhapañcamagāthā* is a delightful compendium of sixteen late morality tales and warnings on incorrect Buddhist practice. It attempts to perform some of the tasks served by the earlier Buddhist story literature, but most of its narratives focus on the esoteric conundrum: the control of individuals at a time of collapsing boundaries, even while Buddhist communities were under great duress. Many factors contributed to the perception of threat experienced in both siddha and monastic centers at this time. Yet Buddhist partisans did not yield the field without serious and protracted attempts to establish a network of communities and a list of rules by which these were to be governed. This chapter examines the ideology of communities in siddha literature, first in terms of the idealized form of siddha maṇḍalas. Afterward, arrangements of siddhas in circular cemeteries and in the various numbering systems, such as eighty-four, are also described, since they exhibit a much greater range of variation and source than are generally understood. The chapter then turns to hagiographical communities, taking as exemplary Vitapāda's retelling of Buddhajñānapāda's travels and study. Siddha communities in India are also ritually described. The discussion accordingly turns to an examination of the sacramental gathering *(gaṇacakra)*, using an early account by one Indrabhūti as an example. Since both these gatherings and the larger communities operated by rules, different examples of the siddha standards of conduct are considered. These standards also required implementation, mostly through the control systems of criticism of transgression and social pressure; the chapter investigates perceptions of behavioral problems. Together, the standards and criticisms tend to give credence to hagiographical episodes depicting lapses, such as those in Nāgabuddhi's text above. The chapter concludes with a reassessment of the imperial model of esoteric Buddhism, finding that the siddha metaphor of becoming the Emperor of Sorcerers *(vidyādharacakravartin)* was in constant negotiation with other models of Buddhist practice. Throughout, this chapter observes the differences between siddha and monastic institutions, along with the reasons for their divergences. A consistent interchange occurred, however, with monks and siddhas appropriating each other's systems and living together from time to time.

SIDDHA MAṆḌALAS, CIRCLES OF GODDESSES

Chapter 4 proposed that Buddhist maṇḍalas be considered the sacralized form of early medieval sāmanta feudalism. In this regard, the relationships between the Buddhas and their families in the various sections of the institutional Buddhist maṇḍalas appear modeled on the political processes of the early medieval period. So within each section of the maṇḍala, the Buddha and his family have an autonomous hierarchy that is capable of assuming the central position of the maṇḍala, should the need arise. Likewise, the hierarchy observed between a superordinate center and the subordinate periphery is a ritualized relationship of central to derivative authority. Entrance into the ritualized relationship occurs through the rite of consecration *(abhiṣeka)*, such that the central Buddha consecrates his retinue, and the meditator becomes identified with the central (or subsidiary Buddhas) through the act of consecration by his master. Chapter 6 demonstrated that this was understood sufficiently to allow for the hagiographical episode of Kukura to place physically the members of King Indrabhūti's retinue in the various positions of the Vajradhātu maṇḍala. Thus the literal enactment of the esoteric narrative as a mythic event (and, we may suspect, in physical reality) within royal circles reinforced the conformity between real and imagined communities.

This conformity, however, depends on the actual form of the institutional maṇḍalas and their descriptive language. Yet some maṇḍalas found in the siddha-related literature appear dissonant with the institutional arrangement. Whereas many maṇḍalas are very much in accordance with the fundamental model, others are far more challenging, especially those maṇḍalas from the *yoginī tantras*. Many of these latter move away from issues of family and the formal political paradigms informing institutional esoterism. Instead they invoke village and even tribal ideals, some of which are visibly displayed in the *yoginī pīṭhas* that still survive as early medieval archaeological sites in the states of Orissa, Chhattisgarh, and Madhya Pradesh. Nevertheless this finding does not mean that the models are necessarily unpolitical, but it does indicate that the clarity of the sāmanta metaphor is minimally adumbrated by competing paradigms.

Although it is not my goal to articulate a rigorous typology of sacred diagrams, siddha literature tends to employ three basic kinds of maṇḍalas. Most in conformity with the institutional arrangement are maṇḍalas found in works eventually to be classified as *mahāyoga tantras:* the *Guhyasamāja*, the *Kṛṣṇayamāri*, the *Vajramahābhairava*, and so on. Their architectures are in a classical fivefold pattern, with central figures like Mañjuvajra surrounded by their immediate family retinues and the four families in the four cardinal directions. Subsidiary divinities, especially the Wrathful Kings *(krodharāja)*, may be placed in intermediate directions, but the political metaphor mostly holds true. These maṇḍalas are still found in palaces, and they still have walls of flaming scepters as globes surrounding their maṇḍalas. They employ much of the same language of consecration as seen in chapter 4. In spatial arrangement and information, they appear on a continuum with the maṇḍalas found in the great institutional works: the *Sarvadurgatipariśodhana*, the *Mahāvairocanābhisambodhitantra*, and so forth. Their siddha distinction appears to come through the accelerated eroticism and violence found in their iconography and attendant ritual descriptions.

In distinction to these are maṇḍalas whose basic premise is that of a single figure. A classic instance is the divinity Siddhaikavīra (Perfect, Unique Hero), identified in the tantra with a form of Mañjuvajra but probably adapted from a non-Buddhist source. The extraordinary emphasis on magical rituals in the tantra—weather, weapons, childbirth, and so on—suggests that Siddhaikavīra has been derived from a local divinity, analogous to Heruka.[2] The designation "unique hero" *(ekavīra)* seemed to have become paradigmatic, and sometimes the term is employed to describe how the meditator visualizes himself (some-

Hevajra maṇḍala[5]

Ghasmarī

Ḍombiṇī Pukkasī

Vetālī Hevajra Gaurī

Caṇḍālī Śavarī

Caurī

Buddhakapāla maṇḍala[6]

Saubhadrā

Pitāmbarā Sauṇḍinī

Pātālavāsinī Buddhakapāla Citrasenā

Ākāśavāsinī Caturbhujā

Kāminī

times with a consort) as he travels through the world while not actively in contemplation *(asamāhita)*.[3] Feminine divinities—Vajrayoginī, Kurukullā, Vajravārāhī, and so on—are also often found as single figures in their ritual descriptions, again possibly a reflection of their origins as local goddesses. Similarly, specific divinities are reduced from their more complex maṇḍalas to a single figure, based on the circumstances. Sahajasaṃvara stands out in my reading, for this divinity appears to be a decidedly secondary form of our old friend Saṃvara, and it followed from the application of the "naturalness" *(sahaja)* discourse to the highest yoga practices.[4]

More interesting is a third variety of maṇḍala: those with a circle of divinities surrounding the central figure. Normatively, the deities found in such circles number eight or multiples of eight and demonstrate an intriguing gender selectivity. Several of these maṇḍalas feature a male figure in the center, surrounded by a group of eight goddesses. This pattern occurs frequently enough to attract our attention as a maṇḍala theme. The standard maṇḍalas for Hevajra and Buddhakapāla, for example, both reflect this arrangement (with north placed at the top as in European maps).

There are others exhibiting this structure, as in the case of Heruka maṇḍalas (Figure 21).[7] Many elements of this variety of maṇḍala are worthy of consideration. First is an all-feminine form, in which Nairātmyā or Mārīcī, for example, is surrounded by other ḍākinīs.[8] These seem not to have been as emphasized, even though Mārīcī was clearly one principal divinity of choice for post-mortem rites.[9] The circle of divinities is also replicated in all-masculine forms as well, with a central figure surrounded by the masculine *ḍākas* or *krodhas*.[10] I know of no form, however, that features a feminine figure in the center surrounded by masculine divinities; they might exist but must be rather rare.

The gender selectivity is important, particularly as it appears so similar to the yoginī temples of sixty-four or eighty-one feminine figures. Both the Buddhist maṇḍalas and the majority of yoginī temples feature an arrangement that seems to prefer groups of eight yoginīs or multiples of eight (64). This also applies to circles of male figures, for the Saṃvara maṇḍalas are predominantly of that variety. In the center of this latter are Cakrasaṃvara and his feminine consort, usually Vajravarāhī; they are surrounded by concentric circles of gods, proceeding outward in radiating zones of mind, speech, and body. Each of these circles has eight figures, making a fundamental maṇḍala of twenty-four, representing the twenty-four divinities (or pairs of divinities) in the twenty-four places of pilgrimage briefly considered in chapter 5. The simple point is that maṇḍalas like these are iterations of the eight divinities or multiples thereof.

FIGURE 21 Saṃvara with a maṇḍala of Ḍākinīs in the background. Bengal, eleventh century. Indian Museum, A25188/9210. *Photo courtesy of the American Institute of Indian Studies*

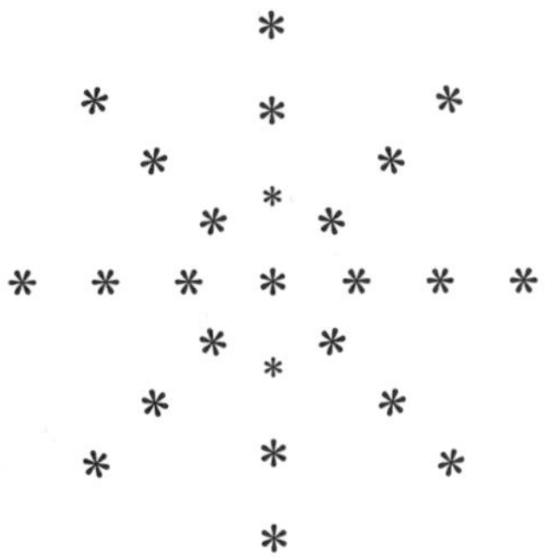

Arrangement of the Cakrasaṃvara maṇḍala

Certainly, earlier analogs may be found in maṇḍalas featuring the eight Great Bodhisattvas, but I believe that the architecture that these particular siddha maṇḍalas employ is informed instead by the old circular sites *(pīṭha)* dedicated to the yoginīs or ḍākinīs.

In this respect it seems that the preference for eight, and the distribution of ḍākinīs in a circle, problematized the fundamental maṇḍala format, especially with respect to family *(kula)*. The institutional maṇḍalas indicated that *kula* was an essential item identifying place and soteriological constituents, so mantras and other practices were considered place- and family-specific. In one sense, the problem of *kula* is a bit curious, since many of the *yoginī tantra* manuals show a definite concern for place and place-relationship. However, this seems sometimes done alongside or even outside the *kula* category. In the *Hevajra Tantra*, for example, *kula* is emphasized (e.g., I.v.5–7), but the term is not introduced when the maṇḍalas of Hevajra are discussed (I.iii; II.v). Instead, at a different point, the question is broached, and the Buddhas of the various families—Vairocana, Akṣobhya and the rest—are artificially brought into the conversation (II.ii.52–61). At one point in the *Hevajra Tantra* goddesses are definitively associated with families: Ḍombī–vajra family, Nartī–lotus family, Caṇḍālī–gem family, Brahmaṇī–Tathāgata family, and Rajakī–karma family (II.iii.62–63). The strange nature of these equivalents is demonstrated by the fact that only Ḍombī (or Ḍombinī, if they are the same) and Caṇḍālī are actually associated with the maṇḍalas specified in the text. Yet even there they do not occupy the positions normally accorded to these families. As a member of the vajra family, Ḍombinī should be in the east instead of the northwest (as she is in the actual maṇḍala), and as a mem-

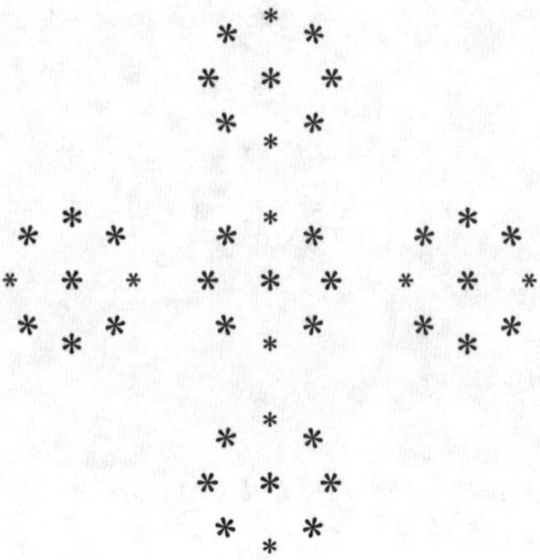

Arrangement of the Pañcaḍāka maṇḍala

ber of the gem family, Caṇḍālī should be in the south instead of the southwest.

These issues are not clarified in some of the consecration texts, such as the *Hevajrasekaprakriyā*. When the disciple is to be assigned a family, it is usually based on his throwing a flower (or garland) into the maṇḍala. However, it is not clear how the text was actually interpreted at the moment of the ritual, since the goddesses' families are not specified in that ritual work either.[11] This may be the reason that other maṇḍalas, such as the Pañcaḍāka maṇḍala, elect to proceed on the multiplication of the circles in a manner different from the *Saṃvara* tradition. In the Pañcaḍāka system, the basic form of the male divinity surrounded by eight female divinities is retained, but there are five such circles. Thus the entire maṇḍala is an aggregate of five maṇḍalas, each assigned the normative value of a Buddha family.[12]

How did this unwieldy synthesis of categories and representations come about? If our later sources are obscure, the earlier *Vidyottama* provides a chapter that I believe is as close as we can come to the process and is a bit less opaque. It describes how the Seven Mothers *(sapta mātaraḥ)*, those autochthonous village or tribal goddesses frequently found in a group in North India, became associated as a circle surrounding the bodhisattva Vajrapāṇi. Characteristically, the *Vidyottama* associates together a mythic event, a mantra, a painting, a practice, and several siddhis as results.

Then, the Seven Mothers that move in the sky, all chattering and laughing, came down to be included in that congregation. They made a triple circumambulation of the assembly and prostrated their heads at the feet of the Lord Buddha.

They then said to the Lord, "Lord, we also would like to make an offering of some mantras to the great bodhisattva Vajrapāṇi."

The Lord replied to those Mothers, "Hey, Rākṣasīs! It is well that you enter the assembly here for the benefit of beings!"

Then, those Mothers offered this mantra to Vajrapāṇi, just as they said they would do:

NAMO BUDDHĀYA NAMO VAJRAPĀṆAYE MAHĀYAKṢASENĀPATAYE
TADYATHĀ HULU HULU LAHU LAHU HAHA TIṢṬHA TIṢṬHA BHRAMA BHRAMA
BANDHA BANDHA MACA ME KAŚCID VIGHNĀṂKARIŚYATE MOHANI
MOHANI NAYATI NAYA MĀLINI VIŚVEŚVARE AMOGHE NAMAS SVĀHĀ

"Now if this spell is simply remembered by a *vidyādhara* accomplished in the best of spells *[vidyottama]*, we Seven Mothers will protect that person up to the distance of a *yojana* [~ 4 miles]. We will indeed correctly protect that person.

"And the various activities associated with the spell will occur. On a clean piece of cotton, paint Vajrapāṇi using paint without a glue binder. Make him ornamented with all ornaments, light blue in color, and having the visage and distemper of a sixteen-year-old. Paint the Seven Mothers surrounding him in a circle. They will be ferocious in appearance.

"Then fast for three days. On the fourteenth day of the bright half of the month, make whatever offerings you can. Be sure to give them [the Mothers] liquor and an offering of meat. Then the *vidyādhara* is to perform a hundred thousand *homa* sacrifices, placing white mustard seeds covered with blood in a fire blazing with khadira wood.

"If you see the painted form of Vajrapāṇi beginning to shake, then the *vidyādhara* should recollect this most excellent of spells. At that time, a woman baring her fangs will come to you. Do not be afraid! Instead say to her, 'Rākṣasī! It is good that you have come! Be sure to recollect that this sacrament has been given to you by Vajradhara [=Vajrapāṇi]!' Having heard that, she will give a cackle and reply, 'It will be done thus!' and she will disappear. Then you continue to make offerings of Tinarare [?] for one day, and all your goals will be accomplished. This will also bestow accomplishment in the spells *[vidyāsiddhi]*."[13]

The scripture goes on to catalogue other rituals and their benefits: overcoming Vināyaka demons and Graha spirits, ruining harvests, spoiling liquor, making an enemy ugly and diseased (but then turning him back again), discovering who one's enemies are, and expelling them. These are all very useful skills, no doubt, and the chapter concludes that these constitute the Mothers' ritual *(mātṛvidhi)*.[14]

Thus the *Vidyottama* depicts sorcerers making flesh and liquor offerings and performing *homa* before a painting of Vajrapāṇi, surrounded by a circle of seven mother goddesses. The fact that the number seven is odd leads to the conclusion that the uncertainty concerning family affiliation of members of the goddesses' circles began with this kind of arrangement. Unlike normative Buddhist (institutional) maṇḍalas, there is no necessary privileging of one direction or member over another—the seven Mothers are simply members of a circle. This is closely analogous to the circular arrangements in the yoginī temples, where the arrangements change from site to site, and in the *yoginī tantra* maṇḍalas, which frequently rearrange the position of individual members in circle to fit different purposes. Finally, we have a commonality of nomenclature. The *Hevajra Tantra* introduces the eight goddesses surrounding Hevajra as a Circle of Mothers *(mātṛcakra)*, and Kāṇha's commentary defines this simply as the maṇḍala of the divinities *(mātṛcakraṃ devatānāṃ maṇḍalaṃ)*.[15]

So are these new circle-type maṇḍalas exhibited in the *yoginī tantras* somehow related to the political models of sāmanta feudalism that inform the other variety of maṇḍalas? I believe this is true only in a derivative sense, not in the primary manner contributing to the formative process of the other kind of maṇḍala. The secondary nature of these is implicit in three ways. First is the emergence of the sāmantization of the gods or their "royalization," as Kulke and Rothermund have termed the process, examined earlier.[16] This was an overall pattern in the erosion of distinctions between kings and gods in medieval India. It is reflected in the highly formal verse forms *(praśasti)* employed in the panegyrics to a king and his lineage, verses that embodied a discourse on the apotheosis of the king. In an analogous manner, religious literature in the early medieval period embodied a discourse on the kingship of the divinities, specifically through the phenomenon of incarnation *(avatāra)*. Inasmuch as these circular maṇḍalas maintained this language—and it is found throughout them—they supported this broader series of conversations in Indian towns and palaces.

Second, as in the case of the new form of consecration, these maṇḍalas are still the object of royal consecration rituals that embody the voice of the court and the accoutrements of royalty. The maṇḍalas still occur in palaces, even if sometimes the palaces are envisioned within the human body. Access is still granted or withheld based on a sacralized coronation with aspersion, a crown, and a scepter. The *yoginī tantra* maṇḍalas, in particular, retain a sense of territorial dominion over pilgrimage sites—whether the twenty-four of the *Saṃvara* system or other arrangements—and over the gods that reside therein. Thus the paradigms of palace, place, and power are resolutely applied in all the *yoginī tantra* maṇḍalas, even if the metaphor is intertwined with other iconologies from Indian village or tribal sites and practices. As seen above, this happened with the siddha consecration ceremonies, so that the king's aspersion was modified to include the erotized consecration ceremonies of sacramental sexuality. In a like manner, the goddess maṇḍalas became embedded in a discourse that implicated regal power and authority, turning the sisterhood into a courtly retinue.

In this vein, there can be no question that the actual form implicates the subordination of the Mothers to Vajrapāṇi, the circle of goddesses to Hevajra and Buddhakapāla. They are his servants, make offerings to him, sing praises in the vernacular literature languages, and become part of his entourage. Thus the sāmantization of Vajrapāṇi in this maṇḍala is effected by his divine status as a superior bodhisattva to the inferior soteriological status of the goddesses, who are mundane *(laukika)* divinities. Ultimately, some (not all) of these implications were carried over to the circles evident in the *yoginī tantras.* In the new Buddhist literature, however, the primary divinity in the center of the maṇḍala may become a goddess as well, apparently demonstrating that the ferocious primacy of the village goddesses has not been entirely lost.

SIDDHAS IN A CIRCLE, SIDDHAS IN A LINE, SIDDHAS IN A MOB

Just as the world is not simply the residence of kings and queens, the maṇḍala is not only the residence of the gods and goddesses. At the margins of the maṇḍala diagram, well outside the palace grounds, are the cemeteries or cremation sites, located at the cardinal and intermediate points of the compass. Like the circle of goddesses, as seen above, they are generally eight in number, each with their specific attributes. Each cemetery has a name, a shape and size, a worldly guardian divinity, and specific trees. In each is found a territorial god *(kṣetrapati)*, an elephant, a snake spirit, a Vajraḍāka, and a stūpa. It is also, supremely, the residence of siddhas attached to each of the eight cemeteries.

It seems that the cremation grounds first appear in the tantras as an afterthought, providing a mundane *(laukika)* component to the entire maṇḍala.

Apparently, the positioning of the worldly gods and other characters in the maṇḍala required a separate series of locales. However, the cemeteries quickly became an important aspect of the *yoginī tantras*, and a genre of cemetery literature developed to describe their various attributes, sounds, meanings, and so forth. Iconographically as well, cemeteries stood as important signposts in the visual record, for, as mundane places, their collective representation became an avenue for artists to blend the sacred and the humorous.

For our purposes, the cemeteries describe idealized communities of siddhas. Their position in tension with the central maṇḍala provides a sense of both contrast and similarity. It describes at once the distance and relationship between siddhas as agents of the new proclamation and the theological objects of their cultus. Without the siddhas, many of the maṇḍalas simply would not have existed, for the new saints constituted the creative impetus behind the movement. Conversely, many of the divinities were simply available in some sense. They were brought from the shadows into the harsh light of Buddhist literature and had their rituals and representations altered in the process. However, the ritual and visual representations of siddhas in cemeteries are not an accurate description of what would be seen on the ground. Rather, it is a new articulation of liminal communities acting as the promoters and providers of a transgressive and polluted spirituality.

Perhaps the most interesting of the cemetery texts is rather late and anomalous in its assignment of names, positions, and so on. It is attributed to Birwa, normally identified as the vernacular name for the mahāsiddha Virūpa, part of whose hagiography was examined for humorous episodes in chapter 6. The text is interesting because it specifies in some detail the attribution of both specific siddhas and their lineages in specific cremation grounds.

Cremation Ground[17]	*Blessed by*	*Community*
Caṇḍogra (E)	Nāgabuddhi	Āryadeva, *Sundarī, and yogins and yoginīs of Nāgārjuna's *Guhyasamāja* system.
*Yamajvāla (S)	Ḍombhiheruka	Avadhūti, *Bhujā, and those following the *Guhyasamāja* and *Kṛṣṇayamāri.*
*Varuṇakapāla (W)	Aśvaghoṣa	Kukuripa, *Hṛdayālaṃkārā, and those following the *Mahāmāyā-tantra.*
*Kuberabhairava (N)	Ācarya *Padmaka	Bhadra, *Kuṭṭakā, and those following the *Hevajra* system of Saroruhavajra.
*Śrīnāyaka (SE)	Saraha	*Guṇakanaka, Padmavajrā, and those following Saraha's system of *Saṃvara.*

Aṭṭahāsa (SW)	Kāṇhapa	Suvarṇavarṇa, *Vaktrakrodhā, and those following the *Dvihṛdaya and Hayagrīva.
Ghorāndhakāra (NW)	Kukuripa	Srotaāpanna, *Kṣetrā, and those following Kukuripa's *Yoginī tantra* system.
Kilikilārava (NE)	Vajravārāhī	Śrīheruka, Nairātmā, and those following *Mahāmāyā* and *Khasama* systems.

Here we have a sense of siddhas in lineages, transmitting their various esoteric systems in specific cremation grounds, surrounded by a vast company of yogins and yoginīs, with their favorite snakes, trees, gods, clouds, and whatnot nearby. The arrangement provides a positive sense of the important lineages according to Birwa as well as the impression that he simply ran out of potential assignees at the end. At Ghorāndhakāra, Kukuripa is repeated, and by the last cemetery, Birwa has lapsed simply into divinities. The easy movement between saint and divinity surely has already begun (as with the god/saint *sidhs* of Himachal Pradesh), and by the end of the text the categories are increasingly open and fluid. Yet the circle at the edge of the maṇḍala also indicates Birwa's late blending of two other categories: a lineage of saints, on one hand, and siddhas in a great group, on the other.

The organization of siddha names and identities into discrete lineages or arrays came rather late in the maturation of esoteric Buddhist literature, perhaps as much as a century after siddhas as a category are noticed in the tantras themselves. Despite clear affirmation that eighth-century individuals were designated as siddhas, our earliest organizational texts were probably translated into Tibetan in the twelfth century and may be from the ninth to eleventh centuries, although solid evidence is lacking for many of the works. The reason for this is that their authors apparently relied on some idea of critical mass—there were simply insufficient siddhas to compound into these compendia of songs, verses, behavior, ritual, and incidentals.

Two types of texts were eventually developed, one describing the siddhas as members of a lineage, the other articulating great groups of siddhas, sometimes numbered and sometimes not. If the distinction between these two is clear in most of the texts, it has not received attention in scholarly studies, which have fixated on a single one of these works, the *Caturaśītisiddhapravṛtti* (Lives of the Eighty-four Siddhas), ascribed to Abhayadattaśrī. It is not immediately evident which of these two types of texts—lineage or group—precedes the other. My intuition, which might be faulty, tells me that the lineage works achieved currency before the other genre, principally because such lineage lists were well known in earlier Indian Buddhism. They may have developed from stories of the preaching of the tantras, and the late eighth- or early ninth-century version of Indrabhūti's receiving the *Sarvabuddhasamāyoga* begins to move in the direction of a lineage.[18] However, the group texts are also well authenticated, with early works focused on the sixteen arhats or the eight great bodhisattvas. There are also texts fulfilling something of both functions, such as those concentrating on the previous Buddhas or on the thousand Buddhas of the good eon, in some ways analogous to Birwa's layout of simultaneous lineages in cemeteries. For their part, the group-related siddha works are somewhat chaotic and make curious reading (being a little thin on plot). Thus, other than Abhayadattaśrī's contribution, they have seldom received the attention they deserve.

Several examples exist of the lineal variety, most notably the lineages collected into the only surviving Sanskrit Buddhist siddha hagiographical text, which has been called the "Sham Sher manuscript."[19] This work emphasizes the "nonreferential cognition" *(amanasikāra)* lineage, of which Maitrīpāda is the primary representative.[20] The work is therefore an eleventh-century work at the earliest, since it concentrates on the notable saint who was the contemporary of Atiśa (982–1054 C.E.). Beyond this text, several others are in the received record. A movement in this direction is found in the list of his teachers given at the beginning of Buddhajñāna's *Dvikramatattvabhāvanā-mukhāgama*, which has been commented on by Vitapāda in his *Sukusuma-dvikramatattva-bhāvanā-mukhāgamavṛtti;* much of its hagiographical narrative is examined below. In a somewhat different manner, the *Sahajasiddhi* ascribed to Indrabhūti includes a longer lineage list at its beginning, and we have to rely on the *Sahajasiddhipaddhati,* by Lhacham Jetsun Pelmo—possibly a Tibetan—to provide us with a narrative.[21] Unfortunately, Buddhajñāna's and Indrabhūti's texts survive only in Tibetan, and both focus on the land of Oḍiyāna and maintain that their lineages began there.

On the other hand, aficionados of the Abhayadattaśrī text will be surprised to learn that the number eighty-four is not universally represented in the siddha group lists. A great spectrum is observed in siddha groupings, from six to three hundred eighty-one names, although this last list is both anomalous and probably Tibetan in composition; the longest authentically Indian list is that of Vajrāsana, which includes eighty-five names. Many of these lists contain irregularities, specifically in the identification of names more than once, and the list of fifty names also has had Marpa the Tibetan translator slipped in for a fifty-first designation. I have no intention of providing a tiresome comparison of the names, but the respective texts are as follows.

Text	To.	Siddhas
Ṣaḍdharmopadeśa	2330	6 (Nāgārjuna and Sukhasiddhi twice)
Nānāsiddhopadeśa	noncanonical	13
dPal u rgyan du tshogs 'khor byas pa'i dus su rnal 'byor pa grub pa thob pa bzhi bcus rdo rje'i mgur bzhengs pa nyams kyi man ngag thig le gser gyi phreng ba	2449	43 (Tilopa twice)
Grub thob lnga bcu'i rtogs pa brjod pa thig le 'od kyi phreng ba	2444	51 (with Marpa)
Lam dri ma myed pa dngul sgong dag pa[22]	noncanonical	54 (*Ghudaripa twice)
Mahāmudrākanakamālā	2454	?
Cittaguhyadohā	2443	79
Abhayadattaśrī	Pe. 5091	84
**Caturaśītisiddhasambodhihṛdaya* of *Vīraprabha	2292	84 (=Abhayadatta's list)
Vajrāsana's *gsol 'deb*	3758	85
rNal 'byor pa thams cad kyi de kho na nyid snang ba zhes bya ba grub pa rnams kyi rdo rje'i mgur	2453	381 (multiple repetitions)

Tucci and Schmidt have independently studied the differences between several of the eighty-four/eighty-five siddha lists, and there is no point in repeating their helpful results.[23] More interesting, however, are some of the differences in the manner in which these lists were gathered together. Most of the lists, in fact, are catalogues—not of siddhas but of their songs of realization or their specific contributions to Buddhist practice. The *Ṣaḍdharmopadeśa* is probably a microcosm of how they were first compiled. It provides teachings or practices of Carya, Nāgārjuna (twice), Lavapa, and Sukhasiddhi (twice). A similar list not translated into Tibetan is included in a Sanskrit manuscript in the Nepal National Archives. Simply entitled *Nānāsiddhopadeśa* (Teachings of Some Siddhas), it contains short meditative instructions that were associated with thirteen siddhas.[24]

However, it was the first-person voice in the elusive songs that ensured their popularity and ultimately led to the kind of compendia seen in the Sikh *Gurugranthsahib.* The compelling immediacy of the first-person expression facilitated their compilation into grand arrangements of eminent personalities. This formula has some exceptions, however, most notably in the Vajrāsana list. This latter is a series of homages to the different siddhas but does include material on their lives or aspects of their realizations, and Vajrāsana is definitely modeling himself after prior hagiographical sources. Vajrāsana's list also shows the degree to which institutionalization continued, since many of the individuals included (such as Asaṅga) had not usually been accorded siddha status and certainly represented peculiar siddha personas. Moreover, because Marpa separated the names from the homages in the *Mahāmudrākanakamālā* and grouped the names into three versified groups, I have not been able to determine exactly how many siddhas were supposed to be represented, particularly as the names have become corrupted in the process of transmission. Also anomalous is the Abhayadattaśrī text, precisely because the names, verses, and hagiographies have all been included.

So, what is the purpose behind these numbers: forty, fifty, fifty-four, eighty, eighty-four, eighty-five, all of which are specified in one or more title? Clearly, they extended beyond the mere Buddhist usage, since fifty siddhas are so designated in the Śākta work, the *Kubjikāmata-tantra*, and a section of the *Skandapurāṇa* is dedicated to enumerating the eighty-four liṅga of Śiva.[25] Even more intriguing are allusions to unidentified numbers of siddhas, as in the case of twenty-one unnamed siddhas being encountered in a vision by Ralo Dorjé Drak (b. 1016).[26] First, and most obviously, such enumerations constitute organizing strategies, statements of completion, and enumerations of the songs that might be sung at an esoteric gathering *(gaṇacakra)* of those following the siddha path. Even when this was admitted by previous scholars, they have emphasized the mystical significance of these numbers, especially the number eighty-four. Buddhists had used this number in a variety of arrays, as in the representation of the eighty-four thousand doors of the Dharma. Yet organizing numbers should also be sought in the early medieval culture to see whether there are analogues that might be of assistance in understanding the field of significance of these numbers for Indian society in that period.

In reality—as might be expected if the sacred/profane dualism that informs much of Indology is put aside—most of these numbers are used elsewhere, in particular in the economic and political organization of Indian villages. Sharma shows that inscriptions and other materials from the early medieval period support the numbers five, ten, twelve, sixteen, twenty-four, forty-two, sixty-four, and so on as specific units of villages within larger political domains, organized as such for the purposes of taxation and control.[27] Whereas the number fifty (as in fifty siddhas) appears unrepresented, the number eighty-four *(caurāsi, caturaśīti)* has special application in this regard, for many of the areas of North India were organized into units of eighty-four throughout the medieval period, and this strategy was retained in places like Chhattisgarh right into the period of the British Raj.[28] This number is also seen as early as the 811/12 C.E. Baroda grant of Karka II, which records the grant to the Brahman named Bhānubhaṭṭa of a village within the Aṅkoṭṭka-caturaśīti, the eighty-four villages known by the designation Aṅkoṭṭka.[29] Thus the numbers eighty-four (siddhas), twenty-four (pilgrimage sites), and so forth were probably generated in the same matrix as Buddhist maṇḍalas: the organizational principles of Indian sāmanta feudalism.

This is certainly seen in sites surviving in isolation from the medieval period, perhaps most particularly in Brahmaur, the old capital of the Gaddi tribal kingdom in the modern state of Himachal Pradesh. There the town square is decorated with temples, mostly from the seventh to the thirteenth centuries (Figure 22). These are said to be the *caurāsi sidh*—the eighty-four siddhas.[30] As in the Maṇḍi employment discussed in chapter 5—and the breezy usage found in Birwa's cemetery text above—the term "siddha" here is simply applied to any of the many divinities. Thus, in Brahmaur, the gods and goddesses are denoted as sidhs and occupy the central place in the square of the old capital, even though no inscriptional evidence indicates that the organization of these temples was understood to be eighty-four when they were built. Nor are there actually eighty-four temples, images, or liṅga present; when I visited the site in 1997, only thirty-one sacred images or liṅga were identifiable, including a 1963 temple to a Jain Digambara saint. The men hanging out in the square all agreed that the square represents the eighty-four sidhs and the nine Nāths, but were at a loss to identify which were the eighty-four. The application of the designation eighty-four, then, may be construed to indicate a site or arrangement in which the number having both religious and political significance unifies these sources of power and authority.

HAGIOGRAPHICAL COMMUNITIES: BUDDHAJÑĀNAPĀDA'S TRAVELS

If ideological communities occupy one zone of the siddha cosmos, real communities may be located in another part of the universe. Because our informa-

FIGURE 22 Brahmaur. Caurāsi-sidh Square, seventh to thirteenth centuries.
Ronald M. Davidson

tion about real siddha communities, however, is impoverished, we must rely on hagiographical congregations to fill in the details, such as they might be ascertained. Unfortunately, undue emphasis has been placed on the work of Abhayadattaśrī, and his text may be important but is by no means definitive. In consideration of the wealth of other sources, and their relative neglect in scholarly literature, it would be appropriate to consider alternative descriptions of Buddhist siddha communities.

The record of Buddhajñānapāda stands out in this regard, not only because of his personal recording in the manner of Śākyamitra but for the attention it has received in subsequent Indian literature. Preeminent is the retelling of Buddhajñānapāda's travels in search of the Dharma by the master Vitapāda. Clearly Vitapāda was a later successor following in Buddhajñānapāda's footsteps, but his virtue is also exhibited in his revelation that he studied those records of his predecessor that no longer survive. His reading, combined with the power of Buddhajñānapāda's vision of the esoteric system, illuminates our task in some measure. For our purposes, we might recollect that not only is the hagiographical remembrance important but Buddhajñānapāda's system of *Guhyasamāja* exegesis—featuring the Mañjuvajra maṇḍala—became one of the two defining systems inherited by most concerned with the *Guhyasamāja* tradition.[31]

The surviving discussion starts with Buddhajñānapāda's monastic career and his study with the preeminent authority on the *Perfection of Insight* scriptures as understood in the late eighth century: Haribhadra. This scholar is, fortunately, to some degree datable, for he states in his own record that he completed his magnum opus on the *Perfection of Insight* during the reign of Dharmapāla (c. 775–812 C.E.).[32] After describing his study with Haribhadra, Buddhajñānapāda embarks on a pilgrimage to learn the new esoteric scriptures being disseminated in the north.

> The place *Guṇodaya is 230 yojanas [~ 920 miles] north of Magadha. It is called the Source of Qualities [*Guṇodaya] because the Ḍākinī's blessing arises out of it. This name is applied to Oḍiyāna. In a section of it is Ratnadvīpa, where was born one who obtained the Great Seal. He is called *Citrarūpa, or is otherwise known as Vilāsavajra. Buddhajñānapāda learned from him many ritual *[kriyā]* and *yoga tantras* and examined them with zeal.
>
> Again in a section of Oḍiyāna was one known as Guneru, who had obtained the Instruction on the Inconceivable Stages *[Acintyakramopadeśa]* and had obtained [a vision of] the Great Yoginī.[33] Buddhajñānapāda went

to his place and propitiated him. He learned many *anuttara yoga tantras*, and learned the teacher's exposition of the sacraments and the consecrations, and immediately set to meditation.

In a dream, a deity explained to Buddhajñānapāda, "In the northern door of Oḍiyāna is a sixteen year old young outcaste girl [mātaṅgī or caṇḍālī] named Jāthig Jvala. She is actually the same as Mahālakṣmī born into a high caste. If you go there, your wish will be accomplished!" Accordingly, he left Guneru's entourage and went to make friends with her, and propitiated her for eight months. He realized then that he had obtained realization in the Great Seal. Since he had been granted some subtle instruction, he attained the siddhi of the god Jambhala.

Then he proceeded to the city of Kanauj in the country of Jālandhara. In one section of that city, he went before Bālipāda, whose thought had become like a river in comprehension of the tantras that principally represent Insight *[prajñātantra]*. He propitiated the teacher and learned the texts, heard his instruction, and assiduously practiced meditation.

About three hundred yojanas [~ 1,200 miles] from Kanauj in the southern direction is the country of Koṅkana. There is a place in Koṅkana called Kāṇherī. Why is it called that? Because it is a place that seems to exist like rootless vines entwined up trees *[anhri]* into the sky *[kha]*. In one part was the Lord of Siddhas, bound to only one more birth *[ekajātipratibaddha]*, whose mind had become like a great river in comprehension of the tantras that principally represent skillful means *[upāyatantra]*. His name was *Rakṣāpāda. Moreover, he was surrounded by his retinue, all of whom had achieved miraculous powers. There was the Brahman Catrata, the Brahman Guhyaparta [? Guhyapatra], the Kṣatriya Mañjuśrī, the Vaiśya Pūnyabhadra, and the Śūdras Dīpaṃkara and Karṇaputra. There were also the prostitutes Āloki and Sādhuśīla. All of their clothing and other necessities were furnished by Devī Vasudhārā. Each day, she would bring to them ten grains *[māṣka]* of gold, half a necklace of pearls, and three hundred cowries. Buddhajñānapāda bowed there at the teacher's feet for nine years, so he also became bound to only one more birth. He obtained the teacher's understanding of the *Samāja Mahātantra* and other works, as well as the yogas associated with the *Samāja Tantra*. Its commentary was the **Yogaśikṣāmāṃsikaputrī Vimalamudrī* [?]. All told, he listened to eighteen texts and practiced them for eighteen months.

Yet he had not obtained the diffusion of the waves of realization, and he told the teacher, "I have not realized it!" But even the teacher replied, "I have not realized it either!" So he somewhat concluded his study, thinking,

> "Others not realizing this would be worthless as well!" So he affixed his seal on the text of the *Samāja*, and, tying it around his neck, he headed north.
>
> Now behind Vajrāsana there was a forest called Kuvaca. Buddhajñānapāda decided, "I'm going to live among those beings that look out of the Bodhimaṇḍa [Bodhgayā temple]. That forest is a terrifying place fairly crawling with bears and tigers of desire, etc. Since I am seeking liberation from those things, for six months I will realize the reality of the teaching present in that forest through meditative ritual, along with the ritual request for instruction in the Dharma."
>
> How did he achieve that realization? There was a monk who was an emanation. That is, in that forest there was a monk who was an emanation of Vajradhara. He had a lower garment made of mouse pelts and would plow the fields with his religious robes made into a kind of hat. He and two gurus lived there along with a nasty woman, her small son, and a dog with blotchy white marks. When Buddhajñānapāda met them, he obtained no sense that they had waves of realization, so the teacher concluded that they simply had no shame.[34]

The narrative continues with the eventual revelation of Mañjughoṣa's maṇḍala to Buddhajñānapāda, who also received from the Bodhisattva of Insight the detailed meditative instructions that were eventually to become the text of the *Dvikramatattvabhāvanā-mukhāgama* (Direct Revelation of the Cultivation of the Reality of the Two Processes). At the conclusion of the vision, both the maṇḍala and Buddhajñānapāda's disreputable companions were revealed as emanations of Mañjughoṣa himself and were withdrawn with him back into space. Buddhajñānapāda then retreated to a mountain cave called Matahranitra (?) a little more than six *yojanas* (~ 25 miles) northeast of Vajrāsana.[35] There, he began his teaching, and Vitapāda indicates that Buddhajñānapāda accrued sixteen great disciples, of whom four were the most important: *Dīpaṃkarabhadra, *Praśāntamitra, *Rāhulabhadra, and Vajramahāsukha.[36] The community was kept alive by daily offerings of seven hundred cowries. Eventually, Buddhajñānapāda returned to his teacher at Kāṇherī and received his blessing.

The hagiographical communities represented here appear to become the new synthesis for Buddhists of many kinds in the early medieval period. By this time small communities seem to have formed in proximity to the large exemplary monasteries, communities composed of both monks and siddha figures (Map 4). This is certainly reflected in Yūkadevī's monastery in early medieval Kashmir, which was divided into two sections, one for monks adhering

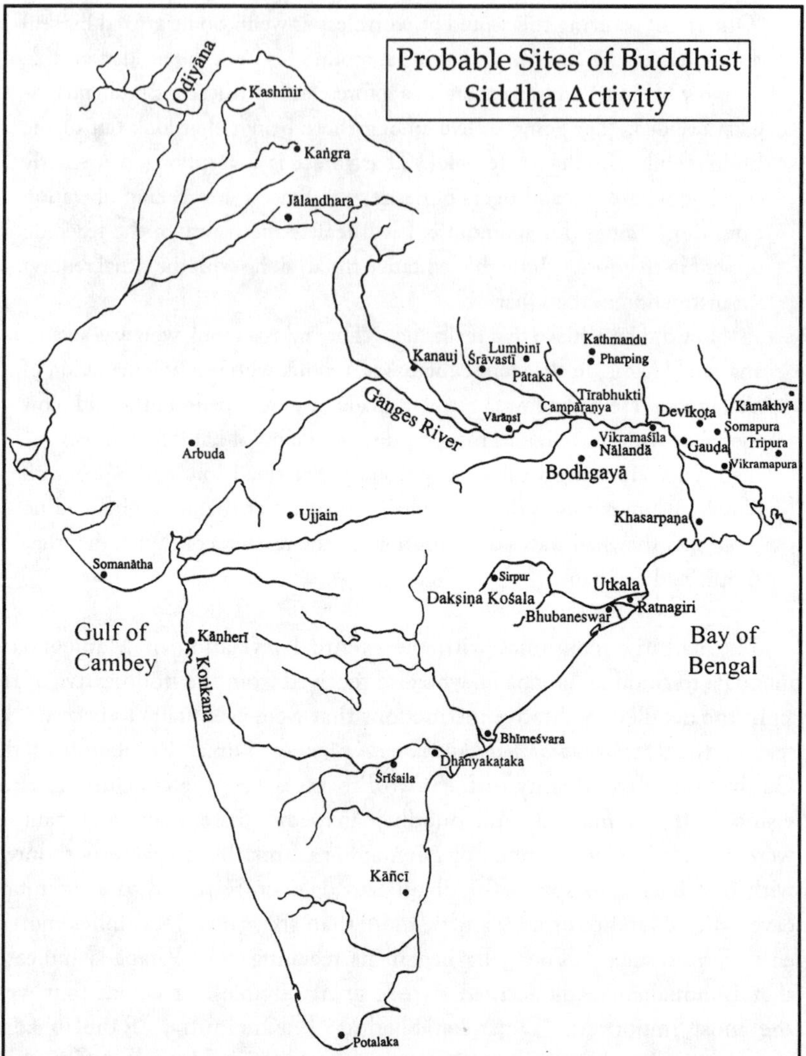

MAP 4 Probable Sites of Buddhist Siddha Activity.
Ronald M. Davidson and Richard Pinto

to the rules of discipline, the other dedicated to "monks" with the accoutrements of householders: wives, children, cattle, and property.[37] Similarly, we see the rather breezy movement from Buddhajñānapāda's presumably monastic study with Haribhadra and Vilāsavajra, to his esoteric study with Guneru, who recommends a sexual involvement with an outcaste yoginī.

From there, Buddhajñānapāda goes south to Kāṇherī, the important Buddhist center in the hills above the modern city of Mumbai (Bombay). The teacher's name given by Vitapāda, *Rakṣāpāda, was not the one that Buddhajñānapāda himself employed. In his own short statement, Buddhajñānapāda indicates that the teacher in Kanauj, Bālipāda (or, Balipāda), and the ācārya in Kāṇherī were one and the same. The multicaste composition of this center in western India is most interesting, as is the identification of the two prostitutes living with the yogins. Although it is difficult to extrapolate from hagiographical sources, it appears that this community, at least, fell back on the old Indian association of ascetics and women of easy virtue, recognized as early as the Mahāvrata rituals and carried on to this day by some Aghoris.[38] Yet this is also probably the same place in Koṅkana where Śākyamitra, undoubtedly a monk, studied the esoteric canon, as seen in his short record translated in chapter 4.

Also informative is the specification of funding—ten grains *(māṣka)* of gold, half a necklace of pearls, and three hundred cowries—and its attribution to the divine providence of Devī Vasudhārā. We do know that the Mahārājamahāvihāra at Kāṇherī of North Koṅkana (Aparānta) continued to receive regal largesse at least as late as 877/878 C.E. under Śilāhāra Kapardin II and still exhibited signs of life as late as the twelfth century.[39] Certainly, there is nothing about the donation of gold, pearls, and cowries that would be inappropriate from a king. Moreover, the interpretation of this community's name is curious. Although the surviving epigraphs make clear that the name "Kāṇherī" is from the Prakrit rendering of Kṛṣṇagiri (Dark Mountain), apparently both Vitapāda and the later Tibetan translation team interpreted it from Sanskrit as "a tree *[aṃhri]* growing in the sky *[kha]*."

After Bālipāda informs Buddhajñānapāda that he himself, although an esoteric teacher, has not achieved the realization of the scriptures he teaches, Buddhajñānapāda returns north and takes retreat in a forest behind Vajrāsana (which Vitapāda interprets as in the northeast, toward Nālandā). Curiously, after his escapades with the outcaste yoginī, he tries to keep his distance from some Buddhist monks and teachers in the forest, for he considers them disreputable. One of these is dressed as a monk while living with a bad-tempered woman, her son, and a dog of poor complexion. The other two in the group are simply said to be "gurus," which could mean almost any kind of teacher, and no further information is provided. The story eventually reclaims the degenerate monk as an emanation of Vajradhara, probably here meaning Vajrapāṇi, for the two names were interchangeable during the eighth and early ninth centuries.[40]

All told, the hagiography supports a sense of the strong involvement of siddha figures with monks in regional centers, away from or in proximity to the larger monastic compounds. Even when he sets up his own teaching establishment, this is evident in the hagiography. The composition of Buddhajñānapāda's four disciples represents their similarly mixed background. Three appear to have monastic names (*Dīpaṃkarabhadra, *Praśāntamitra, *Rāhulabhadra) reflecting ordination in the well-attested –bhadra and –mitra monastic lineages, doubtless from the *Mūlasarvāstivāda Vinaya*. However, the last name, Vajramahāsukha, can only be a siddha appellation. It is extremely unfortunate that the "more extensive" records alluded to by Buddhajñānapāda, and specified by Vitapāda, seem no longer to survive, for they would have provided better information on Nālandā and Vajrāsana, at the very least.[41]

The issue of hagiography, though, would be incomplete without calling into question the self-promotional nature of many siddhas' representations. Chapter 5 began with a quotation from the *Kṛṣṇayamāri-tantra* that provided an idealized portrait of a prototypical siddha. The variety of person depicted is instantly recognizable: free in the world, unconcerned with the slings and arrows of outrageous fortune, at ease in the tribal realms and in the forest. Those at home in Buddhist siddha literature should be familiar with this representation—it has been used frequently in such esoteric systems as the Mahāmudrā of the Tibetan Kagyüpa, where both Tilopa and Nāropā are described in similar terms. In the hagiography of the great Tibetan translator Marpa, for example, the lay scholar goes to India for the last time to seek further instruction from Nāropā, who, he is told, is deceased. Undaunted, Marpa struggles through a jungle, and finally Nāropā appears to him, a veritable cemetery-ornamented Heruka in the primeval forest.[42] Such portraits are also instructive about the degree to which some of our siddha materials have been manipulated by Tibetan scholars, whose personal investments in these representations were overwhelming.

If these images are compared with less subjective accounts, the discontinuity is immediately evident. Some of these statements are found directly in Indian literature. Indeed, chapter 1 began with an extract from the *Mañjuśrīmūlakalpa* describing a Mr. Va—evidently a real Buddhist layman—who was wealthy, worked in the courts of kings, employed mantras and tantras for the protection of the state, and argued incessantly on behalf of the Buddhist cause.

In addition, one of the two popular stories on the preaching of the tantras involved King Indrabhūti and invoked a line of aristocratic individuals. Similarly, some less subjective accounts tell of Nāropā, such as those found in Atiśa's hagiography and in the report of Nagtso Lotsāwa, who was sent to find Atiśa and bring him back to Tibet. While waiting for Atiśa to complete some final tasks at Vikramaśīla, Nagtso went to see Nāropā in Phullahari, in eastern India, before the great siddha's death around 1041 C.E. Supported by a similar description in Atiśa's hagiography, Nagtso's record seems to represent a credible eyewitness account of a paradigmatic siddha.[43]

> Because I went alone as an insignificant monk to invite the Lord Atiśa—and because he tarried for one year in Magadha—I thought that I would go see the Lord Nāropā, since his reputation was so great. I went east from Magadha for a month, as I had heard that the Lord was staying in the monastery known as Phullahari. Very great merit arose from being able to go see him. On the day I arrived, they said some feudal prince had come to pay homage. So I went to the spot, and a great throne had been erected. I sat right in front of it. The whole crowd started buzzing, "The Lord is coming!" I looked and the Lord was physically quite corpulent, with his white hair [stained with henna] bright red, and a vermilion turban bound on. He was being carried [on a palanquin] by four men and chewing betel-leaf. I grabbed his feet and thought, "I should listen to his pronouncements!" Stronger and stronger people, though, pushed me further and further from his seat and finally I was tossed out of the crowd. So, there I saw the lord's face, but did not actually hear his voice.[44]

Collectively, these reports show Nāropā—and other siddhas—not as ferocious Herukas in the wilderness, but as elderly lay gurus and paṇḍitas, who traveled in palanquins and needed assistance simply to walk up stairs. Nagtso indicated that Nāropā's teeth were probably stained red from chewing betel-leaf, which would have given him the dramatic receding gums that afflict habitual users of that mild intoxicant. He was doubtless extremely fat, as Nagtso affirms, and wore a red turban over his long, henna-dyed hair. Nagtso seems to indicate that Nāropā preferred the company of important political personages over that of Buddhist monks, since a local prince's visit preempted the translator from actually speaking with the aging lay scholar. Thus siddhas—and no one was a siddha if Nāropā was not a siddha—apparently manipulated media representations as well as any accomplished purveyor of power could, although certainly much of it was done by their followers. Both the above evidence and others like it make it abundantly clear that siddhas were attributed a spectrum of behavior in the received record, in greater variation than is commonly assumed.

GATHERINGS AND *GAṆACAKRAS*— THE RITUAL COMMUNITY

Religious communities in India, as elsewhere, define themselves around ritual gatherings in which individuals assume positions of importance. Beyond the irregular ritual moments of the consecration and the individual or community meditations, siddha communities defined themselves by a regular gathering of initiates. This gathering was called the *gaṇacakra,* which Snellgrove has labeled the "tantric feast," an appropriate designation in some ways. The term literally means "a group circle," with the first element having great resonance in the period. *Gaṇa,* for example, does mean "a group or following," but also describes Śiva's gang, the hordes of buffoon-like, fat followers who fight over food and are led by Gaṇeśa, Śiva's elephant-headed son, who rides a rat. A *gaṇikā,* conversely, is a prostitute or courtesan, for she also has a retinue, but for decidedly less religious purposes.

Snellgrove has presented *gaṇacakra* descriptions in the two later texts of the *Hevajra Tantra* and the *Saṃvarodaya* and has established the outlines of the rite as it was known to the communities supporting these works.[45] Unfortunately, like ritual descriptions in so many esoteric treatises, these scriptures' specificity leaves something to be desired. The problem of description is often exacerbated by domestication, for as time goes on the later texts devoted to the *gaṇacakra* rite increasingly explain it as either visualized or otherwise sanitized.[46] Other works, though, leave little doubt about the general purpose of its exercise: acquisition of the sorcerer's *(vidyādhara)* powers through the community's sacramental experience of otherwise forbidden items. Among the most detailed of the earlier descriptions is a work dedicated to the *gaṇacakra* rite associated with the *Sarvabuddhasamāyoga-tantra.* Attributed to an Indrabhūti, the text is a relatively early description, in which are provided very specific instructions.

> One who has completed the collections of both merit and wisdom will achieve success in a place appropriate for the specific arrangement of the family *[kula]* for the complete *gaṇacakra.* The place should be one that is perfect as explained in the scripture, or at least a pleasant place like a garden, etc. The time for the *gaṇacakra* is at one of the two twilight periods on the eighth or fourteenth of the waning moon or the eighth or tenth of the

waxing moon. First arrange seats there that are soft and delightful to the touch. They should be covered with cotton cloth on which are printed all kinds of lotuses. These are the completely pure seats. These are the glorious sacraments [*śrīsamaya*] of all the Buddhas. They become the joyful appearance of Vajrasattva. They are the excellent citadels of the Tathāgata. Ornament them with jewels and other ornaments. If you cover the site over with a good canopy, then miraculously there will occur songs and music of the excellent vajra-words, and so forth. Set out fragrant flowers and oil lamps with scented oil. Then you will accomplish the highest bliss that is the ḍākinīs' assembly, the sexual union of all the Buddhas *[sarvabuddha-samāyoga-ḍākinījāla-śaṃvara]*.

Having first correctly asked the Lordly Teacher [Ācāryanātha], then request the followers. With the secret signs of the Buddha, take flowers and admonish these beings. "All you Yogins and Yoginīs! With an intention that is both happy and pure, I pray that you come to my place tonight to perform the *gaṇacakra*!"

"Hey, son, compassionate one!" [they will reply]. Now if they show you the rosary in their hands, then it is to say that "we will come." Since he has moved them to present their rosaries, he becomes sacramental, one with a good vow, a hero, acting for the welfare of others.

Then, there is the evening gathering. Externally they are cleansed: washing with powdered soap and fragrant water, bedecked with flowers, their yoga is purified with the Dharma mantras. Internally, they bathe as well. They are protected and blessed with mantras. The avowed congregation *[samayagaṇa]* is fully renewed in their esoteric promises. They then may gradually enter the ritual enclosure.

In order to test for the secret signs of those having taken the vows, there are the two Agents *[*karmin]* dressed in the blue wrathful ornaments.[47] These two ascertain who knows the signs as they recite spells [to which others are to respond correctly]. They [stand at] the frames of the two doors for the sake of protection, saying:

> Hey, you here, beautified with the blue ornaments of the Wrathful Kings *[krodharāja]*! You Sacramental agents *[*samayavicāraka]*, holders of the Jeweled Club of Accomplishment *[siddhiratnadaṇḍa]*! Heroes and heroines, assemble! I now permit the holy name holders [having received a name with the consecration] in the circle of yoginīs who have beautiful vaginas! OM MAHĀSA[MA]YA HŪṂ | SURATASTĀṂ|[48]

At this time, one of the *Sarvabuddhasamāyoga* maṇḍalas is constructed, and offerings of various varieties are made, including those of fish, meat, and liquor. Everyone meditates, visualizing the gnostic maṇḍala that is propitiated. The offerings are then consumed, for, "There are no false conceptions toward these foods. The Brahman, the dog, and the outcaste all eat together, for they are each of the same nature."[49] Likewise, the yogins and yoginīs engage in ritual intercourse. The yogin is instructed to consider that, without affection toward any of the deities of the maṇḍala, "I am the Mahāheruka!" Having relinquished his own nature, he is to indulge in whatever he likes, without being afflicted by the restraint of his discipline. He is the "Latter-day Buddha," to enjoy himself without fear.[50] After having washed again, the assembly concludes with more meditation and a calling of the divinities for assistance. The divinities are ritually returned to their homes, and the congregation does likewise.

This version of the rite, therefore, calls for four principle actors. First is the master of the rite *(ācārya),* who acts as the leader of the congregation *(gaṇanāyaka).*[51] He is the one charged with conducting the ritual and is ostensibly the teacher of the assembly. The one preparing these offerings, laying out the site, and requesting the performance is normatively identified as the patron *(dānapati).* However, this is primarily seen in other contexts, for there the patron employs the rite as a vehicle to effect the esoteric actions of pacification or increase. In distinction, Indrabhūti's text seems to be addressed to the person in the position of patron, but does not describe him as such, and we have little sense of the rite serving an ulterior motive beyond the sacramental. One of the most interesting sections of the text describes the Agents, called *karmavajrin* in the *Saṃvarodaya Tantra.* They, like all the assembly, are dressed in blue and bedecked with ornaments of the Wrathful Kings. They guard the doorways and allow in only those who know the secret signs, making sure that the participants are cleansed and generally ensuring the maintenance of order.

One problem in understanding the *gaṇacakra* is that there seems to be little precedent for this gathering in the normative rituals of either Mahayana Buddhism or the Hindu Varṇāśramadharma. Its emphasis on sexuality, on eating foods forbidden to caste Hindus, on the use of a circle as a ritual enclosure, and on relative egalitarianism under the leadership of a teacher and his agents all make the *gaṇacakra* stand apart from mainstream practices. Certainly, we see strong continuities with the various *cakra* gatherings of extreme Śaiva or Śākta systems, and the surviving documents also support such assemblies. The *Kulārṇava,* for example, provides a much-abbreviated description of conduct in the cakra, and its various admonitions against the incorrect behavior of others suggest an earlier level of the ritual, against which the text responds.[52] As is evident in other siddha systems, in the case of the *gaṇacakra* we seem to have received descriptions from Śaiva or Śākta sources that are apparently later than the surviving Buddhist works.[53]

It has been suggested that tribal rituals have contributed to such practices as the *gaṇacakra*, yet scholars suggesting such affinities seldom take note of tribal ethnography.[54] It may be the case, for example, that the youth dormitory system found in many groups in Central and East India was a contributor to the *gaṇacakra*. The youth dormitories concentrate adolescents of either sex in close proximity for a specified period of time, so that they form legitimate sexual liaisons with others of their age. Such liaisons, even if stable for a while, do not necessarily entail marriage.[55] The best studied of these is the Ghotul of the Muria of Madhya Pradesh and Bihar; it provides a transitional sense of sexual and group identity for the difficult years between puberty and marriage. Both of our rather extensive studies of the Muria Ghotul have emphasized the web of structured relations and religious responsibilities that ensues for all Ghotul members, so that individuals (theoretically at least) can come to terms with the overwhelming nature of their first sexual experience, if that is their desire.[56] The regular festivals, the specific responsibilities, and the mythological narratives all serve to make the transition smooth for the village, the family, and the individual. The spatial placement of the Ghotul in the precincts of the village simply reinforces its central and inclusive position in the development of Muria society.[57]

We do know that tribal rituals have been viewed with consternation by caste Indians. The offering period to the Goddess Mahāmāyā described in the *Kālikāpurāṇa*, for example, ends with a ritual of ceremonial chaos. Here, people were to deride one another, making rude comments and sexually explicit jokes and generally acting as if there were no rules.[58] This chaotic ritual period is called Śabarotsava, the festival of the Śabaras. Rather than a truly tribal ritual, though, its description suggests the difficulties experienced by caste Hindus in an accurate assessment of the relatively egalitarian values found among tribal peoples. The authors of the *Kālikāpurāṇa* project, instead, hierarchical inversion as the consequence.

However, the *gaṇacakra* in fact serves entirely a different function from the village dormitory, so it is questionable whether the latter contributed in any way. Here, the yogins and their partners become isolated from the larger society, and the *gaṇacakra* serves to reinforce the unique opportunity that these select few have in obtaining awakening beyond the bounds of traditional religious strictures. Instead of a transitional condition, they are confirmed into a mystical society from which there is no retreat. Rather than being a temporary liminal state leading to adulthood, the *gaṇacakra* requires a commitment to a permanent liminal status in which the individual will never be reintegrated into any village anywhere, even though he must observe his fellow ritualists as his immutable brothers and sisters in religion. Thus as yet it is unclear whether any tribal rites actually contributed to the development of the *gaṇacakra* or whether the Buddhist ceremony developed from entirely other local village or regional Kaula or Śaiva rituals.

RULES OF ORDER

Whatever the source of such erotized rituals, Buddhists formulated their identity on rules as well as on rites. Particularly in India, communities define themselves by rules, generally formulated as transgressions in need of ritual atonement. Chapter 4 looked at one list of rather modest restrictions undertaken by the early esoteric meditators associated with the maṇḍalas in the *Mañjuśrīmūlakalpa*. However, while the lists in the first chapters of this text are representative of institutional esoterism, they are by no means authoritative. Other lists of appropriate vows occur, and sometimes different lists are found even within the same tantra. This should come as no surprise, for Buddhist communities have tended to divide and to provide self-definition by means of both their rules and the degree to which these were in fact observed. In the case of monks, certainly, the real observance is always uncertain, in part because there were the other systems explicit in the ideology of the three vows: those of the monk, the bodhisattva, and the *vidyādhara*. Actually, the sorcerers' discipline was not required for community behavior, for the monks were expected to maintain at least an approximate relationship to monastic decorum and, in some monasteries, the bodhisattva vows as well. Although the monastic vows were strained by monks' participation in esoteric communities, more than adequate evidence shows that the vows remained an expectation if not a reality. As a result, over time the perception grew that the discipline of the *vidyādhara* was, for monks, supplemental to both the monastic and Mahayanist rules *(prātimokṣasaṃvara, bodhisattvasaṃvara)*, since secrecy and appropriate behavior during the secret rituals were understood as the primary contributions of the new model.

Conversely, dedicated siddha communities, because they were not principally concerned with monastic behavior, apparently needed specific *vidyādhara* rules to a greater degree than those centers trying to adjudicate the several disciplinary agendas. Consequently, siddha rules have a much greater emphasis on formalization than do the institutional esoteric strictures. Although several specific lists of esoteric vows circulated among siddha communities, two became important: (I) the fourteen root transgressions and (II) the eight gross transgressions (see lists below). These two legal agendas apparently evolved independently, for the two lists contain some redundancy as well as some difference in the meaning of specific items. Interestingly, the individual items are actually numbered in many of the surviving catalogues.[59]

I. *Fourteen* Root Transgressions.

1. Contempt for the teacher.
2. Transgressing the message of the Tathāgata.
3. Anger at members of the feast family.
4. Abandoning loving kindness.
5. Rejecting the thought of awakening.
6. Abusing the three vehicles.
7. Revealing secrets to unprepared people.
8. Disparaging the Victor's body of instruction.
9. Doubt about the pure-natured Dharma.
10. [Improper] love or dispassion toward evil people.
11. Imposition of other than non-duality upon reality.
12. Disparaging those with faith.
13. Not relying on the sacraments and vows.
14. Disparaging insight-filled women.

II. *Eight Gross Transgressions.*

1. Seeking to take a consort who is without sacramental preparation.
2. Relying on unauthorized sacraments.
3. Arguing in the tantric feast.
4. Showing the secret Dharma.
5. Teaching another Dharma to those of faith, causing confusion.
6. Staying with Śrāvakas for seven days.
7. Claiming the status of a *mantrin* without sufficient realization.
8. Teaching secrets to the unprepared.

Certainly, there is some discussion in Buddhist literature about the significance of these items. For example, contempt for the teacher is described in a number of ways, ranging from insults to assaults. Śākyamitra understands contempt as seeing only faults in the preceptor or turning one's back on the master instead of greeting him with a bow to the ground.[60] Likewise, the first gross transgression may simply depict the unseemly circumstance of yogins searching for sexual conquests of any variety—*yakṣīs, rākṣasīs,* animals, or whatever. Some commentators say that the consorts must have physical qualities as described in the tantras, and most texts declare that the ladies are preferable if they have also been consecrated.[61] Still others claim that the female partners of whatever species should be divinely sent; they also council patience to the yogin afflicted by desire.[62] Similarly, the kind of women disparaged is limited to consorts in the tantric feast for some, while others say that the denigration of any woman constitutes an infraction.[63] The redundancy between the lists (or within them) is evident, with I.3 and II.3, or I.7 and II.4 (or II.8), respectively, being virtually the same, a fact taken into account by some commentators. The apparent conflict between nos. I.4 and I.10 of the root transgressions also seems quite apparent. In the former case, one is not to surrender to antagonism toward others, while in the latter case one should not to be content to remain in the company of enemies of the Buddhadharma. Thus I.4 is psychological while I.10 is behavioral. Whatever their difference of opinion on specific transgressions, commentators express broad general agreement on these rules, and almost every exegete who comments on one list also includes the other as well.

Some information can be gleaned from both the lists. First, as already mentioned, their redundancy implies their origins in different sources. This inference is verified to some degree by Mañjuśrīkīrti, who kindly goes out of his way to seek out the scriptural sources for each rule, to the extent that he can. His *Vajrayānamūlāpattiṭīkā-mārgapradīpa*, in fact, makes the comparative study of these rules actually possible and constitutes a remarkable work of traditional scholarship. Concomitant with his analysis, however, is the rather basic observation that neither list of faults appears intact in any single scripture. Both agendas therefore seem to have been synthesized outside the basic scriptural context. Second, it is fairly clear that the rules are written for men. They can be followed only by those who select female consorts, disparage women *per se* (in or out of the tantric feast), and live with the orthodox monks (Śrāvakas) of the conservative monastic traditions for more than seven days. Thus these faults are framed in order to deter potential (and probably actual) sexual predation, misogyny, and sectarian conversion to the path of early Buddhist monasticism.

Finally, we should note the overwhelmingly social nature of these vows. So many of them have to do with behavior in the tantric feast, with teaching or revealing secrets to others, with relations between men and women, with offense to the preceptor, and so forth. Only within the list of fourteen root transgressions are there three rules that appear intellectual or psychological: not to abandon loving kindness (I.4), not to give in to doubt (I.9), and not to consider the elements of reality to be pluralistic (I.11). And yet these agendas are not really complete rules of order, for their focus is on specific kinds of transgressions, such as claiming the status of *mantrin* when it is undeserved. In that regard, the transgressions are curiously similar to the transgressions seen in the early Buddhist rules *(prātimokṣa)*, for one would have difficulty understanding even the idealized monastic life by simply considering the two hundred plus monastic precepts. Both the esoteric strictures, then, as the early Buddhist transgressions, represent special cases, rather than the fundamental operating procedures incumbent on either community.

This section would be incomplete without mentioning that there were other lists of rules that received currency among the siddhas, one of them an intriguing list of fifteen transgressions.[64] It is seldom mentioned even in traditional texts, and I have seen no discussion of it at all in modern scholarly literature. This other list cannot be considered popular, but its treatment by Mañjuśrīkīrti has made it accessible. Each item on the list presents an image in association with an intended explanation.

III. The Fifteen Transgressions.

1. The eye is disinterest in one's own divinity.
2. A moon, passing without the sacraments.
3. Quality, or delight in others' gods.
4. Desire, for the reality of the Vedas
5. Arrowed, one incomplete yet taking disciples.
6. Faculty, focused on worldly Dharma.
7. Mountain, the ethical mountain of killing.
8. Blessing, to teach seeking personal gain.
9. Planets, acting without awakened action.
10. Directions, living in pointless existence.
11. Rudra, the elimination of play (i.e., truth).
12. Sun, the inferior activity (i.e., monks' life).
13. Branch, the thoughts of material things.
14. Earth (vow) may not be always kept.
15. Dharma, or abandoning one's own path.

These are quite peculiar transgressions, and without Mañjuśrīkīrti's explanations I would have little hope of understanding them. Even with the very abbreviated description of the items, as reflected in the presentation here, we can see that this list is much more psychological, in stark contrast to the two groups of rules that gained greatest stature. The consequences of this emphasis carry over into the physical activity implicated in this group of rules. Thus the specifically androcentric nature of the other lists is not replicated in this agenda, although there is little indication that the predominantly male congregation is different in any way. Rules III.2, 5, 6–9, 12, 14, and 15 are definitely concerned with external action, but even then the behavior is addressed in a decidedly different manner, with a stress on the mental or intellectual components of the yogin. Whereas the previous lists emphasized the fault of teaching the unprepared, in this list the focus is on teaching others when one is unprepared (III.5) or has improper motivation (III.8). There is much greater sense of a Buddhist yogin losing the way, either into the Brahmanical fold (III.3–4, 11), into the world (III.1, 2, 6, 8, 13–15), or into inferior Buddhist practice (III.12). Very interesting is III.10, which is actually the antithesis of III.5. In this instance, the yogin is described as fully prepared, but disinterested in teaching others, a sort of latter-day Pratyekabuddha or other self-isolated figure.

One reason that these rules are unreliable guides to the way siddhas actually behaved is that many texts presume that individuals have a great variation in behavior or even that they are expected to change their behavior over time. This latter instance, in particular, shows the consequences of the Buddhist emulation of Pāśupata ideals. A Pāśupata was ideally to move through five stages in his spiritual maturation, with his conduct passing through discrete phases over time. Many Buddhist siddha systems also articulated similar stages in the progression of the individual, generally declaring an antinomian period somewhere in the middle of the practice. Mañjuśrīkīrti provides an interesting focus on variation in Buddhist practice, combined with an idealized depiction of how the yogin is to mature.

> Practice, moreover, is of four varieties. It is said that the beginner is to practice the Samantabhadra conduct. Other scriptures have a different idea and explain that the Samantabhadra conduct is to be applied in other stages as well. If one has obtained a degree of stability [in maṇḍala visualization] then one practices the discipline with a consort *[vidyāvrata]*.[65] As it is explained, those employing mantras should engage this extreme practice for six months or so. Finally, for those who have obtained stability in their meditation, the *Mahākhyānatantra* [?] explains that they should remain in

> the Lordly Conduct [*nāthasamudācāra]. Now, it should be understood that there are two varieties to the path of yoga: reliance on yoga and reliance on the sacraments of skillful means [upāyasamaya]. There are also, however, those who are liberated by yoga even while they rely on the sacraments, and those liberated by the sacraments even while they rely on yoga.[66]

Similar phases of practice were commonly expressed, even if we have little understanding of how often they were actually observed. It is worthwhile, though, to see that twelfth-century Tibetans continued to voice comparable stages of behavior. Drakpa Gyeltsen articulates a similar strategy of passing back and forth between Mahayanist conduct that is entirely beneficial *(samantabhadracaryā)* and that which is radically antinomian *(avadhūtacaryā)*.[67] Thus we can surmise from the record that selected individuals took these transitions as veridical, even if some must have wondered about the necessity to act in so extreme a manner during the middle stages of the path.

SELF-CRITICISM AND CORRECTION

If the siddha propensity for outrageous conduct appears sometimes expressed in the reenactment of Śaiva, village, or other antinomian behaviors, the movement also exhibited a strong self-critical voice. Even though this facet is sometimes overlooked in modern literature, it is certainly evident to readers of siddha documents that each succeeding tangent in the tradition met with a critical response almost as soon as the new direction was expressed. As seen in chapter 6, sometimes criticism was conveyed surreptitiously, through the vehicle of hermeneutical domestication, so that many threatening statements were given a value entirely different from their overt meaning. Criticism is an implied part of this strategy, attributing ignorance to those who would enact forms of conduct as literally as they have been proposed. Here, there is the unspoken intimation that the authors of such contrary instructions should acquiesce to the interpreted (rather than their own original) directions.

Many criticisms, however, were not so subtle, and the contentious nature of the siddha movement is sometimes turned against itself rather than toward other agonistic religious communities. Overall, three kinds of critiques are emphasized in the esoteric literature. In the first, Buddhist yogins are critiqued for exhibiting a level of egotism appropriate to Brahmans, for they have both come to consider themselves divine. In the second, the criticism is voiced that siddhas have become deluded in their obsession with artificial means of meditation, breath control, visualization of letters, or psychic heat, and by the siddhas' search for nubile consorts. Finally, siddhas were criticized for consorting with non-Buddhist yogins and expressing non-Buddhist doctrines.

In the first instance, the potential for publicly enacting the self-glorification inherent in the yogin's visualization of himself as divine was given a devastating review by the anonymous authors of the "commentarial scriptures" within the first century of this doctrine's articulation. The most trenchant critique I have encountered is in the *Sandhivyākaraṇa-tantra*, which is a late eighth- or early ninth-century lengthy expansion on the *Guhyasamāja*, an eighth-century tantra that has been cited throughout our investigation of the siddhas' world. In the middle of a longer discussion of potential problems, the scripture engages in a strong broadside on the self-absorption of mantrins employing the esoteric system for their own personal glorification.

> O, Lord of Secrets! The scholars, having encountered this excellent method, and having correctly grasped its clear significance, will immediately fall into arrogance.
>
> For them, the peace of contemplation and even insight itself will remain distant. Instead, they will say, "A yogin with the quality of the first level of the bodhisattva—that is I!"
>
> They will always delight in egoism, and will indulge in their own deceitful and artificial teachings. Moving along some path other than nirvana, they will quarrel among themselves.
>
> Based on their espousal of the secret mantras, they will contest one against the other; so they have only received Māra's blessing.
>
> If one of them should attain some tiny accomplishment, then with his pride he will think and imagine himself learned.
>
> They will fight in the tantric gathering *[gaṇacakra]* and will act like dogs toward the food in the feast. They just harm the benefit that has resulted from their previous positive karma.
>
> They will say, "Both virtuous and nonvirtuous actions, they are our powers!" Slandering the teacher, who is like the Buddha in person, they will offer him no consideration.
>
> In a second they are angry. In a moment they are greedy. They simply exhibit the behavior of dogs, pigs, and ravens![68]

The resonance of this depiction with the general direction of the tantric rules listed above suggests that the explicit egotism of the esoteric meditative program was a consistent problem. Although such behaviors may not represent the community at large, they certainly seem to be one way to enact the perception of oneself as divine. If the purpose behind the procedure was a sacralization of the world around them—in which all too often warlords acted as if they were gods—it also meant that somehow this idea needed purification as well as sanctification. In fact, the siddhas' texts in particular emphasize the "recollection" of purity, in which the visualized Buddhist divinity is interpreted as a form revealing Buddhist truth statements. Thus the sixteen arms of Hevajra are the sixteen forms of emptiness, his crushing of Śiva is the destruction of the ego, Heruka's twelve implements are the twelve stages of the path leading to absolute awakening, and so forth.[69] Such recollection of purity statements are themselves interpretive devices to fill the liturgical pronouncements of the maṇḍala visualization and its divine representations with the expressly Buddhist content that the divine iconography did not necessarily possess. This recollection of purity was part of a larger overall strategy, along with the rules and the interpretive systems, that allowed the meditator to comprehend the maṇḍala visualizations as specifically Buddhist events, wherein Buddhist rules and expectations would operate.

Even then, individuals are found erecting a critique questioning whether any of these practices were actually efficacious, whether Buddhist-interpreted or not. For these hypercritical siddhas, the visualized forms, the yogic practices, and the sexual congress in the *gaṇacakra*—each and every specific activity enjoined in any of the scriptures—were *prima facie* delusional. For reasons not yet clear to me, this variety of criticism was most explicitly found in works composed in the Apabhraṃśa language, reflecting the *dohā* verse form. Ever since the 1916 publication of the *dohā* collections attributed to Saraha and Kāṇha, their Apabhraṃśa verses have been very popular among Indologists, with repeated treatments and translations of the highly critical Saraha materials in particular. However, this is the tip of the proverbial iceberg, for there are *many* such critical verse collections found in Tibetan translations, most of which have not been noticed.[70] In one versified treatise, attributed to one of the many siddhas using the name Indrabhūti, criticism of other's practices is included in his statement of natural reality, *sahaja.*

> Some claim the self is *sahaja*, and deluded fools make it Īśvara. With their rejection of both conceptual attributes of self and non-self, the Jinas have declared *sahaja* to be the condition of nonduality *[yuganaddhapada].* That is exactly the life of living beings. It is the highest indestructible *[paramākṣara]*, all-pervasive and present in all bodies. However, women, children, cowherds, *mlecchās*, low castes, aquatic life, gods, *yakṣas*, along with *nāgas*,

none of these will understand *sahaja*. Instead, they will wander in the cities of the world.[71]

. . .

Some claim that accomplishment comes from the joining of sexual organs, but even if you are young and apply yourself for a long time until aged, by this you will not achieve *sahaja*. The moment there is a cause, it is error or something very similar. Some [quote] the texts about the enjoyment [body: sambhogakāya], but this is not called *sahaja*. In the middle of the navel is the highest *cakra*. Some practitioners continually meditate on the resplendent form in its midst, but this is not called *sahaja*. The great wheel present at the fontanel—touching it and having bliss drip from it—these are attained by application to the ritual requirement. They are not that called *sahaja*. Some make effort in restricting the "life breath" *[prāṇavāyu*: breathing through the nose], so as to reside [in concentration] at the tip of the nose. Whatever is obtained by this breath restriction—that is not called *sahaja*. Others afflict the body by restricting the wind that evacuates the waste *[āpāṇanvāyu]*, again and again cultivating this practice—but that is not called *sahaja*.[72]

This and other statements contain the message that Buddhist siddhas more than occasionally shared their company with those from the Śaiva and other camps. Nāgabuddhi's **Ardhapañcamagāthā*, with which this chapter begins, is but one expression of the relatively consistent message suggested by the literature: Buddhist yogins were not to frequent non-Buddhist gatherings, they were not to adopt their views, and they were not to accept their divinities, except in a subordinate position in the Buddhist maṇḍalas. Yet it is clear that such prohibitions were an attempt to stem the tide and to redirect existing behavior, rather than to act as the force of law. The reality must have been that Buddhist siddhas, like the other religious companies in medieval India, selectively appropriated ideas and attitudes from almost every level of society found in their environment.

THE IMPERIAL METAPHOR RECONSIDERED: BECOMING THE VIDYĀDHARA-CAKRAVARTIN

If the defining metaphor of the Mantrayāna ritual system is becoming the Universal Ruler, then a reconsideration of how the siddha might be different from the monk seems a desideratum. Their use of new forms of language, the excessively erotic and violent content of their scriptures, their emphasis on pilgrimage and cemetery sites associated with non-Buddhist or tribal peoples, their occasional voicing of hostility toward monastic institutions, their emulation of ghost and tribal behavior, their employment of local glossia—all of these are difficult to explain in light of the imperial metaphor. If the monk's ritual is based on that imperial metaphor, then what can be said of the rituals associated with the siddhas: the circle of offerings *(gaṇacakra)*, the erotic second and third consecrations, the worship of girls before sexual congress, the singing and dancing in their gatherings?

Certainly, the metaphor has become juxtaposed with several others, especially noticeable in the rhetoric of primativeness or naturalness. However, when siddhas explicitly affirmed their goals in their literature, it was still most often modeled after becoming the overlords of the Sorcerers *(vidyādharacakravartin)* or of the gods, in order to gain their powers. Although the goal was sometimes considered metaphorical, at others it was taken as literal, and this is clear in the *Vidyottama-tantra's* discussion of the benefits of several of its practices.

> Then recite the mantra in front of the painting of Vajrapāṇi, until you hear the roar of a lion. Having heard the lion's roar, then demon *[asura]* girls will come—but don't become sexually attracted to them! If you do, then you will not become a lion. Then the demon boys will come and sexually enjoy themselves [with the girls]. If you don't become sexually involved with them, then you will become a lion. Since they desire the lion, eighty Vidyādhara girls will come. And you will have a retinue of four thousand Vidyādharas. Then you can go wherever you want, and you will be the Vidyādhara-cakravartin. But you still haven't obtained dominion with the discus and other implements. So at that time, the vajra, discus, trident, hammer, noose, lance, and club will all come, so that you give a lion's roar as a lion. With this lion's roar, there will arise swords for eighty thousand yojanas [about 320,000 miles]. And whatever Vidyādhara kings are there, they will hear the lion's roar and all fall to the ground. Then you will have power over all those swords. Then you will be the Vidyādhara king, living for an entire eon.[73]

Likewise, the definition of siddha offered in the *Guhyasamāja-tantra* emphasizes a similar model.

> Let him go forth everywhere a siddha—through all the [worlds] as many as sands of the Ganges. Toward each of the highest vows, let him be the lord of sorcerers.[74]

Sometimes the metaphor is expressed by the goal being differentiated from the activity of the mundane ruler, although there are many rituals devised in siddha scriptures to seize real political power. Explaining its version of the imperial dynamic, the *Catuḥpīṭha*, for example, speaks of the siddha becoming an "absolute yogic monarch" *(paramārthayoga-rāja)*, a king of concentration on the absolute as opposed to all those other kings concentrating on worldly life.[75]

Even when the simpler goal of becoming a Vidyādhara is articulated (Figure 23), that Vidyādhara is frequently considered a "lord" *(prabhu)*, a word denoting leadership, chieftainship, dominion, or power. In some places in texts like the *Guhyasamāja*, becoming a Vidyādhara is also equated with Vajradhara (here probably meaning a Vajrapāṇi).

> At his accomplishment of the power of invisibility, etc., he becomes a Vajradhara, a Prabhu.
> At his accomplishment of the power of yakṣa kingship, etc., he becomes a Vidyādhara, a Prabhu.[76]

It is in this light that we should understand the rituals of the siddhas—sexual or otherwise—for they emulate the behaviors that Buddhist siddhas came to associate with achieving the state of, or dominion over, the Sorcerers.[77] If they were not to turn into real lions, as the *Vidyottama* suggests, siddhas were to act like lions in their utter disdain for the conventions of a world that inhibited their freedom.[78] Since the contemporary Indian literature depicted this dominion as achieved by those performing their rites in real or visualized cemeteries, siddhas' ritual systems demonstrate an obsession with this same means. The cemeteries, isolated groves, primal forests, and analogous locales were understood to be the gateways to the Vidyādhara realm, and alternative species of beings—tribal, demonic, kingly, whatever—were understood to be their aids to success. All these elements contributed to the siddhas' practice, whose overarching designation was simply the Vidyādhara discipline *(vidyādhara-saṃvara)*.

Dominion over the Vidyādharas was associated with victory over the gods themselves, and the narrative of subordination of India's great gods is a consistent facet of siddha hagiography and liturgy.[79] This is most definitively seen in some forms of the siddha maṇḍalas, where the circle of vassals is constituted by gods/goddesses (or their surrogates), rather than by other Buddhas, as in the maṇḍalas preferred in institutional esoterism and the more conservative siddha systems. Thus the aspiring siddha visualizes himself as Cakrasaṃvara in the midst of a maṇḍala of Bhairavas conquered and converted to Buddhism.

FIGURE 23
Siddha having achieved sword siddhi and become a Vidyādhara. Ratnagiri, Orissa, eleventh century. Detail of base of Crowned Buddha. Bihar State Museum Arch. no. 6501. *Photo Ronald M. Davidson.*

Analogously, Hevajra is the Heruka in a circle of goddesses, all of whom had been objects of cults but also mythically converted to the Buddhist cause. As seen in the *Vidyottama* above, Vajrapāṇi is shown in the center of the retinue of the seven Mothers *(saptamātṛkā)*, the ancient goddesses whose cults were widely distributed.[80] Even more dramatic is the *Bhūtaḍamara*, which begins with the sly Śiva requesting that Vajrapāṇi kill all the evil ones in the world, a category that normally includes Śiva himself. However, Vajrapāṇi agrees that this is a good idea and instantly slaughters all the other gods (Indra, Brahmā, Viṣṇu, and other available deities), whom he immediately revives with an enormous passing of gas from his anus, a hilarious transformation of the gods into an object of farce.[81] And even taking such statements as necessarily metaphorical is a questionable position. Although the tantric Candrakīrti attempts to turn the *Guhyasamāja*'s definition of a siddha into a metaphor about supremacy above the other divinities in the maṇḍala, the *Bhūtaḍamara* flatly declares that just seeing its own maṇḍala will give total dominion over the real triple universe.[82]

Thus the siddhas were as invested in models of political success as the great Buddhist institutions and their monastic brethren, albeit for somewhat different reasons and employing a modified metaphor. In the one case, the monks were concerned with the images of the ruler of the actual world as they saw it unravel before their eyes. In the other, the siddhas were concerned with the insignia of supernatural powers accorded the Sorcerers. The difference was that the monks knew their rituals to be metaphors, whereas the siddhas showed an ambivalence toward their rites. Sometimes they seemed to realize that they would not become actual emperors of celestial Sorcerers, while at other intervals the tantras state this goal as a bald fact. In either case, the viability of siddha systems hinges on the actual involvement of Buddhists siddhas with real courts of local lords and the siddhas' acquaintance with the ideology of power and supremacy. Whether metaphorical in nature or based on concrete goals, the rituals of coronation yielded dominion within a maṇḍala of vassal figures and conferred control over self and others in a world where hierarchy was not the primary model of social relations, it was the only model.

CONCLUSION: IT'S A SIDDHA'S LIFE

For Buddhist siddhas, community did not immediately involve the grand edifices of institutional monasticism, although siddhas and monks were symbiotically related in small regional centers. Their symbolic communities, the maṇḍalas, both embodied the disparate sources of siddha ideology and demonstrated the problems with their integration into real living arrangements, for they brought together multiple linguistic, cultural, and social forms into a rough collocation. These emphasized cemeteries, palaces, forests, and terrifying locales, although siddhas themselves lived in small congregations in towns and cities. Likewise, siddha rituals, especially the *gaṇacakra*, sought to develop a sense of identity and a structure for the sacraments that were inherently destabilizing. Their emphasis on procedures, on officers in charge of the ritual enclosure, and on correct deportment belie the romantic image of individuals dedicated to personal freedom at any cost.

In the process of institutionalization, these personalities became almost as much literary events as real human beings and became organized as literary personas with the numerical procedures (especially the numbers eighty to eighty-four or eighty-five) already evident in the village and regional political organizations. Thus the economic and political structures of Orissa, Bengal, Chhattisgarh, Jharkand, Madhya Pradesh, Kashmir, Oḍiyāna, and the

Koṅkana coast became the formulae whereby siddhas were organized within institutional literature. By means of this institutionalization of noninstitutional esoterism, the esoteric canon integrated ideas and behaviors derived from Śaiva, Śākta, Saura, Vaiṣṇava, regional divinities, tribal groups, and local cemetery siddha traditions, all on a catch-as-catch-can basis.

The evident spectrum of behavior stemmed from the fact that siddhas came from a variety of backgrounds and did not have a pan-Indic institutional structure to provide the relatively uniform socialization that the Buddhist monasteries afforded the esoteric monks. Yet some had come from an elite background and were well educated at the highest level, but left the monastery or the capital city to engage in a new career of primitive association, free of the strictures incumbent on the resolutely status conscious. Others were from the lowest order and came to the life in a desperate move to make sense of the world that continued to unravel as the gods seemingly supported the capricious conduct of men with swords, power, and wealth.

Siddhas from every level brought both strengths and weaknesses, so the emerging culture of the perfected was constituted by a series of ritual engagements and personal skills, in which charisma and devotion played as important a part as intelligence and naturalness. The siddha process of self-criticism both assisted the communities in their movement into the monastic curricula and revealed the fissures that these communities continued to experience. Notwithstanding their plethora of alternative images, the stated goal of siddhas continued to be the appropriation of power accorded the sorcerers. Their scriptures consistently maintained various versions of the imperial model of dominion over the gods, the sorcerers, and other religious groups.

8

Conclusion: The Esoteric Conundrum

The goal of this discussion has been to place the activities of Buddhist monks and yogins, of wealthy partisans and impoverished outcastes, of tribal peoples and agonistic trickster siddhas, into the dynamic and quickly changing sociopolitical world of the early medieval period of Indian existence. From the demise of the Puṣyabhūtis until the influx of the Ghurids, Buddhist institutions weathered the slings and arrows of outrageous fortune by adapting to and emulating the alterations in public life on the subcontinent. Esoteric Buddhist ideas and practices arose out of the regionalization of Indian polity and religion during this time. Within the confines of India, it represented a moderately successful reorganization of the various religious communities to encounter and overcome the challenges of the period. Whether economic destabilization, population relocation, loss of patronage, the new fluid politics of sāmanta feudalism, or the increasing importance of caste, feudalized gods, and regional identity—all these issues contributed to the genesis and maturation of the Vehicle of Secret Spells.

Buddhist communities were also facing a dramatic change in Buddhist identity through the decline in women's participation, the shift in intellectual values to Brahmanical models, and the loss of both ethical and intellectual centers of gravity. In the face of such challenges, Indian Buddhists responded by appropriating aspects of the sociopolitical sphere, yet this response embodied a tension new to the Buddhist tradition. On one end of the spectrum were those affirming and sacralizing the realpolitik of the day, the Buddhist monks of the great institutions of the Gangetic Valley and, to a limited degree, elsewhere as well. Employing the model of becoming the Supreme Overlord *(rājādhirājā)* or the Universal Ruler *(cākrāvārtin)*, they developed and propagated a meditative system and attendant rituals that displayed a thorough grasp of the ideals and methods of sāmanta feudalism. Constructing sacred Buddhist paradigms of the power relations grounded in the political maṇḍalas surrounding them, they sacralized the observable paradigms of core zones of authority and buffer client states in the relationship between the Buddhas and bodhisattvas in the visualized sacred circles. These power relations were, as in real states, affirmed with the central ritual of the candidates' consecration and the investiture of these candidates into zones of dominion.

The imperial paradigm clearly supported an egoistic perspective, one that had to be domesticated in the matrix of responsibilities and rules of behavior. Exactly this pattern of obligations recreated the spiritual state of the maṇḍala, so that it could become a description of an ideal community, rather than the formula for personal aggrandizement. Under this reinterpretation, the maṇḍala integrated all the figures from a region into a cosmos, one wherein the values and perspectives of the Buddhadharma remained supreme. Accordingly, in monastic hands esoteric Buddhism became another vehicle—added to the rites and vows of the monk and bodhisattva—that socialized neophytes into the codes of conduct expected of the professional religious. Yet it is evident from the literature that attempts to integrate the various esoteric behaviors into the architecture of the Buddhist subculture were not entirely successful. Not only was the monastic regimen occasionally compromised, as in the cases of Virūpa and Maitrīpāda, but the Buddhist reputation for compassion and decorum was by far the most serious casualty.

At the other end of the spectrum was the newly emergent siddha form, a nonmonastic career displacing the Mahayanist devout mercantile laity. The siddhas' goal was individual dominion over the sorcerers, the Vidyādharas, and the gods themselves, those divinities by whose authority the overlord rules. The siddha traditions also imported a politics of dominion and control, but for the benefit of the single siddha and not necessarily for the betterment of the surrounding community. Buddhist siddhas both developed radical meditative techniques not seen before in the Buddhist world and wrapped them in language that was simultaneously playful and ferocious, erotic and destructive. Their Buddhist allegiance caused them to encounter forcefully their Śaiva brethren, so that one facet of Buddhist popular identity became closer to the Śaiva models of the Pāśupatas and Kāpālikas than their prior image, which had been aligned beside the Jaina monks. Siddhas from the Buddhist persuasion became the proponents of regional languages and cultures, of tribal affirmation and of the segmentation of power in medieval India.

Because they did not pass through any single socializing institution that would provide them with common training, behavior, and identity, siddhas represented a wider spectrum of values than heretofore seen in Buddhist saints. They forced monasteries to grapple with the new rituals, to develop new forms of hermeneutics, to comprehend a rapidly evolving iconography, to employ song and dance in offerings to the new forms of the Buddhas, and to become invested in an entirely new canon. Siddhas developed various sexual rituals, new rites for gathering at tantric feasts, and entirely new sets of rules incumbent on those following the vows that sometimes required them to act as insane as others certainly believed them to be. Contentious as ever, the siddha critique of others following the esoteric path is sometimes extreme, but so is the behavior that the tantras espouse, especially those scriptures authored within the siddha community itself. Such extreme behavior was represented by a minority of Buddhists, and there is little indication that there were ever many siddhas. But if these few were accorded the status of siddha, they would have come with a degree of authority not previously granted those flouting the moral codes of Indian life. Ultimately, both monks and siddhas developed a symbiotic relationship in the small regional monasteries located in regional centers, towns, and at the edge of the forest, with the two estates eventually sharing a common syllabus, ritual vocabulary, and a grudging respect for each other's scriptural compositions and spirituality.

The great period for the composition of esoteric scriptures lasted an astonishingly short time. From the mid-seventh century to the mid-eleventh century, the majority of scriptures, commentaries, *ṣāḍḥāṇā* meditative rituals, consecration manuals, esoteric yogic texts, and *ḥōṃā* procedures were composed in India. All our evidence belies a model of slow scriptural compilation, for this material developed so quickly that even lengthy scriptures must have been written and accepted in a matter of a few decades, not over the centuries sometimes proposed. By the late eighth century, even the most extreme scriptures, the *yōgīṇī ṭāṇṭrāṣ*, had begun to be integrated into the ritual curricula in the great monastic centers of North and Central India. By the time the first wave of Tibetans in the new translation period came to India, toward the end of the tenth and beginning of the eleventh centuries, their complete incorporation into the monastic regimen had already been largely effected. In these four short centuries, thousands of texts were written, taught, transmitted, accepted, propagated, and institutionalized. The new forms of hermeneutics to domesticate the extreme varieties of literature were further employed to sponsor the integration of tribal and outcaste models, of antinomian statements and outrageous humor, into the Buddhist canon. A new form of Sanskrit, regional or tantric Sanskrit, was accepted into the Buddhist literary horizon, as was the emergence of ritualized poetic genres in regional languages, especially Apabhraṃśa and Old Beṅgali.

The esoteric conundrum was neither simply the appropriation of Brahmanical models by Buddhist monasteries nor the integration of arguably the most outrageous statements the world has ever seen into the solemn decorum of Buddhist meditative centers. It was not simply the curiosity that some of the most sophisticated intellects in Indian history had accepted tribal and outcaste peoples as romantic simulacra of the Cosmic Buddha. Rather, the conundrum of esoteric Buddhism extends to its modern assessment—the simultaneous scholarly neglect of the Indian basis and fascination with its Tibetan or East Asian secondary developments. As a historical corollary, the other part of its paradox is the popularity and success of the Vehicle of Secret Spells throughout virtually every area of Buddhist influence.

At home, esoteric Buddhism demonstrated tenacious success in India for more than five centuries at a time when the dynamics of the subcontinent were rapidly changing, and Buddhist institutions were in retreat in the Kṛṣṇa River valley and elsewhere. It assisted the maintenance of the great monasteries and stemmed the Śaiva tide sweeping up from the south. It sponsored the development of aesthetic and artistic forms in other countries—such as Tibet, China, Japan, Nan-chao, and Burma—and formulated models of a hierarchical sacred community that survive to the present. It developed some of the most popular rituals ever employed in Buddhist centers and propagated them with a rhetoric of intimacy and secrecy. Indeed, the overwhelming success of the Secret Path has propelled it into a position where it has become perhaps the least secret of all the Buddhist meditative systems.

Appendix: Probable Pāśupata Sites

TEMPLE	LOCATION	APPROXIMATE DATE
Svāmīghāṭ	Mathura (Uttar Pradesh)	fifth century C.E.
{Temple remains}	Mathura (Uttar Pradesh)	fifth century C.E.
Yogeśvarī Cave	by Bombay	525 C.E.
Timbarva	Karvan (Vadodara Dist., Gujurat)	sixth century C.E.
Tilabhāṇḍeśvara	Banaras (U.P.)	sixth century C.E.
Cave 1	Badami (Karnataka)	sixth century C.E.
Indal Deul	Kharod (Bilaspur Dist, M.P.)	650–675 C.E.
Saṅgameśvara	Kudaveli (Krsna & Tungabhadra Riv)	650–680 C.E.
Svarga-Brahma	Alampur (near Kurnool, A.P.)	650–680 C.E.
Siddheśvara	Palari (Raipur Dist., M.P.)	675 C.E.
Rājīvalocan	Rajim (Raipur Dist., M.P.)	seventh century C.E.
Khimeśvara maṭha	Khimeśvar (by Porbandar, Gujurat)	seventh century C.E.
Śiva temple	Dah Parabatiya (Darrang Dist., Assam)	seventh century C.E.
Paraśurāmeśvara	Bhubaneswar (Orissa)	seventh century C.E.
Pañca-Pāṇḍava Caves	Bhubaneswar (Orissa)	seventh century C.E.
Bhāratī Maṭh	Bhubaneswar (Orissa)	seventh century C.E.
Svarṇajāleśvara	Bhubaneswar (Orissa)	seventh century C.E.
Bharateśvara	Bhubaneswar (Orissa)	seventh century C.E.
Pātāleśvara	Paikapada (Koraput Dist., Orissa)	seventh century C.E.
Temple remains	Chittorgarh (Rajasthan)	seventh century C.E.
Rampol Gate	Chittorgarh (Rajasthan)	seventh century C.E.
Śiva temple	Kusuma (Sirohi Dist., Rajasthan)	seventh century C.E.
Temple remains	Gwalior	seventh century C.E.
Lakulīśa temple	Siddhanakolla (by Aihole, A.P.)	690–696 C.E.
Śiva temple	Dhobini (Raipur Dist., M.P.)	700 C.E.
Jambuliṅga temple	Pattadakal (by Aihole, A.P.)	696–720 C.E.
Kaḍasiddheśvara	Pattadakal (by Aihole, A.P.)	695–720 C.E.
Pāpanāth	Pattadakal (by Aihole, A.P.)	720–750 C.E.
Kansuāñ temple	by Kota (Rajasthan)	732 C.E.

TEMPLE	LOCATION	APPROXIMATE DATE
Mahādeva temple	Bithu (Pali Dist., Rajasthan)	725–750 C.E.
Mahānaleśvara sub #2	Menal (Chittorgarh Dist., Rajasthan)	725–750 C.E.
Telī-kā Mandir	Gwalior	725–750 C.E.
Cave 15	Ellora (Aurangabad Dist., Maharashtra)	725–750C.E.
Lakulīśa temple	Jageśvara (Almora Dist., H.P.)	725–750 C.E.
Śiva temple	Lakhamandal (Tehri Garhwal, U.P.)	750 C.E.
Bṛṅgeśvara	Bajrakot (Dhenkanal Dist., Orissa)	750–775 C.E.
Vaitāldeul	Bhubaneswar (Orissa)	eighth century C.E.
Śiśireśvara	Bhubaneswar (Orissa)	eighth century C.E.
Tāleśvara	Bhubaneswar (Orissa)	eighth century C.E.
Maṇikeśvara	Sukleswar (Cuttack Dist., Orissa)	eighth century C.E.
Someśvara	Jajpur (Cuttack Dist., Orissa)	eighth century C.E.
Vīrajā	Jajpur (Cuttack Dist., Orissa)	eighth century C.E.
Simhanātha Mahādeva	Gopinathpur (Cuttack Dist., Orissa)	eighth century C.E.
Sūrya Temple #2	Osian (Jodhpur Dist., Rajasthan)	eighth century C.E.
Kumbhasvāmin	Chittorgarh (Rajasthan)	eighth century C.E.
Nakleśvara	Karvan (Vadodara Dist., Gujurat)	eighth century C.E.
near Sindhvaivamātā	Karvan (Vadodara Dist., Gujurat)	eighth century C.E.
Kāmanāth Mahādeva	Vadodara (Gujurat)	eighth century C.E.
Dhumar Lena (#29)	Ellora (Aurangabad Dist., Maharastra)	eighth century C.E.
Temple 75	Jageśvara (Almora Dist., H.P.)	eighth century C.E.
Śiva temple	Benisagar (Singhbhum Dist., Bihar)	eighth century C.E.
Muṇḍeśvarī	Rohtas Dist. (Bihar)	eighth century C.E.
Unnamed temple	Pattadakal (by Aihole, A.P.)	eighth century C.E.
Cave Temple	Arittapatti (Madurai Dist., Tamilnadu)	eighth century C.E.
Mahabodhi	Bodhgaya (Gaya Dist., Bihar)	800 C.E.
Madhukeśvara	Mukhalingam (Srikakulam Dist., A.P.)	800 C.E.
Śiva temple	Jagatsukh (Kulu Dist., H.P.)	800–825 C.E.
Kāmeśvara	Awa (Pali Dist., Rajasthan)	800–825 C.E.
Madhukeśvara	Mukhalingam (Srikakulam Dist., A.P.)	800–825 C.E.
Śiva temple	Bajinga (Tehri Garhwal, U.P.)	800–825 C.E.
Jaleśvara	Mandalgadh (Chittorgarh, Rajasthan)	850 C.E.
Śiva temples #1 & #2	Jayati (Vizianagaram Dist., A.P.)	850–875 C.E.
Avantīśvara	Avantipur (Kashmir Valley)	855–883 C.E.
Someśvara	Mukhalingam (Srikakulam Dist., A.P.)	ninth century C.E.
Nīlīśvara	Narayanapura (Srikakulam Dist., A.P.)	ninth century C.E.
Vaidyanāth Svāmin	Pushpagiri (Cuddapah Dist., A.P.)	ninth century C.E.
Mallikārjuna	Pattadakal (by Badami, Karnataka)	ninth century C.E.
Nīlakaṇṭha Mahādeva	Adaspur (Prachi Valley, Orissa)	ninth century C.E.
Narasimhanāth	Borogram (Ganjam Dist., Orissa)	ninth century C.E.

TEMPLE	LOCATION	APPROXIMATE DATE
Bhuvaneśvara	Balia (Cuttack Dist., Orissa)	ninth century C.E.
Siddeśvara	Barakar (Barddhaman Dist., W.B.)	ninth century C.E.
Vaidyanāth	Baijnath (Satna Dist., M.P.)	ninth century C.E.
Śiva temple	Marai (Satna Dist., M.P.)	ninth century C.E.
Somanāth	Baramba (Cuttack Dist., Orissa)	ninth century C.E.
Sīmanāth	Baramba (Cuttack Dist., Orissa)	ninth century C.E.
Śiva temple remains	Kara (Allahabad Dist., U.P.)	ninth century C.E.
Śambhunāth	Ghororia (Puri Dist., Orissa)	ninth century C.E.
Śiva temple	Kalinjar (Banda Dist., U.P.)	ninth century C.E.
Śiva temple	Kasba (Baleshwar Dist., Orissa)	ninth century C.E.
Śiva temple	Bhagalpur (Bihar)	900 C.E.
Śiva temple	Pandrethan (Kashmir Valley)	925–950 C.E.
Śiva temple	Payar (Kashmir Valley)	925–975 C.E.
Ekaliṅgajī	Udaipur Dist. (Rajasthan)	971 C.E.
Bhairava temple	Gangua R. (by Bhubaneswar, Orissa)	tenth century C.E.
Baṇeśvara	Bhubaneswar (Orissa)	tenth century C.E.
Mukteśvara	Bhubaneswar (Orissa)	tenth century C.E.
Marīcī Kuṇḍa	Bhubaneswar (Orissa)	tenth century C.E.
Bindu Sarovara (tank)	Bhubaneswar (Orissa)	tenth century C.E.
Śiva temple I & II	Khiching (Mayurbhanj Dist., Orissa)	tenth century C.E.
Indralāth Deul	Ranipur-Jharial (Bolangir Dist., Orissa)	tenth century C.E.
Siddhanāth	Prabhasa (Junagadh Dist. Gujurat)	tenth century C.E.
Somanāth	Prabhasa (Junagadh Dist. Gujurat)	tenth century C.E.
Kapileśvara Mahādeva	Vav (Manas Kantha Dist., Gujurat)	tenth century C.E.
Krakoṭakeśvara	Naresa (Gwalior)	tenth century C.E.
Pitupreteśvara	Naresa (Gwalior)	tenth century C.E.
Temple remains	Dag (Jhalawar Dist., Rajasthan)	eleventh century C.E.
Temple #18	Telkupi (Purulia Dist., W.B.)	eleventh century C.E.
Liṅgarāja	Bhubaneswar (Orissa)	eleventh century C.E.
Rājarāṇi	Bhubaneswar (Orissa)	eleventh century C.E.
Nīlakaṇṭha Mahādeva	Arthuna (Banswara Dist., Rajasthan)	1176 C.E.
Meghesvara	Bhubaneswar (Orissa)	1192–95 C.E.

SOURCE: These sites are culled from Meister and Dhaky 1988–91, Shah 1984, Mitra 1984, Donaldson 1985–87, and Majumdar 1953. Because most of these concern Oriya temples, they may be overrepresented in the table.

A.P.—Andhra Pradesh; H.P.—Himachal Pradesh; M.P.—Madhya Pradesh; U.P.—Uttar Pradesh; W.B.—West Bengal

Glossary

abhiṣeka	Consecration, coronation, or rite for royal investiture
abhicāra	Ritual of magical killing, often through the medium of a homa ritual.
Apabhraṃśa	Middle Indic language of the period, employed by Buddhist siddhas.
Arhatsaṅgha	Community of saints of early Buddhism.
Bodhisattvasaṅgha	Community of bodhisattvas of the Mahayana form of Buddhism.
Buddhakapāla	An important *yoginī-tantra.*
Cakrasaṃvara	An important *yoginī-tantra;* also called *Laghusaṃvara.*
Cakravartin	Universal Ruler, an ideal type of monarch in orthodox Buddhism.
chomā	Lit. "disguise," it means secret signs to accompany coded language.
coded language	The use of specific words *(sandhyā-bhāṣā)* that represent secret meanings.
ḍāka	An autochthonous god; may be divine or demonic; similar krodha.
ḍākinī	An autochthonous goddess; may be divine or demonic; similar yoginī.
datura	A hallucinogen *(esp. datura fastuosa)* used by siddhas in some rituals.
dohā	Form of versification commonly used in Apabhraṃśa and other Prakrits.
early medieval	Period of Indian history, c. 500-1200 C.E.
gaṇacakra	A circle of initiates who gather regularly for esoteric rituals, including sexual activity and the eating of forbidden foods.
Guhyasamāja	An important *mahāyoga-tantra.*
Heruka	Buddhist divinity based on cemetery gods.
Hevajra	Important *yoginī-tantra.*
homa	Fire ritual, an Indian development of the ancient

	Indo-European fire sacrifice; one of the standard media for the four tantric activities.
Kaula	Yogins associated with the worship of a goddess; similar Śākta.
Kāpālika	Extreme form of Śaiva yogin, who carries a skull and *khaṭvāṅga* club.
krodha	An autochthonous god; may be divine or demonic; similar ḍāka.
Madhyamaka	"Middle Way" school of Buddhist philosophy, analogous to Greek Skepticism.
mahāyoga-tantras	Esoteric Buddhist scriptures that reflect siddha practices and ideas.
Mantrayāna	Esoteric Buddhism; similar Vajrayāna.
mantrin	A practitioner of spells (mantra) or a counselor of state secrets (mantra).
***Mārga-phala**	The esoteric tradition of Buddhism among the Sakya in Tibet (Lam-'bras).
Nyingma	The school of Tibetan Buddhism that traces its religious lineage to the Royal Dynastic Period of Tibetan history (c. 650–850 C.E.).
Pāśupata	A sect of Śaiva yogins, most of whom follow the path attributed to Lakulīśa.
pīṭha	A sacred site, possibly tribal in origin, and often dedicated to a goddess.
rākṣasī	Feminine demon frequently encountered in Indian mythology.
Rājādhirāja	The overlord, the one to whom the sāmanta is subordinate.
Śabara	Tribal group, sometimes identified with the modern Saora of Orissa.
Sakya	Tibetan school of Buddhism formed in Sakya Monastery (founded 1073 C.E.) in southwestern Central Tibet.
sāmanta	The major term for a vassal in early medieval Indian politics.
Śaṃvara/Saṃvara	Name employed for divinities in various systems, from Vedic to the late *Cakrasaṃvara* system.
sandhyā-bhāṣā	Coded language, applied either to specific words or as a hermeneutical technique to interpret tantric literature as invariably nonliteral.
Sarvabuddhasamāyoga	An important *yoginī-tantra*.
segmentary state	Form of polity in which units have similar

	structures and form confederations when one becomes dominant; easily segmented in function.
siddha	Perfected—Buddhist saint who is neither a monk nor an ordinary layman.
siddhi	Magical powers attained by the siddha.
śramaṇa	A non-orthodox ascetic, associated with Jaina, Buddhist, or other traditions.
tantra	A word that often indicates a text but may denote specific kinds of performative systems (e.g., an army or a ritual) or a machine (a loom).
tantric karmas	Four activities associated with esoteric rituals, especially the homa: pacification, subduing, increasing, and ritual killing. Sometimes expanded to include a fifth activity, that of seduction rites.
vajra	Scepter or thunderbolt.
Vajrapāṇi	The central bodhisattva of esoteric Buddhism. He wields a vajra as the emblem of his legal authority.
Vidūṣaka	Comical brahman in Sanskrit drama, often depicted as short and stupid.
vidyā	Word indicating one or more meanings: spell, knowledge, ritual consort.
Vidyādhara	Sorcerer or master of vidyā; may live on earth or in a celestial abode.
Vijñānavāda	"Mere Consciousness" school of idealist Buddhist philosophy.
Vinaya	Buddhist rules of discipline that apply to monks and nuns.
yoginī	Ferocious goddesses, at whose sites (pīṭha) human sacrifice was offered; similar ḍākinī.
yoginī-tantras	Esoteric Buddhist scriptures that reflect extreme siddha practices and ideas.

Notes

1. INTRODUCTION: A PLETHORA OF PREMISES

1. In *Mañjuśrīmūlakalpa,* Jayaswal 1934, pp. 61–66; Sastri 1920, pp. 652–653:
adhunā tu pravakṣyāmi dvijānāṃ dharmaśīlinām || 955
mantratantrābhiyogena rājyavṛttim upāśritā |
bhavati sarvaloke 'smiṃ tasmiṃ kāle sudāruṇe || 956
vakārākhyo dvijaḥ śreṣṭha āḍhyo vedapāragaḥ |
semāṃ vasumatīṃ kṛtsnāṃ vicerur vādakāraṇāt || 957
trisamudramahāparyantaṃ paratīrthānāṃ vigrahe rataḥ |
ṣaḍakṣaraṃ mantrajāpī tu abhimukhyo hi vāgyataḥ || 958
kumāro gītavāhy āsīt sattvānāṃ hitakāmyayā |
etasya kalpavisarān mahitaṃ buddhyatandritaḥ || 959
jayaḥ sujayaś caiva kīrttimān śubhamataḥ paraḥ |
kulīno dhārmikaś caiva udyataḥ sādhuḥ mādhavaḥ || 960
madhuḥ sumadhuś caiva siddho madadahanas tathā |
rāghavaḥ śūdravarṇas tu śakajātās tathāpare || 961
te 'pi jāpinaḥ sarve kumārasyeha vāgyataḥ |
te cāpi sādhakāḥ sarve buddhimanto bahuśrutāḥ || 962
āmukhā mantribhis te ca rājyavṛttisamāśritāḥ |
The Tibetan is found To. 543, fols. 325b7–326a7, but is unhelpful in several sections. I presume, like most translators of prophetic sections in Buddhist scriptures, that all the preterite tenses are to be interpreted as futures in the spirit of the text. Phyllis Granoff, whom I thank for corrections and suggestions to the translation of these verses, has suggested emending vākyataḥ of 958d and 962b to vāgyataḥ, a suggestion I find attractive and have accepted. The *Mañjuśrīmūlakalpa* occasionally specifies a six-letter mantra for *Mañjuśrī* (e.g., *Mañjuśrīmūlakalpa,* Shastri 1920, p. 49), but I have not located the specific mantra in mantra section of chapter 2 (*Mañjuśrīmūlakalpa,* Shastri 1920, pp. 25–32); the recitation of the six-letter mantra, OṂ MAṆI PADME HŪṂ, is enjoined in the *Kāraṇḍavyūha-sūtra*, Vaidya 1961, pp. 292–296. Verse 959cd is the most difficult, and the Tibetan is only moderate assistance: cho ga rab 'byam 'di dag las | des ni de phan de la bsten. I have emended

etasyai to etasya and buddhitandritaḥ to buddhyatandritaḥ, so that Mr. Va will not be an idiot. 961b is conjectural by emending siddhaḥ namas tadā to siddho madadahanas tathā, based on a lacuna in the foot and the Tibetan de bzhin grub dang dregs bral dang, although this is rather tentative improvement. Granoff has suggested that the -namas of the current text could be the end of a name, and I have taken this suggestion with the standard equivalent of Tibetan dregs = mada/matta/darpa. However, many alternatives to *Madadahana could be found, and the normative name is Madanadahana, an epithet of Śiva (burner of Mada, i.e., Kāmadeva); this does not fit the foot, though.

2. For the date of the *Mañjuśrīmūlakalpa*, see MATSUNAGA 1985. He points out that this chapter on the prophecy of kings identifies Gopāla, who obtained kingship around 750 C.E.

3. E.g., Wayman 1977; Snellgrove 1987.

4. E.g., Skorupski 1983 and 1994.

5. Przyluski 1923, pp. 317–318.

6. Sanderson 1994, accepted by Strickmann 1996, p. 26; Sanderson's claims are contextualized in chapter 5.

7. Snellgrove 1987; Jong 1984; MATSUNAGA's "Introduction" to the *Guhyasamāja tantra*, pp. vii–xxxi.

8. YORITOMI 1990, pp. 130–144, proposes that the *Mahāvairocanābhisambodhi* be assigned to Orissa on archaeological and art historical grounds, and ties the text to the political history of the Bhaumakaras; cf. Hodge 1994. Strickmann has attempted to relate the relationship between Śaivism and the Buddhist esoteric system (1996, pp. 24–41). As will be clear from this book, Strickmann's proposals were limited by his modest acquaintance with Indian history and society, and by his structuralist presumption that "tantrism" is a single entity. Thus he freely speaks of "un tantrisme taoïste" (pp. 118–126), citing sources composed before the term "tantra" became used in Buddhist circles. The majority of his work, though, is both stimulating and helpful. Samuel attempts to identify various sociological sources for "shamanic" Buddhism, but is vague on specifics of Indian history and society (1993, pp. 427–435).

9. Derrida's hegemonic purpose is explicit (1967, p. 24).

10. E.g., see Foucault's assessment of critical history (1977, pp. 139–168), where he projects what is apparently his own emotional turmoil into an entire discipline.

11. Dirlik et al. 2000, pp. 40–41.

12. Chakrabarty 1992, p. 223.

13. Lopez 1995, pp. 10–12.

14. Brennan 2000, King 1999.

15. Evans 1999, pp. 10, 22–23, 108, 158, 163, 214–216, 220; Murphey 1994, p. 302.

16. See Allen (2000, pp. 30–47, and passim) for the history and evolution of this term, which was coined by Julia Kristeva in her critical essays on Bakhtin.

17. Pollock 1993, p. 111.

18. Thomas C. Patterson, "Archaeologists and Historians Confront Civilization, Relativism and Poststructuralism in the Late Twentieth Century," in Dirlik et al. 2000, pp. 49–64 passim.

19. R. A. Abou-El-Haj, "Historiography in West Asian and North African Studies Since Sa'id's *Orientalism*," in Dirlik et al. 2000, pp. 67–84, esp. pp. 70–71.

20. Evans 1999, p. 109.

21. Etlin 1996, p. 77.

22. Murphey 1994, esp. pp. 263–302.

23. King 1999, pp. 82–95.

24. B. Lewis 1993.

25. The archaeological contributions are not well represented in Kopf (1969), despite Kopf's assessment of the sympathy with which the British "cultural brokers" stimulated the development of Indic institutions during their occupation of that country (ibid., pp. 275–291). For a somewhat extreme critique of Kopf, see King 1999, pp. 86–93. Thomas R. Trautmann has discussed this issue in the context of South Indian linguistics and history ("Inventing the History of South India," in Ali 1999, pp. 36–54). See also Etlin 1996, pp. 114–122.

26. For a discussion of the contributions of one of the more curious characters in this process, Charles Masson, see Possehl 1990.

27. Appiah 1991. In a withering critique, Dirlik has called Western-trained, Western-employed South Asian scholars an "international babu class," similar to the old class of British government employees in India (2000, pp. 10–11).

28. This question is frequently the field of polemics: see Inden 1990, Lopez 1995, and, for this study in particular, the recent polemical critique of Wedemeyer 2001.

29. King 1999, p. 211.

30. *Śatapañcāśatka*, Bailey 1951, vv. 70 and 90, pp. 86, 101; **Mahāyānāvatāra-śāstra,* T.1634.32.36b12–19, commenting on *Catuḥśataka* VIII.5.

31. Pollock 1989 has discussed this issue in the context of Mīmāṃsā.

32. Chakrabarty 1992; King 1999.

33. Pollock has suggested this direction (1993, p. 115).

34. It is unfortunate that the contribution of Petrarch and his followers is even obscure to working historians; see Evans (1996, pp. 14–17, 81), where an excessive estimate of Leopold von Rank is offered, and Foucault (1966, pp. 367–373) shows an inadequate understanding of critical history developed in the Renaissance. On humanists' critical techniques, see Paul Kristeller, "Renaissance Humanism and Classical Antiquity," in Rabil 1988, 1:5–16.

35. For the "mirabilia" genre, see Bloch 1982, pp. 630–636; Jacks 1993, p. 38; Weiss 1969, pp. 6–8; Benson 1982, pp. 353–355. The *Miribilia* was sufficiently popular to be included entirely within two other works of the period—the *Graphia aureae Urbis Romae* (Description of the Golden City of Rome, c. 1155) and an administrative handbook for the Papal Curia *(Liber politicus).*

36. Weiss 1969, pp. 18–20.

37. Green 1982, p. 90; emphasis in original.

38. Bishop 1966, p. 7. Pfeiffer (1976) is particularly emphatic on Petrarch's originality: "We have often been told that humanism arose from the social and political conditions of the consolidated new Italian city states; and it is true that these conditions became more and more favourable to the development and diffusion of Petrarch's ideas. These ideas, however, originated from his own mind; they did not spring from the spirit of the society of his time of which he always spoke with contempt ('mihi semper aetas ista displicuit')" (p. 16). See also Maristella Lorch, "Petrarch, Cicero, and the Classical Pagan Tradition," in Rabil 1988, 1:71–94.

39. Kelley 1988, p. 748.

40. The following material predominantly is taken from Weiss 1969, pp. 48–89.

41. Pfeiffer 1976, p. 27; Jacks 1993, pp. 67–73.

42. Jacks 1993, pp. 89–95.

43. Ibid., pp. 95–99.

44. Ibid., p. 110.

45. Weiss 1969, p. 70; Jacks 1993, pp. 113–121.

46. Kelley 1988, p. 748.

47. Ibid., p. 749.

48. The following material on Bodin is taken from Franklin 1963, pp. 59–79, 137–154; Kelley 1988, pp. 756–758.

49. Kelley 1988, p. 757; Franklin 1963, p. 69.

50. Evans attributes this to von Rank (1996, pp. 14–16, 81), but this is evidently in error, although the elaborate methodology of source criticism certainly was not known to Bodin.

51. Arif Dirlik, "Is There History After Eurocentrism?" in Dirlik et al. 2000, pp. 25–47, esp. pp. 40–43.

52. Schopen has proposed that the modern emphasis on texts is a result of Protestant presuppositions in the study of Buddhism (1991, pp. 19–23). His model, however, appears less than willing to acknowledge that both traditional (India, Tibet, and China) and modern Buddhist scholarship (Japan, China, Tibet, and Thailand) conceive of texts as preeminently important. It would seem that Buddhist studies is influenced by traditional bias of the indigenous informants more than by the values of Protestant Christianity. My experience with Buddhist scholars in India, Nepal, and Tibet has been exclusively textual, with little interest displayed toward epigraphy, archaeology, or other sources.

53. There is an almost complete absence of coins in India after the time of Harṣa until the Mughal period, so numismatics—important to Petrarch—must take a subordinate position, to be supplemented to a lesser degree by the survival of clay monastic sealings.

54. Figueira 1994, pp. 7–17; King 1999, pp. 200–218.

55. Fischer 1970, pp. 74–78.

56. Dietz 1984, pp. 358–399; this letter is considered in chapter 4.

2. PRAYERS IN THE PALACE, SWORDS IN THE TEMPLE: EARLY MEDIEVAL INDIA

1. Fleet (1888, p. 146, line 2): avirbhūtāvalepair avinayapaṭubhir llaṅghitācāra-mārggair mmohād aidaṁyugīnair apaśubharatibhiḥ pīḍyamānā [kṣmā] narendraiḥ |.

2. *Nītisāra* VIII.71: ākīrṇaṃ maṇḍalaṃ sarvaṃ mitrair aribhir eva ca | sarvaḥ svārthaparo lokaḥ kuto madhyasthatā kvacit ||

3. Lin Li-Kouang 1935, p. 84n; *Chen yen tsung chiao shih i*, T.2396.75.431a8–12.

4. This is the subtext behind Romila Thapar's excellent studies of the Mauryas; see Thapar 1997; 1992, pp. 1–22; and 1990, pp. 3–5.

5. For a discussion of some of these issues, see Holden Furber, "The Theme of Imperialism and Colonialism in Modern Historical Writing on India," in Philips 1961, pp. 332–343.

6. Chakrabarty 1992; and the essays on histories in modern colloquial languages collected in Phillips 1961, pp. 429–496.

7. See R. C. Majumdar's "Nationalist Historians," in Philips 1961, pp. 416–428. More recently, it is seen in writers, such as Char (1993), who carry on this tradition.

8. I am following Chattopadhyaya on both the problems and the utility of this nomenclature (1994, pp. 12–37).

9. The best early work on the Ephthalites has been by ENOKI 1959; more recently, see Litvinsky et al. 1996, pp. 135–183.

10. Bhandarkar 1981, pp. 296–305. This conclusion is supported by Litvinsky, "The Hephthalite Empire" (in Litvinsky et al. 1996, p. 141), but has been challenged by Zeimal, "The Kidarite Kingdom in Central Asia" (ibid., pp. 123–124), who maintains that the "Hūṇa" designation was used for all nomadic conquerors and the Kidarites were the most likely candidates at this time.

11. Agrawal 1989, pp. 243, 251.

12. Fleet 1888, p. 257; Agrawal 1989, pp. 239–249.

13. Bhandarkar 1981, pp. 360–364.

14. Sircar 1945, p. 70 n1.

15. Vākāṭaka contributions to art and architecture have been reasserted by the welcome work of Bakker (1997, pp. 58–92).

16. This analysis is inspired by Kulke and Rothermund (1998, pp. 9–11), although it differs in details.

17. The following description of military events is taken largely from Sinha 1977, pp. 81–127; Yazdani 1960, 1:207–232; Agrawal 1989, pp. 250–269; Devahuti 1983, pp. 17–64.

18. The dates are reasonable temporal guideposts to active periods and not meant to indicate anything else.
19. Devahuti 1983, p. 18.
20. Fleet 1888, pp. 200–206.
21. Sircar 1945, p. 70 n5.
22. Stadtner 1976, pp. 32–40; Sinha 1977, pp. 128–137; Devahuti 1983, pp. 53–57.
23. Mirashi 1955, pt. 1, pp. xlv–xlvii.
24. Yazdani 1960, 1:208–209.
25. Devahuti 1983, p. 74.
26. Ibid., pp. 39–44; Sinha 1977, pp. 133–136.
27. Mirashi 1955, pt. 1, pp. xlvii.
28. The genealogy of the Vardhanas is primarily retained in *Harṣacarita* (1918, p. 56), which closely matches the Banskhera Plate; see Bühler 1896–97.
29. *Harṣacarita* 1918, pp. 56–57.
30. Mirashi 1955, pt. 1, pp. xlvii; Yazdani 1960, 1:209–210.
31. Devahuti 1983, pp. 76–77.
32. Ibid., p. 34; cf. Sinha 1977, pp. 128–133.
33. The following material is abstracted from Devahuti 1983, pp. 37–53, 83–91; Sinha 1977, pp. 137–143.
34. Jayaswal 1934, p. 50, text p. 53 v. 723; the defeat of Śaśāṅka was clearly exaggerated in the *Mañjuśrīmūlakalpa.*
35. Śaśāṅka's capital at Karṇasuvarṇa has been discovered in the excavations at Rājbāḍīdāṅgā; see Das 1968.
36. Devahuti 1983, p. 57; we note that the sudden rise in the fortunes of Kharagraha I, Śīlāditya I's successor, after 609 may indicate that he was in charge of this expedition. Kharagraha I begins to issue separate grants in 616.
37. This is his Banskhera copperplate grant; see Bühler 1896–97.
38. Kielhorn 1900–1901a.
39. Yazdani 1960, 1:219.
40. Devahuti 1983, pp. 242–243.
41. Yazdani 1960, 1:221–224.
42. Ibid., pp. 226–228.
43. This episode is examined in detail, taking into account the T'ang sources, by Devahuti (1983, pp. 243–269), in an excellent discussion. Unlike many historians, Devahuti has exhibited an astute command of the Chinese texts. The name of the prince, *Arjuṇa, is one of the possible sources for the Chinese rendering of his name.
44. For the publishing history of Bhāskaravarman's Nidhanpur Grant, see Morrison 1970, p. 161.
45. Sinha 1977, p. 160.
46. Ibid., p. 162; Yazdani 1960, 1:225–226.
47. Wink 1990, p. 201; Meister and Dhaky 1988–91, vol. 2, pt. 1, p. 197.
48. Wink 1990, p. 202.

49. Mirashi 1955, pt. 1, pp. lvi; Puri 1986, p. 44; Wink 1990, p. 208.

50. Mirashi 1955, pt. 1, pp. 137–145.

51. Wink 1990, pp. 242–244.

52. Beckwith 1987, p. 82.

53. Ibid., p. 87; Wink 1990, pp. 242–243.

54. Thaplyal 1985, p. 78 n4; cf. Goetz 1969, pp. 16–19.

55. *Gaüḍavaho,* vv. 414–439.

56. "Introduction," in *Rājataraṅgiṇī,* Stein 1900, 1:90–91; IV.211, 246–264; Goetz 1969, pp. 25–35, 47–65.

57. *Rājataraṅgiṇī,* Stein 1892, 1900, IV.131–180; Goetz makes the claim that, since the names rendered in the *Rājataraṅgiṇī* are sometimes authentic historical personages, the conquest must have been real, since Kalhaṇa could not have invented them (1969, p. 12). He presumes that Kalhaṇa's sources were written by people who could not have fabricated a conquest of known parties, but this is clearly unsustainable. Kalhaṇa has drawn from many dubious and highly mythologized sources, such as the *Nīlamatapurāṇa,* which ascribe fictional events to known persons. Wink uncritically affirmed Goetz's analysis (1990, p. 243).

58. Goetz 1969, p. 21.

59. Mandan has pointed out that the Ellora area was doubtless the early region of the Rāṣṭrakūṭa power, since most of their early inscriptions come from there (1990, p. 33). Moreover, their early patronage of the great Śaiva rock-cut caves and temples of Ellora is in conformity with the idea of a prior homeland as a sacred site after the actual center of power has been moved. Similarly Yazdani 1960, 1:257.

60. Puri 1986, p. 52; Mirashi 1955, pt. 1, p. lvi.

61. Puri 1986, p. 53; Kielhorn 1907–8.

62. Mandan 1990, pp. 50–51; Yazdani 1960, 1:253–256.

63. Mandan 1990, pp. 51–57.

64. Konow 1913–14; Mandan has argued for the king's name Nāgāvaloka of the Hansot plates to apply to Dantidurga, not to Nāgabhaṭa, primarily on the use of -avaloka as a terminal ending in Rāṣṭrakūṭa names (1990, pp. 51–54, 80 n79). Puri (1986, p. 71 n2), however, has already noted that Ojha (1917–18, p. 179 n3) cites the identification of Nāgabhaṭa II as Nāgāvaloka in the Jaina work *Prabhāvaka-carita.* Nāgāvaloka seems to be an acceptable equivalent for Nāgabhaṭa and clearly the Rāṣṭrakūṭas had no proprietary use of the -avaloka designation. Moreover, Nāgāvaloka of the 861 Paṭhārī Pillar Inscription of Parabala appears to identify Nāgabhaṭa I; see Kielhorn 1907–8, p. 250. Sinha appears to think this is Nāgabhaṭa II, however (1977, p. 182).

65. Yazdani 1960, 1:257–259.

66. Mandan 1990, pp. 61–67; Yazdani 1960, 1:258–261.

67. Kielhorn 1896–97, v. 1; in the Bhagalpur Plate of Nārāyaṇapāla (Hultzsch 1886, v. 1) the mātsyanyāya is replaced by kāmakārin, acting on desires without conscience.

68. The Pāla chronology proposed by Susan and John Huntington (1990, p. 542, chart 1) is used here, since it takes into account the existence of Mahendrapāla, whose discovery was announced by Bhattacharya 1988, based on a copper charter.

69. Sinha 1977, p. 172; Majumdar 1971, pp. 96–99; *Mañjuśrīmūlakalpa*, Jayaswal 1934, v. 884.

70. *Mañjuśrīmūlakalpa*, Jayaswal 1934, LIII.884.

71. Mandan 1990, p. 91; *Rājataraṅgiṇī*, Stein 1892, 1900, IV.471.

72. Yazdani 1960, 1:263; Sinha 1977, pp. 176–177.

73. Yazdani 1960, 1:262–264.

74. Ibid., 1:264–265; Mandan 1990.

75. This material is extracted from Mandan 1990, pp. 104–111; Yazdani 1960, 1:268–70; Sinha 1977, pp. 179–182; Puri 1986, pp. 67–70.

76. Yazdani 1960, 1:268–273; Mandan 1990, pp. 108–111.

77. Sinha 1977, p. 184.

78. Ibid., p. 186.

79. Mandan 1990, pp. 116–119; Yazdani 1960, 1:276–279.

80. Puri 1986, p. 86.

81. Mirashi 1955, pt. 1, pp. lxxii–iv.

82. Puri 1986, pp. 90–92.

83. Mandan 1990, pp. 124–125; Yazdani 1960, 1:282–284, 476–480; Mirashi 1955, pt. 1, p. lxxii. Bhīma was Vijayāditya's nephew, not his son.

84. We have records indicating that these three kings claim to have taken control following Devapāla: Majumdar 1971, pp. 119–122; Sinha 1977, pp. 188–190; Bhattacharya 1988. Their claims ignore each other, and Sinha has postulated divided rule for Śūrapāla and Vigrahapāla (1977, p. 191). Mahendrapāla and Śūrapāla were brothers, while Vigrahapāla was the son of Jayapāla, whose line did not pass through Dharmapāla and Devapāla, but by another line to Gopāla.

85. Mandan 1990, p. 126.

86. Puri 1986, p. 103.

87. Mandan 1990, pp. 130–132.

88. Yazdani 1960, 2:481. Previously, virtually all historians maintained that Mahendrapāla invaded Bengal and Bihar and ruled over the Pāla domains as a conqueror. This judgment was based on a series of grants found in these areas identifying the ruler as one Mahendrapāla. This scenario is seriously called into question by Bhattacharya's decifering the plate of the Pāla emperor Mahendrapāla (Bhattacharya 1988). A casual perusal of the grants of "Mahendrapāla," in fact, reveals that two chronologies are employed: one that is normative for the Kanauj state, and one that is normative for the Pāla dynasty. Grants employing the former pertain to lands in Uttar Pradesh, Rajasthan, and west, while grants using the Pāla chronology denote lands in Bihar and Bengal. These disparate chronologies seem to separate these figures, one following the Gurjara-Pratīhāra system, the other the Pāla chronology. See Puri for a list of Mahendrapāla's grants (1986, pp. 221–223).

89. Puri 1986, p. 122; Mandan details an alternative scenario (1990, pp. 128–129).

90. Puri 1986, p. 132.

91. These events are discussed extensively in Mandan 1990, pp. 136–141.

92. Yazdani 1960, 1:288–289.

93. Ibid., pp. 481–487.

94. Puri 1986, pp. 133–148.

95. Yazdani 1960, 1:289–293; Mandan 1990, pp. 141–148.

96. Yazdani 1960, 1:293–297; Mandan 1990, pp. 149–161.

97. Yazdani 1960, 1:297; Mandan 1990, p. 160.

98. Majumdar 1971, pp. 125–126, 205.

99. Ibid., pp. 131, 166–169, 199–206; Sinha 1977, p. 195.

100. Opinions on the origins of the Kambojas are discussed in Majumdar 1971, pp. 172–173.

101. Sinha 1977, pp. 195–197; Majumdar 1971, p. 172.

102. Sinha 1977, pp. 199–201; Majumdar 1971, pp. 131–137.

103. The history of the Chāḷukyas of Kalyāṇī is recounted in Yazdani 1960, 1:315–454.

104. Chattopadhyaya discusses some of the inscriptions concerning the Cāhamānas and Guhilas (1994, pp. 57–88); he provides a bibliography on the Agnikula origin myth (p. 57 n1).

105. Raizul Islam and C. E. Bosworth, "The Delhi Sultanate," in Asimov and Bosworth 1998, pp. 269–291; see also Deyell 1990, pp. 195–219.

106. Mirashi 1955, pt. 1, pp. lxxxix–c.

107. Sinha 1977, pp. 211–243; Majumdar 1971, pp. 199–218.

108. Majumdar 1971, pp. 219–253.

109. Banerji 1963.

110. *MDŚ* VII.89: āhaveṣu mitho 'nyonyaṃ jighāṃsanto mahīkṣitaḥ |
yudhyamānāḥ paraṃ śaktyā svargaṃ yānty aparāṅmukhāḥ ||

111. Scharfe 1993, p. 231; Lingat 1973, pp. 123–132; the *Mahābhārata* is more difficult, but many scholars would agree that the bulk of the current text was completed by 500 C.E.

112. See, for example, Aiyangar's "Introduction" to *Kṛtyakalpataru,* vol. 11 (1943). *Rājadharma-kāṇḍa,* in which all unchivalrous behavior is attributed to Muslims, the East India Company, or His Majesty's Army (pp. 70–72).

113. Brunt 1983, 2:339; cf. Jones 1930, 7:69.

114. In Tibet of the eleventh century, several Indian paṇḍitas were accused of representing themselves in a manner lacking honesty; see Davidson (2002a, forthcoming a, and forthcoming b).

115. Jones 1930, 7:95–99.

116. Keegan 1993, pp. 29, 301.

117. The classic statement by Sharma discusses this in detail (1987, pp. 37, 46, 50, 60, 63, 65, 68, 79, 86, 178–185).

118. Keegan 1993, p. 301.

119. Compare ibid., pp. 139–45, with *Nītisāra* IV.57–61; 7.12.3; cf. Prasad 1989, p. 108.

120. Varady 1979.

121. *Nītisāra* XIX.54–71, passim; cf. *Nītisāra* XVI.

122. *Arthaśāstra* XII.1.19–2.18, 4.4–23.

123. E.g., Chattopadhyaya 1990, p. 71;1994, p. 62.

124. Contamine 1984, pp. 15, 275–276; this effect was clearly evident in medieval Europe.

125. Andrew: "Donald Pearce, a subaltern in the North Nova Scotia Highlanders, recalled how individual battle experiences were just that. 'No one else has really been in the same places as anyone else' he wrote 'and I refuse to play the game of comparing experiences. The whole war seems to be a quite private experience; I mean for everyone. Each man talks about a quite different war from mine, and ultimately everyone is separated from everyone by layers of privacy or egoism'" (1992, p. 58).

126. Mookerji 1928/1972, pp. 162, 233.

127. Hira Lal 1909–10, p. 26.

128. *Siddhaikavīramahātantra*, p. 3; p. 5.1–4: eṣa mantrarājaḥ sarvakalikalahavivādopasargavidhureṣu japtaḥ śāntiṃ karoti | tuṣahomena ca sarvaśāntir bhavati | yathālabdhakusumāni mantram uccārya udake pravāhayet | sarvaśāntiṃ vijayañ ca prāpnoti na saṃśayaḥ | nagaradāhe 'gnisaṃmukhaṃ sthitvā saptāñjalim abhimantrya kṣipet | yasya gṛhasya rakṣitukāmas tasya rakṣāṃ karoti |

129. *Nītisāra* X.3–5 enumerates nineteen reasons for a king to go to war.

130. Kielhorn 1907–8, pp. 253, 255 (verse 15).

131. Willis 1995; 1997, p. 24.

132. *Nītisāra* XVI.3–43.

133. Thakur and Jha 1994, pp. 302–312; see also Sharma 1987, pp. 178–185.

134. *Rājataraṅgiṇī* IV.628. Cf. *MDŚ* VII.123 on the corruption of a king's officials.

135. For a discussion of piracy, see Gopal 1965, pp. 127–130.

136. Chattopadhyaya lists six characteristics of early medieval India: political decentralization, the emergence of landed intermediaries, a change to self-sufficient villages as units of production, the subjection of the peasantry and the proliferation of castes (1994, pp. 10–12).

137. Keegan 1993, p. 142. While we do not have a thorough discussion of this problem in the early medieval period, R. S. Sharma has made a beginning in "Appendix II—Fortified Settlements Under the Pālas and Candellas" (1965/1987, pp. 287–292).

138. *Mahābhārata* 12.74: striyaṃ hatvā brāhmaṇaṃ vāpi pāpaḥ sabhāyāṃ yatra labhate 'nuvādam | rājñaḥ sakāśe na bibheti cāpi tato bhayaṃ jāyate kṣatriyasya || 16 pāpaiḥ pāpe kriyamāṇe 'tivelaṃ tato rudro jāyate deva eṣaḥ | pāpaiḥ pāpāḥ saṃjanayanti rudraṃ tataḥ sarvān sādhvasādhūn hinasti || 17 . . . ātmā rudro hṛdaye

mānavānāṃ svaṃ svaṃ dehaṃ paradehaṃ ca hanti | vātotpātaiḥ sadṛśaṃ rudram āhur dāvair jīmūtaiḥ sadṛśaṃ rūpam asya || 19

I thank Phyllis Granoff for reining in my imagination on this material.

139. Keegan 1993, pp. 3–60, 386–392.

140. *Nītisāra*, X.3–30.

141. Granoff (1984) has made a strong case for the similarity between hagiographies of saints and biographies (hagiographies?) of kings in the medieval period.

142. Fleet 1888, pp. 1–17.

143. Ibid., no. 1, lines 6, 16, and 27.

144. Compare the rather prosaic discussion of the songs and adulation *(gīta, stuti)* generated by *vandanajana* (panegyrists) in line 14 of the Bhitari Stone Pillar Inscription of Skandagupta (Fleet 1888, pp. 52–56). The inscription itself does not provide these verses or songs, but only mentions them in passing; nor does it indicate the identity of the *vandanajana*, who were presumably too insignificant to be so named.

145. Ibid., pp. 79–88.

146. Ibid., pp. 142–150.

147. Ibid., pp. 150–158, line 14.

148. Kielhorn 1900–1901a, v. 5: lakṣmīr bhāvitachāpalāpi cha kṛta śauryeṇa yenātmasādrājāsīj Jayasiṃhavallabha. Translation Kiehhorn's.

149. Kielhorn 1900–1901a, vv. 14–18.

150. Salomon 1996; Mirashi 1955, 1:89, 215–224, etc.; see the discussion in chapter 3.

151. Kielhorn 1900–1901a.

152. Mirashi 1955, 1:224.

153. Huizinga 1950/1955, pp. 89–104.

154. Datta 1989, p. 225.

155. Singh 1993, pp. 294–303.

156. Kulke and Rothermund 1998, pp. 122, 136–138.

157. Williams 1982, pp. 157–158, 174.

158. See Chattopadhyaya 1994, p. 151.

159. Rao indicates that it was probably built by either Chāḷukya Bhīma I (r. 892–921) or Dānārṇava (r. 971–73), and Rao prefers the former as its royal builder (1, p. 1).

160. Li 1993 and Berkemer 1992.

3. THE MEDIEVAL BUDDHIST EXPERIENCE

1. *Mañjuśrīmūlakalpa*, XXXVII.933–935:
pravrajyā dhruvam āsthāya śākyapravacane tadā |
śāsanārthaṃ kariṣyanti mantravādasadāratāḥ || 933

astaṃgate munivare lokaikrāgrasucakṣuṣe |
teṣāṃ kumāra vakṣyāmi śṛṇuṣvaikamanās tadā || 934
yugānte naṣṭe loke śāstupravacane bhuvi |
bhaviṣyanti na sandeho yatayo rājyavṛttinaḥ || 935

Jayaswal (1934) publishes 935a as "ceṣṭa" for "naṣṭe"; emendation based on To. 543, fol. 325a6: ston pa'i gsung rab sa steng du | dus mthar 'jig rten nyams pa na | sdom brtson rgyal po'i tshul gyis ni | 'byung bar 'gyur bar the tshom med |. Note that the Tibetan translators read "rājavṛttinaḥ."

2. Pollock (1996) has called this the transculturation of the Sanskrit cosmopolis, a very stimulating formulation. However, as seen in the question of regional Sanskrit next chapter, Pollock sidesteps the issue of varieties of Sanskrit (1996, p. 201), a position to which he returns (1998, pp. 14–19).

3. Please note particularly the statement found in *Brahmasūtrabhāṣya* to 2.2.32, p. 479: "Alternatively, we see that the Buddha had such animosity to humans that he thought, 'It's possible that they could be deluded by this teaching that has all these internal contradictions!'" (pradveṣo vā prajāsu viruddhārthapratipattyā vimuhyeyur imāḥ prajā iti |).

4. For now classic discussions of the symbiotic relationships between the Samgha and the guilds, see Ray 1986, with relatively weak evidence, and Liu 1988. Much more could be said, however, and, for some of it, see Gernet 1995 and Schopen 1994.

5. See Basak 1919–20, p. 131.

6. See the material collected in Jettmar 1989, 1993.

7. The Kuchean (Tokharian B) Buddhist material has been best studied by French and German scholars; see Thomas 1964, 2:72, XXXII.

8. Humbach 1980, p. 109.

9. *Gaṇḍavyūha*, Suzuki and Idzumi 1949, pp. 225–226.

10. Ray 1994, pp. 153–154.

11. *Daśabhūmika*, Kondo 1936, pp. 28–29; *Varṇārhavarṇastotra*, Hartmann 1987, p. 109; *Bodhicaryāvatāra* I:11 (Buddha), III.30–32 (bodhisattva vow), Vaidya 1960, pp. 8–9, 43. Further references in T. Lewis 1993, pp. 138–142.

12. Gernet: "The needs of the Buddhist communities and laity favored certain businesses—especially those related to construction, the timber trade, dyeing products, and others—and gave rise to or developed certain trades: builders, architects, sculptors, painters, goldsmiths, and copyists all benefited from the religious movement at the same time that agriculture suffered from the requisitioning or hiring of peasants from the great Buddhist construction works" (1995, p. 14).

13. E.g., *Dhammapadaṭṭhakathā*, vol. 1, part 2, pp. 239–248; *Apadāna*, 1:58–59; *Manoratha-pūraṇī (Aṅguttara-nikāya Aṭṭhakathā)*, vol. 1, part i, pp. 209–220; *Paramaṭṭha-dīpanī (Theragāthā-aṭṭhakathā)*, 2:213–216, 236–242.

14. *Divyāvadāna*, pp. 427–428.

15. Pollock 1996, Hinüber 1989, and Salomon 1989 discuss some of the issues of medieval Sanskrit.

16. Gernet 1995, pp. 158–178; Schopen 1994. For the Gāndhārī materials, we must rely on the Niya documents, studied by Agrawala (1955) and, more recently, by Atwood (1991). It may be that the new discoveries in Gāndhārī manuscripts will assist us in understanding patronage issues; see Salomon 1999.

17. E.g., *Rājataraṅgiṇī* IV.628; *Nītisāra* V.82–86; *MDŚ* VII.123.

18. Deyel 1990, pp. 23–43; cf. Shrimali 1991.

19. *Bṛhatkathāślokasaṃgraha* XVIII.203; Lorenzen 1978.

20. Yadzani 1960, 1: 433–436; Gupta 1983–84; Abraham 1988. Indians were apparently poor at handling and breeding horses. Because two of the branches of warfare (cavalry and chariot) required the regular replacement of horses, the horse trade became an intense part of North Indian trade.

21. Jain 1990, p. 181; Jain notes that the guilds at this time became solidified as subcastes and identified as prakṛti-s, that is, they fit into a recognized governmental structure (p. 61). When we do find traders *(vaṇik)* mentioned elsewhere in India, most frequently they are not identified as a formal corporate guild, as in the Anjaneri Plates of Bhogaśakti; Mirashi 1955, pt. 1, I.146–159.

22. Jain 1990, pp. 182–184.

23. Yazdani 1960, 1:433–436; Abraham 1988; Fleet 1881.

24. Summarized by Lin 1935, p. 93.

25. This material is taken from Emmerick 1983.

26. Frye 1984, pp. 341–357;

27. Frye 1975, p. 95.

28. See the essays contained in Asimov and Bosworth 1998, especially pp. 30–94.

29. For a discussion of the importance of the Sogdians and the Sasanian coin finds in the reconstruction of the changing economics of Turfan in the eighth century, see Skaff 1998, pp. 99–104.

30. Mackerras 1990, p. 330.

31. Mackerras suggests others did so, but they remain unspecified (1990, p. 331); he shows the spread of Manichaeism into China principally as a result of Uyghur influence (1972, pp. 42–43). The Manichaeans were also included in the Wu-tsung suppression of Buddhism (840–846 C.E).

32. Elliot and Dowson 1867–77, 1:4; Wink tries unsuccessfully to extend this point into an economic argument (1990, pp. 303–307).

33. Simkin 1968, p. 84.

34. Hourani 1951, pp. 76–77.

35. H. Sastri 1942, pp. 92–102; Barua 1981, pp. 62–64.

36. Beckwith 1977.

37. Evinced by the movement of statuary, Banerji-Sastri (1940) and in inscriptions recorded in Huntington (1984, pp. 203–250) and Fleet 1881.

38. *Śārdūlakarṇāvadāna*, Mukhopadhyaya 1954, esp. pp. 10–12.

39. Inden 1978, pp. 48–49; Inden is, unfortunately, less than completely clear on the evidence for this.

40. Hultzsch 1886, l. 39.

41. See the appendix for Pāśupata temple affiliation.

42. Bhattacharya 1955.

43. See Shah, "Lakulīśa: Śaivite Saint," and Mitra, "Lakulīśa and Early Śaiva Temples in Orissa," in Meister 1984.

44. *Mañjuśrīmūlakalpa*, LIII.680–690, LIII.883; Sastri 1920, pp. 631–632, 647. The verse numbering is from Jayaswal 1934.

45. H. Sastri 1942, p. 91; translation abbreviated with some changes.

46. Mirashi 1955, 1:218; translation abbreviated with some changes; Kielhorn (1888–92b).

47. H. Sastri 1942, pp. 100, 102, v. 33: samasta-śatru-vanitā-vaidhavya-dīkṣā-guruṃ kṛtvā.

48. Hultzsch 1886, pp. 305–306, 308, v. 13; I thank Phyllis Granoff for pointing out the pun on having drunk blood (*pītalohitaḥ*) in the text: bhayād arātibhir yasya raṇamūrddhani visphuran | asir indīvaraśyāmo dadṛśe pītalohitaḥ ||.

49. Wogihara 1930–36, pp. 165–166; Demiéville, "Le bouddhisme de la guerre," reprinted in Demiéville 1973, pp. 261–299, esp. 293; Tatz 1986, pp. 70–71.

50. We note that the phrase used, tasmād rājyaiśvaryādhipatyāc cyāvayati (Wogihara 1930–36, p. 166.16–17), could be used to define the murder of the individual, although it is not interpreted in that sense. See Tatz 1986, p. 215.

51. *Ta t'ang hsi yü chi*, T.2087.893c–894b; Beal 1869, pp. 210–234.

52. Fleet 1888, pp. 52–56.

53. Kielhorn 1892, p. 81: kālaḥ kule vidviṣām.

54. Cf. Banerji 1919–20 and Misra 1934, pp. 40–51.

55. Kielhorn 1892, p. 58; same language in the Nālandā copperplate, but untranslated by H. Sastri (1942, p. 97, v. 12).

56. *Harṣacarita*, Kane 1918, p. 133.

57. Rice 1886, pp. 172, 175, l. 15: tribhuvana-madhya-varttināṃ prāṇināṃ paramakāruṇakathayā bodhisatvopamānasya. I do not follow Rice in reading paramakāruṇikatayā.

58. *Mañjuśrīmūlakalpa*, Jayaswal 1934, vv. 534–535, provides a life in hell for the king "Gomi," whom Jayaswal identifies as Puṣyamitra, vs. a future as a cakravartin for Bālāditya (v. 668).

59. Mitra provides a survey of the more important sites (1971, pp. 198–222).

60. See Das (1993, passim) for a site-by-site analysis of decline; Sharma 1987, pp. 95–100. Amarāvatī is anomalous in that some sculptures were carved but no inscriptions or inhabitation appear during the eighth to eleventh centuries; see Knox 1992, for images. It experienced a slight resurgence from the twelfth through the fourteenth centuries, but it is unclear that occupation was continuous. I thank

Himanshu Ray for calling attention to the sculpture, even though we disagree on its significance.

61. Fleet 1881 and 1889.

62. Gross 1993, pp. 18–24, 90–93; Shaw employs the phrase "androcentric selectivity" in the documents (1994, pp. 12–14, 75–78), dismissing all quantitative evidence as "absurd" and articulates theoretical structures admitting of an uncritical verification of hagiographical sources about women (ibid., p. 78). The kind of careful philological and historical investigation found in Hindu studies, such as Feldhaus 1995, Orr 2000, and Jamison 1996, are all too rare in Buddhist studies, gratifying exceptions include Paul 1980 and Nattier 1991, pp. 28–33.

63. Fischer 1970, pp. 74–78.

64. Orr has presented a model of how such evidence may be assessed (2000, pp. 161–180).

65. An inadequate survey of this material is in Law (1939–40).

66. One only need review Lüders (1912, passim) for entries too numerous to list. An example of the many records that have come to light since Lüders' publication is cited in note 67.

67. Lüders 1961, p. 166:

(mahārājasya) [d](e)vaputrasa Huv[i]ṣkasya sa[ṃ] 30 9 va 3 di 5 etasya[ṃ] purva[y](aṃ) bh[i]khuṇiye Puśaha[th]iniye [a](ṃtevāsi)ni[y](e) bh[i]khuṇiye Budhadevāye Bodhisatvo pratithāpito sahā mātāpitīhi sarvasat[v]ahitasukh[a].

Translation is Lüders's, with minor changes.

68. Bühler 1894, pp. 113–115, 403–407.

69. Bühler's tabulation may actually be an underassessment of women's participation. My own (very rough) evaluation of the much larger body of Sāñcī inscriptions in Marshall and Foucher (1940, 1: 301–383) yields a monks to nuns ratio of 168 : 156 and a laymen to laywomen ration of 208 : 190, or about 52% men to 48% women in both cases. This suggests virtual gender parity at this pre-Gupta site. See also Schopen for an affirmation that early nuns' resources were well reported (1996, pp. 563–565).

70. Falk 1979; unfortunately, Falk's data is insufficient to illustrate this point, since it is drawn almost exclusively from literature.

71. Huntington 1984, appendix, no. 2 (description to fig. 5), pp. 203–204.

72. Ibid., appendix, nos. 7, 8, 16, 21, 22, 23, 25, 43, 45, 55, 60.

73. Banerji-Sastri 1940; by women, inscriptions nos. 4, 20, 22, 53, 56, 58, 59, 84, and 88; by all men, inscriptions nos. 1, 2, 5, 6, 11, 15, 17, 18, 21, 23, 25, 30, 31, 32, 33, 37, 38, 43, 49, 51, 52, 55, 63, 67, 69, 70, 81, 83, 85, 87, 90, 91, and 92. Monks are found in inscriptions nos. 2, 6, 18, 23, 31, 32, 51, 52, 90, 91, and perhaps 69 from the language. While nos. 31 and 32 are perhaps by the same man, the same could be speculated of the women's names in nos. 20 and 56.

74. H. Sastri 1942, pp. 58–64.

75. Ibid., p. 112, no. 78, the name as read by the editor, Chakravarti; Sastri read Karaluka and was uncertain of the reading.

76. Ibid., p. 62.

77. *Nan hai chi kuei nei fa chuan*, T.2125.54.216b11–24; translation TAKAKUSU 1896, p. 80.

78. Quoted in Sawyer 1993, pp. 159 and 178 n2.

79. Miller and Wertz 1976, pp. 11 and 142.

80. Parry 1985, pp. 56 and 73 n11.

81. Denton 1991, pp. 212 n1, 220–225.

82. Sawyer 1993, p. 178 n3.

83. Barrow 1893, p. 224.

84. Ibid., p. 239.

85. Respectively, *Grub thob brgyad cu rtsa bzhi'i gsol 'debs* (To. 3758); **Caturaśīti-siddhābhisamaya* (To. 4317); *Grub thob lnga bcu'i rtogs pa brjod pa thig le 'od kyi phreng ba* (To. 2444); *dPal u rgyan du tshogs 'khor byas pa'i dus su rnal 'byor pa grub pa thob pa bzhi bcus rdo rje'i mgur bzhengs pa nyams kyi man ngag thig le gser gyi phreng ba,* (To. 2449); **Caturaśītisiddhapravṛtti* (Pe. 5091); and **Caturaśītisiddhasambodhihṛdaya* (To. 2292).

86. *Ye shes kyi mkha' 'gro ma sum cu rtsa lnga'i rtogs pa brjod pa* (To. 2450). These Zha-ma lo-tsā-ba materials are discussed in Davidson 2002a.

87. Respectively, the *Cittaguhyadohā* (To. 2443); the **Sarvayogatattvāloka-vikalavajragīti* (To. 2453).

88. *gŹuṅ bshad klog skya ma,* p. 444.

89. I thank Douglas Brooks for a similar observation concerning Śaiva texts; personal communication, April 1996.

90. Shaw 1994, p. 182.

91. *Vyaktabhāvānugata-tattva-siddhi*, pp. 169–172, 176.11.

92. On the problems of extending Western feminist formulae to non-European societies, see Chandra Talpade Mohanty's "Under Western Eyes: Feminist Scholarship and Colonial Discourse," in Mongia 1996, pp. 172–197.

93. Lévi 1937, p. 232; Konow 1907–8.

94. Misra 1934, pp. 40–50; this assumes, with Rajaguru (1955–76), that the Bhauma era began in 739 C.E., a date not universally accepted; Sircar's 831 period inauguration has been accepted by Salomon (1998, pp. 190–191), although I cannot follow him in this opinion.

95. Joan W. Scott has maintained that there are two fundamental fantasies found in feminist histories: the orator and the mother (2001, pp. 293–304). By this she does not mean that these are false, but that feminist historians tend to place themselves as subjects within history. For her, feminist fantasy "is rather the designation of a set of psychic operations by which certain categories of identity are made to elide historical differences and create apparent continuity" (p. 304). I

would have framed this somewhat differently, but the process of projecting self into history seems to be the crux of the matter.

96. On the problems associated with resistance studies, see Florencia E. Mallon, "The Promise and Dilemma of Subaltern Studies: Perspectives from Latin American History," in Dirlik et al. 2000, pp. 191–217.

97. *Harṣacarita,* Kane 1918, p. 140.

98. *Śārdūlakarṇāvadāna*, pp. 11 ff.

99. *Subāhuparipṛcchā,* To. 805, fol. 121a2–3: 'dzum shing 'gro la smra shing zur mig can | yan lang thams cad yid 'phrog byed pa'i gzugs | bu med gzugs ni mtshon cha 'jebs 'dra bas | skye pa'i sems ni mngon du 'phrog par byed ||. This section corresponds to T. 895.18.721c9.

100. See *Vigrahavyāvartanī,* Johnston and Kunst 1978, pt. 1, pp. 21–24, pt. 2, pp. 27–30.

101. *Mūlamadhyamakakārikā,* La Vallée Poussin 1903–13, which includes the *Prasannapadā*, p. 494; *Vigrahavyāvartanī,* Johnston and Kunst 1978, pt. 1, p. 24n.

102. See Groarke 1990, for a nuanced discussion of both the doctrines and problems of skepticism. The extraordinary similarities between Greek skepticism and the Madhymaka position have yet to be thoroughly explored.

103. *Madhyamakāvatāra,* pp. 288–301; Huntington 1989, pp. 177–179; *Mūlamadhyamakakārikā,* La Vallée Poussin 1903–13, pp. 73–74.

104. *Satyadvayavibhaṅga*, Eckel 1987, pp. 137–138.

105. *Rājataraṅgiṇī* III.11–12. The chronology represented here is questionable. The preceptor of the father of her contemporary, Amṛtaprabhā, was evidently a Tibetan named Lo-ston-pa, the teacher of Lo. This is probably gLo-bo, the Tibetan title for Mustang, suggesting a later chronology. As Stein points out (1892, 1:73 n9) a monastery attributed to Amṛtaprabhā was known to the Chinese monk O-k'ung, who took precepts in the valley in 749.

106. *Nan hai chi kuei nei fa ch'uan;* the translation from Takakusu 1896, p. 51 and cf. p. 52; corresponds to T. 2125.54.211c14–19, 212a5–6; we note that a later discussion of this point (Takakusu 1896, p. 93; 218b25–6) is about specifically Chinese monks, but the earlier quotation does not seem to represent a specifically Chinese position; rather, a pitfall of the unexamined concentration on emptiness.

107. For a more recent discussion of the meaning of Śākya Bhikṣu, see Cohen 2000.

108. *Brahmasūtrabhāṣya* to 2.2.5.32: ataś cānupapanno vaināśikatantravyavahāraḥ |.

109. Nāgārjuna's entire discussion of the vindication of his "non assumption of a proposition" is done in the context of the ascertainment of valid sources of reasoning. See *Vigrahavyāvartanī*, passim.

110. Wayman 1958.

111. Cf. *Abhidharmasamuccaya*, pp. 104–106.

112. *Yogācārabhūmi*, Bhattacharya 1957, pp. 118–160; these are placed in the text for the purpose of recognizing incorrect mental application, ayoniśomanskāra.

113. *Abhidharmasamuccaya,* p. 106.4–5: api khalu svahitasukhakāmena vādeṣv abhijnātuṃ pravarttitavyaṃ na paraiḥ vivādaṃ karttuṃ |. This is followed by a lengthy quotation from the seminal *Mahāyānābhidharmasūtra* verifying his position; cf. *Abhidharmasamuccaya-bhāṣyam*, p. 154; and Jinaputra's *Abhidharmasamuccaya-vyākhyā*, Peking 5555, TTP vol. 113.227.3.7.

114. Lamotte 1949, pp. 359–361; Davidson 1990, p. 302.

115. For these standards of authenticity, see Davidson 1990.

116. See the analysis by Snellgrove 1958.

117. Dreyfus 1997, p. 15.

118. *Nan hai chi kuei nei fa chuan*, p. 205a24–b1; TAKAKUSU 1896, pp. 7–8.

119. *Nan hai chi kuei nei fa chuan*, p. 206c1; TAKAKUSU 1896, p. 20. The relative periods of composition of the various *Vinayas* is a disputed matter.

120. A good summary of the introduction of the *Vinaya* into Tibet is in the *Bod rje lha btsan po'i gdung rabs tshig nyung don gsal*, pp. 82–85; cf. *mKhas pa'i dga' ston*, 1: 465–506, for an extended discussion.

121. I thank Gregory Schopen for this latter observation.

122. *Ta t'ang hsi yü chi*, T. 2087.51.923c19; Beal 1869, 2:170.

123. *Nan hai chi kuei nei fa chuan*, pp. 214a4, 227a25–26; TAKAKUSU 1896, pp. 65, 154; *Ta t'ang hsi yü ch'iu fa kao seng chuan,* T.2066.51.6b20; Lahiri 1986, p. 51.

124. See Bhattacharya 1985 and Stewart 1989 for discussions of the site. While I know of no one yet definitively identifying Stupa 3 as the *mūlagandha-kuṭi*, I have little hesitation in making that identification.

125. *Ta t'ang hsi yü ch'iu fa kao seng chuan,* T.2066.51.5c15, 6a29; Lahiri 1986, pp. 53, 58; in this latter place, Lahiri mistranslates the Chinese, which does not read "if you see one, you have seen all the seven," but "if you have seen one, the other seven are similar."

126. *Ta t'ang hsi yü ch'iu fa kao seng chuan,* T.2066.51.5b27; Lahiri 1986, p. 51.

127. *Mūlasarvāstivāda Vinaya, Śayanāsanavastu,* Gnoli 1978, p. 11; cf. Schopen 1994, pp. 529–531; Schopen's attempt to problematize the significance of *pura* : *rtsegs* is in error. The significance of *rtsegs* as a Tibetan building term is well established, meaning "story," as embodied in the gSum-brtsegs at Alchi or in the descriptions of other Tibetan buildings. We also note that the *Śayanāsanavastu's* allowance of a seven-story Perfumed Chamber *(saptapurā gandhakuṭiḥ)* with the five-story monks' chambers is that which we might expect at Nālandā, given the respective site remains and footprints of Stupa 3 and Monastery 1.

128. *Ta t'ang hsi yü ch'iu fa kao seng chuan,* T.2066.51.5b23; Lahiri 1986, p. 51.

129. Sastri 1942, pp. 81, 91, 102, etc.

130. Ibid., passim.

131. Ibid., pp. 103–105.

132. Clearly spelled out in Dutta 1995, pp. 98–114.

133. *Nītisāra* X.4, 8; Davis 1997, pp. 51–87.

134. *sBa bzhed zhabs btags ma*, Stein 1961, pp. 52–53; *sBa bzhed*, 1980, p. 62; *dBa' bzhed*, Wangdu and Diemberger 2000, p. 90.

135. *sBa bzhed*, 1980, p. 50: ma ga dha'i rgyal po'i khab kyi sgo mdun na dha ru rtse do bya ba'i mchod rten gcig gi nang na rgyal po ma skyes dgra'i skal ba |; *sBa bzhed zhabs btags ma* indicates that the purpose is entirely different, for the *caitya* contains "the fortune of the essence of the embodied king": rgyal po gzugs can snying po'i bskal ba, which constitute one Indian measure of the Buddha's relics and bones (Stein 1961, p. 42). *dBa' bzhed* does not contain this material.

4. THE VICTORY OF ESOTERISM AND THE IMPERIAL METAPHOR

1. *Nāmasaṃgītimaṇḍalavidhyākāśavimala*, To. 2543, fol. 13b1–2: sangs rgyas rdo rje 'dzin bcas pas | kun gyis deng khyod dbang bskur bas | khams gsum gyi ni rgyal po che | rgyal ba'i bdag po ston pa yin | deng ni bdud las rnam rgyal te | grong khyer mchog tu rab tu zhugs | khyed rnams kyis ni sangs rgyas nyid | deng nyid the tshom med par 'thob |

2. I employ the terms esoteric Buddhism (Chinese: *mi chiao*), Mantrayāna (*chen yen*) and Vajrayāna interchangeably. Although referring to the system as the resultant vehicle (phalayāna) is acceptable as well, this need not be used here. There is no valid reason for employing any of the modern neologisms—sahajayāna, kālacakrayāna, tantrayāna, and so on—that litter the literature about the esoteric dispensation; they remain unattested in any of our Buddhist sources and appear the result of misunderstandings by modern scholars.

3. This position is especially noticeable in the two primary statements in English, that of Snellgrove (1987) and the introduction to MATSUNAGA's edition of the *Guhyasamāja Tantra* (1978, pp. vii–xxxi).

4. The standard description of Chinese esoterism in English is Chou Yi-Liang 1945. See, as well, Weinstein 1987, pp. 77–89; Orlando 1980; Strickmann 1996. We have to concur with Orzech (1989, 1998) and Strickmann (1983, 1990, 1996), however, that the serious study of Chinese tantrism is in its infancy, and the widespread impression that Chou Yi-Liang has presented all the material is misleading. Both Strickmann's (1996, pp. 41–45) and Orzech's (1998, pp. xiv, 68) recent studies of the intersection of Chinese esoterism and politics appears in support of the model of imperial patronage.

5. For a review of this material, see Kapstein 2000, pp. 25–65.

6. See, especially, the "long roll" of esoteric images painted between 1173 and 1176 (Chapin 1972). Backus (1981, pp. 162 ff.) considers the period in decline, retaining the ideology of the Later Ta-li kingdom.

7. See, for example, Woodward 1981. Strachan interprets Pagan solely in light

of Theravāda tradition, even while acknowledging that the primary artistic and architectural tradition was Pāla and was close in form and aesthetics to Nālandā (1989, pp. 17, 25, 64, etc.; e.g., p. 38, where esoteric figures are illustrated). For another opinion on this period of Burmese history, see Strong 1992, pp. 174–179.

8. This is contra Samuel, who articulates the theory that centralized states prefer non-"shamanic" forms of Buddhism (1993, pp. 390–391). His theory does not accord with our data in India or many other areas; for the earliest mantrin's influence in Chinese state politics, see the biography of Fo T'u-teng in Wright (1990, pp. 34–68).

9. Strickmann has imputed Chinese class associations into Indian society and has misunderstood the metaphorical nature of the ritual enterprise, assuming that those conducting these rituals would represent the aristocratic class (1996, pp. 37–40).

10. See Lamotte 1944–80, 4:1854–1869; Braarvig 1985; Wayman 1975–76; Schopen 1985. We sometimes even find spells in the *Vinaya*, such as an early version of the *Mahāmāyūrīvidyārājñī* in the *Bhaiṣajyavastu* of the *Mūlasarvāstivāda-vinaya;* Dutt 1941–50, vol. 3, part 2, pp. 286–288.

11. Braarvig 1997.

12. Strickmann justifies the term, but with some uneasiness, for he recognizes that "proto-tantric" texts continue to be composed long after the advent of the tantras (1996, p. 130; 2002, pp. 103–109). Methodologically, then, the term "proto-tantric" is a questionable description, and it is not clear that the authors of these works understood other texts as superior. I have chosen only to typify "mature esoterism" as the fundamental change in system and not to speak of the texts that represent a different ideology except as they do not embody the basic metaphor explained later in this chapter.

13. Strickmann affirms Atikūṭa's *Dhāranīsamgraha* as not a literal translation, based on Chinese models intruding into the text (1996, pp. 53, 153; 2002, p. 264). As such, we need to take *Dhāraṇīsaṃgraha* as an important mark in ritualism around 653/54, rather than a translation of a much earlier work. On the maṇḍalas in the *Dhāraṇīsaṃgraha*, see YORITOMI 1990, pp. 81–84.

14. Lin 1935, p. 84n; *Chen yen tsung chiao shih i*, T.2396.75.431a8–12.

15. See Jong's (1984) summary of MATSUNAGA's standard work, p. 100; MATSUNAGA 1978, p. xvii; Chou 1945, p. 265.

16. *Ta t'ang hsi yü chi* T.2087.51.882b13–14; Beal does not represent this section entirely accurately (1869, p. 120). I-ching's involvement with esoteric Buddhism is chronicled in his hagiography, *Sung kao seng chuan,* T.2061.50.710.b8–711.b4.

17. Bodhiruci died in 727. Elements of his hagiography are found in the *Sung kao seng chuan,* T.2061.50.720b4-c12; *Hsü ku chin i ching t'u chi*, T.2152.55.371a28 (identified as Dharmaruci); and *Ta chou k'an ting chung ching mu lu,* T.2153.55.379c29, 380a8, 395a3; 2154.569b13, 570b15. Strickmann 1996, pp. 252–259, and 2002, pp. 254–255; Linrothe 1999, pp. 88–89, 132; and YORITOMI 1990, pp. 46–47, 89–94, discuss some of Bodhiruci's oeuvre.

18. See the material in chapter 5. This is indicated by several quotations to a version of the *Cakrasaṃvara-tantra* in the works of Vilāsavajra, particularly his commentaries on the *Guhyagarbha* and the *Mañjuśrīnāmasaṃgīti*; see Davidson for references (1981, pp. 8–9). We also note that at least one version of the earliest *yoginī tantra,* the *Sarvabuddhasamāyoga* (To. 366) was translated in the Tibetan Royal Dynastic period; its translation is discussed in chapter 5. It is referenced as one of the eighteen tantras of the early Mahāyoga canon; cf. Amoghavajra's *Chin kang ting ching yü ch'ieh shih pa hui chih kuei,* T.869.18.286c9–16 trans. Giebel 1995, pp. 177–182, and Jñānamitra's *Prajñāpāramitā-nayaśatapañcāśatkaṭīkā,* To. 2647, fol. 273a3. I am indebted to Kenneth Eastman for drawing my attention to these works and to Steven Weinberger for reference to Giebel's 1995 translation. KANAOKA (1966, p. 476) has pointed out that Jñānamitra's text appears to be the one listed in the *dKar chag ldan dkar ma;* Lalou 1953, p. 331, no. 523.

19. Examples of this perspective are provided by TSUDA 1978 and 1990.

20. The defense of this position is found in Lessing and Wayman 1968, pp. 164–165.

21. See Davidson 1991, for something of the discussion of Ngor-chen's refutations; they are embodied in his two works examining the ritual systems of texts classified as kriyā and caryā-tantras: the *Bya rgyud spyi'i rnam par bshad pa legs par bshad pa'i rgya mtsho,* and the *sPyod pa'i rgyud spyi'i rnam par gzhags pa legs par bshad pa'i sgron me.*

22. An introduction to polythetic category construction is provided in Lakoff 1987.

23. Murphey for a discussion of the more important research on categories (1994, pp. 10–19); Keil for problems with prototype theory (1989, pp. 26–33).

24. Wittgenstein 1958, § 67.

25. Keil 1989, pp. 83–84, 267–283; Murphey 1994, pp. 14–16.

26. The jump from individual maturation to social maturation of conceptual fields is made by Keil in the articulation of analogies between a child's maturation and the novice/expert distinction (1989, pp. 254–265).

27. Rabe for a consideration of the importance of this work in the socio-political life of the early medieval period (1997, p. 218).

28. *Kāvyamīmāṃsā,* Parashar 2000, pp. 164–179.

29. Snellgrove 1959 articulated some of these considerations with respect to *abhiṣeka,* but did not pursue the metaphor much beyond this point, and was forced to infer "non-Buddhist" influences rather than determine their nature from evidence. I thank Charles Orzech for drawing my attention to this article.

30. The best collection I have seen of Buddhist texts to date is SAKURAI 1996, pp. 407–584.

31. Law 1919 and Inden 1978 are the primary studies, based on entirely different materials.

32. Law 1919, pp. 87–90.

33. *Kṛtyakalpataru,* vol. 11: *Rājadharma-kāṇḍa,* Aiyangar 1943, pp. 9–17. The first scriptural source given by Lakṣmīdhara is not called the **Ādipurāṇa,* but the *Brahmapurāṇa*. It is well known, though, that the received *Brahmapurāṇa* has no connection with the text Lakṣmīdhara quotes as such, but is the old **Ādipurāṇa*. It is extremely common for multiple Indic texts to circulate under a single title or for a single text to be known under multiple titles. The surviving fragments of the old **Ādipurāṇa* have been edited (with the sections included in the *Kṛtyakalpataru*) by Y. IKARI and T. HAYASHI, in IKARI 1994, pp. 83–136.

34. Inden 1978, pp. 41–58.

35. Ibid., pp. 49–55. Cf. the ritual in Heesterman 1957, esp. pp. 63–90, where the "unction festival" is clearly not given much weight in the ceremonial agenda and was principally for the coronation of kings achieving independence for the first time.

36. Schlingloff 1964, textband, p. 41, and references, pp. 194–195; Ruegg 1967; YAMABE 1999, pp. 60–72.

37. *Ch'an mi yao fa ching*, T. 613.15.256c1–15.

38. *Kuan fo san mei hai ching*, T.643.15.664c9–11; I am grateful to YAMABE Nobuyoshi for providing these references to the *Kuan fo san mei hai ching*. See YAMABE 1999, pp. 302–312.

39. *Dhāraṇīsaṃgraha*, T.901.18.799c25–800a2, 802a17-b3, 857b6-c1, 871a1-c6, 875c13–876a5, 889a23–892b20

40. *Daśabhūmika,* KONDO 1936, pp. 178–189; *Laṅkāvatāra,* Bunyiu Nanjio 1923, pp. 1.11, 45.13, 70.3, 100.9, 101.11, 102.13, 103.6, 123.6, 190.17, 322.4, 359.16; these references are from SUZUKI 1934, p. 25b; cf. also the articulation of the *Daśabhūmika* model by Candrakīrti, *Madhyamakāvatāra,* La Vallée Poussin 1907–12, pp. 349–50. For the importance of this myth in the Mahayana legitimization of scripture, see Davidson 1990.

41. Strickmann 1990; idem 1996, pp. 78–87, 98–100, 113–123, 330–332; idem 2002, pp. 113–119, 132–140; the consecration ritual is found T.1331.21.479b5–24.

42. *I tsu fo ting lun wang ching* T.951.19.251b12–252c10. The date is from the *Kai yuan shih chiao mu lu* T.2154.55.569c5, although this text is notoriously unreliable. T.951 and its closely related T.952 are extremely important to demonstrate the transition between the seventh-century material and the rapidly evolving eighth-century synthesis. They, along with the *Subāhuparipṛcchā*, the *Susiddhikara* and the *Mahāvairocanābhisambodhi-vikūrvaṇa,* really demonstrate that transition rather well. YORITOMI (1990, pp. 116–119) discusses the relationship between many of these texts and Atikūṭa's **Dhāraṇīsaṃgraha*. On the question of a "single syllable" (ekākṣara) in the approximately contemporary *Mañjuśrīmūlakalpa*, see Przyluski 1923.

43. *I tsu fo ting lun wang ching*, T. 951.19.250b20–23.

44. *Susiddhikaramahātantrasadhanopāyikapaṭala*, To. 807, fols. 201b3–203b6; T.893.18.

45. Haribhadra's *Abhisamayālaṃkarāloka,* p. 270.13; *dKar chag ldan dkar ma,*

Lalou 1953, p. 326, no. 318; Buddhaguhya's *Vairocanābhisambodhitantrapiṇḍārtha*, To. 2662, fol. 3b4.

46. *Vajrapāṇy-abhiṣeka-mahātantra*, To. 496: de nas rdo rje ldan pa khyod | rdo rje'i chos ni rab brjod pa | sangs rgyas kun gyis khyod lag tu | ting 'dzin 'byung ba'i rdo rje byin | deng nas 'jig rten thams cad kyi | lag na rdo rje rdzul 'phrul che | sdang ba rnams ni tshar bcad dang | bstan pa la ni gnod byed pa | de dag gdul bar bya ba'i phyir | 'dren pa rnams kyis rdo rje byin | ci ltar 'khor los sgyur ba'i rgyal | bdag por bya phyir dbang bskur ba | de bzhin chos rgyal dbang bskur phyir | rdo rje blo ldan dbang bskur brjod |.

47. *Mahāvairocanābhisambodhitantra*, To. 494, fols. 239b2–241a6; cf. Buddhaguhya's *rNam par snang mdzad mngon par byang chub pa'i rgyud chen po'i 'grel bshad*, To. 2663, vol. nyu, fol. 350b.

48. In his *Nāmasaṃgītimaṇḍalavidhyākāśavimala*, To. 2543, fols. 11b1–13b2.

49. Inden 1978, p. 38.

50. *Subāhuparipṛcchā*, To. 805, fols. 122b7–125a5.

51. See Flood 1989, esp. p. 24.

52. Schwab has illustrated that the famous Herakles/Vajrapāṇi of niche V 2 at Tepe Shutur is an excellent example of the Herakles Epitrapezios type, which was believed to be associated with the sculptor Lysippos (1998).

53. *Kuan ting ching*, T.1331.21.515a23-b13. More than twenty years ago, in a graduate seminar at Berkeley Michel Strickmann attracted my attention to this bizarre work, which was the topic of his celebrated article on the *Consecration Scripture* (1990).

54. For one description of the Hevajra system, see Davidson 1992.

55. On esoteric Buddhist texts and spirit possession, see Granoff 1979, pp. 78–79; Strickmann 1996, pp. 213–226.

56. *MDŚ*, VII.5: yasmād eṣāṃ surendrāṇāṃ mātrābho nirmito nṛpaḥ | tasmād abhibhavaty eṣa sarvabhūtāni tejasā ||.

57. See Kulke 1978; 1993, pp. 327–381; the quotation is from p. 365.

58. Pollock 1996, pp. 236–239; 1998, pp. 13, 31–34.

59. Kielhorn 1900–1901a, v. 11; I thank Phyllis Granoff for pointing out to me the subsets of vibhūti.

60. *Nītisāra*, I.4a: sādhubhūtaladevatvam.

61. *Kṛtyakalpataru*, vol. 11: *Rājadharma-kāṇḍa*, Aiyangar 1943, p. 4: aśucir vacanād yasya śucir bhavati pūrusaḥ | śuciś caivāśuciḥ sadyaḥ kathaṃ rājā na daivatam ||. I thank Phyllis Granoff for correcting my translation of this passage.

62. Mañjuśrīmūlakalpa, Sastri 1920, p. 135: paśyed yo hi sa dharmātmā mucyate sarvakilbiṣāt | pañcānantaryakārī 'pi duḥśīlo mandamedhasaḥ ||. I have read with the Tibetan, fol. 175b6: gang gis bdag nyid chen po mthong.

63. Kṛtyakalpataru, vol. 11: Rājadharmakāṇḍa, Aiyangar 1943, pp. 12–13.

64. The normative esoteric definition for maṇḍala is mīlana, a gathering, cognate with Hindi melā/melan; *Guhyasamāja* XVIII.24, *Hevajra Tantra* II.iii.27,

which Snellgrove emended to malana against all the manuscripts for ideological reasons (1959, 1:97n1); *Hevajra Tantra* II.iii.26 calls a maṇḍala the "city composed of Buddhas," sarvabuddhātmakaṃpuraṃ. Strickmann (1996, p. 145), citing Brunner (1986), proposes that the Buddhist maṇḍala form derives exclusively from Śaivite tantric useage, which is unlikely in the face of its political components.

65. *Susiddhikara,* To. 807, fols. 209b2–214a3.

66. *Karuṇāpuṇḍarīka*, YAMADA 1968, 1:67–70; cf. Gómez 1996, pp. 37, 320.

67. Schopen 1977.

68. *Mūlasarvāstivāda Vinaya, Saṅghabhedavastu,* Gnoli 1977, 1:15: kṣetrāṇām adhipatiḥ kṣatāc ca trāyata iti kṣatriyaḥ kṣatriyaḥ samjñodapādi |; *Dīghanikāya,* Rhys Davids and Carpenter 1890–1911, 3:93: khettānaṃ adhipatī ti kho vāseṭṭha khattiyo khattiyo tv eva dutiyaṃ akkharaṃ upanibbattaṃ | (in the middle of defining Mahāsammata, khattiya, and rājā). This is the Buddhist version of the Manu story, used for various reasons; cf. *Mahābhārata, Śāntiparvan*, Sukthankar et al. 1949–50, 12.67.17–38.

69. Edgerton 1953, 2:198b, 201a.

70. See Scharfe: "The relative constancy of Indian social structures and mores over long periods of time makes the particular century in which a certain chapter has been composed often seem irrelevant. But since extensive interpolations in the text cannot be proved, the existing signs of a more recent date that are found in dozens of places must indicate the date of the compilation as a whole. I propose the first or perhaps the second century A.D." (1993, p. 293). This agrees with the employment of siddha explored in chapter 5.

71. This material is taken from *Arthaśāstra* 6.2.2–26 in Kangle 1960; cf. Scharfe 1993, pp. 104–124. Curiously, neither Scharfe nor the other authorities he quotes have directly represented the schematic of the text as it is written. They have taken maṇḍala exclusively in the sense of physical circle as opposed to "spheres of influence"; the *Arthaśāstra* was not drawing exact circles.

72. Chattopadhyaya 1994, pp. 10–37.

73. Kielhorn 1900–1901a, v. 23.

74. Kulke and Rothermund make this observation (1998, p. 126), although it is not entirely clear from their inscriptions; see Singh for a discussion of this point (1993, pp. 66–67).

75. Sharma 1965, p. 1. Wink took strong exception to Sharma's work (1990, pp. 219–223). On the nature of feudalism in general, see Strayer 1965, pp. 11–14; Reynolds 1994, pp. 1–74. Sharma has restated his position recently (2001, pp. 16–118).

76. This is a summary of Fox's ideas based on Stein 1991.

77. *Arthaśāstra*, VII.1.32.

78. *Nītisāra* I.18, IV.1, X.28.

79. Chattopadhyaya 1994, pp. 34–37, 186–202.

80. Ibid., pp. 80–3, 217–221; Sharma 1965, pp. 20–30; Gopal 1965, pp. 263–281; Devahuti 1983, pp. 184–187; Sharma 1996, pp. 62–70; and see Singh, for the most

thorough list of political designations found in a specific locale, in this case Orissa (1993, pp. 321–325). The extent of the list underlines how little we know of the particular powers attached to individual titles under specific administrations.

81. As with the coronation ceremony, Snellgrove recognizes the structural similarity between the maṇḍala and political systems but does not pursue the metaphor: "There is an exact analogy with the gradations of chief ministers, lesser minsters serving staff and messengers, with which a great king seated in state might be supposed to be surrounded." Because it is "profane," though, Snellgrove dismisses the analogy (1987, 1:199).

82. *Sarvatathāgatatattvasaṃgraha*, Chandra 1987, pp. 5–18.

83. *Sarvadurgatipariśodhana-tantra,* Skorupski 1983, sec. 35a, pp. 32, 174.

84. Fleet 1888, p. 168.

85. Bhavnagar Archaeological Dept., pp. 41 (plate II, line 11), 44.

86. Kane 1918, pp. 33–34.

87. *Mayamata,* Dagens 1985, pp. 119–148, 176–203.

88. Meister 1979.

89. *Mānava Dharma Śāstra* VII.119; cf. Doniger and Smith 1991, p. 140 n.

90. Irawati 1953, pp. 50–54.

91. Reported by I-ching in his *Nan hai chi kuei nei fa chuan*, T.2125.216c15; TAKAKUSU 1896, p. 82; noticed in Schopen 1987, p. 199. Unfortunately, this notice relies on the transcription of kula as chü lo, which is not exceptional but the exact identity of the Sanskrit term is difficult to affirm in the absence of Indic attestation.

92. *Mañjuśrīmūlakalpa,* Sastri 1920, p. 327: tathāṣṭakulikā mantrā aṣṭabhyo dikṣu niśritā | uttarāyāṃ diśi sidhyante mantrā vai jinasambhavā || purvadeśe tathā siddhiḥ mantrā vai padmasambhavā | dakṣiṇāpathaṃ niśritya sidhyante kuliśālayāḥ || paścimena gañjaḥ prokto vidiśe maṇikulas tathā | paścime cottare saṃdhau siddhis teṣu prakalpitā || paṣcime dakṣiṇe cāpi saṃdhau yakṣakulas tathā | dakṣiṇe pūrvadigbhāge śrāvakānāṃ mahaujasām || kulākhyaṃ teṣu dṛṣṭaṃ vai tatra sthāneṣu sidhyanti | pūrvottare diśābhāge pratyekānāṃ jinasambhavaṃ || kulākhyaṃ bahumataṃ loke siddhis teṣu tatra vai | adhaś caiva diśābhāge sidhyante sarvalaukikā || pātālapraveśikā mantrā vai sidhyante 'ṣṭakuleṣu ca | lokottarā tathā mantrā uṣṇīṣādyāḥ prakīrtitāḥ || siddhim āyānti te ūrdhvaṃ cakravartijinoditā |. The translation of the obscure Sanskrit takes into account the Tibetan version, To. 543, fols. 323a2–7, and the Chinese of T.1191.20.898b26-c6. There is a textual problem with the line paścimena gañjaḥ prokto, and I have emended the printed gaja to gañja based on the Tibetan mdzod (fol. 232a4). The Chinese renders (898b29) it phonetically, saying that the *na-ja* family is uncertain as to its direction, suggesting that the translators had a poorer text than we.

93. *Mañjuśrīmūlakalpa*, Sastri 1920, p. 326; this is analogous to the depictions of the sinister south in such texts as the *Kāraṇḍavyūha*; see Lienhard 1985 and 1993.

94. On the discussion if worldly (laukika) beings constituted a kula or not, see Ruegg 1964, pp. 79–80.

95. *Nītisāra* XVII.6–7; *Arthaśāstra*:II.4.23.

96. Strickmann (1983) indicates that the earliest description of these activities in Chinese literature is found in the *I tsu fo ting lun wang ching,* said to be translated by Bodhiruci in 709 C.E.; T.951.19.261c. Included is a fifth activity, that of seduction.

97. Homa is another ritual just beginning to receive the attention it is due; see Skorupski 1983 and Strickmann 1983, both in the landmark *Agni* by F. Staal. Skorupski's excellent study has a somewhat misleading title ("Tibetan Homa Rites") for they represent Indian rituals, some in the Tibetan language.

98. E.g., this description is found in the *Pradīpodyotana*, p. 194.24.

99. Skorupski 1994.

100. Bentor 2000.

101. The best description of Vajrapāṇi's position in normative Buddhism remains Lamotte 1966. Snellgrove 1987, 1:134–141, has contributed much.

102. Lamotte 1966, pp. 114–115, 152–153.

103. Sircar 1966, pp. 336–337; the term most consistently employed for Vajrapāṇi is guhyakādhipati.

104. *Kṛtyakalpataru, Rājadharmakāṇḍa*, pp. 101–110; the Yājñavalkya quotation is p. 103.

105. *Mānasollāsa*, I.52–59.

106. *Nītisāra* XII.3, XVI.57; Strickmann 1996, pp. 10, 40, etc., calls attention to the use of the loanword in Chinese as Mandarin from mantrin, but does not place its employment in India as a political office.

107. Ray 1994, pp. 407–410.

108. *Ta t'ang hsi yü chi*, T.2087.51.923a8; Beal 1869, 2:165; Demiéville 1932, pp. 60–61.

109. We see this evidence in the birchbark manuscript of the *Kāraṇḍavyūha*, Mette 1997, p. 97, and we notice the maintenance of this language even in the Newari manuscript transcribed by Mette, p. 143. Meisezahl was also of this opinion in his work on the *Amoghapāśahṛdayadhāraṇī;* see Meisezahl 1962, p. 270. On the topic of birch bark as a manuscript material, see Salomon 1999, pp. 15–22, 57–71, 81–109; Witzel 1994, pp. 6–14. The location of Uḍḍiyāna/Oḍiyāna has been finally affirmed by inscriptions; see KUWAYAMA 1991.

110. *Abhidharmakośabhāsya* VII.47, pp. 424–5.

111. I have in my possession such a manuscript in Tibetan given to me by a Tibetan lama. It is a collection of mantras, much written over and corrected. It is entitled the *Las sgrub rgyun gcod kyi sngags brgya pa, or The Hundred Mantras That Continually Remove Karmic Obscurations*, and is attributed one Mi-pham 'Jam-dpal dgyes-pa'i rdo-rje, one of the pen names of the famous nineteenth–twentieth-century rNying-ma-pa teacher, 'Jam-mgon Mi-pham rgya-mtsho (1846–1912).

112. **Dhāraṇīsaṃgra*, T.901.18.785b3.

113. *Śikṣāsamuccaya*, p. 79.

114. MATSUNAGA, in his introduction to the *Guhyasamāja*, p. IX, identifies the

Dharmaguptaka collection as a *Vidyādhara-piṭaka*, and the issue of vidyādhara is taken up in succeeding chapters. For other issues associated with the *Vidyottama* and related texts, see Stein 1978, pp. 434–439.

115. An esoteric canon said to be the entire *Vajraśekhara* scripture is the subject of Amoghavajra's *Chin kang ting ching yü ch'ieh shih pa hui chih kuei*, T.869, translated Giebel 1995; Yoritomi 1990, pp. 172–179.

116. Cf. Rocher 1986, pp. 30-34. Eastman's 1981 presented but unfortunately unpublished paper is the best investigation of the Buddhist problem to date. Another Indian source affirming a canon of eighteen tantras is Jñānamitra's *Prajñāpāramitā-nayaśatapañcāśatkaṭīkā,* To. 2647, fol. 273a3, and a section of this is translated in chapter 6; this later source is discussed by Kanaoka 1966.

117. On scriptural formulation, see Davidson 1990 and Collins 1990.

118. The conversion of Vajrapani is found throughout North Indian Buddhist literature; Lamotte 1966 for a survey.

119. *Sarvatathāgatatattvasaṃgraha,* Chandra 1987, pp. 5–6: samantabhadratvāt vajrasattvasamādheḥ sudṛḍhatvāc caikaghanaḥ samantabhadramahābodhisattvakāyaḥ saṃbhūya bhagavato vairocanasya hṛdaye sthitvīdam udānam udānayāmāsa | aho samantabhadro 'haṃ dṛḍhasattvaḥ svayaṃbhuvāṃ | yad dṛḍhatvād akāyo 'pi sattvakāyatvam āgataḥ || atha samantabhadramahābodhisattvakāyo bhagavato hṛdayād avatīrya sarvatathāgatānāṃ purataś candramaṇḍalāśrityo bhūtvājñāṃ mārgayāmāsa || atha bhagavān sarvatathāgatajñānasamayavajraṃnāmasamādhiṃsamāpadyasarvatathāgataśīlasamādhiprajñāvimuktivimuktijñānadarśanadharmacakrapravartana-sattvārthamahopāyabalavīryamahājñānasamayam aśeṣānavaśeṣasattvadhātuparitrāṇasarvādhipatya-sarvasukhasaumanasyânubhavanārthaṃ yāvat sarvatathāgatasamatājñānābhijñānuttara-mahāyānābhisamayottamasiddhyavāptiphalahetos tatsarvatathāgatasiddhivajraṃ tasmaisamantabhadrāya mahābodhisattvāya sarvatathāgatacakravartitve sarvabuddhakāyaratnamukuṭapaṭṭābhiṣekeṇâbhiṣicya pāṇibhyām anuprādāt | tataḥ sarvatathāgatair vajrapāṇir vajrapāṇir iti vajranāmābhiṣekeṇâbhiṣiktaḥ || atha vajrapāṇir bodhisattvo mahāsattvo vāmavajragarvollālanatayā tadvajraṃ svahṛdy utkarṣaṇayogena dhārayann idam udānam udānayāmāsa || idaṃ tatsarvabuddhānāṃ siddhivajram anuttaraṃ | ahaṃ mama kare dattaṃ vajraṃ vajre pratiṣṭhitam || iti || I have largely followed Śākyamitra's *Kosalālaṃkāra*, To. 2503, vol. yi, fols. 30a5–33b6. A profitable comparison can be made against the same episode in a slightly different narrative form found in the *Vajrapāṇyabhiṣeka-mahātantra*, To. 496, fols. 25a3–26a3.

120. *Sarvatathāgatatattvasaṃgraha*, Chandra 1987, pp. 56–60; *Vajraśekhara,* To. 480, fols. 236a7–262a7; *Trailokyavijaya*, To. 482, fols. 10a5–13a7; *Candraguhyatilaka*, To. 477, fols. 281a6–287a7; Iyanaga 1985; Snellgrove 1987, 1:134–141; Davidson 1991, 1995b; Stein 1995; Mayer 1998.

121. On this phenomenon, see Mair 1988.

122. E.g., *Trailokyavijaya*, To. 482, fols. 10a5–13a7.

123. *Sādhanamāla* has a sādhana of Trailokyavijaya in this position (1925, 2:511).

124. *Tantrārthāvatāra*, To. 2501, fols. 76b6, 78b5, 79a7.

125. This might be the material we could establish as central for the evolving institutional esoterism if we look at the gsang sngags kyi rgyud and gzungs sections of the *dKar chag ldan dkar ma* (Lalou 1953, pp. 326–328), at the translations into Chinese by the T'ang translators (Chou 1945, passim), and the scriptures specified by Buddhaguhya in his introduction to the *Mahāvairocābhisambodhi*, his *Vairocanābhisambodhitantrapiṇḍārtha*, To. 2662, fol. 3a4–3b6.

126. For example, the doctrinal statements of many of these early tantras emphasizes the issue of the nature of the mind, such as the *Subāhuparipṛcchā*, To. 805, fols. 121b1–122b7, the *Mahāvairocanābhisambodhitantra*, To. 494, fols. 153b1–160a2; *Sarvatathāgatatattvasaṃgraha*, Chandra 1987, p. 4; *Sarvadurgatipariśodhanatantra*, Skorupski 1983, sections 2b–4b, 17b, etc. NAMAI 1997 covers some of this material, which calls into question the estimation that esoteric Buddhism made no contribution to Buddhist doctrine.

127. Mitra 1981, 1:108–138; Linrothe 1999, pp. 252–257. I believe Linrothe's phase stratigraphy suffers from an insufficient consideration of relatively datable esoteric literature.

128. *Chag lo tsā ba'i rnam thar*, Roerich 1959, p. 42; see also *Rwa lo tsā ba'i rnam thar*, p. 71.

129. *Bhoṭasvāmidāsalekha*, Dietz 1984, p. 361.

130. *sBa bzhed*, mGon-po rgyal mtshan 1980, p. 1; *sBa bzhed zhabs btags ma*, Stein 1961, p. 1; this is missing in the *dBa' bzhed*, Wangdu and Diemberger 2000, pp. 23–25.

131. This text has been edited and translated into German in Dietz 1984, pp. 360–365. Her notes are very useful, although I have differed from her translation on small points. I am well aware that the text as it stands cannot be entirely a Royal Dynastic Tibetan production, and sections have been added; see Karmay 1980, p. 9. I do believe, however, that the above material is authentic.

132. The *dKar chag ldan dkar ma*, Lalou 1953, nos. 322, 324, 328, are commentaries on the *Mahāvairocanābhisambodhi*, the *Sarvadurgatipariśodhana*, and the *Dhyānottara*, respectively, but are attributed to Buddhagupta. Yet these are undoubtedly the works of Buddhaguhya (as is probably no. 326, an unidentified commentary on the *Subāhuparipṛcchā)*. While it is possible that he was also known by the name Buddhagupta, I find it equally likely that his name was translated back into Sanskrit by the librarian. Hodge 1994, p. 69, calls attention to *Guhyagarbha* commentaries in the Peking that are attributed to Buddhaguhya. There is much about the Peking *bsTan 'gyur*, that is problematic, however, and these works may require reattribution. Please also see Germano 2002.

133. *kLong chen chos 'byung*, pp. 272–275: babs gsum pa ni | slob dpon sangs rgyas gsang ba gangs ti si la byon pa'i tshe chos gsungs pa rnams yin te | sku che ba'i lo rgyus ni | rgya gar nub phyogs pa'i rgyal rigs chen po zhig yin cing | lan gcig gi tshe rgyal po chen po zhig la sras zhig 'khrungs pa las | rgyal po'i thugs dgongs la

nga'i bu 'di la 'jig rten gyi khams na gang zag mi'i slob dpon du bya ba'i 'os med pas mkhyen rab kyi mnga' bdag 'phags pa 'jam dpal bsgrub tu bcug la de la slob dpon zhu dgos snyam nas | sku rten lugs sku khru gang | gsung rten me tog padma | thugs rten 'o ma spar bu gang gtad de | rgyal pos 'jam dpal gyi sgom lung phog nas bsgrub tu bcug pas rgyal po bsod nams che ba dang | rgyal rigs yin pas zhag drug nas 'grub ste | lugs sku zhal 'dzum pa dang bzhad pa la sogs pa byung | padma'ang sor mar skyes pa 'dra ba byung | 'o ma yang lud la khad pa byung ste rgyal bu'i bsam pa la 'jam dpal 'grub nas 'dug bas siddhi gang la blangs na drag snyam pa'i the tshom skyes pa las | lha nyid bdud 'char ka nag po zhes bya ste | bya nag po chen po zhig tu sprul nas gshogs pa chur bcug pa sa la bsgres te | slob dpon gyi 'gram pa la brgyab pas dar cig brgyal bar gyur te | [brgyal ba] sangs pa dang bltas pas | lugs sku'ang nag log [ger] song | padma yang rnying par [273] song | 'o ma yang bskams la khad par song | [rgyal bu'i bsam pa la] da res siddhi gang la blangs kyang chog pa'i dus su siddhi ma blangs pas lan | de cis nyes snyam na the tshom zos pas lan | de cis lan na thos pa chung bas lan snyam nas | ha cang thos pa chung na yang bdud kyi las su rig par bya ste | nga'am nga lta bu'o gsungs nas | yab rgyal po la zhus nas | rgya gar shar phyogs su paṇḍi ta lnga brgya'i drung du thos pa mdzad du byon pas | khong rigs bzang ba dang | 'jam dpal grub pa'i stobs kyis paṇḍi ta lnga brgya'i mkhyen pa thams cad thogs pa med par thugs su chud cing mkhas pa chen por gyur te khong rigs bzang ba dang mkhas pa'i stobs kyis longs spyod 'du 'dzi mang po 'dus pas g.yengs pa shin tu che ste | skyo ba skyes nas ha cang thos pa che na bdud kyi las su rigs par bya ste | nga'am nga lta bu'o gsungs nas | gangs ti se bya rog gi gdong pa can gser brag bya skyibs bya bar sgom sgrub la byon pa dang de'i dus su bod yul na chos skyong ba'i rgyal po mnga' bdag khri srong lde btsan bzhugs pa dang dus mtshungs nas | gang ti si na rgya gar gyi paṇḍi ta mkhas pa zhig byon nas 'dug zer ba thos nas | lo tsā ba dba' manydzu shrī warma dang | mchims shākya pra bha dang | bran ka ra mu khendra | rtsangs the leg dra dang bzhi la gser phye bre gsum bskur nas gdan 'dren du btang bas | nga sgrub pa'i dam bca' zhig byas nas yod pas bod du mi 'gro gsungs nas | 'byon du ma bzhed | mi 'byon na chos zhu 'tshal zhus pas | chos bshad pa'i dus la bab bam mi bab yi dam gyi lha la dri yis [274] gsungs nas | zhag gsum yi dam lha la gsol ba btab nas dris pas | dus la bab par yi dam lhas lung bstan nas | chos gsung bar gnang ste | gsang sngags kyi chos zab mo bshad pa la sngon la dbang bskur dgos gsungs nas | slob dpon gyis mtsho ma pham g.yu'i maṇḍal bkod pa 'dra ba la | thig sna bskur ba tsam gyis zhi ba rdo rje dbyings kyi dkyil 'khor lha tshogs bzhi bcu ṙtsa gnyis mdun gyi nam mkha' la bkra sa le 'dug pa bang chen pa rnams kyis zhal mthong ba byung | der slob dpon gyis dbang lha la zhu ba'am nga la zhu gsungs pas | khong rnams kyi sems par | lha de nas mi snang bar 'gro bas | sngon la lha la zhu byas pas | slob dpon gyis se gol gtogs pa zhig byas te | lha tshogs rnams thugs kar bsdus nas | khyed bod srin po gdong dmar ba 'di dam tshig shin tu chung bar 'dug ste | chos 'chad pa'i 'brel ba tsam 'dug pas | bshad par bya | gsungs nas mngon par byang chub pa'i rgyud dang | ngan song sbyong rgyud sgrub thabs dang bcas pa |

man ngag a ba ta ra la sogs la yo ga'i chos rnams dang | gzhan yang gsang sngags nang gi sgyu 'phrul gsang ba'i snying po 'grel pa dang bcas pa | man ngag lam rim | slob dpon nyid kyis mdzad pa'i man ngag rdo rje lam rim | khro bo'i lam rim dang | zhi ba drwa chen drwa chung dang | 'bring po la sogs man ngag phra mo mang po dang | bsam gtan phyi ma'i rgya cher 'grel pa dang bcas pa | gsang sngags phyi nang gi chos mang du bsgyur nas byung ba yin no | bang chen pa rnams kyis rgyal po la gsungs pa | rgyal pos lo tsā ba [275] rma gnyags gnyis la bshad | de nas mar sgyu 'phrul gyi brgyud pa spyi mdo dang mthun par gsungs so || Cf. Germano 2002.

134. *Tā ra nā tha'i rgya gar chos 'byung*, Schiefner 1868, pp. 170–171.

135. *Vajravidāraṇadhāraṇyekavīrasādhana*, To. 2926, fol. 330a2, ri gangs can here = himavat. McKay discusses Grunendahl's suggestion that, at the time the *Mahābhārata* was composed, Kailāsa was a mountain located in the Badrinath region of the Garwhal (1998, pp. 169–70). While this is appealing, we appear to lack archaeological evidence for this assignment.

136. Meister and Dhaky describe surviving sites that Buddhaguhya could have visited (1988–91, vol. 2, pt. 2, pp. 92–118).

137. Unfortunately, we have no complete survey of his references. I have noted the following esoteric titles in Buddhaguhya's works, a list instructive but by no means exhaustive. In his *Vairocanābhisambodhitantrapiṇḍārtha*, To. 2662: *Sarvatathāgatatattvasaṃgraha* (ref. fols. 3b3, 13a3–6, 16b2, 34b5–6), *Mahāvairocanābhisambodhitantra* (ref. fols. 10a1, 23a5, 36a1, 36a7), **Trisamayarāja* (ref. fol. 3b4), *Vajrapāṇy-abhiṣeka-mahātantra* (ref. fol. 3b4), *Paramādya* (ref. fol. 3b3), **Samāyoga* (fol. 20b7), **Guhyamaṇḍalopadeśa* (fol. 23a2), **Vajrasamayasamodaya* (fol. 26b4), *Trailokyavijaya* (fol. 26b7–27a1), **Acalamantra* (fol. 27a1), *Subāhuparipṛcchā* (fol. 28a7). In the *Dhyānottara-paṭala-ṭīkā*, To. 2670: **Vajroṣṇīṣatantra* (fols. 3a4, 15a4–7), *Susiddhikara* (fol. 9a4), *Subāhuparipṛcchā* (fol. 9a4–7), *Mahāvairocanābhisambodhitantra* (fols. 9a5–b3, 15b1), *Vajrapāṇy-abhiṣeka-mahātantra* (fol. 9a5–b4), *Vidyādharapiṭaka* (fol. 9a6), *Sarvatathāgatatattvasaṃgraha* (fol. 30b4), *Vajraśekhara* (fol. 30b4–5). In his *Subāhuparipṛcchā-tantra-piṇḍārtha*, To. 2671: "Laukika and Lokottara tantras" (fol. 45a7), *Vidyādharapiṭaka* (fol. 49a4). This latter text (To. 2671) appears an early composition, as reflected in the paucity of references.

138. His discussions of gnosis and emptiness probably lead the way; e.g., *Dhyānottara-paṭala-ṭīkā*, To. 2670, fols. 3a5–4a2,

139. The experience of 'Brog-mi will be covered in my forthcoming work on the Tibetan Renaissance (forthcoming b); see, for example, Grags-pa rgyal-mtshan's *bLa ma brgyud pa bod kyi lo rgyus*, the earliest source on 'Brog-mi's life. Ba-ri's hagiography has been recovered: *bLa ma ba ri lo tsā ba rin chen grags kyi rnam thar*, and covers the late eleventh century. Just as interesting is the thirteenth-century *Rwa lo tsā ba'i rnam thar*, and the Indian portion of the hagiography covers several centers, pp. 67–80.

140. *Nan hai chi kuei nei fa chuan*, T.2125.54.209b20-c11; TAKAKUSU 1896, pp. 38–39.

141. *Bhadracaryāpraṇidhānarājaṭīkā,* To. 4013, fol. 234a3: shākya'i bshes gnyen blo ldan gyis | shākya'i gdung rgyud 'phel ba'i phyir | kun tu bzang po spyod pa yi | rgya cher 'grel pa rab bzang byas |. This text is listed in the *dKar chag ldan dkar ma,* Lalou 1953, no. 559.

142. Cohen 2000.

143. *Kosalālaṃkāra,* To. 2503, fols. 1b5–2a4: grong khyer bzang por sangs rgyas sde zhes grags thob gang | bla ma'i mchog de dang por rab dad mnyes byas te | gnang ba mnos shing cho gas dam tshig thob nas ni | de la shin tu mang thos mang du rnam par dpyad | kong ka nir ni dra mi ḍa dang dbang phyug dpal 'dus dang | chos sde chos kyi 'byung gnas dga' bas bsnyen bkur byas | sa hyer chos kyi rdo rje mchog tu mtshan gsol dang | gtsug tor rdo rje'ang mang du legs par bsnyen bkur byas | yon tan 'byung gnas byang phyogs u rgyan yul grod de | rgyud don de nyid 'dzin rgyal indra bhūti bsnyen | tag kyer grong khyer ka sha la yi slob dpon ni | blo brtan blo gros 'byung gnas tshul mkhas gus pas bsten | bla ma'i zhal nas yang dag man ngag gang las ni | cung zad bdag gis ci rtogs dag pa'i lung gi tshul | 'jig rten rnal 'byor cho gas slob dpon bzhin rim gyis | 'di ni yun ring gnas phyir bdag gis rnam par bsams |

144. *Kao seng fa hsien chuan,* T.2085.51.862b2–11; Legge 1886, pp. 78–9.

145. Pye is both interesting and illuminating on skillful means, although he does not adhere to the idea that the Mahayana introduced any significant change in content and refers to this idea as a "crude interpretation" (1978, p. 33), an assessment with which I cannot agree.

146. *Vairocanābhisambodhitantrapiṇḍārtha,* To. 2662, fol. 2b1–2: gzhan gyi don phun sum tshogs pa ni sku la sogs pa mi zad pa rnam par sprul pa de nyid kyi byin gyi rlabs kyi phyag rgya dang | gsang sngags dang | dkyil 'khor la sogs par brtags pa'i sgo thabs dang bcas par brjod pa yin no |.

147. Ibid., fols. 20b6, 35a5–6, 46b3, 58b3, 59a4, 61a6, 61b4, 63a1, 64b1; *Dhyānottara-paṭala-ṭīkā,* fols. 4b6–7, 10a5.

148. On the simile, and other figures of speech as well, see Gonda 1949.

149. *Ratnagotravibhāga,* Johnston 1950, I.95–133; *Vajracchedikā Prajñāpāramitā,* Conze 1957, p. 62, although there are many other Mahayanist texts that expand on these images.

150. *Triṃśikāvijñaptibhāṣya,* Lévi 1925, pp. 15–20.

151. See, for example, Bhavya's defense of mantras, explored in Braarvig 1997.

152. *Vairocanābhisambodhitantrapiṇḍārtha,* To. 2662, fol. 63b2: de la gsangs sngags mnyes par byed pa'i las dge ba kha cig gi 'bras bu ni srid pa gzhan du mngon par 'grub pa nyid do | kha cig ni bsam pa dang sbyor ba'i dbang gis tshe 'di nyid la rnam par smin par 'gyur te |.

153. We also frequently find the use of √ pariṇām- in various forms; see *Sādhanamālā,* 1925, passim (1:8, 9, etc.)

154. For the Yogācāra literature, see Davidson 1985; for one classic statement in esoteric literature, see *Khasama-tantra-ṭīkā,* 1983, p. 231.

155. *Pīṭhādinirṇaya*, To. 1606, fols. 134b7–135a2: puṃ yi ge la sogs pa'i yi ge yongs su gyur pa las 'khor lo'i rtsibs rnams kyi stongs pa'i nang du gnas la sogs pa'i gnas rnams spyi bo la sogs pa rnams su blta bar bya'o | gnas la sogs pa de rnams su de de'i gnas su son pa'i rtsa rnams de dang de'i lha'i gzugs kyis yongs su gyur pa rnam par gzhag ste bsgom par bya'o | dper na phyi rol du gnas la sogs pa dang nye bar gnas pa'i chu klung gi chu yis gso bar byed pa de bzhin du | lus la yang rtsa rnams kyis sen mo la sogs pa gso bar byed do zhes pa mtshungs pa nyid do |.

156. *Mañjuśrīmūlakalpa*, Sastri 1920, pp. 51–52: vaktavyāś ca iyaṃ bho mahābodhisattvasya mañjuśriyaḥ kumārabhūtasya samayarahsyaṃ mātikramiṣyatha iti | mā bahu apuṇyaṃ prasaviṣyatha iti | sarvamantrāś ca na pratikṣeptavyāḥ | sarvabuddhabodhisattvāś ca na visaṃvādanīyāḥ | gurur ārādhanīyaś ceti | anyathā samayātikramaḥ syāt | mantrāś ca siddhiṃ na gaccheyuḥ | bahu puṇyaṃ syād iti |

157. Bagchi 1945, esp. pp. 145–146, which specifies the transgressions that become impediments to consecration.

158. This burning has been cited in Tibetan political literature; see the *sBa bzhed zhabs btags ma*, Stein 1961, pp. 52–53; *sBa bzhed*, mGon-po rgyal-mtshan 1980, p. 62; *dBa' bzhed*, Wangdu and Diemberger 2000, p. 90.

159. Sastri 1942, pp. 103–105.

160. *Mahākālatantra*, To. 440, fols. 78a2–79a2.

161. See Fussman 1994 for an affirmation that Buddhist doctrine did not substantially change its formulation with the development in Gandhāra. I thank Gregory Schopen for providing me with a copy of this article.

162. Nihom 1994, pp. 151–173; Klimburg-Salter 1997, pp. 207–216; Vitali 1990, pp. 40–51.

5. SIDDHAS AND THE RELIGIOUS LANDSCAPE

1. *Kṛṣṇayamāri-tantra*, Rinpoche and Dvivedi 1992, XI.9–12, p. 73:

mahāṭavīpradeśeṣu āruhya mahiṣottamam |
sarpair ābharaṇaṃ kṛtvā ayovajraṃ tu dhārayet || 9
keśaṃ tu piṅgalaṃ kāryam ūrdhvarūpaṃ viśeṣataḥ |
śiraḥ kapālaiḥ saṃveṣṭya śmaśrau piṅgalam ācaret || 10
hrīḥ ṣṭryādi mantram uccārya ayovajraṃ samudvahet |
siṃhanādaṃ tataḥ kāryaṃ yamārivajraprayogataḥ || 11
kiñcitsāmarthyam ābhujya krīḍayā nagaraṃ viśet |
ṛtyam ca subhagaṃ kāryaṃ ṣāḍavādipragāyanam || 12

The translation supposes that the ochre (piṅgala) smeared in the hair and beard of our siddha friend is that of gorocana; see *Harṣacarita* for its use by Bhairavācārya's disciples, Kane 1918, p. 50. I have accepted the editors' suggestion that 12d read "pragāyanam" instead of "praśāyanam" (Tib., glu blang bya). I thank Phyllis Granoff for suggestions on the translation of these verses.

2. Ruegg 1964, especially pp. 87–90.

3. Sanderson 1994, p. 92.

4. Saussure 1983, pp. 13–15.

5. For a cogent criticism of Saussure's model, see Vološinov 1973, pp. 57–63.

6. White 1996, especially the summary p. 335. As is obvious in the following discussion, I cannot entirely agree with the findings of Professor White's text.

7. For a broad overview, which is not without difficulties, see Mishra 1973.

8. Stein 1980, p. 79; *Ta t'ang hsi yü chi,* Beal 1869, 2:227 ff.

9. The text has been edited and commented on many times. I am using the edition prepared in Barua 1938. I know of no earlier epigraphic mention of siddhas.

10. The tenth-century C.E. Digambara work by Nemicandra, the *Dravva-saṃgaha,* v. 51, defines a siddha as a soul having the shape of a human, but with a body in which the eight forms of karma destroyed.

11. Fleet 1888, pp. 79–88.

12. *Rāmāyana, Yuddhakāṇḍa,* Vaidya 1971, Appendix I, no. 65, pp. 1082–83. For an important recent work on the early solar cult, see Chenet 1993.

13. There are similar references in the surviving works of the second-century Buddhist poet Aśvaghoṣa, the *Saundarananda,* Johnston 1928, X.6, and *Buddhacarita,* Johnston 1936, VII.1, XIV.87.

14. *Arthaśāstra,* Kangle 1960, IV.3.40–44.

15. *Arthaśāstra,* Kangle 1960, IV.5.1–16.

16. *Arthaśāstra,* Kangle 1960, V.1.33–34, XII.2.14.

17. Virtually all of *Arthaśāstra* XII.2 is so dedicated.

18. *Arthaśāstra,* Kangle 1960, V.2.59–63, V.6.48.

19. *Arthaśāstra,* Kangle 1960, V.2.39–41.

20. *Rāmāyana* I.30.14.

21. *Rāmāyana* I.28.2cd: siddhāśrama iti khyātaḥ siddho hy atra mahātapāḥ |

22. *Milindapañha,* Trenckner 1880, IV.1.43–45, pp. 120–121.

23. *Harṣacarita,* Kane 1918, pp. 46–54.

24. Ibid., p. 53: kuntalī kirīṭī hārī keyūrī mekhalī mudgarī khaḍgī. The most normative equipment of the Vidyādhara is the sword. See Hinüber 1978.

25. *Avantisundarīkathā,* Kale 1966, pp. 172–173; this work used to be called the *Daśakumāracarita* before its true identity was discovered; see Rabe 1997.

26. For example, *Bṛhatkathāślokasaṃgraha,* Poddar 1986, XX.97–131.

27. The protest against the excessive reductionism of legitimation theory by Pollock is well merited (1996, pp. 236–239; 1998, pp. 13, 31–34). However, we must also consider—as Pollock does himself—questions of legitimation and its social function must be assessed, even if it cannot be the sole cause for such relations.

28. Lorenzen 1972, pp. 88–90.

29. Ibid., p. 2.

30. Sanderson 1988, pp. 665–666.

31. Hinüber 1992, pp. 35–82.

32. *MDŚ,* VIII.93, XI.72–89; the translation makes this latter section XI.73–90.

33. The *Rucikaraṭīkā;* cited in Tucci 1930, p. 131; Lorenzen 1972, p. 49 n.

34. Sanderson 1988, p. 674; Dyczkowski 1988, p. 38.

35. *Karpūramañjarī* I.22–23 (Know and Lanman, pp. 24–25):
mantāṇa tantāṇa ṇa kiṃ pi jāṇe jhāṇaṃ ca ṇo kiṃ pi guruppasāā |
majjaṃ piāmo mihilaṃ ramāmo mokkhaṃ ca jāmo kulamaggalaggā || 22
avi a raṇḍā caṇḍā dikkhiā dhammadārā majjaṃ maṃsaṃ pijjae khajjae a |
bhikkhā bhojjaṃ cammakhaṇḍaṃ ca sejjā kolo dhammo kassa ṇo bhāi
rammo || 23

36. *Gaüḍavaho* 319 (Suru 1975).

37. Dehejia 1986.

38. These other potential sites include Palodhar (in the Mahesana District of Gujarat), Kamli (close to Siddhpur in Gujarat), Bharuch (Gujarat), Ajmer, Ujjain, and Delhi; see ibid., pp. 67–90.

39. For a summary discussion of the Hirapur site, see Donaldson 1985–87, 1:261–263.

40. Donaldson 1986.

41. For the Siyān inscription of Nayapāla, see Sircar 1971; pp. 47–48, 54; for Udayāditya's Mominabad inscription, see Desai 1962, pp. 94–95.

42. Fleet 1888, p. 76 l. 37.

43. The best discussions to date are by Lorenzen 1972, pp. 173–192; Dyczkowski 1988, pp. 19–26; Bhandarkar 1908; and, perhaps most important, the various articles by Hara (1958, 1973, 1994).

44. Hara 1958; Gonda 1977, pp. 216–224; Lorenzen 1972, pp. 173–192. This material is treated in chapter 3 of the main text: *Pāśupatasūtra*, Sastri 1940, pp. 77 ff.

45. *Pāśupatasūtra*, Sastri 1940, V. 20: siddhayogī na lipyate karmaṇā pātakena va ||.

46. Bhattacharya 1955.

47. Freed and Freed 1993, pp. 15–18, 190–211.

48. On the association of mediumship and spirit possession with esoteric Buddhism, see Granoff 1979, p. 78; Strickmann 1996, pp. 50–52, 215–220; idem 2002, pp. 204–218.

49. Fleet 1888, pp. 260–262.

50. Bühler 1892, pp. 106, 111, v. 27: vaṇik prasiddhas siddhātmajo manyukanāmadheyaḥ |. Bühler, following others, assigns the date of this inscription to 804 C.E., but Vogel reassesses the date to 1204 C.E. (1905–6, p. 22). This 1204 date has been accepted by others, especially Postel et al. (1985, p. 114).

51. Ojha 1917–18.

52. Postel et al. 1985, pp. 250–251, 124, frontispiece.

53. The best study of this phenomenon of which I am aware is that in Campbell (1976, pp. 24, 29, 70), but is much more widespread than the Kangra Valley.

See also Emerson 1920, pp. 118–119, for Maṇḍi State. The term "sidh" also applies to gods, and this usage is already seen in the *Caṇḍamahāroṣaṇa-tantra* 6.196.

54. Campbell 1976, p. 29. Cf. Emerson 1920, p. 112.

55. For Banarsi Bir Babas, see Coccari 1989.

56. See Temple 1884–90 for Punjabi versions of sidh legends; for example, Pūran Bhagat's legends are described on pp. 517–562.

57. This information is based both on Upadhyay 1986 and my own fieldwork in Mandi.

58. Yazdani 1960, 1:438–444; Mishra 1973, pp. 146–153; this popular position is still seen as recently as Sharma 1996, pp. 90–131.

59. *Bhagavadgītā* IX.23: ye 'py anyadevatābhaktā yajante śraddhayā 'anvitāḥ | te 'pi mām eva kaunteya yajanty avidhipūrvakam ||.

60. For example, Chattopadhyaya 1994, pp. 223–232; Singh 1993, pp. 295–303.

61. Stein 1980, pp. 80–81.

62. Mukherjee 1940, pp. 26, 53.

63. Granoff 1986–92 has discussed some of these voices.

64. Granoff 2000, pp. 404–409.

65. For example, *Kṛṣṇayamāri-tantra,* Rinpoche and Dvivedi 1992, XIV.16–18.

66. Ibid., XVII.13: svaparadharmaṃ na dūṣayet.

67. *Vajrapañjara,* To. 419, fol. 54b7–55a1: bcom ldan 'das kyis bka' stsal pa | stong ba snying rje tha dad med | gang du sems ni rab bsgoms pa | 'di ni sangs rgyas chos dang ni | dge 'dun gyi yang bstan pa'o | mu stegs can sun dbyung ba dang | rgol ba rnams tshar gcod pa dang | rang gi sde'i gzhung brjod pa zhes bya ba'i ting nge 'dzin to |

68. *Tillopādadohākoṣa,* pp. 46–77: bamhāvihṇu mahesura devā | bohisattva ma karahu sevā || deva ma pūjahu titya ṇa jāvā | devapūjāhi ṇa mokkha pāvā ||

69. *Guhyasamāja-tantra,* XIII.67–68: sarvatīrtyapravādistambhanavajro nāma samādhiḥ | krodhākāraṃ trivajrāgrān pītakiñjalkasannibhān | girirāja iva sarvān dhyātvā mūrdhni prabhāvayet || 67 buddhasainyam api stambhe mriyate nātra saṃśayaḥ || 68

This interpretation follows *Pradīpodyotana,* Chakravarti 1984, p. 133.

70. Siklós 1996, p. 35.

71. For example, *Kṛṣṇayamāri-tantra* IV.56.

72. E.g., *bLa ma rgya gar ba'i lo rgyus, SKB* III.170.1.1–173.1.6.

73. De 1953.

74. The literature on Vidyādharas is not as extensive as one might want; important are Lüders 1939, Przyluski 1923, Hinüber 1978, Jain 1974, and more recently Granoff 2000, pp. 412–419. To this list may be added the specifically early esoteric affirmation of Vidyādharas as sorcerers, for that is the understanding of the Royal Dynastic Tibetan translators of the *Vidyottama,* who rendered the term as rig-sngags-'chang, rather than the later rig-'dzin; see *Vidyottama-mahātantra,* To. 746, fols. 3b3–4a1, 9a2, 11a4, etc.

75. *Śārdūlakarṇāvadāna*, p. 2; the mention of the mother as a vidyādharī does not seem to be found in the earliest Chinese translations of the work.

76. *Ratnaguṇasañcaya-gāthā* XXVII.5.

77. *Laṅkāvatāra-sūtra*, 1923, p. 248; *Bodhisattvabhūmi*, WOGIHARA 1930–36, p. 359.

78. This usage is sustained as late as Albīrūnī's description, written approximately 1030, when he refers to vidyādharas as "demon-sorcerers"; Sachau 1910, 1:91.

79. *Varṇārhavarṇastotra* II.33 [Hartmann 1987, p. 108]: sarvakleśāmayaghnāya sarvaśalyāpahāriṇe | siddhavidyādharāyâstu bhiṣacchreṣṭhāya te namaḥ ||. I have accepted Hartmann's reconstruction of this verse. Mātṛceta's date would be from his association with Kaniṣka, now usually understood to be active in the first quarter of the second century C.E.

80. Wright indicates that Fo T'u-teng was influential in four areas: agriculture, warfare, medicine, and politics—all good siddha concerns (1990, p. 38); *Bodhisattvabhūmi*, WOGIHARA 1930–36, p. 359.

81. I do not have in mind Samuel's "shamanic" vs. clerical Buddhism, which primarily refers to esoteric vs. exoteric Buddhist practices (Samuel 1993, pp. 3–10). I find Samuel's formulation unhelpful, in part because esoteric Buddhism adheres to neither the ecological nor the phenomenological aspects of normative shamanism. See Hultkrantz 1978 for a thoughtful discussion.

82. *Vajraśekhara*, To. 480, fol. 149a7–b1; Pe. 113, rgyud, nya 170a3–4; quoted in the *Yogaratnamālā* of Kāṇhapa, *Hevajra Tantra,* Snellgrove 1959, 2:104–105: dṛḍhaṃ sāraṃ asauśīṣyam acchedyābhedyalakṣaṇam | adāhi avināśi ca śūnyatā vajram ucyate ||. This verse is also quoted in Munidatta's commentary to the *Caryāgītikośa*, Kværne 1977, pp. 84–85; in the *Advayavajrasaṃgraha*, 1927, p. 23.23–24; and elsewhere. Although this verse of the *Vajraśekhara* has been considered authoritative, it is notable that it comes in the middle of an extended treatise on definitions of esoteric terminology and even includes an entirely different definition of vajra (To. 480, fol. 149b3–4, Pe. 113, fol. 170a7) in conjunction with amoghavajra and vajrakula, much as this one occurred in conjunction with emptiness. Another, probably earlier definition of vajra in the same vein, which may have informed the *Vajraśekhara*, was the *Vajravidāraṇa-dhāraṇī*, 1937, p. 7. This work was very popular at one time, with commentaries and ritual manuals ranging from those attributed to Buddhaguhya to one ascribed to Virūpa; see To. 2678–2687.

83. *Mañjuśrīnāmasaṃgīti* v.1b [Davidson, ed. and trans. 1981, pp. 18, 49, for related literature].

84. For the eroticization of Vajrasattva, see the longer *Sarvabuddhasamāyoga*, To. 366, fols. 152b2, 153a4, 154b3, etc.

85. *Guhyasamāja* XVIII.52: moho dveṣas tathā rāgaḥ sadā vajre ratiḥ sthitā | upāyas tena buddhānām vajrayānam iti smṛtaṃ ||.

86. *Chin kang ting ching yü ch'ieh shih pa hui chih kuei*, T.869.18.286c12–15; Giebel 1995, pp. 181-2; I thank Kenneth Eastman for sharing this point with me.

87. I discuss this material in Davidson 2002b.

88. For example, *Pañcakrama* II.65 (Śākyamitra's section); *Chin kang ting ching yü ch'ieh shih pa hui chih kuei,* T.869.18.286c; *Prajñāpāramitā-nayaśatapañcāśatkaṭīkā,* To. 2647, fol. 273a3; Jñānamitra's work is included in the early ninth-century *dKar chag ldan dkar ma,* Lalou 1953, no. 523; for a discussion of its importance, see KANAOKA 1966. I discuss the Vilāsavajra references in *Mañjuśrīnāmasaṃgīti,* Davidson 1981, pp. 7–8; see also Davidson forthcoming a. The *Laghusaṃvara Tantra,* To. 368, fols. 216a4, 232a5–6, references several other works: the *Tattvasaṃgraha,* the *"Guhyatantra,"* the *Paramādya,* and the *Vajrabhairava Tantra.* This latter is the most intriguing, yet is not as clear as we might like. For a recent translation of five tantras designated as *"Vajrabhairava,"* see Siklós 1996.

89. For example, *Sarvabuddhasamāyoga,* To. 366, fol. 152b6; *Guhyasamāja* VII.21—27, X.14, XI.3, etc., with XV.15–18, 39–48, being particularly interesting; *Laghusamvara,* To. 368, fols. 224a4–b5, 237a4–7, 239b1–4, etc.

90. *Subāhuparipṛcchā,* To. 805, fols. 138b6–139a4; cf. fols. 130b5–131a4 and *Subāhuparipṛcchā-tantrapiṇḍārtha,* To. 2671, fols. 52b6–53a2.

91. *Subāhuparipṛcchā-tantra-piṇḍārtha,* To. 2671, fols. 52b7–53a2.

92. *Dhyānottarapaṭalakrama,* To. 808, fol. 225a6, has a section on controlling various beings, including women, but there appears nothing sexual in the context, and Buddhaguhya treats it as an unremarkable verse; *Dhyānottara-paṭala-ṭīkā,* To. 2670, fol. 34b2.

93. *Guhyasiddhi,* 1987, pp. 50–59; VIII.33 is particularly interesting in this regard.

94. *Vajrayānamūlāpattiṭīkā-mārgapradīpa,* To. 2488, fol. 222a4; this material is translated and discussed in chapter 7.

95. *Jñānasiddhi* XVII.9cd: dharmarājyābhiṣekāgram abhiṣekaṃ niruttaram. Similarly, the *Vajramālābhidhāna-mahāyoga-tantra,* To. 445, fol. 212b2–4.

96. See *Sekatānvayasaṃgraha,* in *Advayavajrasaṃgraha,* 1927, pp. 36–39; To. 2243, fols. 122b4–124b7. Theoretical and synthetic texts dealing with consecration surviving in Tibetan are found in several places in the sDe-dge canon, To. 2243–2244, 2252–2253, 2470, 2472–2477. An exception is *Guhyasiddhi* Ch. III.

97. *Abhiṣekanirukti,* To. 2476, vol. zi, fols. 159b4–168b7; esp. fol. 167a1; cf. *Guhyasiddhi* III.

98. *Bodhipathapradīpa,* Eimer 1978; see also Davidson, trans. 1995.

99. *Subāhuparipṛcchā,* To. 805, fol. 137b2–4; T.895b7–17. In the explanation, I follow the only extensive commentary, the *'Phags pa dpung bzangs kyis zhus ba'i rgyud kyi tshig gi don bshad pa'i brjed byang,* To. 2672. We know almost nothing about this valuable commentary, either its author or its translator, if it was translated. Bu-ston's *bsTan-'gyur* catalogue, the *bsTan 'gyur gyi dkar chag yid bzhin nor bu dbang gi rgyal po'i phreng ba,* p. 520.7, includes the commentary but provides no more information than the title.

100. Buddhaguhya certainly recognizes other siddhis, especially the sword accomplishment; see *Dhyānottara-paṭala-ṭīkā,* To. 2670, fol. 30b5, 37b7; in the for-

mer place he references the *Sarvatathāgatatattvasaṃgraha* and the *Vajraśekhara* as the sources. See also *Vairocanābhisambodhitantrapiṇḍārtha*, To. 2662, fol. 64a7.

101. *Sādhanamālā*, 1925, 2:350; see Lessing and Wayman 1968, pp. 220–221 n; *Pradīpodyotana*, Chakravarti 1984, p. 194; sometimes, as in the latter case, we see "pill manufacture" *gulika* in the place of passing through the earth as a form of siddhi.

102. See the different list produced in Siklós 1996, p. 28n7.

103. *Kṛṣṇayamāri-tantra* IV.45, IX.4 (seeds); *Samputa*, To. 381, fols. 121b5, 128a6; *Saṃvarodaya-tantra* X.36, XXVII.10–14; *Mahākāla-tantra*, in Stablein 1976, pp. 169, 267, 275–277; *Vajramahābhairava-tantra*, in Siklós 1996, p. 83; *Guhyasamāja* XV.81.

104. Harner 1973, pp. 125–147.

105. Sanderson 1994, pp. 94–95; Sanderson (2001) does not bring the issue of the Kāpālikas into the discussion, but simply refers to the proposed sources as Vidyāpīṭha and Kaula (including Krama). Sanderson is certainly to be congratulated for the discovery of the intertextuality between specific works, but we may wonder whether there is a curious theology of scripture that informs his proposals. He does not seem to question the category construction of "Vidyāpīṭha tantras," although the emergence of texts would seem necessarily to predate the category, and Sanderson appears to presume that the category formed as a whole. While it is seldom that a received body of texts reflects no influence at all, this seems to be Sanderson's ultimate position on the Vidyāpīṭha Śaiva scriptures. There is even a prima facie argument *against* the proposed direction of the borrowing, since Sanderson (2001, pp. 44–47) takes as prototypical that a ungrammatical verse of the *Laghusaṃvara* can only be from the *Picumata*, which provides a good Sanskrit reading. Yet this method apparently contradicts the well-known textual procedure of assuming the difficult reading to be the preferred one, summed up by Johann Albrecht Bengel in his famous 1734 dictum, "to the easier reading, the harder is to be preferred" *(proclivi scriptioni praestat ardua)*. As Baird (1992, p. 73) notes, "Behind this principle is the assumption that scribes tend to change (or corrupt) a text in order to make it more readable." As will be clear in chapter 6, the nature of Buddhist tantric Sanskrit must be assessed in the environment of regional Sanskrits, and its later "improvement" was a consistent theme in the Buddhist (and we might suppose Śaiva) context. This direction accords well with the understanding of Goudriaan and Gupta (1981, p. 29), who point out that the later Śaiva and Śākta tantras demonstrate better Sanskrit. Even then, decisions about textual borrowing are best made case by case, rather than corpus by corpus, and I believe that a reciprocal appropriation model (allowing for oral recitation, partial memorization, ritual imitation, individual conversion, etc.) will prove the most fruitful. It is instructive that, while Bühnemann accepts aspects of Sanderson's model, she also finds Buddhist influences within Śaiva scriptures (1999, 2000). I thank Fred Smith for drawing my attention to Sanderson's 2001 article and providing me with a copy.

106. The sources of this version of the myth are discussed in Davidson 1991 and Stein 1995.

107. *Kubjikāmatatantra*, "Introduction," in Goudriaan and Schoterman 1988, pp. 111–112; White 1996, pp. 110–113; Lorenzen 1972, pp. 51–52; the art historical circumstances are explored in Shaw 1997, although his command of the textual material is weak.

108. *Mālatīmādhava* I.15–16, V.1–6, V.21-VI.2, VIII.8, IX.1–7, 41–54, X.16–25.

109. This date is found in the relatively early (800 C.E.) catalogue of Yüan-chao, the *Chen yüan hsin ting shih chiao mu lu*, T.2157.55.974c3; Strickmann has emphasized certain aspects of the text that appear more peripheral than central (1996, pp. 221–231); cf. Lalou 1955.

110. The section actually begins in chapter 6 and continues through chapter 7; *Subāhuparipṛcchā*, To. 805, fols. 129a4–131b2; Subhakarasiṃha's translation obscures the significance, T.895.18.726c29–728a14.

111. Granoff speculates that the mention of Nīlapaṭas (evidently the same as nīlāmbara) by Jayantabhaṭṭa's *Nyāyamañjarī* may identify Jainas (1986–92, p. 297 n), but Ruegg argues for their Buddhist character (1981, pp. 223–224), which the *Subāhuparipṛcchā* appears to support. Albīrūnī, writing about 1030 C.E., notes that Brahmans were forbidden to wear or touch the color blue, and this may be related to the "blue-clad" behavior; Sachau 1910, 2:132. See also Murthy 1987.

112. Chapter 5 of *Subāhuparipṛcchā* is particularly important in this regard: To. 805, fol. 125a4–127b3; T.895.18.725a20–726a18; the term "siddhi" is translated sometimes as *ch'eng-chiu* and other times as *hsi-ti*.

113. *Subāhuparipṛcchā*, To. 805, fol. 123a3: T. 895.18.723a28; compare *Guhyasamāja* XIV.60, which details a similar list of materials to be used in the manufacture of ritual daggers *(kīla)*.

114. *Chin kang ting ching yü ch'ieh shih pa hui chih kuei;* T. 869.18.286c9–16.

115. *Prajñāpāramitā-nayaśatapañcāśatkaṭīkā,* To. 2647, fol. 273a3; as pointed out by KANAOKA 1966, p. 467, Jñānamitra's work is included in the early ninth-century *dKar chag ldan dkar ma,* Lalou 1953, no. 523.

116. KANEKO 1982, no. 207; mTshams-brag manuscript, vol. tsha, fols. 1b1–26a7.

117. A comparison of the texts shows many sections, included within differing chapters, that indicate a common basis for the Tibetan translations of those verses or sections; cf., especially, the maṇḍala arrangement and justification found in the second chapter of the shorter recension, fols. 7b4–12a7, against virtually the same material found in chapter 5 of To. 366, fols. 155b3–159a4. The chapter order and naming, though, is completely different, and we might suspect an earlier version that had no chapter divisions in the manner of the received versions. The prima facie supposition that the shorter text is earlier may be called into question by the presence of rather advanced terminology in the text, e.g., the four kinds of bliss, fol. 3a6. The shorter text, while one-third to one-half the size of the longer version, has eleven chapters (kalpa), whereas To. 366 has ten. *Sarvabuddhasamāyo-*

ga-ḍākinīmāyā-sambara-tantrārthodaraṭīkā, To. 1659, fols. 245a5–248b3, attributed to Indranāla, discusses the question of its preaching and provides contents for both this and its *Uttarottaratantra.* Similarly, the *Suratavajra commentary, *Sarvabuddhasamāyoga-ḍākinīmāyā-sambara-vṛtti-samayogālaṃkāra,* To. 1660, fol. 389 b, discusses the recensions available to him.

118. See KANEKO 1982, nos. 206 (= To. 366) and 207; both versions are included in mTshams-brag, vol. tsha; To. 366 is found in mTshams-brag manuscript, tsha, fols. 58b3–126b3.

119. mTshams-brag, vol. tsha, fols. 26a6–7, represents the shorter text to be the translation of Paṇḍita [?Buddha-] Guhya and 'Brog-mi dPal gyi ye-shes; fol. 126b1 represents the longer text to be the translation of Vajrahāsa and rMa Rin-chen-mchog. The *Sarvabuddhasamāyoga* is not mentioned in the *dKar chag ldan mkhar ma* (Lalou 1953), yet it is quoted in the *bSam gtan mig sgron* of gNubs-chen, pp. 204.6–205.2 and appears in the list of Devaputra as *Kāyatantrasarvabuddhasamayoga;* see Hackin 1924, p. 6; it is mentioned in *Pañcakrama* II.65. It seems to be referenced by Buddhaguhya as well; see chapter 4, n. 137, above.

120. Sanderson 1988. Goudriaan and Gupta (1981, p. 45) believe the *Jayarathayāmala* to be later than Sanderson's chronology allows. Sanderson's informative and detailed discussion (2001, pp. 2–18) concludes: "It is quite possible that by the seventh century most of the literature available to Śaiva scholars in the tenth was already in existence. But it is not until the beginning of the ninth that we have firm evidence of specific texts." We may want to resist, though, the movement from possibility to probability without further evidence.

121. Majumdar 1953, no. 152, pp. 362–382; Cœdès and Dupont 1943–46; Chakravarti 1978 is a two-volume work dedicated to the inscription.

122. For example, Dyczkowski 1988, p. 36; Sanderson 2001, p. 8n; Goudriaan and Gupta 1981, 21.

123. Majumdar 1953, no. 54, pp. 57–60; Chakravarti 1978, 1:127.

124. Majumdar 1953, p. 60, v. 32.

125. Chakravarti 1978, 1:147 n81.

126. *Abhinavagupta's* sources have been detailed by Rastogi 1987, appendices 1, 4, 5, and 9. Sanderson 2001 provides excellent data.

127. For a discussion of this passage, see Sanderson 2001, pp. 10–13, which corrects my earlier *Mañjuśrīnāmasaṃgīti,* Davidson 1981, p. 8n21.

128. *Kālikāpurāṇa* 59.71,77; 60.1, 10, and so on throughout chapters 60, 61, 63, 64, etc.

129. Gross 1992, pp. 127–131.

130. See Huber 1990 for some problems of geography. Mayer (1998, p. 280) has questioned my assertion that we have little validation that these twenty-four sites were specifically Śaiva (1991), but has presented no evidence beyond mythology for such an affirmation.

131. Lorenzen 1972, pp. 21–22; idem 1989; *Bṛhatkathāślokasaṃgraha,* 21.144, 22.228; *Kālikā-purāṇa*, chapter 35.

132. *Bṛhatkathāślokasaṃgraha,* 21.144; Lorenzen 1972, pp. 50–52.

133. Sircar 1948, passim; *Kubjikāmatatantra*, "Introduction," in Goudriaan and Schoterman 1988, pp. 123–126; *Ṣaṭsāhasra Saṃhitā*, Schoterman 1982, pp. 148–50, to name but a few.

134. KUWAYAMA 1991, pp. 269–275.

135. *Hevajra Tantra*, I.vii.12.

136. *Kālikā-purāṇa,* 38.99–161; 64.36.

137. *Ta t'ang hsi yü chi*, T.2087.51.932a14–23 [Beal 1869, 2:233]; Beal observes, "I am disposed, therefore, to think that he did not go farther south than Kanchi. In this case the subsequent account he gives us of Malakûṭa, Mount Malaya, and Potaraka (Potalaka), is derived from hearsay" (2:231n). A more reliable description is the pilgrimage guide found in *Po ta lar 'gro ba'i lam yig*, To. 3756, which mentions its placement in the Malaya Mts., fol. 101a2; this is in accord with v. 7c of the *Potalakāṣṭaka*: malayagiricandanadhūparatim. Cf. Tucci 1949, 2.552–553.

138. *Kāvyamīmāṃsā*, Parashar 2000, pp. 261–262.

139. Chattopadhyaya 1994, p. 61. For Abu's sites, Mehta 1970. According to Suryavanshi 1962, p. 12, the area around Mt. Arbuda was called Abhiradeśa at one time.

140. *Nāṭyaśāstra,* XVII.63

141. Mirashi 1955, 1:233.

142. *Kṛtyakalpataru, Tīrthavivecanakandam,* p. 254.

143. Rocher 1986, pp. 229, 234.

144. McKay 1998, pp. 170–171.

145. Sircar 1948, p. 32.

146. *Pīṭhādinirṇaya,* To. 1606, especially ff. 131a forward.

147. *Pīṭhādinirṇaya,* To. 1606, fol. 132a7-b1: de ci ltar mi 'gal zhe na | gnas dang nye ba'i zhing dag tsha grang dang dngos po dang dngos med bzhin du phan tshun 'gal ba ni ma yin te | gcig la yang ming sna tshogs ji ltar mi 'gal zhes so | 'dir na ga ra dang | pā ṭa li pu ṭa dang | mā la wa sogs gsum ni nye ba'i zhing du gsungs so |. Nagara was considered by Sircar (1971, p. 206) the ancient capital of the region; evidently it was given the name Pāṭaliputa at this time as well.

148. *Mahāmāyūrīvidyārājñī,* SHŪYO 1972, pp. 10–58; these materials were first explored by Lévi 1915.

149. *Mañjuśrīmūlakalpa*, chapter 30 of the received text, Sastri 1920, pp. 325–326; To. 543, fols. 230b7–233a2; T.1191.20.898a18-c24. It is interesting that the Chinese translation does not identify either Cīna or Mahācīna with China, but renders them phonetically instead.

150. *Pāśupatasūtra,* chapter 5, is a lengthy description of Śiva's names; see the introduction to the *Kauṇḍinya-bhāṣya*, in *Pāśupatasūtra,* Sastri 1940, pp. 109–110, for the context.

151. *Kālikā-purāṇa,* 35.10–11; 46.4–10,

152. *Kālikā-purāṇa,* 50.59–147.

153. Shafer 1954, pp. 124–125.

154. This is the opinion of Guha (1991, pp. 2–28); cf. p. 21, where he uses this ethnonym to designation several different tribes, including the Boro, Kachari, Mech, Rabha, Dimasa, Hojai, Hajong, Lalung, Tipra Goro, and probably Chutiyas and Morans.

155. *Subāhuparipṛcchā,* To. 805, fol. 118b6; T.895.18.720a9.

156. *Kālikā-purāṇa,* 63.135–137b: (with minor emendations) śmaśānaṃ herukākhyaṃ ca raktavarṇaṃ bhayaṅkaraṃ | asicarmadharaṃ raudraṃ bhuñjānaṃ manujāmiṣam || tisṛbhir muṇḍamālābhir galadraktābhī rājitam | agninirdagdhavigaladdantapretoparisthitam || pūjayec cintanenaiva śastravāhanabhūṣaṇam |. The text also uses the designation Heruka for a *liṅgam* nearby; *Kālikā-purāṇa,* 67.69, 79.172.

157. *Sarvabuddhasamāyoga,* To. 366. fols. 167a5–168a3, 167a6, 171a6–172b2, 181a6–181b3, 187a1, 188b7–189a1; similarly the shorter *Sarvabuddhasamāyoga,* fols. 6a3–6b3.

158. *Ṛgveda* 1.51.6, 1.59.6, 6.47.21; studied by Parpola 1988, pp. 215, 261-2.

159. *Ṛgveda* 6.31.4, 7.99.5.

160. *Ṛgveda* 4.30.14, 6.26.5.

161. *Arthaśāstra* XIV.3.19.

162. *Sarvabuddhasamāyoga,* To. 366, fol. 151b6–7.

163. Studied by Goudriaan 1973, and in his introduction to the edition and translation of the *Vīṇāśikhatantra,* pp. 18–23; Tumburu also occurs in the *Mañjuśrīmūlakalpa,* references in Goudriaan 1973, p. 85.

164. *Vīṇāśikhatantra* vv. 323–363; the relationship of this section to *Agni Purāṇa* 348 or other sources has yet to be explored. For the Buddhist *ekākṣara* ideology and practices, see Przyluski 1923, p. 305, who specifies T. 956, 1181–82; this idea became reaffirmed in *Mañjuśrīmūlakalpa,* chapters 9, 14, 25–27 (Sastri 1920, pp. 81–84, 129–144, 284–310) and was extended in the 709 C.E. translation of Bodhiruci, *I tsu fo ting lun wang ching* T. 951. The notion of a unique syllable was further the topic of T. 950, 953–958, all of which concern the practice and all were translated from the early to mid-eighth century.

165. *Rudrayāmala,* chapters 37–40, pp. 372–394; Goudriaan and Gupta 1981, p. 87; this material from different sources has been studied in Bharati 1965, pp. 66–79, 238–244.

166. The first thirty chapters of the *Kālikā-purāṇa* are almost exclusively Vaiṣṇava, with a heavy emphasis on the Varāha incarnation; the *Vaiṣṇavītantra* is referenced in *Kālikā-purāṇa* 59.37, 59.68, 60.5, 61.36, and chapters 63, 64 passim, etc.

167. *Sādhanamālā,* "Introduction," in Bhattacharya 1925, 2:cxi–ii; Bhattacharya 1930; the *Rudrayāmala* section is chapter 17 of the received text *Rudrayāmala,* Yogatantra Department 1980, pp. 169–183. For a somewhat different approach to this issue, see Bühnemann 1999, pp. 303 ff., and 2000.

168. *Gorakṣasiddhāntasaṅgraha*, Pāṇḍeya 1973, p. 16: kāpāliko mārgaḥ kim arthaṃ prakaṭīkṛtaḥ ? ity apekṣayayāha viṣṇoś caturviṃśatisaṅkhyākā avatārā jātās te ca kāryānte madonmattā jātāḥ | katham ? yathā 'nte tiryagyonayo jantavaḥ krīḍāḥ kurvanti tathā varāho nṛsiṃhaś cetyādayo bhūdāraṇavanyabhayadānādikaraṇe pravṛttāḥ | puragrāmāditāḍanaṃ keṣāñcit samudrapāto 'pi | tatrāpi kṛṣṇena vyabhicāribhāvo viśeṣeṇa dhṛtaḥ | paraśurāmeṇaikakṣatriyadoṣeṇānekeṣāṃ kṣatriyāṇāṃ nāśaḥ kṛta ityādi viruddhācāropari nāthena kopaṃ kṛtvā caturviṃśatyavatāropari caturviṃśati kāpālikarūpāṇi dhṛtāni | dhṛtvā ca caturviṃśatyavatāraiḥ saha samaraṃ kṛtam | tatra sarveṣām avatārāṇāṃ kapālāni chinnāni kṛtāni | svakarais tāni dhṛtāni | tena kāpālikā jātāḥ |.

169. *Ṣaṭsāhasra Saṃhitā*, Schoterman 1982, pp. 37–38.

170. Dyczkowski 1988, p. 102.

171. *Mūlasarvāstivāda Vinaya*, Gnoli 1977, 1:153, 217–229; 2:295–297.

172. To. 2393: *Tithika tsandalika* = **Tīrthikacāṇḍālika*, fols. 22b7–23a3: rgya gar skad du | ti thi ka tsaṇḍālī ka nā ma | bod skad du | mu stegs kyi gtum mo zhes bya ba | byang chub sems dpa' thal skud can la phyag 'tshal lo | bud med gnas ni dbu rgyan ma | rigs ni gtum mo'i rigs gyur pa | srid pa gsum yang sreg par byed | me lce nam mkhar khyab par byed | a tsin dpal ni gar byed 'gyur | nam mkhar rnge'u chung sa la rnge'u chung brdung | rdo rje me yis rgya mtsho skems | nyi zla gnyis kyang skyabs su gzhug | gar byed dpal gyi a tsin thod pa can | nam mkhar rnge'u chung sa la rnge'u chung brdung | lha dang lha min mi rnams dang | dbang phyug u ma la sogs pa | thams cad ye shes me yis bsregs | gar byed dpal gyi a tsin thod pa can | nam mkhar rnge'u chung sa la rnge'u chung brdung | rnal 'byor ma ni khrid byas nas | mgon po'i gnas su 'jug par byed | 'di lta'i dkyil 'khor glu ru blangs | gar byed dpal ni a tsin thod pa can | nam mkhar rnge'u chung sa la rnge'u chung brdung | mu stegs kyi gtum mo zhes bya ba slob dpon a tsintas mdzad pa rdzogs so ||. The translation presumes that the "little drum" (rnge'u chung) is a ḍamaruka, the drum used by Śaivas and tantric Buddhists, as well as by wandering storytellers and monkey trainers.

173. See note 43 above for references.

174. *Pāśupatasūtra*, Sastri 1940, p. 83; Ingalls 1962, p. 289.

175. Ibid.: atra puruṣākhyaḥ pretaḥ | na mṛtākhyaḥ | kasmāt | ācaraṇopadeśāt | vad iti kiñcidupamā | unmattasadṛśadaridrapuruṣenâtimaladigdhāṅgena rūḍhaśmaśrunakharomadhāriṇā sarvasaṁskāravarjitena bhavitavyam | ato varṇāśramavyucchedo vairāgyotsāhaś ca jāyate | prayojananiṣpattiś ca bhavati avamānādi |. I have followed Ingalls' suggestion (1962, p. 289n19) in reading this passage, which he partially translated.

176. Bhandarkar 1908; *Liṅgapurāṇa* XXIV.124–133, quoted in ibid., p. 154.

177. *Svacchandatantra* XIII.36–38; *Saṃnyāsa-Upaniṣad*, Schrader 1912, p. 154: avyaktaliṅgo 'vyaktācāro bālonmattapiśācavad.

178. Olivelle 1992, pp. 105–112.

179. *Saṃnyāsa-Upaniṣad,* Schrader 1912, pp. 99–102. Note that the description there and in the *Nāradaparivrājakopaniṣad* is exactly the same, with the exception that the *Āśramopaniṣad* leaves "like a demon" (piśācavat) out of the description.

180. Bharati 1970, p. 153.

181. Freed and Freed 1993; it is impossible to praise this study too highly; see also Stanley 1988.

182. Schopen 1992, pp. 8–11.

183. Although Teiser mentions the "interplay between 'Indian' and 'Chinese' aspects in the religion of medieval China" (1988, pp. 15–25), his otherwise excellent treatment takes as a given that it is principally a Chinese phenomenon, discussed under Chinese rubrics, and located primarily in Chinese spatial and temporal domains. By the same token, Maudgalyāyana is only identified by his Indian name a few times; for most of the text, he is "Mu-lien," the Chinese rendering of his very Indian monastic identity. This is a curious reading of a quintessentially Indian concern, which has not received in secondary literature the place it commands in Indian sources.

184. For example, *Vajrapāṇyabhiṣeka-tantra,* To. 496, fols. 100a4–102a2; *Subāhuparipṛcchā,* To. 805, fols. 130a3–132b3.

185. *Subhāṣita-Saṃgraha,* 1904, p. 37 (italics added):
unmattarūpam āsthāya maunībhūtvā samāhitaḥ |
svādhidaivatayogena paryaṭeta piśācavat ||
bhaikṣaparyaṭanārthāya na pātraṃ saṃgrahed vratī |
bhuktojjhitaṃ tu saṃgṛhya rathyākarparamallakaṃ ||
tatraiva paryaṭeta bhikṣāṃ yatamānas tu bhakṣayet |
bhakṣayitvā tu tat tasmiṃs tṛptas tatraiva tat tyajet ||
kaupīnaṃ tu tato dhāryaṃ sphuṭitaṃ jarjarīkṛtaṃ |
digambaro 'thavā bhūtvā paryaṭeta yathecchayā ||
Bendall reads "yatamānam" in the third verse above. The section appears extracted from *Guhyasiddhi* VI.13, 33–35, VII.6.

186. *Amoghapāśahṛdayadhāraṇī,* Meisezahl 1962, p. 322: mahāpaśupativeśadhara (describing Avalokiteśvara); cf. Regamey 1971.

187. *rGyud kyi mngon par rtogs pa rin po che'i ljon shing, SKB* III.48.4.2–49.49.2.3.

188. *Pāśupatasūtra* I.8: hasitagītanṛttaḍuṃḍuṃkāranamaskārajapyopahāreṇopatiṣṭhet |; similar statements in Madhava; cf. Hara 1958, pp. 26–27, and his references to the *Gaṇakārikā* and commentary.

189. Kauṇḍinya's commentary to *Pāśupatasūtra* I.8, p. 13.14–17.

190. Lorenzen 1972, p. 127.

191. *Sarvabuddhasamāyoga,* To. 366, fol. 163b2: khams gsum pa yi rgyal srid che | bdag rtul phod pas mnan nas ni | 'gro ba thams cad rab 'joms par | rta yi gar gyis ston par byed |.

192. *Sarvabuddhasamāyoga,* To. 366, fols. 170b7–171a1: phyag rgya shes pa 'di dag gi | sangs rgyas sprul pa'i glu mchog ni | 'grub par 'gyur ba byed pa'i mchog | las rnams thams cad rab sgrub pa | slong bar byed pa brtan sgrub pa | de bzhin sna tshogs rgyas pa dag | drug pa'i dbyangs kyi glu blangs nas | de ba ta yi glu blang ngo |.

193. Indraji 1881, p. 344; translation his.

194. A recent example is Sharma 1996, p. 105.

195. See the excellent study of this process in Orissa in the work of Eschmann et al. 1978.

196. The antiquity of this practice is evident from its statement as required in *Kālikā-purāṇa* 38.99–161; 64.36.

197. It is dismaying to see that the aggressive activity of the Vishwa Hindu Parishad is characterized as "service" by an anthropologist, who further identifies tribal peoples in Cachar as "tantric" (Danda 1994); this article is a particularly good example of the myopia of Hindu nationalism.

198. *Mahābhārata* 12.59.103; cf. Shafer 1954, p. 18. Sharma's recent discussion (2001, pp. 235–265) is also not well informed on tribal ethnography or languages. See Nath 2001 for a more thoughtful presentation.

199. *Arthaśāstra* 8.4.41–43.

200. *Daśabhūmika*, pp. 28.8, 29.5.

201. *Kirātārjunīye*, Bahadur 1972.

202. *Gaüḍavaho* 336.

203. Elwin also argues for a change in attitude toward tribals in early medieval Sanskrit literature (1955, pp. 17–19).

204. Fleet 1888, p. 293.

205. For example, *Guhyasamāja-tantra* XII.2, 65; *Pradīpodyotana*, Chakravarti 1984, p. 107; cf. the *Kṛṣṇayamāri* quotation at the head of the chapter.

206. For example, *Yogaratnamālā*, in *Hevajra Tantra*, Snellgrove 1959, 2:121; *Mahāmudrā-tilaka*, To. 420, fol. 76a3; *Sampuṭa-tilaka*, To. 382, fol. 159a4. Cf. *Śrī Hevajrapañjikā Muktāvalī*, Tripathi and Negi 2001, p. 168.

207. Shafer tries to derive the term "mleccha" from a Tibeto-Burman word (1954, p. 23), but I find his linguistic analysis unsuccessful; his literary references, though, indicate that the author of one section of the *Mahābhārata* he references applied it to the inhabitants of the Punjab and Bengal (ibid., p. 22). *Mahābhārata* 12.59.103 identifies mlecchas as living in the Vindhyā mountains, which during this period meant much of the area of Maharastra and Madhya Pradesh. Compare the use of "mlecchāṭavī" as a single referent in *Arthaśāstra* 7.10.16. See also Shafer's discussion of other origin myths for mlecchas in the *Mahābhārata;* Shafer 1954, pp. 18–24.

208. I have dealt with the question of *sahaja* in some detail in Davidson 2002b.

209. This Munda language–speaking tribe has currently several hundred thousand members and has been described by both Elwin (1955) and Vitebsky (1992).

210. *Caryāgītikośa,* verse 28 [Kværne 1977, pp. 181–188; Sen 1977, p. 138]:

ūcā ūcā pābata tahñ basaï sabarī bālī |
moraṅgi pīccha parahiṇa sabarī gībata guñjarī mālī ||
umata sabaro pāgala sabaro mā kara gulī guhāḍā |
tohauri ṇia ghariṇī ṇāme sahaja sundarī ||
ṇāṇā tarubara maülila re gaaṇata lāgelī dālī |
ekelī sabarī e baṇa hiṇḍaï karṇa kuṇḍala bajra dhārī ||
tia dhāu khāṭa paṛilā sabaro mahāsukhe seji chāilī |
sabaro bhujaṅga nairāmaṇi dārī pemha rāti pohāilī ||
hia tābolā mahāsuhe kāpura khāi |
suna nairāmaṇi kaṇṭhe laïā mahāsuhe rāti pohāi ||
gurubāka puñcaā bindha ṇia maṇe bānē |
eke śara sandhāṇē bindhaha bindhaha parama ṇibānē ||
umata sabaro garuā roṣe |
giribara sihara sandhi païsante sabaro loṛiba kaïse ||

211. *Kāṇhapādasya dohākoṣa,* no. 25 [Bagchi 1935, p. 133; Shahidullah 1928, pp. 79–80]; baragiri śihara uttuṅga muṇi savare jahiṃ kia bāsa | naü laṃghia pañcāṇaṇehī karibara dūria āsa ||. This verse is also quoted by Munidatta, *Caryāgītikośa,* Kværne 1977, p. 98. My interpretation of the difficult last part is drawn from the commentary of Amitābha, *Śrī-Kṛṣṇavajrapādadohakoṣaṭīkā,* To. 2302, fols. 240b5–241a1.

212. *Kāṇhapādasya dohākoṣa,* Bagchi 1935, commentary to no. 25, p. 133.

213. Tucci 1930, pp. 153–154; Lévi 1930; this material has been studied (from a somewhat different perspective) by Tatz (1987, 1988). A Śabarī ascetic woman is represented in the *Rāmāyana*; cf. Lutgendorf 2001.

214. *mKhas grub khyung po rnal 'byor gyi rnam thar,* 1996, pp. 20–21.

215. *Cittaguhyagambhīrārthagīti,* fol. 83a1. The chronology is defined by Pha-dam-pa's primary translator, Zha-ma lo-tsā-ba Chos kyi rgyal-po (1069–1144).

216. That is, Khyung-po rnal-'byor; for the hagiography of this Śavaripa, see Stearns 1996, pp. 139–141.

217. *Śūnyatādṛṣṭi,* To. 2426, fols. 40a3—40b1: rgya gar skad du | shū nya tā dṛi ṣhṭi nā ma | bod skad du | stong pa nyid kyi lta ba zhes bya ba | spyan ras gzigs dbang phyug la phyag 'tshal lo |

sems kyi rtog rtse chos nyid ni | sa bon nam mkha'i dbyings su smos | bdag med gzhon nus mgul nas 'khyud | gnyid sad byed pa nyid du gnas | spongs shig dor shig bdag smongs so | kye ho bcings ba ma lus pa | sha ba ri bde chen por rol | stong pa'i btsun mo 'khyud byas te | kye ho lus ngag sems smin te | thams cad dus su brtags pa yis | sha ba ri ni myos par 'gyur | dga' ba'i rnam pa thams cad du | sha ba ri ni gnyid log nas | gnyid ni nam mkha'i dbyings su log | kye ho bdag gi de nyid ni | sa bon nam mkhar mnyam par smos | 'bras bu nam mkhar skar chen shar | spongs shig dor shig bdag smongs so | srid pa'i bcings ba'i glang chen bsad |

dbang po lnga yi gtor ma byas | bdag gi sdug bsngal thams cad spangs | spongs shig dor shig bdag rmongs so | nyin mtshan rtag tu gnyid med par | rang gi sems la bya ra byas | de nas skye pa bud med ni | gcig tu dben par song ste gnas | gtso bo 'jig rten mgon pa smra | spongs shig dor shig bdag smongs so | stong pa'i bt-sun mo 'khyud byas te | sha ba ri bde chen por gnas | stong pa nyid kyi lta ba zhes bya ba slob dpon sha ba ris mdzad pa rdzogs so ||

218. Russell 1916, 4:503–504; see also Elwin (1955, pp. 14–33) for a discussion of the relation of the current Saora to the Śabara of literature.

219. *Kṛṣṇayamāri-tantra* XV.1–19, Rinpoche and Dvivedi 1992, pp. 114–117. See also *Sādhanamālā*, 1925, 1: 177, 217, 245–9, 252–3, 250, 308–310. To. 571 (= To. 990, T. 1264), 736 (= To. 995, T. 1384), 3206, 3245, 3360, 3365, 3508, 3509, 3511–13, 3538, 3539, 3540. There are undoubtedly more rituals that might be located in the various tantras, but this list provides a rough idea of the extent of the literature.

220. Kumāracandra's commentary adds that the snake is in her (upper) right hand, with a sword and knife in the other two; in the left three hands are a wheel, a lotus and a skullcap.

221. In *Kṛṣṇayamāri* XV.4b, sphoṭā is translated by the Tibetan translators as a chain, lcags sgrogs, roughly equivalent to the name of the deity carrying it, śṛkhala.

222. *Kṛṣṇayamāri* XV.1–6:

athātaḥ sampravakṣyāmi āryajāṅgulisādhanam |
yena bhāvitamātreṇa jalasyopari caṅkramet ||
trimukhāṃ ṣaḍbhujāṃ pītāṃ phūḥkārabījasaṃbhavām |
sarpahastāṃ mahārūpāṃ mayūravāhanapriyām ||
pūrvato māyūrīṃ likhed dakṣiṇe bhṛkuṭīṃ tathā |
paścime parṇaśabarīm uttare vajraśṛṅkhalām ||
pakṣaṃ kamaṇḍaluṃ śākhāṃ sphoṭāṃ cāpi vibhāvayet |
pītaṃ raktaṃ tathā śyāmaṃ nīlaṃ varṇaprabhedataḥ ||
etā vibhāvayet prājño mantraṃ caiva japet tataḥ | oṃ phūḥ jaḥ ||
mudgarādīn nyased dvāre puṣpādīn koṇake nyaset |
āryajāṅguliyogena jalam ākramyate sadā ||

For the Chinese use of Jāṅguli spells, see Strickmann 2002, pp. 151–156; I thank James Robson for drawing my attention to this passage.

223. Shafer 1954, p. 139.

224. Eschmann et al. 1978, pp. 99–117.

225. Elwin 1955, p. 298.

226. Eschmann et al. 1978, pp. 79–94.

227. *Gaüdavaho* vv. 319–338.

228. *Hevajra Tantra* I.i.31: caṇḍālī jvalitā nābhau | dahati pañcatathāgatān ||
dahati ca locanādīḥ | dagdhe 'haṃ sravate śaśī ||. See Ratnākaraśānti's *Śrī Hevajrapañjikā Muktāvalī*, Tripathi and Negi 2001, pp. 27–28, for an exegesis to this verse.

6. SIDDHAS, LITERATURE, AND LANGUAGE

1. *Śrī-Guhyasamājatantra-nidāna-gurūpadeśana-vyākhyāna*, fol. 90b6–91a1.

2. Ray 1994, pp. 407–410; on p. 410, Ray mentions that Vajrayāna was a forest tradition.

3. Dimock 1966, pp. 95–96.

4. Barrow 1893, pp. 211–212.

5. Gross 1992, pp. 124–135; on p. 135, he mentions the scarcity of jungle sadhus, but attributes their rarity to a decline of habitat. I propose that they were probably always relatively few.

6. On the social composition and role of the sūta, see Rocher 1986, pp. 53–59.

7. *Man ngag gces pa btus pa* contains forty-nine short instructions, although one is by Sa-skya Paṇḍita, a Tibetan; the *Phyag rgya chen po gces pa btus pa'i man ngag* is based on *Man ngag gces pa btus pa* and contains thirty-two short instructions. We also find compendia demonstrating this kind of direction, especially one attributed to an Indian siddha, Pha-dam-pa sangs-rgyas Kamalaśīla. This is the five-volume *Zhi byed snyan rgyud zab byed ma* (Aziz 1979); in it the first and some of the second volumes retain instructions attributed to the Indian saint.

8. These scriptures are found in the Tibetan canon, To. 383–411, 413–415; these thirty-two tantras total about seventy-seven folia.

9. Both of the lengthy *Ḍākārṇava* and the *Vajraḍāka* contain fifty chapters in 110–125 folia in their Tibetan translations.

10. Because of its anomalous position in esoteric literature, the *Kālacakra* and related literature are given less consideration than its importance in Tibet and its recent popularity seem to require.

11. *Guhyasamāja* discussion following XVII.71 (Matsunaga 1978, pp. 108–109).

12. See, for example, the *Guhyasamāja* XVIII.79, 125, 175, Matsunaga 1978.

13. *Hevajra Tantra*, Snellgrove 1959, II.ii.51. Ratnākaraśānti's *Śrī Hevajrapañjikā muktāvalī*, Tripathi and Negi 2001, p. 150, defines the Buddhist heretic as one who accepts the Buddha as teacher but despises the Vajrayāna, which is the essence of his teaching: buddhasya tīrthikā buddhatīrthikāḥ | kathaṃ te buddhasya? buddhasyaiva śāstur abhyupagamāt | kathaṃ tīrthikāḥ? buddhaśāsanasāre 'pi vajrayāne pradveṣāt ||

14. ime dharmāḥ sūtre 'vataranti vinaye saṃdṛśyante dharmatāñ ca na vilomayanti |. For references on this formula, see Davidson 1990, pp. 300–301.

15. *Sarvabuddhasamāyoga*, To. 366, fol. 151b.3: bud med kun gyi sgyu ma'i rgya | 'di ni gnyis med theg pa'i mchog |.

16. *Divyāvadāna*, Vaidya 1959, p. 258.

17. Walleser (1922) has collected and translated the sources.

18. Harrison 1978; Gómez 1995.

19. *Mattavilāsaprahasana*, Lockwood and Bhat 1981, pp. 42–45.

20. *Prajñāpāramitā-nayaśatapañcāśatkaṭīkā*, To. 2647, fols. 272b7–273b2 (with minor emendations): gsung rab 'di'i lo rgyus bshad na | sngon sangs rgyas mi yul na lo brgyad cu bzhugs pa'i tshe na | sarba buddha sa ma yo ga dang | guhya sa manytsa la sogs pas 'dul zhing theg pa de dag gi snod du gyur pa 'dzam bu'i gling gi mi yul na med pas rgyal chen ris bzhi pas sum cu rtsa gsum dang | dga' ldan la sogs pa'i gnas na lha rnams dang bskal pa bzang po'i byang chub sems dpa' la sogs pa snod du gyur nas de'i tshe mdo sde de ni bzhugs so | slad kyis sangs rgyas mya ngan las 'das pa'i 'og tu za hor gyi rgyal po 'khor dang bcas pa ngo mtshar du chos la dad pa dag cig 'dug pa theg pa de'i 'dul skal du gyur cing snod du gyur nas | sarba buddha sa ma yo ga la sogs pa sde chen po bco brgyad phyag na rdo rje'i byin gyi rlabs kyis za hor gyi yul du gshegs pa dang | za hor gyi rgyal po Indra bhū tis mdo sde dag bltas na brda ma phrad nas sngon gyi las kyi dbang gis na mngon par shes pa thob pas bltas na yul gyi dbus yul ma la pa na ā tsārya ku ku ra nyin zhing khyi stong tsam la chos 'chad | mtshan zhing ni khyi de dag la dam tshig longs spyod mdzad pa khyi'i slob dpon mdzad pa zhig bzhugs pa de theg pa'i snod du gyur la | bdag gi 'dul skal du gyur pa yang 'dra nas rgyal pos pho nya btang ste slob dpon gshegs su gsol pa dang | slob dpon de yang sngon gyi las kyi dbang gis na mngon par shes pa lnga dang ldan nas | rgyal po de bdag gi 'dul skal du 'bab bam mi 'bab mdo sde de dag gi snod du bdag gyur ram ma gyur brtags na | bdag gi 'dul skal du yang 'bab | bdag kyang mdo sde'i snod du yang gyur | rgyal po'i the tshom yang sel bar 'gyur mod kyi | 'on kyang mdo sde dag sngar ma bltas na brgya la rgyal po'i the tshom dag ma sel bar gyur na shin du ma legs pas pho nya la slar spring ba | mdo sde dag kho bos sngar blta 'tshal gyis tshur bskur cig ces spring ba dang | de nas mdo sde dag pas gshegs te bltas na mgo mjug gar lta ba'i cha ma mchis na de nyid du lus brdabs te mgon med do | skyab med do zhes bos pa dang dpal rdo rje sems dpa' mngon par gshegs te khyod ci 'dod ces dris pa dang | bdag mdo sde zab mo 'di bltas pa tsam gyis shes par 'dod ces gsol ba dang | de bzhin gnang ngo zhes gsungs nas de nas sarba buddha sa ma yo ga la sogs pa'i glegs bam rnams ma phye bar de dag gi don yid la mngon sum du gsal bar gyur to | de nas slob dpon de za hor gyi yul 'du gshegs nas rgyal po 'khor dang bcas pa rnams la dharmā de dag bshad de | rdo rje sems dpas lung bstan nas rgyal po 'khor dang bcas pa rnams rdo rje dbyings kyi dkyil 'khor ltar sgom du stsal te |.

21. *dKar chag ldan dkar ma*, Lalou 1953, no. 522.

22. *Prajñāpāramitā-nayaśatapañcāśatkaṭīkā*, To. 2647, fol. 274a1.

23. Various forms of this story are encountered widely in siddha literature. A partial list: *Śrī-Tattvapradīpa-mahāyoginī-tantrarāja*, fol. 142b1–6; Jñānavarman's *Śrī-Jñānatilakapañjikā-guhyatattva*, fols. 210b5, 268b1–270b1; *Śrī-Sahajapradīpa-pañjikā*, fols. 197b3–200b4. Cf. *Vajragarbhatantrarājasūtra*, T. 1198.20.542c-548b; trans. in Bagchi 1944. Tibetan versions are found by bSod-nams rtse-mo in the *Rgyud sde spyi'i rnam par gzhag pa*, p. 271.2–2.3; cf. A-mes-zhabs, *Gsang 'dus byung tshul*, pp. 13.4–15.4. In the eleventh century, Zahor is located by Rong-zom chos-kyi bzang-po

to the southeast (!) of Bodhgaya; see Rog Bande, *Grub mtha' so so'i bžed tshul gžuṅ gsal bar ston pa chos 'byuṅ grub mtha' chen po bstan pa'i sgron me*, pp. 43.3–47.4.

24. *Pod ser LL* XI.479.

25. I thank Ken Eastman for attracting my attention to this text and pointing out the issue of Kukura's beastiality.

26. *bLa ma rgya gar ba'i lo rgyus, SKB* III.170.2.3–4.1.

27. *Sahajasiddhi-paddhati*, To. 2211, fols. 6a6–7b2; some of this latter material is in Davidson 2002b.

28. On this school, see Holub 1984.

29. Vidhushekhara Bhattacharya (1928) discusses much of the specifically Mahayanist context; cf. also Ruegg 1989.

30. *rGyud sde spyi'i rnam par gzhag pa, SKB* II.271.2–2.3.

31. For an introduction to these problems, see Broido 1982, 1983, 1984; and Steinkellner 1978.

32. As is so often the case with Indic works, the text is ambiguous as to the speaker's identity from this point on; Padmavajra's commentary makes it clear that Vajrapāṇi is continuing to ask his extended question until the miracle mantra below; *Buddhakapālatantrapañjikā Tattvacandrikā*, To. 1653, fol. 153b7.

33. The phrase rgyud thams cad kyi bdag po'i dbang phyug la appears in the text to apply to Vajrapāṇi, but (possibly based on gender endings) some commentators make these epithets appositive to Lha-mo in the text; see To. *Śrī-Buddhakapālatantrapañjikā Jñānavatī*, 1652.108b2–3; *Śrī-Buddhakapālamahātantrarājaṭīkā Abhayapaddhatiḥ*, To.1654.169.b4–5.

34. The mantras given in the sDe-dge and Peking canons are both corrupt, and I have tried to provide a close approximation of the text. Normatively, one would have recourse to a sādhana in which the mantra would appear, but the *Buddhakapālasādhana* found in *Sādhanamālā*, Bhattacharya 1925, 2:500–503, reproduces another mantra entirely: OṂ MAHĀVAJRO HERUKAVAJRO DHARATU DHARATU MAHĀJÑĀNASPHEṬANE ŚĪGHRAṂ SĀDHAYA STAMBHAYA KĪLAYA HUṂ PHAṬ SVĀHĀ |.

35. *Śrī-Buddhakapāla-yoginī-tantra-rāja*, To. 424, fols. 143a3–144a3: Peking 63, fols. 126b7–128a2:

de nas bcom ldan 'das kyis rdo rje'i tshig gis rdo rje chen po'i gnas su rgyud thams cad dang sngags yang dag par bshad nas | de bzhin gshegs pa thams cad kyi bdag pos rdo rje dang pad ma'i yang dag par sbyar bas btsun mo'i bha gar yongs su mya ngan las 'das so | de yongs su mya ngan las 'das pa mthong nas | byang chub sems dpa' thams cad dang | rnal 'byor ma thams cad rmad du gyur te gcig la gcig lta zhing e ma'o bcom ldang 'das de bzhin gshegs pa thams cad kyi bdag po dkyil 'khor chen po rgyan dang ldan pa'i dbus su ji ltar yongs su mya ngan las 'das |

de nas rnal 'byor ma sna tshogs sde ma la byang chub sems dpa' sems dpa' chen po phyag na rdo rjes 'di skad ces gsol to | lha mo sems can bsod nams dman pa rnams nus pa la zhon par 'gyur ba'i thabs cung zad mchis sam |

gsungs pa | rnal 'byor gyi rgyud la bye ba phrag drug nyid do | rnal 'byor ma'i rgyud la ni bye ba phrag bcu drug nyid do | mdo sde so so la ni bye ba phrag brgyad bcu'o | de bzhin du pha rol tu phyin pa'i theg pa la ni bye ba la bsgres ba'i 'bum phrag lnga'o | 'di dag thams cad ni thub pa'i dbang pos gsungs so | sngags dang bral na ni rgyud kyi nus pa mi snang ste | rgyud la lar ni ci nas sngags bye ba bzlas par gsungs so | bsod nams 'bring po rnams kyis ni sngags 'bum bzlas pas byur bar 'grub par gsungs so | bsod nams che bas khris bzlas pas shin tu myur bar 'grub bo | de ltar rdo rje can chen po rgyud kyi bdag po'i gtso bos gsungs so | bsod nams chung ba'i sems can rnams kyis ni bye ba bzlas par gsungs so | sems can 'bad rtsol chung ba rnams kyis ni 'bum bzlas bar bdag smra'o | sems can sgom pa la zhen pa rnams kyis ni khri kho na bzlas par bya'o | sems can 'dod chags la zhugs pa rnams kyi bzlas pa ji ltar lags | blun po dang lkugs pa'i rigs can rnams kyi sngags kyi grangs ji ltar lags | shin tu dmigs pa'i sngags kyi bzlas pa ji ltar lags | 'di ltar phan tshun smra bas bzlas na dngos grub gzhan du yang 'gyur ro | gal te dman pa'i sems kyis nyon mongs bzhin pas bzlas pa de'i tshe bskal pa skar ma lta bur bye bar yang de la dngos grub med do |

de ltar thos nas rnal 'byor ma sna tshogs sde ma bcom ldan 'das kyi zhal la lta bar byed cing zur mig dang bcas pa'i chags pas bltas te | shin tu khros bas 'jigs par byed cing snying rje'i thugs 'khrugs pas bdud kyi dpung rab tu bcom mo | de ltar zhugs pa'i lha mo chen mo rgyud thams cad kyi bdag po'i dbyang phyug la de na des gzigs pa tsam gyis bcom ldan 'das kyi dbu las sngags byung ngo | OM BUDDHE SIDDHE SUSIDDHE AMṚITA ARJE BUDDHA KAPĀLA SPHOṬANIPĀTAYA TRĀSAYA HŪṂ HO PHAṬ |

de ltar sngags kyi mchog gsan bas sa rim pa bdun gyi 'og tu chud pa'i klu rnams bcom par byas shing phye mar byas nas slar 'ongs te sna tshogs sde ma'i zhal tu zhugs te | pad ma'i nang nas byung nas slar thod par zhugs so | sngags 'di'i mthus klu rnams zhig ste | skrag cing rdul 'byung bar 'gyur ro | nor rgyas la sogs pa'i rdzul 'phrul chen po'i klu thams cad lhags te | stobs kyi rgyu dang | dud skyong dang | 'jog po dang | mtha' yas dang | pad ma dang | pad ma chen po la sogs pa klu chen po rnams dang | gzhan gang yang rung ba dug las byung ba thams cad kyang lhags so |

rnal 'byor ma sna tshogs sde ma la kha phyogs te klu thams cad kyis zhus pa | lha mo bka' ci stsol gi zhig bgyi zhes smra'o | gsungs pa gang yang sangs rgyas nyams su myong ba de ltar gyis shig | de ltar thos pa tsam gyis dkyil 'khor chen po brgyan dang ldan pa'i dbus su bcom ldan 'das kyi thod pa kha phye ste legs bam byung ngo | nam mkha' la sgra byung ngo |

lha mo lha tshogs sde ma zung | sems can kun la phan 'dogs pa |
rgyud 'di rgyal po chen po ste | rnal 'byor ma yi gong na med |
sangs rgyas thod pa zhes bya ba | sems can kun la phan byed pa'o |

de ltar thos nas sna tshogs sde mas glegs bam yang dag par bzhung te | phyag na rdo rje la nye bar gtad do |.

36. *Śrī-Buddhakapālatantrapañjikā Jñānavatī*, To 1652; see bibliography for a complete citation.

37. *Buddhakapālatantrapañjikā Tattvacandrikā*, To. 1653; see bibliography for a complete citation. The title is incorrectly reconstructed by the editors of the Tohoku catalogue as *Buddhakapālatantratattvacandrikāpañjikā: Sangs rgyas thod pa'i rgyud kyi dka' 'grel de kho na nyid kyi zla ba*. This commentary covers only the first two chapters of the tantra. Despite the colophon claiming that the commentary is complete, it is possible that Padmavajra completed the commentary and his exegesis was lost, or was interrupted in the process, or that the tantra only had two chapters at the time of his writing.

38. *Śrī-Buddhakapālamahātantrarājaṭīkā Abhayapaddhatiḥ*, To. 1654; see the bibliography for a complete citation. At least two manuscripts of this work are preserved in South Asia—one in the National Archives of Nepal and one in the Asiatic Society of Calcutta.

39. *Śrī-Buddhakapālatantrapañjikā Jñānavatī*, To. 1652, fol. 104b4–5: gal te yang bcom ldan 'das nyid ston pa po la sogs pa'i gzugs su bzhugs mod kyi | 'on kyang bdag nyid bcom ldan 'das ma'i gzugs su logs su bstan to |. Cf. *Hevajra Tantra* II.ii.39; Davidson 1991, p. 213. Ratnākaraśānti's *Śrī Hevajrapañjikā muktāvalī*, Tripathi and Negi 2001, p. 146, explains this through a hermemeutic of the various bodies of the Buddha. For the verification of Citrasenā's identity, see *Niṣpannayogāvalī*, Bhattacharya 1949, p. 23.

40. *Śrī-Buddhakapālatantrapañjikā Jñānavatī*, To. 1652, fol. 106a4–5: byang chub sems dpa' thams cad de mig la sogs pa'i dbang po drug go |.

41. *Śrī-Buddhakapālatantrapañjikā Jñānavatī*, To. 1652, fol. 106a3–4: mya ngan las 'das pa ni rnam par rtog pa las nges par byung ba ste | de ni chos kyi sku'i rang bzhin zhes bya ba'i tha tshig go || de yong su mya ngan las 'da' ba mthong nas zhes bya ba ni | chos kyi sku de gzigs nas zhes bya ba'i don to |.

42. *Buddhakapālatantrapañjikā Tattvacandrikā*, To. 1653, fol. 152a4–5: de lta bur bcom ldan 'das bde ba chen po'i ngo bor snyoms par zhugs par yongs su snang ba na byang chub sems dpa' la sogs pa rnams ngo mtsar rmad du gyur pa yin par blta'o | da mya ngan las 'das pa mthog ste zhes bya ba la sogs pa ni byang chub sems dpa' la sogs pa rnams dam pa skyes par gyur na ni de kho na nyid kyi mchog rab tu gsal bar rab tu 'byed par mdzad pas so |.

43. *Śrī-Buddhakapālamahātantrarājaṭīkā Abhayapaddhatiḥ*, To. 1654, fol. 168b4: der bcom ldan 'das phyag rgya chen po rdo rje'i gnas kyi shes rab kyis srid pa la mi gnas shing snying rjes zhi ba la mi gnas pa'o zhes pa mi gnas pa'i mya ngan las 'das pas yongs su mya ngan las 'das te | de'i bdag nyid du gyur nas ro gcig pa'i rang bzhin gyis tha dad mtha' dag gis ma reg pa las 'khor ba'i bar du dpag tu med pa'i de bzhin gzhegs pa dang | byang chub sems dpa' dang | rnal 'byor ma dang | 'dod chag dang bral ba dang | phyag rgya dang | dkyil 'khor dang | sngags bye ba phrag brgyad cu po rnams dang lhan cig rnam par rtog pa med par gyur kyang sngon gyi 'phan pa'i dbang las sems can thams cad la ci bya ba'i tshul gyis bzhugs so zhes bya ba'i don to |.

44. E.g., *Grub thob brgyad cu rtsa bzhi'i gsol 'debs*, fol. 110b1–2.

45. *bLa ma rgya gar ba'i lo rgyus*, *SKB* III.170.2.2–5; Guenther 1963, pp. 24–28; Tatz 1987, 1988.

46. Lūhipa is described as a scribe (yi ge pa ? = kāyastha) in the *bDe mchog lu hi pa'i lugs kyi bla ma brgyud pa'i lo rgyus*, *SKB* III.294.1.1; the early lineage hagiography of Ḍombīheruka is (according to the tradition) part of the *bLa ma rgya gar ba'i lo rgyus*, *SKB* III.171.1.6–172.2.2, where the boatman (*ko-mkhan*) was understood to be this siddha; the longer hagiography is preserved in Ngor-chen's *rGyud kyi rgyal po dpal kye rdo rje'i byung tshul dang brgyud pa'i bla ma dam pa rnams kyi rnam par thar pa ngo mtshar rgya mtsho*, *SKB* IX.281.4.6–282.2.4.

47. *Guhyasamāja Mahāguhyatantrarāja*, MATSUNAGA 1978, p. 6 (emphasis added): atha bhagavantaḥ sarvatathāgatāḥ punaḥ samājaṃ āgamya bhagavantaṃ bodhicittavajraṃ sarvatathāgatapūjāspharaṇasamayatattvaratnameghaiḥ sampūjya praṇipatyaivam āhuḥ |

bhāṣasva bhagavan tattvaṃ vajrasārasamuccayam |

sarvatāthāgataṃ guhyaṃ samājaṃ guhyasambhavam || iti

atha bhagavān bodhicittavajras tathāgatas tān sarvatathāgatān evam āha | sādhu sādhu bhagavantaḥ sarvatathāgatāḥ | kin tu sarvatathāgatānām api saṃśayakaro 'yaṃ kuto 'nyeṣām bodhisattvānām iti |.

atha bhagavantaḥ sarvatathāgtā āścaryaprāptā adbhutaprāptāḥ | sarvatathāgatasaṃśayacchettāraṃ bhagavantaṃ sarvatathāgatasvāminaṃ papracchuḥ | yad bhagavān evaṃ guṇaviśiṣṭe 'pi sarvatathāgataparṣadi sarvatathāgatakāyavākcittaguhyaṃ nirdeṣṭuṃ notsahate |.

48. *Kāraṇḍavyūha-sūtra*, Mette 1997, p. 82.8–9; cf. idem, Vaidya 1961, p. 292.17–18.

49. Steinkellner has already discussed some of the principal issues invoked by Candrakīrti in his commentary; see Steinkellner 1978.

50. *Pradīpodyotana*, Chakravarti 1984, p. 22.4–13 (emphasis added): bodhicittavajradharaḥ (text: yo 'dhicittavajradharaḥ) sarvatathāgatān evaṃ vakti | sādhu sādhv ity abhyupagame | abhimatārthadyotakatvāt praśnasya | kin tu śabdo vitarke | sarvatathāgatānām api sandehakaro 'yam iti | ghaṭamānayogino 'tra tathāgatāḥ bodhisattvāś ca draṣṭavyāḥ | na hi kleśavāsanāprahīṇānām buddhabodhisattvānām saṃśayo 'sti | tathāgatā atra ratnapudgalāḥ paripakvakuśalamūlāḥ śrutipāraṅgatā buddhatvābhilāṣiṇo niyatagotrāḥ | guruvaktreṇa vinā teṣām apy aviśayaḥ samājārthaḥ ūhāpagatvāt | kuto 'nyeṣām bodhisattvānām iti? candanādīnām pudgalānāṃ paripakvakuśalamūlānāṃ hīnādhimuktīnāṃ pratipādite 'pi durgrāhyatvād anutsāham āvedayati |.

51. *Guhyasamāja*, MATSUNAGA 1978, XV.39; the conclusion of chapter XV, p. 85, the prose section following XVII.36.

52. *Jñānasiddhi* and *Prajñopāyaviniścayasiddhi* in Bhattacharya 1929.

53. *Guhyasiddhi*, Rinpoche and Dwivedi 1987, p. 5 (emphasis added):

lokācārair vimuktaṃ paramaśivapadaṃ vyāpinaṃ niḥsvabhāvaṃ |

nityotpannaṃ ya[tīndrair] munivaravṛṣabhair vanditaṃ dhyānahīnam |

buddhānām apy agamyaṃ paramuṣitamalaṃ tattva[ta]s taṃ praṇamya |
śrīmatkāyaṃ jinānām kim api padavaraṃ śuddham apy ātmavṛttyā ||

54. For a discussion of this introductory material and its importance to *Guhyasamāja* exegesis, see Wayman 1977.

55. *Guhyasiddhi*, Rinpoche and Dwivedi 1987, pp. 12–13 (emphasis added):
athātaḥ sampravakṣyāmi sādhanaṃ guhyasambhavam |
kiñcit samājamārgeṇa nānyatantrakrameṇa tu || 1||
bāhyatantrakriyāmārgaṃ sarvaṃ tyaktvā 'tidūrataḥ |
sāmnyāyakramayogena yathābhūtaṃ nigadyate || 2||
ācāryā bahavaḥ prāhus tantre saṃgītikārakam |
lokeśaṃ nāyakaṃ vīraṃ śrīsamāje mahādyutim || 3||
vayaṃ tu kevalaṃ brūmo gurupādaprasādataḥ |
abhāvaḥ śrīsamājasya anyasaṃgītikārakaḥ || 4||
sraṣṭā tantrasya hṛdvajro vaktā sa eva deśakaḥ |
abhāvas tāvat anyasya varjitvā mahāsukham || 5||
evaṃ śruteti yad vākyaṃ vijahārapade sthitam |
tat svayaṃ sarvabuddheṣu kathitaṃ cittavajriṇā || 6||
yathāvad bhāṣitaṃ divyaṃ vijahārapadaṃ śubham |
śrīmahāsukhanāthena tathā kiñcid bravīmy aham || 7||
ekasmin parame deśe yathā nirdiṣṭavān prabhuḥ |
buddhānāṃ tantrasadbhāvam svyam eva mahāsukham || 8||
taṃ śrutvā tantrasadbhāvaṃ sarve caiva jinātmajāḥ |
kampitās trāsam āpannās tam ūcuḥ parameśvaram || 9||
kim iyaṃ dharmatā vīra durbhāṣyā bhāṣitā prabho |
atyantaṃ trāsajananī buddhānām api sarvathā || 10||
atyantaguptam udghāṭya vajrayānam anuttaram |
sarvadharmasamaikatvaṃ yat tvayā bhāṣitaṃ prabho || 11||
evam prajalpamānās te sarvabuddhamahaujasaḥ |
prakampya mūrcchām āgamya bodhicitte mano dadhuḥ || 12||
aho guptātiguptasya vajrayānasya deśanā |
niḥsvabhāvasya śuddhasya vidyate yasya nopamā || 13||
tān dṛṣṭvā vajrasattvas tu sarvabuddhān vimūrcchitān |
divyaṃ samādhim āsthāya mahāsukhasukhātmakam || 14||
niyujya ca tato buddhān vajrapadmaprayogataḥ |
paramānandarūpeṇa provāca madhurāṃ giram || 15||

56. Broido 1982, pp. 8 ff.

57. Broido 1982, 1983, 1984; Steinkellner 1978; Wayman 1968; Ruegg 1989; *Caryāgītikośa*, Kværne 1977.

58. *Caryāgītikośa*, Kværne 1977, pp. 81–83:
eka se śuṇḍinī dui ghare sāndhaa | cīa ṇa bākalaa bāruṇī bandhaa ||
sahaje thira karī bāruṇī bandha | je ajarāmara hoi diṛha kāndha ||

daśami duārata cihna dekhiā | āila garāhaka apaṇe bahiā ||
caüśaṭhī ghaṛiye deta pasārā | paiṭhela garāhaka nāhi nisārā ||
eka ghaṛulī sarui nāla | bhaṇanti Biruā thira kari cāla ||

Kværne reads ciana na bakulaa in 1c, but I follow the manuscript and read cīa as the noun. The kind of liquor mentioned, bāruṇī, is not made with yeast. Bāruṇī is a local rot-gut made from sugar, fruit juices, and some vegetable matter, such as bark or grass. The point, then, is that she brews without expected ingredients, such as cīa, not that there is necessarily a paradox built into the song. Kværne has interpreted ghare in 1c as a dual, whereas it is a locative and understood as such in the Tibetan translation and in the verse ascribed to Kāṇha quoted in Munidatta, *Caryāgītikośa,* Kværne 1977, p. 84.

59. Ibid., pp. 84–86.

60. The basic sources for Virūpa's hagiography are the *bLa ma rgya gar ba'i lo rgyus* (drinking episode, *SKB* III.171.2.4–3.1), *Bhir ba pa'i lo rgyus* (a lacuna at the beginning of the episode, pp. 368–9), the *Lam 'bras snyan brgyud* (pp. 419–420), Abhayadattaśrī, **Caturaśītisiddhapravṛtti* (Pe. 5091, fol. 4b2–4b4).

61. *Mattavalāsaprahasana*, Lockwood and Bhat 1981, pp. 30–31: kapālī — priye | paśya paśya | eṣa surāpaṇo yajñavāṭavibhūtim anukaroti | atra hi dhvajastambho yūpaḥ | surā somaḥ | śauṇḍā ṛtvijaḥ | caṣakāś camasāḥ | śūlyamāṃsaprabhṛtaya upadaṃśā havirviśeṣāḥ | mattavacanāni yajūṃṣi | gītāni sāmāni | udaṅkāḥ sruvāḥ | tarṣo 'gniḥ | surāpaṇādhipatir yajamānaḥ |.

62. *Ḍākinījālasaṃvararahasya*, Rinpoche and Dwivedi 1990, p. 1: mahāmudrānurāgeṇa yad akṣaraṃ sukhaṃ caturthaṃ tat punas tathābhiṣekaḥ saṃvarasiddhaye sandhyābhāṣayā cokto bhagavatā |.

63. The equivalents are taken from Wayman 1968.

64. *Hevajra Tantra*, Snellgrove 1959, 2:121.

65. *Saṃdhi-bhāṣā-ṭīkā*, To. 1206, *bstan-'gyur*, rgyud, ja fols. 297a5–301b4.

66. See Wayman 1968, p. 796.

67. *Pāia-Sadda-Mahaṇṇavo,* Seṭh 1963, p. 333. We may observe the derivation chadman > *chaduman > chaumā > chomā ; we also may go chadman > *chandima > *chandima > chaṇḍiā. Seṭh glosses this latter word with the Sanskrit equivalents of channa = hidden, and gupta = covered, secret. Chapter 9 of the *Saṃvarodaya-tantra* also discusses chomā; see *Saṃvarodaya-tantra*, Tsuda 1974, pp. 102–106.

68. *Arthaśāstra*-XII.5.38.

69. *Bṛhatkathāślokasaṃgraha* XXI.27: tridaṇḍipāṇḍarāṅgādipāṣaṇḍaiś chadmakaṅkaṭaiḥ | vārāṇasī mahācaurais tīrthadhvāṅkṣair adhiṣṭhitā ||. Those who have spent time in modern Banares might find themselves wondering whether the city has changed very much.

70. *Sarvabuddhasamāyoga*, To. 366, fols. 184b2–187b1; the entire **chomāmudrā* section goes from 183a4–187b1.

71. *Sampuṭa*, To. 381, fols. 118a5–119b3; the exact meaning of this and many other coded language materials await the critical editing of the available Sanskrit documents.

72. *Catuḥpīṭha-mahāyoginī-tantrarāja*, To. 428, fols. 204a5–205a1.

73. *Buddhakapāla*, To. 424, fols. 156a6–156b2; Peking 63, 141a6–141b2 (emphasis added): sangs rgyas thod pa'i rnal 'byor pa | med par phan tshun smra mi bya | 'on kyang bshad chen de nyid 'di | gcig la gcig gis smra bar bya | rgyud rnams thams cad tu sbas pa | rgyud 'di ru ni gsal bar byed | . . . de ltar dgongs pas bshad pa ni | bder gshegs rnams kyis mi mkhyen no | spyan ma la sogs rnal 'byor ma | rnams kyi khong du mi chud cing | byang chub sems dpa' yul min zhing | bla ma gu pa'i rnal 'byor pas | . . .

74. *Jñānatilaka*, To. 422, fols. 117b3–118a3.

75. *Mahāmudrā-tilaka*, To. 420, fol. 76a3: auḍi ya ṇa gnas la sogs par ni | rnal 'byor ma ni 'dus pa'o | de yi gnas su skad smra ba | gsang ba'i sgra ni yod pa'o |.

76. *Śrī-Buddhakapālatantrapañjikā Jñānavatī*, To. 1652, fol. 132a4: de ltar dgongs pas bshad ces bya ba sogs pa ni go sla'o |.

77. *Śrī-Saṃpuṭatantrarājaṭīkāmnyāyamañjarī*, To. 1198, fol. 229b3–4.

78. Ibid., fols. 229a6–238b4.

79. **Sarvatantranidānamahāguhyaśrīsampuṭatantrarājaṭīkā*, To. 1199, fol. 75b2–7.

80. *Jñānatilakapañjikā-guhyatattva*, To. 1203, fol. 247b1.

81. *Guhyārthaprakāśamahādbhūta*, To. 1200, fol. 138b2–6; I have interpreted the name given as Pa la sa badzra in the retouched xylograph (138b4) as the well-known master Vilāsavajra.

82. Beyond the citations noted in the text, see *Pīṭhādinirṇaya*, To. 1606, fol. 131b3.

83. Wayman 1968.

84. Burrow and Emaneau 1984, nos. 4358, 4541; I am quite aware that Dravidian specialists could provide better etymologies than these.

85. Ibid., no. 1075.

86. Ibid., no. 1719.

87. *Vidyottama*, To. 746, fol. 13a7–13b3; mentioned by Lalou 1956, pp. 292–293.

88. *Mañjuśrīmūlakalpa*, Sastri 1920, p. 326: dakṣiṇāpatham āśritya sidhyante pāpakarminām.

89. Wayman 1968.

90. *Sādhanamālā*, 1925, 1:501.

91. While it appears preserved only in the two Tibetan recensions, neither *Sarvabuddhasamāyoga* version seems to include directly Apabhraṃśa material, although the longer version identifies the use of vajragīti in offerings (To. 366, fol. 169b6), and our received examples of vajragīti are in some form of Apabhraṃśa; see Chaudhuri 1935 on the *Ḍākārṇava*. Ruegg overlooks the employment of Apabhraṃśa in the tantras as Buddhavacana and treats it solely as a śāstric phenomenon (1989, pp. 321–322).

92. Bhayani's essay on the Apabraṃśa in the Appendix, *Kṛṣṇayamāri-tantra*, Rinpoche and Dwivedi 1992, pp. 145–152.

93. Ruegg 1989, p. 321.

94. Ibid., p. 322.

95. This argument of Puṇḍarīka's has also been accepted by Goudriaan (1996, pp. 269–272).

96. Newman 1988, p. 132.

97. D'souza 1992, p. 17.

98. *Nāṭyaśāstra*, Kavi 1926–34, 2:365–378; this material has been edited and translated in Nitti-Dolci 1972, pp. 61–92.

99. *Nāṭyaśāstra*, XVII.1–65; investigated in Nitti-Dolci 1972, pp. 61–92.

100. Schomer 1987; all the articles included in this excellent volume are deserving of attention.

101. Kielhorn 1888–1892a, pp. 164–166.

102. Compare the introduction to the *Kubjikāmatatantra*, Goudriaan and Schoterman 1988, pp. 45–92; Goudriaan and Gupta 1981, pp. 27–31; these latter authorities are critical of the idea that the form of Sanskrit was used for didactical reasons.

103. Goudriaan doubts that we can speak of Tantric Sanskrit in the manner that we can of Epic Sanskrit or Buddhist Hybrid Sanskrit (1996, p. 266). Yet Deshpande has articulated many of the same conventions observable in this regional Sanskrit in his study of modern "priestly Sanskrit" (1996), which I would argue is a similar phenomenon.

104. Especially noticable is the employment of sahaja and citta, this latter instead of the Prakrit ciä; *Kāṇhapādasya dohākoṣa*, nos. 3, 10, 12, 16, 18, 19, 26, 30; *Tillopādadohākoṣa*, nos. 1–3, 5, 8, 10–12, 22, 30; *Sarahapādasya dohākoṣa*, nos. 20, 25, 29, 36–7, 42, 44–6, 57, 63, 72, 77, 83, 85–7, 99, 100, 104–8; *Kṛṣṇayamāri-tantra*, Rinpoche and Dwivedi 1992, pp. 148–149; verses from the *Ḍākārṇava*, in Chaudhuri 1935, pp. 1, 16, 32, 99, 123, 137–138, 141, 143. We also see the variation between "sijja" (ibid., p. 5) and "siddha," in *Kāṇhapādasya dohākoṣa*, no. 19, and *Sarahapādasya dohākoṣa*, no. 80.

105. The lengthy statement in the *Vajrapādasārasaṃgrahapañjikā* occurs in To. 1186, fols. 58b6–62a5. It is useful to note that Pūṇḍarīka also puts forward a similar argument; *Vimalaprabhā*, Upadhyaya 1986, 1:31–32.

106. In fact these were alluded to twice by Pūṇḍarīka (arthaśaraṇatām āśritya), but Newman has overlooked the reference (1988, p. 125); for the position these play in canonical criticism, see Davidson 1990.

107. This is decidedly a different process from the system of transculturation and vernacularization explored by Pollock 1996 and 1998, for Pollock is discussing a "cosmopolis," in which high-status forms were paramount. Still, we might wonder whether Pollock's overlooking the regional forms observed in the smaller areas, like those in Orissa, Madhya Pradesh, and elsewhere, have not contributed to a somewhat reified picture.

108. Colophon to To. 1186, *Chinnamuṇḍasādhana*, To. 1555, fol. 208a3: birba pa yis 'di byes te | sgra yig legs par ma rdzogs kyang | mkha' 'gro ma rnams bzod par rigs |. The circumstance of this colophon becomes clear when we compare it to the surviving Sanskrit texts, edited and discussed in Nihom 1992; Nihom draws parallels between this text and *Sādhanamālā*, nos. 232, 234 and 238, and Bhattacharya 1925, 2:452–533, 455, 458.

109. See Dikshit 1955 and 1956 for his only reporting of the excavation; the excavator discussed some of the bronzes found there in Dikshit 1955–57.

110. Bajpai and Pandey 1978.

111. Ibid., plate XVIIa, incorrectly identified as a Hevajra, even if the eighth-century date is seemingly appropriate.

112. Jain 1969, p. 61, line 11.

113. Vairocanavajra is the translator of *Kāṇhapādasya dohākoṣa*, To. 2301, *bsTan-'gyur*, rgyud, zhi, and identified fol. 230a6. Schaeffer 2000 treats this figure, but his geography is not a clear as it could be.

114. *Rwa lo tsā ba'i rnam thar*, pp. 293–295; this young girl was the daughter of one Kong-po A-rgyal.

115. *Mahāmāyūrī-vidyārājñī-dhāraṇī*, SHŪYO 1972, passim.

116. Morrell 1983, pp. 80–81.

117. Lutgendorf 1991, p. 209; for a consideration of the relationship between oral and literate forms, see Olson and Torrance 1991.

118. On this point, see Blackburn et al. 1989 and Richman 1991.

119. Gitomer 1991, p. 100.

120. Gerow 1977, pp. 226–227, 245–250.

121. *Nāṭyaśāstra*, Kavi 1926–34, 1:11.

122. The best technical study of the comic sentiment to date seems to be Sharma 1941. Although Siegel recognizes both "improprieties and incongruities," he glosses over the difference between Bharata and Abhinavagupta (1987, pp. 12–34).

123. Compare Aristotle's *Poetics* (trans. Janko, 1987, pp. 49–55, 170–174), with *Nāṭyaśāstra* VI.56 prose, Kavi 1926–34, 1:313–314,

124. Fundamental Vidūṣaka discussions are found in Shulman 1985; Kuiper 1979; and Bhatt 1959.

125. *Bhāsanāṭakacakram*, Vetal et al. 1963, vol. 1, section 3, p. 28: kissa aham avedi'o | suṇāhi dāva | athi rāmā'aṇaṃ ṇāma ṇaṭṭasattham | tassiṃ pañca sulo'ā asampuṇṇe saṃvacchare ma'e paṭhidā |

126. Jefferds 1981, p. 73.

127. The use of a fork for blood sacrifice of al least goats at the Ugra-tārā-pīṭha in Bengal is attested in Morinis 1984, pp. 184–185. I have seen the form employed elsewhere, as at Kāmākhyā, Guwahati, Assam. Despite affirmations by some phenomenologists, it is not clear whether this forked stick is developed from the yūpa, the Vedic sacrificial post, or whether it constitutes a separately developed sacrifi-

cial system. *bLa ma brgyud pa'i rnam par thar pa ngo mtshar snang ba* has the antagonists being female, yoginīs rather than yogins (p. 112.5).

128. Ibid., p. 113.2, reads bying (to sink) for bcings (to bind), meaning that Virūpa causes the head to sink to the heart and replaces it with a caitya, hardly understandable given that he grabs the ear between these two activities. It further identifies the name of this state as rNa-`chus lha-mo (the Devī with the Twisted Ear).

129. *bLa ma rgya gar ba'i lo rgyus*, *SKB*, III.172.1.2–2.1: de nas shar phyogs su sa ha dza de wī zhes bya ba rang byung gi tri shū la dang | lha mo tsanti ka'i rang byung gi rdo sku yod pa la phyi rol pa'i rnal 'byor pa rnams kyis mi der khrid pas rang byung gi tri shū la lkog ma la zug nas 'chi | de'i sha las tshogs kyi 'khor lo byed pa yod pa de'i sar slob dpon dpon g.yog gsum gyis byon pa dang | rnal 'byor pa rnams za bar 'dod nas tshogs khang gi nang du bos pas slob dpon gyis g.yog po la dbugs phyir rgyur ma gzhugs par nang du sdoms la sdod cig gsungs nas | slob dpon nyid nang du byon pa dang | rnal 'byor pa de rnams na re | khyod kyi grogs po gnyis po gar song zer | phyi rol na 'dug gsungs pas | tshur khug zer | de khyed rang khug gsungs pas | khong gis bos nas kyang skad med 'dzug gu sug byas pa'i shul na tshur dbugs ngan su su | dri chen 'bur 'bur byung bas 'dis rul nas 'dug zer log pa dang | tri shū la de 'dar yeng yeng 'dug pa dang | slob dpon gyis thal mo gcig brdabs pas de phye mar sil gyis song ngo | de nas lha mo tsanti ka'i sku de par par 'dug pa la sphyi bor thal mo cig brgyab ste mgo bo snying ga'i bar du bcings | rna ba nas bzung nas spyi bor mchod rten zhig bzhag ste rnal 'byor pa rnams brgyal bar gyur to | de nas brgyal bsangs pa dang | rnal 'byor pa rnams na re | khyed nang pa sangs rgyas pa snying rje che ba yin na 'di lta bu byed pa zer ba la | sems can bsad pa'i sha dang khrag dron mos mchod pa ma byed byas pas | de rnams kyis slob dpon gyi zhabs la phyag 'tshal zhing skyabs su song nas sangs rgyas pa'i rnal 'byor par song ngo |.

130. This revelation is the ostensible text of the *Lam 'bras bu dang bcas pa'i gdams ngag dang man ngag tu bcas pa*; for an edition and translation of this work, see Davidson (forthcoming b).

131. The *Catuḥpīṭha-mahāyoginī-tantrarāja*, for example, indicates (fol. 223a6) that the yogins' body becomes like crystal as a result of his practice.

132. *Nāṭyaśāstra* VI:43-45ab, Kavi 1926–34, 1:296:

teṣām utpattihetavaś catvāro rasāḥ | tadyathā śṛṅgāro raudro vīro bībhatsa iti | atra (43)
śṛṅgārād dhi bhaved dhāsyo raudrāc ca karuṇo rasaḥ |
vīrāc caivâdbhutotpattir bībhatsāc ca bhayānakaḥ || (44)
śṛṅgārānukṛtir yā tu sa hāsyas tu prakīrtitaḥ | (45 ab)

133. *Nāṭyaśāstra*, Kavi 1926–34, 1:297: evaṃ tadābhāsatayā prakāraḥ śṛṅgāreṇa sūcitaḥ | tena karuṇādyābhāseṣv api hāsyatvaṃ sarveṣu mantavyam | p. 314: etena sarve rasā hāsye 'ntarbhūtā iti darśita.

134. Ibid.: anaucityapravṛttikṛtam eva hi hāsyavibhāvatvam | taccānaucityaṃ sarvarasānāṃ vibhāvānubhāvādau saṃbhāvyate | tena vyabhicārinām apy eṣaiva vārtā |.

135. Morrell 1983, pp. 15–16.

136. Schopenhauer 1958, 1:59.

137. On Yakṣa lore generally, see Sutherland 1991.

138. The earliest images of Virūpa are from the early thirteenth century. An early Sa-skya-pa painting is illustrated in Kossak and Singer (1998, pp. 136–138), although there are problems with their analysis. The other example is an image in the upper left-hand position on the Dhoti of the colossal Mañjuśrī statue to the right of the gSum-brtsegs lha-khang in Alchi; this Virūpa is almost visible in Goepper (1996, p. 103), but not really identifiable as Virūpa; its identification was done by the author at the site in late July 2000, but no photograph was possible at that time. Interestingly, this Alchi Virūpa is not obese, unlike every other known exemplar and apparently represents a Kashmiri variation, possibly because the Bengali conventions were unknown to the artist, who simply rendered Virūpa like most of the other siddhas with only his attributes differentiating him.

139. Strong 1992, pp. 273–290.

140. Bakhtin 1968, pp. 344–347.

141. Ibid., p. 10.

142. Ibid., p. 317.

143. Buitenen 1958.

144. *Subhāsita-saṃgraha*, in *Le Muséon* 23 (1904): 5n2.

145. *Milindapañha,* IV.1.43–45, Trenckner 1880, pp. 120–121.

7. SIDDHAS, MONKS, AND COMMUNITIES

1. **Ardhapañcamagāthā*, To. 2278, fol. 132b4–b7: gdol pa dza zhes bya ba zhig gis | slob dpon chen po ku ku ri pa la brten te | don dam sems la dmigs pa'o | rdzogs pa'i rim pa phyogs gcig pa bsgoms pa las | chos thams cad brten med du zhen par 'gyur ro | de nas yul dzā lan dha rar | rims nad kyis mi phal cher tshe'i dus byas so | lo tog thams cad ser bas bcom mo | lo lngar char ma bab nas | bram ze gsang tshig mkhan la dris pa dang | sa phyogs 'di ni mi nang pa sang rgyas pa gnas nas | phyi rol gyi grub mtha' gsang bar smra ba la phyogs te gnas pas | bkra mi shis pa sna tshogs byung ste | 'jig rten 'di la gzhan phung zhing | ma 'ongs pa la rang phung bar byed do zhes pa dang | dpal ku ku ri pas thos te | gdol pa dza'i drung du byong nas smras pa |.

2. *Siddhaikavīramahātantra*, especially observable in the first two of the four chapters, pp. 1–14.

3. E.g., *Vajravidāraṇadhāraṇyekavīrasādhana*, To. 2926; Davidson 1992, pp. 123–124.

4. Davidson 2002b.

5. *Hevajra Tantra*, Snellgrove 1959, 1:127; *Niṣpannayogāvalī*, 1949, pp. 40–41, 14–15.

6. *Niṣpannayogāvalī*, 1949, pp. 43–44, 23; there is an expanded Buddhakapāla maṇḍala, in ibid., pp. 47, 30–31.

7. Ibid., pp. 42–43, 20–21.

8. Ibid., pp. 41–42, 52–53, 16–17, 40–41.

9. E.g., at Ratnagiri; Mitra 1981, 1:108–138.

10. Lalou 1936, pp. 332–335.

11. *Hevajrasekaprkriyā*, Finot 1934, p. 24; the language here is reasonably close to that found in the *Saṃkṣiptābhiṣekavidhi*, Sakurai 1996, pp. 411–412.

12. *Niṣpannayogāvalī*, 1949, pp. 72–73, 75–76.

13. *Vidyottama-mahātantra*, To. 746, fols. 48a4–b6: de nas nam mkha' la rgyu ba'i ma mo bdun gyis ca co dang ga zha'i sgra bton nas 'khor de nyid du 'dus par gyur te | 'khor 'dus pa de dag thams cad la lan gsum bskor ba byas nas bcom ldan 'das kyi zhabs la mgo bos phyag 'tshal te bcom ldan 'das la 'di skad ces gsol to | bcom ldan 'das bdag cag gis kyang byang chub sems dpa' chen po lag na rdo rje la gsang sngags kyi shas 'bul bar 'tshal lo | de nas bcom ldan 'das kyis ma mo de dag la 'di skad ces bka' stsal to | sring mo dag gang khyed sems can thams cad la phan pa'i phyir zhugs pa ni legs so legs so | de nas ma mo de dag gis tshigs mthun pā lag na rdo rje la ng sngags phul ba | na mo buddhā ya | na mo badzra pā na ye | ma hā yakṣa se nā pa ta ye | tad ya thā | hu lu hu lu | la hu la hu | ha ha | tiṣṭha tiṣṭha | bhra ma bhra ma | bandha bandha | khā da khā da | ma tsa me kashcid bighnāṃ ka ri shya te | mo ha ni mo ha ni | na ya ti na ya | māli ni bi shwe shwa re | a mo ghe na ma sbā hā | rig sngags 'di dran pa tsam gyis rig pa mchog sgrub pa'i rig sngags 'chang de la bdag cag ma mo bdun gyis dpag tshad gcig gi bar du bsrung bar bgyi | yang dag par so sor bskyab par bgyi'o | rig sngags kyi las rnams 'byung ste ras sar pa la sbyin dang ma 'dres pa'i tshon rtsis lag na rdo rje mdog sngo bsangs la lo bcu drug lon pa'i sha gzugs can rgyan thams cad kyis brgyan pa ma mo bdun gyis bskor bar bri'o | ma mo bdun ni 'jigs pa'i tshul du bsgrub par bya'o | de nas zhag gsum smyang ba byas te mar gyi ngo zhag bcu bzhi la ci nus kyi mchod pa byas te | chang dang sha'i gtor ma yang sbyin par bya'o | de nas rig sngag 'chang gis ri mo'i sku gzugs kyi mdun du seng ldeng gi shing gis me sbar la yungs kar khrag gis bsgos pas lan brgya stong sbyin sreg byas te | de nas ri mo'i sku gzugs 'gul bar mthong na rigs sngags 'chang gis rig pa mchog dran par bya'o | bu med mche ba gtsigs pa yang 'ong bar 'gyur te des 'jigs par mi bya bar sring mo khyod 'ongs pa legs so | rdo rje 'dzin gyis dam tshig byin pa gang yin pa de dran par gyis shig ces smros shig | de skad thos nas ca co'i sgra phyung ste de bzhin du bya'o zhes nas mi snang bar 'gyur ro | de nas nyin gcig bzhin du ti na ra re sbyin par byed cing don thams cad sgrubs te rig sngags kyi dgnos grub kyang sbyin par byed do |.

14. Ibid., fols. 48b6–49b2.

15. *Hevajra Tantra*, Snellgrove 1959, II.v.29; cy. 2:153.

16. Kulke and Rothermund 1998, pp. 136–138; in this description, they are primarily concerned with the intimate connection of divinities to real princes.

17. *Uḍḍiyānaśrīyogayoginīsvabhūtasambhoga-śmaśānakalpa*, To. 1744, passim; these names, their order, and almost everything about the directions assigned are anomalous. Cf. *Saṃvarodaya-tantra*, TSUDA 1974, XVII.36–45; treated by TSUDA 1990; I cannot agree with TSUDA's understanding of the historical circumstances of this material.

18. *Prajñāpāramitā-nayaśatapañcāśatkaṭīkā*, To. 2647, fols. 272b7–273b7.

19. Tatz 1987, 1988.

20. Tucci 1930.

21. *Sahajasiddhi*, To. 2260, fols. 1b1–4; *Sahajasiddhi-paddhati*, To. 2261, fols. 6a5–13b7.

22. There are actually three texts included in the Dam-pa sangs-rgyas collection, the *Zhi byed snyan rgyud zab byed ma* (Aziz 1979), which feature fifty-four names, but all have multiple repetitions. Beyond the above text, I.235.1–242.5, probably the most Indic, there is the *rNal 'byor pho mo lnga bcu rtsa bzhi'i dgongs pa dril ba | lam dri am myed pa gser sgong dag pa'i skor* (I.242.6–247.6), and the *rNal 'byor pho mo lnga bcu rtsa bzhi'i gdams pa yin | lam dri ma myed pa shel sgong dag pa'i skor* (I.247.7–254.8). These latter two texts include the Tibetan translator Rin-chen bzang-po (!) as a siddha.

23. Tucci 1949, 1:227–230; Schmidt 1958, pp. 17–18.

24. This list is found in the manuscript that has been attributed the title of its first work, *Yogāvatārādisaṃgraha*; Nepal National Archives, tṛtīya 366–3, fols. 9b3–11a6. There is also a modern copy of this manuscript placed in the Asiatic Society, ms. G8060.

25. *Kubjikāmata-tantra*, Goudriaan and Schoterman 1988, X.112–130; Rocher 1986, p. 229.

26. *Rwa lo tsā ba'i rnam thar*, p. 265; elsewhere in the same work, Rwa-lo encounters eighty siddhas, pp. 230, 240.

27. Sharma 1965, pp. 86–87, 104–109, 176–188, 213–216, 264.

28. Wills 1919; Chhattisgarh used to be part of Madhya Pradesh, but became a separate state at the end of 2000.

29. Fleet 1883, p. 160, line 46; Sharma 1965 for a synthesis of this and other grants.

30. For a discussion of this locale, see Postel et al. 1985, pp. 28–31, 40–46, 93–97, 121–122, 302.

31. See A mes zhabs, *Gsang 'dus byung tshul*, pp. 37.4–40.3, for his understanding of Buddhajñānapāda's system.

32. *Abhisamayālaṃkārāloka*, Vaidya 1960, p. 558.15.

33. The *Dvikramatattvabhāvanā-mukhāgama*, To. 1853, fol. 2a2, seems to describe Guneru (there written Gunenu) as a male teacher, so this is probably not a title. Otherwise, when Vitapāda's text indicates a teaching received, usually the verb *thob pa* is employed, so the exact significance of this phrase is unclear.

34. *Sukusuma-nāma-dvikramatattvabhāvanā-mukhāgama-vṛtti*, To. 1866, fols.

89b4–90b5: de nas yul dbus las byang du dpag tshad nyis brgya sum cu'i phyogs na yon tan kun 'byung zhes te mkha' 'gro mas byin gyis rlob pa phal cher de las 'byung ba'i phyir | u rgyan gyi yul la bya'o | der bgrod nas de'i phyogs gcig nor bu'i gling du sku 'khrungs pa'i phyag rgya chen po thob pa | dpal sna tshogs gzugs zhes kyang grags pa | slob dpon chen po 'jo sgeg rdo rje zhes bya ba yod de | de la bya ba dang rnal 'byor gyi rgyud mang du thos nas | 'bad pas rnam par dpyad pa yang byas so | yang gnas de nyid kyi phyogs gcig na bsam gyis mi khyab pa'i rim pa'i man ngag thob pa | rnal 'byor ma chen mo de nyid brnyes pa gu ne ru zhes bya ba zhig gnas pa de'i drung du bgrod nas de mnyes par byas te | bla na med pa'i rgyud mang du thos par byas nas | ji skad du gsungs pa'i dam tshig dang dbang la sogs pas bla ma de'i lung thob nas gzod bsgom pa la zhugs so | lhas rmi lam du bstan pa u rgyan gyi gnas de yi byang phyogs kyi chab sgo na | gdol pa'i rigs dzā thig dzwa la zhes bya ba la bu mo lo bcu drug lon pa zhig yod kyis | de ni rigs las skyes [90a] pa'i rnal 'byor ma lakṣmī chen mo zhes bya ba yin gyis der song dang khyod kyi dgongs pa 'grub par 'gyur ro zhes pa dang | 'phral du song nas de dang bshes su 'thams nas | zla ba brgyad kyi bar du mnyes par byas so | des kyang phyag rgya chen po la drod pa yin par rtogs nas | phra mo'i lung stsal ba tsam gyis dpal dzaṃ bha la'i grub pa thob par gyur to | de nas yul dzā lendhar zhes bya ba na grong khyer ka no dzer zhes bya ba yod de | de'i phyogs gcig na shes rab gtso bor byed pa'i rgyud la bsam pa chu klung lta bur gyur pa byis pa chung ba'i zhabs zhes bya ba'i drung du bgrod nas | de mnyes par byas nas de'i gzhung thos shing lung yang thob par byas te bsgom pa yang nan tan du byed do | de nas yul dbus nas lho phyogs su dpag tshad sum brgya yod pa na yul kongka na zhes bya ba yod de | de la nam mkha'i shing ldan zhes bya ste | ci'i phyir zhe na | rtsa ba med par shing rnams la 'khril shing steng du kril pa lta bur gnas pa'o | yul de'i phyogs gcig na thabs gtso bor byed pa'i rgyud la dgongs pa chu klung chen po lta bur gyur pa skye ba gcig gis thogs pa grub pa'i dbyang phyug bsrung ba'i zhabs zhes bya ba gnas te | de yang rdzu 'phrul dang ldan pa'i slob mas bskor ba'o | de dag kyang gang zhe na | bram ze tsa tra ra zhes bya ba dang | bram ze gu hya parta zhes bya ba dang | rgyal rigs manydzu shrī zhes bya ba dang rje'u rigs pūrṇa bha dra zhes bya ba dang | dmangs rigs dī paṃ ka ra zhes bya ba dang | dmangs rigs karṇa pu tra zhes bya ba dang | smad 'tshong ma ā lo ki zhes bya ba dang | smad 'tshong ma sa du shi la zhes bya ba ste | de kun gyi yo byad dang gos zas ni lha mo nor gyi rgyun zhes bya ba des nyi ma re re zhing gser gyis ma sha bcu dang mu tig gi ha ra phyed dang kārṣā paṇa sum brgya sbyor ro | bla ma dam pa de'i drung du lo dgu'i bar du 'dud cing skye ba gcig gis thogs par byas so | 'dus pa'i rgyud chen zhes pa la sogs pa ni bla ma'i dgongs pa ste | de la 'dus pa'i rgyud ni rnal 'gyor rnams so | de'i 'grel pa ni rnal 'byor bslab pa sme sha can gyi bu mo bi ma la mu dri'o | de dang bcas par bco brgyad bar du mnyan [90b] pa ni zla ba bco brgyad kyi bar du bsgrub pa'o | bdag gis ma rtogs pa zhes ba ni rtogs pa'i dba' rlabs ma 'phros pa'o | bla ma chen pos kyang bdag gis kyang ma rtogs zhes gsungs pa dang | thugs cung zad chad nas 'di ma rtogs par gzhan ni don med do par bsams nas | rang gi phyag rgya 'dus pa'i glegs bam du byas nas mgul du btags nas de las byang phyogs su bgrod de | rdo rje gdan gyi rgyab na ku ba tsa zhes bya ba'i tshal yod de der phyin pa'o | de yi dgongs pa ni byang chub kyi snying po las kha phyir bltas pa'i sems can rnams kyi nang na bdag gnas te | de na 'dod chags la sogs pa'i stag dang dred la sogs pa mang zhing shin tu 'jigs pa'i sa ste | bdag de las thar par 'dod pa'i phyir der zla ba drug bskul ba dang bcas pa'i bsgrub pas gnas pa'i chos rnams kyi de bzhin nyid rtogs so zhes so | ji ltar rtogs she na | sprul pa'i dge slong zhes pa la sogs pa'o | de yang rdo rje 'dzin pa chen pos sprul pa'i dge slong byi ba'i sham thabs can chos gos las thod byas pa gcig zhing rmo zhing gnas pa dang | bla ma gnyis te bu chung dang ldan pa'i bud med ngan pa dang | khyi mo dkar ba mtshan ma can no | de rnams dang phrad ba las rtogs pa'i rlabs mi mnga' bas bla mas de rnams la ma khrel to |.

I have emended rtsa ba med par shing rnams la 'khris shing steng du bris pa, to rtsa ba med par shing rnams la 'khril shing steng du kril pa; kha and ba, sa and la are quite similar in manuscripts and easily confused.

35. *Dvikramatattvabhāvanā-mukhāgama*, To. 1853, fol. 16a4, describes it as 50 kroṣa, with the kroṣa normally four to the yojana; however, in *Sukusuma-nāma-dvikramatattvabhāvanā-mukhāgama-vṛtti*, To. 1866, fol. 135a2, Vitapāda translates this into six yojana and two kroṣa, so that we would understand eight kroṣa to the yojana.

36. *Sukusuma-nāma-dvikramatattvabhāvanā-mukhāgama-vṛtti*, To. 1866, fol. 135a5–6.

37. *Rājataraṅgiṇī* III.11–12. The sixth-century chronology represented here appears faulty, and other evidence points to an eighth century date for this monastery; see chapter 3, n. 105.

38. See Gonda 1961 and Parry 1985.

39. Mirashi 1976, pp. xlvii, 6–8.

40. *Mañjuśrīnāmasaṃgīti*, Davidson 1981, p. 18, n. 52, for references on this issue.

41. *Sukusuma-nāma-dvikramatattvabhāvanā-mukhāgama-vṛtti*, To. 1866, fol. 135b3–4: gtam rgyud rgyas par shes byas nas | zhes pa ni bla ma chen po'i gtam rgyud rgyas pa na lendra 'dul ba dang | rdo rje gdan gyi mchod pa byas pa dang | rab tu gnas pa byas pa la sogs pa'i lo rgyus kyis skal ba dang ldan pa cher dad par byas nas | des kyang rang gi 'dod pa'i gzhung la mkhas pa ni bla ma ste |.

42. *Mar pa lo tsā'i rnam thar*, p. 84; Nalanda Translation Committee 1982, p. 85.

43. This date is variously interpreted as 1040 or 1041; the sources are *rNam thar rgyas pa*, Eimer 1979, §§ 231–232; *Deb ther sngon po*, 1984, 1:303, and Roerich 1949, 1:247.

44. *rNal 'byor byang chub seng ge'i dris lan*, *SKB* III.277.4.5–278.2.2: nag tsho lo tsā ba'i zhal nas | nga btsun chung gcig gis jo bo spyan 'dren du phyin tsa na | jo bo ma ga dhār stabs kas lo gcig 'gor bar byung nas | jo bo na ro pa snyan pa che bas zhal blta ba la 'gro snyam ste | ma ga dhā nas zla ba gcig shar lhor phyin pa na | phulla ha ri zhes bya ba'i gtsug lag khang na jo bo bzhugs zhes thos te de blta bar

phyin pas nga bsod nams che bar byung ste | sleb pa'i nyin par jo bo la rgyal phran zhig phyag 'tshal ba yin zer nas phyin pas khri chen po zhig brtsigs nas 'dug pa'i rtsar bsdad | de nas khrom tham cad 'ur langs nas | jo bo byon kyin 'dug zer te bltas pas | jo bo sku bongs che ba | dbu skra dkar ba las thal nas | dmar sang nge ba sindhu ra'i thod bcings pa | mi bzhi tsam gyis bteg nas go la mur gin byon pa mthong | zhabs la 'ju | gsung thos pa[r] bya snyam tsa na | dbang che ches phar phar phul nas tha mar bton | der jo bo'i zhal ni mthong | gsung ni ma thos |.

45. Snellgrove 1987, 1:160–170.

46. The layout of the gaṇacakra maṇḍala provided in Wallace 2001 is a classic example of an idealized form that would be virtually impossible to reproduce (p. 127). It calls for several kinds of tribals, foreigners, and outcastes in its makeup, many of which are seldom found in the same place in medieval India.

47. The text has las mkhan, for which I can find no attested Sanskrit equivalent; *Saṃvarodaya-tantra*, Tsuda 1974, VIII.23, appears to identify this offical as a karmavajrin.

48. *Sarvabuddhasamāyoga-gaṇavidhi*, To. 1672, fols. 195b3–196a4: bsod nams ye shes tshogs rdzogs pas | kun ldan tshogs kyi 'khor lo yi | rigs kyi bkod pa so so'i gnas | phun sum tshogs par bstan pa'am | yang na bde ba'i gnas dag tu | skyed mos tshal la sogs par bsgrub | mar ngo'i brgyad dang bcu bzhi dang | yar ngo'i brgyad dang bcu mtshams gnyis | der ni dang po gdan bshams te | 'jam zhing reg na bde 'gyur ba'i | sna tshogs padma ras kyis g.yogs | de ni thams cad dag pa'i gdan | sangs rgyas kun gyi dam tshig dpal | rdo rje sems dpa'i snang ba bde | de bzhin gshegs pa'i pho brang mchog | rin chen rgyan la sogs pas spras | dril bu rgyal mtshan mchog ldan pa'i | bla re dam pa bres pa na | rdo rje tshig dang mchog la sogs | glu dang sil snyan rnam par 'phrul | me tog bdug pa'i sbyor ba dang | mar me dri la sogs ldan par | sangs rgyas thams cad mnyam sbyor ba'i | mkha' 'gru sgyu ma bde mchog bsgrub | slob dpon mgon la legs zhus nas | phun sum tshogs pa'i rjes 'jug cing | sangs rgyas brda dang ldan pa yis | me tog thogs te 'gro la bskul | rnal 'gyor pho mo thams cad kun | dga' zhing dang ba'i sems bcas kyis | do nub bdag gi gnas dag tu | tshogs kyi cho ga mdzad par gsol | e ma bu ni snying rje che | gal te lag pa'i phreng ston na | 'du bar bya zhes smra ba yin | phreng ba mngon par btang byas nas | dam tshig la gnas brtul zhugs bzang | dpa' bo gzhan don spyod pa'o | de nas nub mo 'dus pa dang | phyi nas 'dag chal dri chab chus | khrus byas me tog gis brgyan cing | rnal 'byor dag chos sngags kyis sbyang | de nas nang gi khrus byas te | sngags kyi bsrungs shing byin brlabs nas | dam tshig tshogs rnams bskang gso zhing | rim bzhin nang du 'gro bar bya | dam tshig brda sogs brtag pa'i phyir | khro bo'i rgyan sngon las mkhan gnyis | rig pa'i sngags brjod thob 'dzin | bsrung ba'i don phyir sgo 'gram gnyis | kye khro rgyal rgyan sngon dag gis mdzes | dam tshig rnam par spyod pa po | dngos grub rin chen dbyug to 'dzin | dpa' bo dpa' mo 'du bar mdzod | mkha' mdzes rnal 'byor ma dkyil du | dam pa'i mtshan ldan bdag thong shig | om ma hā sa ya hūṃ | su ra ta stāṃ |.

49. Ibid., fol. 196b4: 'di la rnam rtog yod ma yin | bram ze khyi dang gdol pa rnams | rang bzhin gcig pas lhan cig bza' |.

50. Ibid., fol. 197a2–3: de dag la ni snying ring nas | snying nas khrag chen 'thungs pa yin | bdag gi ngo bo yongs spangs shing | dka' thub kyis ni gzir mi bya | ci bde bar ni bde bar spyad | 'di ni phyi dus sangs rgyas yin | rnal 'byor longs spyod thams cad la | cis kyang mi 'jigs dga' bar gyis |

51. On these terms, see *Saṃvarodaya-tantra,* VIII.7.

52. *Kulārṇava*, Vidyāratna 1917, VIII.96–111. The practice is not mentioned in the earlier *Kulacūḍāmaṇi*; see Finn 1986, pp. 74–147.

53. Bühnemann has accepted the eleventh to the fifteenth centuries as the date of the *Kulārṇava*'s composition (1992, p. 62). Gupta et al. (1979, p. 155) take the *Kulārṇava* as paradigmatic for this practice; cf. Bharati 1965, pp. 257–261.

54. E.g., Sharma 1996, p. 105.

55. See Elwin 1947, pp. 269–325, for a somewhat dated assessment of this institution.

56. Ibid.; and Gell 1992; cf. Vitebsky 1992, pp. 48–49, and Boal 1982, pp. 20–22.

57. Elwin 1947, pp. 326–332, and Gell 1992, p. 64.

58. *Kālikāpurāṇa,* XLI.17–23.

59. A corrupt version of the Sanskrit of this list is found in the *Mūlāpattayaḥ Sthūlāpattayaḥ* in the *Advayavajrasaṃgraha*, Shastri 1927, p. 13; among the many problems in the text, gotraguṇa (l. 5) should read gotragaṇa, jane pakṣe (l. 7) should be jane 'pakṣe, and iṣṭa- (l. 8) should be duṣṭa. I have relied of the various short texts covering these twenty-two, collectively To. 2478–2488, especially the *Vajrayānamūlāpattiṭikā-mārgapradīpa,* To. 2488, of Mañjuśrīkīrti. This text is provided with an incomplete title both on the title page and in the Tohoku catalogue, but on fol. 231b6 the text is titled: *rdo rje theg pa'i rtsa ba'i ltung ba'i rgya cher 'grel pa lam gyi sgron ma zhes bya ba.*

60. *Pañcakrama,* II.80–81; as noted in MIMAKI and TOMABECHI 1994, this material is also found quoted in the *Subhāṣita-Saṃgraha*, 1903–4, p. 386.

61. Cf. *Hevajra Tantra,* II.viii.2–5.

62. Cf. **Vajrayānacaturdaśamūlāpattiṭikā*, To. 2485, fol. 184a7–b2; **Vajrayānamūlāpattiṭikā*, To. 2486, fol.189a3–b1; *Vajrayānamūlāpattiṭikā-mārgapradīpa*, To. 2488, fols. 219a6–b1. Cf. *Guhyasiddhi*, pp. 50–59.

63. Cf. **Vajrayānacaturdaśamūlāpattiṭikā*, To. 2485, fol. 184a3–5; **Vajrayānamūlāpattiṭikā,* To. 2486, fol. 188b6–189a3; *Vajrayānamūlāpattiṭikā-mārgapradīpa*, To. 2488, fol. 218a5–b1.

64. **Pañcadaśāpatti*, To. 2480; another such list is a list of seven, *Yan lag gi nyes pa bdun pa*, To. 2481; without a commentary, though, its meaning is unclear and the text appears unreliable.

65. *Vidyāvrata* is the topic of chapters 7 and 8 of Padmavajra's *Guhyasiddhi*, Rinpoche and Dwivedi 1987, pp. 50–57. While sexual activity with a consort is its

fundamental feature, it encompasses a wider series of activities, including participation in the tantric feast.

66. *Vajrayānamūlāpattiṭīkā-mārgapradīpa*, To. 2488, fols. 221b7–222a5: spyod pa de yang rnam pa bzhi ste las dang po pas kun tu bzang po'i spyod pa bya bar gsungs te | rgyud gzhan las kun du bzang po'i spyod pa gnas skabs gzhan du yang bstan te dgongs pa gzhan no | cung cad brtan pa thob nas rig pa'i brtul zhugs kyi spyod pa ste | sngags spyod kyis zla ba drug la sogs par bya bar gshad do | brtan pa thob pa rnams kyis mgon po kun du spyod pa la gnas par bya'o zhes bshad pa'i rgyud chen po las bshad do | . . . 'dir rnal 'byor gyi lam rnam pa gnyis su shes par bya ste | rnal 'byor la brten pa dang | thabs kyi dam tshigs la brten pa'o | kha cig dam tshig la brten nas rnal 'byor gyis grol ba yang yod | kha cig rnal 'byor la brten nas dam tshig gis grol ba yang yod |.

67. *rGyud kyi mngon par rtogs pa rin po che'i ljon shing*, *SKB*, III.48.1.4–49.4.5.

68. *Sandhivyākaraṇa-tantra*, To. 444, fol. 161b3–7: gsang ba'i bdag po mkhas rnams kyis | tshul mchog 'di ni rnyed gyur nas | don gsal yang dag rnyed pa dang | de yang nga rgyal dag tu ltung | de rnams ting 'dzin zhi nyid dang | shes rab nyid kyang shin tu ring | rab tu dga' dang ldan pa yis | rnal 'byor pa ni bdag nyid ces | mngon pa'i nga rgyal la rtag dga' | sgyu dang bcos ma'i chos dang ldan | mya ngan 'das dang gzhan 'gro ba | phan tshun dag ni sun yang 'byin | gsang sngags smra ba la brten nas | gcig la gcig ni rtsod par 'gyur | de rnams bdud kyi byin brlabs kyis | gal te dngos grub phra thob na | des ni mngon par rang (sic for nga) rgyal bas | mkhas pa nyam du shes par 'gyur | tshogs pa'i nang du rtsod pa dang | khyi bzhin kha zas la spyod 'gyur | rang las 'bras las byung ba yi | phan pa la ni gnod pa byed | de rnams dge dang mi dge rnams | bdag cag rnams kyi stobs yin zer | mngon sum sangs rgyas 'dra ba yi | slob dpon smod cing bsnyen bkur med | skad cig gcig gis sdang byed cing | de la skad cig gis rjes chags | khyi dang phag dang khwa rnams kyi | spyod pa dag ni ston par byed |.

69. One text dedicated to this description is the *He ru ka'i rnam par dag pa*, To. 1481, attributed to Śraddhākaravarman.

70. While I have emphasized the *Sahajasiddhi*, other examples of a criticism of esoteric conduct are found in works attributed to Virūpa, especially his *Virūpādacaurāsi*, To. 2283, his *Dohakoṣa*, To. 2280, and his *Suniṣprapañcatattvopadeśa*, To. 2020.

71. *Sahajasiddhi*, To. 2260, fols. 2a4–2b2:

la la bdag ni lhan cig skyes | kha cig rmongs pas dbang phyug ste |
bdag bcas ma yin bdag med pa | rtog pa gnyis ni spangs pa nyid |
de ni zung 'jug go 'phang du | rgyal bas lhan cig skyes par gsungs |
de nyid srog chags rnams kyi srog | de nyid mchog tu mi 'gyur ba |
de nyid kun la khyab pa yi | lus kun la ni rnam par gnas |
bud med byis pa ba lang rdzi | kla klo dang ni rigs ngan dang |
chu yi nang gnas sems can dang | lha dang gnod sbyin klur bcas pa'i |
de rnams lhan cig skyes mi shes | 'gro ba'i grong khyer dag tu 'khyam |

72. Ibid., fols. 3a1–4:
kha cig dngos grub dbang gnyis skyes | byis pa yun ring rgan sogs kyis |
'bad pa yis ni thob mi 'gyur |
rgyu dang bcas pa'i skad cig ma | 'khrul dang rnam par 'khrul 'dra ma |
kha cig longs spyod rdzogs pa'i gzhung | de ni lhan cig skyes brjod min |
lte ba'i dbus su 'khor lo mchog | de dbus gzi brjid gzugs can ni |
sgrub pa po yis rtag bsgoms pa | de ni lhan cig skyes brjod min |
spyi bor gnas pa'i 'khor lo che | de la reg dang bde ba 'bab |
bya ba'i rab tu sbyor bas 'thob | de ni lhan cig skyes brjod min |
srog gi rlung ni 'gog pa ru | 'bad pa yis ni gang zhig byed |
sna yi rtse mor rab gzhug bya | de 'gog pa yis gang thob pa |
de ni lhan cig skys brjod min |
thur sel rlung ni 'gog pa yis | lus ni gdung ba byas nas su |
yang nas yang du goms par byed | de ni lhan cig skyes mi brjod |

73. *Vidyottama-mahā-tantra,* To. 746, fols. 12b4–13a1: de nas lag na rdo rje'i mdun du bzlas brjod bgyis te seng ge'i sgra 'byin gyi bar du bgyi'o | seng ge'i sgra thos nas lha ma yin gyi bu mo rnams 'byung ste de dag la 'dod pa bskyed par ma bgyi'o | gal te 'dod pa bskyed na seng ge ni ma mchis so | lha ma yin gyi bu rnams ni mchis te lha ma yin gyi bu rnams kyang yongs su spyad par 'gyur ro | gal te de dag la 'dod pa ma bskyed na seng ger 'gyur te | seng ge la zhen na rig sngags 'chang gi bu mo brgyad cu 'byung ngo | rig sngags 'chang bzhi stong yang g.yog 'khor du 'gyur ro | gang du 'dod pa der mchi'o | rig sngags 'chang gi 'khor los sgyur bar 'gyur ro | 'khor lo la sogs pa'i spyod yul du mi 'gyur ro | gang gi tshe rdo rje dang 'khor lo dang mdung rtse gsum pa dang be con dang | zhags pa dang | mdung thung dang dbyug to rnams mchi ba de'i tshe seng ges seng ga'i sgra 'byin te seng ge'i sgras mtshon pa thams cad dpag tshad brgyad khrir mchi'o | rig sngags 'chang gi rgyal po gang dag seng ge'i sgra thos pa de dag tham cad sa la lhung ngo | mtshon cha de dag thams cad kyang dbang du 'gyur ro | bskal par gnas pa'i rig sngags 'chang gi rgyal por 'gyur ro |.

74. *Guhyasamāja-tantra,* XII.51: vicaret samantataḥ siddho gaṅgāvālukasarvataḥ | sarveṣu samayāgreṣu vidyādharaprabhur bhavet ||. I am relying on the *Pradīpodyotana,* Chakravarti 1984, p. 113, for the interpretation of the first half of the verse.

75. *Catuḥpīṭha-mahāyoginī-tantrarāja,* fol. 27a2.

76. *Guhyasamāja,* XVI.88: antarddhānādisaṃsiddhau bhaved vajradharaḥ prabhuḥ | yakṣarājādisaṃsiddhau bhaved vidyādharaḥ prabhuḥ |. Cf. *Pradīpodyotana,* Chakravarti 1984, p. 199.

77. Cf. *Guhyasamāja,* IX, passim; especially pp. 105, 111.

78. Ibid., XVIII.67–71.

79. Cf. *Guhyasamāja,* XII.9–16.

80. *Vidyottama-mahā-tantra,* fol. 48b2.

81. *Bhūtaḍamara,* fols. 238a3–7

82. Ibid., fol. 249b2–3; cf. *Sandhivyākaraṇa,* fol. 194b5.

Abbreviations

AŚ	*Arthaśāstra*
Asc.	Ascribed to
BEFEO	*Bulletin de l'École Française d'Extrême Orient*
BST	Buddhist Sanskrit Texts series
CAJ	*Central Asiatic Journal*
CII	*Corpus Inscriptionem Indicarum*
EI	*Epigraphia Indica*
GOS	Gaekwad's Oriental Series
HOS	Harvard Oriental Series
HT	*Hevajra Tantra*
IA	*Indian Antiquary*
IHQ	*Indian Historical Quarterly*
IIJ	*Indo-Iranian Journal*
JA	*Journal Asiatique*
JAOS	*Journal of the American Oriental Society*
JIABS	*Journal of the International Association of Buddhist Studies*
JASB	*Journal of the (Royal) Asiatic Society of Bengal*
LL	*Lam 'bras slob bshad*
MCB	*Mélanges chinois et bouddhiques*
MDŚ	*Mānava Dharma Śāstra*
Pe.	Peking canon numbers (SUZUKI 1957)
RBTS	Rare Buddhist Text Series (Sarnath)
SKB	*Sa-skya bKa'-'bum* (Bsod Nams Rgya Mtsho 1969)
T.	*Taishō shinshū daizōkyō* number; TAKAKUSU and WATANABE 1924–34
To.	sDe-dge canon numbers (UI et al. 1934)
TSWS	Tibetan Sanskrit Works Series

Bibliography

The bibliography is ordered as follows: Indic and Ostensibly Indic Tibetan Sources, Chinese Sources, Indigenous Tibetan Sources, Archaeological and Epigraphic Materials, and General Modern Sources. Indic sources are arranged according to the Sanskrit alphabet, with Tibetan titles for which there is no Indic equivalent inserted in Tibetan dictionary order. Indigenous Tibetan sources are also in dictionary order. Chinese sources and general modern sources are ordered according to the Roman alphabet.

INDIC AND OSTENSIBLY INDIC TIBETAN SOURCES

Advayavajrasaṃgraha.

Shastri, Haraprasad, ed. 1927. *Advayavajrasaṃgraha.* GOS, no. 40. Baroda: Oriental Institute.

Apadāna.

Lilley, M., ed. 1925–27. *Apadāna.* London: Oxford University Press for the Pali Text Society.

Abhidharmakośabhāṣya.

Pradhan, Pralhad, ed. 1975. *Abhidharmakośabhāṣyam of Vasubandhu.* TSWS, vol. 8. 2d. rev. ed. Patna: K. P. Jayaswal Research Institute.

Abhidharmasamuccaya.

Pradhan, Pralhad, ed. 1950. *Abhidharma Samuccaya of Asanga.* Santiniketan: Visvabharati. To. 4049; T. 1605.

Abhidharmasamuccaya-bhāṣyam.

Tatia, Nathmal, ed. 1976. *Abhidharmasamuccaya-bhāṣyam.* TSWS, no. 17. Patna: K. P. Jayaswal Research Institute. To. 4053; T. 1606.

Abhidharmasamuccaya-vyākhyā. Asc. Jinaputra. To. 4054. bsTan-'gyur, sems-tsam, li, fols. 117a5–293a7.

Abhiṣekanirukti. Asc. Ratnākaraśānti. To. 2476. bsTan-'gyur, rgyud, zi, fols. 159b4–168b7.

Abhisamayālaṃkārāloka.

Vaidya, P. L., ed. 1960. *Aṣṭasāhasrikā Prajñāpāramitā with Haribhadra's Commentary Called Āloka*. BST, no. 4. Darbhanga: Mithila Institute.

Amoghapāśahṛdayadhāraṇī.

Meisezahl, R. O. 1962. "The Amoghapāśahṛdaya-dhāraṇī: The Early Sanskrit Manuscript of the Ruiunji Critically Edited and Translated." *Monumenta Nipponica* 17:265–328.

Arthaśāstra.

Kangle, R. P., ed. and trans. 1960. *The Kauṭilīya Arthaśāstra*. University of Bombay Studies in Sanskrit, Pakrit, and Pali, nos. 1–3. Bombay: University of Bombay. See Scharfe 1993, below.

**Ardhapañcamagāthā*. Asc. Nāgabuddhi. To. 2278. *bsTan-'gyur*, rgyud, zhi, fols. 128a6–133a4.

Avadānaśatakam.

Vaidya, P. L., ed. 1958. *Avadānaśatakam*. BST, no. 19. Darbhanga: Mithila Institute.

Avantisundarīkathā.

Kale, M. R. 1966. *Daśakumāracarita of Daṇḍin*. Delhi: Motilal Banarsidass.

Uḍḍiyānaśrīyogayoginīsvabhūtasambhoga-śmaśānakalpa. Asc. Birba-pa (Virūpa). To. 1744. *bsTan-*'gyur, rgyud, sha, fols. 111b6–113b2.

Ṛgveda.

Van Nooten, Barend A., and Gary B. Holland. 1994. *Rig Veda: A Metrically Restored Text with an Introduction and Notes*. HOS, vol. 50. Cambridge: Harvard University Press.

Karuṇāpuṇḍarīka.

Yamada, Isshi. 1968. *Karuṇāpuṇḍarīka: The White Lotus of Compassion*. 2 vols. London: School of Oriental and African Studies. Reprint, New Delhi: Heritage, 1989.

Karpūramañjarī.

Konow, Sten, and Charles Rockwell Lanman, ed. and trans. 1901. *Rāja-Çekhara's Karpūra-Mañjarī—A Drama by the Indian Poet Rājaçekhara (About 900 A.D.)*. HOS, vol. 4. Cambridge: Harvard University Press.

Kāṇhapādasya dohākoṣa.

Bagchi, Prabodh Chandra. 1935. *Dohakoṣa. University of Calcutta Journal of the Department of Letters* 28. [Monograph with the surviving anonymous Sanskrit commentary.]

Shahidullah, M. 1928. *Les Chants mystiques de Kāṇha et de Saraha—les Dohā-Koṣa*. Paris: Adrien-Maisonneuve.

Kāraṇḍavyūha-sūtra.

Mette, Adelheid, ed. and trans. 1997. *Die Gilgitfragmente des Kāraṇḍavyūha.* Indica et Tibetica Monographien zu end Sprachen und Literaturen des indo-tibetischen Kulturraumes, no. 29. Swisttal-Odendorf: Indica et Tibetica Verlag.

Vaidya, P. L., ed. 1961. *Mahāyāna-Sūtra-Saṁgraha.* Part 1. BST, no. 17, pp. 258–308. Darbhanga: Mithila Institute.

Kālikāpurāṇa.

Shastri, B. N. 1991–92. *The Kālikāpurāṇa (Text, Introduction & Translation in English).* 3 vols. Delhi: Nag Publishers.

Kāvyamīmāṃsā.

Parashar, Sadhana, ed. and trans. 2000. *Kāvyamīmā ṁ sā of Rājaśekhara: Original Text in Sanskrit and Translation with Explanatory Notes.* New Delhi: D. K. Printworld.

Kāvyālaṅkāra.

Sastry, P. V. Naganatha. 1970. *Kāvyālaṅkāra of Bhāmaha—Edited with English Translation and Notes.* Delhi: Motilal Banarsidass.

Kirātārjunīye.

Bahadur, Kaisher, ed. and trans. 1972. *The Kirātārjunīye by Bhāravi.* Vol. 1. Kathmandu: Ratna Pustak Bhandar.

Kubjikāmata-tantra.

Goudriaan, T., and J. A. Schoterman, eds. 1988. *Kubjikāmatatantra—Kulālikāmnāya Version.* Leiden: E. J. Brill.

Kulārṇava Tantra.

Vidyāratna, Tārānātha, ed. 1917. *Kulārṇava Tantra.* Reprint, Delhi: Motilal Banarsidass, 1965.

Kṛtyakalpataru.

Aiyangar, K. V. Rangaswami, ed. 1942. *Kṛtyakalpataru of Bhaṭṭa Lakṣmīdhara.* Vol. 8: *Tīrthavivecana-kāṇḍa.* GOS, no. 98. Baroda: Oriental Institute.

———. 1943. Idem. Vol. 11: *Rājadharma-kāṇḍa.* GOS, no. 100. Baroda: Oriental Institute.

———. 1950. Idem. Vol. 4: *Śrāddhakāṇḍa.* GOS, no. 110. Baroda: Oriental Institute.

Kṛṣṇayamāri-tantra.

Rinpoche, Samdhong, and Vrajvallabh Dwivedi, eds. 1992. *Kṛṣṇayamāri-tantram with Ratnāvali Pañjikā of Kumāracandra.* RBTS, no. 9. Sarnath: Central Institute of Higher Tibetan Studies.

Kosalālaṃkāra-tattvasaṃgraha-ṭīkā. Śākyamitra. To. 2503. bsTan-'gyur, rgyud, yi, fols. 1b1–245a7, ri, fols. 1b1–202a5.

Khasama-tantraraja. To. 386. *bKa'-'gyur,* rgyud-'bum, ga, fols. 199a7–202a1.

Khasama-tantra-ṭīkā. Ratnākaraśānti.

Upadhyay, Jagannath, ed. 1983. *Khasama-tantra-ṭīkā.* Varanasi: Sampūrṇānanda Samskṛta Viśvavidyālaya. To. 1424. *bsTan-'gyur*, rgyud, wa, fols. 153a3–171a7.

Gaüḍavaho.

Suru, N. G., ed. and trans. 1975. *Gaüḍavaho of Vākpatirāja.* Prakrit Text Society Series, no. 18. Ahmedabad: Prakrit Text Society.

Gaṇḍavyūha.

Suzuki, Daisetz Teitaro, and Hokei Idzumi, eds. 1949. *The Gaṇḍavyūha Sūtra.* 2d rev. ed. Tokyo: Society for the Publication of Sacred Books of the World.

Guhyagarbha-tantra (also known as *Guhyakośa-tantra*). To. 832. *bsTan-'gyur*, rnying rgyud, kha, fols. 110b1–132a7. See Kaneko 1982, no. 187.

Guhyasamāja Mahāguhyatantrarāja.

Matsunaga, Yukei, ed. 1978. *Guhyasamāja Tantra.* Osaka: Toho Shuppan.

Guhyasiddhi. Asc. Padmavajra.

Rinpoche, Samdhong, and Vrajvallabh Dwivedi, eds. 1987. *Guhyādi-Aṣṭasiddhi-Saṅgraha.* RBTS, no. 1, pp. 5–62. Sarnath: Central Institute of Higher Tibetan Studies.

Guhyārthaprakāśamahādbhūta. Asc. Gambhiravajra (Zab-pa'i rdo-rje). To. 1200. *bsTan-'gyur*, rgyud, ja, fols. 111a2–154b1.

Gorakṣasiddhāntasaṅgraha.

Pāṇḍeya, Janārdana Śāstrī, ed. 1973. *Gorakṣasiddhāntasaṅgraha.* Saraswatībhavana-Granthamālā, Vol. 110. Varanasi: Vārāṇaseya Sanskṛta Viśvavidyālaya.

Grub thob brgyad cu rtsa bzhi'i gsol 'debs. Asc. Vajrāsana. To. 3758. *bsTan-'gyur*, rgyud, tshu, fols. 110a6–113b3.

Grub thob lnga bcu'i rtogs pa brjod pa thig le 'od kyi phreng ba. Asc. *Ḍākinī. To. 2444. *bsTan-'gyur*, rgyud, zi, fols. 71b1–74a7.

Caṇḍamahāroṣaṇa-tantra.

George, Christopher S., ed. and trans. 1974. *Caṇḍamahāroṣaṇa-tantra.* New Haven, CT: American Oriental Society. To. 431.

Catuḥpīṭha-mahāyoginī-tantrarāja. To. 428. *bKa'-'gyur*, rgyud-'bum, nga, fols. 181a1–231b5.

Catuḥśataka.

Lang, Karen, ed. and trans. 1981. *Āryadeva's Catuḥśataka: On the Bodhisattva's Cultivation of Merit and Knowledge.* Indiske Studier, no. 7. Copenhagen: Akademisk Forlag.

**Caturaśītisiddhapravṛtti.* Asc. Abhayadattaśrī. Pe. 5091.

Dowman, Keith, trans. 1985. *Masters of Mahamudra: Songs and Histories of the Eighty-Four Buddhist Siddhas.* Albany: State University of New York Press.

Robinson, James B., ed. and trans. 1979. *Buddha's Lions: The Lives of the Eighty-Four Siddhas.* Berkeley: Dharma.

**Caturaśītisiddhasambodhihṛdaya.* Asc. dPa'-bo 'od-gsal (*Vīraprabha). To. 2292. *bsTan-'gyur,* rgyud, zhi, fols. 153a6–158b1.

**Caturaśītisiddhābhisamaya.* Asc. *Śrīsena (dPal gyi sde) of Nepal. To. 4317. Ed. and trans. in Schmidt 1958, pp. 155–169.

Candraguhya-tilaka-mahātantrarāja. To. 477. *bKa'-'gyur,* rgyud-'bum, ja, fols. 247b4–303a7.

Caryāgītikośa.
Kværne, Per. 1977. *An Anthology of Buddhist Tantric Songs: A Study of the Caryāgīti.* Det Norske Videnskaps-Akademi II Hist.-Filos. Klasse Skrifter Ny Serie, no. 14. Oslo: Universitetsforlaget.
Sen, Nilratan. 1977. *Caryāgītikoṣa Facsimile Edition.* Simla: Indian Institute of Advanced Study.

Cittaguhyagambhīrārthagīti. Asc. Śabareśvara. To. 2448. *bsTan-'gyur,* rgyud, zi, fols. 82b1–83a1.

Cittaguhyadohā. Asc. *Ḍākinī. To. 2443. *bsTan-'gyur,* rgyud, zi, fols. 67a3–71a7.

Chinnamuṇḍasādhana. Asc. Birwa. To. 1555. *bsTan-'gyur,* rgyud, za, fols. 206a1–208a4. See Nihom 1992.

Jñānatilaka-tantra. Śrī Jñānatilaka-yoginītantrarāja-paramamahādbhūta. To. 422. *bKa'-'gyur,* rgyud-'bum, nga, fols. 96b6–136b4.

Jñānatilakapañjikā-guhyatattva. Attributed to Jñānaparama. To. 1203. *bsTan-'gyur,* rgyud, ja, fols. 208b1–271b7.

Jñānasiddhi. Asc. Indrabhuti. Edited with *Guhyasiddhi,* pp. 93–157.
Bhattacharya, Benoytosh, ed. 1929. *Two Vajrayana Works.* GOS, no. 44. Baroda: Oriental Institute.

Ḍākārṇava-tantra. Śrī Ḍākārṇavamahāyoginītantrarāja. To. 372. *bKa'-'gyur,* rgyud-'bum, kha, fols. 137a1–264b7. The Apabhraṃśa verses edited in Chaudhuri 1935.

Ḍākinyupadeśaśrotraparamparapīḍācchedanāvavāda. Anon. To. 2286. *bsTan-'gyur,* rgyud, zhi, fols. 145a1–150a2.

Ḍākinījālasaṃvararahasya. Asc. Anaṅga Yogin.
Rinpoche, Samdhong, and Vrajvallabh Dwivedi, eds. 1990. *Ḍākinījālasaṃvararahasya.* RBTS, no. 8. Sarnath: Central Institute of Higher Tibetan Studies.

Tantrārthāvatāra. Asc. Buddhaguhya. To. 2501. *bsTan-'gyur,* rgyud, 'i, fols. 1b1–91b6.

Tillopādadohākoṣa. In Bagchi 1935, with *Kāṇhapādasya dohākoṣa,* pp. 1–4, 41–51.

Tīrthikacāṇḍālīka. Asc. Ācārya Acinta. To. 2393. *bsTan-'gyur*, rgyud, zi, fols. 22b7–23a3. See chapter 5.

Triṃśikāvijñaptibhāsya.

Lévi, Sylvain, ed. 1925. *Vijñaptimātratāsiddhi*. Bibliothèque de l'École des Hautes Études, fasc. 245. Paris: Librairie Ancienne Honoré Champion.

Trailokyavijaya-mahākalparāja. To. 482. *bKa'-'gyur*, gyud 'bum, ta, fols. 10a1–57a7. T. 1171, 1172.

Daśabhūmika.

Kondo, Ryuko, ed. 1936. *Daśabhūmīśvaro Nāma Mahāyānasūtraṃ*. Rinsen Buddhist Text Series II. Reprint, Kyoto: Rinsen Book Company, 1983.

Divyāvadāna.

Vaidya, P. L., ed. 1959. *Divyāvadāna*. BST, no. 20. Darbhanga: Mithila Institute.

Dīghanikāya.

Rhys Davids, T. W., and J. E. Carpenter, eds. 1890–1911. *Dīghanikāya*. 3 vols. London: H. Frowde for the Pali Text Society.

Dohakoṣa. Asc. Birba-pa. To. 2280. *bsTan-'gyur*, rgyud, zhi, fols. 134a1–136a4.

Dravva-saṃgaha. Nemicandra Siddhānta-cakravarttī.

Ghoshal, Sarat Chandra, ed. and trans. 1917. *Dravya-saṃgraha*. The Sacred Books of the Jainas, vol. 1. Arrah: Central Jaina Publishing House.

Dvikramatattvabhāvanā-mukhāgama. Asc. Buddhaśrījñāna. To. 1853. *bsTan-'gyur*, rgyud, di, fols. 1b1–17b2.

Dhammapadaṭṭhakathā.

Smith, H., and H. E. Norman, eds. 1906–1915. *Dhammapadaṭṭhakathā*. 5 vols. London: H. Frowde for the Pali Text Society.

Burlingame, E.W., trans. 1921. *Buddhist Legends*. HOS, nos. 28–30. Cambridge: Harvard University Press.

**Dhāraṇīsamgraha*. Translated 653–654 C.E. by *Atikūṭa. T.901.18.785a1–897b19.

Dhyānottarapaṭalakrama. To. 808. *bKa'-'gyur*, gyud 'bum, wa, fols. 223a1–225b7.

Dhyānottara-paṭala-ṭīkā Asc. Buddhaguhya. To. 2670. *bsTan-'gyur*, rgyud, thu, fols. 1b1–38a3.

Nātyaśāstra.

Kavi, Manavalli Ramakrishna, ed. 1926–34. *Nātyaśāstra with the Commentary of Abhinavagupta*. GOS, nos. 36 and 68. Baroda: Oriental Institute.

Nāmasaṃgītimaṇḍalavidhyākāśavimala. Asc. Mañjuśrīmitra. To. 2543. *bsTan-'gyur*, rgyud, ngu, fols. 1b1–13b6.

rNam par snang mdzad mngon par byang chub pa'i rgyud chen po'i 'grel bshad. Asc.

Buddhaguhya. To. 2663. *bsTan-'gyur*, rgyud, nyu, fols. 65a3–351a7, tu, fols. 1b1–116a7.

Niṣpannayogāvalī. Asc. Abhayākaragupta.

Bhattacharyya, Benoytosh, ed. 1949. *Niṣpannayogāvalī*. GOS, no. 109. Baroda: Oriental Institute.

Nītisāra.

Mitra, Rajendralal, ed. 1982. Revised with English translation by Sisir Kumar Mitra. *The Nītisāra or the Elements of Polity by Kāmandaki*. Bibliotheca Indica, no. 309. Calcutta: Asiatic Society.

Pañcakrama. Asc. Siddha Nāgārjuna.

MIMAKI, Katsumi, and Toru TOMABECHI, eds. 1994. *Pañcakrama—Sanskrit and Tibetan Texts Critically Edited with Verse Index and Facsimile Edition of the Sanskrit Manuscripts*. Bibliotheca Codicum Asiaticorum, no. 8. Tokyo: Centre for East Asian Cultural Studies for UNESCO.

**Pañcadaśāpatti*. Anon. To. 2480. *bsTan-'gyur*, rgyud, zi, fol. 180a3–5; a superior recension of the text is found in Mañjuśrikirti's *Vajrayānamūlāpattiṭīkā-mārgapradīpa*, To. 2488, *bsTan-'gyur*, rgyud, zi, fol. 220b5–7.

Paramaṭṭha-dīpanī (Theragāthā-aṭṭhakathā).

Woodward, F. L., ed. 1940–52. *Paramaṭṭha-dīpanī (Theragāthā-aṭṭhakathā)*. London: Pali Text Society.

Paramādya-mahāyānakalparāja. To. 487. *bKa'-'gyur*, rgyud-'bum, ta, fols. 150b1–173a4. T. 220 (10), 240–4.

Pāiä-Sadda-Mahaṇṇavo.

Seṭh, Paṇḍita Haragovindadās Trikamacand, ed. 1963. *Pāiä-Sadda-Mahaṇṇavo*. Prakrit Text Society series, no. 7. Varanasi: Prakrit Text Society.

Pāśupatasūtra.

Sastri, R. Ananthakrishna, ed. 1940. *Pasupata Sutras with Pancharthabhashya–Kaundinya*. Trivadrum Sanskrit Series no. CXLIII. Trivandrum: Oriental Manuscripts Library of the University of Travancore.

Pīṭhādinirṇaya. Asc. Śakyarakṣita. To. 1606. *bsTan-'gyur*, rgyud, 'a, fols. 130a1–137a7.

Potalakāṣṭaka. Anon.

Pandey, Janardan Shastri, ed. 1994. *Bauddha-Stotra-Saṁgraha*, pp. 123–124. Delhi: Motilal Banarsidass.

Po ta lar 'gro ba'i lam yig. Anon. To. 3756. *bsTan-'gyur*, rgyud, tshu, fols. 100a6–106b6.

Prajñāpāramitā-nayaśatapañcāśatkaṭīkā. Asc. Jñānamitra. To. 2647. *bsTan-'gyur*, rgyud, ju, fols. 272b7–294a5.

Prajñopāyaviniścayasiddhi. Asc. Anaṅgavajra. Edited with *Guhyasiddhi,* pp. 63–88.

Pradīpodyotana.

Chakravarti, Chintaharan, ed. 1984. *Guhyasamājatantrapradīpodyotanaṭīkā-ṣaṭkoṭivyākhyā.* TSWS, no. 25. Patna: Kashi Prasad Jayaswal Research Institute.

dPal u rgyan du tshogs 'khor byas pa'i dus su rnal 'byor pa grub pa thob pa bzhi bcus rdo rje'i mgur bzhengs pa nyams kyi man ngag thig le gser gyi phreng ba. Anon. To. 2449. *bsTan-'gyur,* rgyud, zi, fols. 83a1–85b6.

'Phags pa dpung bzangs kyis zhus ba'i rgyud kyi tshig gi don bshad pa'i brjed byang. Anon. To. 2672. *bsTan-'gyur,* rgyud, thu, fols. 54b7–100b6.

Buddhakapālatantrapañjikā Tattvacandrikā. Asc. Padmavajra. To. 1653 *bsTan-'gyur,* rgyud, ra, fols. 150a3–166a7. [The title is incorrectly reconstructed by UI et al., the editors of the Tohoku catalogue, as *Buddhakapālatantratattvacandrikāpañjikā.]*

Buddhacarita. Asc. Aśvaghosa.

Johnston, E. H., ed. and trans. 1936. *The Buddhacarita: or, Acts of the Buddha.* Reprint, Delhi: Motilal Banarsidass, 1972.

Bṛhatkathāślokasaṃgraha.

Poddar, Ram Prakash, and Neelima Sinha, ed. and trans. 1986. *Buddhasvāmin's Bṛhatkathāślokasaṁgraha with English Translation.* Prācyabhāratī Series, no. 21. Varanasi: Tara Printing Works.

Bodhicaryāvatāra.

Vaidya, P.L., ed. 1960. *Bodhicaryāvatāra of Śāntideva, with the Commentary Pañjika of Prajñākaramati.* BST, no. 12. Darbhanga: Mithila Institute.

Bodhipathapradīpa. Asc. Atiśa Dipaṃkaraśrījñāna. In Eimer 1978 below.

Davidson, trans. 1995a.

Bodhisattvabhūmi.

Wogihara, Unrai, ed. 1930–36. *Bodhisattvabhūmi: A Statement of Whole Course of the Bodhisattva (Being Fifteenth Section of Yogācārabhūmi).* Reprint, Tokyo: Sankibo Buddhist Book Store, 1971. To. 4037; T. 1579. See Tatz 1986.

Brahmasūtrabhāṣya.

Śāstri, Jagadīṣa L., ed. 1980. *Brahmasūtra-śānkarabhāṣyam—With the Commentaries: Bhāṣyaratnaprabhā of Govindānanda, Bhāmatī of Vācaspatimiśra, Nyāya-Nirṇaya of Ānandagiri.* Delhi: Motilal Banarsidass.

Bhadracaryāpraṇidhānarājaṭīkā. Asc. Śākyamitra. To. 4013. *bsTan-'gyur,* mdo 'grel, nyi, fols. 201a4–234a4.

Bhāsanāṭakacakram.

Vetal, Pt. Anantaram Sastri, et al., eds. 1963. *Bhāsanāṭakacakram.* 2 vols. Varanasi: Chowkhamba Sanskrit Series Office.

Bhikṣuṇī-Vinaya.
Roth, Gustav, ed. 1970. *Bhikṣuṇī-Vinaya: Manual of Discipline for Buddhist Nuns.* TSWS, vol. 12. Patna: K. P. Jayaswal Research Institute.

Bhūtaḍamara-mahātantrarāja. To. 747. *bKa'-'gyur,* rgyud-'bum, dza, fols. 238a1–263a7.

Mañjuśrīmūlakalpa.
Sastri, T. Ganapati. 1920. *Āryamañjuśrīmūlakalpa.* Trivandrum: Trivandrum Sanskrit Series. Reprint, Trivandrum: C B H Publications, 1992.
Ch. 53 *(rājavyākaraṇa)* see Jayaswal 1934; cf. MATSUNAGA 1985.

Mañjuśrīnāmasaṃgīti.
Davidson, Ronald M., ed. and trans. 1981. "The *Litany of Names of Mañjuśrī:* Text and Translation of the *Mañjuśrīnāmasaṃgīti.*" In Michel Strickmann, ed., *Tantric and Taoist Studies in Honour of R. A. Stein. MCB* 20:1–69.

Mattavilāsaprahasana.
Lockwood, Michael, and A. Vishnu Bhat, ed. and trans. 1981. *Mattavilāsa Prahasana ("The Farce of Drunken Sport") by King Mahendravikramavarma Pallava.* Madras: Christian Literature Society.

Madhyamakāvatāra.
La Vallée Poussin, Louis de, ed. 1907–12. *Madhyamakāvatāra par Candrakīrti.* Bibliotheca Buddhica, no. IX. Saint-Petersburg: Académie Impériale des Sciences.
Huntington, C. W., trans. 1989. *The Emptiness of Emptiness: An Introduction to Early Indian Mādhyamika.* Honolulu: University of Hawaii Press.

Manoratha-pūraṇī (Aṅguttara-nikāya Aṭṭhakathā).
Walleser, M., and H. Kopp, eds. 1924–1956. *Manoratha-pūraṇī (Aṅguttara-nikāya Aṭṭhakathā).* 5 vols. London: Oxford University Press for Pali Text Society.

Mayamata.
Dagens, Bruno, ed. and trans. 1970–76. *Mayamata—traité sanskrit d'architecture.* Publications de l'Institut Français d'Indologie, nos. 40–I and II. Pondichéry: Institut Français d'Indologie.
———. 1985. *Mayamata—An Indian Treatise on Housing Architecture and Iconography.* New Delhi: Sitaram Bhartia Institute of Science & Research.

Mahākālatantra. To. 440. *bKa'-'gyur,* rgyud-'bum, ca, fols. 45b6–86a7. See Stablein 1976.

Mahābhārata. Śāntiparvan.
Sukthankar, Vishnu S., et al., ed. 1949–50. *Mahābhārata. Śāntiparvan.* 2 parts. Poona: Bhandarkar Oriental Research Institute.

Mahāmāyūrīvidyārājñī.
SHŪYO Takubo, ed. 1972. *Ārya-Mahā-Māyūrī Vidyā-Rājñī.* Tokyo: Sankibo.

Mahāmudrākanakamālā. Asc. Maitripa. To. 2454. *bsTan-'gyur*, rgyud, zi, fols. 115b3–124b3.

**Mahāyānāvatāra-śāstra*. Asc. *Dṛḍhramati. T.1634.32.36a–49c.

Mahāvairocanābhisambodhitantra. Extended title: *Mahāvairocanābhisambodhi-vikurvitādhiṣṭhāna-vaipulyasūtrendrarāja-nāma-dharmaparyāya*. To. 494. *bKa'-'gyur*, rgyud-'bum, tha, fols. 151b2–260a7; T.848.18.1a–55a.

Mālatīmādhava.

Kale, M.R., ed. 1928. *Bhavabhuti's Mālatīmādhava, With the Commentary of Jagaddhara*. Reprint, Delhi: Motilal Banarsidass, 1983.

Mānava Dharma Śāstra.

Shastri, J. L., ed. 1983. *Manusmṛti, With the Sanskrit Commentary Manvartha-Muktāvalī of Kullūka Bhaṭṭa*. Delhi: Motilal Banarsidass.

Doniger, Wendy, and Brian K. Smith, trans. *The Laws of Manu*. London and New York: Penguin Books, 1991.

Mānasollāsa. Asc. Bhūlokamalla Someśvara, and probably written 1131 C.E.

Shrigondekar, G. K., ed. 1925–61. *Mānasollāsa of King Bhūlokamalla Someśvara*. GOS, nos. 28, 64, and 138. Baroda: Oriental Institute.

Milindapañha.

Trenckner, V., ed. 1880. *Milindapañha*. London: Williams and Norgate.

Mūlamadhyamakakārikā.

La Vallée Poussin, Louis de, ed. 1903–1913. *Mūlamadhyamakakārikās de Nāgārjuna avec la Prasannapadā Commentaire de Candrakīrti*. Bibliotheca Buddhica, no. 4. St. Petersburg: l'Académie Impériale des Sciences.

Mūlasarvāstivāda Vinaya.

Dutt, Nalinaksha, ed. 1941–50. *Gilgit Manuscripts*. Vols. 2 and 3. Srinagar: Kashmir Research Department.

Gnoli, Raniero, ed. 1977. *The Gilgit Manuscript of the Saṅghabhedavastu*. Serie Oriental Roma, vol. 49, 2 pts. Rome: Istituto Italiano per il Medio ed Estremo Oriente.

———. 1978. *The Gilgit Manuscript of the Śayanāsanavastu and the Adhikaraṇavastu*. Serie Oriental Roma, vol. 50. Rome: Istituto Italiano per il Medio ed Estremo Oriente.

Ye shes kyi mkha' 'gro ma sum cu rtsa lnga'i rtogs pa brjod pa. Anon. To. 2450. *bsTan-'gyur*, rgyud, zi, fols. 85b6–88a1.

Yogācārabhūmi.

Bhattacharya, Vidushekhara, partially ed. 1957. *The Yogācārabhūmi of Ācārya Asaṅga*. Calcutta: University of Calcutta.

Cf. *Bodhisattvabhūmi*, above, and *Śrāvakabhūmi* below. To. 4035–4042. T. 1579.

Yogāvatārādisaṃgraha. Nepal National Archives, ms. tṛtīya 366–3. Modern copy in the Asiatic Society, ms. G8060.

Ratnaguṇasañcaya-gāthā.
YUYAMA, Akira, ed. 1976. *Prajñā-pāramitā-ratna-guṇasaṃcaya-gāthā (Sanskrit Recension A).* Cambridge: Cambridge University Press.

Ratnagotravibhāga.
Johnston, E. H., ed. 1950. *Ratnagotravibhāga Mahāyānottaratantraśāstra.* Patna: Bihar Research Society.

Ratnamālāvadāna.
TAKAHATA, Kanga, ed. 1954. *Ratnamālāvadāna: A Garland of Precious Gems.* Oriental Library Series D. Vol. 3. Tokyo: Toyo Bunko.

Rājataraṅgiṇī.
Stein, Marc Aurel, ed. 1892. *Kalhaṇa's Rājataraṅgiṇī or the Chronicle of the Kings of Kashmir.* Bombay: n.p.
Stein, Marc Aurel, trans. 1900. *Kalhaṇa's Rājataraṅgiṇī, a Chronicle of the Kings of Kashmir.* 2 vols. Westminster: n.p.

Rāmāyana. Bālakāṇḍa.
Bhatt, G. H., ed. 1960. *Rāmāyana. Bālakāṇḍa.* Baroda: Oriental Institute.
Vaidya, P. L., ed. 1971. *Yuddhakāṇḍa.* Baroda: Oriental Institute.
Shah, Umakant P., ed. 1975. *Uttarakāṇḍa.* Baroda: Oriental Institute.

Rudrayāmala.
Yogatantra Department, ed. 1980. *Rudrayāmala.* Yogatantra-Granthamālā, vol. 7. Varanasi: Sampurnanand Sanskrit Vishvavidyalaya.

Laghusaṃvara-tantra. Tantrarāja-śrīlaghusambara. To. 368. *bKa'-'gyur,* rgyud-'bum, ka, fols. 213b1–246b7.

Laṅkāvatāra-sūtra.
Nanjio, Bunyiu, ed. 1923. *Laṅkāvatāra-sūtra.* Reprint, Bibliotheca Otaniensis, vol. 1. Kyoto: Otani University Press, 1956.

Lam 'bras bu dang bcas pa'i gdams ngag dang man ngag tu bcas pa. Asc. Virūpa. To. 2284. *bsTan-`gyur,* rgyud, zhi, fols. 139a6–142b7.

**Vajragarbhatantrarājasūtra.* T.1198.20.542c-548b. Trans. in Bagchi 1944.

Vajracchedikā Prajñāpāramitā.
Conze, Edward, ed. and trans. 1957. *Vajracchedikā Prajñāpāramitā.* Serie Orientale Roma, no. 13. Rome: Is.M.E.O.

Vajrapañjara. Ḍākinīvajrapañjara-mahātantrarājakalpa. To. 419. *bKa'-'gyur,* rgyud-'bum, nga, fols. 30a4–65b7.

Vajrapāṇy-abhiṣeka-mahātantra. To. 496. *bKa'-'gyur,* rgyud 'bum, da, fols. 1b1–156b7.

Vajrapādasārasaṃgrahapañjikā. Asc. *Yaśaskīrtibhadra (sNyan-grags bzng-po). To. 1186. *bsTan-'gyur,* rgyud, ga, fols. 58b4–146b6.

Vajramahābhairava-tantra. To. 468. Ed. and trans. in Siklós 1996.

Vajramālābhidhāna-mahāyoga-tantra. To. 445. *bKa'-'gyur,* rgyud-'bum, ca, fols. 208a1–277b3.

**Vajrayānacaturdaśamūlāpattiṭīkā.* Asc. Lakṣmīkara. To. 2485. *bsTan-'gyur,* rgyud, zi, fols. 181a5–185a7.

**Vajrayānamūlāpattiṭīkā [rDo rje theg pa'i rtsa ba'i ltung ba'i rgya cher 'grel pa].* Asc. *Garbhapāda (sNying-po-zhabs). To. 2486. *bsTan-'gyur,* rgyud, zi, fols. 185a7–192b6.

Vajrayānamūlāpattiṭīkā-mārgapradīpa. Asc. Mañjuśrīkīrti. To. 2488. *bsTan-'gyur,* rgyud, zi, fols. 197b7–231b7.

Vajrayānasthūlāpatti. Asc. Nāgārjuna. To. 2482. *bsTan-'gyur,* rgyud, zi, fols. 180a2–b3.

Vajravidāraṇa-dhāraṇī.

Iwamoto, Yukata, ed. 1937. *Kleinere Dhāraṇī Texte*, pp. 7–9. Beiträge zur Indologie, no. 2. Kyoto: n.p.

Vajravidāraṇādhāraṇyekavīrasādhana. Asc. Buddhaguhya. To. 2926. *bsTan-'gyur,* rgyud, nu, fols. 329a6–330a3.

Vajraśekhara-mahāguhyayogatantra. To. 480. *bKa'-'gyur,* rgyud-'bum, nya, fols. 142b1–274a5.

Varṇārhavarṇastotra.

Hartmann, Jens-Uwe, ed. 1987. *Das Varṇārhavarṇastotra des Mātṛceṭa.* Sanskrittetexte aus den Turfanfunden, vol. 12. Göttingen: Vandenhoeck & Ruprecht. To. 1138.

Vigrahavyāvartanī.

Johnston, E. H., and Arnold Kunst, ed.; Bhattacharya, Kamaleswar, trans. 1978. *The Dialectical Method of Nāgārjuna.* Delhi: Motilal Banarsidass.

Vidyottama-mahātantra. To. 746. *bKa'-'gyur,* rgyud-'bum, dza, fols. 1b1–237b7.

Vimalaprabhā.

Upadhyaya, Jagannatha, ed. 1986. *Vimalaprabhā.* Bibliotheca Indo-Tibetica Series no. XI. Sarnath: Central Institute for Higher Tibetan Studies.

Virūapādacaurāsi. Asc. Virūpa. To. 2283. *bsTan-'gyur,* rgyud, zhi, fols. 138a4–139a6.

Vīṇāśikhatantra.

Goudriaan, Teun, ed. and trans. 1985. *The Vīṇāśikhatantra: A Śaiva Tantra of the Left Current.* Delhi: Motilal Banarsidass.

Vairocanābhisambodhitantrapiṇḍārtha. Asc. Buddhaguhya. To. 2662. *bsTan-'gyur,* rgyud, nyu, fols. 1–65a.

Vyaktabhāvānugata-tattva-siddhi. Asc. Yogini Cintā. With *Guhyasiddhi*, pp. 169–179.

Śatapañcāśatka.

Bailey, D.R. Shackleton, ed. and trans. 1951. *The Śatapañcāśatka of Mātṛceta.* Cambridge: Cambridge University Press.

Śārdūlakarṇāvadāna.

Mukhopadhyaya, Sujitkumar, ed. 1954. *Śārdūlakarṇāvadāna.* Santiniketan: Viśvabharati. To. 358. T.551, 552, 1300, 1301.

Śikṣāsamuccaya. Asc. Śāntideva.

Vaidya, P.L., ed. 1961. *Śikṣāsamuccaya of Śāntideva.* BST, no. 11. Darbhanga: Mithila Institute. To. 3940. T. 1636.

Śūnyatādṛṣṭi. Asc. Śabaripa. To. 2426. *bsTan-'gyur*, rgyud, zi, fols. 40a3–40b1. Translated in chapter 5.

Śrāvakabhūmi.

Shukla, Karunesha, ed. 1973. *Śrāvakabhūmi of Ācārya Asaṅga.* TSWS, vol. 14. Patna: K. P. Jayaswal Research Institute.

Śrī-Kṛṣṇavajrapādadohakoṣaṭīkā. Asc. *Amitābha. To. 2302. *bsTan-'gyur,* rgyud, zhi, fols. 230a6–242b7.

Śrī-Guhyasamājatantra-nidāna-gurūpadeśana-vyākhyāna. Asc. Vilāsavajra. To. 1910. *bsTan-'gyur,* rgyud, phi, fols. 89b1–97b5.

Śrī-Jñānatilakapañjikā-guhyatattva. Asc. Jñānavarman. To. 1203. *bsTan-'gyur,* rgyud, ja, fols. 208b1–271b7.

Śrī-Tattvapradīpa-mahāyoginī-tantrarāja. To. 423. *bKa'-'gyur,* rgyud-'bum, nga, fols. 136b5–142b7.

Śrī-Buddhakapāla-yoginī-tantra-rāja. To. 424. *bKa'-'gyur,* rgyud-'bum, nga, fols. 143a1–167a5; Pe. 63. bKa'-'gyur, rgyud-'bum, da, fols. 126b4–153a6.

Śrī-Buddhakapālatantrapañjikā Jñānavatī. Asc. Saraha. To 1652. *bsTan-'gyur,* rgyud, ra, fols. 104b1–150a2.

Śrī-Buddhakapālamahātantrarajaṭīkā Abhayapaddhatiḥ. Asc. Abhayākaragupta. To. 1654, *bsTan-'gyur,* rgyud, ra, fols. 166b1–255b3. Manuscript Asiatic Society no. 3827; Nepal National Archives, ms. pañca 21.

Śrī-Saṃpuṭatantrarājaṭīkāmnyāyamañjarī. Asc. Abhayākaragupta. To. 1198. *bsTan-'gyur,* rgyud, cha, fols. 1b1–316a7.

Śrī-Sahajapradīpa-pañjikā. Asc. *Vajragupta. To. 1202. *bsTan-'gyur,* rgyud, ja, fols. 160a1–208b1.

Śrī Hevajrapañjikā muktāvalī. Asc. Ratnākaraśānti.

Tripathi, Ram Shankar, and Thakur Sain Negi, eds. 2001. *Hevajratantram with Muktāvalīpañjikā of Mahāpaṇḍitācārya Ratnākaraśānti.* Bibliotheca Indo-Tibetica Series, XLVIII. Sarnath: Central Institute of Higher Tibetan Studies. To. 1189. *bsTan-'gyur*, rgyud, ga, fols. 221a1–297a7.

Ṣaṭsāhasra Saṃhitā.

Schoterman, J. A. 1982. *The Ṣaṭsāhasra Saṃhitā: Chapters 1–5.* Orientalia Rheno-Traiectina, vol. 27. Leiden: Brill.

Ṣaḍdharmopadeśa. Asc. Tillipa. To. 2330. *bsTan-'gyur,* rgyud, zhi, fols. 270a7–271a3.

Saṃvarodaya-tantra.

Tsuda, Shinichi, ed. and trans. 1974. *The Saṁvarodaya-Tantra—Selected Chapters.* Tokyo: Hokuseido Press.

Saṃkṣiptābhiṣekavidhi. Asc. Vāgīśvarakirti. In Sakurai 1996, ed., pp. 407–441.

Satyadvayavibhaṅga.

Eckel, Malcolm David, ed. and trans. 1987. *Jñānagarbha's Commentary on the Distinction Between the Two Truths.* Albany: State University of New York Press.

Saṃdhi-bhāṣā-ṭīkā. Asc. Nāgārjunapāda. To. 1206. *bsTan-'gyur,* rgyud, ja fols. 297a5–301b4.

Sandhivyākaraṇa-tantra. To. 444. *bKa'-'gyur,* rgyud-'bum, ca, fols. 158a1–207b7.

Saṃnyāsa-upaniṣad.

Schrader, F. Otto, ed. 1912. *The Minor Upanisads—Vol 1: Saṃnyāsa-Upaniṣads.* Madras: Adyar Library.

Olivelle, Patrick, trans. 1992. *Saṃnyāsa Upaniṣads: Hindu Scriptures on Asceticism and Renunciation.* Oxford: Oxford University Press.

Sampuṭa. Sampuṭodbhava. To. 381. *bKa'-'gyur,* rgyud-'bum, ga, fols. 73b1–158b7; Pe. 26. bKa'-'gyur, rgyud-'bum, ga, fols. 244a2–330a5. Partially edited and described in Skorupski 1996.

Sampuṭa-tilaka. To. 382. *bKa'-'gyur,* rgyud-'bum, ga, fols. 158b7–184a7.

Sarahapādasya dohākoṣa. Published with the surviving commentary in Bagchi 1935 and published and translated in Shahidullah 1928; see *Kāṇhapādasya dohākoṣa.*

Sarvatathāgatatattvasaṃgraha. To. 479; T. 882.

Chandra, Lokesh, ed. 1987. *Sarva-Tathāgata-Tattva-Saṅgraha.* Delhi: Motilal Banarsidass.

Yamada, Isshi, ed. 1980. *Sarva-tathāgata-Tattvasaṅgraha: A Critical Edition Based on a Sanskrit Manuscript and Chinese and Tibetan Translations.* New Delhi: International Academy of Indian Culture.

See Iyanaga 1985 for a discussion of the textual transmission.

**Sarvatantranidānamahāguhyaśrīsampuṭatantrarājaṭīkā.* Asc. Vīravajra. To. 1199. *bsTan-'gyur,* rgyud, ja, fols. 1b1–111a2.

Sarvadurgatipariśodhana-tantra.

Skorupski, Tadeusz, ed. 1983. *The Sarvadurgatipariśodhana Tantra—Elimination of All Evil Destinies.* Delhi: Motilal Banarsidass.

Sarvabuddhasamāyoga, or *Sarvabuddhasamāyoga-ḍākinījāla-sambara-nāma-uttara-tantra.* (longer recension) To. 366. *bKa'-'gyur,* rgyud-'bum, ka, fols. 151b1–193a6.

Sarvabuddhasamāyoga-gaṇavidhi. Asc. Indrabhūti. To. 1672. *bsTan-'gyur,* rgyud, la, fols. 195a7–199a4.

Sarvabuddhasamāyoga-ḍākinīmāyā-sambara-tantrārthodaraṭīkā. Asc. Indranāla (brGya-byin sdong-po). To. 1659. *bsTan-'gyur,* rgyud, ra, fols. 245a1–389a5. Commentary to To. 366.

Sarvabuddhasamāyoga-ḍākinīmāyā-sambara-vṛtti-samayogālaṃkāra. Asc. *Suratavajra (Rab-tu dga'-ba'i rdo-rje). To. 1660. *bsTan-'gyur,* rgyud, ra, fols. 389a5–439a7. Commentary to To. 366.

Sarvabuddhasamāyoga-tantrarāja (shorter recension). rNying ma rgyud 'bum, mTshams-brag ms., vol. tsha, fols. 1b1–26a7. Kaneko *1982*, no. 207. References are to the *mTshams-brag.*

**Sarvayogatattvāloka-vikalavajragīti.* Anon. To. 2453. *bsTan-'gyur,* rgyud, zi, fols. 92b1–115b3.

Sahajasiddhi. Asc. Indrabhūti. To. 2260. *bsTan-'gyur,* rgyud, zhi, fols. 1b1–4a3; Pe. 3107. *bsTan-'gyur* rgyud-'grel, tsi, fols. 1b1–4b7.

Sahajasiddhi-paddhati. Asc. Lha-lcam rje-btsun-ma dpal-mo (? = *Devībhaṭṭāri-kāśrī). To. 2261. *bsTan-'gyur,* rgyud, zhi, fols. 4a3–25a1; Pe. *3108*. *bsTan-'gyur,* rgyud-'grel, tsi, fols. 4b8–29a7.

Sādhanamālā.

Bhattacharya, Benoytosh, ed. 1925. *Sādhanamālā.* GOS, nos. 26, 41. Baroda: Oriental Institute. Reprint, Baroda: Oriental Institute, 1968.

Siddhaikavīramahātantra.

Pandey, Janardan, ed. 1998. *Siddhaikavīramahātantra.* RBTS, no. 20. Sarnath: Central Institute of Higher Tibetan Studies.

Sukusuma-nāma-dvikramatattvabhāvanā-mukhāgama-vṛtti. Asc. Vitapāda. To. 1866. *bsTan-'gyur,* rgyud, di, fols. 87a3–139b3.

Suniṣprapañcatattvopadeśa. Asc. Virūpa. To. 2020. *bsTan-'gyur,* rgyud, tsi, fols. 81a7–84a6.

Subāhuparipṛcchā. T.895.18.719a–746b, translated by Shan-wu-wei in 726 C.E.; To. 805. *bKa'-'gyur,* rgyud-'bum, wa, fols. 118a–140b.

Subāhuparipṛcchā-tantra-piṇḍārtha. Asc. Buddhaguhya. To. 2671. *bsTan-'gyur,* rgyud, thu, fols. 38a3–54b7.

Subhāṣita-Saṃgraha.

Bendall, Cecil, ed. 1903–4. *Subhāṣita-Saṃgraha.* In *Le Muséon* 22 (1903): 375–402; 23 (1904): 1–46, 245–274.

Susiddhikara-mahātantrasādhanopāyikapaṭala. To. 807. *bKa'-'gyur,* rgyud-'bum, wa, 168a1–222b7; T.893.18.603a-633c.

Saundarananda.

Johnston, E. H. 1928. *The Saundarananda of Aśvaghoṣa.* Reprint, Delhi: Motilal Banarsidass, 1975.

Hartmann, Jen-Uwe. 1988. *Neue Aśvaghoṣa- und Mātṛceṭa-Fragmente aus Ostturkistan,* pp. 18–23. Nachrichten der Akademie der Wissenschaften in Göttingen I. Philologische-Historische Klasse, no. 2. [includes new fragments and bibliography.]

Svacchandatantra.

Yogatantra Department, ed. 1992. *Śrī Svacchandatantra with the Commentary 'Uddyota' by Mahāmāheśvara Śrī Kṣemarāja.* Yogatantra-Granthamālā, vol. 19. 5 parts. Varanasi: Sampurnanand Sanskrit Vishvavidyalaya.

Harṣacarita.

Kane, P. V., ed. 1918. *The Harshacarita of Bāṇabhaṭṭa.* Bombay: Nirnaya Sagar. Reprint, Delhi: Motilal Banarsidas, 1986.

He ru ka'i rnam par dag pa. Asc. Śraddhākaravarman. To. 1481. *bsTan-'gyur,* rgyud, zha, fols. 125a3–128b4.

Hevajra Tantra.

Snellgrove, David L. 1959. *The Hevajra Tantra: A Critical Study.* London Oriental Series, vol. 6. 2 pts. London: Oxford University Press. [Includes the *Yogaratnamālā* of Kāṇhapāda.]

Hevajrasekaprakriyā. In Finot 1934, pp. 19–31.

CHINESE SOURCES

Ch'an mi yao fa ching. T. 613.15.242a–267c. Translation asc. Kumārajīva between 402 and 412 C.E.

Chen yen tsung chiao shih i. T.2396.75.374a–450a.

Chen yüan hsin ting shih chiao mu lu. T.2157.55.771a–1048a. Composed in 800 C.E. by Yüan-chao.

Chin kang ting ching yü ch'ieh shih pa hui chih kuei. T.869.18.284c–287c. Translation asc. Amoghavajra between 746 and 774 C.E..

Hsü ku chin i ching t'u chi. T. 2152.55. Compiled by Chih Sheng in 730 C.E.

I tsu fo ting lun wang ching. T.951.19.224a–263b. Translation asc. Bodhiruci in 709 C.E.

K'ai yuan shih chiao mu lu. T.2154.55. Compiled by Chih Sheng in 730 C.E.

Kao seng fa hsien chuan. T.2085.51.857a–866c.
Legge, James, trans. 1886. *A Record of Buddhistic Kingdoms.* Oxford: Clarendon Press.

Kuan fo san mei hai ching. T.643.15.645c–697a.

Kuan ting ching. T.1331.21.495a–536b. Translation asc. Śrīmitra, 317–322 C.E. See Strickmann 1990.

Nan hai chi kuei nei fa chuan. I-ching. T. 2125.54.204c–234a.
Takakusu, Junjiro, trans. 1896. *A Record of the Buddhist Religion as Practice in India and the Malay Archipelago* (A.D. 671–695). London: Clarendon Press.

Sung kao sung chuan. Tsan Ning, completed in 988 C.E. T. 2061.50.709a–900a.

Ta chou k'an ting chung ching mu lu. T. 2153.55. Compiled by Ming Chuan in 695 C.E.

Ta t'ang hsi yü chi. Hsüan-tsang. T.2087.51.
Beal, Samuel, trans. 1869. *Si-yu-ki: Buddhist Records of the Western World.* London: Kegan Paul, Trench, and Trübner.

Ta t'ang hsi yü ch'iu fa kao seng chuan. I-ching. T.2066.51.1a–12b.
Lahiri, Latika, trans. 1986. *Chinese Monks in India.* Reprint, Delhi: Motilal Banarsidass, 1995.

INDIGENOUS TIBETAN SOURCES

kLong chen chos 'byung. Asc. (probably apocraphally) kLong-chen rab-'byams-pa (1308–1363). Lhasa: Bod ljongs bod yig dpe rnying dpe skrun khang, 1991.

dKar chag ldan dkar ma. Pho brang stod thang ldan dkar gyi chos 'gyur ro cog gi dkar chag. To. 4364.
Lalou, Marcelle. 1953. "Les Textes bouddhiques au temps du Roi Khri-sroṅ-lde-bcan," *JA* 241, no. 3: 313–353.

mKhas grub khyung po rnal 'byor gyi rnam thar. Anon.
bSod nams tshe brtan, ed. 1996. *Shangs pa bka' brgyud pa bla rabs kyi rnam thar.* Lhasa: Bod ljongs bod yig dpe rnying dpe skrun khang.

mKhas pa'i dga' ston. dPa' bo gtsug lang phreng ba; written 1545–1564 C.E.
Dam pa'i chos kyi 'khor lo bsgyur ba rnams kyi byung ba gsal bar byed pa mkhas pa'i dga' ston. 2 vols. Beijing: Mi rigs dpe skrun khang, 1986.

Grub mtha' so so'i bźed tshul gźuṅ gsal bar ston pa chos 'byuṅ grub mtha' chen po bstan pa'i sgron me. Rog Bande Shes-rab-'od. Leh, Ladakh: Tshul Khrims-Jam dbyang, 1971?

rGyud kyi rgyal po dpal kye rdo rje'i byung tshul dang brgyud pa'i bla ma dam pa rnams kyi rnam par thar pa ngo mtshar rgya mtsho. Written 1525 C.E. Ngor-chen Kun-dga' bzang-po. *SKB* IX.278.1.1–284.3.3.

rGyud kyi mngon par rtogs pa rin po che'i ljon shing. Grags-pa rgyal-mtshan. *SKB III.1–70.1.*

rGyud sde spyi'i rnam par gzhag pa. bSod-nams rtse-mo. *SKB* II.1–37.

Chag lo tsā ba'i rnam thar. 'Ju-ba Chos-dar.
Roerich, G. N., ed. and trans. 1959. *Biography of Dharmasvamin (Chag lo-tsa-ba Chos-rje-dpal).* Historical Researches Series, vol. 2. Patna: K. P. Jayaswal Research Institute.

rNying ma rgyud 'bum. mTshams-brag manuscript.
The mTshams-Brag Manuscript of the rNying-ma rgyud 'bum. Thimphu, Bhutan: National Library, 1981.

rNying ma rgyud 'bum. gTing-skyes manuscript.
The Collected Tantras of the Ancient School of Tibetan Buddhism. Thimbu, Bhutan: Dil mgo mkhyen brtse, 1973.
See KANEKO 1982, for a catalogue of the gTing-skyes.

Tā ra nā tha'i rgya gar chos 'byung.
Schiefner, Antonius, ed. 1868. *Târanâthæ de Doctrinæ Buddhicæ in India Propagatione.* St. Petersburg: Imprimerie Academiæ Scientiarum.

bsTan 'gyur gyi dkar chag yid bzhin nor bu dbang gi rgyal po'i phreng ba. Bu-ston Rin-chen-grub (1290–1364 C.E.).
Chandra, Lokesh, ed. 1971. *The Collected Works of Bu-Ston.* Śata-Piṭaka Series, vol. 60, part 26, pp. 401–643. New Delhi: International Academy of Indian Culture.

Deb ther sngon po. 1984. 'Gos lo-tsā-ba gZhon-nu dpal (written between 1476 and 1478 c.e.). 2 vols. Chengdu: Si khron mi rigs dpe skrun khang.
Roerich, George N., trans. 1949. *The Blue Annals.* Royal Asiatic Society of Bengal Monograph Series, no. 7. 2 vols. Calcutta: Royal Asiatic Society of Bengal.

bDe mchog lu hi pa'i lugs kyi bla ma brgyud pa'i lo rgyus. Grags-pa rgyal-mtshan. *SKB* III.293.2–298.4.

rNam thar rgyas pa.
Eimer, Helmut, ed. and trans. 1979. *Rnam Thar Rgyas Pa: Materialien zu einer Biographie des Atiśa (Dīpaṃkaraśrījñāna).* Asiatische Forschungen, no. 67. Wiesbaden: Otto Harrassowitz.

rNal 'byor byang chub seng ge'i dris lan. Grags-pa rgyal-mtshan. *SKB* III.276.4.1–278.2.7.

Pod ser. First compiled by Grags-pa rgyal-mtshan, with many additions. *LL* XI.

sPyod pa'i rgyud spyi'i rnam par gzhags pa legs par bshad pa'i sgron me. Completed by Ngor-chen Kun-dga' bzang-po in 1420 C.E. *SKB* X.248.3.1–265.4.2.

Phyag rgya chen po gces pa btus pa'i man ngag. Collection attributed to Grags-pa rgyal-mtshan. *SKB* IV.302.3.1–311.4.5.

Bod rje lha btsan po'i gdung rabs tshig nyung don gsal. Kaḥ-thog mkhan-po Tshe-dbang nor-bu (written 1745 C.E.). In *Bod kyi lo rgyus deb ther khag lnga,* pp. 55–86. Lhasa: Bod ljongs bod yig dpe rnying dpe skrun khang, 1990.

Bhir ba pa'i lo rgyus. In *gŽuṅ bsad Klog skya ma and Other Related Esoteric Texts,* pp. 347–404.

Bya rgyud spyi'i rnam par bshad pa legs par bshad pa'i rgya mtsho. Completed by Ngor-chen in 1420 C.E. *SKB* X.265.4.2–319.1.6.

bLa ma rgya gar ba'i lo rgyus. Grags-pa rgyal-mtshan. *SKB* III.170.1.1–173.1.6; *LL* I.2.1–14.4; *LL* XI.581–594.

bLa ma brgyud pa bod kyi lo rgyus. Grags-pa rgyal-mtshan. *SKB* III.173.1.7–174.1.7; *LL* I.14–18; *LL* XI.594–599.

bLa ma brgyud pa'i rnam par thar pa ngo mtshar snang ba. Asc. bLa-ma Dam-pa bSod-nams rgyal-mtshan (1312–1375), *LL* XVI.2–121.

bLa ma ba ri lo tsā ba rin chen grags kyi rnam thar. bSod-nams rtse-mo. *Sa skya'i rje btsun gong ma rnam lnga'i gsung ma phyi gsar rnyed,* 1:255–266.

dBa' bzhed.

Wangdu, Pasang, and Hildegard Diemberger, ed. and trans. 2000. *dBa' bzhed: The Royal Narrative Concerning the Bringing of the Buddha's Doctrine to Tibet.* Österreichische Akademie der Wissenschaften, Philosophisch-Historische Klasse, Denkschriften, no. 219. Vienna: Verlag der Österreichischen Akademie der Wissenschaften.

sBa bzhed.

mGon-po rgyal-mtshan, ed. 1980. *sBa bzhed.* Beijing: Mi rigs dpe skrun khang.

sBa bzhed zhabs btags ma.

Stein, Rolf A., ed. 1961. *Une chronique ancienne de bSam-yas: sBa-bźed.* Publications de l'Institut des Hautes Études Chinoises, Textes et documents, no. 1. Paris: Institut de Hautes Études Chinoises.

Man ngag gces pa btus pa. Compiled by Sa-chen Kun-dga' snying-po (1092–1158). dPal sa skya pa'i man ngag gces pa btus pa rin po che'i phreng ba. *SKB* I.268.2.1–281.2.6.

Mar pa lo tsā'i rnam thar. Asc. Khrag-'thung rgyal-po (gTsang-smyong he-ru-ka, 1452–1507).

Mar pa lo tsā'i rnam thar. 1983. Chengdu: Si khron mi rigs dpe skrun khang.

Nalanda Translation Committee, trans. 1982. *The Life of Marpa the Translator.* Boston and London: Shambhala.

Zhi byed snyan rgyud zab byed ma.

Aziz, Barbara Nimri, ed. 1979. *The Tradition of Pha Dam-pa Saṅs-rgyas:*

A Treasured Collection of His Teachings Transmitted by Thugs-sras Kun-dga'. 5 vols. Thimphu: Druk Sherik Parkhang.

gŹuṅ bsad Klog skya ma and Other Related Esoteric Sa-skya-pa Texts. 1975. Tashi Dorje, ed. Dolanji, Himachal Pradesh: Tibetan Bompo Monastic Centre.

Rwa lo tsā ba'i rnam thar. Attributed to Rwa ye-shes seng-ge.

mThu stobs dbang phyug rje btsun rwa lo tsā ba'i rnam par thar pa kun khyab snyan pa'i snga sgra. 1989. Xining: mTsho sngon mi rigs dpe skrun khang.

Lam 'bras snyan brgyud. In gŹuṅ bsad Klog skya ma and Other Related Esoteric Texts, pp. 405–590.

Lam 'bras slob bshad.

Sa-skya Khri-'dzin Ngag gi dbang phyug, ed. 1983–84. *Lam 'bras slob bshad.* 31 vols. Dehra Dun: Sakya Centre.

Sa skya bka' 'bum.

Bsod Nams Rgya Mtsho, ed. 1968. *The Complete Works of the Great Masters of the Sa Skya Sect of the Tibetan Buddhism.* 14 vols. Tokyo: Toyo Bunko.

Sa skya'i rje btsun gong ma rnam lnga'i gsung ma phyi gsar rnyed. bSod-nams tshe-'phel et al., eds. 3 vols. n.p. (Lhasa?), n.d. (late 1980s). [Copy provided courtesy of E. Gene Smith and the Tibetan Buddhist Resource Center, Cambridge, MA.]

Sras don ma. Sa-chen Kun-dga' snying-po. *Lam 'bras gzhung bshad sras don ma. LL XII.1–446.*

Gsang 'dus byung tshul. dPal gsang ba 'dus pa'i dam pa'i chos byung ba'i tshul legs par bshad pa gsang 'dus chos kun gsal pa'i nyin byed. 1985. A mes zhabs Ngag-dbang kun-dga' bsod-nams. Dehra Dun: Sakya Centre.

bSam gtan mig sgron. Asc. gNubs-chen sangs-rgyas ye-shes.

Rnal 'Byor Mig Gi Bsam Gtan or Bsam Gtan Mig Sgron. 1974. Leh: Khor-gdoṅ Gter-sprul Chi-med-rig-'dzin.

ARCHÆOLOGICAL AND EPIGRAPHIC MATERIALS

Bajpai, K. D., and S. K. Pandey. 1978. *Malhar: 1975–76.* Sagar: University of Sagar.

Bakker, Hans T. 1997. *The Vākāṭakas: An Essay in Hindu Iconology.* Gonda Indological Studies, vol. 5. Groningen: Egbert Forsten.

Banerji, R. D. 1917–18. "The Bangarh Grant of Mahi-Pala I: The 9th Year." *EI* 14:324–330.

———. 1919–20. "Neulpur Grant of Subhakara: The 8th year." *EI* 15:1–8.

Banerji-Sastri, A. 1940. "Ninety-three Inscriptions on the Kurkihar Bronzes." *Journal of the Bihar and Orissa Research Society* 26, no. 3:236–251, 299–308.

Barua, B. M. 1938. "Hathigumpha Inscription of Kharavela." *IHQ* 19:459–485.

Barua, Dipak K. 1981. *Buddha Gaya Temple: Its History.* Buddha Gaya, Bihar: Buddha Gaya Temple Management Committee.

Basak, Radhagovinda. 1919–20. "The Five Damodarpur Copper-Plate Inscriptions of the Gupta Period." *EI* 15:113–145.

Berkemer, George. 1992. "The 'Centre Out There' as State Archive: The Temple of Siṃhācalam." In Hans Bakker, ed., *The Sacred Centre as the Focus of Political Interest,* pp. 119–130. Groningen Oriental Studies, vol. 6. Groningen: Egbert Forsten.

Bhandarkar, Devadatta R. 1908. "An Ekliṅgî Stone Inscription and the Origin and History of the Lakulīśa Sect." *Journal of the Bombay Branch of the Royal Asiatic Society* 22:151–167.

———. 1981. "Inscriptions of the Early Gupta Kings." In Bahadurchand Chhabra and Govind Swamirao Gai, ed., *CII,* III. New Delhi: Archæological Survey of India.

Bhattacharya, Gouriswar. 1985. "The Newly Discovered Buddhist Temple at Nalanda." In Janine Schotsmans and Maurizio Taddei, eds., *South Asian Archæology 1983.* Istituto Universitario Orientale Series Minor, vol. 23. Naples: Istituto Universitario Orientale.

———. 1988. "The New Pāla Ruler Mahendrapāla: Discovery of a Valuable Charter." *South Asian Studies* 4:71–73.

Bhavnagar Archæological Department, ed. n.d. *A Collection of Prakrit and Sanskrit Inscriptions.* Bhaabnagar, Gujarat: State Printing Press.

Bühler, G. 1892. "Two Prasastis of Baijnātha." *EI* 1:97–118.

———. 1894. "Further Inscriptions from Sanchi." *EI* 2:366–408; "Votive Inscriptions from the Sanchi Stupas." *EI* 2:87–116.

———. 1896–97. "Banskhera Plate of Harsha, [Year 22]." *EI* 4:208–211.

Chakravarti, Adhir. 1978. *The Sdok Kak Thom Inscription—A Study of Indo-Khmèr Civilization.* Calcutta Sanskrit College Research Series, no. 111. 2 vols. Calcutta: Sanskrit College.

Chapin, Helen B. 1972. *A Long Roll of Buddhist Images.* Ascona, Switzerland: Artibus Asiæ.

Cœdès, G., and P. Dupont. 1943–46. "Les stèles de Sdök Käk Thom, Phnoṃ Sandak et Prāḥ Vihār." *BEFEO* 43:56–154.

Das, Jithendra. 1993. *The Buddhist Architecture in Andhra.* New Delhi: Books & Books.

Das, Sudhir Ranjan. 1968. *Rājbāḍīdāṅgā: 1962.* Asiatic Society Monograph Series, vol. 14. Calcutta: Asiatic Society.

De, S. C. 1953. "A Śiva Liṅga Inscribed with Buddhist Dhāraṇī from Soro." *Orissa Historical Research Journal* 1:271–273.

Dehejia, Vidya. 1986. *Yoginī Cult and Temples, A Tantric Tradition.* New Delhi: National Museum.

Desai, P. B. 1962. *Select Stone Inscriptions of Andhra Pradesh.* Andhra Pradesh Governement Archæology Series, no. 9. Hyderabad, India: Government of Andhra Pradesh.

Dikshit, Moreshwar G. 1955. "Excavation at Sirpur, District Raipur." *Indian Archæology 1954–55*:24–26.

———. 1955–57. "Some Buddhist Bronzes from Sirpur, Madhya Pradesh." *Bulletin of the Prince of Wales Museum of Western India* 5:1–11.

———. 1956. "Excavation at Sirpur, District Raipur." *Indian Archæology 1955–56*:26–27.

Donaldson, Thomas E. 1985–87. *Hindu Temple Art of Orissa.* 3 vols. Leiden: E. J. Brill.

———. 1986. "Erotic Rituals on Orissan Temples." *East and West* 36:137–182.

Fleet, John Faithfull. 1881. "Sanskrit and Old-Canarese Inscriptions, No. CXVI." *IA* 10:185–190.

———. 1883. "Sanskrit and Old-Canarese Inscriptions." *IA* 12:156–165.

———. 1888. *Inscriptions of the Early Gupta Kings. CII*, III. Calcutta: Government of India.

———. 1889. "Belur Inscription of the Time of Jayasimha III—Saka Samvat 944." *IA* 18:270–275.

Flood, F. B. 1989. "Herakles and the 'Perpetual Acolyte' of the Buddha: Some Observations on the Iconography of Vajrapani in Gandharan Art." *South Asian Studies* 5:17–27.

Goepper, Roger. 1996. *Alchi: Ladakh's Hidden Buddhist Sanctuary—the Sumtsek.* London: Serindia.

Hira Lal, Rai Bahadur. 1909–10. "Kuruspal Stone Inscription of Somesvaradeva." *EI* 10:25–31.

Hultzsch, E. 1886. "The Bhagalpur Plate of Narayanapala." *IA* 15:304–310.

Humbach, Helmut. 1980. "Hybrid Sanskrit in the Gilgit Brāhmī Inscriptions." *Studien zur Indologie und Iranistik* 5, no. 6:99–121.

Huntington, Susan L. 1984. *The "Pala-Sena" Schools of Sculpture.* Studies in South Asian Culture, vol. 10. Leiden: E. J. Brill.

Huntington, Susan L., and John C. Huntington. 1990. *Leaves from the* Bodhi *Tree: The Art of Pala India (8th–12th Centuries) and Its International Legacy.* Dayton, Seattle, and Washington: Dayton Art Institute in Association with the University of Washington Press.

Indraji, Pandit Bhagwânlâl. 1881. "An Inscription at Gayâ Dated in the Year 1813 of Buddha's Nirvâna, with Two Others of the Same Period." *IA* 10:341–347.

Jain, Balchandra. 1969. "Sirpur Inscription of Acharya Buddhaghosha." *EI* 38:2:59–62.

Jettmar, Karl, ed. 1989. *Antiquities of Northern Pakistan: Reports and Studies.* Vol. 1, pts. 1–2. Mainz: Philipp von Zabern.

———. 1993. *Antiquities of Northern Pakistan: Reports and Studies.* Vol. 2. Mainz: Philipp von Zabern.

Kielhorn, F. 1886. "The Sasbahu Temple Inscription of Mahipala, of Vikrama-Saṁvat 1150." *IA* 15:33–46.

———. 1888–92a. "Siyadoni Stone Inscription." *EI* 1:162–179.

———. 1888–92b. "Bilhari Stone Inscription of the Rulers of Chedi." *EI* 1:251–270.

———. 1892. "Mungir Copper-Plate Grant of Devapaladeva." *IA* 21:253–258.

———. 1896–97. "Khālimpur Plate of Dharmapāladēva, [Year 32]." *EI* 4:243–254.

———. 1900–1901a. "Aihoḷe Inscription of Pulikēśin II, Śaka-Saṁvat 556." *EI* 6:1–12.

———. 1900–1901b. "Rādhanpur Plates of Gōvinda III, Śaka Saṁvat 730." *EI* 6:239–251.

———. 1907–8. "Paṭhārī Pillar Inscription of Parabala, [Vikrama] Saṁvat 917." *EI* 9:248–256.

Kinnard, Jacob N. 2000. "The Polyvalent *Pādas* of Viṣṇu and the Buddha." *History of Religions* 40:32–57.

Klimburg-Salter, Deborah E. 1997. *Tabo: A Lamp for the Kingdom.* New York: Thames and Hudson.

Knox, Robert. 1992. *Amaravati: Buddhist Sculpture from the Great Stūpa.* London: British Museum Press.

Konow, Sten. 1907–8. "Sarnath Inscription of Kumaradevi." *EI* 9:319–328.

———. 1913–14. "Hānsōṭ Plates of Chāhmāna Bhartṛivaḍḍha, Saṁvat 813." *EI* 12:197–204.

Kossak, Steven M., and Jane Casey Singer. 1998. *Sacred Visions: Early Paintings from Central Tibet.* New York: Metropolitan Museum of Art.

KUWAYAMA, Shoshin. 1991. "L'inscription du Gaṇeśa de Gardez et la chronologie des Turki-Ṣāhi." *JA* 279:267–287.

Law, Bimala Churn. 1939–40. "Bhikshunis in Indian Inscriptions." *EI* 25:31–34.

Lévi, Sylvain. 1937. "Les Donations religieuses de rois de Valabhî." In Paul Hartman, ed., *Mémorial Sylvain Lévi,* pp. 218–234. Paris: Imprimerie Nationale.

Linda, Mary F. 1993. "Temples of Stone, Centers of Culture: Sacred Space in Early Medieval Kaliṅga." In Howard Spodek and Doris Meth Srinivasan, eds., *Urban Form and Meaning in South Asia: The Shaping of Cities from Prehistoric to Precolonial Times,* pp. 145–162. Studies in the History of Art, no. 31. Washington: National Gallery of Art.

Linrothe, Rob. 1999. *Ruthless Compassion: Wrathful Deities in Early Indo-Tibetan Esoteric Buddhist Art.* Boston: Shambhala.

Lüders, Heinrich. 1912. *A List of Brahmi Inscriptions from the Earliest Times to about* A.D. 400 with the Exception of Those of Asoka. Appendix to *EI* 10. New Delhi: Government of India Press. Reprint, New Delhi: Government of India Press, 1959.

———. 1961. *Mathurā Inscriptions.* Klaus L. Janert, ed. Abhandlungen der Akademie der Wissenschaften in Göttingen Philologisch-Historische Kalsse, Dritte Folge, no. 47. Göttingen: Vandenhoeck and Ruprecht.

Majumdar, B. P. 1953. "Lakulīśa Pāśupatas and Their Temples in Mediaeval India." *Journal of the Bihar Research Society* 39:1–9.

Majumdar, R. C. 1953. *Inscriptions of Kambuja.* Calcutta: Asiatic Society.

Marshall, John and Alfred Foucher. 1940. *The Monuments of Sāñcī.* 3 vols. London: Probsthain.

Meister, Michael W. 1979. "Maṇḍala and Practice in Nāgara Architecture in North India." *JAOS* 99:204–219.

———. 1984. *Discourses on Śiva: Proceedings of a Symposium on the Nature of Religious Imagery.* Philadelphia: University of Pennsylvania Press.

Meister, Michael W., and M. A. Dhaky, eds. 1988–91. *Encyclopædia of Indian Temple Architecture.* 4 vols. in 8 parts. Princeton and New Delhi: Princeton University Press and the American Institute of Indian Studies.

Mirashi, Vasudeva Vishnu. 1955. "Inscriptions of the Kalachuri-Chedi Era." In *CII,* IV. 2 parts. Ootacamund, India: Government Epigraphist for India.

———. 1976. *Inscriptions of the Silaharas.* In *CII,* VI. New Delhi: Archæological Survey of India.

Misra, Binayak. 1934. *Orissa Under the Bhauma Kings.* Calcutta: Viswamitra Press.

Mitra, Debala. 1971. *Buddhist Monuments.* Calcutta: Sahitya Samshad.

———. 1981. *Ratnagiri (1958–61).* Memoirs of the Archaeological Survey of India, no. 80. 2 vols. New Delhi: Archaeological Survey of India.

———. 1984. "Lakulīśa and Early Śaiva Temples in Orissa." In Meister 1984, pp. 103–118.

Morrison, Barrie M. 1970. *Political Centers and Cultural Regions in Early Bengal.* Association for Asian Studies: Monographs and Papers, no. 25. Tucson: University of Arizona Press.

Mookerji, Radha Kumud. 1928. *Asoka.* Reprint, Delhi: Motilal Banarsidass, 1972.

Ojha, Gaurishankar Hirachand. 1917–18. "Partābgarh Inscription of the Time of [the Pratihāra] King Mahēndrapāla II of Mahōdaya, Saṁvat 1003." *EI* 14:176–188.

Postel, M., A. Neven, and K. Mankodi. 1985. *Antiquities of Himachal.* Bombay: Project for Indian Cultural Studies.

Rajaguru, Satyanarayan. 1955–76. *Inscriptions of Orissa.* 5 vols. Bhubaneswar, Orissa: Orissa State Muesum.

Rao, M. Rama. 1964. *Eastern Cāḷukyan Temples of Āndhra Dēśa.* Andhra Pradesh Government Archæological Series, no. 19. Hyderabad: Government of Andhra Pradesh.

Rice, Lewis. 1886. "Mudyanur Plates of Saka 261 of the Bana King Malladeva-Nandivarman." *Indian Antiquary* 15:172–177.

Salomon, Richard. 1990. "New Evidence for a Gāndhārī Origin of the Arapacana Syllabary." *JAOS* 110:255–273.

———. 1996. "British Museum Stone Inscription of the Tripurī Kalacuri Prince Valleka." *IIJ* 39:133–161.

———. 1998. *Indian Epigraphy—A Guide to the Study of Inscriptions in Sanskrit, Prakrit, and the Other Indo-Aryan Languages.* New York and Oxford: Oxford University Press.

———. 1999. *Ancient Buddhist Scrolls from Gandhāra—The British Library Kharoṣṭhī Fragments.* Seattle: University of Washington Press.

Sastri, Hirananda. 1942. *Nalanda and Its Epigraphic Material.* Memoirs of the Archæological Survey of India. Delhi: Archæological Survey of India.

Schwab, Katherine A. 1998. "The Lysippan Herakles as Vajrapani in Hadda." In Olga Palagia and William Coulson, eds., *Regional Schools in Hellenistic Sculpture*, pp. 27–33. Oxbow Monograph, no. 90. Oxford: Oxbow Books.

Shah, U. P. "Lakulīśa: Śaivite Saint." In Meister 1984, pp. 92–102.

Shaw, Richard. 1997. "Srisailam: Centre of the Siddhas." *South Asian Studies* 13:161–178.

Sircar, Dinesh Chandra. 1948. "The Śākta Pīṭhas." *JASB Letters* 14:1–108.

———. 1971. "Siyān Stone Slab Inscription of Nayapāla." *EI* 39:39–56.

Skaff, Jonathan Karam. 1998. "Sasanian and Arab-Sasanian Silver Coins from Turfan: Their Relationship to International Trade and the Local Economy." *Asia Major* 11:67–115.

Stadtner, Donald Martin. 1976. "From Sirpur to Rājim: The Art of Kosala During the Seventh Century." Ph.D. diss., University of California, Berkeley.

Stewart, Mary L. 1989. *Nālandā Mahāvihāra—A Study of an Indian Pāla Period Buddhist Site and British Historical Archæology, 1861–1938.* BAR International Series, no. 524. Oxford: BAR.

Strachan, Paul. 1989. *Imperial Pagan: Art and Architecture of Burma.* Reprint, Honolulu: University of Hawaii Press, 1991(?).

Thaplyal, Kiran Kumar. 1985. *Inscriptions of the Maukharis, later Guptas, Pusyabhutis, and Yasovarman of Kanauj.* Delhi: Indian Council of Historical Research.

Upadhyay, Neelmani. 1986. *Temples of Mandi.* Mandi, Himachal Pradesh: Rupendra.

van der Veer, Peter. 1992. "Ayodhya and Somnath: Eternal Shrines, Contested Histories." *Social Research* 59:85–109.

Vitali, Roberto. 1990. *Early Temples of Central Tibet.* London: Serindia Publications.

Vogel, J. Ph. 1905–6. "Ancient Monuments of Kāṇgrā Ruined in the Earthquake." *Archæological Survey of Indian, Annual Report* 1905–6:10–27.

Williams, Joanna Gottfried. 1982. *The Art of Gupta India: Empire and Province.* Princeton: Princeton University Press.

Willis, Michael D. 1995. "Some Notes on the Palaces of the Imperial Gurjara Pratīhāras." *Journal of the Royal Asiatic Society*, 3d ser. 5, no. 3:351–360.

———. 1997. *Temples of Gopakṣetra.* London: British Museum.

Woodward, Hiram W. 1981. "Tantric Buddhism at Angkor Thom." *Ars Orientalis* 12:57–67 + plates.

GENERAL MODERN SOURCES

Abraham, Meera. 1988. *Two Medieval Merchant Guilds of South India.* Delhi: Manohar Publications.

Agrawal, Ashvini. 1989. *Rise and Fall of the Imperial Guptas.* Delhi: Motilal Banarsidass.

Agrawala, Ratna Chandra. 1955. "Religious Conditions as Depicted in the Niya Documents from Central Asia." *Journal of the Greater India Society* 14:13–54.

Ali, Daud, ed. 1999. *Invoking the Past: The Uses of History in South Asia.* New Delhi: Oxford University Press.

Allen, Graham. 2000. *Intertextuality.* New York: Routledge.

Andrew, Bill. 1992. "The Soldier and the Battle." In David A. Charters et al., eds., *Military History and Military Profession*, pp. 57–72. Westport and London: Praeger.

Appiah, Kwame Anthony. 1991. "Is the Post- in Postmodernism the Post- in Postcolonial?" *Critical Inquiry* 17:336–357.

Aristotle. 1987. *Poetics.* Richard Janko, trans. Indianapolis, IN: Hackett.

Asimov, M. S., and C. E. Bosworth, eds. 1998. *The Age of Achievement: A.D. 750 to the End of the Fifteenth Century; Part One, The Historical, Social and Economic Setting.* History of Civilizations of Central Asia, vol. 4. Paris: UNESCO.

Atwood, Christopher. 1991. "Life in Third–Fourth Century Cadh'ota: A Survey of Information Gathered from the Prakrit Documents Found North of Mingeng (Niyä)." *CAJ* 35:161–199.

Backus, Charles. 1981. *The Nan-chao Kingdom and T'ang China's Southestern Frontier.* Cambridge: Cambridge University Press.

Bagchi, Prabhodha Chandra. 1944. "Vajragarbhatantrarājasūtra: A New Work of King Indrabodhi." *Sino-Indian Studies* 1, no. 1:22–59.

———. 1945. "Bodhisattva-śila of Śubhākarasiṃha." *Sino-Indian Studies* 1, no. 3:132–160.

Baird, William. 1992. *History of New Testament Research. Volume One: From Deism to Tübingen.* Minneapolis: Fortress Press.

Bakhtin, M. M. 1968. *Rabelais and His World.* Trans. Hélène Iswolsky. Bloomington: Indiana University Press, 1984.

Banerji, Adris. 1963. "Eastern Expansion of the Gāhaḍavāla Kingdom." *Journal of the Asiatic Society* 5, nos. 3–4:105–111.

Barrow, H. W. 1893. "On Aghoris and Aghorapanthis." *Journal of the Anthropological Society of Bombay* 3:197–251.

Beckwith, Christopher I. 1977. "Tibet and the Early Medieval *Florissance* in Eurasia: A Preliminary Note on the Economic History of the Tibetan Empire." *CAJ* 21:89–104.

———. 1987. *The Tibetan Empire in Central Asia.* Princeton: Princeton University Press.

Benson, Robert L. 1982. "Political *Renovatio:* Two Models from Roman Antiquity." In Robert L. Benson et al., eds., *Renaissance and Renewal in the Twelfth Century,* pp. 339–386. Cambridge: Harvard University Press.

Bentor, Yael. 2000. "Interiorized Fire Rituals in India and Tibet." *Journal of the American Oriental Society* 120:594–613.

Bergson, Henri. 1911. *Laughter, An Essay on the Meaning of the Comic.* C. Brereton and F. Rothwell, trans. New York: Macmillan.

Bharati, Agehananda. 1965. *The Tantric Tradition.* London: Rider.

———. 1970. *The Ochre Robe: An Autobiography.* Garden City, NY: Doubleday.

Bhatt, G. K. 1959. *The Vidūṣaka.* Ahmedabad, Gujarat: New Order Book Company.

Bhattacharya, Benoytosh. 1930. "Buddhist Deities in Hindu Garb." In *Proceedings and Transactions of the Fifth Indian Oriental Conference,* vol. 2, pp. 1277–1298. Lahore: University of the Panjab.

Bhattacharya, Kamaleswar. 1955. "La secte des Pāçupata dans l'ancien Cambodge." *JA* 243:479–490.

Bhattacharya, Vidhushekhara. 1928. "Sandhābhāṣā." *IHQ* 4:287–296.

Bishop, Morris. 1966. *Letters from Petrarch.* Bloomington and London: Indiana University Press.

Blackburn, Stuart H., et al., eds. 1989. *Oral Epics in India.* Berkeley: University of California Press.

Bloch, Herbert. 1982. "The New Fascination with Ancient Rome." In Benson et al. 1982, pp. 615–636.

Boal, Barbara M. 1982. *The Konds—Human Sacrifice and Religious Change.* Warminster, Wilts, UK: Aris and Phillips.

Braarvig, Jens. 1985. "*Dhāraṇī* and *Pratibhāna:* Memory and Eloquence of the Bodhisattvas." *JIABS* 8:17–29.

———. 1997. "Bhavya on Mantras: Apologetic Endeavors on Behalf of Mahāyāna." *Studia Indologiczne* 4:31–39.

Brennan, Timothy. 2000. "The Illusion of a Future: *Orientalism* as a Traveling Theory." *Critical Inquiry* 26:558–583.

Broido, Michael. 1982. "Does Tibetan Hermeneutics Throw Any Light on *Sandhābhāṣā?*" *Journal of the Tibet Society* 2:5–39.

———. 1983. "*bshad thabs:* Some Tibetan Methods of Explaining the Tantras." In Ernst Steinkellner and Helmut Tauscher, eds., *Contributions on Tibetan and Buddhist Religion and Philosophy,* vol. 2, pp. 15–45. Vienna: Universität Wien.

———. 1984. "Abhiprāya and Implication in Tibetan Linguistics." *Journal of Indian Philosophy* 12:1–33.

Brunner, Hélène. 1986. "*Maṇḍala* et *yantra* dans le śivaïsme āgamique." In André Padoux, ed., *Mantras et diagrammes rituels dans l'hindouïsme,* pp. 11–35. Paris: Editions du Centre National de la Recherche Scientifique.

Brunt, P.A., trans. 1976. *Arrian: History of Alexander and Indica.* Loeb Classical Library, no. 236. 2 vols. Cambridge: Harvard University Press.

Bühnemann, Gudrun. 1992. "On Puraścaraṇa: Kulārṇavatantra, Chapter 15." In Teun Goudriaan, ed., *Ritual and Speculation in Early Tantrism: Studies in Honor of André Padoux,* pp. 61–106. Albany: State University of New York Press.

———. 1999. "Buddhist Deities and Mantras in the Hindu Tantras: I. The *Tantrasārasaṃgraha* and the *Īśānaśivagurudevapaddhati.*" *IIJ* 42:303–334.

———. 2000. "Buddhist Deities and Mantras in the Hindu Tantras: II. The *Śrīvidyārṇavatantra* and the *Tantrasāra.*" *IIJ* 43/1: 27–48.

Buitenen, Hans van. 1958. "The Indian Hero as Vidyādhara." *Journal of American Folklore* 71:305–311.

Burrow, T., and M. B. Emeneau. 1984. *A Dravidian Etymological Dictionary.* 2d ed. Oxford: Oxford University Press.

Bury, R. G. 1926. *Plato: Laws.* Leob Classical Library. 2 vols. Cambridge: Harvard University Press.

Caillat, Colette, ed. 1989. *Dialectes dans les littératures indo-aryennes.* Publications de l'Institut de Civilisation Indienne, no. 55. Paris: Éditions e. de Boccard.

Campbell, J. Gabriel. 1976. *Saints and Householders: A Study of Hindu Ritual and Myth Among the Kangra Rajputs.* Kathmandu: Ratna Pustak Bhandar.

Chakrabarty, Dipesh. 1992. "Postcoloniality and the Artifice of History: Who Speaks for 'Indian' Pasts?" *Representations* 37:1–26. Reprinted in Mongia 1996, pp. 223–247.

Char, S. V. Desika. 1993. *Caste, Religion and Country: A View of Ancient and Medieval India.* New Delhi: Orient Longman.

Chattopadhyaya, Brajadulal. 1990. *Aspects of Rural Settlements and Rural Society in Early Medieval India.* Calcutta and New Delhi: K. P. Bagchi.

———. 1994. *The Making of Early Medieval India.* Delhi: Oxford University Press.

Chaudhuri, Nagendra N. 1935. *Ḍākārṇavaḥ—Studies in the Apabhraṃśa Texts of the Ḍākārṇava.* Calcutta Sanskrit Series, no. 10. Calcutta: Metropolitan Printing and Publishing House.

Chenet, François. 1993. "Le Sauras de l'Inde: le brilliant échec d'une identité religieuse inclusiviste?" *JA* 281:317–392.

Chou Yi-Liang. 1945. "Tantrism in China." *Harvard Journal of Asiatic Studies* 8:241–332.

Coccari, Diane M. 1989. "Protection and Identity: Banaras's Bīr Babas as Neighborhood Guardian Deities." In Sandria B. Freitag, ed., *Culture and Power in Banaras: Community, Performance, and Environment, 1800–1980*, pp. 130–146. Berkeley: University of California Press.

Cohen, Richard S. 2000. "Kinsmen of the Son: Śākyabhikṣus and the Institutionalization of the Bodhisattva Ideal." *History of Religions* 40, no. 1:1–31.

Collins, Steven. 1990. "On the Very Idea of a Pali Canon." *Journal of the Pali Text Society* 15:89–126.

Contamine, Philippe. 1984. *War in the Middle Ages.* Michael Jones, trans. Oxford: Basil Blackwell.

Danda, Dipali G. 1994. "Method of Hinduization in North Cachar." *Journal of the Indian Anthropological Society* 29:143–49.

Datta, Swati. 1989. *Migrant Brāhmaṇas in Northern India: Their Settlement and General Impact c.* A.D. 475–1030. Delhi: Motilal Banarsidass.

Davidson, Ronald M. 1985. "Buddhist Systems of Transformation: *Āśraya-parivṛtti / parāvṛtti* Among the Yogācāra." Ph.D. diss., University of California, Berkeley.

———. 1990. "An Introduction to the Standards of Scriptural Authenticity in Indian Buddhism." In Robert E. Buswell, ed., *Chinese Buddhist Apocrypha*, pp. 291–325. Honolulu: University of Hawaii Press.

———. 1991. "Reflections on the Maheśvara Subjugation Myth: Indic Materials, Sa-skya-pa Apologetics, and the Birth of Heruka." *JIABS* 14, no. 2:197–235.

———. 1992. "Preliminary Studies on Hevajra's *Abhisamaya* and the *Lam-'bras Tshogs-bshad.*" In Steven D. Goodman and Ronald M. Davidson, eds., *Tibetan Buddhism: Reason and Revelation,* pp. 107–132, 176–184. Albany: State University of New York Press.

———. 1995a. "Atiśa's *A Lamp for the Path to Awakening.*" In Donald Lopez, ed., *Buddhism: In Practice,* pp. 290–301. Princeton: Princeton University Press.

———. 1995b. "The Bodhisattva Vajrapāṇi's Subjugation of Śiva." In Donald Lopez, ed., *Religions of India: In Practice*, pp. 547–555. Princeton: Princeton University Press.

———. 1999. "Masquerading as Pramāṇa: Esoteric Buddhism and Epistemological Nomenclature." In Katsura Shoryu, ed., *Dharmakīrti's Thought and Its Impact on Indian and Tibetan Philosophy—Proceedings of the Third International Conference on Dharmakīrti and Pramāṇa,* pp. 25–35. Vienna: Österreichischen Akademie der Wissenschaften.

———. 2002a. "Gsar-ma Apocrypha: Gray Texts, Oral Traditions, and the Creation of Orthodoxy." In Helmut Eimer and David Germano, eds., *The Many Canons of Tibetan Buddhism,* pp. 203–224. Leiden: Brill.

———. 2002b. "Reframing *Sahaja*: Genre, Representation, Ritual and Lineage." *Journal of Indian Philosophy* 30: 45–83.

———. forthcoming a. "Vajras at Thirty Paces: Authority, Lineage, and Religious Conflict in gSar-'gyur Central Tibet." In Elliot Sperling, ed., *Proceedings of the Eighth Seminar of the International Association of Tibetan Studies.* Bloomington: Indiana University Press.

———. forthcoming b. *Tibetan Renaissance: Indian Yogins, Solemn Clansmen and the Rise of Sakya.*

Davis, Richard H. 1997. *Lives of Indian Images.* Princeton: Princeton University Press.

Demiéville, Paul. 1924. "Les versions chinoises du Milindapañha." *BEFEO* 24:1–264.

———. 1932. "L'origine des sectes bouddhiques d'après Paramartha." *MCB* 1:15–64.

———. 1973. *Choix d'études bouddhiques (1929–1970).* Leiden: E. J. Brill.

Denton, Lynn Teskey. 1991. "Varieties of Hindu Female Asceticism." In Leslie 1991, pp. 211–231.

Derrida, Jacques. 1967. *of Grammatology.* Gayatri Chakravorty Spivak, trans. Baltimore: Johns Hopkins University Press, 1974.

Deshpande, Madhav M. 1996. "Contextualizing the Eternal Language: Features of Priestly Sanskrit." In Houben 1996, pp. 401–436.

Devahuti, D. 1983. *Harsha—A Political Study.* 2d rev. ed. Delhi: Oxford University Press.

Deyell, John S. 1990. *Living Without Silver: The Monetary History of Early Medieval North India.* Delhi: Oxford University Press.

Dietz, Siglinde. 1984. *Die Buddhistische Briefliteratur Indiens—Nach dem tibetischen Tanjur herausgegeben, übersetzt und erläutert.* Asiatische Forschungen, no. 84. Wiesbaden: Otto Harrassowitz.

Dimock, Edward C., Jr. 1966. *The Place of the Hidden Moon: Erotic Mysticism in the Vaiṣṇava-sahajiyā Cult of Bengal.* Chicago: University of Chicago Press.

Dirlik, Arif, et al., eds. 2000. *History After the Three Worlds: Post-Eurocentric Historiographies.* Lanham, Boulder, New York, and Oxford: Rowman and Littlefield.

Dowman, Keith. 1985. *Masters of Mahamudra: Songs and Histories of the Eighty-Four Buddhist Siddhas.* Albany: State University of New York Press.

Dreyfus, Georges B. J. 1997. *Recognizing Reality—Dharmakīrti's Philosophy and Its Tibetan Interpretations.* Albany: State University of New York Press.

D'souza, Jean. 1992. "Dimensions of South Asia as a Sociolinguistic Area." In Edward C. Dimock et al., eds., *Dimensions of Sociolinguistics in South Asia: Papers in Memory of Gerald B. Kelly.* New Delhi: Oxford University Press.

Dutta, Saroj. 1995. *Land System in Northern India, c.* A.D. *400–c.* A.D. *700.* New Delhi: Munshiram Manoharlal.

Dyczkowski, Mark S. G. 1988. *The Canon of the Śaivāgama and the Kubjikā Tantras of the Western Kaula Tradition.* Albany: State University of New York Press.

Eastman, Kenneth W. 1981. "The Eighteen Tantras of the Vajraśekhara/ Māyājāla." Paper presented at the 26th International Conference of Orientalists in Japan, May 8.

Eck, Diana. 1982. *Banaras: City of Light.* New York: Alfred Knopf.

Edgerton, Franklin. 1953. *Buddhist Hybrid Sanskrit Grammar and Dictionary.* New Haven: Yale University Press. 2 vols.

Eimer, Helmut, ed. and trans. 1978. *Bodhipathapradīpa: Ein Lehrgedicht de Atiśa (Dīpaṃkaraśrījñāna) in der Tibetischen Überlieferung.* Asiatische Forschungen, no. 59. Wiesbaden: Otto Harrassowitz.

Elliot, H. M., and John Dowson. 1867–77. *The History of India, as Told by Its Own Historians: The Muhammadan Period.* 8 vols. London: Trübner.

Elwin, Verrier. 1947. *The Muria and Their Ghotul.* Bombay: Oxford University Press.

———. 1955. *The Religion of an Indian Tribe.* Bombay: Oxford University Press.

Emerson, H.W., ed. 1920. *Punjab Gazetteers: Mandi State.* Lahore: Superintendent, Government Printing, Punjab.

Emmerick, R. E. 1983. "Buddhism Among Iranian Peoples." In Ehsan Yarshater, ed., *The Cambridge History of Iran: The Seleucid, Parthian and Sasanian Periods,* vol. 3, part 2, pp. 949–964. Cambridge: Cambridge University Press.

Enoki, Kazuo. 1959. "On the Nationality of the Ephthalites." *Memoirs of the Research Department of the Toyo Bunko* 18:1–58.

Eschmann, Anncharlott, Hermann Kulke, and Gaya Charan Tripathi, ed. 1978. *The Cult of Jagannath and the Regional Tradition of Orissa.* South Asia Institute, Heidelberg University, South Asian Studies, no. 8. New Delhi: Manohar. Reprint, New Delhi: Manohar, 1986.

Etlin, Richard A. 1996. *In Defense of Humanism: Value in the Arts and Letters.* Cambridge and New York: Cambridge University Press.

Evans, Richard J. 1999. *In Defense of History.* 2d rev. ed. New York and London: W. W. Norton.

Falk, Nancy Auer. 1979. "The Case of the Vanishing Nuns: The Fruits of Ambivalence in Ancient Indian Buddhism." In Nancy Falk and Rita Gross, eds., *Unspoken Worlds: Women's Religious Lives in Non-Western Cultures,* pp. 207–224. San Francisco: Harper & Row.

Feldhaus, Anne. 1995. *Water and Womanhood: Religious Meaning of Rivers in Maharashtra.* New York and Oxford: Oxford University Press.

Figueira, Dorothy M. 1994. *The Exotic: A Decadent Quest.* Albany: State University of New York Press.

Finn, Louise M. 1986. *The Kulacūḍāmaṇi Tantra and the Vāmakeśvara Tantra with the Jayaratha Commentary.* Wiesbaden: Harrassowitz.

Finot, Louis. 1934. "Manuscrits sanskrits de Sādhana retrouvés en Chine." *Journal Asiatique* 225:1–86.

Fischer, David Hackett. 1970. *Historians' Fallacies—Toward a Logic of Historical Thought.* New York: Harper and Row.

Foucault, Michel. 1966. *The Order of Things: An Archæology of the Human Sciences.* [English edition, New York: Random House, 1970.]

———. 1977. *Language, Counter-Memory, Practice: Selected Essays and Interviews.* Ithaca: Cornell University Press.

Fowler, Harold N., and W. R. M. Lamb. 1925. *Plato: The Statesman, Philebus, and Ion.* Leob Classical Library. Cambridge: Harvard University Press.

Franklin, Julian H. 1963. *Jean Bodin and the Sixteenth-Century Revolution in the Methodology of Law and History.* New York: Columbia University Press.

Freed, Ruth S., and Stanley A. Freed. 1993. *Ghosts: Life and Death in North India.* American Museum of Natural History, Anthropological Papers, no. 72. New York: American Museum of Natural History.

Frye, Richard N. 1975. *The Golden Age of Persia: The Arabs in the East.* London: Weidenfeld and Nicolson.

———. 1984. *The History of Ancient Iran.* Munich: C. H. Becksche Verlagsbuchhandlung.

Fussman, Gérard. 1994. "Upāya-kauśalya: L'implantation du bouddhisme au Gandhāra." In Fumimasa Fukui and Gérard Fussman, eds., *Bouddhisme et cultures locales: Quelques cas de réciproques adaptations,* pp. 17–51. Paris: École française d'Extrême-Orient.

Gell, Simeran M. S. 1992. *The* Ghotul *in Muria Society.* Studies in Anthropology and History, vol. 7. Philadelphia: Harwood Academic.

Germano, David. 2002. "The Seven Descents and the Early History of Rnying ma Transmissions." In Helmut Eimer and David Germano, eds., *The Many Canons of Tibetan Buddhism,* pp. 225–263. Leiden: Brill.

Gernet, Jacques. 1995. *Buddhism in Chinese Society: An Economic History from the Fifth to the Tenth Centuries.* Franciscus Verellen, trans. New York: Columbia University Press. [Rev. edition of his *Les aspects économiques du bouddhisme dans la société chinoise du Ve au Xe siècle* (Hanoi, 1956).]

Gerow, Edwin. 1977. *Indian Poetics.* A History of Indian Literature, vol. 5, part 3. Wiesbaden: Otto Harrassowitz.

Giebel, Rolf W. 1995. "The *Chin-kang-ting ching yü-ch'ieh shih-pa-hui chih-kuei*: An Annotated Translation." *Journal of Naritasan Institute for Buddhist Studies* 18:107-201.

Gitomer, David L. 1991. "Such as a Face Without a Nose: The Comic Body in Sanskrit Literature." *Journal of South Asian Literature* 26, nos. 1–2:78–110.

Goetz, Hermann. 1969. *Studies in the History and Art of Kashmir and the Indian Himalaya.* Universität Heidelberg Studien Institut Schriftenreihe, no. 4. Wiesbaden: Harrassowitz.

Gómez, Luis O. 1995. "The Whole Universe as a Sutra." In Donald Lopez, *Buddhism—In Practice,* pp. 107–112. Princeton: Princeton University Press.

———. 1996. *The Land of Bliss: The Paradise of the Buddha of Measureless Light.* Honolulu: University of Hawaii Press.
Gonda, Jan. 1949. *Remarks on Similes in Sanskrit Literature.* Leiden: E. J. Brill.
———. 1961. "Ascetics and Courtesans." *Adyar Library Bulletin* 25:78–102.
———. 1977. *Medieval Religious Literature in Sanskrit.* A History of Indian Literature, vol. 2, part 1. Wiesbaden: Otto Harrassowitz.
Gopal, Lallanji. 1965. *The Economic Life of Northern India, c.* A.D. 700–1200. Delhi: Motilal Banarsidass. 2d rev. ed., Delhi: Motilal Banarsidass, 1989.
Goudriaan, Teun. 1973. "Tumburu and His Sisters." *Wiener Zeitschrift für die Kunde Sudasiens* 17: 49–95.
———. 1996. "Speech of the Gurus: Instances of Treatment of Sanskrit in Tantric Literature." In Houben 1996, pp. 267–274.
Goudriaan, Teun, and Sanjukta Gupta. 1981. *Hindu Tantric and Śākta Literature.* A History of Indian Literature, vol. 2, part 2. Wiesbaden: Otto Harrassowitz.
Granoff, Phyllis. 1979. "Maheśvara/Mahākāla: A Unique Buddhist Image from Kaśmīr." *Artibus Asiae* 41:64–82.
———. 1984. "Holy Warriors: A Preliminary Study of Some Biographies of Saints and Kings in the Classical Indian Tradition." *Journal of Indian Philosophy* 12:291–303.
———. 1986–92. "Tolerance in the Tantras: Its Form and Function." *Journal of Oriental Research, Madras* 56–62:283–302.
———. 2000. "Other People's Rituals: Ritual Eclecticism in Early Medieval Indian Religious." *Journal of Indian Philosophy* 28, no. 4:399–424.
Green, Thomas M. 1982. *The Light in Troy: Imitation and Discovery in Renaissance Poetry.* New Haven and London: Yale University Press.
———. 1988. "Petrarch and the Humanist Hermeneutic." In Harold Bloom, ed., *Petrarch*, pp. 103–123. New York and Philadelphia: Chelsea House.
Groarke, Leo. 1990. *Greek Scepticism: Anti-Realist Trends in Ancient Thought.* Montreal and Kingston: McGill-Queen's University Press.
Gross, Rita M. 1993. *Buddhism After Patriarchy: A Feminist History, Analysis, and Reconstruction of Buddhism.* Albany: State University of New York Press.
Gross, Robert Lewis. 1992. *The Sādhus of India: A Study of Hindu Asceticism.* Jaipur and New Delhi: Rawat Publications.
Guenther, Herbert V. 1963. *The Life and Teaching of Nāropa.* Oxford: Clarendon Press.
Guha, Amalendu. 1991. *Medieval and Early Colonial Assam: Society, Polity, Economy.* Calcutta and New Delhi: K. P. Bagchi.
Gupta, Chitrarekha. 1983–84. "Horse Trade in North India: Some Reflections on Socio-Economic Life." *Journal of Ancient Indian History* 14:186–206.
Gupta, Sanjukta, et al. 1979. *Hindu Tantrism.* Leiden: Brill.
Hackin, Joseph. 1924. *Formulaire sanscrit-tibétain du Xe siècle.* Mission Pelliot en

Asie Centrale, Série Petit in Octavo, vol. 2. Paris: Librarie Orientaliste Paul Geuthner.

HARA, Minoru. 1958. "Nakulīśa-Pāśupata-Darśanam." *IIJ* 2:8–32.

———. 1973. "Pāśupata and Sāṃkhya-Yoga." *Journal of Oriental Research* (Madras) 34–35:76–87.

———. 1994. "Pāśupata Studies II." *Weiner Zeitschrift für die Kunde Südasiens* 3:323–335.

Harner, Michael J., ed. 1973. *Hallucinogens and Shamanism.* New York: Oxford University Press.

Harrison, Paul M. 1978. "Buddhānusmṛti in the Pratyutpanna-Buddha-Saṃmukhāvasthita-Samādhi-sūtra." *Journal of Indian Philosophy* 6:35–57.

Heesterman, J. C. 1957. *The Ancient Indian Royal Consecration: The Rājasūya Described According to the Yajus Texts and Annotated.* The Hague: Mouton.

Hinüber, Oskar von. 1978. "Das Schwert des Vidyādhara." *Wiener Zeitschrift für die Kunde Südasiens* 22:45–48.

———. 1989. "Origin and Varieties of Buddhist Sanskrit." In Caillat 1989, pp. 341–367.

———. 1992. *Sprachentwicklung und Kulturgeschichte—Ein Beitrag zur materiellen Kultur des buddhistischen Klosterlebens.* Abhandlungen der Geistes-und Sozialwissenschaftlichen Klasse Jahrgang 1992, no. 6. Stuttgart: Franz Steiner Verlag.

Hodge, Stephen. 1994. "Considerations on the Dating and Geographical Origins of the *Mahāvairocanābhisaṃbodhi-sūtra.*" In Tadeusz Skorupski and Ulrich Pagel, eds., *The Buddhist Forum, Vol. III: Papers in Honour and Appreciation of Professor David Seyfort Ruegg's Contribution to Indological, Buddhist, and Tibetan Studies,* pp. 57–83. London: School of Oriental and African Studies.

Holub, Robert C. 1984. *Reception Theory: A Critical Introduction.* London and New York: Methuen.

Houben, Jan E. M., ed. 1996. *Ideology and Status of Sanskrit: Contributions to the History of the Sanskrit Language.* Brill's Indological Library, vol. 13. Leiden: E. J. Brill.

Hourani, George F. 1951. *Arab Seafaring.* Rev. and expanded by John Carswell, Princeton: Princeton University Press, 1995.

Huber, Toni. 1990. "Where Exactly Are Cāritra, Devikoṭa and Himavat? A Sacred Geography Controversy and the Development of Tantric Buddhist Pilgrimage Sites in Tibet." *Kailash: A Journal of Himalayan Studies* 16, nos. 3–4:121–164.

Huizinga, Johan. 1950. *Homo Ludens: A Study of the Play Element in Culture.* Boston: Beacon Press. Reprint, Boston: Beacon Press, 1955.

Hultkrantz, Ake. 1978. "Ecological and Phenomenological Aspects of Shamanism." In V. Diószegi and M. Hoppál, eds., *Shamanism in Siberia,* pp. 27–58. Budapest: Akadémiai Kiadó.

IKARI, Yasuke, ed. 1994. *A Study of the Nīlamata: Aspects of Hinduism in Ancient Kashmir.* Kyoto: Institute for Research in Humanities, Kyoto University.

Inden, Ronald. 1978. "Ritual, Authority, and Cyclic Time in Hindu Kingship." In J. F. Richards, ed., *Kingship and Authority in South Asia,* pp. 41–91. Madison: University of Wisconsin-Madison. Reprint, Delhi: Oxford University Press, 1998.

———. 1990. *Imagining India.* Oxford: Basil Blackwell.

Ingalls, Daniel H. H. 1962. "Cynics and Pāśupatas: The Seeking of Dishonor." *Harvard Theological Review* 55, no. 4:281–298.

Irawati, Karvé. 1953. *Kinship Organization in India.* Deccan College Monograph Series, no. 11. Poona: Deccan College Research Institute.

IYANAGA, Nobumi. 1985. "Récits de la soumission de Maheśvara par Trailokyavijaya: d'après les sources chinoises et japonaises." In Michel Strickmann, ed., *Tantric and Taoist Studies in Honour of R.A. Stein. MCB* 22:633–745.

Jacks, Philip. 1993. *The Antiquarian and the Myth of Antiquity: The Origins of Rome in Renaissance Thought.* Cambridge and New York: Cambridge University Press.

Jain, Beena. 1990. *Guild Organization in Northern India (From Earliest Times to 1200 A.D.).* Delhi: Pratibha Prakashan.

Jain, J. C. 1974. "Vidyādharas in the Vasudevahiṇḍi." *Journal of the Oriental Institute of Baroda* 24:120–127.

Jamison, Stephanie W. 1996. *Sacrificed Wife/Sacrificer's Wife: Women, Ritual, and Hospitality in Ancient India.* New York and Oxford: Oxford University Press.

Jayaswal, Kashi P. 1934. *An Imperial History of India in a Sanskrit Text.* With the Sanskrit text [of the *Mañjuśrīmūlakalpa*]. Revised by Ven. Rāhula Sāṅkṛityāyana. Lahore: Motilal Banarsidass. Reprint, Patna: Eastern Book House, 1988.

Jefferds, Keith N. 1981. "Vidūṣaka Versus Fool: A Functional Analysis." *Journal of South Asian Literature* 16:61–73.

Jha, Amal Kumar, ed. 1991. *Coinage, Trade and Economy, January 8th–11th, 1991: Third International Colloquium.* Nashik, Maharastra: Indian Institute of Research in Numismatic Studies.

Jones, Horace L. 1930. *The Geography of Strabo.* Leob Classical Library. 8 vols. London: William Heinemann.

Jong, J. W. de. 1984. "A New History of Tantric Literature in India." *Acta Indologica* [Naratasan Shinshoji] 6:91–113.

KANAOKA, Shūyū. 1966. "Kukurāja." *Journal of Indian and Buddhist Studies* 15:467–458.

KANEKO, Eiichi. 1982. *Ko-Tantora zenshū kaidai mokuroku.* Tokyo: Kokusho Kankōkai.

Kapstein, Matthew T. 2000. *The Tibetan Assimilation of Buddhism: Conversion, Contestation, and Memory.* New York: Oxford University Press.

Karmay, Samten Gyaltsen. 1980. "An Open Letter of Pho-brang Zhi-ba-'od to the Buddhists in Tibet." *Tibet Journal* 5:3–28.

Keegan, John. 1993. *A History of Warfare.* New York: Alfred A. Knopf.

Keil, Frank C. 1989. *Concepts, Kinds, and Cognitive Development.* Cambridge, MA: MIT Press.

Kelley, Donald R. 1988. "The Theory of History." In Charles B. Schmitt et al., eds., *The Cambridge History of Renaissance Philosophy,* pp. 746–761. Cambridge and New York: Cambridge University Press.

King, Richard 1999. *Orientalism and Religion: Postcolonial Theory, India and the "Mystic East."* London and New York: Routledge.

Kopf, David. 1969. *British Orientalism and the Bengal Renaissance: The Dynamics of Indian Modernization, 1773–1835.* Berkeley: University of California Press.

Kuiper, F. B. J. 1979. *Varuṇa and Vidūṣaka: On the Origin of the Sanskrit Drama.* Amsterdam: North-Holland.

Kulke, Hermann. 1978. *The Devarāja Cult.* Data Paper, no. 108. Ithaca: Department of Asian Studies, Cornell University. Reprinted as "The Devaraja Cult: Legitimation and Apotheosis of the Ruler in the Kingdom of Angkor" in Kulke 1993, pp. 327–381.

———. 1993. *Kings and Cults: State Formation and Legitimation in India and Southeast Asia.* Delhi: Manohar.

Kulke, Hermann, and Dietmar Rothermund. 1998. *A History of India.* Rev. ed. London and New York: Routledge.

Kumar, Dharma, and Tapan Raychaudhuri, eds. 1982. *The Cambridge Economic History of India.* 2 vols. Cambridge: Cambridge University Press.

Kværne, Per. 1975. "On the Concept of Sahaja in Indian Buddhist Tantric Literature." *Tememos* 11:88–135.

Lakoff, George. 1987. *Women, Fire, and Dangerous Things.* Chicago: University of Chicago Press.

Lalou, Marcelle. 1936. "Mañjuśrīmūlakalpa et Tārāmūlakalpa." *Harvard Journal of Asian Studies* 1:327–349.

——— 1955. "A la Recherche du Vidyādharapiṭaka: le cycle du *Subāhuparipṛcchā-tantra.*" In Gadjin M. NAGAO and Josho NOZAWA, eds., *Studies in Indology and Buddhology: Presented in Honour of Professor Susumu Yamaguchi on the Occasion of His Sixtieth Birthday,* pp. 68–72. Kyogo: Hozokan.

———. 1956. "Four Notes on Vajrapani." *Adyar Library Bulletin* 20:287–293.

Lamotte, Etienne. 1949. "La critique d'interprétation dans le bouddhisme." *Annuaire de l'Institut de Philologie et d'Histoire Orientales et Slaves* 9:341–361.

———. 1944–80. *Le traité de la grande vertu de sagesse.* Publications de l'Institut Orientaliste de Louvain. 5 vols. Louvain: Institut Orientaliste.

———. 1966. "Vajrapāṇi en Inde." In *Mélanges de Sinologie offerts à Monsieur Paul Demiéville.* Bibliothèque de l'Institut des Hautes Études Chinoises, vol. 20, pp. 113–159. Paris: Presses Universitaires de France.

Law, Narendra Nath. 1919. "Ancient Hindu Coronation and Allied Ceremonials." *IA* 48: 84–95.

Leslie, Julia, ed. 1991. *Roles and Rituals for Hindu Women* Rutherford, Madison, and Teaneck, NJ: Fairleigh Dickinson University Press.

Lessing, Ferdinand D., and Alex Wayman. 1968. *Mkhas Grub Rje'i Fundamentals of the Buddhist Tantras.* Indo-Iranian Monographs, vol. 8. The Hague: Mouton.

Lévi, Sylvain. 1915. "Le catalogue géographique des Yakṣa dans la Mahā-māyūrī." *JA* series 11, vol. 5:19–138.

———. 1930. "Un nouveau document sur le bouddhisme de basse époque dans l'Inde." *Bulletin of the School of Oriental and African Studies* 6:418–429.

Lewis, Bernard. 1993. *Islam and the West.* New York and Oxford: Oxford University Press.

Lewis, Todd T. 1993. "Newar-Tibetan Trade and the Domestication of *Siṃhalasārthabāhu Avadāna.*" *History of Religions* 33:135–160.

Lienhard, Siegfried. 1985. *Die Abenteuer des Kaufmanns Simhala. Eine nepalische Bilderrolle aus der Sammulung des Museums für Indische Kunst Berlin.* Berlin: Das Museum für Indische Kunst Berlin.

———. 1993. "Avalokiteśvara in the Wick of the Night-Lamp." *IIJ* 36:93–104.

Ligeti, Louis, ed. 1978. *Proceedings of the Csoma de Körös Memorial Symposium (Held at Mátrafüred, Hungary 24–30 September 1976).* Bibliotheca Orientalis Hungarica, vol. 23. Budapest: Akadémiai Kiadó.

Lin, Li-Kouang. 1935. "Punyodaya (Na-T'i), un propagateur du tantrisme en Chine et au Cambodge à l'époque de Hiuan-tsang." *JA* 227:83–100.

Lingat, Robert. 1973. *The Classical Law of India.* Berkeley: University of California Press.

Litvinsky, B. A., et al., eds. 1996. *The Crossroads of Civilizations: A.D. 250 to 750.* History of Civilizations of Central Asia, vol. 3. Paris: UNESCO.

Liu, Xinru. 1988. *Ancient India and Ancient China: Trade and Religious Exchanges A.D. 1–600.* Delhi: Oxford University Press.

Lopez, Donald, Jr., ed. 1995. *Curators of the Buddha: The Study of Buddhism Under Colonialism.* Chicago: University of Chicago Press.

Lorenzen, David N. 1972. *The Kāpālikas and Kālāmukhas: Two Lost Śaivite Sects.* Berkeley and Los Angeles: University of California Press.

———. 1978. "Warrior Ascetics in Indian History." *JAOS* 98:61–75.

———. 1989. "New Data on the Kāpālikas." In Alf Hiltebeitel, ed., *Criminal Gods and Demon Devotees,* pp. 231–238. Albany: State University of New York Press.

Lüders, Heinrich. 1939. "Die Vidyadharas in der buddhistischen Literatur und Kunst." *Zeitschrift der Deutschen Morgenländischen Gesellschaft* 93:89–104.

Lutgendorf, Philip. 1991. *The Life of a Text: Performing the* Rāmcaritmānas *of Tulsidas.* Berkeley: University of California Press.

———. 2001. "Dining Out at Lake Pampa: The Shabari Episode in Multiple Ramayanas." In Paula Richman, ed., *Questioning Ramayanas: A South Asian Tradition*, pp. 119–136. Berkeley: University of California Press.

Mackerras, Colin 1972. *The Uighur Empire According to the T'ang Dynastic Histories: A Study in Sino-Uighur Relations, 744–840*. Columbia: University of South Carolina Press.

———. 1990. "The Uighurs." In Denis Sinor, ed., *The Cambridge History of Early Inner Asia*, pp. 317–342. Cambridge: Cambridge University Press.

Mair, Victor H. 1988. *Painting and Performance: Chinese Picture Recitation and Its Indian Genesis*. Honolulu: University of Hawaii Press.

Majumdar, Ramesh Chandra. 1971. *History of Ancient Bengal*. Calcutta: G. Bharadwaj.

Majumdar, Ramesh Chandra, and Anant Sadashiv Altekar. 1946. *The Vakataka-Gupta Age (Circa 200–550 A.D.)*. Banaras, Uttar Pradesh: Motilal Banarsidass.

Mandan, A. P. 1990. *The History of the Rastrakutas*. New Delhi: Harman.

MATSUNAGA, Yukei. 1985. "On the Date of the Mañjuśrīmūlakalpa." In Michel Strickmann, ed., *Tantric and Taoist Studies in Honour of R.A. Stein. MCB* 22:882–894.

Mayer, Robert. 1998. "The Figure of Maheśvara/Rudra in the rÑiṅ-ma-pa Tantric Tradition." *JIABS* 21:271–310.

McKay, Alex. 1998. "Kailas-Manasarovar in 'Classical' (Hindu) and Colonial Sources: Asceticism, Power, and Pilgrimage." In Alex McKay, ed., *Pilgrimage in Tibet*, pp. 165–183. Richmond, Surrey, UK: Curzon Press.

Mehta, Jodh Singh. 1970. *Abu to Udaipur: Celestial Simla to City of Sunrise*. Delhi: Motilal Banarsidass.

Millar, Susanna. 1974. *The Psychology of Play*. New York: Jason Aronson.

Miller, David M., and Dorothy C. Wertz. 1976. *Hindu Monastic Life: The Monks and Monasteries of Bhubaneswar*. Montreal and London: McGill-Queen's University Press.

Mishra, Vibhuti Bhushan. 1973. *Religious Beliefs and Practices of North India During the Early Mediæval Period*. Handbuch der Orientalistik, Zweite Abteilung: Indien. Leiden: E. J. Brill.

Mongia, Padmini, ed. 1996. *Contemporary Postcolonial Theory: A Reader*. London, New York, Sydney, and Auckland: Arnold.

Morinis, E. A. 1984. *Pilgrimage in the Hindu Tradition*. Delhi: Oxford University Press.

Morrell, John. 1983. *Taking Laughter Seriously*. Albany: State University of New York Press.

Mukherjee, P. 1940. *The History of Medieval Vaishnavism in Orissa*. Calcutta: R. Chatterjee.

Murphey, Murray G. 1994. *Philosophical Foundations of Historical Knowledge*. Albany: State University of New York Press.

Murthy, M. Chidananda. 1987. "Nilapatas—A Relatively Unknown Religious Sect of Medieval India." In A. V. Narasimha Murthy and K. V. Ramesh, eds., *Giridharaśrī—Essays on Indology, Dr. G. S. Dikshit Felicitation Volume*, pp. 209–216. Delhi: Agam Kala Prakashan.

Namai, Chishō Mamoru. 1997. "On *bodhicittabhāvanā* in the Esoteric Buddhist Tradition." In Helmut Krasser et al., eds., *Tibetan Studies—Proceedings of the 7th Seminar of the International Association for Tibetan Studies, Graz 1995*, pp. 657–668. Vienna: Verlag der Österreichischen Akademie der Wissenschaften.

Nath, Vijay. 2001. *Purāṇas and Acculturation: A Historico-Anthropological Perspective.* New Delhi: Munshiram Manoharlal Publishers.

Nattier, Jan. 1991. *Once Upon a Future Time: Studies in a Buddhist Prophecy of Decline.* Berkeley: Asian Humanities Press.

Newman, John. 1988. "Buddhist Sanskrit in the Kālackara Tantra." *JIABS* 11:123–140.

Nihom, Max. 1992. "The Goddess with the Severed Head: A Recension of Sādhanamālā 232, 234, and 238 Attributed to the Siddhācārya Virūpā." In A. W. van den Hoek et al., eds., *Ritual, State and History in South Asia: Essays in Honour of J. C. Heesterman*, pp. 222–243. Leiden, New York, and Cologne: E. J. Brill.

———. 1994. *Studies in Indian and Indo-Indonesian Tantrism: The Kuñjarakarṇadharmakathana and the Yogatantra.* Publications of the De Nobili Research Library, vol. 21. Vienna: Institute of Indology, University of Vienna.

Nitti-Dolci, Luigia. 1972. *The Prākṛita Grammarians.* Prabhākara Jhā, trans. Delhi: Motilal Banarsidass.

Olson, David R., and Nancy Torrance, eds. 1991. *Literacy and Orality.* Cambridge: Cambridge University Press.

Orlando, Raffaello. 1980. "The Last Will of Amoghavajra." *Annali Istituto Orientale di Napoli* 40:89–113.

Orr, Leslie C. 2000. *Donors, Devotees, and Daughters of God: Temple Women in Medieval Tamilnadu.* New York and Oxford: Oxford University Press.

Orzech, Charles D. 1989. "Seeing Chen-Yen Buddhism: Traditional Scholarship and the Vajrayāna in China." *History of Religions* 29:87–114.

———. 1998. *Politics and Transcendent Wisdom: The Scripture for Humane Kings in the Creation of Chinese Buddhism.* University Park: Pennsylvania State University Press.

Parpola, Asko. 1988. "The Coming of the Aryans to Iran and India and the Cultural and Ethnic Identity of the Dāsas." *Studia Orientalia* (Helsinki) 64:194–302.

Parry, Jonathan P. 1985. "The Aghori Ascetics of Benares." In Richard Burghart and Audrey Cantlie, eds., *Indian Religion.* Collected Papers on South Asia, no. 7, pp. 51–78. New York: St. Martin's Press.

———. 1994. *Death in Banaras.* Cambridge: Cambridge University Press.

Paul, Diana Mary. 1980. *The Buddhist Feminine Ideal: Queen Śrīmālā and the Tathāgatagarbha.* American Academy of Religion Dissertation Series, no. 30. Missoula, MT: Scholars Press.

Pfeiffer, Rudolf. 1976. *History of Classical Scholarship from 1300 to 1850.* Oxford: Clarendon Press.

Philips, C. H., ed. 1961. *Historians of India, Pakistan and Ceylon.* London: Oxford University Press.

Pollock, Sheldon. 1989. "Mīmāṃsā and the Problem of History in Traditional India." *Journal of the American Oriental Society* 109:603–11.

———. 1993. "Deep Orientalism? Notes on Sanskrit and Power Beyond the Raj." In Carol A. Breckenridge and Peter van der Veer, eds., *Orientalism and the Postcolonial Predicament,* pp. 76–113. Philadelphia: University of Pennsylvania Press.

———. 1996. "The Sanskirt Cosmopolis, 300–1300 C.E.: Transculturation, Vernacularization, and the Question of Ideology." In Houben 1996, pp. 197–247.

———. 1998. "The Cosmopolitan Vernacular." *Journal of Asian Studies* 57:6–37.

Possehl, Gregory L. 1990. "An Archaeological Adventurer in Afghanistan: Charles Masson." *South Asian Studies* 6:111–124.

Prasad, Om Prakash. 1989. *Decay and Revival of Urban Centres in Medieval South India (c.* A.D. 600–1200). New Delhi: Commonwealth.

Przyluski, Jean. 1923. "Les Vidyārāja: Contribution à l'histoire de la magie dans les sects mahāyānistes." *BEFEO* 23:301–318.

Puri, Baij Nath. 1986. *The History of the Gurjara-Pratihāras.* 2d rev. and enlarged ed. New Delhi: Munshiram Manoharlal.

Pye, Michael. 1978. *Skilful Means: A Concept in Mahayana Buddhism.* London: Gerald Duckworth.

Rabe, Michael D. 1997. "The Māmallapuram *Praśasti:* A Panegyric in Figures." *Artibus Asiæ* 57:189–241.

Rabil, Albert, ed. 1988. *Renaissance Humanism: Foundations, Forms, and Legacy.* 3 vols. Philadelphia: University of Pennsylvania Press.

Rastogi, Navjivan. 1987. *Introduction to the Tantrāloka: A Study in Structure.* Delhi: Motilal Banarsidass.

Ray, Himanshu Prabha. 1986. *Monastery and Guild: Commerce Under the Sātavāhanas.* Delhi: Oxford University Press.

———. 1994. *The Winds of Change: Buddhism and the Maritime Links of Early South Asia.* Delhi: Oxford University Press.

Ray, Reginald A. 1994. *Buddhist Saints in India: A Study in Buddhist Values and Orientations.* New York and Oxford: Oxford University Press.

Regamey, Constantin. 1971. "Motifs vichnouïtes et śivaites dans le Kāraṇḍavyūha." In *Études tibétaines dédiées à la mémoire de Marcelle Lalou,* pp. 411–432. Paris: Librairie d'Amérique et d'Orient.

Reynolds, Susan. 1994. *Fiefs and Vassals: The Medieval Evidence Reinterpreted.* Oxford: Oxford University Press.

Richman, Paula, ed. 1991. *Many Ramayanas: The Diversity of a Narrative Tradition in South Asia.* Berkeley: University of California Press.

Robinson, James B. 1979. *Buddha's Lions: The Lives of the Eighty-four Siddhas.* Berkeley: Dharma.

Rocher, Ludo. 1986. *The Purāṇas.* Vol. 2, part 3: *A History of Indian Literature.* Wiesbaden: Otto Harrassowitz.

Ruegg, David Seyfort. 1964. "Sur les rapports entre le bouddhisme et le 'substrat religieux' indien et tibétain." *JA* 252:77–95.

———. 1967. "On a Yoga Treatise in Sanskrit from Qïzïl." *JAOS* 87:157–165.

———. 1981. "Deux problèmes d'exégèse et de pratique tantriques." In Michel Strickmann, ed., *Tantric and Taoist Studies in Honour of R.A. Stein. MCB* 20:212–226.

———. 1989. "Allusiveness and Obliqueness in Buddhist Texts: *Saṃdhā, Saṃdhi, Saṃdhyā* and *Abhisaṃdhi.*" In Caillat 1989, pp. 294–328.

Russell, R. V. 1916. *The Tribes and Castes of the Central Provinces of India.* Assisted by Rai Bahadur Hira Lal. 4 vols. London: Macmillan. Reprint, Oosterhout, the Netherlands: Anthropological Publications, 1969.

Sachau, Edward C. 1910. *Alberuni's India—An Account of the Religion, Philosophy, Literature, Geography, Chronology, Astronomy, Customs, Laws and Astrology of India About A.D. 1030.* 2 vols. London: Kegan Paul, Trench, and Trubner.

Sakurai, Munenobu. 1996. *Indo mikkyōgirei kyenkyū.* Kyoto: Hōzōgan.

Salomon, Richard. 1989. "Linguistic Variability in Post-Vedic Sanskrit." In Caillat 1989, pp. 275–294.

———. 1999. *Ancient Buddhist Scrolls from Gandhāra: The British Library Kharoṣṭhī Fragments.* Seattle: University of Washington Press.

Samuel, Geoffrey. 1993. *Civilized Shamans: Buddhism in Tibetan Societies.* Washington and London: Smithsonian Institution Press.

Sanderson, Alexis. 1988. Śaivism and the Tantric Traditions." In S. Sutherland et al., eds., *The World's Religions,* pp. 660–704. London: Routledge & Kegan Paul.

———. 1994. "Vajrayāna: Origin and Function." In Dhammakaya Foundation, ed., *Buddhism into the Year 2000,* pp. 87–102. Bangkok and Los Angeles: Dhammakaya Foundation.

———. 2001. "History Through Textual Criticism in the Study of Śaivism, the Pañcarātra, and the Buddhist Yoginītantras." In François Grimal, ed., *Les sources et le temps,* pp. 1–47. Pondicherry: École française d'Extrême Orient.

Saussure, Ferdinand de. 1983. *Course in General Linguistics.* La Salle, IL: Open Court.

Sawyer, Dana W. 1993. "The Monastic Structure of Banarsi Dandi Sadhus." In Bradley R. Hertel and Cynthia Ann Humes, eds., *Living Banaras: Hindu Religion in Cultural Context,* pp. 159–180. Albany: State University of New York Press.

Schaeffer, Kurtis R. 2000. "The Religious Career of Vairocanavajra—A Twelfth-

Century Indian Buddhist Master from Daksiṇa Kośala." *Journal of Indian Philosophy* 28, no. 4:361–384.

Scharfe, Harmut. 1993. *Investigations in Kauṭalya's Manual of Political Science.* Wiesbaden: Harrassowitz.

Schlingloff, Dieter. 1964. *Ein Buddhistisches Yogalehrbuch.* Sanskrittexte aus den Turfanfunden, no. 7. 2 vols. Berlin: Akademie-Verlag.

Schmidt, Toni. 1958. *The Eighty-five Siddhas.* Sino-Swedish Expedition, no. 42. Stockholm: Statens Ethnografiska Museum.

Schomer, Karine. 1987. "The *Dohā* as a Vehicle of Sant Teachings." In Karine Schomer and W. H. McLeod, eds., *The Sants: Studies in a Devotional Tradition of India,* pp. 61–90. Berkeley: Berkeley Religious Studies Series.

Schopen, Gregory. 1977. "Sukhāvatī as a Generalized Religious Goal in Sanskrit Mahāyāna Sūtra Literature." *IIJ* 19:177–210.

———. 1985. "The Bodhigarbhālaṅkāralakṣa and Vimaloṣṇīṣa Dhāraṇīs in Indian Inscriptions." *Wiener Zeitschrift für die Kunde Südasiens* 29:119–149.

———. 1987. "Burial *'Ad Sanctos'* and the Physical Presence of the Buddha in Early Indian Buddhism." *Religion* 17:193–225.

———. 1990. "The Buddha as an Owner of Property and Permanent Resident in Medieval Indian Monasteries." *Journal of Indian Philosophy* 18:181–217.

———. 1991. "Archæology and Protestant Presuppositions in the Study of Indian Buddhism." *History of Religions* 31:1–23.

———. 1992. "On Avoiding Ghosts and Social Censure: Monastic Funerals in the Mūlasarvāstivāda-Vinaya." *Journal of Indian Philosophy* 20:1–39.

———. 1994. "Doing Business for the Lord: Lending on Interest and Written Loan Contracts in the *Mūlasarvāstivāda-vinaya.*" *JAOS* 114:527–554.

———. 1994a. "Ritual Rights and Bones of Contention: More on Monastic Funerals and Relics in the *Mūlasarvāstivāda-vinaya." Journal of Indian Philosophy* 22:31–80.

———. 1996. "The Suppression of Nuns and the Ritual Murder of Their Special Dead in Two Buddhist Monastic Texts." *Journal of Indian Philosophy* 24:563–592.

Schopenhauer, Arthur. 1958. *The World as Will and Representation.* E. F. J. Payne, trans. 2 vols. Indian Hills, CO: Falcon's Wing Press.

Scott, Joan W. 2001. "Fantasy Echo: History and the Construction of Identity." *Critical Inquiry* 27:284–304.

Shafer, Robert. 1954. *Ethnography of Ancient India.* Wiesbaden: Otto Harrassowitz.

Shahidullah, M. 1928. *Les chants mystiques de Kāṇha et de Saraha—les Dohā-Koṣa.* Paris: Adrien-Maisonneuve.

Sharma, Har Dutt. 1941. "Hāsya as a Rasa in Sanskrit Rhetoric and Literature." *Annals of the Bhandarkar Oriental Research Institute* 22:103–115.

Sharma, Ram Sharan. 1965. *Indian Feudalism—c. 300–1200.* Calcutta: University of Calcutta. Reprint, Calcutta: University of Calcutta, 1987.

———. 1987. *Urban Decay in India (c. 300–c. 1000).* New Delhi: Munshiram

Manoharlal.
———. 2001. *Early Medieval Indian Society: A Study in Feudalisation.* Calcutta: Orient Longman Limited.
Sharma, Shanta Rani. 1996. *Society and Culture in Rajasthan: c. A.D. 700–900.* Delhi: Pragati.
Shaw, Miranda. 1994. *Passionate Enlightenment.* Princeton: Princeton University Press.
Shorey, Paul. 1933. *Plato: The Republic.* Leob Classical Library. 2 vols. Cambridge: Harvard University Press.
Shrimali, Krishna Mohan. 1991. "Cash Nexus on Western Coast, c. A.D. 850–1250: A Study of the Śilāhāras." In Jha 1991, pp. 178–193.
Shulman, David Dean. 1985. *The King and the Clown in South Indian Myth and Poetry.* Princeton: Princeton University Press.
Siegel, Lee. 1987. *Laughing Matters: Comic Tradition in India.* Chicago and London: University of Chicago Press.
Siklós, Bulcsu. 1996. *The Vajrabhairava Tantras: Tibetan and Mongolian Versions, English Translation and Annotations.* Buddhica Britannica Series Continua, no. 7. Tring, UK: Institute of Buddhist Studies.
Simkin, C. G. F. 1968. *The Traditional Trade of Asia.* London: Oxford University Press.
Singh, Upinder. 1993. *Kings, Brāhmaṇas and Temples in Orissa: An Epigraphic Study A.D. 300–1147.* New Delhi: Munshiram Manoharlal.
Sinha, Bindeshwari Prasad. 1977. *Dynastic History of Magadha, Circa 450–1200 A.D.* New Delhi: Abhinav.
Sircar, Dinesh Chandra. 1945. "The Maukharis and the Later Guptas." *Journal of the Royal Asiatic Society of Bengal, Letters* 11:69–74.
———. 1966. *Indian Epigraphical Glossary.* Delhi: Motilal Banarsidass.
———. 1971. *Studies in the Geography of Ancient and Medieval India.* Delhi: Motilal Banarsidass.
Skorupski, Tadeusz. 1983. "Tibetan Homa Rites." In Staal 1983, pp. 403–417.
———. 1994. "*Jyotirmañjarī:* Abhayākaragupta's Commentary on Homa Rites." *Mikkyō bunka kenkyūsho kiyō* 8:206–236.
———. 1996. "*The Sampuṭa-tantra*—Sanskrit and Tibetan Versions of Chapter One." In Tadeusz Skorupski, ed., *The Buddhist Forum, Vol. IV: Seminar Papers 1994–1996,* pp. 191–244. London: School of Oriental and African Studies.
Snellgrove, David L. 1958. "Note on the *Adhyāśayasaṃcodanasūtra.*" *Bulletin of the School of Oriental and African Studies* 21:620–623.
———. 1959. "The Notion of Divine Kingship in Tantric Buddhism." In *La Regalità Sacra—Contributi al Tema dell' VIII Congresso Internazionale di Storia delle Religioni,* pp. 204–218. Leiden: E. J. Brill.
———. 1987. *Indo-Tibetan Buddhism: Indian Buddhists and Their Tibetan Successors.* 2 vols. Boston: Shambhala.
Staal, Frits, ed. 1983. *Agni: The Vedic Ritual of the Fire Altar.* 2 vols. Berkeley:

Asian Humanities Press.

Stanley, John M. 1988. "Gods, Ghosts, and Possession." In Eleanor Zelliot and Maxine Berntsen, eds., *The Experience of Hinduism: Essays on the Religion in Maharashtra,* pp. 26–59. Albany: State University of New York Press.

Stablein, William George. 1976. "The Mahākālatantra: A Theory of Ritual Blessings and Tantric Medicine." Ph.D. diss., Columbia University.

Stearns, Cyrus. 1996. "The Life and Tibetan Legacy of the Indian *Mahāpaṇḍita* Vibhūticandra." *JIABS* 19:127–171.

Stein, Burton. 1980. *Peasant State and Society in Medieval South India.* Delhi: Oxford University Press.

———. 1991. "The Segmentary State: Interim Reflections." *Puruṣārtha* 13:217–237.

Stein, Rolf A. 1995. "La soumission de Rudra et autres contes tantriques." *JA* 283:121–160.

Steinkellner, Ernst. 1978. "Remarks on Tantristic Hermeneutics." In Ligeti 1978, pp. 445–458.

Strayer, Joseph R. 1965. *Feudalism.* Princeton: D. van Nostrand.

Strickmann, Michel. 1983. "Homa in East Asia." In Staal 1983, pp. 418–455.

———. 1990. "The *Consecration Sūtra:* A Buddhist Book of Spells." In Robert E. Buswell, ed., *Chinese Buddhist Apocrypha,* pp. 75–118. Honolulu: University of Hawaii Press.

———. 1996. *Mantras et mandarins: Le bouddhisme tantrique en Chine.* Bibliothèque des Sciences humaines. Paris: Gallimard.

———. 2002. *Chinese Magical Medicine.* Bernard Faure, ed. Stanford: Stanford University Press.

Strong, John S. 1992. *The Legend and Cult of Upagupta.* Princeton: Princeton University Press.

Suryavanshi, Bhagwan Singh. 1962. *The Abhiras: Their History and Culture.* M.S. University Archaeology and Ancient History Series, no. 6. Baroda: M.S. University of Baroda.

Sutherland, Gail Hinich. 1991. *The Disguises of the Demon: The Development of the Yakṣa in Hinduism and Buddhism.* Albany: State University of New York Press.

Suzuki, Daisetz Teitaro. 1934. *An Index to the Lankavatara Sutra.* 2d rev. ed. Kyoto: Sanskrit Buddhist Texts Publishing Society.

———. 1957. *The Tibetan Tripitaka: Peking Edition.* Tokyo-Kyoto: Tibetan Tripitaka Research Institute.

Tagore, Rabindranath. 1938a. *Candālikā.* In Amiya Chakravarty, ed., *A Tagore Reader,* pp. 169–179. New York: Macmillan, 1961.

———. 1938b. *Chandālikā Nṛtyanātya.* Shyamara Devi, trans. *Orient Review* (January–February 1956).

Takakusu, Junjirō, and Kaigyoku Watanabe, eds. 1924–34. *Taishō shinshū daizōkyō.* Tokyo: Taishō issaikyō kankōkai.

Tatz, Mark. 1986. *Asanga's Chapter on Ethics with the Commentary of Tsong-*

Kha-Pa, The Basic Path to Awakening, The Complete Bodhisattva. Lewiston, NY: Edwin Mellen Press.

———. 1987. "The Life of the Siddha-Philosopher Maitrīgupta." *JAOS* 107:695–711.

———. 1988. "Maitrī-pa and Atiśa." In Helga Uebach and Jampa L. Panglung, eds., *Tibetan Studies: Proceedings of the 4th Seminar of the International Association for Tibetan Studies, Schloss Hohenkammer—Munich 1985,* pp. 473–481. Munich: Bayerische Akademie der Wissenschaften.

Teiser, Stephen F. 1988. *The Ghost Festival in Medieval China.* Princeton: Princeton University Press.

Temple, Richard Carnac. 1884–90. *Legends of the Punjab.* 3 vols. Bombay: Education Society's Press.

Thakur, Vijay Kumar, and Kalpana Jha. 1994. "Towns and Trade in the Samarāichchakahā: Text and Context." In N. N. Bhattacharya, ed., *Jainism and Prakrit in Ancient and Medieval India: Essays for Prof. Jagdish Chandra Jain,* pp. 295–324. New Delhi: Manohar.

Thapar, Romila. 1990. *From Lineage to State: Social Formations in the Mid-First Millennium* B.C. in the Ganga Valley. Delhi: Oxford University Press.

———. 1992. *Interpreting Early India.* Delhi: Oxford University Press.

———. 1997. *Aśoka and the Decline of the Mauryas.* 2d rev. ed. Delhi: Oxford University Press.

Thomas, Werner. 1964. *Tocharisches Elementarbuch.* 2 vols. Heidelberg: Carl Winter.

Torrance, Robert M. 1978. *The Comic Hero.* Cambridge: Harvard University Press.

TSUDA, Shinichi. 1978. *A Critical Tantrism.* Memoirs of the Research Department of the Toyo Bunko, no. 36. Tokyo: Toyo Bunko.

———. 1990. "The Cult of śmaśāna, the Realities of Tantra." In Teun Goudriaan, ed., *The Sanskrit Tradition and Tantrism,* pp. 96–108. Leiden, New York, Copenhagen, and Cologne: E. J. Brill.

Tucci, Giuseppe. 1930. "Animadversiones Indicæ." *JASB* 26:125–160.

———. 1949. *Tibetan Painted Scrolls.* Rome: La Libreria Dello Stato. 3 vols. Reprint, Bangkok: SDI, 1999.

———. 1958. *Minor Buddhist Texts.* Serie Orientale Roma, no. 9. 2 vols. Rome: IsMEO.

UI, Hakuju, et al., eds. 1934. *A Complete Catalogue of the Tibetan Buddhist Canons (BKaḥ-ḥgyur and Bstan-ḥgyur).* Sendai: Tôhoku Imperial University.

Varady, Robert Gabriel. 1979. "North Indian Banjaras: Their Evolution as Transporters." *South Asia* (Australia) 2:1–18.

Vitebsky, Peirs. 1992. *Dialogues with the Dead: The Discussion of Mortality Among the Sora of Eastern India.* Cambridge: Cambridge University Press.

Voloéinov, V. N. 1973. *Marxism and the Philosophy of Language.* New York and London: Seminar Press.

Waldschmidt, Ernst. 1981. "Bemerkungen zu einer zentralasiatischen Sanskrit-Version des Virūpā-Avadāna." In K. Bruhn and A. Wezler, eds., *Studien zum Jainismus und Buddhismus. Gedenkscrift für Ludwig Alsdorf*, pp. 341–358. Wiesbaden: Otto Harrassowitz.

Wallace, Vesna A. 2001. *The Inner Kālacakratantra: A Buddhist Tantric View of the Individual.* Oxford and New York: Oxford University Press.

Walleser, Max. 1922. "The Life of Nāgārjuna from Tibetan and Chinese Sources." *Asia Major* (Hirth Anniversary volume):421–455.

Wayman, Alex. 1958. "The Rules of Debate According to Asaṅga." *JAOS* 78:29–40.

———. 1968. "Concerning Saṃdhā-bhāṣā/Saṃdhi-bhāṣā/Saṃdhyā-bhāṣā." In *Mélanges d'indianisme à la mémoire de Louis Renou*, pp. 789–796. Publications de l'Institut de Civilisation Indienne, no. 28. Paris: Éditions e. de Boccard.

———. 1975–76. "The Significance of Mantras, from the Veda Down to Buddhist Tantric Practice." *Indologica Taurinensia* 3–4:483–497.

———. 1977. *Yoga of the Guhyasamājatantra: The Arcane Lore of Forty Verses.* Delhi: Motilal Banarsidass.

Wedemeyer, Christian K. 2001. "Tropes, Typologies, and Turnarounds: A Brief Genealogy of the Historiography of Tantric Buddhism." *History of Religions* 41:223–259.

Weinstein, Stanley. 1987. *Buddhism Under the T'ang.* Cambridge: Cambridge University Press.

Weiss, Roberto. 1969. *The Renaissance Discovery of Classical Antiquity.* Oxford: Basil Blackwell.

White, David Gordon. 1996. *The Alchemical Body.* Chicago and London: University of Chicago Press.

Wills, C. U. 1919. "The Territorial System of the Rajput Kingdoms of Mediæval Chhattisgarh." *JASB* 15:197–262.

Wink, André. 1990. *Al-Hind: The Making of the Indo-Islamic World.* Vol. 1. Leiden: E. J. Brill.

Wittgenstein, Ludwig. 1958. *Philosophical Investigations.* G. E. M. Anscombe, trans. 3d ed. New York: Macmillan.

Witzel, Michael. 1994. "Kashmiri Manuscripts and Pronunciation." In IKARI 1994, pp. 1–53.

Wright, Arthur F. 1990. *Studies in Chinese Buddhism.* New Haven and London: Yale University Press.

Yazdani, G., ed. 1960. *The Early History of the Deccan.* 2 vols. London: Oxford University Press.

YAMABE, Nobuyoshi. 1999. " 'The Sūtra on the Ocean-Like Samādhi of the Visualization of the Buddha': The Interfusion of the Chinese and Indian Cultures in Central Asia as Reflected in a Fifth Century Apocryphal Sūtra." Ph.D. diss., Yale University.

YORITOMI, Motohiro. 1990. *Mikkyōbutsu no kenkyū.* Kyoto: Hōzōgan.

Index

PERSONAL NAMES

TEXTS

GENERAL INDEX